IFIP Advances in Information and Communication Technology 492

IFIP – The International Federation for Information Processing

IFIP was founded in 1960 under the auspices of UNESCO, following the first World Computer Congress held in Paris the previous year. A federation for societies working in information processing, IFIP's aim is two-fold: to support information processing in the countries of its members and to encourage technology transfer to developing nations. As its mission statement clearly states:

> *IFIP is the global non-profit federation of societies of ICT professionals that aims at achieving a worldwide professional and socially responsible development and application of information and communication technologies.*

IFIP is a non-profit-making organization, run almost solely by 2500 volunteers. It operates through a number of technical committees and working groups, which organize events and publications. IFIP's events range from large international open conferences to working conferences and local seminars.

The flagship event is the IFIP World Computer Congress, at which both invited and contributed papers are presented. Contributed papers are rigorously refereed and the rejection rate is high.

As with the Congress, participation in the open conferences is open to all and papers may be invited or submitted. Again, submitted papers are stringently refereed.

The working conferences are structured differently. They are usually run by a working group and attendance is generally smaller and occasionally by invitation only. Their purpose is to create an atmosphere conducive to innovation and development. Refereeing is also rigorous and papers are subjected to extensive group discussion.

Publications arising from IFIP events vary. The papers presented at the IFIP World Computer Congress and at open conferences are published as conference proceedings, while the results of the working conferences are often published as collections of selected and edited papers.

IFIP distinguishes three types of institutional membership: Country Representative Members, Members at Large, and Associate Members. The type of organization that can apply for membership is a wide variety and includes national or international societies of individual computer scientists/ICT professionals, associations or federations of such societies, government institutions/government related organizations, national or international research institutes or consortia, universities, academies of sciences, companies, national or international associations or federations of companies.

More information about this series at http://www.springer.com/series/6102

Ramy Harik · Louis Rivest
Alain Bernard · Benoit Eynard
Abdelaziz Bouras (Eds.)

Product Lifecycle Management for Digital Transformation of Industries

13th IFIP WG 5.1 International Conference, PLM 2016
Columbia, SC, USA, July 11–13, 2016
Revised Selected Papers

Springer

Editors
Ramy Harik
University of South Carolina
Columbia, SC
USA

Louis Rivest
École de Technologie Supérieure
Montreal, QC
Canada

Alain Bernard
Ecole Centrale de Nantes
Nantes
France

Benoit Eynard
Université de Technologie de Compiègne
Compiègne
France

Abdelaziz Bouras
Qatar University
Doha
Qatar

ISSN 1868-4238 ISSN 1868-422X (electronic)
IFIP Advances in Information and Communication Technology
ISBN 978-3-319-54659-9 ISBN 978-3-319-54660-5 (eBook)
DOI 10.1007/978-3-319-54660-5

Library of Congress Control Number: 2017933873

Printed on acid-free paper

This Springer imprint is published by Springer Nature
The registered company is Springer International Publishing AG
The registered company address is: Gewerbestrasse 11, 6330 Cham, Switzerland

Preface

In the wake of the fourth Industrial Revolution, commonly known as Industry 4.0, the need for optimization and automation-enabling tools and methodologies is growing steadily. PLM continues to merge together parallel and discontinued aspects of product ideation, design, manufacturing, support, recycling, and many other trades. This is facilitating industry cross-integration, reducing costs and increasing sustainability in complex environments empowering product lifecycle management for digital transformation of industries. The ability to neutralize product data and embed viewpoint integration is not new and has been researched since the explosion of CAD/CAM tools. This is what makes PLM particularly current and sets it as a need, especially for the next few decades where cyber-physical systems and cross-functional processes will only surge.

The IFIP International Conference on Product Lifecycle Management (www.plmconference.org) started in 2003 and since then it has been held yearly around the world and has facilitated the exchange and discussion of the most up-to-date information on product lifecycle management among professionals from academia and industry. This is the official conference of the IFIP Working Group WG 5.1 "Global product development for the whole lifecycle" (www.ifip-wg51.org), and IFIP PLM 2016 was held in Columbia, South Carolina, USA, during July 10–13, 2016.

Product lifecycle management, also known as PLM, is an integrated business approach to the collaborative creation, management, and dissemination of engineering data throughout the extended enterprises that create, manufacture, and operate engineered products and systems.

IFIP PLM 2016 marked the 13th anniversary of the conference, which continues its progress at an excellent rate both in terms of quality and quantity. The topics covered in the program include digital transformation of industries, big data analytics, building information modeling (BIM), cloud computing and mobile PLM, collaborative development architectures, cyber-physical systems (CPS), Industry 4.0, interoperability and systems integration, knowledge sharing, re-use and preservation, lean product development, lifecycle assessment and sustainability, metrics, standards and regulation, PLM and innovation, social networks impact, supply chain and value chain integration, traceability and performance.

One of the objectives of the conference is to provide a platform for experts to discuss and share their success in applying advanced concepts in their respective fields. The IFIP PLM 2016 conference included an outstanding technical program, with distinguished keynote speeches on current development and future visions from Karthik Ramani (Purdue University), Edward Griffor (NIST), Priyanka Gandhi (Amazon Web Services), Jiani Zhang (IBM Watson Internet of Things), Jim Doxey (Dropbox), Alain Bernard (Ecole Centrale Nantes), as well as an insightful tour of the premium McNAIR Laboratories. The conference also offered a great opportunity to young and aspiring researchers to present their research proposals and on-going work during a dedicated PhD Workshop on the preconference day. This regular workshop is designed to support students in their networking activities and help them build their future community.

This book, organized in 14 chapters, is composed of selected enhanced papers presented at the IFIP PLM 2016 conference. It is part of the *IFIP Advances in Information and Communication Technology* (AICT) series that publishes state-of-the-art results in the sciences and technologies of information and communication. In addition to this conference, the *International Journal of Product Lifecycle Management* (IJPLM) is the official journal of the WG5.1 (www.inderscience.com/ijplm).

On behalf of the conference, we thank all the authors, sessions chairs, reviewers, and keynote speakers for their help and support in achieving a great conference. Our gratitude goes to the University of South Carolina, The McNAIR Center for Aerospace Innovation and Research, The College of Engineering and Computing at USC, The Office of Economic Engagement at the University of South Carolina, the Department of Mechanical Engineering at USC, and our sponsors Dassault Systemes, Ingersoll Machine Tools, HAAS, and Ingersoll Cutting tools.

We hope this book serves as a step forward in this exciting area of PLM and we look forward to meeting you at the next PLM conference in Seville, Spain, during July 9–12, 2017 (www.plm-conference.org).

February 2017 Ramy Harik

Organization

Program Chairs

Ramy Harik	University of South Carolina, USA
Louis Rivest	ETS Montréal, Canada

General Chair

Balan Gurumoorthy	IISc Bangalore, India

Steering Committee

Alain Bernard (Chair)	ECN Nantes, France
Abdelaziz Bouras	Qatar University, Qatar
Benoît Eynard	UTC Compiègne, France
Sebti Foufou	Qatar University, Qatar
Shuichi Fukuda	Hon. Professor, Japan
Chris McMahon	University of Bristol, UK
Sergio Terzi	Politecnico di Milano, Italy
K.-D. Thoben	University of Bremen, Germany

Scientific Committee

Améziane Aoussat, France
Romeo Bandinelli, Italy
Alain Bernard, France
Nikolaos Bilalis, Greece
Abdelaziz Bouras, Qatar
Nopasit Chakpitak, Thailand
Paolo Chiabert, Italy
Umberto Cugini, Italy
Christophe Danjou, Canada
Eduardo De Senzi Zancul, Brazil
Frederic Demolly, France
Debashish Dutta, USA
Benoit Eynard, France
Sebti Foufou, Qatar
Shuichi Fukuda, Japan
Philippe Girard, France
Balan Gurumoorthy, India
Rafiq Hamad, Canada
Ramy Harik, USA
Nathan Hartman, USA
Peter Hehenberger, Austria
Paul Hong, USA
George Huang, Hong Kong, SAR China
Julie Jupp, Australia
Hannu Kärkkäinen, Finland
Addis Kidane, USA
Dimitris Kiritsis, Switzerland
Hannele Lampela, Finland
Julien Le Duigou, France
Jong Gyun Lim, Korea
Wen Feng Lu, Singapore
Johan Malmqvist, Sweden
Nicolas Maranzana, France
Mihaita Matei, Canada
Alison Mc Kay, UK
Chris Mc Mahon, UK

Frédéric Noël, France
Felix Nyffenegger, Switzerland
Yacine Ouzrout, France
Hervé Panetto, France
Young Won Won Park, Japan
Henk Jan Pels, The Netherlands
Margherita Peruzzini, Italy
Virgilio Quintana, Canada
Sudarsan Rachuri, USA
Louis Rivest, Canada
Monica Rossi, Italy
Lionel Roucoules, France
Nickolas S. Sapidis, Greece
Joel Sauza Bedolla, Italy
Michael Schabacker, Germany
Frédéric Segonds, France
Anneli Silventoinen, Finland
Alexander Smirnov, Russia
Joshua Tarbutton, USA
Sergio Terzi, Italy
Klaus-Dieter Thoben, Germany
Vince Thomson, Canada
Sandor Vajna, Germany
Darli Vieira, Canada
Singh Vishal, Finland
Bob Young, UK

Local Committee

Chair

Joshua Tarbutton University of South Carolina, USA

Webmaster

Christophe Danjou ETS Montréal, Canada

Registration

Pete Windham University of South Carolina, USA

Administrative Assistant

Angel Anderson University of South Carolina, USA

Program and Graphic Design

Samar Mouawad

General

Liudas Panavas
Alex Zuloaga

Doctoral Workshop

Yacine Ouzrout (Chair) Lyon University, France
Monica Rossi (Co-chair) Politecnico di Milano, Italy

Contents

PLM and Innovation

PLM Tools

Cloud Computing and PLM Tools

Traceability and Performance

Building Information Modeling

Knowledge Sharing, Re-use and Preservation

Industrial Knowledge Management Tools Applied to Engineering Education

Joel Sauza-Bedolla(✉), Carlo Rosso, Gianluca D'Antonio, Paolo Chiabert, and Vittorio Romagnoli

Politecnico di Torino, Corso Duca degli Abruzzi 24, 10129 Torino, Italy
{joel.sauza, carlo.rosso, gianluca.dantonio, paolo.chiabert, vittorio.romagnoli}@polito.it

Abstract. Knowledge is a major source of competitive advantage. Hence, industry has developed tools to capture and reuse its knowledge in the development of new projects and products. Information practices and learning strategies, as Knowledge Management, are gaining acceptance also in the field of education. However, the use of these tools are limited to staff applications and they are not being employed in the university core business: education. This paper shows how a tool to build and validate internal combustion engines, developed in industry, has been successfully integrated into a university course. The learning process has being greatly enriched by the use of this application. Evidence on the planned improvements are also presented.

Keywords: Knowledge management · Engineering education · Internal combustion engines

1 Introduction

The dynamism of the new market has created a competitive incentive among many companies to consolidate their knowledge assets as a means of creating value that is sustainable over time [1]. Since knowledge resides within the brain of employees, firms have developed various strategies to create organizational knowledge through leveraging employees' knowledge [2]. Among them, Knowledge Management (KM) involves any activity related to the capture, use and sharing of knowledge by the organisation [3]. KM practices can include the handling of key documents, expertise directories, lessons-learned databases, best practices and communities of practice that reflect and deliver knowledge to learners at a particular time of need [4].

The enterprise final objective is to build and deliver great products that customers are excited to buy. In the actual global conditions, companies have to fulfil many market requirements and some of them are in conflict with each other, for example car manufacturers have to design new engines with increased power that satisfy stricter pollution standards. Therefore, it is important to develop and validate, during the product conceptual phase, several product alternatives that take into account those conflicts and to select the optimal solution. The decision making process needs to be supported with IT tools.

R. Harik et al. (Eds.): PLM 2016, IFIP AICT 492, pp. 3–12, 2016.
DOI: 10.1007/978-3-319-54660-5_1

In this contribution, the innovative principles of a tool to design and validate internal combustion engines are presented. The tool has been developed using a KM method in an industrial environment. Nonetheless, it is of primary importance to introduce automotive engineering students to the same industrial methods and to the use of the same tools. Therefore, the KM-based tool has be introduced in a university course.

The remainder of this paper is structured as follows: Sect. 2 presents the revision of the state of the art of KM tools in industry and education. Next, the innovative principles embedded in the tool, Engine Paradigm (EP), are summarized in Sect. 3. In Sect. 4, a description of the activities necessary for the correct introduction of the tool in a university curricula is provided. The course deployment and results are discussed in Sects. 5 and 6 respectively. Finally, conclusive remarks are discussed in Sect. 7.

2 State of the Art

KM is a trend topic and it has been extensively used in industry. There is evidence of its recent successful application in sectors such as aerospace [5], shipbuilding [6], wind generation and naval engineering [7]. In particular, KM has undoubtedly made strong inroads in the automobile industry [8]. In 2004 FIAT (now FCA Group) started a research to capture designer's knowledge in the first steps of engine concept design. The resulting tool, EP, is a knowledge driven accelerator conceived for developing diesel and gasoline engines.

Even if initially KM appeared to be adopted only in large, multinational and international companies [9], now it has become the underlying source for successful organisations regardless of their size and geographical locations [10]. KM is beneficial in fields such as banking, telecommunications, production, manufacturing, and even the public sectors [11]. There is even evidence of the use of KM in the management of cultural heritage [12]. Among all these sectors, higher education institutions are exposed increasingly to marketplace pressures similarly to other industrial businesses. Hence, information practices and learning strategies, as KM, are gaining acceptance in education [13]. However, KM practices in universities are often limited to the storage and dissemination of lecture slides and other relevant materials in virtual learning environments [14]. Universities have not employed KM in its core business: education.

Politecnico di Torino has introduced KM to the issues related to automotive engine design. The course of Powertrain Components Design provides students with the necessary knowledge for the structural design, sizing and verification of main engine components by using analytical, semi-empirical and numerical approaches. These tasks allow students to perform calculations, but they might not have a graphical representation of their analysis. Modelling all the elements of the engine would become a time consuming task, focused on calculation rather than designing activities; further, students may lose the global picture of the designer activity.

Therefore, as first attempt, an instrument to generate a 3D parametric CAD model was developed; it provides the designer with a first simplified vision of the engine components [15]. However, even if this solution was a promising method, it presented some drawbacks. As a matter of fact, the developed software was devoted to teaching purposes and lacked completely industrial practical knowledge.

In the next sections, this paper presents the tool and implementation in a university course.

3 Engine Paradigm

A paradigm is a set of assumptions, concepts, values, and practices that constitute a way of viewing reality for the community that shares them, especially in an intellectual discipline [16]. Figure 1 shows the general paradigm process that has served as a framework for the study of the design practice in FCA. The model consists, firstly, in capturing knowledge by analysing previous projects. Next, it is necessary to formalize and store the common knowledge. Then, the final aim of the framework is to reuse the captured knowledge in new projects. However, in order to keep the knowledge at the state of the art, the model needs to be updated frequently.

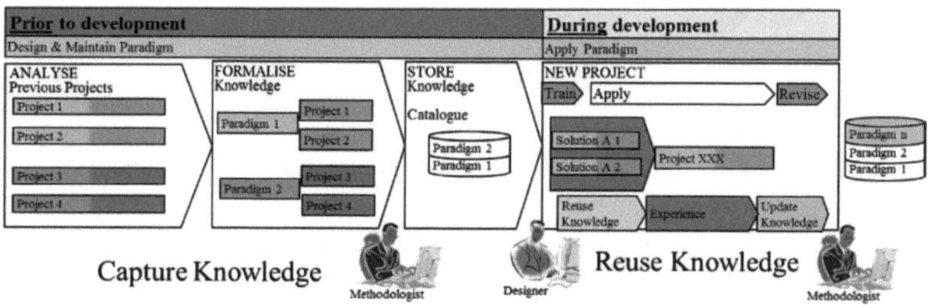

Fig. 1. Paradigm approach

The paradigm approach has been applied to organize and capture the "technical skills" of people during the product development process of FCA, with the aim of increasing their average performance without blocking individual creativity. It is an infrastructure built and integrated into the CAD software Nx. It was developed by Vittorio Romagnoli (former FGA worker) and Domenico Giannetto (SIEMENS Industry Software – Italy). The development process of an engine was thoroughly studied, a group of 8 people (consisting in developers and expert designers) met one or two times per week over a period of 5 years. The study resulted in an infrastructure that allows to easily to conceive, validate and compare several combustion engine alternatives. The same principles were employed in the development of Die Paradigm (DP), which is currently being used by FCA. The main objectives of EP are twofold: first, to model directly the key components of an engine; second, to define and validate several product alternatives.

Modelling

The EP application is installed as an add-on of the CAD software and it requires a special license for its use. The EP assembly is made up of simplified components. The management of these components (insertion/removal in the assembly, control of their size and characteristics) is performed via defined User Interfaces (UI). At first, the components are created as copies (templates) of parts that exist in a library. Both the part library and UI can be easily modified and/or extended.

The main engine assembly consists of four functional groups (FG). Each FG is built by adding the parts that conforms the sub-assembly. Furthermore, each part is composed of smaller modules. In Fig. 2 the FG crankshaft-conrod is presented. It is composed by four modules: counterweight (shown in orange), no counterweight, distribution terminal and flywheel. The modular strategy allows the system to easily respond to modifications. The actual configuration is a 4 cylinder engine and if the number of cylinders is extended or reduced the system automatically adds or eliminates modules.

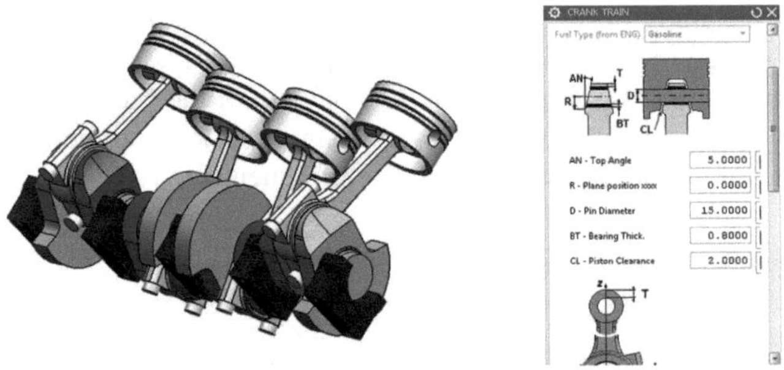

Fig. 2. User interface and functional groups (Color figure online)

EP makes extensive use of parametric models that are computer representations of a design constructed with geometrical entities. Each entity has several attributes (properties): some of them are fixed (constraints); others can vary (parameters) [17]. The generation of a geometry defined by dimensions, parameters, attributes and rules keep the coherence of the design. This information is used, at a higher level, to propagate data between different layers of the assembly (interpart expressions) and to create associative copies of geometry between parts (wave links). EP consistently supports the parametric design of parts and assemblies: its structure allows keeping the design consistent with the constraints and thus increasing the designer ability to explore ideas by reducing the tedium of rework. The system allows creating the geometry of a complete engine from a scratch in a matter of minutes (a skilled user employs 15 min. while a new user requires 3 h). Figure 3 shows a complete example of an engine developed with the support of EP.

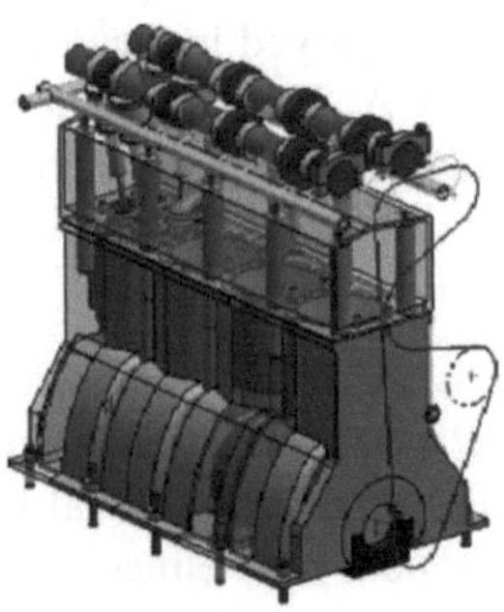

Fig. 3. Engine paradigm

Product Validation

Once the geometry has been created, the concept of the best engine configuration amongst several options must be validated. Starting from the preliminary product requirements, designers follow their train of thought, perform calculations and use technical languages to describe a potential solution. The design process is iterative and reaches the final solution after several loops, as part of the required data is not available at the beginning. At this stage the designer needs a project dashboard that monitors the current status of the product alternatives in terms of values and checks performed.

EP is able to control and maintain the consistency between several part-sketches belonging to different parts managed in the product study. Figure 4a shows the main Engine data dashboard that contains all the information that can be modified at the main assembly level. Figure 4b presents a particular frame of the Engine General Data. The designer can change the values of all the different parameters. Some of these inputs are not independent with each other; the unconstrained changes may lead to a condition where constraints are not respected. Hence, a set of checkers (green circle in the picture) have been implemented to help the designer to quickly evaluate if entered values are meaningful. Moreover, it is possible to fix the value of an important parameter (see the green lock of Fig. 4c) once it has been determined. In this case, the designer can continue to explore solutions with the certainty that this input cannot be changed.

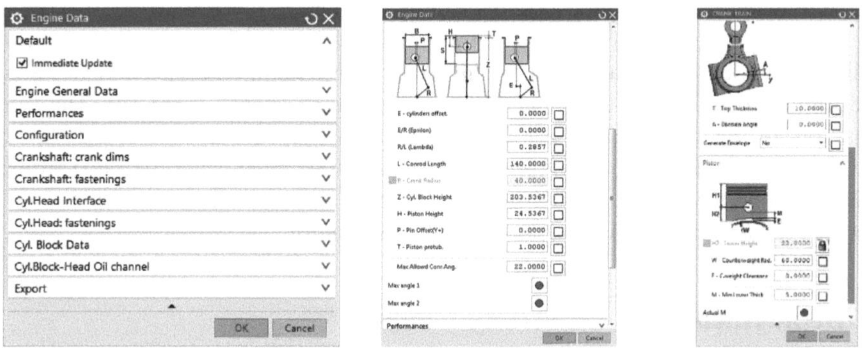

a) b) c)

Fig. 4. (a) Main engine data (b) Engine general data overview (c) Checker (Color figure online)

The system also allows to quickly configure products alternatives while assuring compliance with international standards or industrial best practices. Figure 5a shows two possible valve arrangements; the designer will choose the best solution according to the intake/exhaust location. Once the general schema has been defined, the distance between valves and between valves and engine head walls must be considered. This particular requirement is regulated by a FCA best practice. The system automatically calculates such distance (which is the result of the valve's angle) and shows a green flag (Fig. 5b) if the requirement is met. Finally, the 3D geometry is regenerated (Fig. 5c).

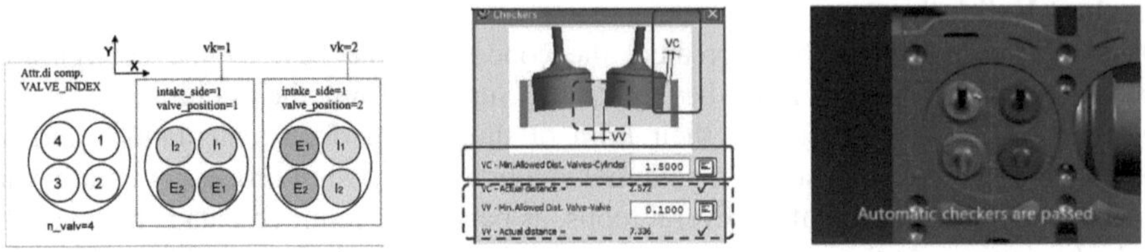

a) b) c)

Fig. 5. (a) Valve arrangement (b) Valve angle checker (c) Regenerated model (Color figure online)

4 System Upgrading and Pilot Test

EP was originally developed in a previous Nx version (Unigraphics) and, since the development was stopped in 2009, it was not sustained over time. It was then necessary to analyse the porting of the old structure to a newer version. As stated before, a similar tool, Die Paradigm (DP), was developed soon after EP ended. It was decided to use the existing DP infrastructure in order to reduce the development time. Several meetings were necessary to agree the best strategy both from the technical point of view, with SIEMENS Industry Software – Italy, and from the property rights, with FCA. The complete updating of the tool took over three months.

After the successful EP upgrading, training on the use of the tool was necessary for all the stakeholders that participate to the project. The training consisted in two phases. The former included the complete development of an engine using EP. The overall behaviour of the structure was tested and several issues were identified and corrected. The latter consisted in the development of a custom example using the same structure. This was done to allow a better comprehension on the basic function of the tool. The tool was then installed and distributed in the laboratories.

5 Deployment in a University Course

The M.Sc. course of Powertrain Components Design is included in the 2nd year of the automotive engineering curriculum in Politecnico di Torino. Approximately 40 students attend it each year. The course has a total duration of 100 h. Approximately, 60 h are used for theoretical aspects concerning engine and transmission design, while the remaining time is employed for laboratory activities. The laboratory practice is divided in the course's main topics: 20 h for powertrain concepts and 20 h for components design. EP is used in the latter section.

Students that attend this course come from different universities, different countries and different backgrounds (mechanical engineering, automotive engineering, production systems, etc.).

The goal of the practice is to design an engine while respecting the following constrains: (i) 4 cylinder gasoline engine, (ii) overall displacement around 1.2 ltrs and

(iii) power delivery 70 kW. Moreover, the development of the engine should take place as it is done in actual industrial practices, thus collaborative work is required. Students are requested to create a common engine; still each student faces different challenges and responsibilities. The group division and assignments are reported in Table 1. The course chair defined the group division randomly. The only driving criterion was to avoid more than three people from the same country, in order to allow student's interaction and integration.

Table 1. Group subdivision for engine design practice

Group	Goals	People
Project management	Definition of the engine layout and management of the group activities	2
Piston	Design of the piston, evaluation of piston slap, thermal analysis of the piston for defining the proper size, rings conformability	6
Piston pin	Design of the pin. Static and fatigue verification	2
Connecting rod	Design of con-rod, considering bearing and screws	6
Crankshaft	Flywheel, crank, check, crank pin and journal pin. Analytical analysis of torsional behaviour, potential mass damper usage, lubrication, drawing of the solution. Static and modal finite element verification. Definition of journal bearing	12
Crankcase	Definition of the geometry and of the construction philosophy, evaluation of water circuit, drawing and static verification. Liner dimensioning	5
Oil pan	Drawing, modal analysis, optimization procedure	4
Cylinder head	Dimensioning and drawing, static analysis. Definition of the valvetrain and drivetrain system, valve spring definition	5
Manifold	Design of intake and exhaust manifold, computation of exhaust manifold	3

6 Results

At the end of the course, students presented their results. The evaluation of this presentation counts for a third of the final score. Additionally, direct student interview was performed to obtain feedback on the course. An interesting and useful discussion took place and pros and cons were highlighted.

Positive Aspects

Mainly, the course achieved its objectives satisfactorily and the contents of the course were considered original by the majority of students. The teaching method and material given were highly appreciated. EP allowed the students of the group to provide a complete assembly of the engine in less than 4 weeks. The main constraints, described in Sect. 5 were respected. All the groups successfully developed the requested tasks on time. The obtained result is visible in Fig. 6.

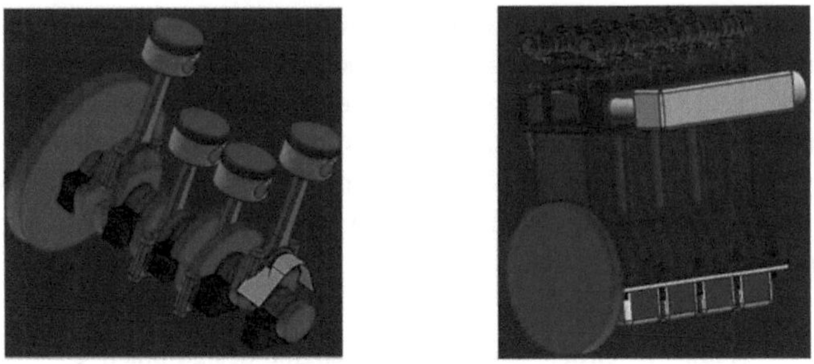

Fig. 6. Engine designed by the students

EP allowed the students to reach a first design attempt of the overall engine in the established 20 h of laboratory. On the contrary, the practice on powertrain concepts did not reach similar results, even if the same amount of time to this task were employed. This fact highlights the didactic relevance of EP.

In addition, students appreciated the easy and fast mounting of parts thanks to templates. The easiness of the UI was also greatly appreciated. Though, the most relevant aspect was the possibility to rapidly change all important engine parameters.

Future Improvements

The laboratory infrastructure is only composed by 32-bits computers while the CAD system requires exclusively 64-bits machines. In order to by-pass this problem, a set of virtual machines were installed and distributed over the 32-bit machines. The infrastructure worked correctly but performed rather slow, especially when working with big assemblies.

One non-technological aspect that affected the development of the exercise is the previous knowledge on the CAD system. The M.Sc. course is attended by students that have heterogeneous education and not all of them were confident with the use of the CAD tool. Such students tried to develop their parts in other systems and they found difficult the integration with EP.

Another issue that restrains the didactic objectives it the engine architecture: EP is limited to in-line engines because when it was created, there were no plans of developing other kinds of engines. Moreover, EP lacks of some important components such as the oil pan, intake and exhaust manifolds, valvetrain activation systems and oil pump. It is important to highlight that these components were designed by the students and they can be now imported to the EP library and to the UI. In addition, some sketches of the existing components must be changed in order to increase the geometrical control. For example, the counterweight opening angle should be included in the UI in order to quickly modify the counterweight mass.

The most important aspect regards the collaborative work. At this stage, EP works in a standalone version and it is not integrated to any Product Lifecyle Management (PLM) system. For this reason, each group worked independently and, after completing the study, communicated the final information to the project management team. This is a major issue that needs to be addressed immediately to assure a correct working method.

7 Conclusions

In this paper the introduction of an industrial Knowledge Management tool in a high level education institution was presented. This contribution extends the state of the art by showing evidence that the tool has been employed for didactic purposes and not only in staff applications. In fact, the use of Engine Paradigm in the course of Powertrain Components Design allowed students to take effective decisions while developing an engine. Students were exposed to the complexity of developing a product with the help of an actual industrial application. The tool facilitated the evaluation of several design alternatives while reducing the tedium of rework. The results obtained, compared to a similar exercise performed in the same course (same students), are really promising.

The experience gained in this first application has allowed authors to identify strengths, weaknesses and improvement opportunities. On one hand, positive aspects assures the goodness of the teaching strategies. On the other hand, the identified opportunities are now being studied. The proposed improvements comes from both students and professors. The embedded knowledge defined by its creators it is now being enriched with the actual requirements of the university.

References

1. Gold, A.H., Malhotra, A., Segars, A.H.: Knowledge management: an organizational capabilities perspective. J. Manag. Inf. Syst. **18**(1), 185–214 (2015). doi:10.1080/07421222.2001.11045669
2. Birasnav, M.: Knowledge management and organizational performance in the service industry: the role of transformational leadership beyond the effects of transactional leadership. J. Bus. Res. **67**, 1622–1629 (2014). doi:10.1016/j.jbusres.2013.09.006
3. Organisation for Economic Co-operation and Development: Oslo Manual - Guidelies for Collecting and Interpreting Innovation Data, 3rd edn. OECD and Eurostat (2005). ISBN: 92-64-01308-3
4. Bielawsky, L., Metcalf, D.: Blended Elearning: Integrating Knowledge, Performance Support, and Online Learning. HRD Press (2002). ISBN: 978-0874258608
5. La Rocca, G., van Tooren, M.J.L.: Knowledge-based engineering to support aircraft multidisciplinary design and optimization. Proc. Inst. Mech. Eng. Part G: J. Aerosp. Eng. **224**(9), 1041–1055 (2010). doi:10.1243/09544100JAERO592
6. Hiekata, K., Grau, M., Stjepandić, J.: Cross-domain collaboration in shipbuilding. In: The IFIP WG5.1 11th International Conference on Product Lifecycle Management – PLM14, Yokohama, Japan (2014)
7. Ford, G., Igba, J., McMahon, C., Alemzadeh, K., Rowley, C., Henningsen, K.: Knowledge management: a cross sectorial comparison of wind generation and naval engineering. In: Fukuda, S., Bernard, A., Gurumoorthy, B., Bouras, A. (eds.) PLM 2014. IAICT, vol. 442, pp. 129–138. Springer, Heidelberg (2014). doi:10.1007/978-3-662-45937-9_14
8. Sukumaran, S., Shetty, M.V.: Knowledge management in automobile: application of a value chain approach using KM tools. In: Internet Technology and Secured Transactions, London (2009). doi:10.1109/ICITST.2009.5402554

9. Wong, K.Y.: Critical success factors for implementing knowledge management in small and medium enterprises. Ind. Manag. Data Syst. **105**(3), 261–279 (2005). doi:10.1108/02635570510590101
10. Okunoye, A., Karsten, H.: Where the global needs the local: variation in enablers in the knowledge management process. J. Glob. Inf. Technol. Manag. **5**(3), 12–31 (2002). doi:10.1080/1097198X.2002.10856329
11. Omotayo, F.O.: Knowledge management as an important tool in organisational management: a review of literature. Libr. Philos. Pract. (e-journal), Paper 1238 (2015). http://digitalcommons.unl.edu/libphilprac/1238
12. Hervy, B., Laroche, F., Bernard, A., Kerouanton, J.-L.: Co-working for knowledge management in cultural heritage: towards a PLM for museum. In: 10th IFIP WG 5.1 International Conference, PLM 2013, Nantes (2013). doi:10.1007/978-3-642-41501-2_32
13. Petrides, L.A., Nodine, T.R.: Knowledge Management in Education: Defining the Landscape. Institute for the Study of Knowledge Management in Education, Half Moon Bay (2003)
14. Leung, N., Shamsub, H., Tsang, N., Au, B.: Enhancing learning experience of coursework students in higher education: a knowledge management methodology. In: EDULEARN 2014 Proceedings (2014). http://hdl.handle.net/1959.3/397253
15. Rosso, C., Delprete, C., Bonisoli, E., Tornincasa, S.: Integrated CAD/CAE functional design for engine components and assembly. SAE Technical Paper, p. 12 (2011). doi:10.4271/2011-01-1071
16. Kuhn, T.S.: The Structure of Scientific Revolutions. The University of Chicago (1962). ISBN: 978-0226458083
17. Barrios-Hernandez, C.R.: Thinking parametric design: introducing parametric Gaudi. Des. Stud. **21**(2), 99–107 (2006). doi:10.1016/j.destud.2005.11.006

Enhancing Domain Specific Sentiment Lexicon for Issue Identification

Madhusudanan N(✉), B. Gurumoorthy, and Amaresh Chakrabarti

Virtual Reality Lab, Centre for Product Design and Manufacturing,
Indian Institute of Science, Bangalore, India
{madhu, bgm, ac123}@cpdm.iisc.ernet.in

Abstract. The research work reported here is part of a larger project aimed at acquiring knowledge about issues in assembly, from documents. In order to do so, the first step is to identify the presence of issues. For this, sentiment analysis is proposed as a means. The presence of issues is proposed to be found by detecting negative sentiment. However, general English sentiment lexicons are not enough to detect negative sentiment in specialized domains, in this case, aircraft assembly. This paper studies an existing sentiment analysis tool, and creates an enhanced sentiment lexicon on the basis of the performance of the tool. The enhanced domain lexicon is proposed as the solution to identifying domain specific issues.

Keywords: Natural language text · Issues in assembly · Sentiment analysis

1 Introduction

Knowledge is an important asset in an organization and is generated through many complex processes. Hence it is useful to capture and reuse this knowledge, especially where it can improve time or costs. The aim of the research, which the present work is a part of, is to acquire knowledge about manufacturing - in particular, knowledge of assembly issues from documents. Such acquired knowledge is intended to be used to detect potential issues in current or future assembly plans. The domain under study is assembly of aircraft structures. The knowledge to be acquired is that of issues that arise in assembly stage of manufacturing. This knowledge is then expected to be fed back to assembly planners to foresee issues in their current assembly plans. In the context of a product's lifecycle, this amounts to reuse of knowledge from a later stage of the lifecycle in an earlier stage. Such a reuse of knowledge is an important factor for PLM systems [1].

The overall process of acquiring knowledge is shown in Fig. 1, and the focus of this paper is shown in the dotted rectangle. From previous assembly processes, documents about problems in assembly may have been generated. These input documents are processed in the first step to segregate portions of documents that are related to aircraft assembly. Among these relevant portions, issues or problems that are present in the text are to be identified. This implies finding parts of text that talk about these issues in the domain. Once such issues are identified, the causes of these issues and

R. Harik et al. (Eds.): PLM 2016, IFIP AICT 492, pp. 13–21, 2016.
DOI: 10.1007/978-3-319-54660-5_2

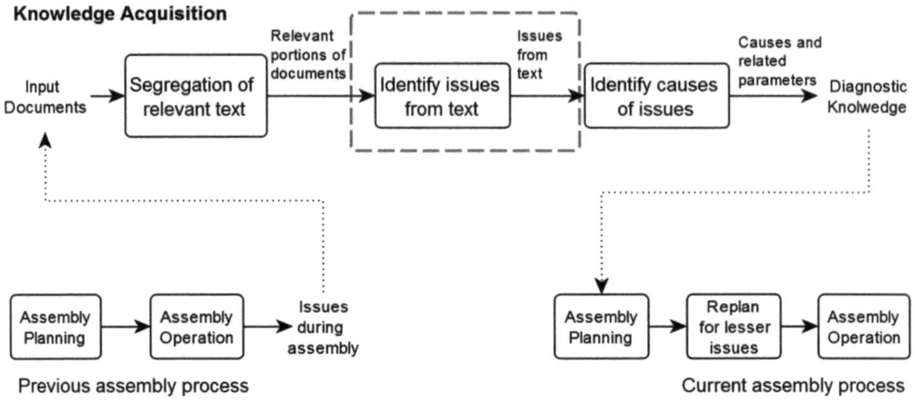

Fig. 1. Overview of the process to acquire knowledge of issues

parameters related to these causes are to be found. This knowledge about issues, their causes, and the parameters leading to the causes, should be structured as diagnostic knowledge. This structured knowledge would become the source for predicting assembly issues in the current assembly process.

To illustrate the knowledge reuse, consider an example where a document has been written about problems faced during an earlier assembly operation. An issue that a *particular riveting gun does not provide enough force for clean riveting* (although specifications say otherwise) is described in this document. Hence a riveting gun with a higher force specification is prescribed. If there is another assembly that is currently in the planning stage, and it also involves riveting, knowledge of this issue is relevant. Hence the planners can using a riveting gun of a higher force in practice and thus avoid a revision in assembly planning, due to this knowledge being available beforehand.

In order to identify issues from text, the first step is to identify sections that talk about issues. In an earlier paper [2], the authors have evaluated various methods and finally identified two possible means for such an identification. As a more practical solution, the method of sentiment analysis, which is a set of natural language processing techniques, was chosen.

1.1 Sentiment Analysis

Sentiment analysis (SA) is a set of natural language processing techniques whose aim is to determine whether a given piece of text is carrying a positive, negative, or neutral sentiment [3] (i.e. the sentiment polarity of the text), and a numeric value to indicate the strength of the sentiment. For example, '*happy*' is positive, '*very happy*' is more positive, and '*not happy*' is negative. Sentiment analysis has found use in domains like movie reviews, and consumer electronics [4]. Sentiment can be calculated at various levels in text - at document, sentence, phrase or word-levels.

1.2 Research Problem

Although sentiment analysis is useful, adapting it to a specific domain is not a straightforward process. This process of adapting this technique to the domain of aircraft assembly is described in this paper.

The contribution of this paper is a means of enhancing domain lexicon in the field of aircraft assembly, in order to detect negative sentiment in documents. Such a negative sentiment, it is hoped, will be linked to a potential problem description in the document of interest.

2 Tools for Sentiment Analysis

2.1 Different Types of Sentiment Analysis Tools

There are two major groups of sentiment analysis techniques, depending on the practical application [5]. The first group is that of supervised classification methods based on training with large amounts of positive and negative text. The second group is to construct lexicons of predefined words for a given sentiment task in a domain. Both these groups of methods have their distinct advantages and disadvantages. For example, the former is sensitive to training data supplied (and hence can adapt well to a domain, given enough data), but it also demands the availability of large amounts of data. The latter does not necessitate such labelling of data, but requires detailed study to build suitable sets of positive and negative words.

The need for large amount of training data is also prevalent in the domain of aircraft assembly. The currently available limited set of sources of documents are from the World Wide Web, and there is no single coherent source of such data.

2.2 Choice of Tool

Due to the difficulties in finding sufficiently large training data in the domain of interest, we chose a lexicon-based approach to our task of identifying sections mentioning issues in text. From the available choices in this approach, two tools, namely SentiWordNet [6] and SO-CAL [3] were considered. SentiWordNet is a lexicon based on WordNet with sentiment values assigned to words. SO-CAL, on the other hand, is based on a detailed theory of how sentiment is not just dependent on single words, but also gets modified, using valence shifters [7]. Since this could judge overall sentiment for sentences, SO-CAL has been used as the tool for Sentiment Analysis in this research. For further details on this tool, readers are referred to Taboada et al. [3].

3 Shortcomings of General Sentiment Lexicons

As mentioned in the previous section, we now have a choice of a Sentiment Analysis (SA) tool to identify locations in text where issues are being described. The next step in the research was to verify if the lexicon, which was developed for a general English language texts (or for a different domain) would be still applicable to the domain of aircraft assembly. As mentioned in Kanayama and Nasukawa [8], it is more difficult to prepare domain dependent lexicons than domain independent ones.

Fahrni and Klenner [9] have developed a combination of target nouns and adjectives that bear sentiment. This requires large, organized resources such as Wikipedia, and documents which bear the correct sentiment polarities (i.e. whether the text is positive, negative or neutral) for the objects. We are currently not having such resources for the domain of aircraft assembly. Denecke [10] compared lexicon based methods with machine learning based methods, concluding that the latter were better with SentiWordNet scores, doing well in multi-domain classification. However, sentence level sentiment was not studied, and machine learning based methods require labelled training data. Yue et al. [11] proposed an optimization based method to learn target-specific sentiment words by combining multiple knowledge sources. It, however assumes the availability of *aspects* (set of words describing a topic), either from experts or from an automatic method, which requires it to be combined for operation. This method is also capable of handling clause level sentiment. Muhammed et al. [12] attempted to extend a general lexicon to a social media lexicon and then combining the general lexicon with the domain-specific lexicon. This, once again, was dependant on a distant supervision dataset to be labelled and available. Ohana et al. [13] suggest the use of many different lexicons with a score adjustment based on term frequencies, in order to improve domain-independent sentiment classification. However, there are no directions to generate a lexicon for a given domain, in the absence of one.

As seen in the various methods discussed above there are several practical issues in adapting them, such as the availability of training data, or availability of other information that complements the lexicon building process. From a practical perspective, the simplest, yet useful method seemed to be to extend the lexicon manually for the chosen SA tool.

3.1 Study of Existing Lexicon on Domain Documents

In order to understand the current performance of the chosen SA tool on domain specific documents, a set of documents was initially chosen. These were documents available over the World Wide Web, and were about issues in manufacturing. SO-CAL was then used to analyze these documents, and the results were studied.

For every sentence, the researchers compared the polarity of sentiment assigned, with what was perceived to be the actual polarity. It is important to state here that the strength of sentiment (how strongly positive/negative) could not be considered, as that requires considerably more subjects and efforts to arrive at commonly agreed numbers.

A total of 357 sentences from 5 different documents were studied. Out of these, true positives and true negatives, as well as false positives and false negatives were identified. When we say "True Positive" here, it means that the sentence was positive in sentiment, and was also marked positive by the SA tool. The numbers are presented in Table 1. Since the original focus is to identify only negative sections of text, even sentences with SO-CAL score 0 were considered positive for this study (24 sentences were indecisive, hence they were not counted here).

Table 1. Initial performance of the tool, without adding any specific domain lexicon.

		Classification by SA tool	
		Positive	Negative
Classification by researchers	Positive	144 (TP)	20 (FN)
	Negative	68 (FP)	101 (TN)

Some examples of these four categories were:

True Positive (TP):
"*A good rule to be used is that the number of blind rivets needs to be increased roughly in the proportion of 5 blind rivets for 3 solid rivets.*"

True Negative (TN):
"*In my opinion, this defeats the purpose of these rivets in the first place.*"

False Positive (FP):
"*But the mechanics say managers keep pressuring them to fix the planes faster.*"

False Negative (FN):
"*From race cars to airplanes, the blind rivet is the fastener of choice for joining sheet metal.*" (It may be noted that the word 'blind' triggers the classification as negative sentiment)

3.2 Inadequacies of General Sentiment Lexicons

As seen in Table 1, it was observed that there are large number cases where the negative (or positive) sentiment in a sentence is correctly identified by the SA tool. However, there were still other cases where it was not identified correctly (68 and 20 sentences for the positive and negative cases by tool). Each of these cases where the assigned sentiment did not match the opinion of the researchers was studied. The observations were classified into the following categories:

- Ambiguity of word meaning: The sense of a word differs, based on the context in which it is used. For example, the word '*issue*' was marked negative even when it was used in the context of a magazine's date. Also, domain-specific use is a huge contributor to ambiguity, since a term that is used in general English would have a different meaning in manufacturing. For example, a '*blind*' rivet is not negative in meaning; '*upset*' a rivet is not negative either; however, '*crossed*' wires is negative. At times, this can be seen more as domain-specific meaning, rather than ambiguity.
- Missing entries in the lexicon: There were many words in the SA tool's in-built lexicon which did not have a corresponding entry for sentiment score. Fortunately, SO-CAL provides a list of such missing entries which cannot be scored, for a corresponding Part-Of-Speech. Some examples were '*non-conformance*', '*openness*', and '*carcinogenic*'. Also missing are certain entries that are phrases indicative of sentiment, such as '*got to our head*' and '*build up*'.

- Clause level sentiment change: In the current work, the unit chosen is sentences, since the SA tool being used can handle sentences. However, even within sentences, there may be opposing sentiments in different clauses, which are finally summed up. For example, consider the following sentence:
  'The program had been the gold standard of industrial design tools in the 1980s but was only capable of producing two-dimensional blueprints'.
  In this sentence, the first part of the sentence appears to be largely positive whereas the second part is negative, and they are connected by what is called as the 'but' connective in literature [14].

4 Enhancing Lexicon for Domain Specificity

The previous section described various reasons as to why a general sentiment lexicon did not perform as expected on text that is specific to a domain. In this section, we describe means of resolving some of these concerns.

The list of missing entries was the first means for improving the lexicon to result in better sentiment analysis. SO-CAL outputs a list of words that could be resolved by its tagger, but marked as missing in its dictionaries. The list is classified into four categories on the basis of part-of-speech, namely nouns, verbs, adjectives and adverbs. For the initial set of 5 chosen documents, this list consisted of 2160 nouns, 1080 verbs, 484 adjectives, and 152 adverbs. This list was then collected and manually analyzed. The objective was to assign a single number (between −5 and +5) to each word that indicates its sentiment specific to the current domain. The sentiment values were only *prior* values, which meant they were values for context-independent use of the words.

4.1 Assignment of Domain-Specific Sentiment Values

Based on the above list, assignment of sentiment value for the list of words was to be chosen. Since there was no specific guideline that was available, we chose the following scheme to assign these values. Since the maximum sentiment value was +5 and minimum was −5, we decided to limit our values between +4 and −4 for the extreme cases, with one point for a buffer. Some generic guidelines were,

- If the word indicates high efficiency, or solution to a problem, it was given a score of 4 ("*much-lauded*").
- If it reflects cause for improvements or progress, it was given a score of 2 ("*completion*").
- An object description of name was given a neutral score ("*hydraulic*").
- If something is not hazardous but still problematic, it got a score of −2 ("*inaccessible*").
- If there is a hazard involved the word got a score of −4 ("*burst*").
- Any word which was felt to be in between these categories was given an appropriate middle value, although such a value is subjective.

4.2 Evaluating the Effects of Adding User Lexicon

The user specific dictionary was then tested. This first iteration of testing involved testing the effects only for the additional dictionary. The same set of documents were run through SO-CAL, after configuring it to use the additional dictionary. The results of this first iteration of testing are shown in Table 2 (Please note that the 'Zero'th iteration in the table refers to testing without any domain lexicon being added, from Table 1).

Table 2. Effects of enhanced dictionary (first, second iteration) and changed settings (second iteration)

Iteration	TP	TN	FP	FN	Others
Zero	144	101	68	20	24
First	140	112	57	24	24
Second	145	138	31	19	24

There was improvement in terms of reduced False Positives and False Negatives. There was also an increase in True negatives However, there was also a minor reduction in number of True Positives.

The FN and FP cases were then analysed using the same approach described in Sect. 3.1. Multiple reasons were identified for the current performance of the tool. Some of the sentiment values needed a modification for the sentence level sentiment to be reflected correctly. In other cases, we realized that not only the specialized dictionary, but also the settings of the tool itself had played a role in deciding sentiment. These settings were related to the ignoring of sentiment words if they were in quotes or in irrealis mode (e.g. "*may* forget"). However, for our purposes both these modes were required to be present. Also, to a minor extent, some words from the existing SO-CAL dictionary itself had to be assigned a modified score, so that their prior sentiment is appropriate for the domain.

In the second iteration, there were three changes made in the analysis: the modified extra dictionary added by the user (19 instances), ignoring the quotes and irrealis factors (15 instances), and a small number of modifications to the original sentiment dictionary (2 instances). SO-CAL was again re-run on the same test documents. The results can be found in the third row of Table 2.

It is observed that the best improvements are present in the True Negatives and False Positives. Between the initial state and the second iteration the number of true negatives has increased by 37 instances, which is a 10.3% improvement over the total number of sentences. Similarly the number of false positives has fallen by the same number of instances.

5 Conclusions

This paper has discussed a method to improve the performance of a sentiment classification tool for the domain of aircraft assembly. Since there is a specific purpose for which sentiment analysis was used (to detect the presence of issues), the study focused more on the negative sentiment identification.

The study led to two means of improving the performance of the tool for the domain of aircraft assembly. The first is the construction of a dictionary of sentiment terms with prior sentiments assigned to them. The second was, to a lesser extent, the ignoring of *irrealis* and *modal* factors in text. By testing the tool's performance on sample documents from the domain of interest repeatedly over two iterations, the dictionary has also been improved. Though we expected a larger number of modifications in the original English dictionary, there were not many that were eventually made.

The results clearly establish the feasibility of the tool to perform well to detect negative sentiment in domain specific documents. This would enable us to detect presence of issues by using sentiment analysis as the method of choice.

6 Future Work

The research reported in this paper can be subjected to many improvements. As discussed in Sect. 4.2, the major improvement that is immediately possible is to assign finely tuned values of sentiment priors to words in the dictionaries. The number of entries in the dictionary will have to increase once more documents are studied, and might reach a steady state once a large number of documents have been studied.

From a larger perspective, an important part would be to have target specific sentiment lexicon, and a means to use it. The sentiment value of a word may be of two types - prior, or context (target) dependant. We have currently addressed only the prior values in the aircraft assembly domain. As seen in the example of "cold pizza" vs "cold coke" by Fahrni and Klenner [9], it is necessary to associate specific words which are context (target) sensitive. Although there were no concrete cases in our test examples which suffered because of this, we can foresee that this may well be a problem (e.g. "*blind rivets*" is not negative, but "*blind spot*" is).

The other issue, seen in some cases, is that of ambiguity of word sense (By "*late*" autumn…). This is a commonly occurring issue during processing of natural language text, and methods like Word Sense Disambiguation (WSD) are suggested as means to resolve it.

From the perspective of creating the domain specific sentiment dictionary, creating a lexicon in a manual way is usually subjective and might be prone to errors. Automatic methods, many of which have also been described in literature here, may be used to improve the size and quality of the dictionary, since it remains to be seen how the size of the dictionary would grow over larger numbers of documents.

Acknowledgments. The authors are very grateful to Prof. Maite Taboada of the Simon Fraser University for making available the SO-CAL tool and the in-built dictionaries of SO-CAL for our research purposes, since the tool is the foundation for building the sentiment analysis work. This project was carried out with funding from The Boeing Company USA, under SID Project PC 36030.

References

1. Ameri, F., Dutta, D.: Product lifecycle management: closing the knowledge loops. Comput.-Aided Des. Appl. **2**(5), 577–590 (2005)
2. Madhusudanan, N., Gurumoorthy, B., Chakrabarti, A.: Evaluation of methods to identify assembly issues in text. In: Bouras, A., Eynard, B., Foufou, S., Thoben, K.-D. (eds.) PLM 2015. IAICT, vol. 467, pp. 495–504. Springer, Heidelberg (2016). doi:10.1007/978-3-319-33111-9_45
3. Taboada, M., et al.: Lexicon-based methods for sentiment analysis. Comput. linguist. **37**(2), 267–307 (2011)
4. Blitzer, J., Dredze, M., Pereira, F.: Biographies, bollywood, boom-boxes and blenders: domain adaptation for sentiment classification. In: ACL, vol. 7 (2007)
5. Gonçalves, P., et al.: Comparing and combining sentiment analysis methods. In: Proceedings of the first ACM Conference on Online Social Networks. ACM (2013)
6. Baccianella, S., Esuli, A., Sebastiani, F.: SentiWordNet 3.0: an enhanced lexical resource for sentiment analysis and opinion mining. In: LREC, vol. 10 (2010)
7. Polanyi, L., Zaenen, A.: Contextual valence shifters. In: Shanahan, J.G., Qu, Y., Wiebe, J. (eds.) Computing Attitude and Affect in Text: Theory and Applications, vol. 20, pp. 1–10. Springer, Heidelberg (2006)
8. Kanayama, H., Nasukawa, T.: Fully automatic lexicon expansion for domain-oriented sentiment analysis. In: Proceedings of the 2006 Conference on Empirical Methods in Natural Language Processing. Association for Computational Linguistics (2006)
9. Fahrni, A., Klenner, M.: Old wine or warm beer: target-specific sentiment analysis of adjectives. In: Proceedings of the Symposium on Affective Language in Human and Machine. AISB (2008)
10. Denecke, K.: Are SentiWordNet scores suited for multi-domain sentiment classification? In: Fourth International Conference on Digital Information Management, ICDIM 2009. IEEE (2009)
11. Lu, Y., et al.: Automatic construction of a context-aware sentiment lexicon: an optimization approach. In: Proceedings of the 20th International Conference on World Wide Web. ACM (2011)
12. Muhammad, A., et al.: Domain-based lexicon enhancement for sentiment analysis. In: SMA@ BCS-SGAI (2013)
13. Ohana, B., Tierney, B., Delany, S.-J.: Domain independent sentiment classification with many lexicons. In: 2011 IEEE Workshops of International Conference on Advanced Information Networking and Applications (WAINA). IEEE (2011)
14. Hatzivassiloglou, V., McKeown, K.R.: Predicting the semantic orientation of adjectives. In: Proceedings of the 35th Annual Meeting of the Association for Computational Linguistics and Eighth Conference of the European Chapter of the Association for Computational Linguistics. Association for Computational Linguistics (1997)

Knowledge Management and Big Data: Opportunities and Challenges for Small and Medium Enterprises (SME)

Patrick Mbassegue[1(✉)], Ma-Lorena Escandon-Quintanilla[2], and Mickaël Gardoni[2]

[1] Ecole Polytechnique, Montreal, Canada
Patrick.mbassegue@polymtl.ca
[2] Ecole de Technologie Supérieure, Montreal, Canada
Ma-lorena.escandon-quintanilla.1@etsmtl.net,
Mickael.gardoni@etsmtl.ca

Abstract. Whenever a new technology is made available, it is worth finding possible uses in different domains. The advancement of information technologies now enables a wealth of information to be digitally collected and exploited for knowledge management and reused for further knowledge creation. Big data enables organizations to capitalize on large amounts of data by bringing together different sources of information to find trends and knowledge that are only visible with large amounts of data. This knowledge can then be applied for knowledge exploration, exploitation and decision making.

Keywords: Knowledge management · Big data · Data analytics · SME Small medium enterprises

1 Introduction

Knowledge management allows companies to make the most out of the information they collect and generate. However, it relies on an ongoing effort by companies to keep their records, and process them continuously. It requires dedicated resources to explore the information generated outside organizational borders to remain competitive and be able to react to environmental changes.

New information technologies now make it possible to build a knowledge based which can include internal and external information, and provide insights and knowledge which can only be detected when large amounts of data are being studied.

In this paper, we discuss the link between big data tools and techniques and how they can support a knowledge management effort in a small or medium enterprise, as well as the challenges they might face when undergoing such efforts.

R. Harik et al. (Eds.): PLM 2016, IFIP AICT 492, pp. 22–31, 2016.
DOI: 10.1007/978-3-319-54660-5_3

2 Big Data and Managerial Implications

2.1 The Concept of Big Data

Big data stems from our current ability to generate exponential volumes of data. Data is everywhere and growing at an exponential rate (Lynch [1]; Tweed [2]; Delort [3]). It comes from individuals, groups, organizations, networks, connected objects, etc. (McKinsey [4]). However, it is necessary to find ways to make data more accessible (Dove and Jones [5]).

The current threshold of a big data set is about an exabyte, or a quintillion bytes" (Howkins [6]). Nonetheless, Howkins [6] explains that the criteria for big data is not only the size, but the variety in the data, the potential relationships between the data and the need for new tools to be able to exploit the data (see also Maniyka et al., 2001 in Kabir and Carayannis) [7]. Because data can be reused and analyzed in different ways to find new insights, companies need to take advantage of the wealth of data by using it in a more creative fashion (Howkins) [6].

The produced data is distinguished by a number of characteristics, also known as the 5Vs: volume, variety, velocity, veracity and value (Laney [8]; Koutroumpis and Leiponer [9]). The combination of these characteristics shows the richness they entail for organizations, especially for decision making.

The data also allows for a more precise understanding of phenomena and the discovery of relationships that exist between variables; to not only identify the linear causalities, but also the cross-effects between the variables involved in an observed phenomenon (Beyer and Laney [10]). Indeed, we not only try to understand what happens at time t, but also to identify the trend and what will materialize at t + 1. The predictive dimension, and consequently an ability to manage uncertainty, is sought: what is beneficial to the manager to successfully accomplish the primary tasks of management: plan, organize, manage, and control (POMC).

2.2 Big Data Needs SMEs

For organizations, the presence of this much data represents a challenge, as well as potential new opportunities (George et al. [11]). Consequently, SMEs face the same challenges and issues as large organizations concerning the need for information, to process it, and use it to make decisions. In this sense, SMEs are subject to a large volume of internal data (which they generate and/or collect) just as much as external (data produced in their specific industry, as well as for the overall business ecosystem). The data affecting SMEs is increasingly large; they are collected in real time from various sources (Liebowitz [12]; Tweed [2]). For SMEs, the imperatives of Big data are situated in 3 levels: internal environment, external environment and organizational performance.

Internally, SMEs are structured in different departments or functions, each of which generate and collect important volumes of data, but different in nature. For example, the data generated and collected in marketing department is different from the data in production, finance, human resources or supply management. All these data are necessary and essential to generate value (Delport [3]). SMEs need an infrastructure adapted to optimally exploit its data; in that way Big data attributes can reconcile all these disparate data and enable their processing on a common basis. It enables the optimization of exploitation activities.

The daily management practices show that the diversity of functions and data induces a managerial structural division which has a negative impact on the quality of decisions. However, the functions that make up the organizational structure are the basis and the architecture that enable SMEs to offer products and services customers expect.

Externally, SMEs are found in an environment that creates pressures to which they must develop adaptation strategies and solutions. However, this environment produces an exponential amount of data on different levels based on economic, political, competitive, technological, social and demographic variables (McKinsey [4]; George et al. [11]). To ensure its survival and especially improve its competitive position, SMEs must collect, process and integrate external data in decision making.

The market competition has expanded and is not limited by geographic boundaries; therefore, ignoring it will contribute to weaken the basis on which decisions are taken by SMEs. Moreover, the consideration of a large and diverse volume of data enables a better understanding of customers, the quality of the service provided, and its relevance to each of the specific groups of consumers. Thus, based on a critical mass of diverse data, external to the organization, SMEs can better understand its ecosystem, environment and offer products and services that serve its various market segments (Chan [13]; George et al. [11]).

Based on these environmental constraints, SMEs need to consider all the data at their disposal, both to optimize the foundation of its operations and the combination of its internal resources to improve its external position and its ability to provide the answers needed by its clients.

3 Knowledge Management and Managerial Implications

3.1 Knowledge Management Concept and Activities

The concept of KM or knowledge management is subject of different representations, particularly among sociologists (Latour [14]), philosophers of science (Polanyi [15]), economists (Winter and Nelson [16]), industrial economists (Porter [17]), promoters of knowledge engineering (Tarondeau [18]; Ermine [19]) and strategic management (Wernerfelt [20]; Barney [21]; Wright and van Wijk [22]). Despite these differences, it appears that knowledge becomes a source of income that allows a firm to stand out in its market or markets. Therefore, knowledge prevails as much at individual and collective levels (service, department, division) as at an organizational level (Lebowitz [23]; Alavi and Leidner [24]).

Knowledge management activities correspond to different organizational aspects, namely managerial practices, material and technical structures that enable the identification, processing and dissemination of knowledge (Veybel and Prieur [25]; Ling [26]). In this case, we are talking more of a global knowledge management that takes into account different aspects namely: 1- The implementation process of activities, material and organizational infrastructure; 2- From which the players in the organization develop collaborative relationships, partnerships and exchanges; 3- The development, coding, creation, acquisition, storage, processing and use of knowledge; 4- By relying on human relations and organizational support, relationship, material and technology.

The overall management of knowledge should lead to a situation that favors organizational performance. The latter is generated by the emergence of a new culture and practices based on the exploitation of organizational knowledge. KM also allows the organization to eventually build a competitive advantage and improve or maintain its competitive position.

Managers then have the mandate to build the organizational capacity to develop a competitive advantage that is materialized by a better competitive position. Knowledge thus becomes a matter of strategic interest. The resources mobilized by the organization must allow the creation of value in a context of increasingly competitive markets. To do this, managers must seek different ways to promote the creation of value; it is necessary to master and apply individual and collective intelligence based on the combination of available knowledge. KM is therefore one of the critical ingredients to create value, especially in today's economy which is increasingly intangible and service based.

3.2 Knowledge Management and Needs for SMEs

KM is recognized by many as a framework of choice for organizations to create value: What about small and medium-sized enterprises (SMEs)? SMEs, beyond their relative weight in the ecosystem, are characterized by other dimensions. They are generally small in size and concentrated in specific market segments (Marchesnay and Julien [27]). Their income depends on a limited number of market segments, products or services, makes them especially vulnerable. There are less diversified than large organizations (Julien [28]). All these dimensions weaken the SME.

Furthermore, management is often concentrated in the hands of the founder who also serves as senior manager or CEO. The CEO not only has the authority because he or she controls the capital, but also the legitimacy of being the founder (Julien [28]; OCDE [29]). Because of its position and its multi-dimensional role, the place of the founder is critical. The success and performance of the SME will depend on his/her potential, abilities and knowledge.

In terms of management practices, it appears that the strategic fragility of the SME is also characterized by the practice of solving problems day to day without relying systematically on previous experiences (Asmaa [30]). Thus, the accumulated experiences held by the few employees who are part of the SME may not be taken into account.

In the SME, all structural features related to production or service delivery system predominate. But what characterizes the organizational performance is the structural balance between structure strategy and the ability of leaders to take into account the dynamics of the environment by offering answers (products or services) expected by potential customers.

Indeed, based on the findings relating to the SME management practices, KM is an indispensable framework to be effective and efficient. Effectiveness is induced by KM to the extent that identification activities will help better identify the needs of clients. Efficiency is induced by the capitalization of both internal and external knowledge. The capitalization of knowledge contributes to the optimization of the resources mobilized to provide products and services. This optimization of resources also has an impact on the costs of goods and services, because based on the capitalization and enhancement of knowledge it is possible to find innovative solutions to improve quality and productivity (Mbassegue et al. [31]).

KM for the SME is critical because it will help adopt management practices that will allow combining all critical resources, namely its processes and knowledge. Building a collective and organizational intelligence, permitted because of KM, promotes the emergence of shared practices of assimilated knowledge, mastered and produced by all actors of the SME.

4 The Basis of Knowledge Management and Big Data Integration

4.1 Association of Knowledge Management and Big Data: Strategic and Operational Necessity

Starting with Nonaka and Takeuchi [32], the domain of Knowledge Management has been engaged in researching the way knowledge is created and transmitted within companies. This domain evolved to include the adoption of computer systems to support different aspects of KM. KM is at the service of the organization, particularly for value creation. In this sense, it's important to characterize knowledge management activities and big date dimensions to find a common base for integration. On one side, knowledge activities means identify, capture, store, analyze, disseminate, share and develop new solutions and innovative solutions which contribute to this creation of value. On the other side the characterization of Big Data is established from 5 dimensions (volume, velocity, variety, veracity, value), which are necessary to the creation of value (Laney [8]).

The combination of KM and Big data is necessary because of the reality of SME management and the inputs for basic value creation. The base of KM is about to manage knowledge. Therefore, knowledge cycle is characterized by three elements: the data, which when contextualized becomes information, and in turn information becomes knowledge when processed. Data is therefore the first material from which we arrive at knowledge of different kinds, following the application of various transformational knowledge (algorithms, artificial intelligence base, etc.) recognized as the basis of analysis (or analytics) and treatments made with the support of information technologies (Sathi [33]; Minelli et al. [34]). The achieved knowledge is usable, structured and, mostly, generates value for the organization. This whole cycle embodied elements from Big data characteristics and dimensions relating to KM activities which in fine contributes to the global performance of the SME (Fig. 1).

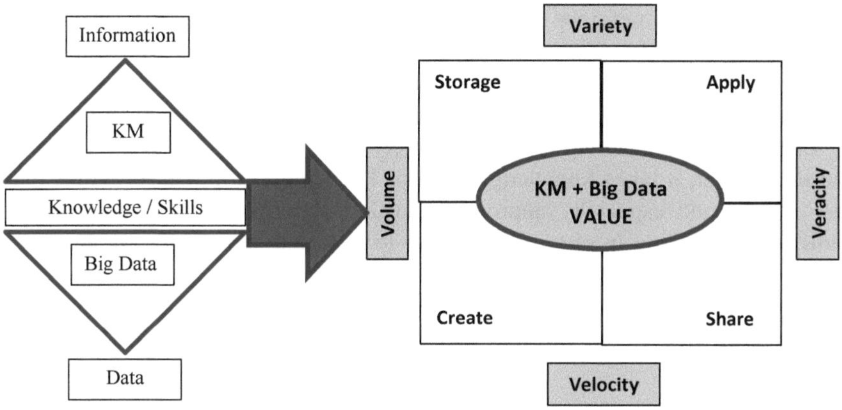

Fig. 1. Integration of KM and big data

Conceptually, the model of the processing chain (income, input, throughput, output, outcome) is as relevant in situations of KM as Big Data. Indeed, this conceptual model helps to understand how the SME identifies needs it wants to respond, what resources to mobilize and the products and services to offer in this regard. For this model to materialize in an effective performance, the data collected must be important, varied, voluminous, and collected in a systematic manner. The SME will develop effective processing capacity of inputs into outputs, with the purpose of creating value. Including large quantities of data nourishes the process level activities: that which characterizes the nature of KM as well as Big Data (Bose [35]).

Moreover, whether at the beginning of the organizational value chain model (income, input), for processing (process), or at the outlet (output, outcome), the need for large quantities and varied data is necessary so managers can take on the challenge that is theirs, namely achieving arbitrations that will lead to the optimal allocation of scarce resources, and to create value. This is the real result sought by the SME when implementing initiatives combining KM and big data (Rothberg and Erickson [36]; Sathi [33]).

Baesens [37] underlines others aspects of the link between knowledge management and big data. Figure 2 depicts this analytics process. In this model, the first step is the gathering of data from different sources, followed by the data selection, cleaning and transformation, to provide users with the data analyzed in patterns. It is up to the users to obtain insights from the patterns.

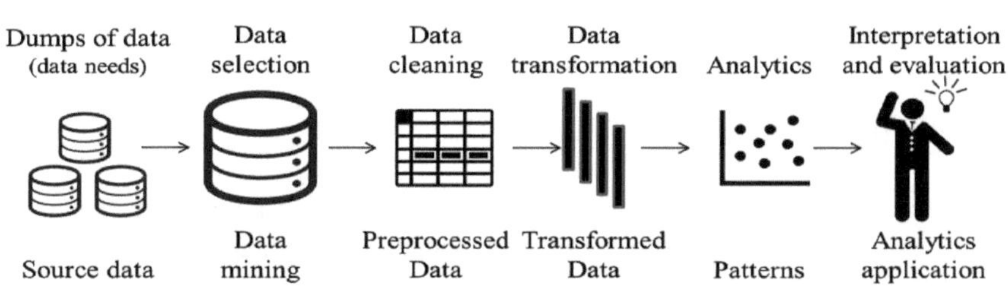

Fig. 2. The analytics process model (Baesens [37])

In sum, these dimensions are functionally nested in each other. Data mining, processing and transformation will lead to the discover patterns and structures that can make sense of the data. Because there are different types of data, a greater volume means more matches, which will rich the potential application and exploitation (Bose [35]; Erickson and Rotheberg [38]). To succeed in this operation and the extraction of value in the data, it takes knowledge or prior knowledge. Big data provides the necessary variety and especially appropriate analytical tools to make a more efficient organization by setting in place an initiative to treat and exploit diverse data.

4.2 Potential Benefits of the Knowledge Management and Big Data Integration

Benefits stemming from the combination of KM and Big data can be assigned to three key activities: knowledge exploitation, knowledge exploration and decision making. We talk about exploitation when we discuss the efforts in an organization to take advantage of internal resources to improve the solutions offered. In using KM to exploit internal resources, the effort of linking it with Big data could result in a better understanding of the current market segment. In turn, this understanding can be applied to:

- Improve current users' satisfaction
- Build a knowledge base from previous product development efforts

Knowledge Exploration refers to the activities performed by an organization to find out about knowledge outside the frontiers of the company. It means keeping track of competitors, news, research and trends that might affect their operations. By including external data sources as an input for the organizational effort of combining KM and Big data, the insights of this exploration can lead to:

- The identification of potential new products/services
- The identification of complementary resources (opportunities for collaboration, new suppliers)

To make decisions, organizational leaders need to rely on different variables (sales, income, number of customers, customer geography, market segments, employee skills and productivity, etc.). In practice, however, managers are limited to a few variables in their decision making process, ignoring the wealth contained in the important volume of data available to them. Big data processes, infrastructure and attributes, combined with the relatively low cost of data processing thus pave the way for new business models that are available to organizations, especially SMEs with limited resources which could take advantage of better business opportunities.

5 Challenges and Future Work

The challenges faced by SME concerning the integration of knowledge management activities and big data occurred at two levels, namely on data and organizational basis.

5.1 Data Challenges

External data comes from different sources, including social networks, connected objects, research publications, and institutional databases. This impressive production of available data is as much a threat as it is an opportunity.

A great challenge for SMEs is being able to maintain their data sources up to date, and to have access to external data which is behind a pay-wall. Social media companies have understood the value of data and, thus making it difficult for smaller companies to access social media information. Patents are also usually not easily accessible. A way for companies to access this data is to find a vendor from which to license an access to only the information it requires.

A second challenge related to data is the processing of the information. Once the company has surmounted the access challenge, it must then be able to define the right process to be performed on the data. Since resources are scarce in SMEs, the organization has two options to do this processing, assign an internal resource, or resort to a provider. Both options have advantages and disadvantages. Having an internal resource means that the organization can experiment with the questions it wants answers to, but it is a constant expense. Having a provider will drive the managers to figure out the questions before commissioning the development, but the company can profit from professionals who might be able to gear them in new directions.

A third challenge in terms of the data is the insight. As mentioned before, the data is useful when it is being interpreted by someone who has sufficient knowledge of the domain to be able to understand and read the weak signals that can indicate a new trend.

5.2 Organizational Challenges

It is necessary that the different functions are effective and efficient and contribute to organizational performance. The fact is that operations are so predominant, that there is a tendency to put limited resources to other functions, including client management, promotion, market segmentation, etc. But the need to create value leads the SME to use the knowledge from all functions.

To be able to profit from it, processing these data requires systematic collection, and a consistent information infrastructure. The purpose is to give a dynamic character to the data and to highlight the evolutionary aspect.

5.3 Future Work

To better evaluate the efforts implemented in SMEs to combine big data with knowledge management, the first step is to identify the kind of project the organization want to put in place in a short term period and long term. More than that, SME must be able to establish the link between these projects and the performance of the firm. The purpose is to understand practically how the integration of big data and knowledge management activities contribute to the organizational performance. To do so, we plan to conduct a survey with SME.

The results of the survey will provide an insight to the measures taken and the considerations regarding internal and external data, as well as the strategies to manage the knowledge base (in-house versus outsource of information systems).

6 Conclusion

SMEs interested in gaining insights and knowledge from internal and external information can turn to new technologies such as big data. The use of this technology will enable the organization to improve their competitiveness by figuring insights in the weak signals of future trends. The knowledge attained from these efforts can lead to the identification of new products, services and complementary resources.

Nonetheless, many aspects need to be taken into account in the implementation of such an initiative. Considerations regarding the data to be analyzed must be taken into account, as the data needs to be reliable. The new tools will allow size and speed of the data to not be a factor; it is the processing that will take center stage, asking the right questions is what will provide the advantage.

References

1. Lynch, C.: Big data: how do your data grow? Nature **455**(4), 28–29 (2008)
2. Tweed, K.: Smart Meters Deliver 1 Billion Data Points Daily (2013). http://www.greentechmedia.com/articles/. Accessed 29 Mar
3. Delort, P.: Le big data. Collection Que sais-je? PUF, Paris (2015)
4. McKinsey Global Institute: Big Data: The Next Frontier for Innovation, Competition and Productivity. McKinsey & Company (2011)
5. Dove, G., Jones, S.: Using information visualization to support creativity in service design workshops. In: Proceedings Service Design and Innovation Conference (2014)
6. Howkins, J.: The Creative Economy: How People Make Money from Ideas. Penguin, United Kingdom (2002)
7. Kabir, N., Carayannis, E.: Big data, tacit knowledge and organizational competitiveness. J. Intell. Stud. Bus. **3**(3), 54–62 (2013)
8. Laney, D.: 3D Data Management: Controlling Data volume, Velocity and variety (2001). https://blogs.gartner.com/doug-laney/files/. Accessed 29 Mar
9. Koutroumpis, P., Leiponen, A.: Understanding the value of big data. In: IEEE Conference on Big Data, Sillicon Valley, CA, October 2013
10. Beyer, M.A., Laney, D.: The Importance of Big Data: A Definition (2012). https://www.gartner.com/doc/2057415. Accessed 3 Apr 2016
11. George, G., Hass, M.R., Pentland, A.: Big data and management. Acad. Manag. J. **57**(2), 321–326 (2014)
12. Liebowitz, J.: Big Data and Business Analytics. CRC Press, Boca Raton (2013)
13. Chan, J.O.: The big data customer knowledge management. Commun. IIMA **14**(3) (2014). http://scholarworks.lib.csusb.edu/ciima/vol14/iss3/5. Accessed 31 Mar
14. Latour, B.: Science in Action: How to Follow Scientists and Engineers Through Society. Harvard University Press, Cambridge (1987)
15. Polanyi, M.: The Tacit Dimension. Anchor Books, New York (1966)

16. Winter, S.G., Nelson, R.: An Evolutionary Theory of Economic Change. Belknap Press, Cambridge (1982)
17. Porter, M.E.: From competitive advantage to corporate strategy. Harvard Bus. Rev. **65**, 43–59 (1987)
18. Tarondeau, J.-C.: Le Management des Savoirs. Que sais-je? PUF, Paris (1998)
19. Ermine, J.L.: Les systèmes de connaissance, 2nd edn. Hermès Science Publication, Paris (2000)
20. Wenerfelt, B.: A resource-based view of the firm. Strateg. Manag. J. **5**, 171–180 (1984)
21. Barney, J.: Firm resources and sustained competitive advantage. J. Manag. **17**(1), 99–120 (1991)
22. Wright, R.W., van Wijk, G.: Les principes du management des ressources fondées sur le savoir. Revue Française de Gestion. **21**, 70–75 (1995)
23. Liebowitz, J.: Knowledge Management Handbook. CRC Press, Boca Raton (1999)
24. Alavi, M., Leidner, D.: Knowledge management and knowledge management systems: conceptual foundations and research issues. MIS Q. **25**(1), 107–136 (2001)
25. Veybel, L., Prieur, P.: Le knowledge management dans tous ses états. La gestion de la connaissance au service de la performance. Éditions d'Organisation, Paris (2003)
26. Ling, L.S.: Defining knowledge management activities from information communication technologies (ICTs) perspective. J. Organ. Knowl. **2011**, 1–10 (2011)
27. Marchesnay, M., Julien, P.A.: The small business as a transaction space. J. Entrepreneuship **2**, 111 (1990)
28. Julien, P.A.: Les PME Bilan et perspectives, 3rd edn, p. 551. Presses Inter-universitaires et Économica, Paris (2002)
29. OCDE: Perspectives de l'OCDE sur les PME et l'entrepreneuriat. OCDE, Paris (2005)
30. Asmaa, G.: L'impact de la capitalisation des connaissances sur les projets d'innovation: développement de produits nouveaux au sein des PME. Mémoire de Maîtrise en gestion de projet. Université du Québec à Rimouski (2010)
31. Mbassegue, P., Nogning, F.L., Gardoni, M.: A conceptual model to assess KM and innovation projects: a need for an unified framework. In: Bouras, A., Eynard, B., Foufou, S., Thoben, K.-D. (eds.) PLM 2015. IAICT, vol. 467, pp. 444–458. Springer, Heidelberg (2016). doi:10.1007/978-3-319-33111-9_41
32. Nonaka, I., Takeuchi, H.: The Knowledge Creating Company: How Japanese Companies Create The Dynamics of Innovation. Oxford University Press, New York (1995)
33. Sathi, A.: Big Data Analytics: Disruptive Technologies for Changing the Game. MC Press, Boise (2012)
34. Minelli, M., Chambers, M., Dhiraj, A.: Big Data, Big Analytics: Emerging Business Intelligence and Analytic Trends for Today's Businesses. Wiley, New Jersey (2013)
35. Bose, R.: Advanced analytics; opportunities and challenges. Ind. Manag. Data Syst. **109**(2), 155–172 (2009)
36. Rothberg, H., Erickson, S.: From Knowledge to Intelligence: Creating Competitive Advantage in the Next Economy. Elsevier Butterworth-Heinemann, Woburn (2005)
37. Baesens, B.: Analytics in a Big Data World. Wiley, Hoboken (2014)
38. Erickson, S., Rothberg, H.: Big data and knowledge management: establishing a conceptual foundation. Electron. J. Knowl. Manag. **12**(2), 108–116 (2014)

Ergonomic Considerations in Product Design Through PLM Technologies

Carolina Marroquín(✉), Melisa Gaviria, and Ricardo Mejía-Gutiérrez

Design Engineering Research Group (GRID),
Universidad EAFIT, Medellín, Colombia
{cmarroqu,mgavirl9,rmejiag}@eafit.edu.co

Abstract. This article presents an integration of a product design methodology with emphasis in ergonomics with PLM. The articulation requires a comparative overview of the management levels offered by both approaches. PLM focuses on procedural activities and task performance and supports the ergonomic design methodology into a project and process management level in which decisions and control claims a mayor role. As result, workflow and indicators solutions attached to PLM strategy approach are structured accordingly to particular needs of the methodology in question.

Keywords: Product Lifecycle Management · Product design · Ergonomics · Design methodology · Business Process Modeling

1 Introduction

Product development balances the interactions between context, artifacts and users in the performance of an activity to generate wellbeing. Ergonomics aims to apply knowledge of human abilities, human limitations, and other human characteristics in the design [1]. Ergonomics, integrated with the design process, provide the tools to assist a more reliable design [2, 3]. Although, design methodologies include ergonomic criteria to optimize the product successful coupling with ergonomic needs of the end users, when addressing projects with high ergonomic expectations these criteria are often insufficient. Moreover, ergonomic methods are not necessarily applied by designers and engineers on a regular basis, which increases the need of a closed follow up and a strict guidance to gather appropriate information for ergonomic analysis [4]. Such needs can be support with Product Lifecycle Management (PLM) strategy that allow industries to align their intellectual capital in order to create products more efficiently, integrating the complex dynamics around product development [5] creating synergy in collaborative work, concurrent engineering, process management and project management methods to support the product development decision making process. This ensures benefits related to accelerated product development [6], change management, traceability, extended enterprise and knowledge management capabilities.

PLM tools are usually adapted with pre-configured applications or modules to guide a basic implementation. However, specialized working methodologies and strategies need a more detailed configuration, according to the complexity of processes, projects and information management. As the context of this work is the usability and

R. Harik et al. (Eds.): PLM 2016, IFIP AICT 492, pp. 32–42, 2016.
DOI: 10.1007/978-3-319-54660-5_4

product/user interaction, the research intends to integrate these aspects into a product development process. Consequently, the work will be supported in an Ergonomic Oriented Design Methodology (EODM) for which it can be found in the literature different alternatives, such as the ones proposed by Rincon [7]; Stanton et al. [8]; and Hoyos et al. [9]. For the present work, the EODM corresponds to the H2A[1] methodology proposed by Hoyos et al. 2015, as it was selected in terms of its completeness and design oriented approach which include balance between the interactions of human-artifact-environment dimensions solved through the application of ergonomic methods and tools such as biomechanics analysis, RULA assessments, cognitive ergonomic evaluation lists among others [9]. The objective was to experience the implementation of an EODM following a PLM strategy. The emphasis requires adaptations to the process, project support and monitoring. To enable the integration of the methodology into the PLM strategy, an analysis in the structure of the EODM and the PLM software must be done.

2 Background

The EODM is used in the local market for specialized consultancy, in recent cases was applied in two separate projects (1) the redesign of a working space for the musicians of a symphonic orchestra and (2) a small appliance redesign for a local appliance industry. The projects comprised conception to conceptual design stages. During the 4 month application, weaknesses such as, difficulty to update schedules, missing information resulting from the lack of information management mechanisms, difficulty to sort out between the different documents and absence of communication strategies to enhance collaborative work were noticeable. Moreover, the complexity of the EODM demands a complete focus on the coordination operative task such as verification of the information updates, constant meetings to solve questions over the design activities, assigned time to verify activities deliverables and a dedicated time to gather and analyze the results from each stage, leaving little time to create and implement proactive improvement strategies that ensure successful outcomes during the course of the project.

The applications showed that, the EODM requires support during management, given that while product design projects vary on scope and complexity, product development decisions remain consistent [10]. Hence, a PLM approach may resolve the issues through automated guidance, smart follow ups and knowledge management applications.

PLM offers managerial capabilities to product development process. To take advantages of such versatile capabilities, the PLM strategy relies on Business Process Modeling tools to revise and adapt their current working process according to suggestions from the PLM strategy. This processes might be represented with a graphic model using Event-Driven Process Chain (EPC) diagrams that integrate the interactions

[1] H2A: H2A methodology stands for "*Hombre-Artefacto-Ambiente*" (human-artefact-environment); Hence, the name takes the first letter of the word and the 2 capital A's. This methodology is a result of previous work within the authors' research group.

between activities, decision events, information and roles, providing a chain of function and logical connectors [11, 12] that facilitates logical understanding of the general system. The analysis of the resulting model gives insights in to the most efficient way to integrate the entities in to a holistic process that adds value to the customer [13]. In addition, PLM solutions provide a series of specialized pre-configured modules that provide managerial capabilities. Once the software is acquire, a process of configuration must take place in order to load the product lifecycle used in the organization, under the PLM strategy conditions. For this article, authors worked with *Aras Innovator* (AI) from Aras Corporation as the selected PLM software, due to its open source benefits, which include high flexibility to adapt unique workflows and projects configuration among other specialized arrangements.

Despite the capabilities of PLM strategy there are little details reported in regards of the use in ergonomics oriented developments. Projects with such orientations are often supported by tools attached to CAD and simulations software's [14], only a few approaches focus on the capabilities of PLM itself [4, 15], focusing on the extraction of ergonomics information from PLM and the use of tools and expert knowledge to support design. However, the application of a complete ergonomic oriented working methodology for design, supported under PLM dimensions of process, organization, tools and resources are yet to be addressed.

3 Analysis of the Ergonomic Approach with PLM Concepts

In order to articulate a PLM strategy that may be able to support a design methodology with emphasis on ergonomics, four dimensions are considered: Process, Information, Organization, and Resources [16]. This method seeks to integrate the PLM strategy and PLM software requirements for data management in a holistic way. As mentioned in Sect. 1, this research work uses the H2A [9] as design methodology with emphasis in ergonomics. Consequently, the aforementioned dimensions were aligned with the EODM approach:

- *Information:* The EODM includes the creation of CAD first approximations to concept design. The data associated with product, such as drawings, parts and images is available for use.
- *Resources:* technological tools to support the EODM
- *Process*: The EODM is not articulated, by default, as a management process. However the EODM structure has implicit in the description of stages, activities and overall structure, a general process. Following Business Process modeling (BPM) methods and tools, the general workflows can be identified and made explicit. This enables PLM software configuration and allow the EODM management in an operational level (project) and a management level (workflow).
- *Organization*: The product development activities depend on the capabilities and skills of the teams. In order to understand the people dynamics into the proposed EODM a characterization of the human aspect was performed based on interactions and contributions. This information is the input to configure the software users, identities (groups of users) and permissions.

Identifying and analyzing the mentioned dimensions, is the easiest way to understand the EODM in a PLM environment. EODM was implemented in PLM as a new "Module". To do so, some hierarchical differences were found in terms of how to refer to modules, activities, tasks, etc. and its equivalence with the structure of the EODM (phases, activities, etc.). Those structures differ; hence, a comparison was made to find a way to articulate the methodology and the software as shown in Fig. 1. As it can be seen, a set of hierarchical levels can be identified in each side. Each level is associated with a level of the structure. Thus, the taxonomy levels can be named as LevelNumber$_{Structure}$ (Example: $L1_{H2A}$ or $L1_{PLM}$). Consequently, they can be identified as follows:

- $L1_{H2A} = L1_{PLM}$ = Ergonomics
- $L2_{H2A} = L3_{H2A}$ = Stages (not managed in PLM)
- $L3_{H2A} = L2_{PLM}$ = Phases
- $L3_{H2A} = L3_{PLM}$ = Workflow activities
- $L3_{H2A} = L4_{PLM}$ = Workflow task
- $L4_{H2A} = L5_{PLM}$ = Project schedule
- $L5_{H2A} = L6_{PLM}$ = Project activity
- $L6_{H2A} = L7_{PLM}$ = Project task

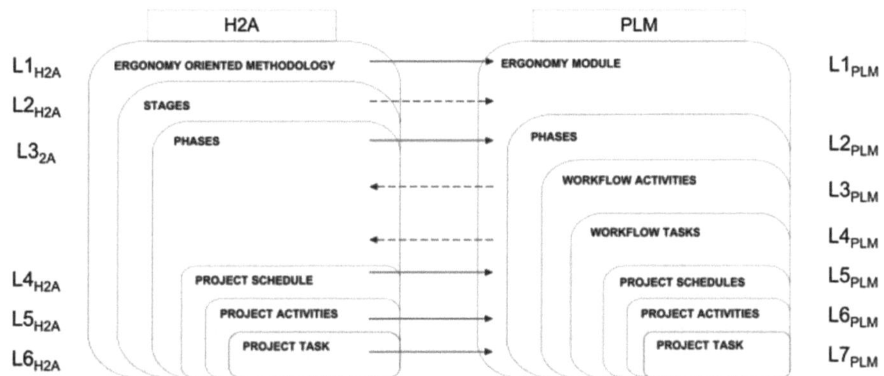

Fig. 1. Articulation of the EODM (H2A) to the PLM (AI) strategy

The EODM (corresponding to the H2A) is organized in five management levels ($L1_{H2A}$ to $L5_{H2A}$); unlike the PLM software where two additional levels exist ($L1_{PLM}$ to $L7_{PLM}$). However, they do not match at the hierarchical level. Two main differences are evidenced:

- The absence in PLM of an equivalent to $L1_{H2A}$, called "stages" is not present in the PLM software $L2_{H2A} \neq L2_{PLM}$.
- PLM adds workflow configurations at $L3_{PLM}$ and $L4_{PLM}$ to assist management.

The absence of an equivalent $L2_{H2A}$ in PLM is due to its use in EODM as midpoint control, which can be managed differently in PLM. On the other hand, $L3_{PLM}$ is subdivided, given that the EODM was implemented by workflows that include a new level of managing activities.

The EODM does not include coordination activities, however PLM offers workflow modules to support management, thus, $L3_{PLM}$ and $L4_{PLM}$ in which workflow activities such as planning, revision and correction loops are integrated sources of guidance for the coordination team. Also, project schedule creation became a mandatory automated workflow task rather than an isolated activity launched by human will, need or believe, this ensures that all projects regardless of instruction will use project Gantts and schedules for activity completion.

The PLM software images presented in the article correspond to the module created for application in the local context, hence the images are only shown for demonstrative purposes and its contents are further explained on the body of the presented work.

4 Ergonomic Module Implementation in PLM

The implementation principle set the EODM to be managed through a main workflow that coordinates activities of planning, execution, evaluation and delivery of each phase. An EPC model named "coordination workflow" was created for the five phases. This model was implemented in AI, using the workflow module as shown in Fig. 2.

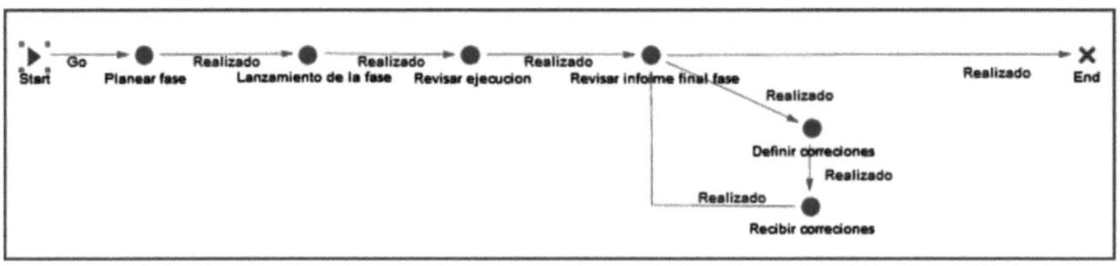

Fig. 2. Workflow map for phase management in AI

The workflow is built with activities and transitions. Each activity is defined with a sequence of tasks necessary to achieve successful completion and subsequent approval as depicted in Fig. 3. Additionally, a decision must take place after every tasks is completed.

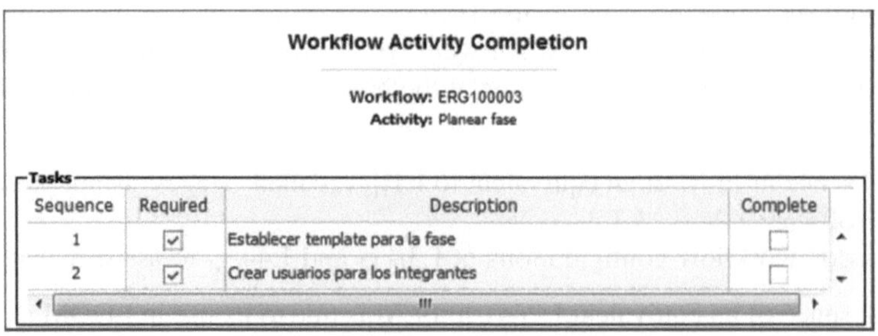

Fig. 3. Workflow decisions in AI

The design project itself is managed through the AI's "Project Management" Module which is automatically activated from the workflow in an activity named "phase revision of execution". A project's Work Breakdown Structure (WBS) is suggested by the EODM in every phase. Thus, a total of 6 phases and 53 activities are pre-configured in the software templates, with a suggested predecessor assignation. The use of the activities suggested in the WBS allows rational decision making regarding the ergonomic approach of the project (See Fig. 4).

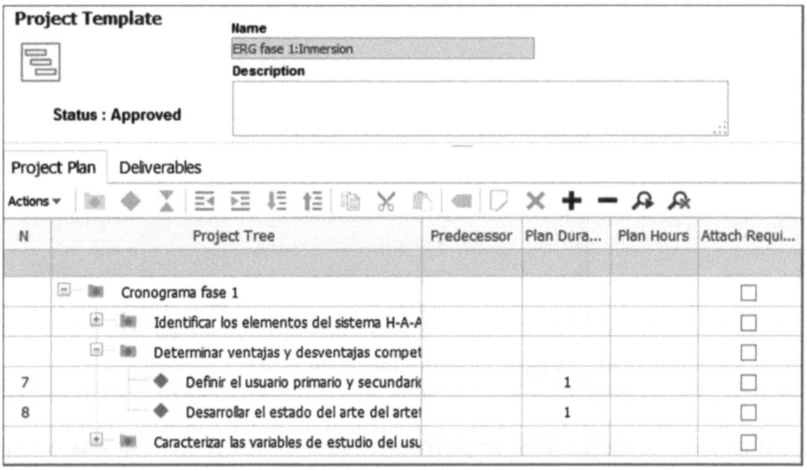

Fig. 4. Project break down structure in AI

In terms of "document management", usually design projects base their body of knowledge on CAD files. However, the PLM, as an evolution of Product Data Management (PDM) systems, fosters the management of the whole lifecycle documentation. For that purpose, four additional types of documents (Manuals, Procedures, Templates, Records) were implemented according to the ISO-9000 standard [17]. Additionally, as PLM strategies recommends, a nomenclature was built in order to facilitate document retrieval. The Prefix was the initial of the type of document, followed by the project type (ERG) and the suffix is a consecutive number (*e.g.* F-ERG-23). The EODM, under its standardization purposes, suggests 30 templates to register the activities completion (to obtain project's "Records") and two manuals to clarify to users the stages and the interactions in them.

The files are centralized in the PLM database and available for access accordingly to permissions assigned to each role. In PLM the distribution of responsibilities goes according to their skills, authority and resources, this is implemented as Gantt Charts and Workflows not only through activity assignment, but also through permissions definition over the decisions and access to the entire system. Thus, an external party will have a limited view of the product lifecycle, whereas a project manager will have view, vote and access to every step of the product development project. The organizational structure proposed in the EODM is composed of two categories (Internal &

External) with seven roles, where three of them (Coordinator, Advisor and Designer) are internal staff directly related to the product development and the other four (User, Client, Expert and Third party) are external stakeholders that remained outside the PLM software. Figure 5 shows the implementation of this structure in AI for permission assignation and workflow configuration.

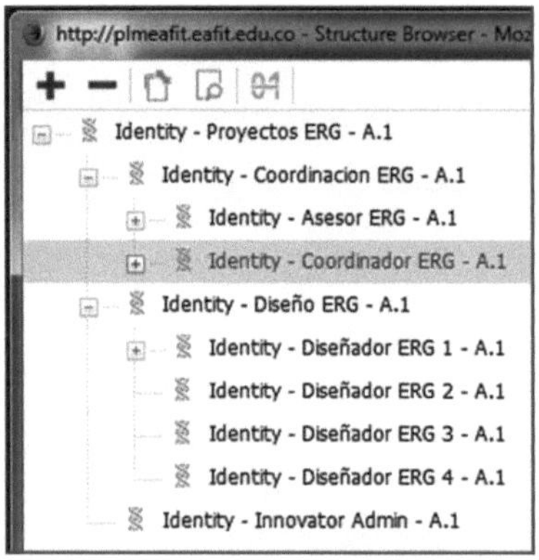

Fig. 5. Identity hierarchy in AI

As a final step on the EODM implementation, a monitoring view was considered. Ergonomics and management indicators were identified and selected from the literature about performance indicators [18, 19]. Six quantitative indicators were selected for the PLM software and they are detailed in Table 1.

Table 1. Management indicators

Item	Name	Equation	Scale (unit of measure)
1	Project deviation	(Real weeks of execution)/(Planned weeks of execution)*100	# Weeks
2	Phase deviation	(Real execution days)/(Planned execution days)-1	# Days
3	Activities on time	(Activities executed)/(Activities planned)	# Activities
4	Delivery performance	(Real weeks needed to delivery)/(Planned weeks to delivery)	# Weeks
5	Tutoring compliance	(Executed tutoring)/(Planned tutoring)	# Tutoring
6	% of executed activities (Executed activities)/(Programmed Schedule)		# Activities

The purpose of those indicators is explained below:

- *Project deviation*: It quantifies the delays on the complete project schedule
- *Phase deviation*: It represents the delays associated with the planned schedule of every phase and the real progress of the execution.
- *Activities on time*: Sets which activities were conducted within the expected time.
- *Delivery performance*: Quantifies compliance with the milestones in each phase.
- *Tutoring Compliance*: It represents the points of tutoring by a consultant or an advisor regarding project development.
- *Percentage of executed activities*: Quantifies the percentage of activities executed within the implemented schedule, the activities discarded multiple times should be reviewed.

In addition to the performance indicators, ergonomic metrics for physical and cognitive assessment were established based on the RULA method [20]. This enabled to record information related to posture, effort, movement and repetition of movements, providing insights about the reduction of the ergonomic risk.

The indicator proves the efficiency of the new design and the advantages over commercial products. The indicators were structured before implementing them in the software to get a first insight in the variable association and the meta-data needed to support each measure. Finally, the indicator web form to capture ergonomic product data was implemented in AI, as shown in Fig. 6.

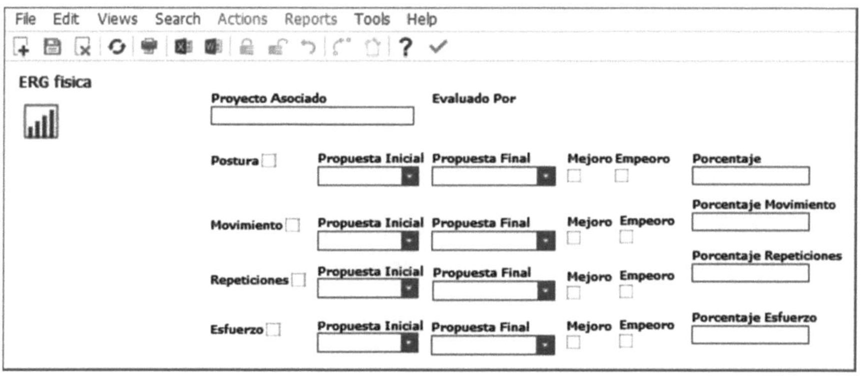

Fig. 6. Ergonomic factors indicators form in AI

5 Results

Once the Ergonomic module was finished, a test environment was set in order to validate (i) the proper performance of the lifecycles and workflows (ii) ensure the automated assignations compliance and (iii) test the interactions between lifecycles, workflows, projects and information. Eight tests were executed focusing in the automated workflow and verifying the proper activities assignation, the trajectories of the decisions and the permissions, as well as identities synergy. The identified software mistakes (such us unlinked activities, workflow nomenclature, lifecycle malfunctioning, mistaken assignations, etc.) were corrected progressively in every testing cycle. The final balance of the PLM "ergonomics module" is shown in Table 2 were it is evidenced how the EODM proposes items that were successfully implemented in the PLM module in AI.

Table 2. Articulations from the PLM strategy to the EODM

	EODM proposals	PLM implementation	Module completeness
Template schedule	6	6	100%
Activities supported in schedules	40	53	133%
Delivery points	6	6	100%
System document	32	32	100%

The second row shows the additions made to the methodology into the PLM module. This is related to the enhancement of management capabilities, thus control points and explicit decision-making strategies were added by incorporating a main workflow to control all phases under the same parameters. This is an effort to increase operability consistency. The PLM strategy enhances the items shown in Fig. 7.

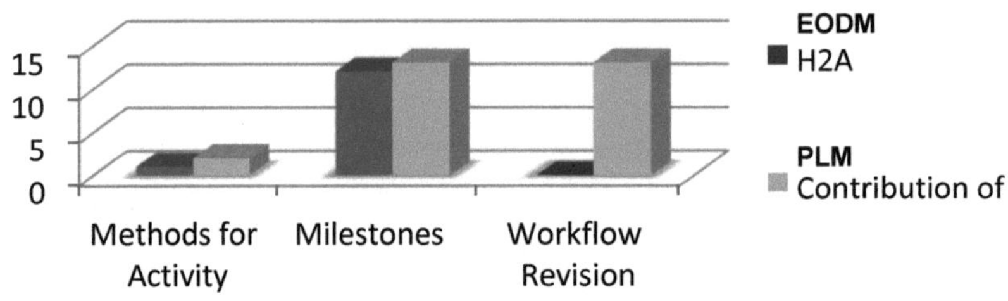

Fig. 7. Detail on the activities supported in schedules

Finally, after the PLM Ergonomics Module was implemented, activities from the EODM may now be controlled, not only through schedules but also through a new workflow for high level management. The milestones increased in 8% due to milestone addition. Six management indicators and two ergonomic tables, enables control over the execution and the end results in terms of ergonomic aspects in the product design. During the software configuration 32 documents were created, as well as 30 templates and 2 manuals that consolidates the complete content of the EODM. Additionally, 53 activities were automated and supported in the software.

6 Conclusions

The adoption of any working method or methodology to PLM software must be articulated under the PLM strategy and technological requirements. Thus, the implementation in the software requires previous understanding of the methodology and a restructuration to fit the levels and requirements of PLM strategy concerning the four dimensions: people, project, product and processes. The PLM module effectively allows recording all lifecycle information generated in the design process, creating traceability of design activities and generates an understanding of the decisions made. The configured module enables to monitor the activities of a project schedule in real time. This result in consistency and availability of information to identify significant deviations from schedules, thus strategic actions might be proactive.

Specific knowledge is required in the field of Business Process, Project Management and Product Development Process in order to achieve a successful integrated implementation of a PLM module. Communication between the software administrators and the responsible of the strategy must be direct; otherwise, efforts will be made in separated fronts causing compatibility issues between software configuration and the methodologies to be supported.

The proposed indicators, both at managerial and technical level, in particular in terms of ergonomics, should be implemented to assess long-term effectiveness. The approach of both types of indicators facilitates decision-making and it is recommended the graphical representations on the PLM software. Further implementations will ensure the collaborative effectiveness of the EODM Supported under a PLM approach. All suggested indicators are quantitative due to the numeric nature of the web templates. As further research, the implementation of qualitative indicators is an action to be included. This involves creating qualitative templates within the software with value ranges lead to a measurable and comparable level.

Acknowledgments. Special thanks to Colciencias (Colombian Administrative Department of Science, Technology and Innovation) and EAFIT University, who jointly sponsored the "Young Researchers Program" trough the call "*Conv. No. 617-2013*".

References

1. BCPE: Board of Certification in Professional Ergonomics (2016)
2. Cecilia, F.: Ergonomía para el Diseño. Editorial Designio, SA de CV, México, DF (2001)
3. Rubin, J., Chisnell, D.: Handbook of Usability Testing: How to Plan. Design and Conduct Effective Tests. Wiley, Hoboken (2008)
4. Kim, G.Y., Do Noh, S., Rim, Y.H., Mun, J.H.: XML-based concurrent and integrated ergonomic analysis in PLM. Int. J. Adv. Manuf. Technol. **39**, 1045–1060 (2008)
5. Jun, H.-B., Kiritsis, D., Xirouchakis, P.: Research issues on closed-loop PLM. Comput. Ind. **58**, 855–868 (2007)
6. Grieves, M.: Product Lifecycle Management: Driving the Next Generation of Lean Thinking. McGraw Hill, New York (2006)

7. Rincón, O.: Ergonomía y procesos de diseño. Consideraciones Metodológicas para el Desarrollo de Sistemas y Productos. Editorial Pontificia Universidad Javeriana, pp. 38–41 (2010)
8. Stanton, N.A., Young, M.S., Harvey, C.: Guide to Methodology in Ergonomics: Designing for Human Use. CRC Press, Boca Raton (2014)
9. Hoyos-Ruiz, J., Martínez-Cadavid, J., Osorio-Gómez, G., Mejía-Gutiérrez, R.: Implementation of ergonomic aspects throughout the engineering design process: human-artefact-context analysis. Int. J. Interact. Des. Manuf. (IJIDeM), 1–15 (2015)
10. Krishnan, V., Ulrich, K.T.: Product development decisions: a review of the literature. Manage. Sci. **47**, 1 (2001)
11. Tsai, A., Jiacun, W., Tepfenhart, W., Rosea, D.: EPC workflow model to WIFA model conversion. In: IEEE International Conference on Systems, Man and Cybernetics, SMC 2006, pp. 2758–2763 (2006)
12. van der Aalst, W.M.P.: Formalization and verification of event-driven process chains. Inf. Softw. Technol. **41**, 639–650 (1999)
13. Davis, R., Brabänder, E.: An Introduction to BPM. In: Davis, R., Brabänder, E. (eds.) ARIS Design Platform, pp. 1–12. Springer, Heidelberg (2007)
14. Annarumma, M., Pappalardo, M., Naddeo, A.: Methodology development of human task simulation as PLM solution related to OCRA ergonomic analysis. In: Cascini, G. (ed.) CAI 2008. TIFIP, vol. 277, pp. 19–29. Springer, Heidelberg (2008). doi:10.1007/978-0-387-09697-1_2
15. Mahdjoub, M., Monticolo, D., Gomes, S., Sagot, J.-C.: A collaborative design for usability approach supported by virtual reality and a multi-agent system embedded in a PLM environment. Comput. Aided Des. **42**, 402–413 (2010)
16. Peñaranda, N., Mejía, R., Romero, D., Molina, A.: Implementation of product lifecycle management tools using enterprise integration engineering and action-research. Int. J. Comput. Integr. Manuf. **23**, 853–875 (2010)
17. Peach, R.W.: The ISO 9000 Handbook. Irwin Professional Publishing, Burr Ridge (1995)
18. Dominguez Giraldo, G.: Indicadores de Gestión y Resultados: Un enfoque sistémico. Biblioteca Jurídica, Bogotá (2004)
19. Beltran, J.J.M.: Indicadores de gestión: guía práctica para estructurar acertadamente esta herramienta clave para el logro de la competitividad: 3R (1999)
20. Corlett, E.: Rapid upper limb assessment (RULA). In: The Occupational Ergonomics Handbook, p. 437 (1998)

KBE-PLM Integration Schema for Engineering Knowledge Re-use and Design Automation

Jullius Cho[1(✉)], Thomas Vosgien[2], Thorsten Prante[2], and Detlef Gerhard[1]

[1] TU Wien, Vienna, Austria
{jullius.cho,detlef.gerhard}@tuwien.ac.at
[2] V-Research GmbH, Dornbirn, Austria
{thomas.vosgien,thorsten.prante}@v-research.at

Abstract. The re-use of product knowledge is vital to the development of Knowledge-Based Engineering (KBE) systems and to the deployment of Product Lifecycle Management (PLM) strategies. This paper addresses the challenges related to KBE-PLM systems integration in order to unlock engineering knowledge from proprietary representations and to manage the lifecycle of KBE models as well as their usage by different design automation applications. Essential constituents of product knowledge are identified and analyzed and the concepts of design intent and design rationale are re-introduced as key enablers to re-use this product knowledge in the appropriate KBE context. The paper introduces a KBE-PLM integration framework including a platform-independent Open KBE repository structured according to the KBE-PLM integration schema. This schema is a multi-layer neutral product and knowledge data model designed for integrating information from parameterized Computer-Aided Design (CAD) models, rule-based KBE systems and PLM systems.

Keywords: Knowledge-based engineering · Design automation · Knowledge re-use · Design intent · Design rationale

1 Introduction

As part of the implementation of PLM strategies, contemporary computer-based tools should provide engineers with means to better handle the processes involved across the product lifecycle. Within this context, there is considerable pressure on engineers to improve their product development processes in order to deliver complex and high-quality products and services to the market rapidly and at low cost [1]. One approach to achieving this improvement is engineering design automation, where interdependent engineering design processes are subject to partial or full automation. If the focus of the automation is on repetitive tasks, this is called Knowledge-Based Engineering (KBE) [2]. For its implementation, product and process engineering knowledge needs to be identified, acquired, formalized, processed and re-used. However, on the one hand, knowledge acquisition is still a bottleneck and, on the other hand, the formalized engineering knowledge is too often encapsulated in CAD models

R. Harik et al. (Eds.): PLM 2016, IFIP AICT 492, pp. 43–55, 2016.
DOI: 10.1007/978-3-319-54660-5_5

and inference engines of KBE systems, which are not easily accessible outside vendor-specific application environments. Thus, re-use of formalized knowledge across KBE applications, and even within the same KBE application across time, is an issue. This is reflected in the following shortcomings of KBE as identified in [2]: First, case-based, ad hoc development of KBE applications, second, a tendency toward development of 'black-box' applications (i.e. formalized knowledge is not explained or contextualized, so not related to design intent – with some exceptions such as [3]) and, third, generally, a lack of knowledge re-use is observed – where these three reported shortcomings are interrelated. Compared with this, PLM support entails the modeling, capturing, manipulating, exchanging and using of information all along product life cycle decision making processes, across all application domains [4]. Therefore, a strong focus of a PLM strategy should be on knowledge re-use and it doesn't come as a surprise that integration of KBE and PLM systems has been identified to provide advantages [5, 6] for product development. For instance, the following deficiency could therewith be overcome: Although many CAD systems provide basic design automation capabilities which allow parts, assemblies, and drawings to be parametrically generated and changed, the capabilities for consistent changes to product configurations generally remain restricted because knowledge in repositories of KBE systems is not linked to the product information/definition managed in PLM systems [5]. Still, there are major challenges for overall KBE-PLM integration and its interoperability enabler: one, the "ability to unlock engineering knowledge from proprietary representations" and, two, the ability to manage the lifecycle of KBE models" [6]. Overcoming these challenges will result in improved support for the development and maintenance of KBE systems for design automation and hence for the overall engineering design process efficiency. In this paper, we propose a KBE-PLM integration framework enabling to retrieve and integrate the information and knowledge from CAD, KBE and PLM systems in order to store and manage them in a platform independent Open KBE repository structured according to the KBE-PLM integration schema. The goal is to be able to re-use this knowledge for different KBE applications for design automation. Section 2 discusses relevant background and state of the art. The architecture of the framework and the KBE-PLM integration schema are presented in Sect. 4 and discussed in Sect. 5, before concluding the paper and presenting lines of possible future work.

2 Background

2.1 Product Knowledge, Design Intent and Design Rationale

There are several methodologies which have been developed and/or used for the design, development and deployment of KBE systems, such as MOKA [7], CommonKADS [8], and KNOMAD [9]. While most of them have addressed the issue of knowledge capture and structuring/formalization, none of them has yet integrated the concepts of design intent and design rationale to facilitate better re-use. According to [10], product knowledge includes function, structure and behavior models of an artifact along with product specifications, requirements, and constraints and includes various kinds of relationships between parts and assemblies [11]. This definition is in line with the Function-Behavior-Structure (FBS) framework proposed by [12]. In [11], the authors also include design process knowledge as part of the product knowledge, which can be encoded as methods in a product representation and provides mechanisms for realizing design details at various stages of the product lifecycle and in [10] process knowledge is defined as design rules, strategies, automated model mappings, analysis scripts and problem-solving algorithms. In making the connection between product and design knowledge on the one hand and design intent and design rationale on the other, it must be noted that there is some ambiguity regarding the definitions of the two later terms [11]. While design intent is captured in a set of functional and non-functional requirements, the design rationale encapsulates both the semantics and conditions for all the mappings and transformations from requirements to architecture (i.e. structure) [14]. Thus, design rationale relates to and describes the process of designing ('design logic') and is related to the design intent which represents the reason(s) that justify design decisions. In this paper, design intent and rationale will be defined as follows (see Sect. 3.2): design intent is a concept that, based on a specific usage context, enables one to know which product structural representation and related design rationale to use to fulfill a specific functional intent. Design rationale refers to the design rules, automated model mappings, analysis scripts and problem-solving algorithms required to fulfill a specific intent.

2.2 Model-Based Definition (MBD) and KBE-PLM Systems Integration

The central concept embodied in MBD is that the 3D product model is the most appropriate vehicle for delivering all of the detailed product information necessary for downstream organizations to perform their portion of the product creation [13]: CAD models are enriched with explicit and implicit knowledge which needs to be extracted, formalized and managed for re-use in different contexts. However, extracting knowledge encapsulated in CAD models remains a challenge. Gerhard and Lutz [14] propose a knowledge acquisition and knowledge formalization assistant (KAFA) which employs the design structure matrix technique to capture product knowledge directly from CAD models and enable experts to formalize the design logic. Using CAD models as the main container of product knowledge stresses the necessity to be able to extract and re-use this knowledge in heterogeneous environments such as KBE and PLM systems. However, current MBD approaches do not address the development of neutral product data representations which enable links between representations of product definition, design intent and design rationale. Combining both MBD and KBE-PLM approaches is required to efficiently encapsulate design knowledge in CAD models and at the same time to extract the knowledge for re-use in faster platform-independent KBE systems development or in the appropriate design context and related activities.

2.3 KBE-PLM Systems Interoperability

An example of a standardized modeling framework is the Model-Driven Architecture (MDA) for portability, interoperability and reusability between IT systems [15].

In order to achieve integration and interoperability, transparent access to proprietary data and services is needed. Moreover, a neutral representation of product information will help to increase interoperability. Truyen [16] addresses these concerns and specifies three default viewpoints on a system: computational independence, platform independence and platform specific models. Correspondingly, the framework proposed in this paper (Sect. 3), needs to be CAD, PLM and KBE systems independent. Thus, we have considered the following:

- Neutral product data representations to ensure data interoperability between CAD and PLM systems.
- Neutral knowledge representations to ensure the interoperability between KBE systems.
- A CAD abstraction layer enabling managing multi-CAD APIs giving access to the various CAD systems capabilities and enable inference engines to be CAD independent.

There are works dedicated to the exchange of data between CAD and PDM systems as well as the exchange of CAD and configuration data information between KBE and PLM systems such as [17]. The Standard for the Exchange of Product Model Data (STEP)[1] covers many aspects of product data exchange in the context of product development. The emerging STEP Application Protocol (AP) AP242 [18] merges AP203 and AP214 which are currently the most implemented for CAD data exchange between existing commercial CAD systems. The PDM Schema is a core set of entities in STEP that support the mapping of concepts for Product Data Management (PDM) systems interoperability integrating different STEP generic and application resources among which Parts 41 (fundamentals of product description and support), 42 (geometric and topological representation), and 44 (product structure configuration). The transfer of associated geometric interrelationships, parameters, and constraints, which is of particular importance to our proposal and which is not yet implemented in any application, is addressed by the Integrated-Application Resource 108 [19] and also in [20]. In [21], the author proposes a multi-layer design analysis systems integration framework integrating various concepts defined in the aforementioned STEP AP and parts as well as concepts from other neutral product data representations such as the CPM [22]. However, these endeavors have not solved the problem of being able to explicitly and unambiguously share geometric parameters and the design intent/design rational for knowledge re-use.

Concerning neutral KBE knowledge representations, some knowledge sharing initiatives in the beginning of the 90's have led to the implementation of some neutral knowledge formats in specific KBE applications such as the Knowledge Query and Manipulation Language (KQML) [23] and the Knowledge Interchange Format (KIF) [24]. However the adoption and implementation of these formats are restricted to few applications and their development and maintenance seem to have been stopped.

[1] NB: To respect the length requirement of the paper, some of the mentioned parts of the ISO STEP standard are not in the reference list.

More recently, the Rule Interchange Format (RIF) [25] has been developed to enable knowledge representation and information processing on the Web.

Very few works can be found in the literature regarding the development of platform-independent KBE systems. However we can quote the recent work from [26] in which authors propose a software framework using ontologies for representing design knowledge and for implementing platform-independent KBE systems within the aerospace industry. An essential element of the proposed framework and which will also be required for our framework is the use of APIs and GUIs that enables direct integration and communication between a KBE knowledge base, different CAD systems, GUI application and end-user.

Finally, in 2006, the Object Management Group (OMG) submitted a Request for Proposal for an international standard for KBE Services for PLM [27]. This standard intended to facilitate the integration of KBE applications in a PLM environment. To date, no answer to this RFP and no OMG specification for KBE services exist. This paper do not pretend to answer the request for proposal, but the framework and the schema presented in the next section could serve as a basis for future work in that direction.

3 The KBE-PLM Integration Framework and Schema

The proposed KBE-PLM integration framework presented in Sect. 3.1 is a federated platform-independent KBE environment enabling to retrieve and integrate the information and knowledge from CAD, KBE and PLM systems in order to store and manage them in a platform independent Open KBE repository. The goal is to be able to re-use this knowledge for different KBE applications for design automation. It also ensures a reintegration of the KBE-processed knowledge within various PLM systems repositories for further re-use in downstream design activities. Considering an MBD approach for supporting KBE-PLM systems integration, we assume that most design knowledge and related design rationale (design logic) are encapsulated respectively in CAD models and in KBE systems inference engine scripts. The Open KBE repository is structured according to the KBE-PLM integration schema introduced in Sect. 3.2. This schema depicts a concept for representing in a neutral way a configured product definition, the explicit knowledge encapsulated in parameterized CAD models and the implicit knowledge related to the design intent and rationale of these models.

3.1 Architecture of the KBE-PLM Integration Framework

The KBE-PLM integration framework architecture, shown in Fig. 1, has been specified using the open enterprise modeling standard ArchiMate [28] developed by The Open Group. The framework mainly comprises a Transformation Engine including a Multi-CAD API Manager, an Open KBE Repository (the server), and an Open KBE Client. ‘Open’ is used in the sense of neutral. The transformation engine encompasses a set of translator libraries. These enable the transformation of native data inputs extracted from PLM system (such as PDM and ERP systems) as well as from KBE

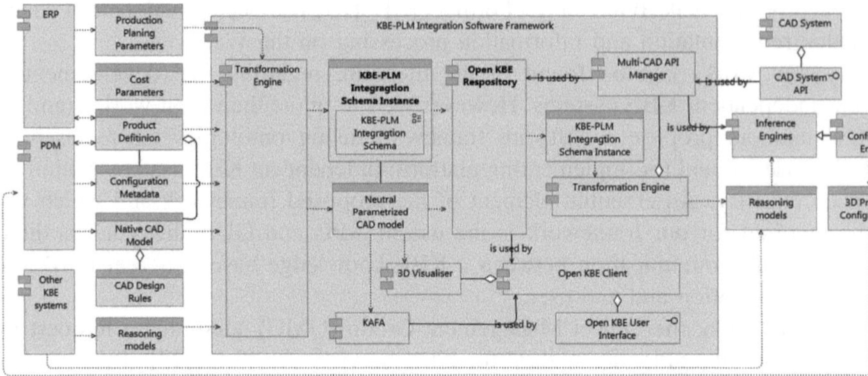

Fig. 1. KBE-PLM integration framework architecture described in ArchiMate.

systems. The nature of these inputs will depend on the addressed use case scenarios that the framework will support. The goal of the translators is to make these inputs compliant with the proposed KBE-PLM integration schema. Once the data inputs are transformed according to the schema, they can be stored in the Open KBE Repository and be interpreted and processed by the other framework components. For instance, the product structure and knowledge encapsulated in CAD parameterized assembly models can be extracted with the help of the Knowledge Acquisition and Formalization Assistant (KAFA) [14]. KAFA automatically reads the structure, components and parameters of a CAD model and generates a component-parameters design structure matrix (DSM). It extends the functionality of DSM methods by providing simple and intuitive means to enable the engineer to formalize the configuration and design logic in textual and executable forms.

The component and parameter dependencies and formalized rules defined in KAFA should enrich the Open KBE Repository according to the schema. The Open KBE client includes a user interface (UI) to access and request the Open KBE repository as well as a configurable 3D visualizer enabling to display the CAD geometry with the "fit-for-purpose" information (dimension, tolerances, parameters, rules, etc.). This UI should enable framework users to drive the required transformations for:

- translating the instantiated KBE-PLM Integration Schema and related reasoning models so that they can be processed by the right inference engine;
- driving the automation procedure in the appropriate CAD system through the use of the Multi-CAD API Manager;
- translating the outputs of the inference engine into the appropriate format so that new product definitions can be reintegrated in the various PLM systems.

3.2 The KBE-PLM Integration Schema

The KBE-PLM Integration Schema is an abstract model with system-independent and language-independent semantics. The schema defines a neutral product data and knowledge representation enabling the exchange of parameterized CAD assembly models and related design intent and rationale. It also associates the geometric representation and rationale to a specific usage context integrating information such as configuration management data, version history and the KBE application that process the design rationale. Figure 2 shows a Unified Modeling Language (UML) class diagram of the top abstraction level of the KBE-PLM Integration Schema. The structure of the schema is aligned with the modeling principles defined in STEP integrated and generic application resources and is also based on the premise that a product artifact has a form, a particular function and a behavior. The *Product Model* is the base abstract class for all entities that constitute the definition of a product. It is a master model containing data common to all configurations and versions of a system constituent. One *Product Model* has one or more *Product Definitions* and represents an abstract entity gathering all the characteristics and design information of a *Product Model*. The three *Product Definition* sub-types which are *Functional Definition*, *Structural Definition* and *Behavioral Definition* respectively gather the product functional variables, structural design variables and behavioral features of a *Product Model*.

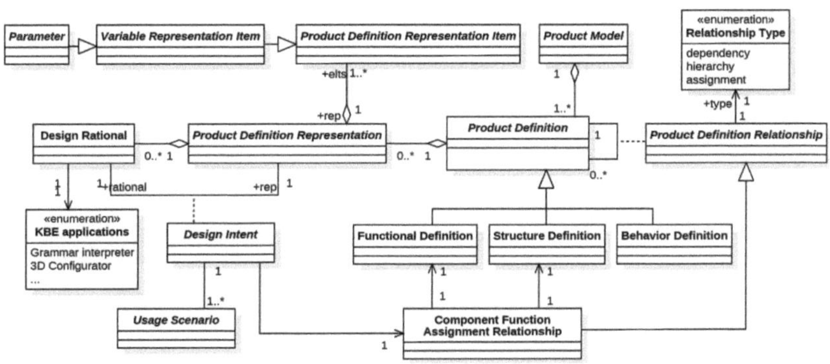

Fig. 2. KBE-PLM integration schema – top abstraction level.

A *Product Definition* consists of a set of *Product Definition Representations* (e.g. CAD models) and properties (e.g. mass and material properties). The product definition relationship entity enables to set up different types of relationship (dependency, hierarchical, etc.) so as to have traceability and consistency between the functional, structural and behavioral definition of a component. The ***Design Intent*** is a concept that, based on a specific usage context (defined by the *Usage Scenario* entity), enables the designer or engineer to know which product structural representation and related design rationale to use to fulfill a specific functional intent. The functional intent (defined by the *Component Function Assignment Relationship*) allows linking one *Functional Definition* to one *Structure Definition* to know what are the functions and related design requirements this structural definition intends to fulfill. Concretely, the design intent allows linking a specific *Product Definition Representation* to a specific

Design Rationale and the related *KBE application* that can process it. Figure 3 shows a more detailed level of the schema depicted in Fig. 2, focusing on instantiations of some of the abstract classes directed at:

- representing a parameterized CAD assembly model;
- representing the KBE rules through the use of the abstract class Variational Representation Item, the instances of which are the Parameters and Explicit Constraints defining the mathematical functions between parameters;
- defining the specific relationships between a geometric model and its topological elements, its design rationale, functional requirements and design parameters.

To represent an assembly model an *Assembly Component Usage* (sub-type of *Product Relationship*) describes which components are present in each parent assembly component as well as its relative *Position*. A *Structure Definition* also aggregates a set of *Properties* class which can be *Item Property* or *Shape Dependent Property*. The Structure Definition also aggregates *Structure Model(s)* which is an abstract class defining various models derived from the *Structure Definition*. In Fig. 3 below, only the *Geometric Model* is considered.

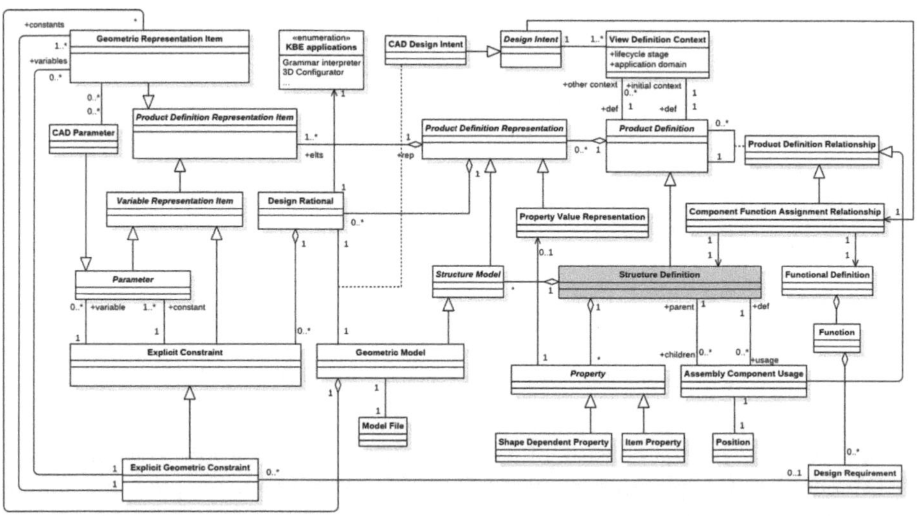

Fig. 3. KBE-PLM integration schema – CAD assembly models, CAD design intent, design rationale and parameterization.

A *Geometric Model* is an aggregation of *Geometric Representation Items* (topological element of the CAD model). In the STEP and Feature Based Parametric Modeling paradigms, the *Geometric Representation Items* are driven by parameters and constraints. In this schema the constraints (represented by the *Explicit Constraint* entity) define the dependency rules and the mathematical functions (as defined in ISO10303-50) between *Parameters*. In the above schema, there is a complex but necessary inheritance structure to manage and link these *Geometric Representation Items* to their related parameters and constraints. This inheritance mechanism is necessary to further extend the schema and to define constraints and/or rules between other types of parameters and product definition representation items from other types of product definition representations (behavioral representation or item property representations). The *Geometric Representation Item* entity and the *Variational Representation Item* entity are direct sub-class of the *Product Definition Representation Items* (which are the constituting elements of a representation whatever its type). The *Parameter* and *Explicit Constraint* entity are both sub-types of the *Variational Representation Item* entity. The abstract *Explicit Constraint* entity links a set of constant and variable parameters. The *Explicit Geometric Constraint* entity is the "instantiable" sub-type for linking a set of constant and variable CAD model parameters that are related to the some topological elements (*Geometric Representation Item*) of the CAD model.

Finally to integrate configuration context information with the Product Definition and its Design Intent, the proposed KBE-PLM integration schema is actually a multi-layer schema as the one defined by Vosgien [21]. As shown in Fig. 4, it integrates a system definition layer and a configuration layer in order to be able to ensure the interoperability with PDM systems through standardized data exchange. A *Configuration* is a product variant (or Configuration Item in ISO10303-44), i.e. the identification of a particular variant of a product. A product variant is defined with respect to the product class (product concept in ISO10303-44), i.e. the class of similar products of which it is a member.

Concretely, Fig. 4 shows the data model enabling to build, capture and modify the various product configurations and how they are linked to their constituting elements (Assembly Component Usage of Product Definitions) through the concept of

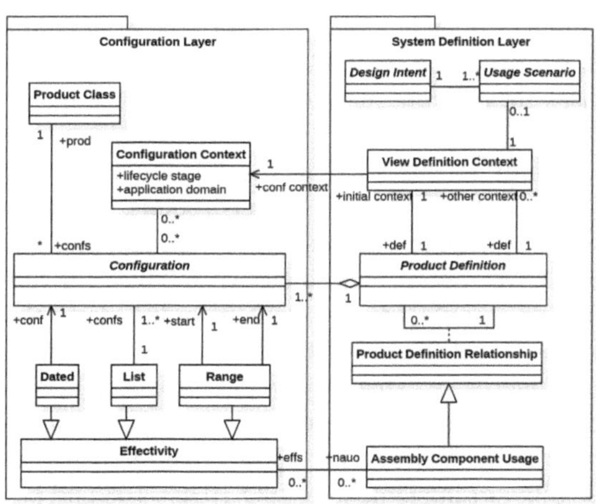

Fig. 4. KBE-PLM integration schema – integration of configuration context information with the product definition and its design intent. (adapted from [31])

"Effectivity". *Effectivity* is the key concept for linking the system Product Definitions to the appropriate product configurations in which they are valid as defined in. Instances of *Effectivity* may be applied to any *Product Definition* instances (or *Assembly Component Usage*). The *View_Definition_Context* defines the context in which the *Product Definition* of a product model is valid. A *View Definition Context* is the grouping of a *Configuration_Context* (defining the application domain(s) and the life cycle stage(s) in which a *Product Definition* is valid). In order to specify the usage and potential re-use of a representation with a design rationale in a specific configuration context, the *Design Intent* entity is linked to one *Usage Scenario* which refers to at least one *View Definition Context Definition.*

Summarizing, the core contribution of this schema is built on the *Design Intent* entity and its instantiation for CAD models (the *CAD Design Intent*) defining the proper defined relationships between a CAD model, its design rationale and its KBE usage scenario.

4 Discussion

The KBE-PLM integration framework and schema have been presented above. The schema has to be enriched with all *Geometric Representation Item* sub-types in order to be able to represent and exchange any kind of geometric model. The construction history has not been taken into account yet in the schema but will have to be addressed in future work. The feasibility of implementing such a data model will be demonstrated in future work addressing several test cases (see next section). With respect to the implementation of the framework components, we face some heavy refactoring work based on a number industry-strength prototypes of configurators and design automation systems developed by V-Research in earlier and current industrial research projects as part of COMET ProDSS [29] and AEDA K-Projects (see below). We also have a KAFA prototype from TU Wien, and the neutral CAD-model representation is part of the first author's PhD project. The Multi-CAD API Manager is already operational with bidirectional interfaces (at different maturity levels) to three major CAD systems and was developed by V-Research.

The major limitation of the presented approach is the need to develop a large set of interfaces for CAD/KBE/PLM systems to incorporate them into the framework. Moreover, any evolution in these systems will entail adapting these interfaces to the evolved systems, e.g. CAD systems and their APIs. Thus, for full-potential leverage, standardization initiatives would be important in order to involve industrialists and software vendors in the development of the standard and in the implementation and maintenance of these interfaces. That is why the proposed KBE integration schema could serve as a basis to re-launch research work targeted on answering the OMG request for proposal "KBE services for PLM". Additionally, it could be used to demonstrate the feasibility of implementing ISO 10303-108 and be able to use this part of the schema in both PLM and KBE repositories.

5 Conclusion and Way Forward

The proposed KBE-PLM integration framework presented in Sect. 3.1 is a federated platform-independent KBE environment permitting to retrieve and integrate the information and knowledge from CAD, KBE and PLM systems. The goal is to be able to re-use this knowledge for different KBE applications for design automation. It also ensures a re-integration of the KBE-processed knowledge within various PLM systems repositories for further re-use in downstream design activities. The framework encompasses a platform-independent Open KBE repository structured according to the KBE-PLM integration schema introduced in Sect. 3.2. This schema depicts a concept for representing, in a neutral way, configured product definitions, the explicit knowledge encapsulated in parameterized CAD models and the implicit knowledge related to the design intent and rationale of these models. The work presented here only represents a starting point. The following issues will be addressed in future work. As mentioned, we are currently reviewing use-case scenario candidates and will correspondingly capture industrial test case (TC) datasets. These datasets will be used to demonstrate the feasibility to instantiate the proposed schema and implement such a platform-independent KBE repository generating a data base with the data model. Then a first client prototype will be developed to be able to enrich and request this database. Hence, KAFA will be extended to automate the extraction of the knowledge from the TC datasets, and the database will be enriched automatically. The Multi-CAD API Manager CADAL (CAD Abstraction Layer) is an ongoing development effort at V-Research.

Acknowledgments. This work was supported by the K-Project 'Advanced Engineering Design Automation' (AEDA) that is financed under the COMET (COMpetence centers for Excellent Technologies) funding scheme of the Austrian Research Promotion Agency.

References

1. Brown, S.L., Eisenhardt, K.M.: Product development: past research, present findings, and future directions. Acad. Manage. Rev. **20**(2), 343–378 (1995)
2. Verhagen, W.J.C., Bermell-Garcia, P., van Dijk, R.E.C., Curran, R.: A critical review of knowledge-based engineering: an identification of research challenges. Adv. Eng. Inform. **26** (1), 5–15 (2012)
3. Kim, J., Pratt, M.J., Iyer, R.G., Sriram, R.D.: Standardized data exchange of CAD models with design intent. Comput.-Aided Des. **40**(7), 760–777 (2008)
4. Rachuri, S., Subrahmanian, E., Bouras, A., Fenves, S.J., Foufou, S., Sriram, R.D.: Information sharing and exchange in the context of product lifecycle management: role of standards. Comput.-Aided Des. **40**(7), 789–800 (2008)
5. Catic, A., Malmqvist, J.: Towards integration of KBE and PLM. In: Proceedings of the International Conference on Engineering Design (ICED 2007) (2007)
6. Bermell-Garcia, P., Fan, I.-S.: Practitioner requirements for integrated knowledge-based engineering in product lifecycle management. Int. J. Prod. Lifecycle Manag. **3**(1), 3–20 (2008)

7. Stokes, M.: Managing Engineering Knowledge: MOKA - Methodology for Knowledge Based Engineering Applications. Professional Engineering Publication, London (2001)
8. Schreiber, G.: Knowledge Engineering and Management: The CommonKADS Methodology. MIT Press, Cambridge (2000)
9. Curran, R., Verhagen, W.J.C., van Tooren, M.J.L., van der Laan, T.H.: A multidisciplinary implementation methodology for knowledge based engineering: KNOMAD. Expert Syst. Appl. **37**(11), 7336–7350 (2010)
10. Hoisl, F., Shea, K., Helms, B., et al.: Towards representing, evolving and networking engineering knowledge for computational design synthesis. In: The 10th International Design Conference on Proceedings DESIGN 2008, Dubrovnik, Croatia (2008)
11. Chandrasegaran, S.K., Ramani, K., Sriram, R.D., Horváth, I., Bernard, A., Harik, R.F., Gao, W.: The evolution, challenges, and future of knowledge representation in product design systems. Comput.-Aided Des. **45**(2), 204–228 (2013)
12. Gero, J.S., Kannengiesser, U.: The situated function–behaviour–structure framework. Des. Stud. **25**(4), 373–391 (2004)
13. Quintana, V., Rivest, L., Pellerin, R., Venne, F., Kheddouci, F.: Will model-based definition replace engineering drawings throughout the product lifecycle? A global perspective from aerospace industry. Comput. Ind. **61**(5), 497–508 (2010)
14. Gerhard, D., Lutz, C.: IT-based configuration and dimensioning of customer specific products – towards a framework for implementing knowledge based design assistant systems. In: 68-6: Proceedings of the 18th International Conference on Engineering Design, ICED 2011 (2011)
15. Object Management Group: Model Driven Architecture (MDA) (2014)
16. Truyen, F.: The Fast Guide to Model Driven Architecture the Basics of Model Driven Architecture. Cephas Consulting Corporation, Tustin (2006)
17. Pablo, B.-G., Ip-Shing, F., Adrian, M. et al.: Towards the semantic interoperability between Kbe and PLM systems. Guidelines for a Decision Support Method Adapted to NPD Processes (2007)
18. ISO 10303-242: Industrial Automation Systems and Integration - Product Data Representation and Exchange - Part 242: Application Protocol: Managed Model-Based 3D Engineering (2014)
19. ISO 10303-108:2005: Industrial Automation Systems and Integration – Product Data Representation and Exchange – Part 108: Integrated Application Resource: Parameterization and Constraints for Explicit Geometric Product Models (2005)
20. Lee, H.C., Gaikwad, P.K., Adédjouma, S.A., Azehoun-Pazou, G., Tall, K., Mboup, M.L., Farssi, S.M., Diop, I., Diop, A.K., Sissoko, G. et al.: Strategies for using STEP in parametric design. Strategies **2**(4) (2013)
21. Vosgien, T.: Model-based system engineering enabling design-analysis data integration in digital design environments: application to collaborative aeronautics simulation-based design process and turbojet integration studies. Ph.D. thesis, Ecole Centrale Paris (2015)
22. Fenves, S.J., Foufou, S., Bock, C., Sriram, R.D.: CPM2: a core model for product data. J. Comput. Inf. Sci. Eng. **8**(1), 014501 (2008)
23. Finin, T., McKay, D., Fritzson, R.: An overview of KQML: a knowledge query and manipulation language. Citeseer (1992)
24. Genesereth, M.R., Fikes, R.E. et al.: Knowledge interchange format-version 3.0: reference manual (1992)
25. Kifer, M.: Rule interchange format: the framework. In: Calvanese, D., Lausen, G. (eds.) RR 2008. LNCS, vol. 5341, pp. 1–11. Springer, Heidelberg (2008). doi:10.1007/978-3-540-88737-9_1

26. Sanya, I.O., Shehab, E.M.: An ontology framework for developing platform-independent knowledge-based engineering systems in the aerospace industry. Int. J. Prod. Res. **52**(20), 6192–6215 (2014)
27. Fan, I.-S., Bermell-Garcia, P.: International standard development for knowledge based engineering services for product lifecycle management. Concurr. Eng. **16**(4), 271–277 (2008)
28. Lankhorst, M.,M., Proper, H.,A., Jonkers, H.: The architecture of the ArchiMate language. In: Halpin, T., Krogstie, J., Nurcan, S., Proper, E., Schmidt, R., Soffer, P., Ukor, R. (eds.) BPMDS/EMMSAD -2009. LNBIP, vol. 29, pp. 367–380. Springer, Heidelberg (2009). doi:10.1007/978-3-642-01862-6_30
29. Frank, G., Entner, D., Prante, T., Khachatouri, V., Schwarz, M.: Towards a generic framework of engineering design automation for creating complex CAD models. Int. J. Adv. Syst. Meas. **7**(1, 2), 179–192 (2014)

On the Use of Process Mining and Machine Learning to Support Decision Making in Systems Design

Widad Es-Soufi(✉), Esma Yahia, and Lionel Roucoules

Arts et Métiers ParisTech, CNRS, LSIS, 2 cours des Arts et Métiers, 13617 Aix en Provence, France
{Widad.ES-SOUFI,Esma.YAHIA,Lionel.ROUCOULES}@ensam.eu

Abstract. Research on process mining and machine learning techniques has recently received a significant amount of attention by product development and management communities. Indeed, these techniques allow both an automatic process and activity discovery and thus are high added value services that help reusing knowledge to support decision-making. This paper proposes a double layer framework aiming to identify the most significant process patterns to be executed depending on the design context. Simultaneously, it proposes the most significant parameters for each activity of the considered process pattern. The framework is applied on a specific design example and is partially implemented.

Keywords: Collaborative design process · Process mining · Supervised classification · Process patterns · Decision-making

1 Introduction

The product design is a purposeful, constrained and decision making process [1]. Indeed, companies aim at satisfying their clients by proposing innovative products. Thus, a multidisciplinary group of engineers work in collaboration in order to propose the products that best meet the clients' requirements. However, current practises and software do not allow one to document the decisions that were taken as well as the rejected design choices. Hence, engineers lose a considerable amount of time while retrieving the design decisions when changes are occurring [2].

Our research is interested in product design that is a process in which a high added value output (i.e. product) is produced. To solve the problem of decisions retrieval, authors have already proposed in [3, 4] a collaborative design process meta-model to capitalize the design rationale. Authors proposed to gather and archive all the design process executions' traces, that conforms to a trace meta-model, in a trace base. The trace meta-model describes the design process knowledge that needs to be captured and saved for a further analysis. In this paper, authors propose a generic method that couples mining and learning techniques in order to assist engineers in their decision-making processes. Indeed, through a process traces analysis, the most suitable design activities to be executed are identified. Then, for each activity, the most convenient design choices are identified. Authors assume that this objective can be achieved using Process mining

R. Harik et al. (Eds.): PLM 2016, IFIP AICT 492, pp. 56–66, 2016.
DOI: 10.1007/978-3-319-54660-5_6

(PM) and machine learning (ML) techniques. Indeed, PM allows one to explore the design process from past executions by generating the different process patterns based on the occurrence of activities in the trace data base. Whereas, ML techniques allow one to extract knowledge from data that is collected in the trace data base and thus, help predicting future data according to the new design context.

This paper is organized as follows. In Sect. 2, the relevant research tackling the process mining for process discovery, as well as the machine learning for activity parameters prediction are introduced. Related works are presented in Sect. 3. In Sect. 4, the decision-making support technique is introduced and then tested on a case study in Sect. 5. Finally, future work is discussed and the paper is concluded.

2 Literature Review on Process Mining and Machine Learning

PM is a research field that supports process understanding and improvements, it derives from the field of data mining that is fully concentrated on data and thus cannot provide a complete description of the end-to-end process [5]. This discipline helps to automatically extract the hidden useful knowledge from the recorded event logs generated by information systems. In [6], the author distinguishes three types of applications in process mining: *discovery*, *conformance* and *enhancement*. In this present work, authors are more interested in the *discovery* application of PM.

Process Discovery allows one to automatically generate the process model from the event log by analysing the observed behaviour from the recorded events (i.e. trace), and without using any a-priori information out of the event log. Through this application, PM allows one to extract the patterns which frequently occur in a design process. The pattern concept was first introduced in [7] as an entity that describes both a frequent problem and the solution that was considered to resolve it. In the context of software design, different specific patterns among component, composite, etc. were defined in order to describe the frequent solutions that resolve software design problems [8]. In [9], authors reuse these patterns to build product models during the product information system specification. In our context, the pattern concept is slightly different since it refers to a possible end-to-end design process execution that encapsulates the process information (i.e. who did what, when, where, why and how defined in [4]).

ML consists in "*building computer programs able to construct new knowledge or to improve already possessed knowledge by using input information*" [10]. The starting point in machine learning is a data set that consists of a set of data records (also called instance, observation or case). An instance is described by a n-dimensional attribute vector $X = (X_1, X_2, \ldots, X_n)$ and has a target attribute Y called the class or label. Most learning problems fall into one of four categories: supervised, unsupervised, semi supervised or reinforcement learning. A brief summary is provided of each.

Supervised learning: this kind of machine learning is a two steps process. The learning step uses a labelled data set, where the label Y of each attributes vector X is known, to build and evaluate a classification model (i.e. classifier). The Prediction step uses the already constructed classification model to predict class labels for given real-world data

[11]. Supervised learning has two tasks: *supervised classification* where the label Y is a discrete set (True/False), and *regression* where the label Y is a continuous number.

Unsupervised learning: in this type of machine learning, labels in the data set are unknown. The task consists in exploring the data set and identifying data groups by the exploratory analysis and then gathering them in groups called clusters [12].

Semi supervised learning: this technique makes use of both supervised and unsupervised learning and has two tasks. First, the *semi supervised classification* uses a data set that contains both labelled and unlabelled data, the goal is to train a classifier from both of them. Second, the *constrained clustering* uses a training data that consists of unlabelled data as well as a-priori information about clusters such as must-link and cannot-link constraints [13].

Reinforcement learning: this technique combines the field of programming and supervised learning. The goal is to develop learners or software agents that learn from their own experience and from the feedback of environment which may be expressed by a reward or punishment [14].

ML in product design is defined as the learning methods that can be applied to the acquisition of knowledge [15]. In [16], authors introduce a method that allows one to automate the generation of the key design parameters, they use a ML genetic algorithm [17] to select the optimal design among a set of trial designs and thus produce designs with higher performance gains. In [18], authors show that the commercial success of a product depends not only on its functionality but also on its physical appearance that may meet or not the consumer's expectations. Authors use ML techniques to predict the consumer response to any product form. In [19], authors introduce a hybrid algorithm linking ML and search techniques. It uses the capitalized expert knowledge from past optimizations and allows one to select the project scenarios in the early product design phase. In [20], authors aim to adapt CAD models for numerical simulations by simplifying or removing some features of the designed product, this is called the CAD models preparation process. Authors use ML based techniques to predict the features that can be removed or simplified in a new CAD model based on the past expertise knowledge. In [21], authors propose a method that couples the fuzzy theory with the ML techniques to approximate the product design duration as it is constrained by several random factors and is not a forecast problem.

3 Literature Review on Coupling PM and ML

Many research works link both PM and ML techniques. In [22], authors propose a tool that supports collaborative writing of an electronic document. The tool uses ML techniques for extracting document changes as well as PM techniques for extracting event logs, that capture the user's behaviour, and then generating the process model. In [23], authors use the Case Data Extraction mining plugin (PM technique) to extract the case data of the dyeing log, and the association rule mining (ML technique) to find relationships between the extracted data. Our work is closely related to [24], where the authors propose a method for discovering business rules. The PM is first used to analyse the information in event log by identifying the category of users that performs the activity and then ML is used to analyse the context information existing in the event log to discover the set of possible activity parameters' values.

The studied works use ML techniques to extract the knowledge from data and find relationships between them. Afterwards, they use PM techniques to identify the process model from the recorded event log. The work reported in this paper adopts the same logic and, in addition, presents a double process analysis. Indeed, authors start by discovering the process' possible patterns using PM. Then, for each pattern, authors predict the activity possible parameters using the supervised classification (ML technique). The most suitable pattern and activity parameters are then proposed to the decision-maker according to the design context.

4 Double Layer Framework for Decision-Making Support

In the context of product design, the proposal distinguishes two types of decision-making (Fig. 1): The global decision-making (expressed in BPMN [25]) and the local decision-making (expressed in IDEF0[1]).

Global decision-making: when working or reworking on a product design, the engineer has the choice to perform some activities before others. The different gateways (And, Or, Xor) [25, Sect. 8.3.9] are used to control how the process flows and, thus, give rise to several possible executions (Fig. 1). The global decision-making consists in automatically proposing a ranking of the most significant patterns (i.e. set of ordered activities), that match the design context.

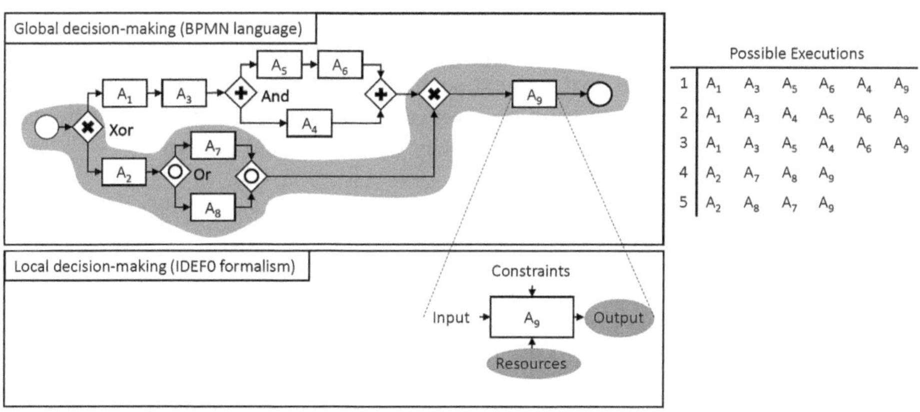

Fig. 1. Global and local decision-making (in grey, the decisions that have been taken)

Local decision-making: when dealing with the product design process, two main types of activities are distinguished: modelling and decision activities. On the one hand, the

[1] https://en.wikipedia.org/wiki/IDEF0.

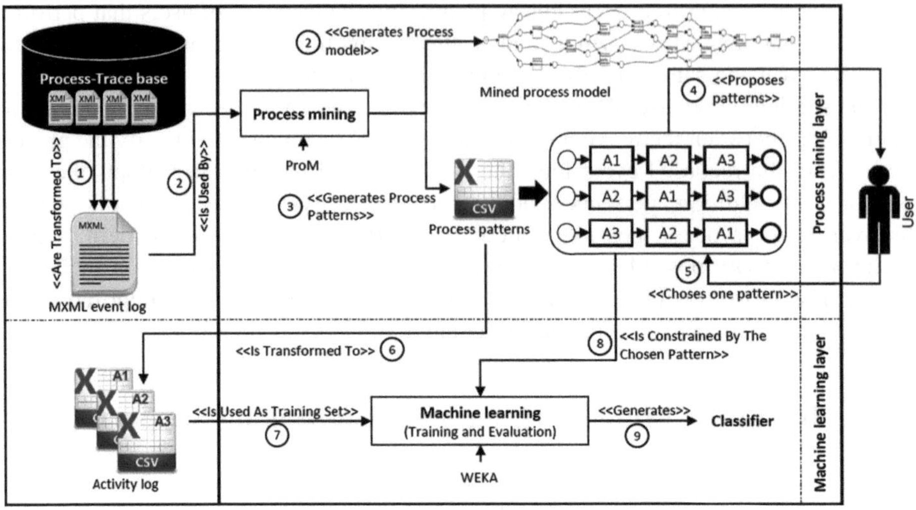

Fig. 2. Overview of the proposal

modelling activity transforms an input into output, by taking in consideration the imposed design constraints, and by using some resources (human, documentary, software, etc.). On the other hand, the *decision activity* consists in choosing one or several solutions among all the design alternatives by taking into account the constraints and using some resources. The local decision-making consists in predicting the most relevant resources for the modelling and decision activities. In addition, it consists in predicting the output (i.e. Decision) in the case of the decision activity (Fig. 1).

The double layer framework shown in Fig. 2 represents the proposal of this research. In the process mining layer, the goal is to extract the most frequent patterns of the product design process. In the machine learning layer, the goal is to predict the most frequent parameters, given the context, for each activity of the selected pattern.

4.1 Process Mining Layer

The starting point of PM is some information about the past executions of design processes in the form of event logs that could be expressed in XES format (eXtensible Event Stream) or MXML format (Mining eXtensible Markup Language). In this paper, authors use MXML as it is an XML-based syntax format and has a meta model [26]. In the process mining layer (Fig. 2), authors start by transforming the process executions' traces contained in the Process-Trace base [3], where each trace is a single past execution of the process and is expressed in XMI format (XML Metadata Interchange). Indeed, the trace is considered as an instance of the trace meta-model proposed in [4], that is implemented in the Eclipse environment[2], and whose instantiation generates a

[2] https://eclipse.org/.

XMI trace. The transformation consists in a translation of all the traces into a MXML event log. This latter stores the information related to several executions of the process, each execution refers to a case (i.e. trace) and contains ordered events where each event refers to an activity of the process [26]. Event logs should conform to the MXML meta model but may store additional information. In our context, an event log contains the basic elements described in the MXML meta model [26] as well as the concepts of the process meta model identified in [4].

There are many mining software tools that help to discover event logs, authors can cite, inter alia, Mylnvenio[3], ProM[4] and Disco[5]. In this present work authors use ProM as it is a free and open source process mining tool that supports the development of PM plugins. ProM allows the *process discovery* by generating process models from the input event log. In addition, it allows the process patterns discovery by identifying the most frequent patterns in a process through the pattern abstraction visualization [27]. Mined patterns can be filtered depending on certain parameters including their apparition frequency in the process and their size (i.e. number of contained activities) and they can be exported in CSV format. Hence, during a new execution of the process, authors propose the mined patterns classified according to their frequency. The user chooses one of them and its choice constrains the machine learning layer.

4.2 Machine Learning Layer

In this layer, authors aim at predicting the resources to be used and/or the decision to be considered for each activity of the chosen process pattern. In this context, the most relevant learning technique, among those presented in Sect. 2, is the supervised classification, since its objective is to learn from known values to predict new ones. There are several machine learning tools that support supervised classification, authors chose Weka[6] since it is a free and open source framework, simple to use and well documented. As it is considered, each time, only one activity of the process pattern while applying the supervised classification algorithms with Weka, a training set for this considered activity is constructed in order to start the supervised classification process (Fig. 3). Thus, the different executions of each activity are extracted from the CSV file of the mined process patterns and saved separately in an activity log in CSV format. The training set is constructed as following: X is the input attributes vector that describes the properties of the activity and Y is the output variable. The training set can be pre-processed in case some attributes of the vector X need to be eliminated [28].

The next step is to select a supervised classification algorithm (i.e. classifier) among naïve Bayes, decision tree, SVM, neural nets, etc. and apply it on the training set. After being trained, the selected algorithms are evaluated by using a testing set, where Y is unknown for each attributes vector X. The most accurate classifier will be then used to

[3] https://www.my-invenio.com/.

[4] http://www.promtools.org/.

[5] https://fluxicon.com/disco/.

[6] http://www.cs.waikato.ac.nz/ml/weka/downloading.html.

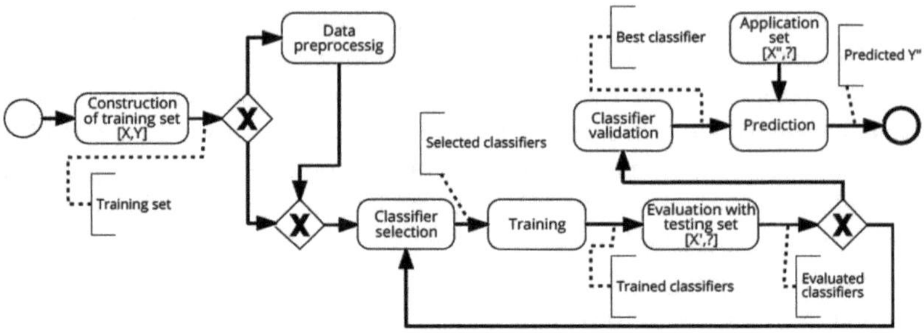

Fig. 3. Process of the supervised classification

predict the desired variable during a new activity execution. The evaluation of supervised classification algorithms is not addressed in this paper since authors assume that the decision tree algorithm is the most suitable in our context.

5 Case Study: Application on an Electric Torch Design Process

The example considered in this study is an electric torch design process (Fig. 4). First, the engineer has the choice to begin the process with one of the fourth activities: "External functional analysis", "Internal functional analysis", "Nomenclature" or

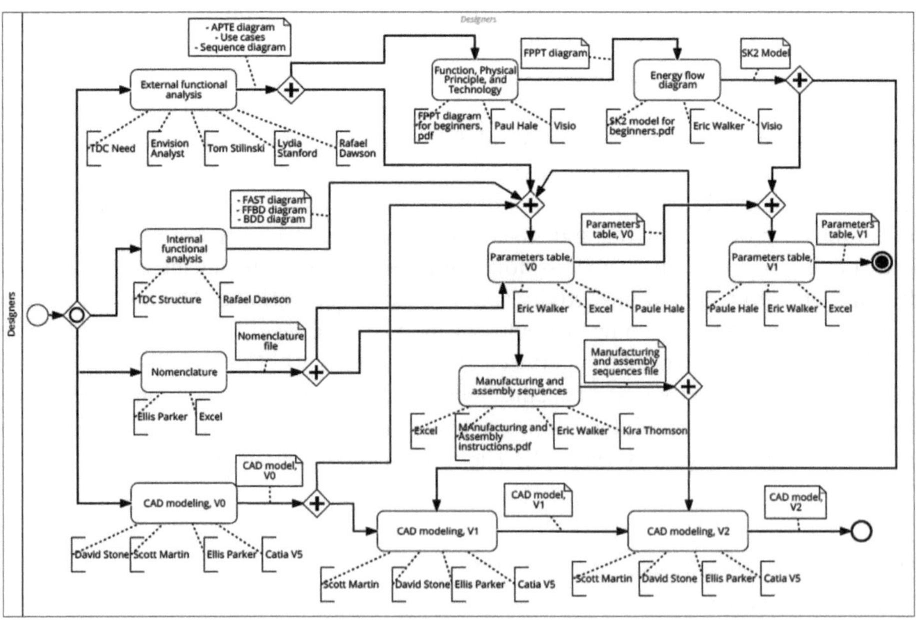

Fig. 4. Electric torch design process in BPMN formalism

"CAD modelling V0". Second, after performing the previous fourth activities, he can either perform the "Function, Physical principle and technology" activity or the "Manufacturing and assembly sequences" activity. After that, he has the possibility to choose to begin with creating the "Parameters table V0" or the "Energy flow diagram". Finally, he has the choice to perform the "Parameters table V1" or "CAD modelling V1". Note that there are several different possible executions.

Process mining phase: in order to derive the process patterns to be followed, ProM is used to analyse the past executions (in MXML format) and then extracts the most frequent patterns (Fig. 5). In this example, the first pattern proposed by ProM contains four activities (i.e. pattern alphabet), and in 90% of the cases, the "Parameters table V1" activity is followed by "CAD modelling V1" activity which is followed by the "CAD modelling V2" activity that concludes the process. The patterns proposed by ProM are classified by their apparition frequency and can be exported in CSV format (Fig. 6). The engineer chooses, then, the most suitable pattern; where the first is the most frequently used in this design context.

Pattern Alphabet	Pattern Sequence Set	Alphabet Count	Instance Count (%)
CAD modeling V2-complete CAD modeling V1-complete Parameters table V1-complete EndProcess-complete	Parameters table V1-complete CAD modeling V1-complete CAD modeling V2-complete EndProcess-complete	9	90
CAD modeling V2-complete CAD modeling V1-complete Parameters table V1-complete Parameters table V0-complete Energy flow diagram-complete Manufacturing and assembly sequences-complete EndProcess-complete Function, Physical principle and technology-complete	Function, Physical principle and technology-complete Manufacturing and assembly sequences-complete Energy flow diagram-complete Parameters table V0-complete Parameters table V1-complete CAD modeling V1-complete CAD modeling V2-complete EndProcess-complete	7	70

Fig. 5. Frequent patterns (only two are presented) in the electric torch design process

case	event	startTime	completeTime	Input	Documentary reso	Software resou	Human resource	Output	Internal Control
	CreateProcess	1/2/2016 9:00	1/2/2016 9:00						
	External functional analysis	1/2/2016 10:15	1/2/2016 10:15			TDC Need	Tom Stilinski	APTE diagram	
	Internal functional analysis	1/2/2016 11:15	1/2/2016 11:15			TDC Structure	Rafael Dawson	FAST diagram	
	Nomenclature	1/2/2016 12:15	1/2/2016 12:15			Excel	Ellis Parker	Nomenclature file	
	CAD modeling V0	1/2/2016 13:15	1/2/2016 13:15			Catia V5	Ellis Parker	CAD model V0	
	Function, Physical principle and te	1/2/2016 14:15	1/2/2016 14:15		FPPT diagram for	Visio	Paul Hale	FPPT diagram	APTE diagram
1	Manufacturing and assembly sequ	1/2/2016 15:15	1/2/2016 15:15		Manufacturing an	Excel	Eric Walker	Manufacturing a	Nomenclature file
	Energy flow diagram	1/2/2016 16:15	1/2/2016 16:15		SK2 model for beg	Visio	Eric Walker	Sk2 model	FPPT diagram
	Parameters table V0	1/2/2016 17:15	1/2/2016 17:15		Nomenclature file	Excel	Paul Hale	Parameters table	Manufacturing and assembly sequence file
	Parameters table V1	1/2/2016 18:15	1/2/2016 18:15		Nomenclature file	Excel	Paul Hale	Parameters table	Parameters table V0
	CAD modeling V1	1/2/2016 19:15	1/2/2016 19:15	CAD model	Nomenclature file	Catia V5	Ellis Parker	CAD model V1	Sk2 model
	CAD modeling V2	1/2/2016 20:15	1/2/2016 20:15	CAD model	Nomenclature file	Catia V5	Ellis Parker	CAD model V2	Manufacturing and assembly sequence file
	EndProcess	1/2/2016 20:30	1/2/2016 20:30						
	CreateProcess	1/2/2016 9:00	1/2/2016 9:00						
	Internal functional analysis	1/2/2016 10:15	1/2/2016 10:15			TDC Structure	Rafael Dawson	FAST diagram	
	External functional analysis	1/2/2016 11:15	1/2/2016 11:15			TDC Need	Tom Stilinski	APTE diagram	
	Nomenclature	1/2/2016 12:15	1/2/2016 12:15			Excel	Ellis Parker	Nomenclature file	
	CAD modeling V0	1/2/2016 13:15	1/2/2016 13:15			Catia V5	Ellis Parker	CAD model V0	
	Function, Physical principle and te	1/2/2016 14:15	1/2/2016 14:15		FPPT diagram for	Visio	Paul Hale	FPPT diagram	APTE diagram
2	Manufacturing and assembly sequ	1/2/2016 15:15	1/2/2016 15:15		Manufacturing an	Excel	Eric Walker	Manufacturing a	Nomenclature file
	Energy flow diagram	1/2/2016 16:15	1/2/2016 16:15		SK2 model for beg	Visio	Eric Walker	Sk2 model	FPPT diagram
	Parameters table V0	1/2/2016 17:15	1/2/2016 17:15		Nomenclature file	Excel	Paul Hale	Parameters table	Manufacturing and assembly sequence file
	Parameters table V1	1/2/2016 18:15	1/2/2016 18:15		Nomenclature file	Excel	Paul Hale	Parameters table	Parameters table V0
	CAD modeling V1	1/2/2016 19:15	1/2/2016 19:15	CAD model	Nomenclature file	Catia V5	Ellis Parker	CAD model V1	Sk2 model
	CAD modeling V2	1/2/2016 20:15	1/2/2016 20:15	CAD model	Nomenclature file	Catia V5	Ellis Parker	CAD model V2	Manufacturing and assembly sequence file
	EndProcess	1/2/2016 20:30	1/2/2016 20:30						

Fig. 6. Exported process patterns (only two are presented)

Machine learning phase: for each activity of the chosen process pattern, authors aim to propose the parameters (resources and/or decision) to be considered while performing the activity. Weka is used since it provides many supervised classification algorithms which can be trained by the training set that refers to the activity log. In this study, authors use the J48 decision tree classifier which is an implementation of the C4.5 algorithm that generates decision trees [29]. After being trained and tested, the algorithm allows predicting the desired activity parameters' value, in Fig. 7 an example of the software resource that is used to perform the "External functional analysis" activity is presented. In this example, the prediction takes into account the human resource that performs the activity and the start time of the execution of the activity. For example, the J48 algorithm is 77.6% sure that Tom Stilinski uses TDC Need to perform the "External functional analysis" activity at 9.25 AM o'clock.

Instance	Human Resource	Start Time	Software
1	Tom Stilinski	09:25	?
2	Lydia Stanford	10:25	?
3	Rafael Dawson	14:15	?
4	Lydia Stanford	17:30	?
5	Rafael Dawson	07:45	?

```
=== Predictions on test set ===

 inst#     actual  predicted error prediction
     1        1:?  1:TDCNeed       0.776
     2        1:?  1:TDCNeed       0.742
     3        1:? 2:EnvisionAnalyst         0.997
     4        1:?  1:TDCNeed       0.742
     5        1:? 2:EnvisionAnalyst         0.997
```

Fig. 7. The software resource prediction for the "External functional analysis" activity

6 Conclusion and Future Work

The objective of this research is to propose a decision-making support technique that aids engineers, during the design or redesign of a product. Through the proposed technique, the past design executions are analysed and the most relevant design patterns to be followed are proposed. In addition, for each activity of the considered design process, the most suitable resources and/or decision are proposed. The proposed technique illustrates the feasibility of the assumption about the use of PM and ML in the decision-making support. It has been illustrated on a case study where only *And* and *Or* (with true conditions) gateways are considered. Future work consists in addressing the design processes containing the *Xor/Or* gateways that give rise to several patterns, where only the one that satisfies the condition must be executed. The objective is to automatically propose, in a new design context, the process pattern in which all the *Xor/Or* gateways' conditions are satisfied. Future work also consists in studying the impact of the proposal on design processes with respect to some performance indicators such as development time, changes propagation, etc.

Acknowledgments. This research takes part of a national collaborative project (Gontrand) that aims at supervising a smart gas grid. Authors would like to thank the companies REGAZ, GDS and GRDF for their collaboration.

References

1. Gero, J.S.: Creativity, emergence and evolution in design. Knowl. Based Syst. **9**(7), 435–448 (1996)
2. Ullman, D.G.: The Mechanical Design Process. McGraw-Hill Higher Education, New York (2003)
3. Roucoules, L., Yahia, E., Es-Soufi, W., Tichkiewitch, S.: Engineering design memory for design rationale and change management toward innovation. CIRP Ann. Manuf. Tech. **65** (1), 193–196 (2016)
4. Es-Soufi, W., Yahia, E., Roucoules, L.: Collaborative design and supervision processes meta-model for rationale capitalization. In: Eynard, B., Nigrelli, V., Oliveri, S.M., Peris-Fajarnes, G., Rizzuti, S. (eds.) Advances on Mechanics, Design Engineering and Manufacturing, pp. 1123–1130. Springer, Heidelberg (2017)
5. van der Aalst, W.M.P.: Process Mining: Discovery, Conformance and Enhancement of Business Processes. Springer, Heidelberg (2011)
6. van der Aalst, W.M.P.: Process mining: overview and opportunities. ACM Trans. Manag. Inf. Syst. (TMIS) **3**(2), 7 (2012)
7. Alexander, C., Ishikawa, S., Silverstein, M.: A Pattern Language: Towns, Buildings, Construction. Oxford University Press, New York (1977)
8. Gamma, E., Helm, R., Johnson, R., Vlissides, J.: Design Patterns: Elements of Reusable Object-Oriented Software. Pearson Education, Upper Saddle River (1994)
9. Gzara, L., Rieu, D., Tollenaere, M.: Product information systems engineering: an approach for building product models by reuse of patterns. Robot. Comput. Integr. Manuf. **19**(3), 239–261 (2003)
10. Kodratoff, Y., Michalski, R.S., Carbonell, J.G., Mitchell, T.M.: Machine Learning: An Artificial Intelligence Approach. Morgan Kaufmann, San Mateo (1990)
11. Han, J., Kamber, M., Pei, J.: Data Mining: Concepts and Techniques. Elsevier Science, Amsterdam (2011)
12. Albalate, A., Minker, W.: Semi-supervised and Unsupervised Machine Learning: Novel Strategies. Wiley, New York (2013)
13. Zhu, X., Goldberg, A.B.: Introduction to semi-supervised learning. Synth. Lect. Artif. Intell. Mach. Learn. **3**(1), 1–130 (2009)
14. Kulkarni, P.: Reinforcement and systemic machine learning for decision making. Wiley, New York (2012)
15. Sim, S.K., Duffy, A.H.B.: A foundation for machine learning in design. AI EDAM **12**(02), 193–209 (1998)
16. Tong, S.S., Powell, D., Cornett, D.: Engineous: a unified method for design automation, optimization, and integration. In: Artificial Intelligence in Engineering Design, vol. III, pp. 235–254 (1992)
17. Goldberg, D.E.: Genetic Algorithms in Search, Optimization and Machine Learning, 1st edn. Addison-Wesley Longman Publishing Co., Inc., Boston (1989)
18. Chen, H.-Y., Chang, H.-C.: Consumers' perception-oriented product form design using multiple regression analysis and backpropagation neural network. Artif. Intell. Eng. Des. Anal. Manuf. **30**(01), 64–77 (2016)
19. Pitiot, P., Coudert, T., Geneste, L., Baron, C.: Hybridation of Bayesian networks and evolutionary algorithms for multi-objective optimization in an integrated product design and project management context. Eng. Appl. Artif. Intell. **23**(5), 830–843 (2010)
20. Danglade, F., Pernot, J.-P., Véron, P.: On the use of machine learning to defeature CAD models for simulation. Comput. Aided Des. Appl. **11**(3), 358–368 (2014)

21. Yan, H.S., Xu, D.: An approach to estimating product design time based on fuzzy ν-support vector machine. IEEE Trans. Neural Netw. **18**(3), 721–731 (2007)
22. Reimann, P., Calvo, R., Yacef, K., Southavilay, V.: Comprehensive computational support for collaborative learning from writing. In: International Conference on Computers in Education (ICCE), Putrajaya, Malaysia (2010)
23. Saravanan, M., Rama Sree, R.: Application of mining algorithms using ProM and Weka tools. IJCST **2**(3), 331–337 (2011)
24. Crerie, R., Baião, F.A., Santoro, F.M.: Discovering business rules through process mining. In: Halpin, T., Krogstie, J., Nurcan, S., Proper, E., Schmidt, R., Soffer, P., Ukor, R. (eds.) BPMDS/EMMSAD -2009. LNBIP, vol. 29, pp. 136–148. Springer, Heidelberg (2009). doi:10.1007/978-3-642-01862-6_12
25. Object Management Group: Business Process Model and Notation (BPMN) Version 2.0, January 2011
26. van Dongen, B.F., van der Aalst, W.M.P.: A meta model for process mining data. EMOI-INTEROP **160**, 30 (2005)
27. Jagadeesh Chandra Bose, R.P., van der Aalst, W.M.P.: Abstractions in process mining: a taxonomy of patterns. In: Dayal, U., Eder, J., Koehler, J., Reijers, H.A. (eds.) BPM 2009. LNCS, vol. 5701, pp. 159–175. Springer, Heidelberg (2009). doi:10.1007/978-3-642-03848-8_12
28. Witten, I.H., Frank, E., Trigg, L., Hall, M., Holmes, G., Cunningham, S.J.: Weka: practical machine learning tools and techniques with Java implementations (1999)
29. Quinlan, J.R.: C4.5: Programs for Machine Learning. Morgan Kaufmann Publishers Inc., San Francisco (1993)

Collaborative Development Architectures

Static Product Structures: An Industrial Standard on the Wane

Stefan Kehl[1(✉)], Carsten Hesselmann[1], Patrick D. Stiefel[2], and Jörg P. Müller[1]

[1] Department of Informatics, Clausthal University of Technology, Clausthal-Zellerfeld, Germany
{stefan.kehl, carsten.hesselmann, joerg.mueller}@tu-clausthal.de
[2] Volkswagen Group, Wolfsburg, Germany
patrick.stiefel@volkswagen.de

Abstract. This paper aims at closing the gap between early phases (e.g. design) and later phases (e.g. procurement or production) of the Product Development Process (PDP) by proposing a Virtual Product Model (VPM) as a *collection* of individual components (VPMCs) without the need for a static structure. Based on an analysis of the requirements on product development in the automotive industry, the main problems we observe are limited transparency, limited continuity, and limited reusability throughout different phases of the PDP. Virtual Product Model Components (VPMCs) can be used in *different products* and allow the reflection of *changes throughout the PDP* as well as the derivation of *domain-specific views* on the overall product at runtime. We illustrate these concepts by use case scenarios derived from an analysis of automotive product development practices.

1 Introduction

Over the past years, the complexity of industrial products has been increasing due to rising expectations from customers and the resulting higher variety. E.g. in the automotive industry the number of possible variants is skyrocketing and has reached a level at which "the number of theoretical possible Vehicle Variants is higher than the number of sold Cars" [9]. This trend is often referred to as *mass customization*. According to Tseng and Jiao [18], it is about "producing goods and services to meet individual customer's needs with near mass production efficiency". With this "explosion of potential offering variety" [5] many issues arise such as (i) the traceability of parts (and their geometric representation) used in multiple products, (ii) a comprehensive way to manage changes on components, and (iii) an effective structuring of product models which supports reusability, continuity and transparency [13] and need to be addressed in order to preserve success on the market and meet both new technological and customer requirements. Some practitioners propose concepts, like the modularization of complex products [7, 12], to share common parts in multiple products and product lines regarding their individual components [2].

R. Harik et al. (Eds.): PLM 2016, IFIP AICT 492, pp. 69–78, 2016.
DOI: 10.1007/978-3-319-54660-5_7

In practice static product structures, such as Bill of Materials (BOMs) (see Sect. 2), are still heavily used as the data backbone for Product Lifecycle Management (PLM)-systems [1]. E.g. in [17], Tekin described an approach to use multiple static product structures for different stages of the PDP. Structures which are used later during the PDP (so called *As Built Bill of Materials (ABOMs)*) rely on previous ones like Manufacturing Bill of Materials (MBOMs) and are reconciled with Engineering Bill of Materials (EBOMs). Chatras et al. argue in [5] that managing complex product models with BOMs is no longer an adequate solution because of the current scale of diversity.

Besides considering the aspect of *how to structure a virtual product model* much work focuses on the engineering perspective of the product development process [7, 10, 12]. Within the MOKA product model [15] constraints which represent design restrictions are described. Among other things, those constraints can be used to model product choices and to define the order in which design decisions are made. Others like [16] take mechatronic aspects of the engineering processes into account. Furthermore, much attention has been paid to the field of engineering change management or the impact of geometrical changes of components on each other and the overall product [11]. In [1] a method for an automated structuring of geometric product data in a two step procedure is presented which can be used on 3D Computer Aided Design (CAD) models.

We propose a new way of modeling a product without employing a static product structure as the backbone of the Product Data Management (PDM) system. We achieve this by introducing a Virtual Product Model (VPM) that allows the derivation of specialized views at runtime (e.g. a BOM) and that is based on VPMCs. A VPMC is a collection of data elements from different departments (e.g. design or procurement) that describe a single component. By assigning a VPMC to a product, context-specific instances of this VPMC and of the data elements are instantiated in the following denoted as VPMC-U.

The structure of this paper is as follows: In Sect. 2, we describe the current practice in managing BOM data and design data in the automotive industry. In Sect. 3, we describe the concept of the VPM, how VPMCs can be used to provide design data (based on industrial use cases), and how views on the VPM can be derived. In Sect. 4, we illustrate, that the VPM contains (at least) the same information as the EBOM presented in Sect. 2 by providing an algorithm to transform a set of VPMCs and their context specific instances (VPMC-U) into an EBOM. Finally, we conclude with a summary and outline avenues of future work.

2 State-of-Practice in Providing Design Data

In practice, static product structures, such as BOMs, are used to provide a data backbone for PLM systems [1]. E.g. for automobile Original Equipment Manufacturers (OEMs) multiple types of product structures are important. Two of the most relevant ones are: (i) An EBOM to organize a product's design data and (ii) a MBOM that focuses on manufacturing part sequences. In the following we focus on EBOMs.

The main goal of an EBOM is to integrate design data into a BOM. For *releasing* design data (appending the corresponding data elements to an EBOM), a BOM-based approach is no longer an adequate solution [5], because of the static and inflexible nature of an EBOM and the current scale of diversity. Such an EBOM has to meet requirements of all domain experts (from different departments like virtual prototyping, tool manufacturing, procurement) participating in the PDP. Therefore, the size of the structure easily gets unmanageable. Thus, PLM roll-out projects may fail, when designers are expected to use such an *overloaded* EBOM. Furthermore, transformations of static structures are computational complex and therefore very time-consuming.

The most important contribution of designers within the PDP is the so called *part-geometry alignment* that connects a part (logistical, BOM-oriented element that carries organizational information such as suppliers and procurement channels) and a revision of a geometry (design-oriented collection of 3DCAD-Files and several 2D-Drawings that carry information about the geometric characteristics of a part). In this paper we assume, that the relations between geometry revisions and parts are provided by the designer. Nevertheless, in previous work [3] we proposed an agent-based approach to (partly) automate such alignments. This part-geometry alignment can be used in one or multiple *contexts* (generic term for a collaborative developed product or derivative of a product).

A typical product structure that represents a context (see Fig. 1(a)) consists of *nodes* (to structure the virtual product) and BOM items (parts), that specify a component of the virtual product in the context of the EBOM. In order to model different derivatives of the same product (e.g. sedan, roadster, station wagon), the so called *technical validity* of those parts (part variance) is attached to the structure. E.g. the variance rule $(BODY = SW) \wedge (HD = LEFT)$ describes the validity for a *station wagon* with *left-hand drive*.

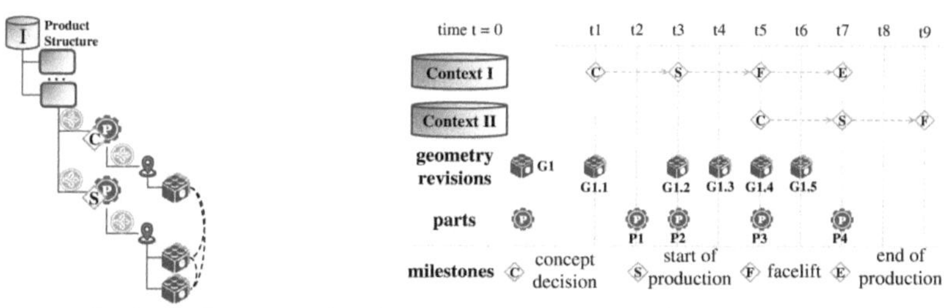

(a) Static product structures (b) Context specific and disjoint milestones of geometries and parts

Fig. 1. Current practice in providing design data using a static product structure

Furthermore, the validity of a part according to the context-specific PDP can be defined by assigning *milestones* to the part-node, where a milestone marks the attainment of a specific stage of the PDP. For each milestone the components have to meet predefined characteristics and quality requirements. For Digital MockUp (DMU) a geometry- and context-specific *position* needs to be defined (e.g. the four *rims* of a car are positioned differently and *POS = FrontLeft* describes the left front wheel). In order to be able to differentiate between these alternate positions (e.g. to use only one positioned geometry for collision detection), *position variance* needs to be applied to the structure.

Taking the requirements above into account, such an EBOM easily gets unmanageable, due to its size and number of levels. They are the result of integrating multiple domains into a single structure. In contrast, the VPM provides the possibility to derive domain specific views based on the consolidated product data.

3 Providing Design Data Using VPMCs

In this section we discuss the concept of the VPM based on VPMCs and their context-specific usages. In Sect. 3.2 we introduce the basic concept, and the differences between VPMCs and their context-specific *usages*. Section 3.3 shows how use cases derived from the automotive industry, can be performed based on VPMCs. These use cases cover the evolution of a component over time and its usage in different contexts (derivatives or even products) with temporally disjoint PDPs (see Fig. 1(b)). Finally, Sect. 3.4 explains how to derive domain specific views on our VPM.

3.1 Use Case: Aligning Design and Logistic Data

Changes on a component usually result in changes on the geometric representation. In practice not every change on the geometry (new revision) is reflected on the part-geometry alignment, because (i) parts do not depend on the geometric level exclusively, but on changes regarding the procurement (or other organizational matters) as well; and (ii) not every geometry revision fulfills the quality requirements for post-design phases of the PDP. Taking into account the parallel and temporal independent development of multiple contexts (derivatives or products) different revisions of the component (and therefore of the geometry) might be valid for different context-specific milestones. Example:

The component *rim* evolves over time *t* (see Fig. 1(b)). At milestone *concept decision* of the context *I* (*sedan*) in $t = 1$ only the first geometry revision of this *rim* is available. At this point there is no need for aligning a part, because organizational information (such as suppliers) are needed not until the production planning starts at $t = 2$.

In $t = 3$ (milestone *start of the production* of context *I*) the latest part geometry alignment consists of the second geometry revision *G1.2* and part *P2* (e.g. *silver rim*). Therefore, this alignment can be assigned to the *sedan* (context *I*) for milestone *S*. In $t = 4$ a new geometry revision has been development, but no part is assigned, because milestone *S* (*start of production*) of context *I* has past, and neither milestone *F* (*facelift*) of context *I* nor a crucial milestone of another context has been reached (see Fig. 1(b)).

The development of the *roadster* (second context *II*) starts at $t = 5$. At this point there are four different revisions of the geometry. The newest part is *P3* (*black rim*). Therefore, the fourth geometry and the part *P3* are assigned to the context *roadster* for milestone *C*.

3.2 Virtual Product Model Component and VPMC-U

As mentioned in Sect. 2, parts, geometries, the relation(s) between them, and context-specific information appended to these relations are the basis for components of the VPM. The set of these information regarding a single component is defined as a VPMC. Due to geometry being the most characterizing element (in contrast parts carry much organizational information and may differ according to market conditions), each VPMC is geometrically unique.

A VPMC evolves over time, because product development is not a linear process, but a continuous sequence of changes [4, 6, 8, 14]. Taking into account the efforts of most practitioners to increase the commonality of different products [2], a component is most likely *used* in multiple contexts. In the following we refer to this context-specific objects as VPMC-Us. Accordingly, a VPMC is related to multiple VPMC-Us. Because VPMCs contain parts and geometries, these elements are related to multiple *part usages*/*geometry usages* as well. These usages are related again to other context-specific elements such as milestones, the positions of the geometry in that context, and variance expressions regarding the geometrical (on the geometry usage) or technical validity (on the part usage). A VPMC itself has no relation to any context, but to several VPMC-Us; each VPMC-U serves as a collector for the context specific elements. The number of VPMC-Us depends on (i) the number of contexts the VPMC is used in, (ii) the number of occurrences of that VPMC in each context (e.g. a car typically has four tires), and (iii) the number of updates *inside* a VPMC-U (traceability - see Sect. 3.3). Yet other elements of the VPM are predefined, structured, and tree-like *views*. The leaves of such a tree are classified. This classification is related to the class of the VPMCs. E.g. one leaf contains all components of the class *rim*. Therefore, all VPMCs with a relation to this class can be assigned to the *rim* node. Applying this concept to VPMC-Us provides a context-specific and dynamic view based on VPMCs and classified views (see Sect. 3.4). Figure 2 illustrates the differences between VPMCs and VPMC-Us.

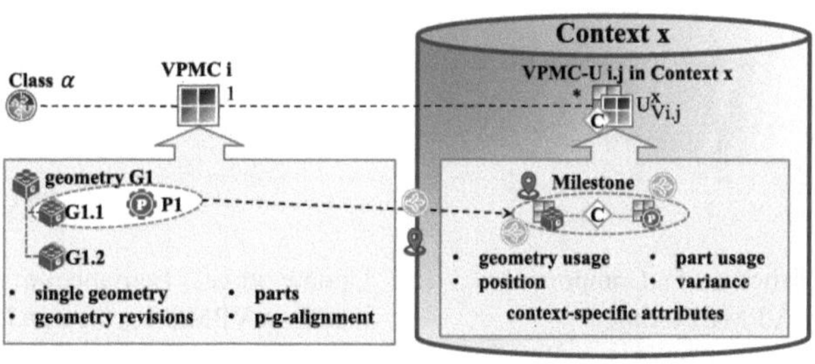

Fig. 2. Concept of VPMCs, VPMC-Us, and dynamic views

In summary a VPMC is a reusable component with a unique geometry. It contains the following data elements: (i) A single geometry with several revisions (to trace changes on the geometry); (ii) multiple parts that are realized by the geometry revisions; (iii) relations between geometry revisions and their parts (part-geometry alignment); and (iv) a reference to a class (classification of VPMCs).

Furthermore, a VPMC-U is a context-specific instance of a VPMC. It contains the following data elements: (i) A geometry usage with a relation to a geometry revision; (ii) the position of this geometry revision in the context; (iii) variance rules, that describe the validity of the geometry; (iv) several alternate geometry usages because of different positions; (v) a part usage that represents the part in that context; (vi) variance rules (on the part usage) that describe the technical validity of the part; and (vii) a milestone that defines the stage of the PDP the VPMC-U is released for.

3.3 Reflecting Changes of Components Using VPMCs

In this section we discuss the data model of VPMCs and their context-specific usages (VPMC-Us) capable of managing the evolution of a component (especially their containing part-geometry alignments) in relation to context-specific and disjoint milestones (Fig. 1(b)).

At first the designer creates a new geometry *G1* representing the *rim* of the previous example. Thus a new VPMC is instantiated. Furthermore, the designer provides a class α, that specifies the "type" of the VPMC (e.g. *rim*).

At $t = 1$ (see Fig. 3(a)) the designer assigns *G1.1* of the geometry *G1* at a context-specific position for milestone *C* in context *I* (sedan). Therefore, the following data elements are instantiated: (i) A new VPMC-U $U^I_{V1.1}$ that serves as a collector for the context-specific occurrences of the VPMC; (ii) a geometry usage $U^1_{G1.1}$ that represents the current version of the *rim* in the sedan; and (iii) a node representing the position with a relation to the geometry usage $U^1_{G1.1}$.

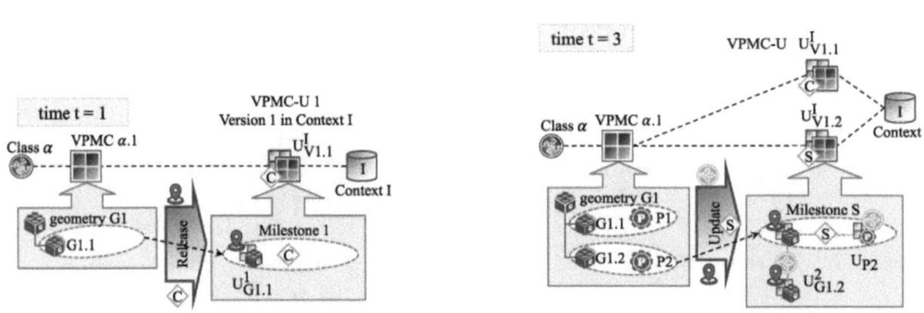

(a) Release Process of a Component Based on VPMCs a time *t=1*

(b) Update process (variance) of a component based on VPMCs at time *t=3*

Fig. 3. Providing design data using VPMCs

At $t = 2$ a new part (*silver rim*) is associated to the geometry revision *G1.1*. The VPMC-U $U^I_{V1.1}$ can be updated automatically, because the part-geometry alignment is unique. The data elements created are: Firstly, a new part usage U_{P1} that represents the *silver rim* in the sedan (context *I*). Because of the existing relation between the geometry revision and the part, the corresponding usages are related to each other. Furthermore, both usages share the same validity for milestone *C*. Secondly, a variance expression that describes the validity of the part in relation to different configurations of context *I*. E.g. this specific *silver rim* might only be valid for cars with a costly equipment package. This variance expression is related to the part usage directly.

At $t = 3$ (see Fig. 3(b)) the geometry of the *silver rim* is updated (*G1.2*), a new part *P2* (*black rim*) is provided, and both are aligned to each other. These usages (and there the collector $U^{I}_{V1.2}$) are valid for the sedan's milestone *S*. The first position of the geometry revision, the validities on the geometry usage $U^{1}_{G1.2}$ and/or the part usage U_{P2}, can be taken from the previous VPMC-U or, on behalf of the designer, replaced by new information. Furthermore, there might be an alternate position of the geometry revision (e.g. to model the *rim* turned right or the front left *rim*). The data elements created are: (i) a geometry revision *G1.2*, a part *P2*, and an alignment between these elements, (ii) a VPMC-U valid for milestone *S* with a relation to the VPMC, (iii) a new part usage U_{P2} for the part *P2*. The variance expression of this part usage is taken from the part usage of the previous VPMC-U $U^{I}_{V1.1}$, and (iv) two new geometry usages $U^{1}_{G1.2}$ and $U^{2}_{G1.2}$ for the geometry revision *G1.2*. The position of the first geometry usage is taken from the geometry usage $U^{1}_{G1.1}$ of the previous VPMC-U $U^{I}_{V1.1}$ the alternative position and the variance rule are provided.

In summary this approach leads (for one VPMC) to a set of context-specific VPMC-Us with different validities. Each VPMC-U describes the current state of the related VPMC in a specific context at a particular point of the context's PDP. The separation of components into context-free (VPMC) and context specific (VPMC-U) elements, enables the development of a component to be independent of its actual usages. This solves the problem of using the same component (VPMC) in different contexts with disjoint PDPs mentioned at the beginning of Sect. 3.

3.4 Domain-Specific Views on a VPM

One of the main advantages of our VPM is the possibility to create *views* at runtime (see Sect. 3.2) by assigning VPMC-Us to leaf nodes of arbitrary structures based on their classification. Therefore, the computational complex transformation (see Sect. 2) mentioned in Sect. 2 are obsolete.

Furthermore, these *views* can either be context-specific (see Fig. 4(a)) or a collection of VPMC-Us of different contexts by adding context-specific nodes subordinated to the classified nodes of the arbitrary structures (see Fig. 4(b)).

The relation between the context-specific nodes and the VPMC-Us can be derived, because every VPMC-U knows the context it is assigned to. Therefore, this approach can be used to calculate structures at runtime, that describe the share of common parts in different contexts. Moreover, by selecting only the data elements of the VPMC-Us relevant for a specific domain (e.g. parts for purchasers or geometries for designers) these views become *domain-specific* (see the right side of Fig. 1(a)).

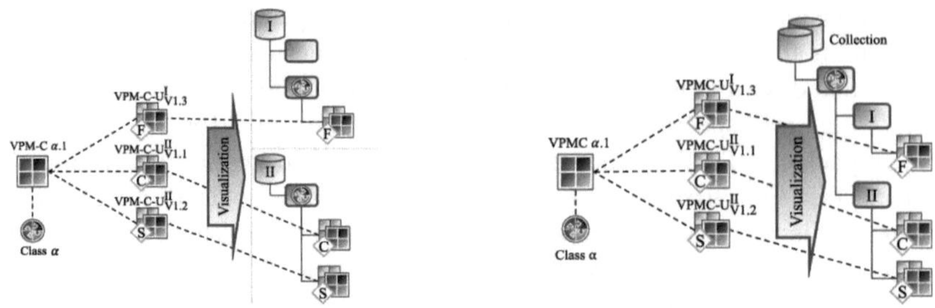

(a) Context-specific views on VPMCs (b) Collection of context-specific views

Fig. 4. Deriving views from a VPM

4 Evaluation

To evaluate the information content of a product model based on VPMCs, in the following we describe an algorithm to transform a VPM into an EBOM illustrated in Sect. 2. It is unlikely, that this algorithm is used in practice, because of the ability of the VPM to create dynamic views at runtime, but it shows that the VPM contains (at least) the same information as an EBOM. See Fig. 5 for an illustration of the transformation and Algorithm 1 for a description in pseudo code.

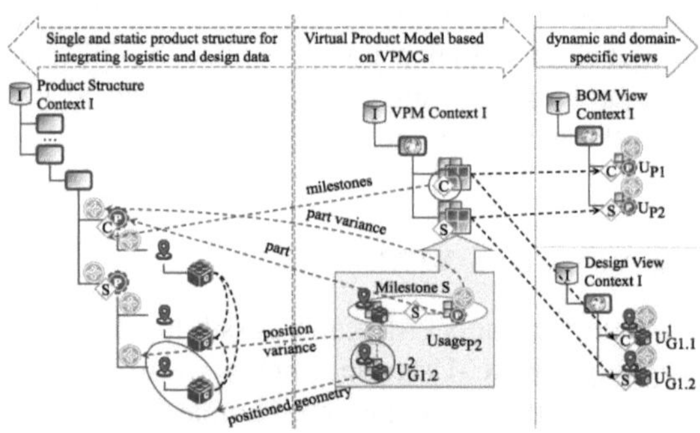

Fig. 5. Static product structure vs. domain-specific and dynamic views on VPMCs

The algorithm takes a mapping from *classes* to nodes of the EBOM and a context as an input. For each class of the mapping the corresponding node of the EBOM is determined using the given mapping. For each VPMC-U of the current class a new part-node is generated, the validities (variance and milestone) are retrieved from the VPMC-U, and assigned to the new part-node. Next a node representing the *first position* of the VPMC-U's geometry revision and the revision itself are appended. The final steps are to iterate over all alternate positions of the VPMC-U's geometry, to create nodes that represent these positions, to set the geometric validity according to the VPMC-U, and to append the geometry revisions.

Algorithm 1 VPM2ProductStructure Transformation

```
procedure transformVPMCs2Structure(Mapping: Class → Node, Context context)
    for all Class class : mapping.getClasses() do                         ▷ all classes of VPMCs
        Node node = mapping.getNode(class)                                 ▷ get node in the structure
        for all VPMC-U vpmcu: context.getVPMCUsages() do
            if vpmcu.getVPMC().getClass() == class then                    ▷ check class membership
                Node partNode = node.appendPart(vpmcu.getPartUsage(), node)    ▷ part
                partNode.setVariance(vpmcu.getPartVariance())                  ▷ part variance
                partNode.setValidity(vpmcu.getMilestone())                     ▷ milestone
                                                         ▷ append first geometry in first position
                Node posNode = partNode.addPositionedGeometry(vpmcu.getGeometryUsage())
                                                         ▷ add alternate positions
                for all GeometryUsage altGeoUsage: geoUsage.getAlternatives() do
                                      ▷ add position node and geometry revision from geometry-usage
                    Node altPosNode = partNode.addPositionedGeometry(altGeoUsage)
                    altPosNode.setVariance(altGeoUsage.getPositionVariance())
```

5 Conclusion

In this paper, we described a data model for managing the development of complex products, where several domain experts take part in the development of new products and each domain has its own and specialized view on an overall product model. We proposed a novel *Virtual Product Model (VPM)* that supports *reusability*, *transparency*, and *continuity*. Each component of our VPM is modeled as a combination of context-free *parts*, *geometries* (Virtual Product Model Component (VPMC)), and their context-specific counterparts, *part usages*, *geometry usages* extended with *milestones* and *variance-expressions* and combined in a VPMC-U. As we pointed out in [13], the VPMCs are extended by domain experts within their specialized views throughout the Product Development Process (PDP). Therefore, the approach presented in this paper allows the derivation of specialized views (BOM or design oriented) on a single product or on a collection of multiple contexts. This reduces the amount of information each domain expert is required to manage.

To summarize, the main contributions of this paper are: (i) an analysis of an industrial use case to determine the minimal set elements needed in a Product Data Management (PDM)-System to support the development process, (ii) a conceptual definition (based on the use case analysis) of VPMCs and their elements to support the release process of design information, and (iv) the derivation of specialized and user-related views on the VPM.

Future work will focus on (i) an agent based model to handle the dependencies between elements of VPMC [3], and (ii) methods for Feature Model Analysis to increase the transparency regarding the reuse of individual components in different products.

References

1. Adolphy, S., Grosser, H., Kirsch, L., Stark, R.: Method for automated structuring of product data and its applications. Procedia CIRP **38**, 153–158 (2015)

2. Benavides, D., Segura, S., Ruiz-Cortés, A.: Automated analysis of feature models 20 years later: a literature review. Inf. Syst. **35**(6), 615–636 (2010)
3. Bender, J., Kehl, S., Müller, J.P.: A comparison of agent-based coordination architecture variants for automotive product change management. In: Müller, J., Ketter, W., Kaminka, G., Wagner, G., Bulling, N. (eds.) MATES 2015. LNCS, vol. 9433, pp. 249–267. Springer International Publishing, Cham (2015). doi:10.1007/978-3-319-27343-3_14
4. Bucciarelli, L.L.: Designing engineers. Inside technology, Institute of Technology (1994)
5. Chatras, C., Giard, V., Sali, M.: High variety impacts on bill of materials structure: carmakers case study. IFAC-PapersOnLine **48**(3), 1067–1072 (2015)
6. Cheng, H., Chu, X.: A network-based assessment approach for change impacts on complex product. J. Intell. Manuf. **23**(4), 1419–1431 (2012)
7. Clarkson, J.P., Simons, C., Eckert, C.: Predicting change propagation in complex design. In: ASME 2001 Design Engineering Technical Conferences and Computers and Information in Engineering Conference, Pittsburgh, Pennsylvania (2001)
8. Cross, N.: Engineering Design Methods: Strategies for Product Design, 3rd edn. Wiley, Chichester (2005)
9. Kees, M., Seibertz, A.: Compositional variant management and its application in embedded software development, 29 April 2010
10. Galle, P.: The ontology of Gero's FBS model of designing. Des. Stud. **30**(4), 321–339 (2009)
11. Hamraz, B., Caldwell, N.H.M., Clarkson, P.J.: A holistic categorization framework for literature on engineering change management. Syst. Eng. **16**(4), 473–505 (2012)
12. Jarratt, T., Eckert, C.M., Caldwell, N., Clarkson, P.J.: Engineering change: an overview and perspective on the literature. Res. Eng. Des. **22**(2), 103–124 (2011)
13. Kehl, S., Stiefel, P., Müller, J.P.: Changes on changes: towards an agent-based approach for managing complexity in decentralized product development. In: International Conference on Engineering Design (ICED 2015), Milan, Italy, vol. 3, pp. 219–228 (2015)
14. McMahon, C.A.: Observations on modes of incremental change in design. J. Eng. Des. **5**(3), 195–209 (1994)
15. Oldham, K., Kneebone, S., Callot, M., Murton, A., Brimble, R.: MOKA - a methodology and tools oriented to knowledge-based engineering. In: Proceedings of the Conference on Integration in Manufacturing, Göteborg, Sweden, 6–8 October 1998, vol. 8, p. 198 (1998)
16. Roucoules, L., Noel, F., Teissandier, D., Lombard, M., Debarbouille, G., Girard, P., Merlo, C., Eynard, B.: IPPOP: an open source collaborative design platform to link product, design process and industrial organisation information. In: 6th International Conference on Integrated Design and Manufacturing in Mechanical Engineering, IDMME 2006, p. CDROM (2006)
17. Tekin, E.: A method for traceability and "as-built product structure" in aerospace industry. Procedia CIRP **17**, 351–355 (2014)
18. Tseng, M.M., Jiao, J.: Mass customization: 25. In: Handbook of Industrial Engineering, pp. 684–709. Wiley (2007)

A Lightweight Approach to Manage Engineering Parameters in Mechatronic Design Processes

Lukas Weingartner[1(✉)], Peter Hehenberger[1], Michael Friedl[2], Andreas Kellner[1], Stefan Boschert[3], and Roland Rosen[3]

[1] Institute of Mechatronic Design and Production, Johannes Kepler University Linz, Linz, Austria
{lukas.weingartner,peter.hehenberger, andreas.kellner}@jku.at

[2] Institute of Machine Design and Hydraulic Drives, Johannes Kepler University Linz, Linz, Austria
michael.friedl@jku.at

[3] Siemens Corporate Technology, Munich, Germany
{stefan.boschert,roland.rosen}@siemens.com

Abstract. In mechatronic design processes the exchange of information between stakeholders from different disciplines is essential to enable simultaneous engineering and a successful integration of domain specific subsystems. Although there is a comprehensive range of methodologies and tools to support collaboration, intentions to implement a central data management platform covering all stakeholders often do not succeed. Reasons are the heterogeneous model landscape, the variety of stand-alone authoring tools, departments', disciplines' or companies' boundaries and a lack of flexibility of established solutions regarding the support of unpredictable and quickly changing design processes. This paper focuses on the management of individual parameters and parameter instances (values) within a multi-disciplinary development team. The presented lightweight approach can extend existing methods and data management infrastructure by adding functionalities to provide access to individual parameters using a dedicated database. The procedure is shown by the example of a technical mechanism.

Keywords: Mechatronic design process · Engineering parameter management · Parameter database · Data exchange process · Model management

1 Introduction

During the course of the multi-firm project SyMMDe [1], mechatronic design processes of four different companies were analyzed in detail and presented in the form of model dependency maps [2]. From this point of view, every model needs input parameters and generates results (e.g., output parameters in various forms) for a particular purpose. Heterogeneous models on various hierarchical levels are usually created and implemented within specific authoring systems (e.g., CAx-tools) by different stakeholders

R. Harik et al. (Eds.): PLM 2016, IFIP AICT 492, pp. 79–88, 2016.
DOI: 10.1007/978-3-319-54660-5_8

and experts (e.g., from the disciplines of mechanics, electronics and software). In most cases, models (e.g., parametric geometry models) are stored using a kind of file-based model storage. There is a wide range of software solutions (e.g., file systems, "PDM - product data management" systems, "ECM - enterprise content management" systems) to manage (mostly proprietary) files within a central platform covering essential functionalities like versioning, access management, configuration management, and much more. For pragmatic reasons like performance advantages and interoperability, individual model storage systems can be settled locally at the expert's computer or close to the authoring systems (e.g., team data management). From our observations, there is usually no overall (e.g., company-wide) consistent model backbone for all kinds of models. Although tailor-made configured PLM systems can meet these challenges in principle, in many cases their potential has not yet been exhausted, since only a limited scope (e.g., PDM aspects) of possible functionalities is used, without covering all stakeholders and models.

During mechatronic modeling processes, different types of parameters appear. As discussed in [3], a discipline-specific component can consist of a user-defined part described by design parameters and a standardized part described by configuration parameters. In addition to product descriptive parameters (including, for example, process parameters in process models) there are many other parameters that are relevant for the various discipline-specific models (e.g., regarding rules and know-how, or solver parameters and settings in simulation processes). The subset of parameters that influence more than one stakeholder or rather multiple models play a significant role across the product development process. It is essential that all stakeholders gain a common understanding of these important parameters. Globally unique and therefore complex names and descriptions of all parameters used are usually inconvenient. Experts from the different disciplines naturally have varied interpretations and views at the system and demand their own naming conventions. If the parameter management concept fails to unify these different views or to regulate access on the parameters, redundancies and consistency problems may follow. To achieve a close integration of domain specific subsystems, domain experts with diversified knowledge and skills often are in typical conflicts of interests. Conflicting objectives and targets concerning subsystems force stakeholders to negotiate about parameters (e.g., available design space). Therefore, parameter and parameter values can change several times due to improvements or coordination between stakeholders. Such engineering changes can have various triggers (e.g., unforeseeable events) and arise throughout the whole design process [4]. To enable an integration of components and solutions developed from several disciplines, substantial main parameters must be defined and made available to all stakeholders. Lacking access to a central parameter management system often leads to mainly spread, unregulated, and not standardized information exchange (e.g., using telephone, post-it notes, social media, email or additional stand-alone groupware or project management applications). Despite the availability of PLM tools, one commonly used mostly manual and file-based method is to manage parameters in rather simple lists with ordinary spreadsheet tools. Although this is a proper solution for documentation purposes, problems occur if multiple users have frequent change requests, as in the case of usual iterations during design processes. Figure 1 shows a comparison of the basic mechanisms with a central database (type 3) and without (type 1 and 2).

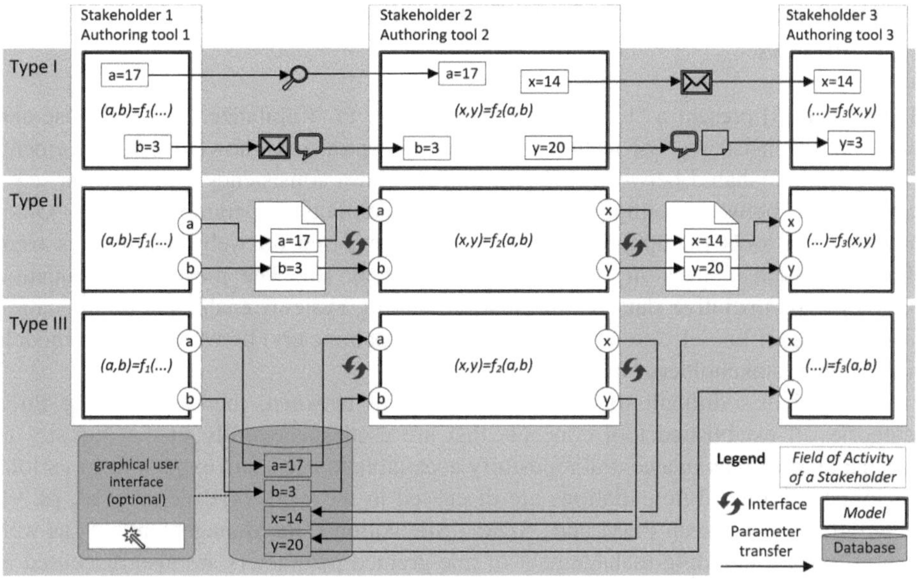

Fig. 1. This example shows three models (*f1*, *f2*, *f3*) and three basic types of information exchange (parameter values of *a*, *b*, *x*, *y*) between different stakeholders and authoring tools: (I) Manual exchange of parameter values. (II) File-based exchange of parameter values. (III) Parameter value exchange using a central repository with an additional graphical user interface.

The aim of this paper is to introduce and implement a methodology that covers the following needs and requirements related to parameter management as observed during typical interdisciplinary development processes at our industrial examples: (i) Access to individual parameters across multiple models (e.g., from proprietary files), without having to use the respective authoring system, e.g., by different stakeholders across multiple departments/locations. (ii) Multi-user access including rights management. (iii) Management of parameters including capabilities to keep an overview by using metadata and attributes or functionalities like filtering and highlighting of major and product defining parameters. (iv) Representation of relationships between parameters and possibilities to analyze impacts in the case of changes. (v) Traceability and history of changes including the possibility to add knowledge regarding decision making (e.g., rules) and documentation about decisions made (e.g., implicit assumptions, findings, reasons for occurring iterations). (vi) Several models (e.g., on different hierarchical levels created in specific authoring tools) should be able to access individual parameters using simple adapters and interfaces without the need of an additional overall authoring tool. (vii) Widespread introduction of the parameter management system should be possible, e.g., by using thin clients or web interfaces. (viii) Ability to extend and customize the platform using standardized tools or common programming languages. (ix) No adverse impacts and limitations on the established development process and flexibility to deal with highly dynamic changes within the development process.

2 Discussion of Established Methodologies and Tool Concepts

Badin et al. [5] present a "KCModel" methodology to "Capitalize, Trace, Re-use and ensure the Consistency" of technical data using centralized knowledge management. Parameters are shared between different models and a consistency management (e.g., expert rules) between configurations can detect conflicts in parameter values. Other concepts and tools to support collaborative design based on web technologies were already introduced back in 2002 by Riboulet et al. [6]. The presented application "CoDISS" (cooperative data & information sharing system) enables communication (e.g., sharing of knowledge, concepts and related parameters) between various models and different stakeholders [7].

Although it's difficult to draw a clear line in between, there are mainly three categories of established tool concepts that are used successfully in the industry to manage product data in a central repository accessible to users and experts from various disciplines. Similar differentiations are discussed in the work of Panchal et al. [8, 9]. Differentiations between PDM and "SDM - Simulation Data Management" [5] as well as weaknesses regarding management of fine grained parameters are also discussed in [10]. Each of the following three options has strengths and weaknesses in different applications.

The *first option* ("model backbone") are IT systems that focus on file-based product data management to enable collaboration between the stakeholders. There are powerful options to classify and structure the files by using metadata or structural modeling, but their focus is not to manage fine grained information like individual parameters within the files. The most commonly used concepts and tools can be grouped under the headings ECM, "DMS - document management system" and PDM as a part of "PLM - product lifecycle management". Prominent representatives in the field of mechatronic engineering tools are, e.g., Siemens Teamcenter® [11] or Dassault Systèmes ENOVIA® [12]. PLM systems (as an extension of PDM systems) even provide possibilities to extract and exchange fine-grained information and parameters from files, e.g., to initiate and execute customized and purpose-built workflows or simulation processes. Some authoring systems can be seamlessly integrated including bidirectional associativity of attributes and parameter values. However, the common fundamental PLM tool concepts are not designed or intended to support highly dynamic engineering processes of different models *on a parameter level*. Functionalities to analyze changes of parameter values and their impact within the model landscape are the aim of additional tools (e.g., requirements management and systems engineering applications), that can be connected to or installed within the PLM system. Clearly defined processes – even on parameter-level – are well-supported by tool adapters and workflows customized by PLM experts. To set up quick changing processes (e.g., experimental simulation processes) domain experts need ability and flexibility to implement specific processes by their own, e.g., using an end-user-friendly interface.

This leads to a *second option* ("model-based workflow management"), that is provided by systems and tools that focus on models and parameter exchange to realize workflows. So-called "PIDO - process integration and design optimization" frameworks or SDM solutions have to deal with a huge amount of individual parameters. Within a framework workflows consisting of interconnected (mainly external) models can be defined and executed. This means that parameters from different sources can be connected and exchanged within the tool environment. In the area of simulation processes, the second option is well suited for a limited number of users. The central simulation process model within the framework (usually a proprietary system platform) allows to run preconfigured simulations and calculations including parameter studies or optimization. The simulations can run at the local machine, without the need to connect to a server, which causes improved performance in some cases. Prominent simulation environments like Siemens LMS Imagine.Lab™ Amesim with Sysdm [11] or MathWorks® MATLAB® Simulink® [13] provide extensive possibilities to manage parameters within the associated environment.

A *third option* ("descriptive system model") is to build a model that contains essential knowledge (parameters, relationships, rules). Such approaches can be implemented using (model based) systems engineering methodologies and modelling languages (e.g., SysML) [14]. A major advantage of general-purpose modeling languages like SysML is the standardization, which is a basis for a tool-neutral integration. A well-known problem is that systems engineering tools follow a generic approach and must be adapted to fit concrete applications. Like a survey [15] pointed out, the large learning curve to understand SysML is a large inhibitor. In traditional engineering disciplines, only few domain experts have sufficient knowledge in this kind of modeling, mainly inspired by computer science (e.g., UML). From our observations, the role of systems engineers is not widespread introduced in industry at the present time. In the recent past, tool vendors developed modeling applications that enable analysis and execution of diagrams, e.g., SysML parametric diagrams, including expressions in form of constraints [14] and management of instances.

As a conclusion, there are many individual solutions but no universal parameter management approach, which meets all the requirements as stated in Sect. 1. The objective was now to develop a powerful but not overloaded ("lightweight") approach, that can be adapted and used productively with reasonable implementation effort, e.g., as a supplement to established design processes.

3 Generic Methodology for Lightweight Parameter Management

Bearing in mind that parameters only get a meaning and a significance in conjunction with models, the following approach is based on a separation of models and parameters and values. There are advantages (e.g., regarding transparency and simplified access to parameters) if models and parameters are considered in separate terms and also get technically implemented separately (e.g., in different databases). As mentioned above, models are nowadays managed successfully using different methodologies and tools (e.g., PLM systems) within a "model backbone". In addition, to manage fine grained parameters, a "parameter backbone" is introduced. In contrast to other approaches, already existing models do not have to be changed and there is only one additional data model necessary, but no centralized knowledge configuration model or dependency model between parameters. Any information (e.g., functional or mathematical relations) how OUT-parameters are generated from the IN-parameters are provided by existing models.

Figure 2 describes the basic methodology by the example of two models that are created with different (non-integrated) authoring systems. Once stakeholder 1 creates "model 1" using a specific tool, the model is transferred to the "model backbone" (e.g., a common model management system). In addition to this task, the essential parameters are transferred to a separate "parameter backbone" (e.g., by manual input or by using tailored interfaces). These essential parameters can be identified by the fact, that they are generated as (interim) results for a particular purpose and they are used several times as inputs for different models. If parameters appear only once within the development process (e.g., as an input for one downstream model within a seamless tool chain), the central storage may be not appropriate. For every parameter supplementing attributes (e.g., description, context information) need to be specified. Dependent on the type of every attribute, that user task can also be achieved either manually, (semi-)automatically or supported by using functionalities of the parameter backbone (e.g., DBMS "database management system") like (automatic) creation of unique IDs, access and change logs, or versioning. One important attribute that needs to be defined is which model generated the parameter. If stakeholder 2 starts creating "model 2" using another authoring system, the parameter management system provides access to already entered parameters. It is essential, that parameters can be found and identified due to unique attributes. There are supporting functionalities to retrieve the desired parameters, like using filtering by multiple criteria such as parameter name, description, creation date, creator, owner and/or many other context information. To establish the link between "model 2" and every required parameter, attributes are set. Every user of the parameter backbone now has the information, who (which model) generates and which models utilize the parameters. This information is helpful to estimate effects on other models in case of parameter changes. If "model 2" generates further essential parameters, they can be taken into account in the same way.

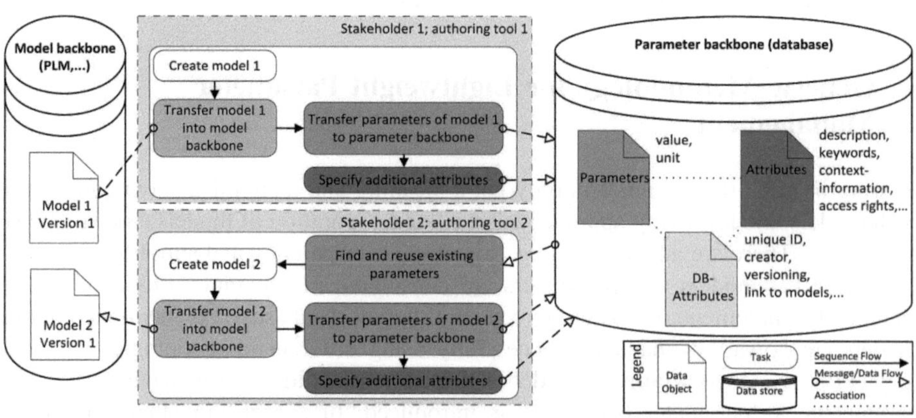

Fig. 2. Example how to use the introduced methodology in case of two models created by two stakeholders using different authoring tools.

To implement the parameter management approach (e.g., in an enterprise), a well-designed data model is a prerequisite for a transparent and performant implementation (e.g., within a DBMS). To develop the data model, at first an overview of the parameters and parameter types to be managed must be created. Parameters (and parameter values) are usually spread and redundantly stored at different locations within physical files, that contain a particular selection (view) of parameters. Pragmatic reasons for the occurrence of such parameter sets can be: (i) Software tools need certain machine-readable file formats that can be imported/exported. (ii) Sets contain all parameters that belong to a model. (iii) Sets contain parameters structured by areas of responsibility (e.g., due to expert knowledge or organizational reasons). (iv) Sets contain all relevant parameters that relate to a subsystem (e.g., parameters that are relevant to production). If parameters appear multiple times within different files, all influences have to be considered in the database concept. At the implementation of a central parameter backbone, required views can be provided using adequate attributes to allow grouping or filtering. As an example, there are 10000 essential parameters necessary to describe a certain machine tool. Thereof a set of 50 parameters belong to an electric motor of a drivetrain (e.g., type, manufacturer, power, weight, nominal speed). Various stakeholders from mechanical, electrical and automation departments need different views at these motor parameters. While some of the parameters are created and solely used by one department, other parameters (e.g., like the nominal speed) play an important role for all stakeholders. At this point, the approach brings enormous advantages, since all departments have access to current parameter data (following specified rules) including history and transparency (regarding affected stakeholders and dependent models). To sort or filter parameters, additional attributes like responsible department, project name, assembly can be defined easily. In case of using a relational database for the implementation, there are significant advantages in terms of consistency, transparency and data integrity. Relations between separate tables containing sets of essential parameters (e.g., common motor parameters) avoid data duplication and make changes easier.

4 Example: Implementation of a Parameter Management System

The presented methodology is currently under test in industrial case studies in the field of mechatronic product development. The parameter management system is implemented using MySQL™ [16] as a DBMS and Visual Studio [17] VBA programming to build a graphical user interface for user login, manual parameter/attribute input or manipulation and to visualize database queries. In following example of the development of a mechanism, there are many models used by different stakeholders from different departments. A first stakeholder uses a model to perform a two dimensional multi criteria optimization of a mechanism using MATLAB® [13]. The output parameters of this model are characteristic dimensions (e.g., L_1 = 350 mm … length of connection rod) that can be stored within the database using the ODBC API. In addition to every parameter, further corresponding attributes must be defined by using the following relations: “Model” (list and description of models used), “Units”, “Projects”,

"Visualization" (e.g., a sketch to show the context information of a parameter or even a lightweight representation for example based on a JT visualization format [18]), "Person" (general user management) and "Status" (e.g., to indicate a release status of a parameter). These relations are shown in Fig. 3 with an exemplary data model.

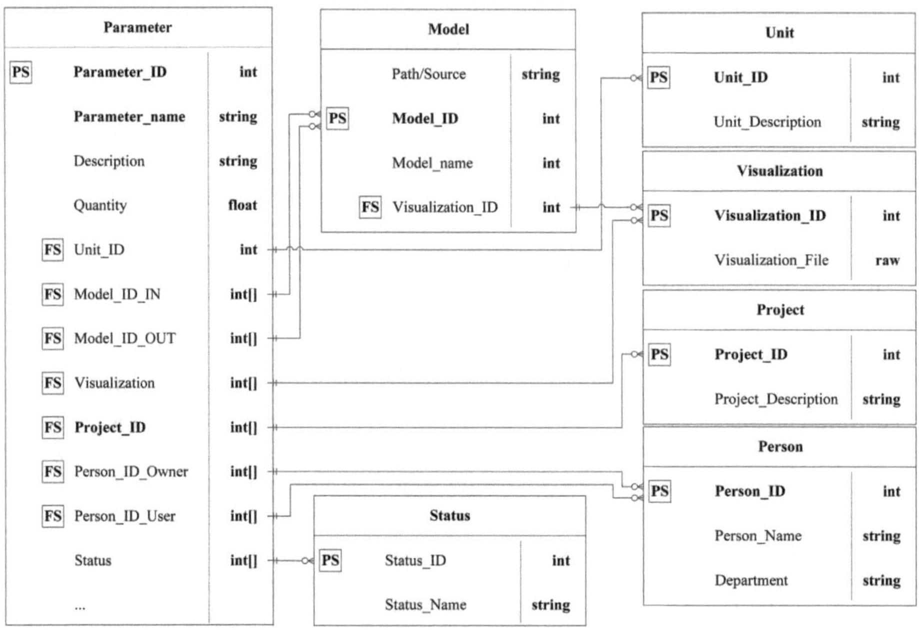

Fig. 3. Data model as a description of individual parameters and assigned attributes using relations (crow's foot database notation).

Based on the created database information, a second stakeholder is able to identify and reuse essential parameters to parameterize a CAD representation of the mechanism. This three-dimensional model is used to perform a collision check using the advanced capabilities of the Siemens NX™ CAD system. Input-parameters are loaded semi-automatically by the help of NX journaling functionalities to import expressions. Solutions of the collision check are also stored as parameters within the database, since they are important for other stakeholders. This means, every user of the parameter backbone has access to all actual parameter values, even without having access to the discipline-specific models (e.g., 3D-CAD model), and without the need to open the models within specific authoring systems.

Figure 4 shows the prototype of the graphical user interface to create and manipulate individual parameters like the displayed parameter "L1". In the lower area, a database viewer shows the query results depending on actual filter settings. The button "load model list" gives access to a separate list of models, that can be linked to the parameter. Write access (e.g., to parameter values) can be limited (e.g., to the "owner"/ creator of the parameter) by generating access permissions, e.g., using the MySQL Access Privilege System and/or GUI programming.

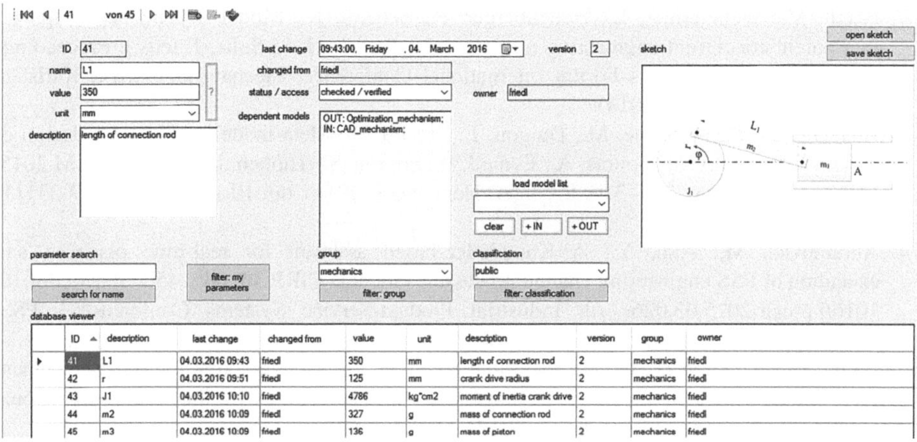

Fig. 4. Prototype of a graphical user interface to access the parameter backbone.

5 Summary and Conclusion

The presented approach essentially fulfills the initial requirements regarding parameter management, as described in Sect. 1. The exemplary implementation is done using a DBMS. Interfaces between models (authoring tools) and the central database are set up using several APIs. Although, the attempts to keep it lightweight lead to deliberate limitations regarding traceability. The approach shows direct effects to subsequent models in case of parameter value changes, but effects over several models in series are not displayable, since all the information about parameter correlations remain within the models. Nevertheless, first implementations showed that the presented methodology brings transparency into multi-disciplinary development processes. Several users get access to parameter values and receive now additional information about relationships between parameters and models considering responsibilities of stakeholders, after a reasonably small effort in implementation. A difficulty that has to be addressed in future work is to keep the parameter values synchronized, also considering release status and access permissions. It is not always possible to design models in a way that they can handle input parameters or directly link to the parameter database. As a result, parameter values are stored within the models that are probably not up-to-date. Here a notification mechanism could be implemented, to inform the responsible stakeholder to update the model in case of relevant parameter changes.

Acknowledgments. This work has been supported by the Austrian COMET-K2 programme of the Linz Center of Mechatronics (LCM), and was funded by the Austrian federal government and the federal state of Upper Austria.

References

1. SyMMDe - System Models for Mechatronic Design: Multi-Firm-Project, Johannes Kepler University Linz (2013–2016). http://symmde.jku.at. Accessed 15 Apr 2016

2. Friedl, M., Weingartner, L., Hehenberger, P., Scheidl, R.: Model dependency maps for transparent concurrent engineering processes, In: De Vin, L.J., Solis, J. (eds.): Proceedings of the 14th Mechatronics Forum International Conference, Mechatronics 2014, Karlstad, Sweden, pp. 614–621 (2014)
3. Hehenberger, P., Bricogne, M., Duigou, J., Eynard, B.: Meta-model of PLM for design of systems of systems. In: Bouras, A., Eynard, B., Foufou, S., Thoben, K.-D. (eds.) PLM 2015. IAICT, vol. 467, pp. 301–310. Springer, Heidelberg (2016). doi:10.1007/978-3-319-33111-9_28
4. Abramovici, M., Aidi, Y.: A Knowledge-based assistant for real-time planning and execution of PSS engineering change processes. Procedia CIRP **30**, 445–450 (2015). doi:10.1016/j.procir.2015.03.026. 7th Industrial Product-Service Systems Conference - PSS, Industry Transformation for Sustainability and Business
5. Badin, J., Chamoret, D., Gomes, S., Monticolo, D.: Knowledge configuration management for product design and numerical simulation. In: Proceedings of the 18th International Conference on Engineering Design (ICED 11), Denmark (2011)
6. Riboulet, V., Marin, P., Noël, F., Delinchant, B., Gerbaud, L.: Tools for dynamic sharing of collaborative design information. In: Gogu, G., Coutellier, D., Chedmail, P., Ray, P. (eds.) Recent Advances in Integrated Design and Manufacturing in Mechanical Engineering, pp. 493–502. Springer Netherlands, Dordrecht (2003). doi:10.1007/978-94-017-0161-7_48
7. Vu-Thi, H., Marin, P., Noël, F.: Integrating product model and whiteboard to ease collaborative work in global product development. In: Bernard, A. (ed.) Global Product Development, pp. 217–226. Springer, Heidelberg (2011). doi:10.1007/978-3-642-15973-2_21
8. Panchal, J.H., Fernández, M.G., Paredis, C.J.J., Allen, J.K., Mistree, F.: A modular decision-centric approach for reusable design processes. Concurr. Eng. **17**, 5–19 (2009). doi:10.1177/1063293X09102251
9. Panchal, J.H., Fernández, M.G., Allen, J.K., Paredis, C.J.J., Mistree, F.: Facilitating meta-design via separation of problem, product, and process information. In: ASME International Mechanical Engineering Congress and Exposition, Orlando, pp. 49–62 (2005)
10. Penciuc, D., Durupt, A., Belkadi, F., Eynard, B., Rowson, H.: Towards a PLM interoperability for a collaborative design support system. In: 8th International Conference on Digital Enterprise Technology – DET, Procedia CIRP 25, vol. 42, pp. 369–376, (2014). doi:10.1016/j.procir.2014.10.051
11. SIEMENS LMS Imagine.Lab™ System Synthesis software, NX™ software and Teamcenter® software. http://www.plm.automation.siemens.com. Accessed 15 Apr 2016
12. Enovia software Dassault Systèmes http://www.3ds.com. Accessed 15 Apr 2016
13. MathWorks® software. https://www.mathworks.com. Accessed 15 Apr 2016
14. Sakairi, T., Palachi, E., Cohen, C., Hatsutori, Y., Shimizu, J., Miyashita, H.: Model based control system design using SysML, simulink, and computer algebra system. J. Control Sci. Eng. **2013** (2013). Article ID 485380, doi:10.1155/2013/485380
15. Bone, M., Cloutier, R.: The current state of model based systems engineering: survey results from the OMG™ SysML request for information 2009. In: 8th Conference on Systems Engineering Research, Hoboken (2010)
16. MySQL™. https://www.mysql.com. Accessed 15 Apr 2016
17. Microsoft Visual Studio software. http://www.visualstudio.com. Accessed 15 Apr 2016
18. Ding, L., Ball, A., Matthews, J., McMahon, C.A., Patel, M.: Product representation in lightweight formats for product lifecycle management (PLM). In: 2007 4th International Conference on Digital Enterprise Technology, Bath (2007)

Improvement of Multidisciplinary Integration in Design of Complex Systems by Implementing Knowledge-Based Engineering

Chen Zheng[1(✉)], Matthieu Bricogne[1], Julien Le Duigou[1], Peter Hehenberger[2], Sandor Vajna[3], and Benoît Eynard[1]

[1] Department of Mechanical Systems Engineering, Sorbonne Universités, Université de Technologie de Compiègne, UMR CNRS 7337 Roberval, CS 60319, 60203 Compiègne Cedex, France
{chen.zheng,matthieu.bricogne,julien.le-duigou, benoit.eynard}@utc.fr

[2] Institute of Mechatronic Design and Production, Johannes Kepler University Linz, Linz, Austria
peter.hehenberger@jku.at

[3] Faculty of Mechanical Engineering, Otto-von-Guericke University Magdeburg, 39106 Magdeburg, Germany
sandor.vajna@ovgu.de

Abstract. Interface in one complex system represents the logical or physical relationship integrating the components of the complex system or the components with their environment. It plays a quite significant role to guarantee the components designed by the designers of different disciplines integrate correctly in order to achieve the multidisciplinary integration. This paper presents an interface knowledge base to capitalise the design data and rules related to the interfaces. A knowledge-based engineering (KBE) design methodology in which the interface knowledge base is implemented is then proposed to help the designers to improve the multidisciplinary integration during the detailed design phase of complex systems. This KBE design methodology is finally demonstrated by a case study based on a partial discharge (PD) detection system.

Keywords: Design methodology · Knowledge-based engineering · Complex systems · Interface model · Multidisciplinary integration

1 Introduction

Current development trends indicate that systems become increasingly complex due to the constantly changing requirements and the introduction of new technologies. Pure mechanical systems that generate certain motions or transfer forces or torques, have been used for a long time. Since the beginning of 20th century, control systems have been introduced to manipulate the variables of mechanical systems. This kind of evolution allows fulfilling much more functions compared with a pure mechanical system.

R. Harik et al. (Eds.): PLM 2016, IFIP AICT 492, pp. 89–98, 2016.
DOI: 10.1007/978-3-319-54660-5_9

In 1969, the Yaskawa Electric Corporation coined the term "Mechatronics" as a combination of mechanical systems and electronic systems [1]. After the 1970s, the meaning of Mechatronics has been broadened to include software and computation. From then on, more disciplines, such as optical, hydraulic, pneumatic, telecommunication disciplines, etc., have been gradually integrated into products and systems. During the 1990s, driven by the development of information and communication technologies, systems are influenced by some new development trends shifting towards information processing associated with personal computers processing [2]. In this context, various types of complex systems, such as embedded systems, Cyber-Physical Systems (CPS), Internet of Things (IoT), Systems of Systems (SoS), etc., have been proposed and studied.

The above introduction reveals that the design of complex systems encompasses a wide range of disciplines. Therefore increasing attention has been paid to the multidisciplinary integration. The multidisciplinary integration not only requires the synergic integration of involved disciplines, but also focuses on the designers' activities of the whole design process [3]. During the detailed design phase of complex systems, components are usually designed in parallel by designers of different disciplines.

The interface is at the heart of the multidisciplinary nature for the design of complex systems [4]. The interface in the complex systems refers to the logical or physical relationships integrating the components of one system or the components with their environment, which can be used to describe the interactions of the components designed by different disciplines [5]. This paper presents a knowledge-based engineering (KBE) methodology, in which the interface model is considered as the key part to help the designers to improve the multidisciplinary integration. Two new features are provided by the proposed KBE design methodology. First, it has the capability to capture and organise the design data related to the interface and store the data in a structured base in order to achieve the reuse of knowledge. Second, it provides an automated compatibility test to guarantee the correction of different components. By applying the two features proposed by the KBE design methodology, both the synergistic integration of the components in one complex system and the integration of the several involved disciplines during the design process become more integrated, so that the multidisciplinary integration of complex systems can be improved.

The paper is organised as follows. Section 2 presents a review of related work. Section 3 firstly introduces the interface model which is considered as the key part of the proposed KBE design methodology. Then, an overview of the proposed KBE design methodology is presented. A case study based on a partial discharge (PD) detection system will be introduced in Sect. 4 to demonstrate the proposed KBE design methodology. Finally, the authors draw the conclusions in Sect. 5.

2 Related Work

The design of complex systems in which several disciplines are involved requires the extension of knowledge used by to include more disciplines. In order to achieve the multidisciplinary integration, some multidisciplinary design methodologies have been presented. Many researchers focus on the methodologies based on CAD to help the designers for the multidisciplinary design. For example, Lefèvre et al. [6] extract the geometric information from a CAD representation of the control component of a motor fan to simulate the dissipation by Ansys Fluent. Biahmou et al. [7] propose a methodology to translate a CAD model into behaviour simulation models created in MATLAB/Simulink. The methodologies based on CAD only focus on the product dimensions, geometric and surface contour and product materials, but neglect the design data and rules that can be reused during the detailed design phase [8].

KBE has some origins in CAD, and moreover, it can be used to capture and apply discipline-specific knowledge and expertise in order to facilitate solving problems [9]. Therefore KBE has been widely adopted for the design of discipline-specific systems, especially in mechanical engineering discipline. Sapuan and Abdalla [9] develop knowledge-based system for the material selection for the design of mechanical systems, Chapman and Pinfold [10] describe an application of a KBE approach for the rapid design and analysis of mechanical s of automobiles and Yang et al. [11] propose a KBE methodology for the design of ship decks. As to other disciplines, KBE can also be used to assist the design process. Aurum et al. [12] point out the importance of knowledge during the software engineering process and propose a structured model to manage the software engineering knowledge. In the electronic engineering discipline, Wang et al. [13] discuss the possibility to apply KBE to the rapid design of process chambers of integrated circuits.

This literature review shows that KBE can be used as an effective support for the discipline-specific design. Nowadays, by considering the specialities of the multidisciplinary design, the KBE has been gradually implemented in the design of complex systems. Chen et al. [14] propose a knowledge-based framework for the conceptual design phase of multidisciplinary systems. La Rocca and van Tooren [15] develop conceptual aircraft design applications based on KBE. Tian and Voskuijl [16] integrate the knowledge related to Electronic systems into the application developed by La Rocca and van Tooren to support the conceptual design of mechatronic systems. The literature review shows that most of the studies on those design methodologies based on KBE focus on the conceptual design phase. How to achieve the collaboration of designers from different disciplines during the detailed design phase has not been discussed.

Considering the limitations of related works on the multidisciplinary integration for the design of complex system, the authors propose a KBE design methodology in which the interface model is implemented to help the designers to improve the multidisciplinary integration during the detailed design phase for complex systems. Next section will present the details of the proposed design methodology.

3 KBE Design Methodology

The KBE design methodology presented in the paper implements the interface model as the key part to help the designers to improve the multidisciplinary integration during the detailed design phase of complex systems. The knowledge base is used to collect the design data, rules, experiences and other knowledge. In the paper, the authors propose a knowledge base which stores the design data and rules related to the interface by instantiating the interface model. This interface model will be firstly introduced in this section.

3.1 Interface Model

The authors propose the interface model to deal with the problem of multidisciplinary integration [17]. This interface model not only provides a structured base to store the design data related to the interface in order to achieve the knowledge reuse, but also offers compatibility rules to the designers in order to guarantee that different components integrate correctly (Fig. 1).

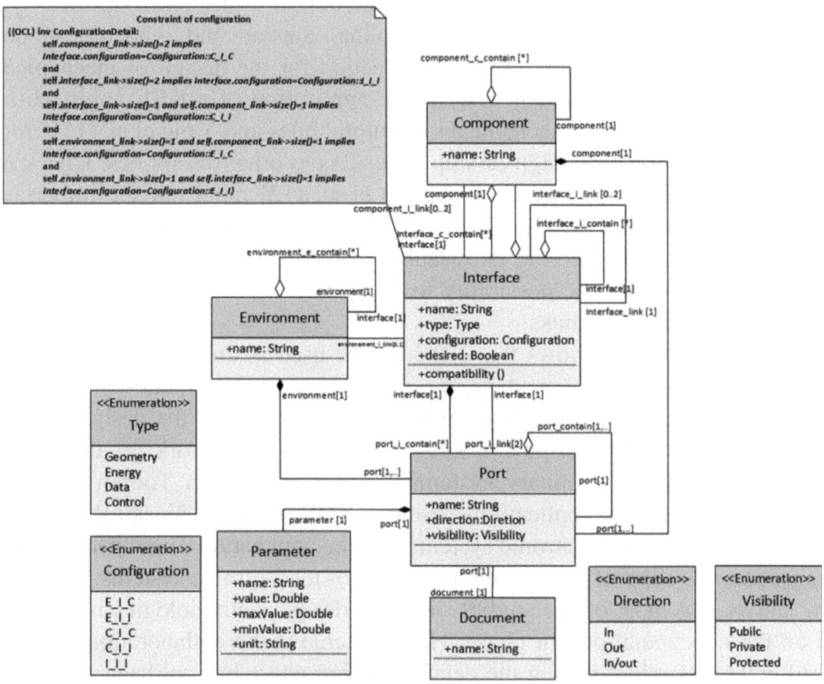

Fig. 1. UML class diagram of interface

First, the proposed interface model provides a structured base to store the design data related to the interface in order to achieve the knowledge reuse. It contains classes to define the attributes of one interface and its ports. The term "port" is considered as the primary location through which one element of a system interacts with other elements. The interface attributes are defined by taking into consideration of three different features: **type**, **configuration** and **desired/undesired**. **Type** attribute focuses on which types of transfer (geometric, energy, control or data) occur through one interface. **Configuration** attribute describes which elements are linked by the interface. **Desired/undesired** attribute expresses whether the interface creates positive effects (e.g. data or energy transmission) or unintended side-effects (e.g. heat, magnetic fields, vibration and other side effects. In summary, the attributes contained in the interface model provide a common representation for the interfaces defined by design teams of different disciplines.

Second, the interface model offers the compatibility rules to the designers to guarantee the different components integrate correctly. The method **compatibility()** is contained by the class **Interface** to check the compatibility of the interface. One example is cited here to illustrate the compatibility test method. Two components (Component 1 and Component 2) are connected by an interface (Interface) through the ports (CP1 and CP2). Two compatibility rules are presented as follows.

$$\begin{aligned} &CP1.Parameters1.value = CP2.Parameters2.value \\ &CP1.Parameters1.unit = CP2.Parameters2.unit \end{aligned} \tag{1}$$

$$\begin{aligned} &CP1.Parameters1.value < CP2.Parameters2.maxValue \\ &CP1.Parameters1.value > CP2.Parameters2.minValue \\ &CP1.Parameters1.unit = CP2.Parameters2.unit \end{aligned} \tag{2}$$

CP1.Parameter1 represents the parameter stored in the class **Parameter** of the port **CP1**, and ***CP2.Parameter2*** is the parameter of port **CP2**. In the compatibility **Rule 1**, in order to ensure the two components integrate with each other correctly, both the value and the unit of the parameters of **CP1** and **CP2** should be equal. However, sometimes the design parameter of one port is not specified by an exact value accurately. The compatibility **Rule 2** is used to illustrate that case. If the port **CP2** specifies the parameter by using an interval (***minValue***, ***maxValue***), the parameter of ***CP1*** should satisfy that ***CP1.Parameter1.value*** ∈ ***(CP2.Parameters2.minValue, CP2. Parameters2.maxValue)***.

The interface knowledge base being dealt in this paper is based on the previous interface model. Next sub-section will present the interface knowledge base and the KBE design methodology based on the interface knowledge base.

3.2 Interface Knowledge Base in Detailed Design Phase

In this paper, a knowledge-based engineering approach is applied to the detailed design phase of complex systems. The designers should capitalise the design input parameters including the interface data and compatibility rules from the heterogeneous and multidisciplinary sources and store them into the interface knowledge base. The flow chart based on the interface knowledge base is shown in Fig. 2, which mainly illustrates how the knowledge-based engineering approach can help the designers to improve the multidisciplinary integration during the detailed design phase.

Before entering the detailed design phase, the system designers have defined the architecture of the complex system [18]. In other words, the system designers should decompose the architecture recursively until the standard components or the components that have to be designed by the designers of discipline-specific teams. At the beginning of the detailed design phase, the designers of different disciplines carry out their design process for the discipline-specific components. The designers capture the design data and capitalise the design rules related to the interfaces generated or proposed during the design process of discipline-specific components. Then the interface

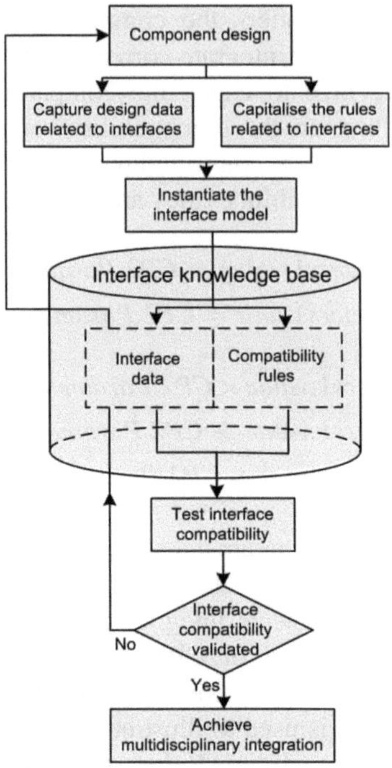

Fig. 2. Flow chart of detailed design phase based on interface knowledge base

model is instantiated by the design data and the rules and stored in the interface knowledge base. Once the model of an interface has been instantiated and stored in the interface knowledge base, the interface compatibility should be checked by using the compatibility rules in order to guarantee the different components integrate correctly. If the components prove to be incompatible with each other, the iterative process should be carried on. In the iterative process, the designers take the design data stored in the interface knowledge base to redesign the components in order to solve the incompatibility problems.

In this section, the interface knowledge base and the design methodology based on it have been presented. Knowledge bases are generally presented as a way to store design knowledge such as design data and design rules. The interface knowledge promotes the multidisciplinary integration by ensuring that the interfaces compatibility rules are respected. A case study is proposed by means of a partial discharge (PD) detection system to demonstrate the KBE methodology.

4 Case Study

The case study chosen to demonstrate the KBE methodology in this section is a partial discharge (PD) detection system. This PD detection system is designed to detect the partial discharge in gas insulated switchgear (GIS). GIS is a new type of high voltage switchgear that has been widely used in electric power systems. Although the reliability of GIS is high, any insulation defect that occurs without warning may result in damage to neighbouring equipment, customer dissatisfaction, disruption to economic activity, and the imposition of regulatory fines [19]. The PD detection system has been widely applied in GIS to detect the partial discharge in the GIS in order to avoid the risk of insulation accident. The PD detection system is considered as a complex system integrating synergistically the electrical/electronic system, mechanical parts, information processing and telecommunication technology, so the design of the system requires a multidisciplinary integration. Moreover, PD detection system has a number of variants according to the different internal structures or the voltage classes of the GIS. Similar design of the variants can directly reuse the knowledge base including the design data and rules, which can significantly shorten the design cycle to achieve the goal of rapid design and improve the quality, efficiency of design and production. Figure 3 shows the principle of the PD detection system. The PD signal can be captured by an ultra-high frequency sensor and transferred by the coaxial transmission line to the signal pre-processing sub-system where the analogue PD signal will be filtered, amplified and eventually converted to the digital data. Such digital data will be acquired and further processed. The processing results will be used for diagnostic purposes and control the operation state of the GIS.

The principle of the PD detection system indicates that different disciplines are involved in the design process. For example, the ultra-high frequency sensor to capture the PD signal is designed by the telecommunication team, whereas the coaxial wave line and the signal pre-processing sub-system are chosen and designed by the electronic team. Therefore the integration of the ultra-high frequency sensor and the coaxial transmission line will be chosen in order to demonstrate the proposed KBE based design methodology more clearly.

The ultra-high frequency sensor plays a crucial role to the accuracy and sensitivity of detection in the PD detection system [19]. It is designed by the designers of telecommunication team due to their rich experiences in antenna design. The designers of telecommunication team adopt the planar equiangular spiral antenna (PESA) as the ultra-high frequency sensor to capture the PD signal due to its ultra wideband feature. By considering the internal structure of the GIS and the electromagnetic wave's bandwidth created by the PD signal, the designers design the PESA with bandwidth from 700 MHz to more than 3 GHz, and its outside radius is 109 mm and initial radius is 2 mm. The software ANSYS[1] is used for modelling and simulation of the PESA, and the simulation result shows that the impedance of the antenna is about 135 Ω. The designers of the electronic team choose the standard coaxial transmission line to transfer the PD signal captured by the ultra-high frequency sensor, whose impedance is 50 Ω.

The demonstrator based on the KBE methodology has been developed by making use of the 3DEXPERIENCE platform[2]. The two components, i.e., the ultra-high frequency sensor and the coaxial transmission line (two blue boxes) and the interface between them (purple box) are presented by the demonstrator on the top of Fig. 4.

---

[1] http://www.ansys.com/.

[2] http://www.3ds.com/about-3ds/3dexperience-platform/.

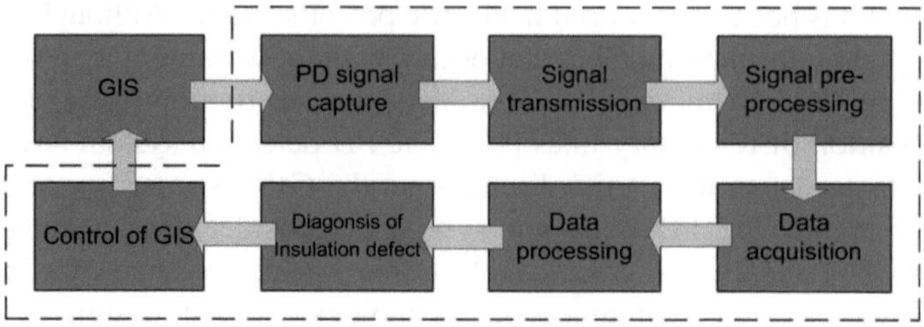

Fig. 3. Principle of PD detection system

The UML class diagram below the interface I1 in Fig. 4 shows the instance of the interface by considering the design data related to the interface. The attributes of the interface I1 and the ports' parameters linked to I1 are transferred into a structured representation by the demonstrator (shown on the left side and at the bottom of Fig. 4) and stored in the Interface knowledge base (shown in the centre of Fig. 4). The rule to check the compatibility of the interface I1 is processed by the Knowledgeware workbench of the 3DEXPERIENCE platform. The check result of interface compatibility (shown on the right side of Fig. 4) indicates that the interface between the ultra-high frequency sensor and the coaxial transmission line is incompatible, because the impedance of the ultra-high frequency sensor is different from that of the coaxial

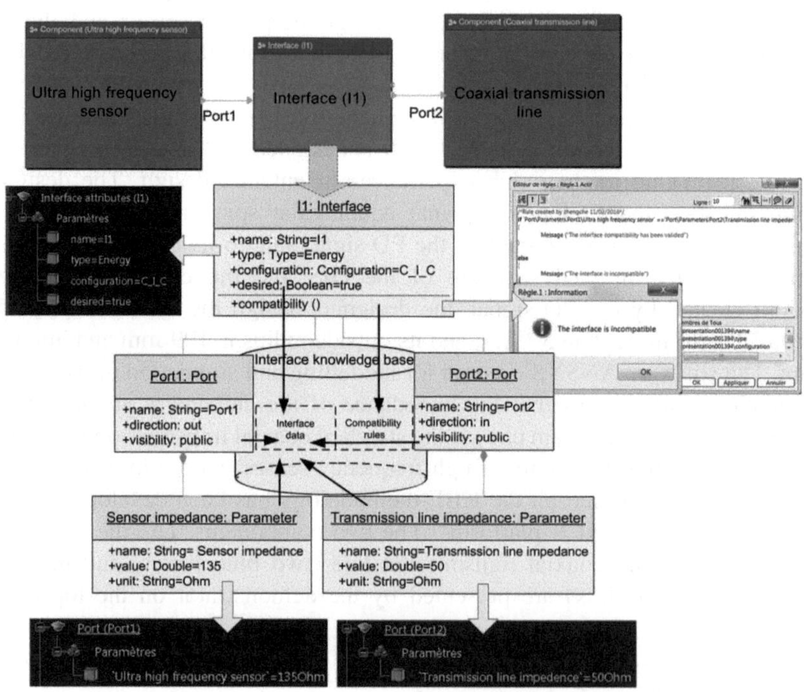

Fig. 4. Instantiation of the interface model and interface knowledge base (Color figure online)

transmission line. The difference of the impedances between the ultra-high frequency sensor and the coaxial transmission line implies that the two components do not match with each other, which affects the transmission of the PD signal negatively [20].

The flow chart in Fig. 2 shows that if the components prove to be incompatible with each other, the iterative process should be carried on. The designers should consider the design data related to the incompatible interface stored in the interface knowledge base. A micro-strip impedance transformer is designed by the designers of the telecommunication team which can change the impedance from 135 Ω to 50 Ω will be added between the ultra-high frequency sensor and the coaxial transmission line. After applying the incompatibility problem solution during the iterative process, a micro-strip impedance transformer is added between the ultra-high frequency sensor and the coaxial transmission line.

5 Conclusion

This paper presents a KBE methodology to help the designers to improve the multidisciplinary integration during the design process of complex systems. The interface knowledge base that is constructed and based on the interface model is implemented in the KBE methodology. It not only has the capability to capture the design data related to the interface and to store them in a structured base in order to achieve the knowledge reuse, but it provides an automated compatibility test to guarantee the different components integrate correctly as well. A PD measurement system has been chosen as case study to demonstrate how the KBE methodology can support efficiently the detailed design phase of complex systems by making use of a demonstrator developed based on the 3DEXPERIENCE platform. By applying the two features proposed by the KBE based design methodology, both the synergistic integration of the components in one complex system and the integration of the several involved disciplines during the design process will become more integrated, so that the multidisciplinary integration of complex systems can be improved.

The literature review in Sect. 2 has shown that some design applications based on the KBE have been developed for the conceptual design phase of multidisciplinary systems; while the KBE methodology proposed in the paper focuses on the detailed design phase. However, little attention has been paid to the link between the conceptual design phase and the detailed design phase, i.e., the system architecture definition. How to use the KBE approach to support the architecture definition should be further studied in the future.

Acknowledgement. This work has been partially supported by the Doctoral Program of Chinese Scholarship Council and the Austrian Center of Competence in Mechatronics (ACCM)/Linz Center of Mechatronics (LCM) in the framework of the Austrian COMET program. It also takes place in the scientific strategy of Labex MS2T supported by the ANR - French National Agency for Research.

References

1. Carryer, J.E., Ohline, R.M., Kenny, T.W.: Introduction to Mechatronic Design. Prentice Hall, Boston (2011)
2. Marwedel, P.: Embedded System Design: Embedded Systems Foundations of Cyber-Physical Systems. Springer, Dordrecht (2011)
3. Zheng, C., Bricogne, M., Le Duigou, J., Eynard, B.: Survey on mechatronic engineering: a focus on design methods and product models. Adv. Eng. Inform. **28**, 241–257 (2014)
4. Fosse, E., Delp, C.L.: Systems engineering interfaces: a model based approach. In: 2013 IEEE Aerospace Conference, Big Sky (2013)
5. Liang, V.C., Paredis, C.J.J.: A port ontology for conceptual design of systems. J. Comput. Inf. Sci. Eng. **4**, 206–217 (2004)
6. Lefèvre, J., Charles, S., Bosch-Mauchand, M., Eynard, B., Padiolleau, E.: Multidisciplinary modelling and simulation for mechatronic design. J. Des. Res. **12**, 127–144 (2014)
7. Biahmou, A., Frohlich, A., Stjepandic, J.: Improving interoperability in mechatronic product development. In: Proceedings of the International Conference on Product Lifecycle Management, Bremen (2010)
8. Kulon, J., Broomhead, P., Mynors, D.J.: Applying knowledge-based engineering to traditional manufacturing design. Int. J. Adv. Manuf. Technol. **30**, 945–951 (2006)
9. Sapuan, S.M.: A knowledge-based system for materials selection in mechanical engineering design. Mater. Des. **22**, 687–695 (2001)
10. Chapman, C.B., Pinfold, M.: The application of a knowledge based engineering approach to the rapid design and analysis of an automotive structure. Adv. Eng. Softw. **32**, 903–912 (2001)
11. Yang, H.Z., Chen, J.F., Ma, N., Wang, D.Y.: Implementation of knowledge-based engineering methodology in ship structural design. Comput. Des. **44**, 196–202 (2012)
12. Aurum, A., Jeffery, R., Wohlin, C., Handzic, M.: Managing Software Engineering Knowledge. Springer, Heidelberg (2013)
13. Wang, K.S., Lin, J., Cheng, J., Ji, L.H.: Investigation on the development of knowledge-based engineering and its application in rapid design of process chamber of IC equipment. Appl. Mech. Mater. **373**, 2147–2155 (2013)
14. Chen, Y., Liu, Z.L., Xie, Y.B.: A knowledge-based framework for creative conceptual design of multi-disciplinary systems. Comput. Des. **44**, 146–153 (2012)
15. La Rocca, G., van Tooren, M.J.: Knowledge-based engineering to support aircraft multidisciplinary design and optimization. J. Aerosp. Eng. **224**, 1041–1055 (2010)
16. Tian, F., Voskuijl, M.: Mechatronic design and optimization using knowledge based engineering applied to an inherently unstable and unmanned aerial vehicle. IEEE/ASME Trans. Mechatron. **21**, 542–554 (2015). doi:10.1109/TMECH.2015.2441832
17. Zheng, C., Le Duigou, J., Bricogne, M., Eynard, B.: Multidisciplinary interface model for design of mechatronic systems. Comput. Ind. **76**, 24–37 (2016)
18. Sage, A.P., Rouse, W.B.: Handbook of Systems Engineering and Management. Wiley, Hoboken (2009)
19. Judd, M.D., Yang, L., Hunter, I.B.B.: Partial discharge monitoring of power transformers using UHF sensors. IEEE Electr. Insul. Mag. **21**, 5–14 (2005)
20. Zheng, C., Li, T.: Development of an exponential tapered impedance transformer for UHF-PD sensor. In: 1st International Conference on Electric Power Equipment, Xi'an (2011)

A Business Collaborative Decision Making System for Network of SMEs

Muhammad Naeem[1(✉)], Néjib Moalla[1], Yacine Ouzrout[1], and Abdelaziz Bouras[2]

[1] Decision and Information for Production Systems (DISP), University Lumière Lyon 2, Lyon, France
{Muhammad.Naeem,Nejib.Moalla, Yacine.Ouzrout}@univ-lyon2.fr

[2] CSE Department, Qatar University, Doha, Qatar
abdelaziz.bouras@qu.edu.qa

Abstract. The enterprise collaboration has gain much popularity and strength with the inception of digital revolution. The concept of enterprise collaboration has observed a dynamic and evolving phenomenon of value added chain. This phenomenon under the convergence of information technology has placed a remarkable impact on decision-making processes within enterprises. The enterprises are involved in establishing a common window of collaborative network where the principle enterprise decides the synthesis of the incoming opportunity. In this study, we have shown how the decision-making capability can be improved by means of analytics of vast amount of data during enterprise collaboration. The proposed system has adopted prescriptive analysis across enterprise resources. The outcome of proposed system addresses the individual and collaborative enterprise capability within enterprise network. Our proposed knowledge based decision making model provides a self-adaptive solution for enterprise collaborative services.

Keywords: Big data · Enterprise collaboration · Opportunity analysis · Capability evaluation · Data asset

1 Introduction

Since the inception of shift of paradigm of manufacturing from 'whole' product to 'integrated' product, the Small and Medium Enterprises (SMEs) are facing operational challenges in turbulent environment [1]. This phenomenon is directing the SMEs towards improving the quality of decision-making process. The dynamic and in time momentum of quality aware decision making process has shaped itself into a part and parcel of the enterprise management. The information support for decision-making processes at all levels of the enterprise is inevitable. Moreover, the organizational arrangement of the processes are becoming increasingly important. The processes in the enterprises are meant to produce data all the time. The accumulation of data across the business processes leads to the technical challenge of handling Big Data (BD) in enterprises in a value-driven course of action. Big Data amounts not only towards data

R. Harik et al. (Eds.): PLM 2016, IFIP AICT 492, pp. 99–107, 2016.
DOI: 10.1007/978-3-319-54660-5_10

gathering but, most of all, data processing, organization and its visualization. All of these are in fact substantial for obtaining business improvements.

Data warehouses are a conventional means of storing and processing BD. Data warehouse environment is traditionally a production driven, equipped with highly managed service level agreements [2]. This environment certifies timely generation of managerial reports as well as dashboards. Certainly, it is a cost effective job where a skilled person is required to organize newly generated data source. Such an idea is marked by the persistent granular data along its traceable history in the data warehouse system. This conventional approach plays in an environment of highly structured data warehouse [2]. We have proposed an added value to this traditional approach in business analysis coined by our earlier big data framework [1, 3].

We present a simple case scenario (see the Fig. 1) for the requirement of collaborative network. An enterprise is receiving large number of projects. There is a likelihood of any project to be an opportunity. We already described that the competitive environment is pushing enterprises to leverage more and more attractable versatility in the products. Under normal circumstances, numerous projects are deemed to be inappropriate because the enterprise has no mechanism to extrapolate the level or degree of collaborative effort required in transforming the 'risky' projects into acceptable projects. The decision making system can first reduce the timing for initial assessment and classification of the acceptance of the projects; henceforth the rate of the profitable projects is significantly increased. The motivation is to establish an in house decision making facility of enterprise collaboration where the data anonymity is also maintained. The reason for establishing the enterprise collaboration coined by data anonymity is marked by the fact that the enterprises are always prone to be sensitive in exposing their data pertaining to its internal business processes.

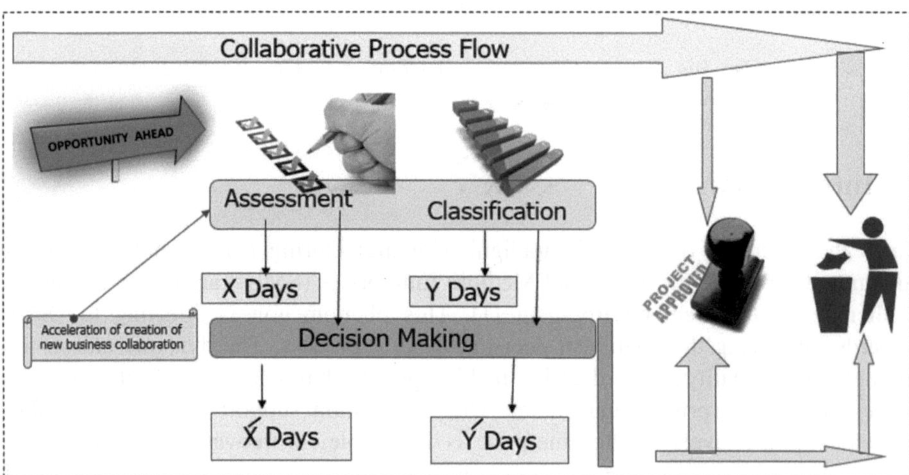

Fig. 1. A motivational scenario of early response by means of enterprise collaborative decision making.

Our approach is to generate a step forward analytic sandbox with the slogan of loading whatever data is available from internal and external data sources. The idea is to perform more data profiling, refining, transformation, identifying and generating new composite metrics. Keeping in view of this added value, the proposed system takes the structured data as well as Computer Aided Design (CAD) design resource file STandard for the Exchange of Product model data (STEP) [4] file and integrate both of them for the purpose of a "Forehand Analysis". Here the term "Forehand Analysis" refers to the situation in which firstly an enterprise is receiving sufficient number of projects. Secondly, each project may or may not be a profitable opportunity or waste of time depending on its context. Thirdly, the enterprise needs to produce a positive or negative response as soon as possible.

The remaining paper is organized into three sections. The Sect. 2 is related to conceptual and pragmatic work related to the theme of this study. In Sect. 3, we have shown our methodology. The Sect. 4 is dedicated to explanation of a holistic approach using all components in Sect. 3. The paper in last section is concluded with some recommendations and future extensions.

2 Related Work

We have drawn a specialized taxonomy of application of BD in decision making of enterprise collaboration. The applications of BD analytics can be classified into three broader categories including descriptive, predictive and prescriptive analytics.

The term "descriptive analytics" briefly refers to "What has been done". The descriptive analytics is carried out in two situations. The first situation is a frequency based approach usually obtained by means of aggregation across source data. The second is on demand as in case of on-line analytical processing. The descriptive analysis is characterized by the identification of problems by means of drilling down into the ongoing processes, their technical and functional detail within the organization. We have noticed that most the work in this category is performed in social alliance [5], strategies in financial alliance [6], internationalization [7], supply chain [8], and unexpected events management in the context of hierarchical production planning [9] and others [10].

The predictive analytics is aimed towards identifying what is happing in future or what type of new instance can be generated. It is also coined by inference mechanism in data analytics. Apart from this, it can also be used for granular level grouping of the existing instances in shape of a complex tree or graph [11]. It can be used for the inference and forecasting purpose as well [12–14]. The Table 1 is showing the detail for the collaborative work performed in the area of communication enabling and logistic industry.

Some researchers have also defined another type of analytics known as prescriptive analysis [15–17]. Its scope is broader but at the same time it draws the cumulative effect of complexity. It is aimed towards the exploitation of data as well as the algorithms to find the most appropriate (or nearest) decisions targeting objectives and requirement related to high volume of data and its versatile nature. It can be briefly described as "What is suggested to be done". It is know that BD has already provided an umbrella of

Table 1. Big data analytic in enterprise collaboration

	Descriptive	Predictive	Prescriptive
Enterprise collaboration strategy	- Supply chain [8] - Social alliance [5] - Financial alliance [6]	- Forest enterprises [11]	- Collaboration requirement [16]
Enterprise collaboration planning	- Work flow, mappings between activities in process models [10] - Internationalization [7]	- Communication enabling [12]	- Safety management [15]
Enterprise collaboration operation	- Unexpected events management in the context of hierarchical production planning [9]	- Logistic industry [14] - Content management [13]	-

NoSQL where complex structures or semi structured can be handled by means of storage into key value, column family database, document family and graphical database. The Industries are producing more and more versatile nature of data. This aspect accentuates the needs of leveraging the NoSQL technologies for descriptive and predictive learning. Both of these learning analytics play a vital role in helping companies realizing effective decisions in the strategic direction of the organization. We argue that a more holistic approach by means of utilizing these two fundamental learning system accompanied by knowledge base learning can realize into a best course of learning action namely prescriptive analysis. It qualifies the problem of enterprise collaboration a good candidate under the prescriptive analysis. But on the other hand, one can conclude from the literature review that operational level enterprise collaboration in perspective analysis is still missing.

To extend the concept of perspective level data analytics in enterprise collaboration, we introduced the non-conventional resources other than relational data. The CAD model can be considered for the purpose of identification of explicit or implicit manufacturing capabilities. Since the inception of the concept of PLM and the emergence of the STEP CAD format [4], the research community has been motivated to introduce the mechanism of extracting the low level geometric entities of a product design. The STEP format holds a specific structure which is typically used to facilitate process planning and manufacturing activities [4].

3 Proposed Methodology

We previously pointed out gaps in the coherent implementation of the data analytics in the pursuit of enterprise collaboration. Our methodology is based on the conceptual design to bring out a prescriptive analysis suitable for the decision making. We shall propose the generic steps to obtain the idea formulated on the basis of the gap identified in the literature review. The Fig. 2 is showing the steps for the treatment and analysis of the incoming project from the stream of opportunities. The STEP [4] file is analyzed into two parts/section. One section (plastic) is related to the manufacturing domain of enterprise and the second component is the realm of metal production. The metal production facility is the business of another organization which is a potential partner enterprise as well. To complete this project, both of the enterprises are in need of a profit oriented collaboration. Our system will analyze the design structure (available from STEP resources).

However, synthesis of STEP resource is insufficient till it is backed up by other data, specially the transformation performed by BD analytics. We in our system adopt this data from the Supplier Relationship Management (SRM), Product Life cycle Management (PLM), Customer Resource Management (CRM) and Enterprise Resource Planning (ERP) in an iterative way. From a historical perspective of information system application, ERP is comprised of several integrated modules. These include logistics, procurements, sales, marketing, human resources and finance supporting intra organizational collaboration. SRM extends its scope to include market information with focus upon order management for improving product availability and enhancing customer satisfaction. All of these structured data provides the array of transactions related to customer, product, costing, taxation and timing records related to the previous similar projects. A combine analysis of both of these stream of resources is likely to produce the classification as shown in the classification instances in the Fig. 2.

The Capability Evaluator (CE) is the technical transformation component. This component is based on statistical descriptive or predictive analysis. Each CE outcomes a classification illustrating the capability of each enterprise individually. It is useful that we explain the components responsible for the analysis of structured data. The generic

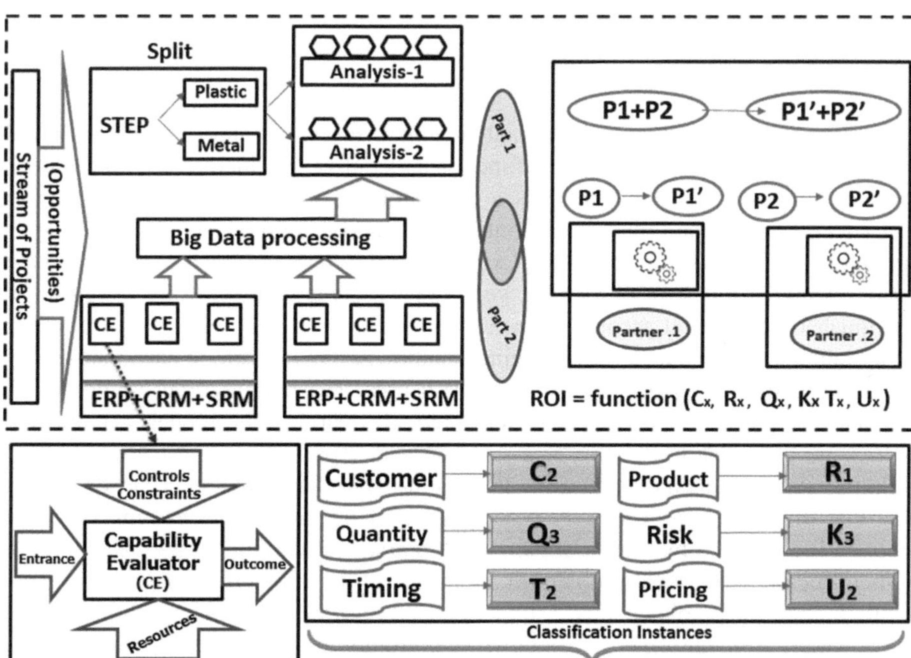

Fig. 2. Methodology of classification of technical and functional characteristics during decision making treatment for enterprise collaboration.

functionality and specification of every component is characterized by consumption of input resources. It operates on the input by means of given resources under certain constraints and controls. Each component produces an output which functions the classification system of the enterprise capacity in specific context of the system. We shall discuss a few CE components with its functional capability and technical specification as shown in Tables 2 and 3.

Table 2. Capability evaluator – parameters for product wise ranked list of partner

Inputs (entrance)	Controls constraints	Outcome	Resources
- List of partner - Specific opportunity	- Last x months of business with each partner	- Ranked list of partner (general) - Ranked list of partner (for a specific opportunity/project)	- Partners - Orders - Quotation

Table 3. Capability evaluator – parameters for risk likelihood (outcome: causation risk model)

Inputs (entrance)	Controls constraints	Resources
History of specific - Product item - Customer - Potential partner	- Change in the price of the raw material - New taxation and levies (if any) - Environmentally affected production process - Intrinsic level of the design of the product - Profit margin - Insurance liability/coverage	- Sentiment analysis - Project detail - Product design

Ranking the partner is an important treatment in establishing the enterprise collaborative facility. To illustrate the functional detail of product wise ranked list of partners. Let us assume that there is a collection of orders placed by the potential customers. Each of the orders itself contains a detail of the product. The input for the ranking is not limited to merely the placement of the fresh orders. It also incorporates the previous list of the orders which were either regretted, successfully completed or just finished with trivial accomplishments.

In ranking, given a query, the ranking function assigns a score to each partner, and ranks the partner in descending order of the scores. The ranking order represents the relevance of partner with respect to the query. In learning the model, a number of queries are provided; each query is associated with a perfect ranking list of partner; a ranking function is then created using the training data. This process is carried out in a way that the model can precisely predict the ranking lists in the training data. The problem is addressed by means of pair-wise approach as carried out by Cao et al. [18] in their document retrieval problem or by means of a ranking modeling.

Risk is an inevitable characteristic associated with every incoming opportunity. It varies widely from customer to customer, opportunity to opportunity. It demands an in depth understanding of other related factors. An in depth understanding of overall risk assessment is likely to help predict the likelihood and cost of incoming opportunity. Numerous conditions contribute to the frequency and severity of the associated risks.

These include ignoring the drastic change in the price of the raw material, new taxation and levies (if any), environmentally affected production process, intrinsic level of the design of the product, profit margin, insurance liability/coverage etc. The goal of this module is to provide a realistic assessment based on the characteristics of the incoming opportunity in the shape of a project.

4 Holistic Enterprise Collaboration

In previous section, we provided two higher level of CE in Tables 2 and 3. We have termed the descriptive level of CE in Level 1 (CE.L1) and those which require a higher level of course of action are placed under the category of CE in Level 2 (CE.L2). In our research the final objective of decision making for an incoming opportunity (project) is not limited to only two CE.L2. In-fact, there are numerous such CE.

The collective and accumulative effect of all of these CE irrespective of their level plays a non-trivial role in determination of a prescriptive decision making system. The outcome of these CE are shaped in either the classification such as C_x, Q_x, R_x, T_x etc., (see the Fig. 1 for their interaction and outcome). All of these CE return an assessment in the shape of Return of Investment (*RoI*) as can be defined:

$$RoI = f(CE_1, CE_2) \tag{1}$$

The *RoI* (defined in Eq. 1) is certainly an essential transformation for the decision making. Here question arises how this prescriptive analysis in form of *RoI* can be achieved. The answer is provided by means of ontological modelling. The Table 4 is showing the mapping, interaction and evolution of knowledge base. The interaction is focused on ontological engineering of the CE interoperability and domain knowledge representation (shown in Fig. 3). A repository of semantically encoded rules using SWRL queries for dynamic decision making will bring forward the decision about the suitability of an incoming opportunity. The whole decision making system is not only dynamic but also iterative. The continuous evolution and refinement of core value

Table 4. A partial overview of mapping of knowledge base (BD analytics) to ontology schema.

Property/relationship across T-Box	Knowledge base from CE
In-house/partner mechanical processes	Aggregated numeric value (L1)
In-house/partner cost	Frequency based value (L1)
In-house/partner timing	Time series analysis (L2)
Partner recommendation index	Random forest prediction (L2)
x months business volume with partner	Frequency based value (L1)
Change in the price of the raw material	Frequency based value (L1)
Taxation/levies	Frequency based value (L1)
Risk factor	Naive Bayes prediction (L2)
Customer classification	Frequency based value (L1)
Collaboration level	Regression analysis (L2)
Churn index	Random forest prediction (L2)

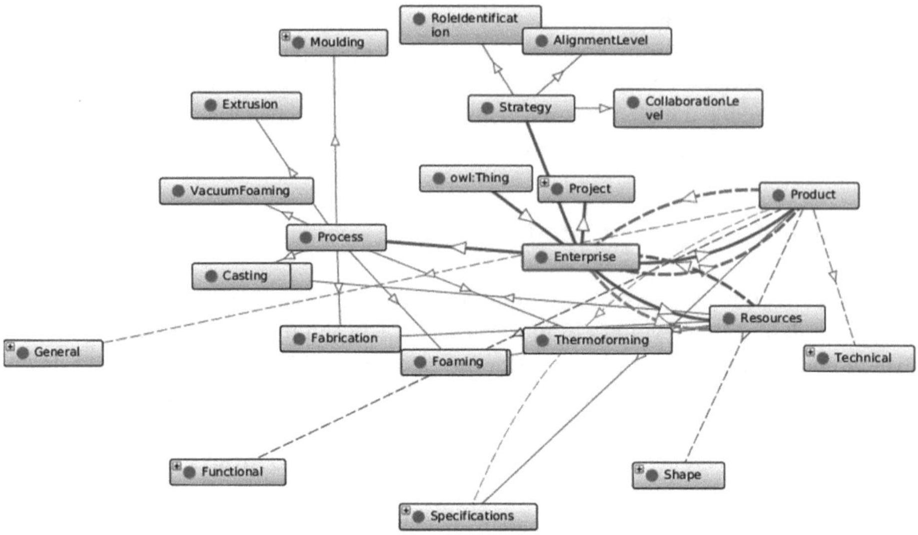

Fig. 3. A top level concept view of enterprise collaboration value ontology.

ontology gives a clear advantage of those system which either use conventional database system or connect the knowledge base directly to the underlying first level (raw) data.

5 Conclusion

The idea of enterprise collaboration is gaining a strategic position. This position is triggered by the ineluctable need of the enterprises to revitalize their chain of manufacturing with optimized utilization of underlying resources. Modern infrastructure of information technology is characterized by complex set of hardware, software along with its underlying enterprise policies and solutions processed with organizational resource. This complexity exercises an influence on the decision making of enterprise management and its collaborative effort. Given the contemporary collaborative operations, it is not a straight forward process to establish a strong connection between functional exploitation of versatile large amount of data and quality of decisions. To cope up this challenge, we have proposed a system treating various transformation and translation of BD capabilities into a dynamic decision making system. The outcome of this study is a decision making system across demands of versatile products. We have shown how the system can enhance support of the networked enterprise in timely creation and participation in collaborative environment by means of facilitating an infrastructure. The infrastructure is aimed towards discovery, capturing, delivery and application of this knowledge to create collaboration in improvement of operational efficiency. A possible extension to this work lies in the preservation of the decision making rules in such a shape which can facilitate the forthcoming opportunities and projects.

References

1. Naeem, M., Moalla, N., Bouaras, A., Ouzrout, Y.: Opportunity analysis for enterprise collaboration between network of SMEs (2015)
2. Kościelniak, H., Puto, A.: BIG DATA in decision making processes of enterprises. Procedia Comput. Sci. **65**, 1052–1058 (2015)
3. Naeem, M., Moalla, N., Ouzrout, Y., Bouras, A.: Weaving trending, costing and recommendations using big data analytic: an enterprise capability evaluator. In: Mertins, K., Jardim-Gonçalves, R., Popplewell, K., Mendonça, J.P. (eds.) Enterprise Interoperability VII. PIC, vol. 8, pp. 163–173. Springer, Heidelberg (2016). doi:10.1007/978-3-319-30957-6_13
4. Iso, I.S.: 10303-1 TC184/SC4: Product Data Representation and Exchange-Part 11: The EXPRESS Language Reference Manual (1994)
5. Sakarya, S., Bodur, M., Yildirim-Öktem, Ö., Selekler-Göksen, N.: Social alliances: business and social enterprise collaboration for social transformation. J. Bus. Res. **65**, 1710–1720 (2012)
6. Kaya, N.: Corporate entrepreneurship, generic competitive strategies, and firm performance in small and medium-sized enterprises. Procedia-Soc. Behav. Sci. **207**, 662–668 (2015)
7. Costa, E., Soares, A.L., de Sousa, J.P.: Information, knowledge and collaboration management in the internationalisation of SMEs: a systematic literature review. Int. J. Inf. Manag. **36**, 557–569 (2016)
8. van Hoof, B., Thiell, M.: Collaboration capacity for sustainable supply chain management: small and medium-sized enterprises in Mexico. J. Clean. Prod. **67**, 239–248 (2014)
9. Vargas, A., Boza, A., Patel, S., Patel, D., Cuenca, L., Ortiz, A.: Inter-enterprise architecture as a tool to empower decision-making in hierarchical collaborative production planning. Data Knowl. Eng. **105**, 5–22 (2015)
10. Tan, W., Li, L., Xu, W., Yang, F., Jiang, C., Yang, L., Choi, J.: A role-oriented service system architecture for enterprise process collaboration. Comput. Oper. Res. **39**, 1893–1900 (2012)
11. Ambrose-Oji, B., Lawrence, A., Stewart, A.: Community based forest enterprises in Britain: two organising typologies. For. Policy Econ. **58**, 65–74 (2015)
12. Kolberg, M., Buford, J.F., Dhara, K., Wu, X., Krishnaswamy, V.: Feature interaction in a federated communications-enabled collaboration platform. Comput. Netw. **57**, 2410–2428 (2013)
13. Nof, S.Y., Morel, G., Monostori, L., Molina, A., Filip, F.: From plant and logistics control to multi-enterprise collaboration. Ann. Rev. Control **30**, 55–68 (2006)
14. Pateman, H., Cahoon, S., Chen, S.-L.: The role and value of collaboration in the logistics industry: an empirical study in australia. Asian J. Shipp. Log. **32**, 33–40 (2016)
15. Niskanen, T., Louhelainen, K., Hirvonen, M.L.: Results of the Finnish national survey investigating safety management, collaboration and work environment in the chemical industry. Safety Sci. **70**, 233–245 (2014)
16. To, C.K.M., Ko, K.K.B.: Problematizing the collaboration process in a knowledge-development context. J. Bus. Res. **69**, 1604–1609 (2016)
17. Wang, G., Gunasekaran, A., Ngai, E.W.T., Papadopoulos, T.: Big data analytics in logistics and supply chain management: certain investigations for research and applications. Int. J. Prod. Econ. **176**, 98–110 (2016)
18. Cao, Z., Qin, T., Liu, T.-Y., Tsai, M.-F., Li, H.: Learning to rank: from pairwise approach to listwise approach. In: Proceedings of the 24th International Conference on Machine Learning, pp. 129–136. ACM (2007)

Agile and Project-Planned Methods in Multidisciplinary Product Design

Benjamin Guérineau[1(✉)], Louis Rivest[2], Matthieu Bricogne[1], and Alexandre Durupt[1]

[1] Sorbonne Universités, Université de Technologie de Compiègne, CNRS, UMR 7337 Roberval, Centre de Recherche Royallieu - CS 60 319, 60 203 Compiègne Cedex, France
{benjamin.guerineau, matthieu.bricogne, alexandre.durupt}@utc.fr

[2] Laboratoire Numérix, Ecole de Technologie Supérieure, Montréal, Canada
louis.rivest@etsmtl.ca

Abstract. This paper presents a method introducing Agile practices in project planned methodology in the context of a multidisciplinary product design. These multidisciplinary products can be Mechatronics or Cyber-Physical-Systems. Various design methodologies and types of project architecture already exist. Some of them are focused on a micro-level, whereas others are on a macro-level. Our proposition is focused on the macro-level. Agile and project-planned methods are presented and analyzed before looking at a possible hybridization. Hybrid solutions already exist, but this paper formalizes a project architecture to combine the advantages of project-planned and Agile methods and to describe the relative PLM position.

Keywords: PLM · Multidisciplinary design methodology · Agile · Project-planned

1 Introduction

This paper investigates the design methodology and project organization used to design multidisciplinary products. A multidisciplinary product is defined as a product which involves different domains (e.g. mechanics, electronics, computer science, optics, chemistry, etc.). An example of a multidisciplinary product is Mechatronics, which appeared in the late 1960s in Japan, and is defined as the synergetic approach of mechanics, electronics and information technology (IT) [1, 2]. Cyber Physical Systems (CPS) are another type of multidisciplinary products. Introduced more recently in the 2000s [3], CPS can be defined as "physical and engineered systems whose operations are monitored, coordinated, controlled, and integrated by a computing and communication core" [4]. Some business sectors like the automotive or aeronautical industry have developed strong interest in CPS and Mechatronics. These developments have reached a high level of complexity driven by the perpetual growth of customers' expectations, as these have involved diverse disciplines (e.g. mechanics, electronics,

R. Harik et al. (Eds.): PLM 2016, IFIP AICT 492, pp. 108–118, 2016.
DOI: 10.1007/978-3-319-54660-5_11

and computer science) and the incorporation of the continual technological advances in these domains to meet those expectations.

CPS and Mechatronics are two domains where the design methodologies remain discipline-dependent. This heterogeneity generally leads to poorly integrated products [5], mainly because the methods have generally been developed to address the needs of a given discipline; very and few of the existing methods were initially developed to cope with multidisciplinary approaches. In some companies, methodologies have adapted to cope with this complexity, even though most design methods were first developed for a specific domain (e.g. electronics, mechanics, or software development). Our objective is not to create a design methodology or a new organizational structure but to propose mixing some existing methods to meet specific needs. To support this mixing, an organizational model is proposed. Its aim is to promote multidisciplinary integration, leading to a better collaboration for product design. This proposition falls within the scope of Product Lifecycle Management (PLM).

PLM is an approach to support this complexity, including the design methodology and the complete product life cycle [6, 7]. PLM is defined as "the business activity of managing, in the most effective way, a company's products all the way across their lifecycles; from the very first idea for a product all the way through until it is retired and disposed of" by [8]. PLM is thus an approach that supports the collaborative process for product development, from its first draft to the end of its life.

Several approaches are used for product development, although this paper is focused on Agile methods and project-planned (PP) methods, also called plan-driven methods. Agile methods were selected because of their growing implementation in companies which see their potential as a new approach to product development. The PP method is highlighted because of its frequent utilization in hardware (HW) product development. Agile methods arose from software (SW) development and are defined as "the ability to react rapidly to changes in the environment, whether expected or not" [9]. PP methods are a popular way of designing and manufacturing a product in hardware product development, and offers a rigorous framework to the process. These methods each have their own advantages and drawbacks. Hybrid models have also been explored [10], and this solution will be investigated further.

Moreover, in a multidisciplinary product development methodology, a domain is often dominant and its background is instilled in the design project. CPS have a SW and IT background, and Mechatronics comes from the HW side and is an evolution of electromechanics products [5]. Thus, because of CPS' SW-oriented-background, the engineers, the design process, the design methodology, the procedures and everything in relation with the project are both IT- and SW-oriented. This particularity should be taken into account: this environment is their hallmark and changing it by massively introducing techniques from a HW development background could introduce resistance to change, as well as being incredibly difficult. Moreover, their working habits appear to be efficient and they do not have an interest in changing them.

After introducing the context, this paper focuses on different design methodologies that are able to provide a framework for multidisciplinary product development. The second section proposes an overview of Agile and PP methods and discusses a hybridization option. The third section is our proposition based on the hybridization of the Agile and the PP methods. We end with our conclusion and an overview of promising future work.

2 Agile, Project-Planned and Hybrid Methods

This section presents the Agile, PP and hybrid methods, including their advantages and their limits. In a hybrid approach, the added value expected from combining two (or more) approaches is much higher than if they were utilized separately. This is the main motivation for using hybrid methods; their practicality has already led to the exploration of their incorporation in multidisciplinary product design and especially for CPS and Mechatronics products.

2.1 Agile Methods

Agile methods, noted in plural form as there are several methods (e.g. Scrum [11], Extreme programming [12], etc.), appeared in the late 80s and at the beginning of the 90s in SW development, their adoption supported by the general dissatisfaction with the "heavyweight approaches" in use [13]. Those too-rigid methods with their heavy frameworks were perceived as inefficient and did not add any notable value. Agile methods, instead, focus more on the product rather than on how it is produced and all of the associated documentation.

In our CPS and Mechatronics context, the market, the expectations of the customers and the resulting requirements can all change quickly, and thus Agile methods would be the best option for meeting those challenges and to react efficiently to changes. The current methods can present as too rigid to deal effectively with these types of challenges.

Another advantage of Agile methods is their bottom-up approach [5]. The reverse is the top-down approach, which is used in the analysis of PP's described in the next section. This bottom-up approach reflects how teams really work. Team members are directly linked to customers and their requirements, thus, solutions are not imposed by the head of a project and can arise from the relationships between customers and team members. This approach is, from our point of view, a bottom-up scheme. This scheme stimulates and supports creativity and new ideas, leading to innovations even at a final stage. In the current very competitive market, Agile methods and how they support innovation is a solution to make products more distinguishable. According to Highsmith: "Agile development defines […] a capability to balance flexibility and structure, a capability to draw creativity and innovation out of a development team" [14]. Thus, innovation can also be stimulated by the flexibility provided by Agile methods.

Having listed the main advantages, the Agile method's limits are presented next. Among their limits, as highlighted in [13] and [15], is the problem of how this method can be applied to large-scale companies and projects: all the principles cannot be respected. For example, the involvement of all stakeholders is needed, especially that of major clients, and the associated communication task in large-scale projects can be insurmountable. In most cases it is understood that the customer is the final user, although in some cases, the customer can be different from the user. It is the project members' responsibility to identify all the stakeholders and to involve them in the development process. Another point involves communication in an extended enterprise context. When a project is highly collaborative and involves many partners a strong communication network is needed. Sommerville [13] focuses on the security and safety aspects in development. This perspective is addressed in the third section. Agile methods are not yet widespread in HW domains, but some work has already been done to analyze the relationship between Agile methods and HW [16, 17]. We should note that in HW it could be more difficult to address late requirement changes. Moreover, in a HW or in a physical product development, a production line is often designed or modified concurrently. As a consequence, late changes could incur a significant cost and thus an overall view is needed to analyze the situation and make the best decision in terms of a project's durability and return on investments (ROI). A possible solution to allow for and manage late changes without significantly affecting a project's global cost could be to introduce modularity, as is often done in SW engineering. The product would then be developed in a modular approach and so a particular attention should be paid to the interfaces. However, if this modular approach is overdeveloped, product integration can be hindered.

Finally, in Agile methods, the focus is on the product and not on the documentation. The associated lack of documentation is rarely acceptable for a physical product [13], where it is normally required, especially in terms of maintenance. If the documentation is to provide a user guide, an exception is made by some smartphones which are delivered with no documentation because they are considered to be intuitive, however for other hi-tech or large Mechatronics and CPS products, this lack of documentation is not conceivable.

This section has presented a brief state of the art on Agile methods, their strengths and their limitations. In the next section, the PP methods are evaluated in terms of their advantages and their limits.

2.2 Project-Planned/Plan-Driven Methods

Project-planned (PP), also called Plan-driven [13] methods, were first introduced in the 1980s [18]. The philosophy of this method could appear as quite antagonist to that of Agile methods: whereas Agile methods are flexible, PP methods appear as more rigid. Another difference is that they are reference-document-based [5]. At the beginning of a project, reference documents are submitted in order to have a common objective and to position the project into a specific direction. These reference documents are built with project management references such as Product Breakdown Structure (PBS), Work Breakdown Structure (WBS), Organization Breakdown Structure (OBS) and Cost Breakdown Structure (CBS) [18]. These references are provided in order to define the hierarchical architecture of the product (with PBS), the link between the planned work and the team members (with WBS), the organizational structure of the project with the different actors (with OBS) and the cost distribution (with CBS). These references provide the rigid framework that is required in certain large-scale or medium-scale product design processes to fix a common view and objectives. PP is also based on the milestones and associated deliverables determined by project leaders in the early stages of a project. Each stage also has its own objectives in terms of costs, time and product performance. Managers measure a project's progress by checking the deliverables' progress. Earned value management [18] is often used to determine if a project is running late or not. In this methodology, the major decisions emerge from the head of the project, based on their application of these reference tools, and thus this method is considered to be a top-down approach [5]. Moreover, in a generic design approach, projects are based on templates to capitalize on knowledge from past projects.

After introducing the main concepts of PP, this paragraph investigates the advantages of PP's methods. PP is mainly applied in HW product development. PP can also be applied in SW engineering for large developments, or when there are serious security, safety and reliability concerns (e.g. when developing an operating system or an embedded SW for an aircraft or in a spaceship). Sommerville [13] recommends that for "critical systems", "embedded systems where the SW depends on HW development" or for "very large systems where development may involve teams working in different locations" PP is preferable because Agile methods cannot be fully applied. Some of the documents provided by PP have important advantages for the course of a project. For example, WBS allows task parallelization and avoids overloading team members [5]. When a strict organization is needed, with a "very detailed specification and design before moving to implementation" [13], as is the case for some Mechatronics and CPS developments, Sommerville advises using PP methods.

Having mentioned the advantages associated with PP, we address its limits. One of its limits is the development of risk management for projects to rationalize their execution [5]. This rationalization influences the stages and deliverables, which can now be standardized. Finally, it induces a highly rigid organization that impedes initiatives and innovation. When the top-down approach is over-developed, the empowerment and the decisional power of the team members and of some managers is low, which will badly impact any impetus for innovation. Moreover, the task force organization does not contribute to any significant reduction in the compartmentalization of the different disciplines. This point has an important impact in a multidisciplinary context where disciplines have to communicate to efficiently produce a highly integrated product [5]. Finally, due to compartmentalization, only a few people in a project will have a global view of a project and its problems.

After analyzing two of the main current product design methodologies, highlighting the limits and the advantages of each methodology, hybridization is discussed next.

2.3 Hybrid Methods

As presented in the previous sections, each method has its advantages and its limits. Hybridization could be a way to get more from these methods; to select the most important characteristics of each method and to merge the two together. Hybridization has already been experimented with in [10], in an association of Scrum (an Agile method) and Stage-gate methods, which are very close to PP. That study was conducted on different companies from different business sectors. They all adapted some of the principles from Scrum, although they do not have the same level of hybridization.

The authors in [10] quote Ovesen's studies on the implementation of a Scrum solution into a "traditional" organization and the analysis of the implementation of Scrum in different types of companies [19]. Ovesen observed that "all companies deploy a Stage-Gate process-control model in combination with the Scrum framework" and that "none of the seven companies comply 100% with the rules of Scrum". This emphasizes that hybridization is tested often in companies because it can bring new elements that increase a companies' efficiency and flexibility. This observation is also supported in [10], where the authors state "companies significantly improve product development (PD) performance after implementation [of Scrum], but the Agile framework is merged into the existing PD standards rather than replacing them."

Based on the previous observations, the two methods appear to be antagonistic but are in fact complementary. Detecting possible model clashes and synergies is an important step to realize before building and implementing a hybrid model [15]. Boehm and Turner suggest that companies "develop management and architectural practices for hybrid agile and plan-driven methods" [15] in order to overcome the Agile methods' barriers.

Table 1 was prepared as a means to compare and summarize these methods' ability to deal with criteria selected to highlight the methods' advantages and limits. Table 1 is built on the literature review exposed in previous sections. Agile and PP methods' limits and advantages are indicated in the first two columns, and the Hybrid method's column is filled with what is expected by merging the first two. A "++" or "+" is indicated when a method is, respectively, completely or partly suitable to a particular criteria. When the drawbacks of a method are incapacitating or cannot fulfill the criteria, a "–" is indicated.

The proposed criteria were selected to cover some of the specific aspects of project organization: a projects' scale, type of product developed, management aspects, dealing with changes and "non-functional requirements" [13]. The financial aspects are deliberately not taken up in this study but that is envisioned for future works. The proposed model is macro-level focused, to be further detailed up to a micro level with

Table 1. Agile, project-planned and hybrid methods for multidisciplinary design.

Criteria	Methodology		
	Agile methods	Project-planned	Hybrid
Large-scale projects	–	++	++
Medium-scale projects	+	++	++
Small-scale projects	++	+	+
SW development	++	+	+
HW development	+	++	++
Multidisciplinary development	+	+	++
Strategic level decision-making power	–	++	+
Tactical level decision-making power	+	+	+
Operational decision-making power	++	–	++
Reaction to late/unexpected changes	++	–	+
Dealing with non-functional requirements	–	++	+

metrics to obtain the information required for efficient project management. Large, medium and small-scale projects: a particular attention is paid to determine if a method is suitable for different project scales. A large-scale project would not be managed in the same manner as a small one. Whereas large projects need a rigid framework, a small one could be easily supported by Agile methods.

Dealing with late/unexpected changes is linked to customer involvement and meeting frequencies. Agile methods provide a framework that allows late changes to be managed, due to their significant customer involvement and daily meetings. A Hybrid approach must integrate this aspect to be able to incorporate late changes. In an industrial context customers are at the core of product design. The product must meet the customers' needs and their expectations, which could change during the design process. Another point is that when a modification has to be made in a SW domain, it is not as expensive as a similar-scale modification in a HW domain. Late changes are always a challenge, but Agile methods cope with them efficiently in the SW domain.

Strategic-tactical-operational decision power is linked to top-down and bottom-up approaches. In a top-down approach, the strategic level has a strong decision-making power. It sets the objectives and makes most of the decisions during meetings. Technical solutions are virtually frozen and innovation does not have much opportunity to be expressed. In contrast, the bottom-up approach offers more decision-making power and initiatives to the teams members at the operational level. Due to this flexibility and decentralized decision-making power, innovation can be expressed much more easily. A significant rigidity will impede innovation and technical solutions, but is needed to set clear and common objectives. This is emphasized by Bricogne: "[PP] allows little opportunity for initiatives and innovations, it does not spur regular tradeoff between the different disciplines and is thus considered to be relatively "rigid"" [5]. However, too much flexibility and decentralized decision-making power can slow down a project.

SW/HW/Multidisciplinary development are analyzed to determine if a method can deal with SW and HW design and a combination of both.

When dealing with non-functional requirements (e.g. security, reliability), Agile methods are not the most suitable methods to use 'as is' [13, 15]. Instead, they would require some modification to cope with security and reliability, both of which are important in CPS and Mechatronics.

Finally, the ideal hybrid method would be where the limits of one method are counterbalanced by the advantages of the other and vice versa. Several authors share the view that hybridization can increase efficiency and is a way to implement Agile methods in a company. The observations made in this section emphasize the need to develop and implement hybrid methods in a multidisciplinary product design to take maximum advantage of Agile and PP methods. Hybridization cannot be the perfect answer to all of a project's needs, even though it does allow Agile and PP methods to overcome their respective barriers. Our vision of Agile-PP hybridization is exposed in the next section.

3 An Organizational Model of a Hybrid Agile-PP Approach

This section presents our proposition, illustrated in Fig. 1, which is a macro-level-hybrid model. Agile and PP methods are hybridized as a way to optimize their advantages and overcome their limits.

Four main areas are shown in Fig. 1: the hierarchical levels are on the left; a slider which can move towards Agile or PP methods is on the right; between the two is the core of our proposition, the hybridization between PP and Agile methods; and the PLM, which provides a global framework, is at the bottom.

Our proposition is mainly focused on utilizing both top-down and bottom-up approaches and deciding how best to combine them. This proposed model could be an answer to the development of medium- and large-scale projects by integrating Agile methods to stimulate innovation and support bottom-up initiatives to create a dynamism, and PP methods to provide a rigid framework for a common global project view.

The hierarchical levels are the strategic, tactical, and operational levels [19]. The strategic level defines the global objectives and makes the decisions that can affect a company's longevity. This level is mainly represented by the company's directors, which can be grouped as a steering committee who monitor a project. Project leaders can also be encountered at this level, depending on their decisional power. The tactical level is an intermediate one. This is where the "structures and resources" [19] needed to match the objectives set by the strategic level are defined here. Depending on a company's organization, this level is represented by project leaders and/or by team leaders. Project leaders have an overview of the project and can be viewed as global project managers. Team leaders are in charge of a project team. Finally, the third level is the operational level, where the decisions are applied and which is charged with the

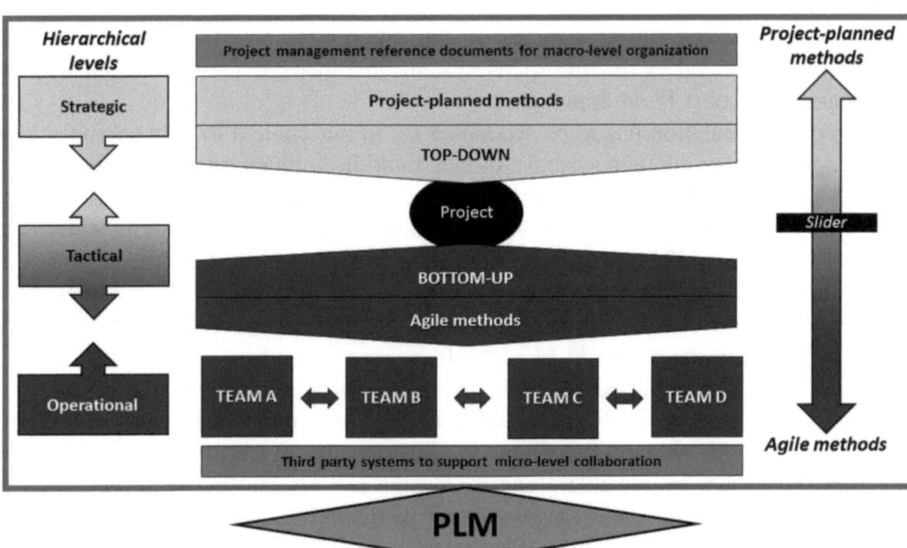

Fig. 1. Macro-level-hybrid model.

design's execution [19]. This hierarchical model is top-down oriented, although applying Agile methods' principles at the operational and tactical level is expected to stimulate some bottom-up communication and to assign more decisional power to these levels. Moreover, in our multidisciplinary context, the team's composition must be considered. Ovesen [20] proposes three types of team composition: a large and extremely cross-functional team, multiple smaller functional teams, and multiple cross-functional teams.

In addition to the hybridization at the tactical and operational levels, at the strategic level the PP method is implemented with its rigid framework. The global project is structured by project management reference documents (e.g. PBS, PDP, CBS, WBS, Gantt Planning, etc.). Moreover, in a PLM approach, our macro-task allocation would be provided by a macro-workflow. A classical workflow allocates a task to a person, whereas our vision of a macro-workflow only allocates macro-tasks to the team leaders, to give them an objective. A project's global objectives and vision are set and shared to all of the project's members. The aim of this top-down structure is to provide a framework to set the boundaries and offer a common vision. The long and short-term objectives and financial aspects are discussed at this level.

On the bottom of Fig. 1, at the operational level, Agile methods are preferred. These are applied to small teams to avoid large-scale problems and to respect the communication principle. In this organization, with independent small teams, the macro tasks are given by PP and the project subdivision made by PBS and WBS. Once these tasks are given by the macro-level workflow, the teams are completely independent, and an Agile method is used to manage the operational level of the project. The team leader links the team's work with the customers' requirements. Hence, the teams are mainly customer-focused. The teams' tasks evolve with the evolution of the customers' requirements. Each team is independent during the Agile process flow; system architects, helped by Software Configuration Management (SCM), check the interfaces and the impacts of changes on the different levels. This micro-level collaboration is supported by the third-party systems that manage a project's data and that are integrated in most PLM approaches.

Moreover, simulation has to be accounted for in our context to help engineers and technicians to design efficient systems. In fact, multidisciplinary product design such as Mechatronics or CPS cannot be managed without using simulation. Products are becoming more and more complex and simulation is the best way to efficiently deal with that complexity [21]. Moreover, according to Ottino et al. [22], managing simulation data is a key factor in being competitive and reducing time-to-market. This management could be done by implementing a Simulation Lifecycle Management (SLM) approach in the macro PLM context.

Finally, because a project is often developed in a context of uncertainty, our approach is aimed at being dynamic and not static, and thus it is flexible. A slider is shown on the right side of the figure to illustrate the dynamism of the proposed approach. The slider is movable along the design process and between the stages to deal with company, team and environmental particularities. It can slide towards the Agile or PP methods, indicating the balance between bottom-up and top-down approaches as well as the balance between rigidity and flexibility, and thus how much innovation is stimulated or not.

For example, if the project deviates too much from the global direction and that is not desired, moving the slider towards PP (the global organization will be more oriented toward PP methods) to provide more rigidity and rigor in order to reframe the project could be necessary. On the contrary, if team members do not manage to circumvent a patent, or to create a technological gap to produce a major competitive advantage, moving the slider towards Agile methods could be a solution to increase flexibility and to stimulate innovation. The possibility of moving the slider aims to face the scope of possible situations that a project manager can face along the project. Maintaining an ideal balance between too much rigidity and too much flexibility is the goal. This can be done by relying on project leaders' experience and by using metrics to adapt the balance. The balance between Agile and PP methods can be changed during the course of a project. This decision, which will impact the project, should be taken during regular meetings between the steering committee, project leaders and team managers at the strategic level.

4 Conclusion and Future Work

This paper proposes a representation of an Agile-PP-hybrid-approach. This type of hybridization has been explored by Ovesen [20] and Sommer et al. [10] and is already being tested in some companies. PP and Agile methods are two approaches that can appear to be in opposition although they are actually complementary. Agile methods bring new elements to PP and PP can provide elements to overcome the Agile methods' limits.

Our model aims to formalize a possible hybridization between Agile and PP methods by combining the main advantages of both methods and using those to overcome their respective limits. The PP method is used to achieve a macro-rigid-framework to give a project its global direction (at the strategic level). Agile methods are used at the operational and tactical levels to provide the requisite flexibility to encourage innovation for technical solutions. The model aims to combine top-down and bottom-up approaches for multidisciplinary large- and medium-scale product development.

A project evolves in an uncertain environment, and thus our model should be dynamic. For the moment, it is the project team's responsibility to find the right balance and to position the slider between Agile and PP approaches. A part of our future work is to refine our representation so as to focus on the micro-level project aspects by determining metrics with which to measure a project's data. These data would be measured to facilitate the monitoring of a project in order to make suitable decisions and to even change the direction of a project as needed.

Finally, multidisciplinary product design is very specific to the interactions that can exist between the domains. Our proposition can provide a framework for multidisciplinary product design which then needs to be refined and detailed up to the micro-level. It will be interesting to observe if Mechatronics and CPS design needs to be de-coupled, and at which level of the approach the de-coupling is most likely to occur.

References

1. Abramovici, M., Bellalouna, F.: Integration and complexity management within the mechatronics product development. In: Advances in Life Cycle Engineering for Sustainable Manufacturing Businesses (2007). doi:10.1007/978-1-84628-935-4_20
2. Harashima, F., Tomizuka, M., Fukuda, T.: Mechatronics - what is it, why, and how? IEEE/ASME Trans. Mechatron. **1**, 1–4 (1996)
3. Baheti, R., Gill, H.: Cyber-physical systems. Impact Control Technol. 161–166 (2011). doi:10.1145/1795194.1795205
4. Rajkumar, R.: A cyber-physical future. Proc. IEEE **100**, 1309–1312 (2012). doi:10.1109/JPROC.2012.2189915
5. Bricogne, M.: Méthode Agile pour la conception collaborative multidisciplinaire de systèmes intégrés: application à la Mécatronique. Université de Technologie de Compiègne (2015)
6. Bergsjö, D.: Management of Mechatronic Product Data in PLM Systems. Chalmers University of Technology, Göteborg (2007)
7. Sellgren, U., Törngren, M., Malvius, D., Biehl, M.: PLM for mechatronics integration. In: Proceedings of the 6th International Product Lifecycle Management Conference (PLM 2009) (2009)
8. Stark, J.: Product Lifecycle Management (2015). doi:10.1007/978-3-319-17440-2
9. Matthews, P.C., Lomas, C.D.W., Armoutis, N.D., Maropoulos, P.G.: Foundations of an agile design methodology. Int. J. Agile Manufact. **9**, 29–37 (2006)
10. Sommer, A.F., Dukovska-Popovska, I., Steger-Jensen, K.: Agile product development governance – on governing the emerging scrum/stage-gate hybrids. In: Grabot, B., Vallespir, B., Gomes, S., Bouras, A., Kiritsis, D. (eds.) APMS 2014. IAICT, vol. 438, pp. 184–191. Springer, Heidelberg (2014). doi:10.1007/978-3-662-44739-0_23
11. Schwaber, K., Sutherland, J.: The scrum guide. Scrum.org (2011)
12. Beck, K.: Extreme Programming Explained: Embrace Change. Addison-Wesley Professional, Boston (2000)
13. Sommerville, I.: Software Engineering, 9th edn. Pearson, London (2010)
14. Highsmith, J.: What is agile software development? J. Defense Softw. Eng. **15**, 4–9 (2002). doi:10.1109/MC.2007.73
15. Boehm, B., Turner, R.: Management challenges to implementing agile processes in traditional development organizations. IEEE Softw. **22**, 30–39 (2005). doi:10.1109/MS.2005.129
16. Ronkainen, J., Abrahamsson, P.: Software development under stringent hardware constraints: do agile methods have a chance? In: Marchesi, M., Succi, G. (eds.) XP 2003. LNCS, vol. 2675, pp. 73–79. Springer, Heidelberg (2003). doi:10.1007/3-540-44870-5_10
17. Huang, P.M., Darrin, A.G., Knuth, A.A.: Agile hardware and software system engineering for innovation. In: 2012 IEEE Aerospace Conference. IEEE, Big Sky (2012)
18. Gidel, T., Zonghero, W.: Management de projet: Approfondissements. Lavoisier, Cachan (2006)
19. Girard, P., Doumeingts, G.: Modelling the engineering design system to improve performance. Comput. Ind. Eng. **46**, 43–67 (2004). doi:10.1016/j.cie.2003.09.008
20. Ovesen, N.: The Challenges of Becoming Agile: Implementing and Conducting Scrum in Integrated Product Development. Aalborg University, Aalborg (2012)
21. CIMdata: Simulation Lifecycle Management - More than data management for simulation. Ann Arbor, Michigan (2011)
22. Ottino, A., Duigou, J.L.E., Vosgien, T., Figay, N., Lardeur, P., Eynard, B.: Gestion et réutilisation des données de simulation: vers une approche de vérification et validation des modèles. 22ème Congrès Français de Mécanique (2015). doi:10.13140/RG.2.1.2295.1440

Interoperability and Systems Integration

Flat Versus Hierarchical Information Models in PLM Standardization Frameworks

Sylvere Krima and Joshua Lubell(✉)

National Institute of Standards and Technology, Gaithersburg, MD, USA
{krimas, lubell}@nist.gov

Abstract. Smart manufacturing requires digital product data to be shared and exchanged among numerous engineering applications and information systems. But no single product data standard can satisfy every integration scenario. Customizable standardization frameworks for Product Lifecycle Management (PLM) attempt to address this problem by allowing users to add new information structures to an existing data model in a controlled manner. A PLM information model may be either flat or hierarchical. We discuss two approaches. One is based on ISO 10303-239 as an exemplar for customizing flat models. The other is based on Open Application Group Integration Specification (OAGIS) as an exemplar for customizing hierarchical models. We evaluate the two approaches and observe that the type of model strongly influences how well the PLM standardization framework meets each evaluation criterion, and that the best choice is use-case dependent.

Keywords: Open Application Group Integration Specification · Product Life Cycle Support · Reference Data Library · Core Components · Information modeling

1 Introduction

Smart manufacturing, which is information-intensive and requires advanced communication and network technologies [1], requires that digital product data be shared and exchanged among numerous engineering applications and information systems. Standardized information models for Product Lifecycle Management (PLM) aim to help manufacturers meet these requirements. Terzi et al. define PLM as "a product-centric, lifecycle-oriented business model," enabled by information technology, in which "product data are shared among actors, processes and organizations in the different phases of the product lifecycle for achieving desired performances and sustainability for the product and related services." [2] Manufacturers are under pressure not only to bring to market ever more complex products but also to bring them faster and cheaper. Doing so requires product information that can be used by many different participants in the product realization process. To help meet these requirements, standards bodies,

---

R. Harik et al. (Eds.): PLM 2016, IFIP AICT 492, pp. 121–133, 2016.
DOI: 10.1007/978-3-319-54660-5_12

industry groups, and consortia have standardized a number of product information models targeted to a particular integration scenario. Examples include the Object Management Group (OMG) PLM Services [3, 4] and the ISO 10303-242 Business Object Model [5, 6], both of whose scope is limited to design engineering data.

To remain competitive, manufacturers are using PLM data to optimize their proprietary business processes throughout the product lifecycle. To maximize the benefits of PLM, manufacturers must map their proprietary processes to the standardized PLM models. Unfortunately, due to the complexity of today's products and processes, no single standardized PLM model can satisfy every use case. Moreover, the ever-evolving product data requirements pose a serious technological challenge. Why? Because currently, it is not possible to define, in advance, information structures flexible enough to meet such changing requirements [7]. Developing such structures requires a new approach that allows users to integrate new information structures into an existing information model. The need for that kind of capability has led to the development of frameworks that software implementers can use to customize interoperable PLM standards.

To enable the creation of such standards, a PLM standardization framework must include:

- An initial, generic information model capable of representing a broad spectrum of products and related industrial data. This model's semantics are too abstract to be used directly for a real-world scenario, but are intended to be consistent with any scenario-specific application [8].
- A methodology for customizing the initial information model to meet the requirements of a particular scenario-specific use case.

The initial information model may be *flat* or *hierarchical*. Although one can conceive of an initial information model having both flat and hierarchical parts, we know of no existing PLM standardization framework with this characteristic. Our definitions, adapted from Zimmermann [9], are as follows. We define a flat information model as having objects that are accessible from one another and are arranged as peers. For such models, the framework provides a means for referencing external classification taxonomies that refine the meaning of concepts in the model. The reference ensures compatible exchange forms, since all implementations share the underlying model (see left hand side of Fig. 1). Moreover, as the figure illustrates, constructing a model meeting the requirements of a specific business process requires two operations: identifying the appropriate subset of the initial model and referencing the appropriate business context information from the external information source.

We define a hierarchical information model as a tree-like structure where objects can contain other objects or collections of objects. For such models, the framework provides mechanisms for building extensions of the underlying model by adding new concepts and relationships to the initial information model. Creating an extension is usually straightforward since it does not require any additional modeling methodologies or implementation methods beyond those used to create the initial information model. However, because extensions add new concepts and relationships to the initial model, different implementations of the same extensions may be incompatible – when, for example, independent organizations doing similar work make different modeling

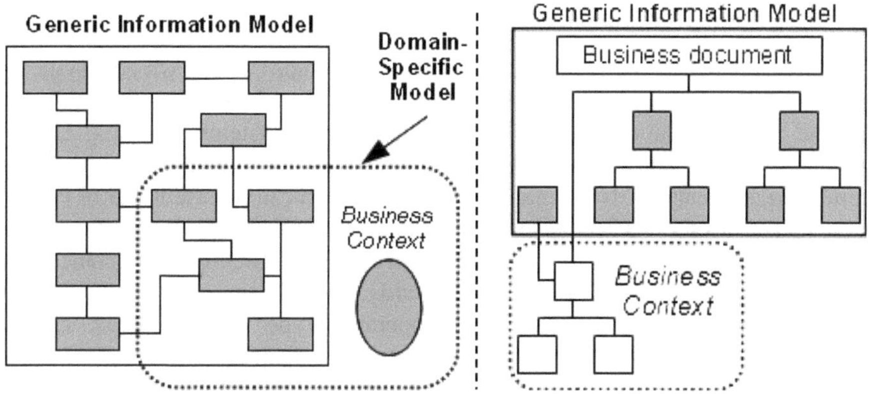

Fig. 1. Customization of flat (*left*) and hierarchical (*right*) models.

choices. The right hand side of Fig. 1 shows a "business document" exchange form as an aggregation of data elements. The business document is analogous to the union of the information model and business context shown on the left hand side of Fig. 1. The extension shown implements the addition of a new substructure that reuses an existing data element and includes additional, business-context information.

In this paper, we compare the flat and hierarchical PLM standardization frameworks, with a focus on customizability. We choose the Product Life Cycle Support (PLCS) framework [10] for developing data exchange specifications using ISO 10303-239 [11] as an exemplar of the flat approach[1]. We choose the Open Application Group Integration Specification (OAGIS) [12] as an exemplar of the hierarchical approach. In the following sections, we provide an overview of the customization approaches used in flat and hierarchical PLM standardization frameworks, justify our choices of PLCS and OAGIS as exemplars, evaluate the two, and make two observations. First, the type of model strongly influences how well the framework meets each evaluation criterion. Second, the best choice is use-case dependent. We note that this paper's focus is limited to customization. Other important characteristics of PLM standardization frameworks, such as the quality of the initial information model and impact of changes to the initial information on existing implementations are not discussed.

2 Related Work and Existing Customization Approaches

A key goal of PLM is to align engineering processes, such as design and manufacturing, with more business-focused activities such as sales, inventory control, and enterprise resource planning (ERP). In this section, we review previous efforts in classifying PLM standards and in harmonizing product information with electronic business ("e-business") information standards, and then describe the "Reference Data Libraries" and "Core Components" customization approaches.

[1] The PLCS framework, introduced in Sect. 2, is not part of ISO 10303-239. However, both are commonly referred to as "PLCS" (a source of confusion).

2.1 PLM Standards Landscape and Harmonization

The PLM standards typology of Rachuri et al. [13] includes Type Two and Type Three standards. Type Two standards define information models specific to a domain of discourse. An example of a Type Two standard is the Systems Modeling Language (SysML) [14], a graphical language intended for (but not limited to) use in Systems Engineering applications. No single Type Two standard can represent "all of PLM." In our context, "all of PLM" includes all information pertaining to products, processes, and services that make up the entire product lifecycle – beginning with detailed design and ending with disposal. Type Three standards are architectural frameworks, which are standards for creating families of interoperable Type Two standards. The PLM frameworks we evaluate in this paper are Type Three standards.

Paviot et al. [15] determined that the ISO 10303-239 (Product Life Cycle Support, PLCS) [11] Type Two standard is – unlike many other Type Two standards – customizable by design. Since customization is inevitable, PLCS must be tailored to fit both the scope and the granularity of a specific PLM domain. This observation is critically important because, without such flexibility, a developer of a Type Two standard must choose between scope and granularity. The flexibility of PLCS enables the ISO 10303-239 information model – a Type Two standard – to serve as the foundation of a Type Three PLM framework. We choose PLCS as an exemplar flat framework (i.e., one with a flat information model) both because of its flexibility and because the PLCS framework includes a methodology for customization of the ISO 10303-239 information model using Reference Data Libraries, discussed in 2.2.

Successful deployment of PLM requires both product metadata standards and e-business standards [4]. Fiorentini and Rachuri [16] investigated methods for sharing PLM data among engineering and business software applications. Their research focused specifically on the OMG PLM Services [3], a Type Two standard. Fiorentini and Rachuri selected OAGIS [12] as the e-business standard with which to harmonize the OMG PLM Services. OAGIS is a critical standard for application-to-application and business-to-business integration [17]. By successfully mapping portions of the OAGIS Engineering Change Management concepts to OMG PLM Services concepts, their research demonstrated the feasibility of harmonizing product design data standards with OAGIS. Since the PLCS scope is a superset of the OMG PLM Services, and both have information models based on ISO 10303 [4], it follows that (1) portions of PLCS and OAGIS can be harmonized and (2) portions of PLCS implementations and OAGIS implementations can be made interoperable with one another. Based on this conclusion, as well as the broad scope and widespread adoption of OAGIS relative to other e-business frameworks [18], we choose OAGIS as the exemplar for e-business frameworks with a hierarchical model.

2.2 Customization and Reference Data Libraries

The Reference Data Library (RDL) approach aims to enable controlled customizability without sacrificing breadth. A RDL is an externally-defined, controlled vocabulary for specializing concepts in an underlying schema [19]. For example, consider a concept

Person defined in a generic information model and the Person's specialization in an accompanying RDL. The RDL specifies a taxonomy that enables specialization of a Person instance as a Customer, an Employee, or other concepts. The RDL approach assumes the existence of an underlying information model with a wide scope – the generic information model. Such a model, however, is too abstract to be verified by subject matter experts associated with a specific integration scenario. That makes the model difficult to implement, and use.

To overcome these difficulties, the RDL approach allows users to work with any subset of the original information model by defining scenario-specific subsets of the underlying information model. These subsets use *templates* to define how information-model entities and their attributes will be instantiated. A template is a predicate with a signature specifying arguments and their types [20]. Templates are critical elements of the RDL approach because they apply an integration scenario and an externally-defined controlled vocabulary directly to the underlying schema. A template also may invoke other templates, providing a means of modularizing and combining integration patterns. Templates should not be seen as a means of customizing an information model, but rather as a way of customizing its use.

The PLCS framework, as proposed by the Organization for the Advancement of Structured Information Standards (OASIS) PLCS Technical Committee (TC) [21], employs the RDL approach. The underlying information model for PLCS is ISO 10303-239. The TC has developed guidance for defining RDLs using the Web Ontology Language (OWL) [22] and templates as SysML block and parametric diagrams[2,3].

2.3 Extensions Using Core Components

The Core Components approach to extension is based on the Core Components Technical Specification (CCTS) [23] standard, which provides the foundation for several XML-based e-business standards, including OAGIS. CCTS-based e-business schemas use a hierarchical modeling pattern. Customization involves (1) identifying the relevant components, (2) associating them with a selection of the components contained in the generic document, (3) interpreting the components to their business-specific use, and (4) selecting from the generic fields those fields that can represent the business-specific information units that describe those components. Customization can also add components to the document, or add fields to a component. This process creates new artifacts, based on a business-specific terminology and representation of the information. This customization is known as *extension* because users can extend the initial artifacts, in addition to restricting some and leaving others unused.

---

[2] This guidance is not an OASIS standard, but rather a Committee Specification that has been approved only by the members of the TC and not by the entire OASIS membership.

[3] The PLCS TC uses SysML for this (atypical) purpose because they found the SysML notation useful for representing templates and their relationships with other templates. They also wanted to take advantage of existing SysML software tools.

Revisiting our previous RDL example, we specify an extension by applying the four steps from the preceding paragraph. First, we determine that (1) a `Customer` concept is necessary to represent our business information requirements. We next determine that (2) `Person` is the CCTS concept closest to `Customer`. We then determine that (3) a `Customer` needs, in addition to a `Person`'s fields, an `id` field. Finally, we (4) extend this component by adding an `id` field.

OAGIS facilitates integration of disparate business systems by defining a standardized architecture for representing Business Object Documents (BODs), the messages to be exchanged. OAGIS has historically been solely XML-based. OAGIS 10, the newest version of the standard, encourages a more model-driven approach, allowing for alternative methods for specifying and implementing BODs [1][4]. BOD data contains the message content, represented as a verb-noun pair. The verb identifies an action performed on a noun. The noun identifies the business-specific information that is exchanged. Nouns are made of extensible building blocks called components, as in CCTS.

Despite the large number of nouns and components, OAGIS BODs by themselves cannot support every possible message exchange. Therefore, OAGIS provides a variety of customization mechanisms. Component Open Extension, introduced in OAGIS 10, is a simple mechanism that does not require any changes to the OAGIS XML schema definitions. Overlay Extension, an XML implementation of the CCTS customization mechanism, provides OAGIS users with more flexibility – but requires modifications to the BOD schema definitions.

3 Use Cases and Evaluation Criteria

In this section, we discuss two use cases for PLM standards: data exchange and data sharing. We then identify two PLM-related requirements and assessment criteria to evaluate the PLCS and OAGIS frameworks with respect to the use cases. *Data exchange* enables the transfer of information from one processing entity to another. Exchange requires translating that information from the source schema into an instance of a target schema. Successful exchange means that the translation must reflect the source information as accurately as possible [24]. Because it typically involves few, if any, time constraints, data exchange is often considered to be a batch operation. *Data sharing*, on the other hand, requires real-time access to the information source [4]. Data sharing's technical requirements differ from those of data exchange in that the information provider must expose data requested by the consumers on demand. A PLM standardization framework can provide the pieces needed to standardize interfaces for product data sharing.

Having discussed our proposed use cases, we now consider two capabilities a PLM standardization framework needs to best support them. These capabilities all facilitate interoperability, which Ray and Jones [25] define as the ability of disparate software

[4] However, since the developers of OAGIS have not yet provided customization guidance for implementing such an approach, this paper's discussion of OAGIS extension is XML-specific. Non-XML BOD extension guidance is planned for future OAGIS versions.

applications to share digital technical and business data efficiently and without errors. Chen [26] developed a more expansive characterization enumerating the following interoperability concerns: data, services, processes, and business. As discussed in 2.1, PLM frameworks are Type Three standards used to create families of interoperable Type Two standards. PLM framework customization methods must address interoperability concerns while also allowing family members' data models to retain business-specific terms and definitions.

Controlled customization is a process intended to limit the introduction of inconsistencies and to facilitate interoperability. Data exchange requires controlled customization to maintain data quality during translation. Controlled customization limits the possibility of introducing inconsistency – and breaking interoperability – when tailoring an initial information model for implementation. Controlled customization accomplishes this goal by restricting the set of potentially customizable concepts from the initial information model to those that minimize the likelihood for inconsistency. Since a PLM standardization framework's initial information model is very large, and never used as a whole, customization is a necessary and often complex process. Controlled customization requires defining a subset of the original concepts that can be customized. Defining this subset requires an understanding of the information requirements of the downstream lifecycle processes that will use the results of the customization.

Unlike data exchange, data sharing happens within the scope of a specific context: the business transaction the data sharing supports. Because of data sharing's ephemeral nature, guarding against long-term inconsistencies is not an issue. Therefore, data sharing does not require controlled customization. It does, however, require the development of software interfaces specific to a particular business domain. Such interfaces can be specified as a collection of standardized *business objects*.

Business objects, when combined with standards for product metadata and recent advances in service-oriented architecture (SOA) technology, create new integration possibilities [4]. Each business object encapsulates all of the product information in a specific transaction. A business object model [27] results from an implementation method that uses a domain-specific, transaction-oriented vocabulary, which hides the complexity and reduces the granularity of the underlying information model.

A business object instance automatically instantiates the underlying generic concepts and their relationships. These instantiations result from an invertible mapping between the business object model and the underlying information model. This

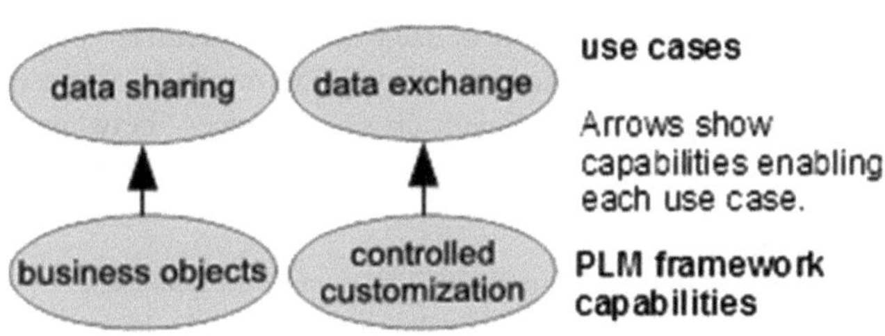

Fig. 2. Use cases and capabilities.

mapping is defined unambiguously and is computer interpretable, enabling interoperable business object model implementations.

Figure 2 summarizes the dependency relationships discussed in the preceding paragraphs between use cases and PLM standardization framework capabilities.

4 Evaluation of PLCS and OAGIS

We now assess the PLCS and OAGIS frameworks with respect to their business object creation and controlled customization capabilities. We favor native support of a capability by the information model because lack of native support often results in a new layer of complexity, in the form of implementation-specific guidance or a parallel information model. For illustrative purposes, we use representation of a Bill of Material (BOM) as a recurring example. Our example uses the OAGIS `BOM` noun and the PLCS `PhysicalBreakdown` template. ISO 10303-239 defines a physical breakdown as "the partitioning of a product into a set of related physical elements so as to form explicit, parent-child views that comprise the product elements."

The PLCS framework uses templates for encapsulating ISO 10303-239 concepts into business objects. Templates are used in conjunction with the Platform Specific Model (PSM), an implementation model derived from the ISO 10303-239 information model. The PSM is available from PLCSlib [10], an online environment created for the development and use of PLCS templates. Templates are defined using SysML diagrams[5].

Unlike PLCS, OAGIS has a native mechanism for representing business objects, namely the OAGIS BODs. Because BODs are composed of nouns representing business objects and verbs representing actions performed on business objects, the OAGIS BODs are well-suited for representing engineering and business processes[6] [4]. The OAGIS framework follows the CCTS methodology and uses standardized components as building blocks for defining BODs. BOD developers extend low-level components to support domain-specific information, combining them together to create domain-specific objects, the OAGIS nouns.

For example, consider the OAGIS `BOM` noun. As shown on the left hand side of Fig. 3, this noun comprises four elements: a header (`BOMHeader`), the item data (`BOMItemData`), the product option(s) (`BOMOption`) and classifiers of the product option(s) (`BOMOptionClass`). `BOMHeader` is partially expanded to show child elements used in an extension. In this figure, the BOM is a set of part descriptions, where each part is identified by a `BOMItemData`, and the additional elements provide specific information about the part as it is used in this structure.

The right hand side of Fig. 3 shows how a BOM might be represented using the PLCS PSM. The thick arrows indicate cross-references between PSM objects. `ExchangeContextClassLibrary` points to a RDL. `ExternalOWLClass`

[5] We refer readers to PLCSlib for details on the PLCS template methodology.

[6] Because the BOD schemas contain many weakly-typed optional elements, OAGIS users are encouraged to add constraints to their BOD implementations. The OAGIS standard provides guidance on adding constraints to XML schema definitions.

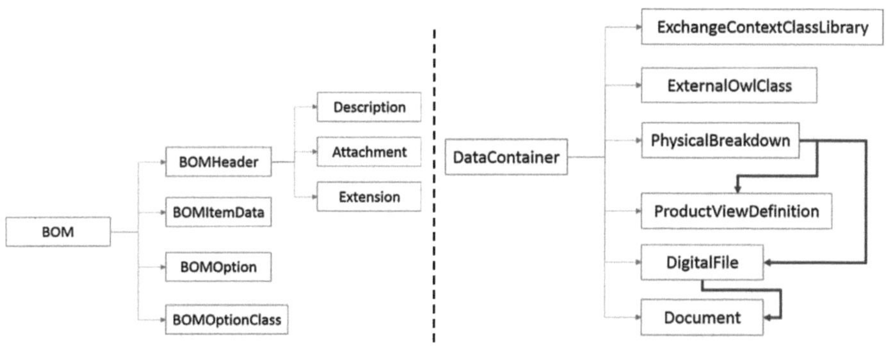

Fig. 3. BOM represented in OAGIS (*left*) and using PLCS PSM (*right*).

points to an RDL class. The rest of the PSM objects result from following the guidance specified in the PLCSlib `PhysicalBreakdown` template. The other PSM objects represent generic concepts. These concepts include cross-references to other `ExternalOWLClass` objects (omitted from Fig. 3 to reduce clutter).

The flat structure is a consequence of the RDL approach, which requires that the initial information model be abstract and that business-specific classification be done in an external class library. This external classification gives rise to fewer composition relationships, but more association relationships. For example, the OAGIS `BOM` noun is composed of a header, item data, and information regarding options. However, the PSM `PhysicalBreakdown` object is too abstract for the initial model to make any assumptions about its composition. In PLCS, as in any other RDL-based framework, a less-abstract concept such as a BOM is defined in a RDL rather than in the initial information model. Additionally, the BOM object must be linked to the elements of its composition, which are modeled as independent (external) objects. As we will discuss in Sect. 5, information model flatness in the RDL approach has advantages that could offset the impact on business object complexity.

To achieve controlled customization, RDLs customize concepts in the initial information model using information external to that model. Instances of customizable concepts contain links to external references through a property designed specifically for the purpose. A RDL-based framework, such as PLCS, controls customization at the information model level by providing only a limited set of concepts with the "external references" property.

Extension is a customization method that enlarges the initial information model to support new requirements. Extensions introduce new concepts and relationships. Controlling the use of extensions requires policies limiting extension to specific parts of the initial model and prohibiting extensions elsewhere. To do so, a CCTS-based framework such as OAGIS must control editorial rights of its information artifacts. This control cannot be done at the information model level; instead, it must be done at the implementation level using an implementation-dependent method. OAGIS specifies its information artifacts as XML schemas spanning a directory tree that contains multiple directories and files. OAGIS allows only certain definitions in certain files to be modified. Moreover, OAGIS provides XML-specific rules on how to specify the modifications.

To summarize, PLCS supports specialization using external references and controls customization by having hooks in the PSM for pointing to an RDL. OAGIS supports extension but not external references. It controls customization through XML-specific and directory structure-specific policies that allow only certain concepts to be extended. Because the PSM natively controls customization, controlled customization in PLCS is not tied to a specific implementation method, as is the case with OAGIS.

Table 1 presents our evaluation results:

Table 1. Summary of evaluation results.

	RDL based	Core Components based
Business objects	Represents business objects as templates, in the form of SysML diagrams in the case of PLCS	Hierarchical XML element representation is naturally amenable to creation of business objects
Controlled customization	The information model is designed in a way such that only a certain set of its entities can be specialized within the RDLs	Lower level concepts cannot be extended, but higher-level concepts can be. OAGIS provides a variety of XML-based extension methods

5 Native Support as a Metric for Framework Capabilities

Based on our assessment in Sect. 4, we observe inherent tradeoffs that depend on whether the PLM standardization framework's information model is flat or hierarchical. If the model is flat, as is the case with the RDL approach, then it controls customization directly. A flat information model limits the possibilities for redundancies or inconsistencies when exchanging data. For example, a flat file will not have two real-world products (individuals) with the same product model each containing a separate copy of that product model in their information content. In PLM, the individual and the product model are both first class objects. Therefore, a flat representation is advantageous for keeping the product model metadata and the individual model's metadata separate from one another. However, a flat information model is not natively a business object model. To support a business object model implementation, additional guidance is needed. In the PLCS framework, the template methodology provides this guidance, but it increases the complexity of standards development and deployment. Complexity increases from the additional difficulties in the creation of business object models.

On the other hand, if the PLM standardization framework's information model is hierarchical, as is the case with CCTS-based e-business frameworks, then it is natively a business object model. A hierarchical information model supports business objects "for free" because they require less cross-referencing. However, in the e-business frameworks, the individuals rather than their product models are the primary focus. As a result, redundant or inconsistent product models are possible. Also, the information model does not natively control customization, so additional implementation-specific, controlled customization methods must be provided. For OAGIS, these methods include the Component Open and Overlay Extensions.

Terzi et al. [2] observed that product development and ERP, which are both within the scope of PLM, have fundamentally different information requirements. Product development is iterative, recursive, and requires a detailed and precise representation of the product model. The ISO 10303-239 information model and its PLCS PSM derivative are based upon the concepts of *product* and *activity* [15]. A product can either be an individual real-world product, such as a manufactured automobile, or it may be a model of a (to-be-manufactured) product. An activity describes the occurrence of an action such as a design, manufacturing, or support operation or process. Using these two concepts, the ISO 10303-239 information model is able to represent assemblies, lifecycle information, product history, process plans, and schedules. ERP, on the other hand, involves a chain of repetitive operations and requires *transactional data*, defined by McGilvray [28] as data associated with an event or business process. OAGIS represents these repetitive operations as verbs. The OAGIS BODs encapsulate transactional data natively as business objects.

A concept in an information model cannot be both flat and hierarchical. Therefore, the same concept cannot natively support both controlled customization and business objects. To overcome this difficulty, a PLM standardization framework needs to provide additional implementation guidance, which results in added complexity for users. With respect to the two capabilities – business objects and controlled customization – we observe that there is no perfect framework. Consideration of native support, combined with Fig. 2 and Table 1, can help prospective users to determine the right framework to meet their requirements.

6 Conclusion

In this paper we discussed PLM standardization frameworks and their customization mechanisms. To represent business-specific information in a multitude of integration scenarios, the framework must enable customization and interoperability simultaneously. Our literature review identified two recurrent customization mechanisms. The first is extension, which adds to the initial set of concepts and relationships of the standard information model. The second is specialization, which uses classifiers from external sources to refine generic concepts into business-specific concepts. We also identified two primary approaches, RDL and CCTS, and we investigated an exemplary framework for each approach, PLCS and OAGIS respectively. We then described two key capabilities that PLM standards frameworks should support in order to meet requirements for the use cases of data exchange and data sharing. Figure 2 summarized how the capabilities relate to the use cases.

We conclude that (1) choice of framework should take use case into account, (2) no single framework is best for both use cases, and (3) it is better for a framework's information model to natively support a capability than for the framework to require additional technology to implement the capability. As shown in Fig. 2, data sharing depends on support for business objects. Therefore, a CCTS-based framework such as OAGIS, with its native support for business objects, is a good choice to support data sharing. Likewise, an RDL-based framework such as PLCS with its native support for controlled customization, is a good candidate to support data exchange.

A significant limitation of the research is the lack of an industrial example with realistic PLM data. Applying such an example to our evaluation of PLCS and OAGIS would add more rigor to our conclusions. Another follow-on to the research discussed in this paper would be to expand upon Fiorentini and Rachuri's harmonization and integration work. Their research covered only one use case – engineering change management (ECM). Pilot implementations of additional use cases exploiting other PLM disciplines where engineering and e-business concerns meet – such as logistics support and maintenance - could lead to useful lessons learned. Experience gained could not only result in improved metrics for evaluating PLM standardization frameworks, but also enable improvements to the frameworks themselves. Other possible follow-ons include evaluation of the RDL and CCTS approaches with respect to how well they support additional use cases such as long-term data retention, and exploration of the feasibility of combining both approaches within a single framework.

Acknowledgments. We wish to thank Jay Ganguli, Peter Denno, Albert Jones, and KC Morris for their insightful feedback on earlier drafts of this paper.

References

1. Ivezic, N., Kulvatunyou, B., Srinivasan, V.: On architecting and composing through-life engineering information services to enable smart manufacturing. Procedia CIRP **22**, 45–52 (2014)
2. Terzi, S., Bouras, A., Dutta, D., Garetti, M., Kiritsis, D.: Product lifecycle management – from its history to its new role. Int. J. Prod. Lifecycle Manag. **4**, 360–389 (2010)
3. OMG Product Lifecycle Management Services, v2.1. Object Management Group (2011)
4. Srinivasan, V.: An integration framework for product lifecycle management. Comput.-Aided Des. **43**, 464–478 (2011)
5. ISO 10303-242:2014. Industrial automation systems and integration – product data representation and exchange – part 242: application protocol: managed model-based 3D engineering
6. Katzenbach, A., Handschuh, S., Vettermann, S.: JT format (ISO 14306) and AP 242 (ISO 10303): the step to the next generation collaborative product creation. In: Kovács, G., Kochan, D. (eds.) NEW PROLAMAT 2013. IAICT, vol. 411, pp. 41–52. Springer, Heidelberg (2013). doi:10.1007/978-3-642-41329-2_6
7. Krima, S., Feeney, A.B., Foufou, S.: Dynamic customisation, validation and integration of product data models using semantic web tools. Int. J. Prod. Lifecycle Manag. **7**, 38–53 (2014)
8. Fenves, S.J., Foufou, S., Bock, C., Sriram, R.D.: CPM2: a core model for product data. J. Comput. Inf. Sci. Eng. **8**, 014501 (2008)
9. Zimmermann, T.: Information Architecture. http://www14.informatik.tu-muenchen.de/konferenzen/Jass05/courses/6/Papers/03.pdf
10. PLCSlib. http://www.plcs.org/plcslib
11. ISO 10303-239:2012. Industrial automation systems and integration – product data representation and exchange – part 239: application protocol: product life cycle support
12. Open Applications Group Integration Specification (OAGIS) Release 10.1. Open Applications Group (2014)

13. Rachuri, S., Subrahmanian, E., Bouras, A., Fenves, S.J., Foufou, S., Sriram, R.D.: Information sharing and exchange in the context of product lifecycle management: role of standards. Comput.-Aided Des. **40**, 789–800 (2008)
14. OMG Systems Modeling Language (OMG SysML). Version 1.3. Object Management Group (2012)
15. Paviot, T., Cheutet, V., Lamouri, S.: A PLCS framework for PDM/ERP interoperability. Int. J. Prod. Lifecycle Manag. **5**, 295 (2011)
16. Fiorentini, X., Rachuri, S.: STEP-OAGIS Harmonization Joint Working Group: PDM Subgroup Interim Report (2009)
17. Lu, Y., Morris, K.C., Frechette, S.: Standards landscape and directions for smart manufacturing systems. In: 2015 IEEE International Conference on Automation Science and Engineering (CASE), pp. 998–1005 (2015)
18. Lampathaki, F., Mouzakitis, S., Gionis, G., Charalabidis, Y., Askounis, D.: Business to business interoperability: a current review of XML data integration standards. Comput. Stand. Interfaces **31**, 1045–1055 (2009)
19. Price, D., Bodington, R.: Applying semantic web technology to the life cycle support of complex engineering assets. In: McIlraith, S.A., Plexousakis, D., Harmelen, F. (eds.) ISWC 2004. LNCS, vol. 3298, pp. 812–822. Springer, Heidelberg (2004). doi:10.1007/978-3-540-30475-3_56
20. ISO/TS 15926-7:2011. Industrial automation systems and integration — integration of life-cycle data for process plants including oil and gas production facilities — part 7: implementation methods for the integration of distributed systems: template methodology
21. OASIS Product Life Cycle Support (PLCS) TC | OASIS. https://www.oasis-open.org
22. OWL 2 Web Ontology Language Document Overview (Second Edition) (2012)
23. UN/CEFACT Core Components Technical Specification Version 3.0. United Nations Centre for Trade Facilitation and Electronic Business (2009)
24. Fagin, R., Kolaitis, P.G., Miller, R.J., Popa, L.: Data exchange: semantics and query answering. Theor. Comput. Sci. **336**, 89–124 (2005)
25. Ray, S.R., Jones, A.T.: Manufacturing interoperability. J. Intell. Manufact. **17**, 681–688 (2006)
26. Chen, D.: Enterprise interoperability framework. In: Proceedings of the Open Interop Workshop on Enterprise Modelling and Ontologies for Interoperability, Luxembourg (2006)
27. Hunten, K.A., Feeney, A.B.: Business object models for industrial data standards. Presented at the ASME 2011 International Design Engineering Technical Conferences and Computers and Information in Engineering Conference (2011)
28. McGilvray, D.: Executing Data Quality Projects: Ten Steps to Quality Data and Trusted Information (TM). Morgan Kaufmann, Burlington (2010)

An Onto-Based Interoperability Framework for the Connection of PLM and Production Capability Tools

Maxime Lafleur[1], Walter Terkaj[2], Farouk Belkadi[3(✉)], Marcello Urgo[4], Alain Bernard[3], and Marcello Colledani[4]

[1] AUDROS Technology, 41 rue de la cite, 69003 Lyon, France
[2] ITIA-CNR, Institute of Industrial Technologies and Automation, via Bassini 15, 20133 Milan, Italy
[3] Ecole Centrale de Nantes – IRCCyN – UMR CNRS 6597, 1 rue de la Noë, 44300 Nantes, France
farouk.belkadi@irccyn.ec-nantes.fr
[4] Department of Mechanical Engineering, Politecnico di Milano, via La Masa 1, 20156 Milan, Italy

Abstract. This paper proposes a model-driven interoperability framework as a technical support of co-evolution strategy of product structure and production systems with a frugal innovation perspective. Based on the modularity concept, the role of this framework is to connect possible product modules managed in the Product Life cycle Management tool to all possible production capabilities managed on the Manufacturing Process Management tool, and able to realize each module. This will help designers to define the optimal product architecture based on technical features of modules regarding the functional requirements as well as the optimal production strategy.

Keywords: Interoperability · Co-evolution · Modularity · Production capabilities

1 Introduction

To reach economic sustainability in context of hard competitiveness, companies extend their resource optimization strategy across the whole value chain, including the consideration of product, processes and production systems co-evolution as well as change propagation and decisions' interdependencies. According to Tolio et al. [1], the term "co-evolution" represents the "ability to strategically and operationally manage the propagation of engineering changes to gain competitive advantage from the resulting market and regulatory dynamics".

The success of any co-evolution strategy should be based on robust models ensuring the global consistency between all development stages, from product design to production network configuration. Modularity concept is laid out in the literature as a potential solution to handle co-evolution [2] because of its property to decompose a complex system into independent but interconnected parts that can be treated as conceptual, logical, physical or organizational units. This is the scope of the modular approach developed in ProRegio project to support frugal innovation process [3].

R. Harik et al. (Eds.): PLM 2016, IFIP AICT 492, pp. 134–145, 2016.
DOI: 10.1007/978-3-319-54660-5_13

According to this approach, a critical task on using modularity for co-evolution perspective is the definition of the mapping strategy between designed product modules and related possible production capabilities, which inform about the standard manufacturing processes and technologies able to provide the designed module with the desired features.

In practice, the problem of mapping between product modules and related production capabilities can be extended to the more generic problem of system interoperability that aim to support the communication between two or more systems at conceptual, organizational and/or technical level [4]. The first category of tools is dedicated to store and manage product architectures and features, based on a modular organization. PLM systems are the main accepted tool for such a topic. The second category of tools aims to support process and manufacturing data. Manufacturing process management (MPM) and Enterprise Resource Planning (ERP) are currently used to reach this goal. Thus, the mapping of product modules and production capabilities requires the connection of PLM systems and MPM/ERP tools. In addition, even if a PLM tool includes few manufacturing data, the adopted semantic is not already conforming to the semantic used by the MPM. The success of any co-evolution strategy requires then robust semantic interoperability between the concepts used by involved software tools.

This paper investigates how a semantic interoperability framework (based on the Virtual Factory Framework - VFF [5]) can be integrated with a commercial PLM tool (i.e. Audros PLM [6]) to facilitate the exchange of information needed to support a co-evolution strategy between product architecture and production system. Audros solution is French PLM systems which provide a set of flexible tools able to be adapted to any functional domain through an intelligent merge of the business process model, the data model generator and the user interface design.

The next section presents a survey of the literature related to the problem of interoperability between enterprise software; the VFF and PLM tools taken into considerations are also described. Section 3 describes the proposed model-driven approach used for the definition of the connector framework. The last section describes the mapping and query mechanisms used for the implementation of the interoperability between the RDF store (used for the assessment of production capabilities) and the Audros tool.

2 Literature Survey

Even if the PLM tools are greatly evolving in terms of efficiency and functionalities, there is still a gap between technologies for product design and production system design that jeopardize the realization of a proper digital factory platform. In particular, the generation and management of digital factory data is a key problem. Lee and Noh [7] suggested creating digital factory models on the basis of an information data model taking advantage as much as possible on the data schemas provided by the STEP standard. Zhai et al. [8] identified the need of a proper Virtual Factory Data Management System (VFDMS) within their Integrated Simulation Method aimed at supporting Virtual Factory Engineering. Other approaches have been proposed in the scope of the Core Manufacturing Simulation Data initiative proposed by NIST [9]. Indeed, proper enabling technologies are still being investigated by academics to fulfil the concepts sketched by the early literature works, whereas large ICT players in the market propose all-comprehensive software suites that still lack full integration [10] and/or are not affordable for a large share of industrial companies. The digital tools available in large software suites are typically missing to support an effective interoperability, both between tools belonging to different suites and sometimes also between tools of the same suite.

A solution to the interoperability problem, both at academic and industrial level, is represented by the use of Semantic Web technologies and ontology that offers advantages like (1) key enablers for interoperability, data distribution, extensibility of the data model, querying, and reasoning; (2) the re-use of general purpose technologies for data storage, consistency checking and knowledge inference. Indeed, ontologies can help to meet the goals of (meta-)modelling and interoperability [11].

Several works have proposed ontology-based approaches to facilitate the data exchange between design and other engineering activities in collaborative tasks. For instance, Barbau et al. [12] presented the OntoSTEP initiative dealing with the conversion of EXPRESS schemas to OWL (Web Ontology Language), focusing in particular on the semantic enrichment of product models by adding behavioral and functionality concepts to the more traditional geometry concepts (as in the STEP-family standard).

Ontology-based models are also proposed to support data structuring and interoperability in PLM field [13]. Panetto et al. [14] have proposed the ONTO-PDM framework, as a common core model to provide an interoperability solution between product data (encapsulated in PLM) and manufacturing process management (MPM) applications. An ontology-based approach to support the factory design is represented by the Virtual Factory Framework (VFF) [5]; Colledani et al. [15] showed how the VFF approach can be employed to support the design and performance evaluation of a production system to quickly assess its production capability.

The next section takes advantages from the ontology-based VFF approach to build a software connector mapping between product modules and production capabilities.

3 Semantic Mapping of Product Module to Production Capability

During the product design process, a solution is defined based on technical characteristics implementing the product functions but also on the optimal production strategy. Designers should analyze all possible modules able to answer one product function as well the related manufacturing alternatives (M.A.) producing the modules.

3.1 The Connector Framework

Taking into consideration the constraints coming from production technologies during the product design process has a potential benefit but, within the PLM system, the M.A. must be connected to a product module and characterized by a list of production resources (a set of machines, a real system, etc.) able to manufacture the module. Therefore, the production capabilities linked to a M.A. must be considered from the earlier times of the design stage, to help the selection of the best product modules. This implies the need to assess the production capabilities for each M.A. of a single module, but also for its integration into the whole production network.

Herein, the data about a production system are formalized according to an ontology-based data model, named Virtual Factory Data Model (VFDM), that was first developed in the scope of VFF project to formalize the concepts of building, product, process and resource while taking into consideration geometric, physical and technological characteristics of the factory that are required to support its planning processes [16]. The VFDM acts as a semantic repository supporting MPM applications to represent the characteristics and classify the types of a manufacturing system in terms of products types, manufacturing processes, and involved resources. The current version of the VFDM [17] is mainly based and extends Industry Foundation Classes (IFC) standard [18], automatically converted from an EXPRESS schema specification into an OWL ontology (named *ifcOWL*) [19].

Thus, a production system is formalized as an RDF graph according to the VFDM ontology. RDF graphs can be serialized into files or can be stored into more advanced storage solutions (named triplestore or RDF store) providing also remote access and SPARQL endpoint to ease the input/output data exchanges (Fig. 1). The VFDM facilitates the interoperability between different software tools if they are endowed with a specific a software connector taking care of input/output data conversion from the ontology format to proprietary data structures and vice-versa.

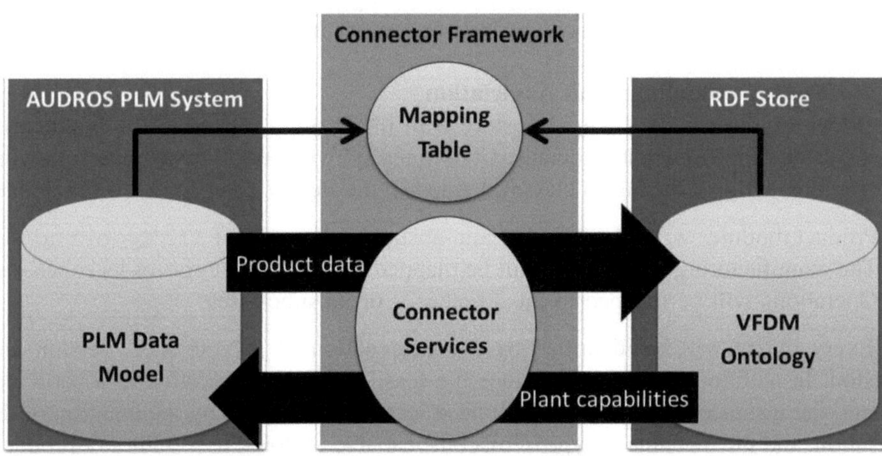

Fig. 1. Global interoperability scheme

Since both the scope of product design and production system design are very broad, the mapping of data and the interactions between the two systems of data storage must be limited and flexible. For instance, data will be transferred from the PLM system to the RDF store as soon as a M.A. or a product module is created or modified. Specifically, in a PLM system, the completion of the validation workflow to endorse and formalize the new (or first) version of an M.A is the right moment to disseminate information within the connected Information Systems.

3.2 Semantic Interoperability Between Audros and VFDM-Based Models

Semantic interoperability concerns the definition of concepts and relationships supporting the communication between heterogeneous data models. For this, the concept matching strategy and data exchange processes are defined in this section.

3.2.1 Exchange Process Definition

Based on the specification presented in previous paragraphs, two processes of communication must be defined, the import of the capabilities into the PLM system and the export of product and M.A. information to an RDF store having VFDM as reference ontological model, which includes classes, types and rules.

The import is triggered by the product specification validation and must take place before the design office receives the go for product definition. The systems will query production capabilities for each M.A. of each module compatible for every function the product will answer. A query will consist of the interrogation of the RDF store for currently capable systems. It will retrieve which production systems are able to execute a process plan, i.e. all its nested process steps.

The query, as is, executes the assessments taking in consideration all the process plans and production systems that are defined in the ontological model. The query will return a table containing, for each line, a production system, a process plan and a Boolean variable representing the capability.

Finally, the export of object types is required to extend the content of the RDF store. The module, as a product, and the M.A. as a process plan is characterized by the M.A. operations (reference, machines, and operation time) and Operations sequence.

3.2.2 Concept Matching and Association

The PLM system can feed the RDF store with information related to the product, its processes and their operations details. Consequently, we naturally make the following associations, while referring to classes defined in the ifcOWL version of IFC standard

- Product modules will be mapped to non-abstract subclasses of `IfcTypeProduct`
- The manufacturing alternatives will be mapped to `IfcTaskType` or its subclasses
- Operations will be mapped to the `IfcTask` or its subclasses.

Every object will be identified by a concatenation of its reference, version and revision. In addition, in order to deduce the feasibility of an operation in a particular system, the instances of `IfcTask` will need to be characterized by the duration of the operation, and the machine or type of machine capable of doing it. Modules or products are exported only to characterize what a manufacturing alternative realize. Finally, the instances of `IfcTaskType` are mostly characterized by their operations. This considerations lead to the mapping shown in the diagram of Fig. 2.

A final mapping issue concerns the relation between concepts. It is relatively easy to identify equivalent concepts between the two systems, but the relationships are managed in a different way. For instance, while in the PLM system there is a direct link between a M.A. and its module, in the ifcOWL ontology the link between an instance of `IfcTypeProduct` and an instance of `IfcTaskType` must go through an instance of the objectified relationship `IfcRelAssignsToProduct`.

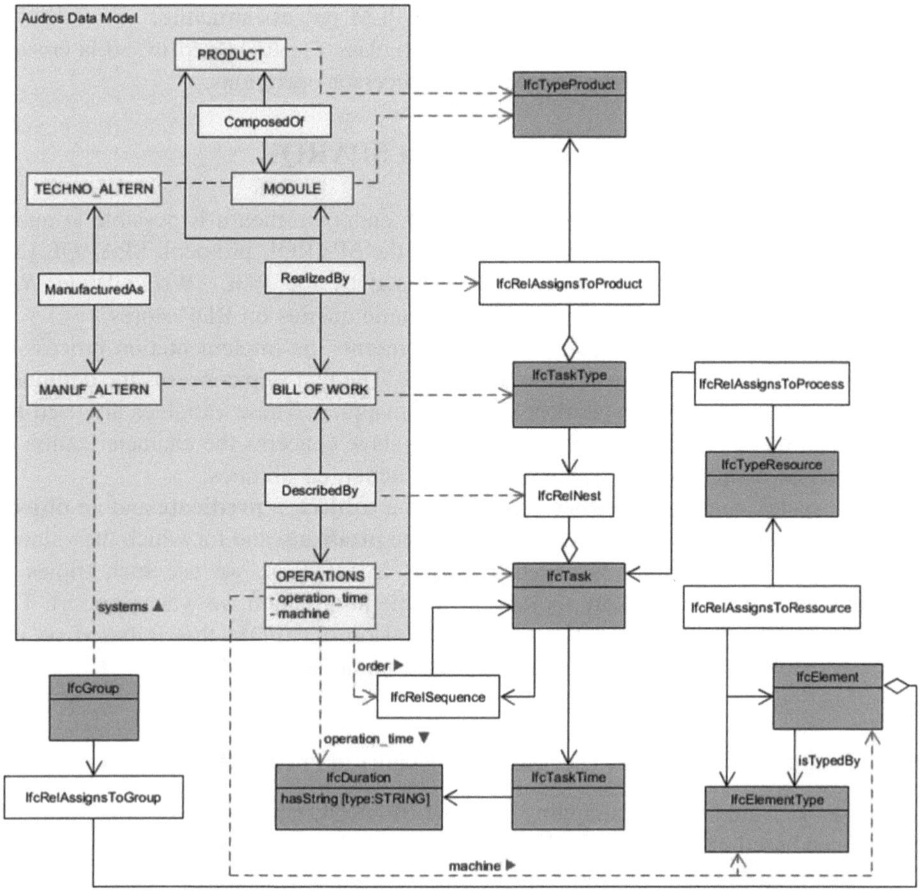

Fig. 2. Semantic interoperability between Audros data model and VFDM ontology mainly based on ifcOWL.

Therefore, the following mapping rules are specified in the proposed method:

- To declare a module:
  - An instance of a subclass of `IfcTypeProduct` is declared
- To declare a M.A.:
  - An instance of `IfcTaskType` is declared to represent a process plan.
  - An instance of the objectified relationship class `IfcRelAssignsToProduct` is generated and linked to the instances of `IfcTypeProduct` and `IfcTaskType`.
- To declare operations:
  - Each of operation is declared as an instance of `IfcTask` (or a subclass) to represent the steps in the process plan.
  - An instance of the objectified relationship class `IfcRelNest` is also declared to link the process plan to its operations.

- The order of operation is extracted from PLM process structure.
- An instance of the objectified relationship class `IfcRelSequence` is created to link each pair of direct predecessor/successor operations.

4 Implementation Strategy Based on SPARQL

If the employed RDF store provides a SPARQL endpoint, then it is possible to query and update the knowledge base remotely using the SPARQL protocol. SPARQL [20, 21] is a query language developed and validated by the W3C (World Wide Web Consortium) allowing reading and writing semantic queries on RDF stores.

Using the SPARQL protocol, this section presents the implementation process of different mapping rules defined in the Sect. 3.2.2. The first step concerns the definition of mapping variables that implement concepts' mapping. These variables are used for the declaration of prefixes and objects. The last stage concerns the characterization of operations necessary for the assessment of production capabilities.

RDF syntax consists of **triples** composed of a **subject**, a **predicate** and an **object**. A **subject** possesses a property represented by the **predicate** and for which the value is the **object**. A set of triples is called a **graph**. In SPARQL we use such triples to describe the information we are looking for or the information we want to insert. The following query examples refer to the latest version of VFDM that is based on the ifcOWL ontology. The OWL language is based on and extends RDF.

4.1 Product and Related Processes Data Export to "Feed" the RDF Store

To implement the semantic mapping with the SPARQL language, mapping variables are defined based on PLM and RDF store objects ID (Table 1). Except for `moduleID`,

Table 1. Definition of mapping variable

Variable name	Description
`graphName`	URI of the graph where to insert data
`moduleID`	Concatenation of the PLM object reference, version and revision to identify the instance of `ArtifactType` (a subclass of `IfcTypeProduct`).
`manufAlterID`	Concatenation of the PLM object reference, version and revision to identify the instance of `IfcTaskType`.
`opeID`	Concatenation of the PLM object reference, version and revision to identify the instance of `IfcTask`.
`relProdProcID`	ID of the relation object between a module/product and its M.A.
`relProcOpeID`	ID of the relation object between a M.A and its operations.
`relSeqOpeID`	ID of the relation object describing the sequence between 2 operations.
`durationID`	ID of the duration object characterizing an operation.
`tasktimeID`	ID of the time definition characterizing an operation.
`relOpeResID`	ID of the relation object between an operation and is production resource object.
`prodResID`	ID of a production resource object.
`relResMachineID`	ID of the relation object between a production resource and a machine.
`machineID`	ID of the machine as an instance of `MachineTool` (a subclass of `IfcElement`)

manufAlterID and opeID, all the IDs characterize concepts exclusive to the RDF store. For reuse possibility those IDs will be constructed based on the objects they link and the type of property/relation they characterize. Thus it will be possible to retrieve them for further modification. (i.e. declaring new M.A for existing module).

4.1.1 Prefixes Definition

The prefixes below are required in the following statement; <graphName> represents a new RDF graph where data are exported from the PLM system.

```
PREFIX list: <https://w3id.org/list#>
PREFIX express: <https://w3id.org/express#>
PREFIX xsd: <http://www.w3.org/2001/XMLSchema#>
PREFIX ifc: <http://ifcowl.openbimstandards.org/IFC4_ADD1#>
PREFIX factory: <http://www.h2020-proregio.eu/Factory#>
PREFIX PROnto: <graphName>
```

4.1.2 Declaration of an Object

In order to declare an object in the ontology, we must declare it as a NamedIndividual and type it to the class it belongs, e.g. ArtifactType (i.e. a subclass of IfcTypeProduct) in the case of a product module.

```
PROnto:<moduleID> a owl:NamedIndividual , factory:ArtifactType .
```

Declaration of the Link Between a Module and a M.A. The relation is represented by an instance of IfcRelAssignsToProduct characterized by links with both module and M.A.

```
PROnto:<manufAlterID> a owl:NamedIndividual , ifc:IfcTaskType .
PROnto:<relProdProcID> a owl:NamedIndividual,ifc:IfcRelAssignsToProduct;
        ifc:relatingProduct_IfcRelAssignsToProduct PROnto:<moduleID> ;
        ifc:relatedObjects_IfcRelAssigns PROnto:<manufAlterID> .
```

Declaration of the Link Between a M.A. and its Operations. This relation is enabled through the creation of an instance of IfcRelNests that groups all the operations belonging to the M.A.

```
PROnto:<manufAlterID_item> a owl:NamedIndividual , ifc:IfcObjectDefinition_List.
PROnto:<opeID> a owl:NamedIndividual , ifc:IfcTask .
PROnto:<relProcOpeID> a owl:NamedIndividual , ifc:IfcRelNests ;
        ifc:relatingObject_IfcRelNests PROnto:<manufAlterID> ;
        ifc:relatedObjects_IfcRelNests PROnto:<manufAlterID_item> .
PROnto:<manufAlterID_item> list:hasContents PROnto:<opeID> .
```

Nevertheless, to transcribe the sequence, an instance of another objectified relationship class is needed: IfcRelSequence. This instance will link an operation to its predecessor, independently to any other association.

```
PROnto:<relSeqOpeID> rdf:type owl:NamedIndividual , ifc:IfcRelSequence ;
        ifc:relatingProcess_IfcRelSequence PROnto:<opeID_1> ;
        ifc:relatedProcess_IfcRelSequence PROnto:<opeID_2> .
```

4.1.3 Characterization of Operations

Associate Time to Operation. To characterize an operation by its duration, we declare:

- Duration instance (IfcDuration) carrying a string value representing the duration.
- Task time instance (IfcTaskTime) linked to the operation instance (IfcTask).

```
PROnto:<durationID> a owl:NamedIndividual , ifc:IfcDuration ;
        express:hasString "PT10S"^^xsd:string .
PROnto:<tasktimeID> a owl:NamedIndividual , ifc:IfcTaskTime ;
        ifc:scheduleDuration_IfcTaskTime PROnto:<durationID> .
PROnto:<opeID> ifc:taskTime_IfcTask PROnto:<tasktimeID> .
```

Associate Machine/Machine Type with Operation. To link an operation to the machine tool that can execute it, we declare:

- A production resource instance (IfcTypeResource).
- A machine tool instance (MachineTool as a subclass of IfcElement) or an instance of machine tool type (MachineToolType as a subclass of IfcElementType).
- Two instances of objectified relationship classes linking the operation with the production resource and then the machine.

```
PROnto:<prodResID> a owl:NamedIndividual , ifc:IfcTypeResource .
PROnto:<machineID> a owl:NamedIndividual , factory:MachineTool .
PROnto:<relOpeResID> a owl:NamedIndividual , ifc:IfcRelAssignsToProcess;
      ifc:relatingProcess_IfcRelAssignsToProcess PROnto:<opeID> ;
      ifc:relatedObjects_IfcRelAssigns PROnto:<prodResID> .
PROnto:<relResMachineID> a owl:NamedIndividual,
                         ifc:IfcRelAssignsToResource ;
      ifc:relatingResource_IfcRelAssignsToResource PROnto:<prodResID> ;
      ifc:relatedObjects_IfcRelAssigns PROnto:<machineID> .
```

4.1.4 Production Capabilities Assessment

The plant capability assessment will consist of the following SPARQL query that is designed under the following assumptions:

- only one level of nesting in the process plan, i.e. the process steps of the process plan are not further nested;
- a system is a group of elements, e.g. machine tools;
- elements are not decomposed;
- a system is not decomposed into sub-systems.

Most, if not all, of these assumptions can be relaxed in the future, by upgrading the content of the query.

```
SELECT DISTINCT ?pplan ?sys (if(?npstepPP=count(distinct ?pstep),"true","false" )
as ?assessment)
WHERE {
    VALUES ?pplan {PRonto:<manufAlterID>}.a
    VALUES ?sys {PRonto:<systemID>}.b
    ?sys rdf:type/rdfs:subClassOf* factory:TransformationSystem .
    ?sys (ifc:isGroupedBy_IfcGroup|^ifc:relatingGroup_IfcRelAssignsToGroup)/
(ifc:relatedObjects_IfcRelAssigns|^ifc:hasAssignments_IfcObjectDefinition) ?elem .
    ?res (^ifc:relatingResource_IfcRelAssignsToResource)/
(ifc:relatedObjects_IfcRelAssigns|^ifc:hasAssignments_IfcObjectDefinition) ?elem .
    ?pstep (^ifc:relatingProcess_IfcRelAssignsToProcess)/
(ifc:relatedObjects_IfcRelAssigns|^ifc:hasAssignments_IfcObjectDefinition) ?res .
    ?pplan (ifc:isNestedBy_IfcObjectDefinition|
^ifc:relatingObject_IfcRelNests)/(ifc:relatedObjects_IfcRelNests)/
list:hasNext*/list:hasContents ?pstep .
    {
        SELECT ?pplan (count(distinct ?pstep) as ?npstepPP)
            WHERE {
            ?pplan rdf:type/rdfs:subClassOf* ifc:IfcTaskType .
            ?pplan (ifc:isNestedBy_IfcObjectDefinition|
^ifc:relatingObject_IfcRelNests)/(ifc:relatedObjects_IfcRelNests)/list:hasNext*/li
st:hasContents ?pstep .
        }
        GROUP BY ?pplan
    }
} GROUP BY ?sys ?npstepPP ?pplan
```

[a] This constraint allows restricting the capability assessment to a subset of process plans
[b] This constraint allows restricting the capability assessment to a subset of systems

5 Conclusion

The presented approach allows an asynchronous and flexible data exchange between a PLM system and an RDF store and gives an answer to the problem of interoperability between corporate information systems. The strength of this approach comes from the use of standards as the ifcOWL ontology and SPARQL language. In future work, we foresee studying the possibility to develop domain ontology to better represent manufacturing-specific concepts while taking advantage of ifcOWL and SPARQL standards.

Being developed in the project "ProRegio", the approach will be prototypically implemented together with industrial partners in several use cases. Thus, its feasibility and potentiality to support co-evolution strategy can be test on real use cases. Further works will concerns the extension of the mapping table with the ontology models to support more complex interoperability situations including other tools than MPM.

Acknowledgments. The presented results were conducted within the project "ProRegio" entitled "customer-driven design of product-services and production networks to adapt to regional market requirements". This project has received funding from the European Union's Horizon 2020 research and innovation program under grant agreement no. 636966. The authors would like thank the industrial partners involved in this research.

References

1. Tolio, T., Ceglarek, D., ElMaraghy, H.A., Fischer, A., Hu, S.J., Laperrière, L., Newman, S.T., Váncza, J.: SPECIES - co-evolution of products, processes and production systems. CIRP Ann. Manuf. Technol. **59**(2), 672–693 (2010)
2. Sako, M.: Modularity and outsourcing: the nature of co-evolution of product architecture and organisation architecture in the global automotive industry. In: The Business of Systems Integration, pp. 229–253. Oxford University Press, New York (2005)
3. Belkadi, F., Buergin, J., Kumar Gupta, R., Zhang, Y., Bernard, A., Lanza, G., Colledani, M., Urgo, M.: Co-definition of product structure and production network for frugal innovation perspectives: towards a modular-based approach. In: 26th CIRP Design Conference, Stockholm Sweden, 15–17 June 2016
4. Penciuc, D., Durupt, A., Belkadi, F., Eynard, B., Rowson, H.: Towards a PLM interoperability for a collaborative design support system. In: 8th International Conference on Digital Enterprise Technology, DET, Stuttgart, Germany, 25–28 March 2014
5. Kádár, B., Terkaj, W., Sacco, M.: Semantic virtual factory supporting interoperable modelling and evaluation of production systems. CIRP Ann. Manuf. Technol. **62**(1), 443–446 (2013)
6. Audros Company. http://www.audros.fr/en/
7. Lee, K.I., Noh, S.D.: Virtual manufacturing system—a test-bed of engineering activities. CIRP Ann. Manuf. Technol. **46**(1), 347–350 (1997)
8. Zhai, W., Fan, X., Yan, J., Zhu, P.: An integrated simulation method to support virtual factory engineering. Int. J. CAD/CAM **2**(1), 39–44 (2002)
9. Bloomfield, R., Mazhari, E., Hawkins, J., Son, Y.J.: Interoperability of manufacturing applications using the Core Manufacturing Simulation Data (CMSD) standard information model. Comput. Ind. Eng. **62**(4), 1065–1079 (2012)
10. Chen, D., Kjellberg, T., Euler, A.: Software tools for the digital factory – an evaluation and discussion. In: Huang, G.Q., Mak, K.L., Maropoulos, P.G. (eds.) 6th CIRP-Sponsored International Conference on Digital Enterprise Technology. AINSC, vol. 66, pp. 803–812. Springer, Heidelberg (2010)
11. Agyapong-Kodua, K., Lohse, N., Darlington, R., Ratchev, S.: Review of semantic modelling technologies in support of virtual factory design. Int. J. Prod. Res. **51**(14), 4388–4404 (2013)

12. Barbau, R., Krima, S., Rachuri, S., Narayanan, A., Fiorentini, X., Foufou, S., Sriram, R.D.: OntoSTEP: enriching product model data using ontologies. Comput.-Aided Des. **44**(6), 575–590 (2012)
13. Bruno, G., Villa, A.: The exploitation of an ontology-based model of PLM from a SME point of view. Manuf. Model. Manag. Control **7**(1), 1447–1452 (2013)
14. Panetto, H., Dassisti, M., Tursi, A.: ONTO-PLM: product-driven ONTOlogy for product data management interoperability within manufacturing process environment. Adv. Eng. Inform. **26**(2), 334–348 (2012)
15. Colledani, M., Pedrielli, G., Terkaj, W., Urgo, M.: Integrated virtual platform for manufacturing systems design. Procedia CIRP **7**, 425–430 (2013)
16. Terkaj, W., Pedrielli, G., Sacco, M.: Virtual factory data model. In: Workshop on Ontology and Semantic Web for Manufacturing, OSEMA, CEUR Workshop Proceedings, vol. 886, pp. 29–43 (2012)
17. Pellegrinelli, S., Terkaj, W., Urgo, M.A.: Concept for a pallet configuration approach using zero-point clamping systems. Procedia CIRP **41**, 123–128 (2016)
18. Liebich, T., Adachi, Y., Forester, J., Hyvarinen, J., Richter, S., Chipman, T., Weise, M., Wix, J.: Industry Foundation Classes IFC4 Official Release (2013). http://www.buildingsmart-tech.org/ifc/IFC4/final/html/
19. Pauwels, P., Terkaj, W.: EXPRESS to OWL for construction industry: towards a recommendable and usable ifcOWL ontology. Autom. Constr. **63**, 100–133 (2016)
20. W3C. SPARQL Query Language for RDF. n.d. https://www.w3.org/TR/rdf-sparql-query/
21. Kollia, I., Glimm, B., Horrocks, I.: SPARQL query answering over OWL ontologies. In: Antoniou, G., Grobelnik, M., Simperl, E., Parsia, B., Plexousakis, D., Leenheer, P., Pan, J. (eds.) ESWC 2011. LNCS, vol. 6643, pp. 382–396. Springer, Heidelberg (2011). doi:10.1007/978-3-642-21034-1_26

Model-Based Engineering for the Integration of Manufacturing Systems with Advanced Analytics

David Lechevalier[1], Anantha Narayanan[2], Sudarsan Rachuri[3], Sebti Foufou[4], and Y. Tina Lee[5(✉)]

[1] Le2i, Université de Bourgogne, Dijon, France
david_lechevalier@etu.u-bourgogne.fr
[2] University of Maryland, College Park, MD, USA
anantha@umd.edu
[3] Advanced Manufacturing Office,
Department of Energy, Office of Energy Efficiency and Renewable Energy, Washington, DC, USA
sudarsan.rachuri@hq.doe.gov
sudarsan.rachuri@ee.doe.gov
[4] CSE Department, College of Engineering, Qatar University, Doha, Qatar
sfoufou@qu.edu.qa
[5] Systems Integration Division, National Institute of Standards and Technology, Gaithersburg, MD, USA
yung-tsun.lee@nist.gov

Abstract. To employ data analytics effectively and efficiently on manufacturing systems, engineers and data scientists need to collaborate closely to bring their domain knowledge together. In this paper, we introduce a domain-specific modeling approach to integrate a manufacturing system model with advanced analytics, in particular neural networks, to model predictions. Our approach combines a set of meta-models and transformation rules based on the domain knowledge of manufacturing engineers and data scientists. Our approach uses a model of a manufacturing process and its associated data as inputs, and generates a trained neural network model as an output to predict a quantity of interest. This paper presents the domain-specific knowledge that the approach should employ, the formal workflow of the approach, and a milling process use case to illustrate the proposed approach. We also discuss potential extensions of the approach.

Keywords: Data analytics · Meta-model · Neural network · Manufacturing process · Predictive modeling

1 Introduction

The manufacturing industry generates large amounts of data on products, processes, and resources, among other things. Data analytics provide the capabilities needed to extract insights and make predictions from these data. The potential impacts of data

R. Harik et al. (Eds.): PLM 2016, IFIP AICT 492, pp. 146–157, 2016.
DOI: 10.1007/978-3-319-54660-5_14

analytics on manufacturing-systems efficiency include a reduction of production cost and time across all manufacturing levels [1, 2]. Data scientists and manufacturing engineers often collaborate when using data analytics to solve process-specific problems to improve product quality [3, 4], equipment efficiency [5, 6], and resource efficiency [7, 8]. However, these collaborations require a significant amount of time and effort to merge the expertise from these two domains. In [9], the authors present a domain-specific framework to address this challenge. The framework (1) identifies the main components and interfaces that must be implemented to improve communication between these domains and (2) facilitates the application of data analytics in manufacturing. In this paper, we introduce an implementation of some of the components and interfaces that will be a part of this framework.

Our approach focuses on using data analytics – specifically neural networks (NNs) – for predicting a set of manufacturing-process-related performance metrics. There are three main contributions of this paper. First, we provide meta-models to represent manufacturing processes and NNs. Second, we describe an algorithm to generate a trained NN automatically from a manufacturing process model and data. Third, we discuss a tool to export the NN in two standard formats: the Predictive Model Markup Language (PMML) [10] and the Portable Format for Analytics (PFA) [11].

The paper is organized as follows. Section 2 presents the domain-specific knowledge required from the manufacturing and data-science domains to generate NNs for manufacturing processes. It also introduces the approach to generate NNs automatically. Section 3 describes, in more detail, two components of the proposed approach: a manufacturing meta-model and transformation rules to generate an NN. Section 4 presents a process-level manufacturing use case to illustrate the capabilities of the approach.

2 Domain Specific Knowledge from Neural Networks and Manufacturing Processes

In this section, we discuss the knowledge required from manufacturing engineers and data scientists to apply NNs to manufacturing processes. We review applications of NNs in manufacturing processes, and devise a methodology based on the common practice of data scientists.

2.1 Manufacturing Domain Knowledge

To identify the required manufacturing-domain knowledge, we studied several research efforts on the applications of data analytics (DA) to manufacturing processes. In [12], the authors apply analytics to detect faults in the alignment of a cap to the base part of a product. In [13–15], the authors predict product quality using three DA algorithms: Bayesian networks (BNs), linear regression, and NNs. In [16], the authors describe a way to predict the need for equipment repair using BNs. In [15], the authors used NNs to study surface roughness in a milling process. They identified surface roughness as the performance metric of interest. They also identified spindle speed, feed rate, depth of cut, and the vibration average per revolution as the process variables that have the most impact on surface roughness. They collected 492 data samples to train and validate the NN. Each application followed a similar workflow: (1) identify the performance metric to be studied, (2) identify the variables that impact this target quantity, and (3) use test data to build an analytical model to predict the performance metric from the process variables. We used this same workflow in our work.

2.2 Data Science Domain Knowledge

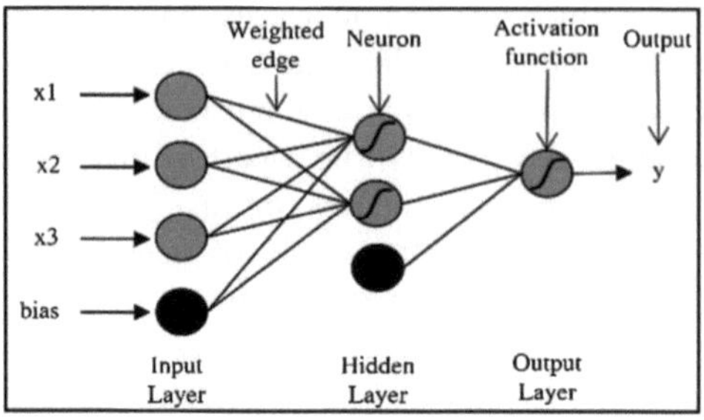

Fig. 1. Structure of a neural network

To understand the knowledge required from a data scientist to apply data analytics techniques to build an NN, it is important to understand how an NN is built. Figure 1 presents the main elements and the structure of an NN. An NN is composed of an input layer, zero or more hidden layers, and an output layer. Each layer contains at least one neuron. All layers except the output layer contain a bias neuron (shown in black). Weighted edges fully connect neurons in different layers. From a mathematical viewpoint, NNs can be viewed as a set of nonlinear basis functions (the activation functions), with free parameters (the adjustable weights). Training the NN is about adjusting the weights to minimize the error between the output value of the NN and the known, real, output value for a given data sample [17].

As noted above, the first step in building the NN involves selecting the input variables relevant to the performance metric. This step is called *feature selection* and defines the number of input neurons of the NN. There is one input neuron for each input variable. The second step is to determine the number of hidden layers and the number of neurons in each layer. In general, one hidden layer is sufficient [18] for the class of problems related to manufacturing processes. The number of hidden neurons has an impact on the NN accuracy, thus data scientists define this number very carefully. Finally, the output neuron represents the variable that we are trying to predict, which we call the quantity of interest. For example, a performance metric such as energy consumption may be the quantity of interest in a manufacturing scenario.

Based on these reviews, our approach needs to define the input neurons based on the process variables, define the optimal number of hidden neurons for an NN with one hidden layer, and finally define the output neuron for the quantity of interest.

2.3 Integration of Manufacturing and Data Science Domain Models

After identifying the required knowledge from manufacturing engineers and data scientists, we describe our approach and how it contributes to the framework defined in [9]. Figure 2 summarizes the workflow of our approach. In this figure, meta-models (Ⓐ and Ⓑ) are in gray, models (①, ③ and ⑤) are in yellow, and software solutions

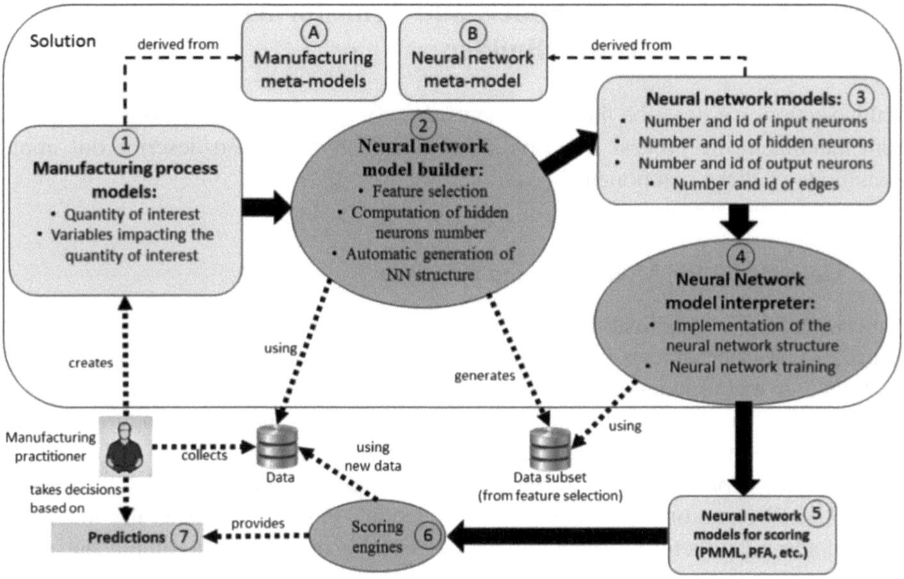

Fig. 2. Formal workflow of the approach

(②, ④ and ⑥) are in blue. The dashed arrows represent actions defined in the related label. The solid arrows show the use of models as input or output of the software solutions.

Box Ⓐ represents our manufacturing meta-model that captures the manufacturing knowledge. This meta-model defines the concepts, rules and constraints needed to represent a manufacturing process. Using the meta-model, a manufacturing engineer is able to build a manufacturing process model ① to define the quantities of interest and the variables involved in the manufacturing process. Note, we provide an interface to collect data related to the manufacturing process.

Taking the manufacturing process model and data as inputs, an NN model builder ② embeds a set of algorithms to run a feature selection that (1) optimizes the number of input neurons, (2) computes the optimal number of hidden neurons, and (3) builds the optimal structure of the NN ③. This NN structure is recorded using an NN meta-model contained in the meta-model repository. The NN meta-model and NN model interpreter are presented in [19]. The NN model interpreter ④ generates a trained NN. This NN is exported as a PMML or PFA file ⑤ that is ready to use for prediction with new data. A scoring engine ⑥ provides predictions ⑦ using the PMML file and new data. Scoring is the process of using a model to make predictions about the behavior of a quantity of interest. A manufacturing engineer makes decisions based on these predictions to control the manufacturing process under investigation.

3 Manufacturing Meta-models and Transformation Rules of the Neural Network Builder

In this section, we describe the components, Ⓐ, Ⓑ and ② in Fig. 2, to generate NNs from manufacturing process descriptions automatically. We also describe our implementations of these components.

3.1 Meta-model for Manufacturing Processes

A meta-model is a graphical description of concepts and their relationships, which can be used to describe objects or instances of those concepts in a particular domain. We developed a meta-model for describing manufacturing processes in a way that is helpful to build an NN. A manufacturing engineer builds a manufacturing model using the meta-model to provide the required knowledge identified in Sect. 2.1. Since the purpose of the approach is to use data-driven techniques (in this case NNs), there are no physics-based equations associated with the model. Figure 3 presents the main concepts of the manufacturing meta-model. Please note that this is a simple but a reasonable representation of the domain model. The notation in Figs. 3 and 4 is based on Unified Modeling Language Class Diagrams [20], where the rectangles represent concepts occurring in the domain, and the lines represent relationships between the concepts. A line with a solid diamond represents a containment relationship, with a numerical range at one end denoting the number of allowed instances. For example, in Fig. 3, a *ManufacturingModel* can contain 0 or more instances of *Manufacturing Process*.

The annotation <<Model>> is used to identify first class objects, while the annotation <<Connection>> is used to represent edges, flows, or associations.

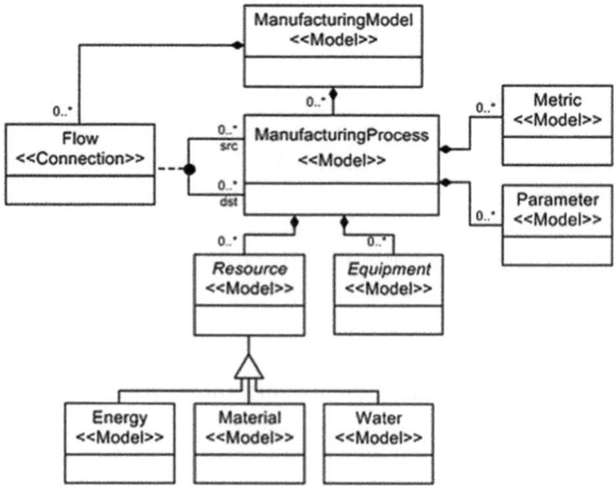

Fig. 3. Manufacturing meta-model

ManufacturingModel is a high level concept that allows the description of a manufacturing model that is composed of *Flows* and *ManufacturingProcess* concepts. The *Flow* concept represents connections between instances of the *ManufacturingProcess* concept. A *ManufacturingProcess* is composed of *Resource* and *Equipment* concepts, which allow the manufacturer to include resource or equipment parameters as variables of the manufacturing process. *ManufacturingProcess* also contains the concepts of *Parameter* and *Metric*. Metric is used to define a quantity of interest in the manufacturing process. Parameters are the variables that can impact the metric for a manufacturing process.

In the UML notation, an empty triangle is used to denote specialization, where one concept may be specialized into many sub-concepts. As shown in Fig. 3, the *Resource* concept is extended to define different types of resources: energy, water, and material. The manufacturing meta-model can also be extended to define other kinds of resources such as labor.

3.2 Meta-model for Neural Networks

Figure 4 shows the neural network meta-model (NNMM) presented in [19]. The NNMM represents different types of NNs through various abstractions. A *NeuralNetworkModel* concept is composed of *Neuron* and *Edge* concepts. A *Neuron* can be one of four types: *InputNeuron*, *HiddenNeuron*, *BiasNeuron*, and *OutputNeuron*. An *Edge* can be a *VisibleEdge* or a *HiddenEdge*. A *VisibleEdge* is used to represent an edge between an input neuron and a hidden neuron, between a hidden neuron and an output neuron, or between a bias neuron and an output neuron. Edges between two hidden neurons, or between a bias neuron and a hidden neuron are represented using *HiddenEdge*.

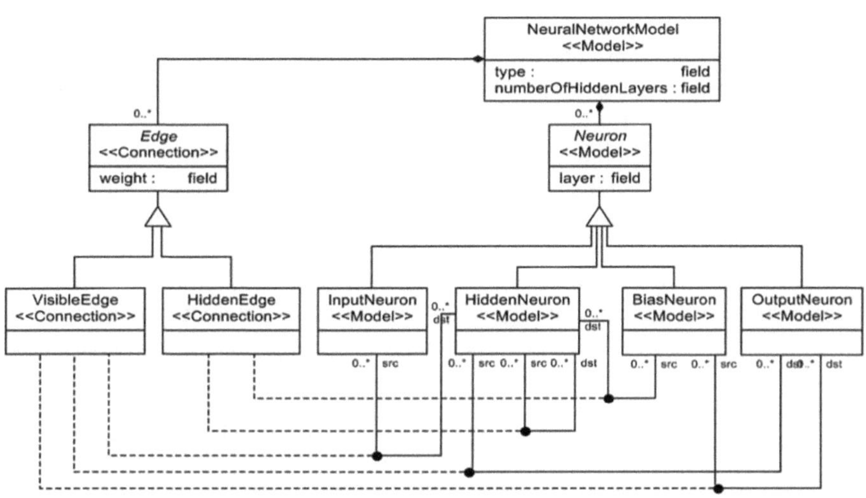

Fig. 4. Neural network meta-model [19]

3.3 Transformation Rules to Generate an NN from a Manufacturing Model

We developed a set of transformation rules to generate an NN model from a manufacturing model. Together, these rules represent a step-by-step process to build an NN from the input model and the data provided by a manufacturing engineer. We embedded these rules into the NN model builder, so that they can be applied to any type of manufacturing process model. The result of applying these rules is an untrained NN model, which is built based from the NN meta-model described above, and an input data set for training. Figure 5 presents the workflow and the transformation rules of the NN model builder, identified as ② in Fig. 2.

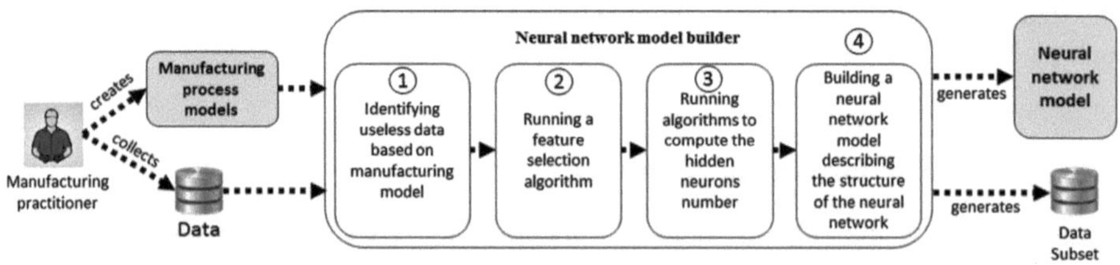

Fig. 5. Workflow of the NN model builder

The NN model builder takes the manufacturing process model and data provided by the manufacturing engineer as inputs. In the builder, Step 1 identifies those variables that the manufacturer listed as impacting the quantity of interest in the manufacturing model. The identified variables are compared with the variables present in the data set. The variables that are not identified in the manufacturing model are then removed. Step 1 takes advantage of the manufacturing expertise that the manufacturing engineer provides in the model.

Step 2 uses the feature-selection algorithm and a real data set to identify those variables that do not contribute to the quantity of interest based on a data set. This algorithm takes the variables provided from Step 1 and removes the variables that do not contribute from the list.

During Step 3, the builder runs an algorithm to optimize the number of hidden neurons for the NN. Several reports document the studies associated with optimizing the number of hidden neurons and putting them all into a single hidden layer. Sheela and Deepa [21], for example, analyzes the performance of the different optimization methods described in different reports – that is, their ability to predict the actual optimal number of hidden neurons. Our algorithm applies these different methods and computes the number that appeared most frequently. That number is the one selected for the NN. As we mentioned previously, one hidden layer is sufficient for manufacturing process-related problems, and the algorithm is implemented to build one hidden layer. This algorithm, however, can easily be modified to build NNs with more than one hidden layer.

In Step 4, the builder generates the NN instance model and a data set as outputs. The NN instance model describes the structure of the NN, and must be trained in order to predict the quantity of interest. The output data set is a subset of the input data set. The input data set variables that do not impact the quantity of interest are not included in the output data set.

Using the output data set, the NN model interpreter [19] performs the NN training and updates the weights on the NN instance model. It also generates a PMML or PFA file containing the trained NN model.

4 Use Case

In this section, we show how our implementation of the proposed approach is used in a typical manufacturing scenario. For our approach, manufacturing engineers build a model of the process they wish to study using the meta-model described earlier. Next, they collect test data by conducting experiments or from other sources. Finally, they use the automated tools described in Fig. 2 to generate an NN for their process. This NN can be used to make future decisions without having to conduct physical experiments to determine target values.

4.1 Scenario Description

This case study focuses on predicting the energy consumed by a milling machine tool. The data set used in this case study was generated in [22] from a total of 18 parts machined with 196 face milling, 108 contouring, 54 slotting and pocketing, 16 spiraling and 32 drilling operations. We focused on face milling in this use case. The series of machining operations were performed. Data was collected using power meters and different sensors, and then stored in a database. We use the collected data as test data to build an NN model to predict power consumption for different combinations of machining parameters.

The test data includes the timestamp, power demand, feed rate, spindle speed, depth of cut, cutting direction, cutting strategy, cutting ratio, cutting volume, and length of cut in the 3 axis, referred as cutX, cutY and cutZ. As described below, we first built a manufacturing process model based on our case study, then identified the optimal process parameters and the metric of interest.

4.2 Building the Manufacturing Process Model

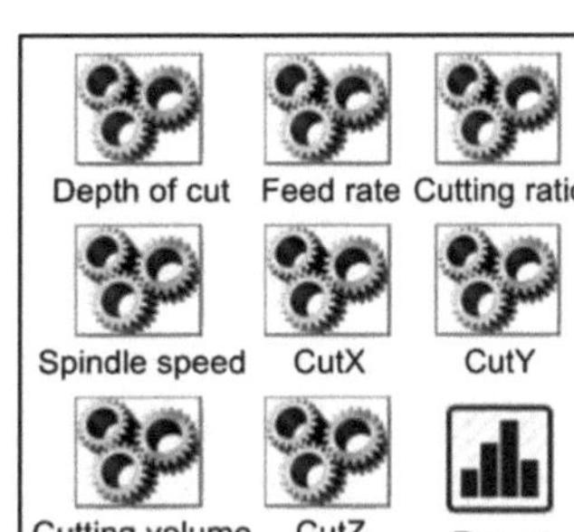

Fig. 6. Manufacturing model

Figure 6 shows the manufacturing process model that we built for the milling process. This model contains the parameters that the manufacturing engineer has specified as contributing to the quantity of interest. In this model, we defined power as the quantity of interest. We defined feed rate, spindle speed, depth of cut, cutting ratio, cutting volume, cutX, cutY, and cutZ as parameters that impact the power consumption. During this step, the manufacturers use their domain expertise to list only those parameters that they think will have a significant impact on their power consumption. The test data and the manufacturing model are the inputs to our next step, which performs feature selection and generates the NN.

4.3 Generating the Neural Network for Prediction

In the next step, the manufacturing engineer executes the NN model builder using both the manufacturing model (in Fig. 6) and the test data as inputs. Our algorithm, takes those inputs and generates a trained NN. It does this using two pieces of software: the NN model builder and the NN model interpreter.

The NN model builder identifies the quantity of interest (the selected performance metric) from the manufacturing model. In this case, it is power. The NN model builder prunes the data set by removing the data that were omitted in the manufacturing model. In our case, it removes the cutting direction and cutting strategy variables from the data set since these are not present in the manufacturing model in Fig. 6. Next, the feature selection algorithm is executed. It uses the test data to identify and remove parameters that have an insignificant impact on the target variable. In our example, feed rate, depth of cut, cutX, and cutY were found not to have a significant effect on power; therefore, these parameters are not considered when building the NN.

The NN model builder then displays which variables were removed (1) based on the manufacturing model and (2) using the feature selection algorithm. Then the builder saves the new data set in a location identified by the manufacturing engineer. Figure 7 shows the resulting NN model, an automatically generated instance of the NNMM which is shown in Fig. 4.

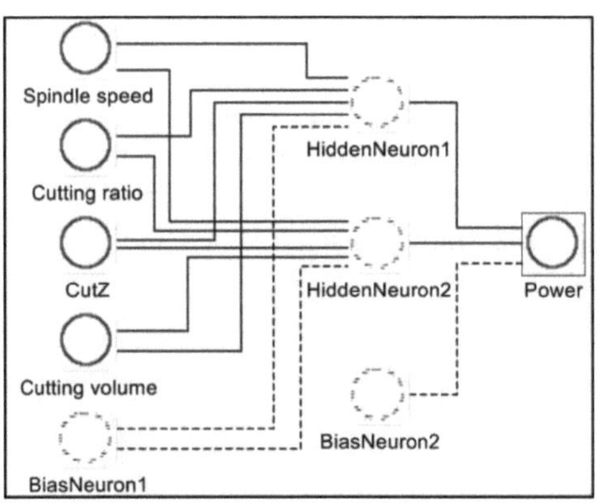

Fig. 7. Neural network model

In this NN model, the NN model builder keeps four variables: spindle speed, cutting ratio, cutting volume and cutZ. They are defined as input neurons in the NN. The algorithm computes that two hidden neurons are optimal in this model. Power is defined as the output neuron in the NN. Finally, the builder adds a bias neuron for every layer except the output layer to build a correct NN.

The NN model builder generates the structure model the NN. It still needs to be trained (i.e. weights must be assigned to the edges to make correct predictions). To generate the weights, the structural NN must be trained with the test data. The NN model and the test data are inputs to the NN model interpreter. The interpreter generates a trained NN based on the structure described in the NN model and the test data. The NN is generated as a standard PMML file. Several off-the-shelf data analytics tools can read this PMML file.

The manufacturer can now use this NN to predict the energy consumption of the milling machine under different conditions. This allows the manufacturer to perform different tests and make decisions, without having to physically execute experiments on the machine.

5 Summary and Future Work

In this paper, we proposed an approach to generate an NN to predict performance metrics for manufacturing processes. This approach provides capabilities to collect the required manufacturing knowledge and to use that knowledge to build NN models to predict the performance metrics for different values of the process parameters. This can be used to optimize performance by finding the best values for the process parameters.

We first reviewed the applications of data analytics to manufacturing processes for identifying the steps taken by data scientists to create NNs. We then developed and implemented the components needed to provide the capabilities required by this approach. Part of that approach is developing a manufacturing meta-model. The meta-model allows manufacturing engineers to provide a set of the most important process parameters – those have the most impact on performance – in a manufacturing model. In addition to this meta-model, we implemented an NN model builder to automatically build an NN model from a manufacturing model and data provided by manufacturing engineers. The NN model builder provides (1) a feature-selection algorithm based on the test data and (2) an NN model generator that generates the structure of the NN. From the generated NN structure, an NN model interpreter produces a trained NN in a standard format. Using a scoring engine, the trained NN can then be used to predict the quantity of interest.

We illustrated the capabilities of our implementation using a realistic manufacturing scenario. In this scenario, an NN is trained to predict energy use during a particular milling process. A manufacturing engineer provides a manufacturing model used as input to the NN builder. The implemented algorithms finally generate a trained NN that can be used with new data for predicting energy consumption.

This paper presented an initial description and implementation of an approach to generate predictive models for manufacturing applications. We implemented a translator (the NN model builder) to generate neural networks automatically. More translators will be implemented in future work to generate other types of predictive models. In practice, manufacturing processes and their interactions with their surrounding environment are complex. In order to generate reliable prediction models for practical scenarios, our meta-models and translators must be extended to account for other parameters and constraints that affect manufacturing processes. Future work lies in four directions. The first is to extend the manufacturing meta-model to enable the representation of problems in greater detail, and at different manufacturing levels such as assembly. Next, add new steps to the NN model builder to improve its accuracy. Third, include a scoring engine. Fourth, extend the framework to include different analytical techniques such as Bayesian networks. Capabilities to build BN models could enable the application of uncertainty quantification in manufacturing [23].

Acknowledgement. The research in this paper was supported by National Institute of Standards and Technology's Foreign Guest Researcher Program, and Cooperative Agreement No. 70NANB14H250.

References

1. Manyika, J., Chui, M., Brown, B., Bughin, J., Dobbs, R., Roxburgh, C., Byers, A.H.: Big Data: The Next Frontier for Innovation, Competition, and Productivity. McKinsey (2011)
2. Brown, B., Chui, M., Manyika, J.: Are you ready for the era of 'big data'. McKinsey Q. **4**(1), 24–35 (2011)
3. Erzurumlu, T., Oktem, H.: Comparison of response surface model with neural network in determining the surface quality of moulded parts. Mater. Des. **28**(2), 459–465 (2007)
4. Zhai, L.Y., Khoo, L.P., Fok, S.C.: Feature extraction using rough set theory and genetic algorithms—an application for the simplification of product quality evaluation. Comput. Ind. Eng. **43**(4), 661–676 (2002)
5. Dabbas, R.M., Chen, H.N.: Mining semiconductor manufacturing data for productivity improvement—an integrated relational database approach. Comput. Ind. **45**(1), 29–44 (2001)
6. Chien, C.F., Diaz, A.C., Lan, Y.B.: A data mining approach for analyzing semiconductor MES and FDC data to enhance overall usage effectiveness (OUE). Int. J. Comput. Intell. Syst. **7**(sup2), 52–65 (2014)
7. Shin, S.J., Woo, J., Rachuri, S.: Predictive analytics model for power consumption in manufacturing. Procedia CIRP **15**, 153–158 (2014)
8. Gupta, D., Gopalakrishnan, B.: Energy sensitive machining parameter optimisation. Int. J. Ind. Syst. Eng. **5**(4), 405–423 (2010)
9. Lechevalier, D., Narayanan, A., Rachuri, S.: Towards a domain-specific framework for predictive analytics in manufacturing. In: 2014 IEEE International Conference on Big Data (Big Data), pp. 987–995. IEEE (2014)
10. PMML v4.2.1. http://dmg.org/pmml/pmml-v4-2-1.html. Accessed 1 May 2016
11. PFA v0.8.1. http://dmg.org/pfa/index.html. Accessed 1 May 2016
12. Wolbrecht, E., D'ambrosio, B., Paasch, R., Kirby, D.: Monitoring and diagnosis of a multistage manufacturing process using Bayesian networks. Ai Edam **14**(01), 53–67 (2000)
13. Correa, M., Bielza, C., de Ramirez, M.J., Alique, J.R.: A Bayesian network model for surface roughness prediction in the machining process. Int. J. Syst. Sci. **39**(12), 1181–1192 (2008)
14. Abouelatta, O.B., Madl, J.: Surface roughness prediction based on cutting parameters and tool vibrations in turning operations. J. Mater. Process. Technol. **118**(1), 269–277 (2001)
15. Tsai, Y.H., Chen, J.C., Lou, S.J.: An in-process surface recognition system based on neural networks in end milling cutting operations. Int. J. Mach. Tools Manuf. **39**(4), 583–605 (1999)
16. Kurz, D., Kaspar, J., Pilz, J.: Dynamic maintenance in semiconductor manufacturing using Bayesian networks. In: 2011 IEEE Conference on Automation Science and Engineering (CASE), pp. 238–243. IEEE (2011)
17. Haykin, S.: Neural Networks: A Comprehensive Foundation. Prentice Hall (2004)
18. Heaton, J.: Introduction to Neural Networks with Java. Heaton Research Inc., St. Louis (2008)

19. Lechevalier, D., Hudak, S., Ak, R., Lee, Y.T., Foufou, S.: A neural network meta-model and its application for manufacturing. In: 2015 IEEE International Conference on Big Data (Big Data), pp. 1428–1435. IEEE (2015)
20. Unified Modeling Language. http://www.uml.org. Accessed 1 May 2016
21. Sheela, K.G., Deepa, S.N.: Review on methods to fix number of hidden neurons in neural networks. Mathematical Problems in Engineering (2013)
22. Park, J., et al.: A generalized data-driven energy prediction model with uncertainty for a milling machine tool using Gaussian Process. In: ASME 2015 International Manufacturing Science and Engineering Conference (2015)
23. Nannapaneni, S., Mahadevan, S.: Uncertainty quantification in performance evaluation of manufacturing processes. In: 2014 IEEE International Conference on Big Data (Big Data). IEEE (2014)

Proposal of a Model-Driven Ontology for Product Development Process Interoperability and Information Sharing

Anderson Luis Szejka[1,2,3(✉)], Osiris Canciglieri Júnior[1], Eduardo Rocha Loures[1], Hervé Panetto[2,3], and Alexis Aubry[2,3]

[1] Production and Systems Engineering Graduate Program, Pontifical Catholic University of Paraná, Curitiba, Brazil
{anderson.szejka, osiris.canciglieri, eduardo.loures}@pucpr.br
[2] Centre de Recherche en Automatique de Nancy, University of Lorraine, Vandoeuvre-lès-Nancy Cedex, France
{herve.panetto, alexis.aubry}@univ-lorraine.fr
[3] CNRS/CRAN UMR 7039, Vandoeuvre-lès-Nancy Cedex, France

Abstract. The semantic interoperability of information has become increasingly important in Product Development Process (PDP) to support different phases during the product development. This article presents a proposal of an Interoperable Product Design and Manufacturing System (IPDMS) concept based on a set of engineering domain ontologies and sematic mapping approaches. The concept explores the potentials of semantic well-defined core-foundations in a Semantic Web ontology language. The formal core-foundations can be specialised to perform application view in Product or Manufacturing Model. The application view is used to support the information sharing between product design and manufacturing and verify the accordance with product requirements. A preliminary experimental has been realised, using a test case to share information from the design to manufacturing of an injection moulding plastic. As results, it was identified potential benefits and limitations. The mains contributions are: semantic interoperability during information sharing in PDP and analysis of inconsistencies in PDP.

Keywords: Integrated product development process · Transdisciplinary engineering · Semantic interoperability · Formal model · Model-driven ontology

1 Introduction

The complexity of Product Development Process (PDP) has increased over the years to meet the customer's needs. This process requires continuous information sharing with different groups within institutional boundaries as well as across multiple organisations. Thus, the current PDP's approaches of information exchange have been based on the product master models, as detailed in [1, 2]. These approaches have a strict information structure, but mistakes and misinterpretation issues have been identified across different PDP phases [3, 4]. This occurs because PDP has a set of transdisciplinary activities and

R. Harik et al. (Eds.): PLM 2016, IFIP AICT 492, pp. 158–168, 2016.
DOI: 10.1007/978-3-319-54660-5_15

multiple viewpoints that generate semantic obstacles without interoperability. The lack of interoperability is expensive for several globally distributed companies as discussed by [5].

Several resourceful efforts have been fostered to integrate solutions, following product master models through the definition of common information models. This is the way that international standards have been providing basis for product information exchange, e.g. STEP PLCS (ISO 10303). Related works such as OntoSTEP [6], OntoSTEP-NC [7], PRONOIA [8], and Semantic Annotation applied to PLM [9] indicate that there is a tendency to explore the use of Semantic Web ontology languages, like the Web Ontology Language (OWL), to model the knowledge of product models. However, a significant problem is to work with multiple domains since it is necessary to find effective and technical methods for semantically map information across related domains during the PDP. It is also evident that current works do not entirely address the rules to establish an analysis of product requirements, defined by the costumer alongside the product design and manufacturing. Product requirements define the constraints and characteristics of a product and its information must be effectively shared across different phases of PDP without losing any meaning [10].

Based on this context, this paper proposes a model-driven ontology concept to formally structured a product design and manufacturing interoperability system and the establishment of the main rules for the information and knowledge sharing to achieve the semantic interoperability in the PDP. Thus, the main contributions of this research are highlighted as: (i) improvement in product design and manufacturing information and knowledge sharing; (ii) interoperability between multiple domains; (iii) continuous analysis of product constraints across the PDP.

2 Technological Background

Product Life Cycle (PLC) describes every phase a product goes through, from the first definition into retired and disposal. It is composed by different phases such as: (i) Conception; (ii) Development; (iii) Manufacturing/Production; (iv) Utilization/Maintenance; and (v) Retirement/Disposal. While PLC has a holistic view of whole phases of Product, PDP has a set of multidisciplinary activities structured to transform market opportunities, customers' needs and technological constraints in products [2]. PDP is complex because information from multiple knowledge fields are simultaneously shared and exchanged through heterogeneous groups that may jointly function in institutional limits and across multiple organisations [11]. Although, PDP has a full view of product, providing information support to different phases of product development, misinterpretation and mistakes has been identified in it, highlighting mainly in the design and manufacturing phases [12]. According to Rozenfeld et al. [2], the activities of design and manufacturing are most costly (85% of product final cost). Therefore, in a modern PDP, design and manufacturing information and knowledge handling must be efficiently shared across different phases of PDP.

This is a typical semantic interoperability problem for which the meaning associated to the captured information and knowledge must be effectively shared across systems without any loss of the meaning and intent of the information and knowledge during the exchange process [13]. The most common way to support information sharing has been to explore integrated solutions through defining common information models [14, 15]. In this way, improved information sharing is being investigated through constructing formal ontologies [16] in different domains of application such as engineering, medicine, dentistry, business, etc. Some related works.

Gruber [17] originally defines ontology as an "explicit specification of conceptualization". Another important definition is provided by ISO 18629:2005 [18] that ontology is "a lexicon of specialised terminology along with some specification of the meaning of the terms in the lexicon", where lexicon is the vocabulary of a language. Ontologies can be classified according to their degree of expressiveness. Simple ontologies, for example, involving only taxonomy of concepts and basic relations, are referred to as lightweight ontologies. Ontologies with concepts and relations as a lightweight ontology enriched with axioms in the form of constraints are classified as heavyweight ontology. According to [19], axioms are used to clarify the intended meaning of the terms gathered on the ontology. However, ontologies are usually limited to the purpose of its application and it has limited reusability outside the scope of its application. Thus, ontology integration is an important task to achieve different levels of integration. Ontology integration is the process of finding commonalities between two different ontologies O and O′ and deriving in a new ontology O″ [19]. Based on this, three approaches for combining heterogeneous ontologies can be distinguished: (i) Ontology Inclusion; (ii) Ontology Mapping; and (iii) Ontology Merging.

Although, ontologies create semantic formalisms, a expressive problem is how to work with multiple ontologies of multiple domains to provide an effective mapping information across them [20]. Ontology mapping has been a key direction to tackle semantic heterogeneity issues across ontologies, intending to promote semantic interoperability. Several categories of ontology mapping methods have been suggested [21, 22], but there is a common consensus over the types of methods that can be applied. These types are: (i) Merging; (ii) Transformation; (iii) Alignment; and (iv) Articulation. Related works as [21, 22] present significant results on using matching techniques that use the semantics of logic-based systems, which employ upper ontologies. Therefore, this work uses the structure of product development process, ontologies and ontologies mapping ontologies to extract and enrich information to support the information sharing across PDP design and manufacturing phases in a transdisciplinary environment and in accordance to the customer's needs.

3 Interoperable Product Design and Manufacturing System Concept

Semantic interoperability is achieved when the meaning associated to the information and knowledge captured in computational form can be effectively exchanged across systems without losing any meaning and intent of the information and knowledge during the exchange process [13]. Additionally, IEEE [23] defines interoperability as the capacity of two or more systems to exchange information and to use the information that has been shared. Therefore, it is necessary to develop model-driven to semantic interoperability that provides balance and integrates multiple domain work and developers team with distinct viewpoints to allow the information exchange in a computational form across different phases of PDP.

In this context, Fig. 1 depicts the Interoperable Product Design and Manufacturing System (IPDMS) concept to support the information exchange in a computational form across three different phases of PDP. The concept uses a semantically well-defined core of concepts and constraints to instantiate the information in the application view and link them to with the semantic rules. Thus, the architecture of IPDMS is composed by four views: (i) Foundation View; (ii) Application View; (iii) Semantic Reconciliation View; and (iv) Constraints View. The three phases of PDP are exposed on Detail A of Fig. 1: (i) Conceptual Design Phase; (ii) Tooling Design Phase; and (iii) Manufacturing Design Phase. IPDMS works based on formal models and semantic reconciliation trough the semantic mapping concepts. The implication of each part of the IPDMS concept is next explained.

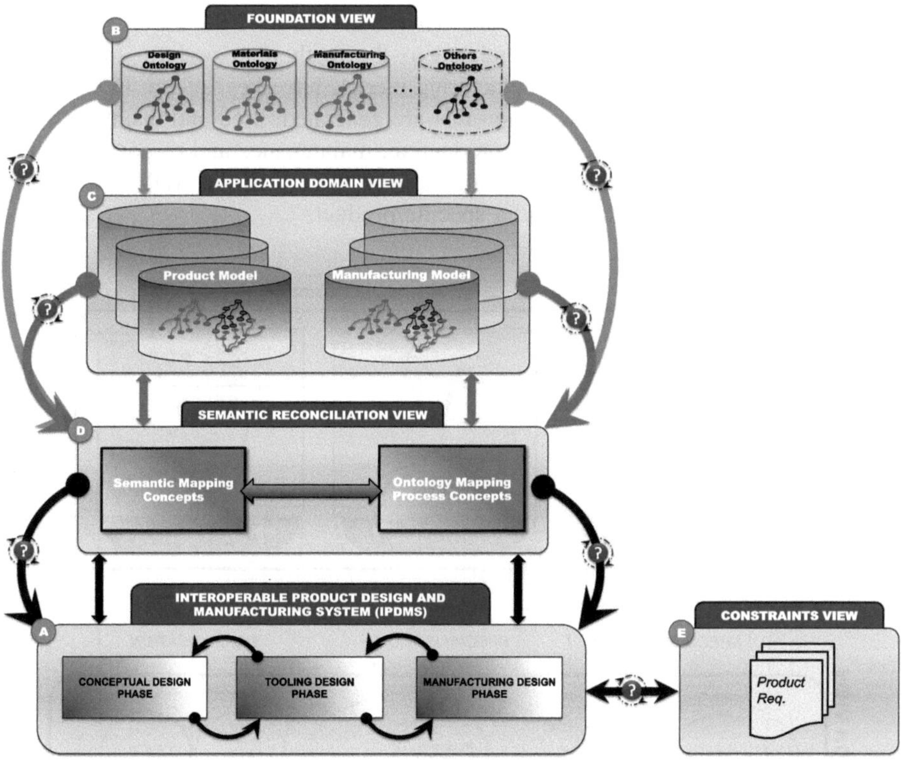

Fig. 1. Architecture of the Interoperable Product Design and Manufacturing System (IPDMS) Concept.

3.1 Foundation View and Application Domain View

The Foundation View (FV), detail B of Fig. 1, gathers and expressively represents concepts of different domains in a formal models at a relatively high level of abstraction. FV has Product Design Core, Tolerances Core, Materials Core, Manufacturing Core, etc. Common Logic Based formalism is used to govern the way that the concepts can be formalised at the computational level.

In this way, we are using the ontologies approach to structure the FV, but we are not building ontologies. Thus, two distinct procedures to formalize the concepts based on ontological approaches are been used: (i) standards and information model in UML structure are formalize in a lightweight representation; and (ii) representations already published in ontology libraries, such as [DAML, OWL: Library, JOWL, DBpedia] are analysed and integrated to the FV. For both procedures, it is used Web Ontology Language (OWL) [24] with axioms rules in Semantic Web Rule Language (SWRL) [25].

The cores in FV can be individually specialized in the Application Domain View (ADV) to meet the needs of specifics Product Design and Manufacture domains. Thus, the ADV was structured in Product Model and Manufacturing Model, as illustrate in Detail C of Fig. 1. A product model may be defined as an information model that stores information related to a specific product. The same occurs with the manufacturing model that has specific information related to the method to perform the product. According to [13], product and manufacturing models have key role on PDP because they hold and share product information that are generated, used and maintained over the process of design, manufacturing, production, maintenance and disposal. Figure 2 illustrates an example of three specialisations from the FV to the ADV to create the semantic links between concepts and a specific product.

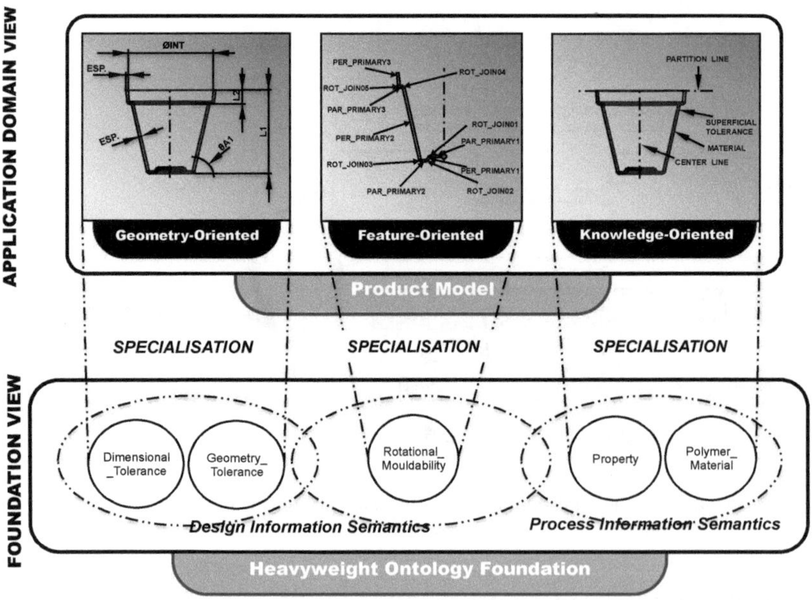

Fig. 2. Link between foundation view and application domain view.

3.2 Semantic Reconciliation View

Several transdisciplinary information are shared across different phases of PDP and need to be integrated to other models in the ADP to verify possible inconsistencies. In the event that these models need to interoperate with the intention of sharing knowledge, domain semantics need to be reconciled. Semantic Reconciliation View (SRV), detail D of Fig. 1, covers relevant applied ontology-based techniques enabling the reconciliation of domain semantics.

These techniques work segments of known ontology matching methods such as: (i) the computation of contexts for domain ontologies [26]; (ii) ontology mapping [21, 22]; and (iii) semantic alignment [27]. Based on this, Fig. 3 illustrates the basic concepts involved in the mapping of domain models at the SRV. The process of semantic reconciliation can be performed between pairs of models at a time, as can be encountered in almost all-current ontology mapping frameworks and methodologies [21]. Context Adjustment involves a first stage of contexts adjustments (namespaces in this case) of two domain models which are to be reconciled. Following this stage is a simple ontology intersection process, where both models are intact loaded on to a single specialise ontology. The last procedure in the SRV is the semantic alignment, where semantic mapping concepts are loaded into the intersected models.

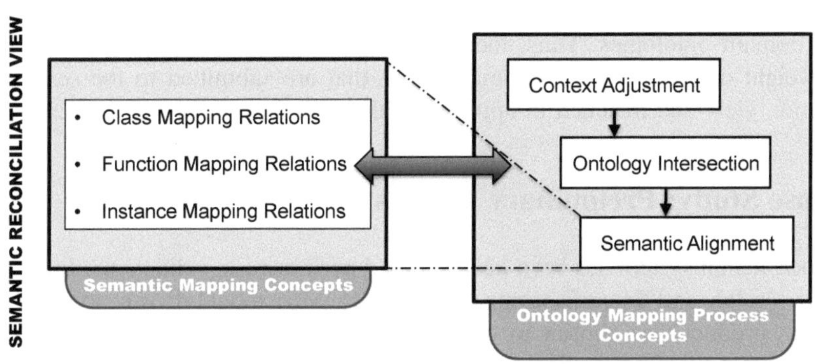

Fig. 3. Stages of semantic reconciliation view.

3.3 Constraints View

The Constraints View (CV), detail E of Fig. 1, gathers the restrictions for developing the product based on the Product Requirements defined by the customer's needs and technological specifications. Requirement is a statement from the stakeholder's needs to define a product; system or process characteristics and it must be unambiguous, clear, unique, consistent, stand-alone and verifiable [10]. Additionally, according to ISO/IEC 15288 [28], a requirement must be complete, coherent, unique, feasible, traceable and verifiable. Each requirement matches a single part of the future product, system or process and is grouped in an appropriate combination of textual statement views. Based on that, product requirements are used to create constraints rules to govern the way to develop the product and verify the consistency of the product design

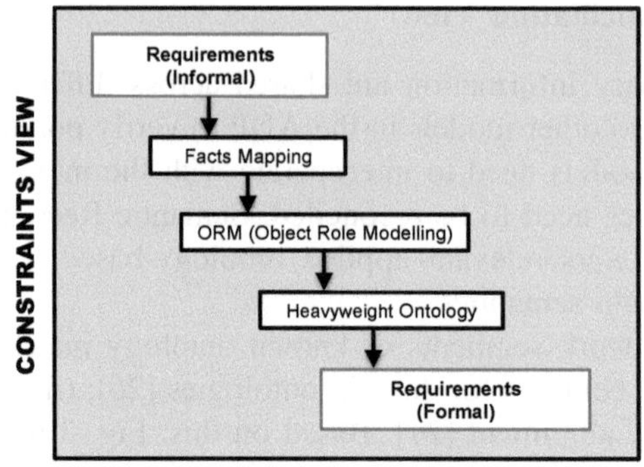

Fig. 4. Phases of constraints view.

and manufacturing. Figure 4 presents the main concepts involved to add these requirements in the IPDMS.

Firstly, the main facts are manually mapped in the requirement statement and modelling in a Conceptual Graphical approach as discussed by [4]. For this modelling is used the ORM (Object Role Modelling) that is a fully communication oriented information modelling method rooted in NIAM (Natural language Information Analysis Method) [29]. According to [30], ORM has been used in ontology engineering to model domain ontologies. Thus, the product requirements in ORM are translated to heavyweight ontologies with axiomatic rules that are submitted to the semantic reconciliation view and matched in application domain view.

4 Case Study: Preliminary Results

An experimental system has been designed and performed to validate the Interoperable Product Design and Manufacturing System (IPDMS) model-driven approach and a rotational product was chosen to explore it. The product is a polystyrene cup with thermal conservation properties, as illustrated at the left side of Fig. 5. The figure also presents a simple demonstration of the IPDMS concept, supporting the information sharing from product concept design phase to product tooling design phase.

This test case explores the material and dimension information sharing to reduce the problems with product shrinkage, which is inherent in the injection moulding process. Shrinkage occurs because the density of polymer varies from the processing temperature to the ambient temperature. According to [31], during the injection moulding, the variation in shrinkage creates internal stress. If the internal stress are high enough to overcome the structural integrity of the product, the product are going to wrap upon ejection from the mould or crack with external load during the extraction. Therefore, during the conception design and tooling design phases is necessary to share and transform information of the material properties and dimensions. This is a semantic obstacle because the meaning information found in the product concept must be effectively shared to product tooling design.

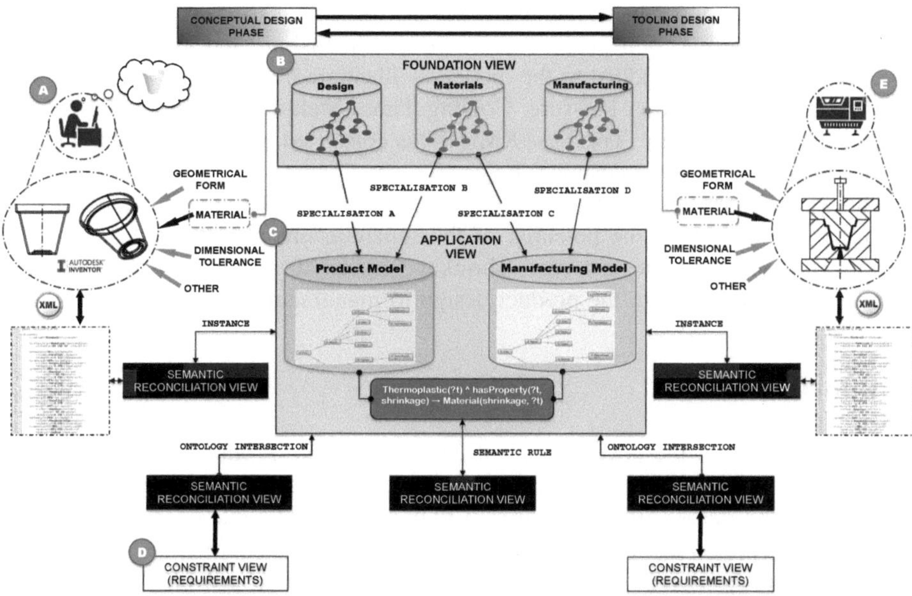

Fig. 5. IPDMS experimental demonstration system.

The IPDMS experimental demonstration is illustrates in Fig. 5. The product dimensions and geometry are extracted from the product modelled in CAD (Computer Aided Design) and structured in a XML file as illustrated on detail A of Fig. 5. The XML file has the context alignment in the Semantic Reconciliation View that identifies the main concepts and search in the foundation view the core ontologies, detail B of Fig. 5, related to the information extracted from the CAD. In this test case, the ontologies specialized in the product model are material core ontology and design core ontology and the ontologies specialized in the manufacturing model are material core ontology and manufacturing core ontology. The core ontologies identified in the foundation view are specialized in the Product Model and in the Manufacturing Model of the Application View, as shown on detail C of Fig. 5 and instantiated with the specific information extracted from the CAD model.

Additionally Requirements, Specifications and Technological Constraints are added to the models through the constraint view, detail D of Fig. 5, such as: Material Name, Maximum Temperature, Liquid Type, Injection Process Type, etc. These new information are semantically reconciled and intersections occur between the constraint ontology and specialized ontologies. Thus, new semantic rules are established between the both ontologies through the SWRL (Semantic Web Rule Language) and shrinkage properties are embedded in the models. Moreover, concept mapping are established between the Product Model Ontology and Manufacturing Ontology Model as well as Semantic Rules in SWRL.

According to the set of formal information and rules defined in the specialized ontologies in product and manufacturing model, a new xml file is created and is responsible for the product tooling design, as show on detail E of Fig. 5. Part of the product tooling design can be automatically performed, respecting the rules of the shrinkage process, injection process and product dimensions and tolerance. Furthermore, constraints can be added to the model, as illustrated on Detail F of Fig. 5, such as: Machine type, Injection Pressure, Cooling Time, Melt Temperature, Mould Temperature, Holding Pressure. This new XML file is converted to a CAD file and the new 3D model with the tooling design is built.

This preliminary test case shows the performance of the IPDMS concept. The preliminary results show the potential of the semantic interoperability to reduce the semantic obstacles. In the test case, shrinkage issues were solved by a structured information exchange from the product design to manufacturing.

5 Conclusion

This paper presented the development of an Interoperable Product Design and Manufacturing System (IPDMS) concept that are able to exchange information from multiple domains across different phases of PDP in a semantic interoperability manner. The IPDMS supports the product developers, providing structured and formal information as well as transforming automatically information based on the knowledge added to the system.

The IPDMS concept uses a semantically well-defined core concepts and constraints, modelling in ontologies, to instantiate the information in the application view and constraint by semantic rules. The concept architecture has four different views: (i) Foundation View, (ii) Application View, (iii) Reconciliation View and Constraint View. The Foundation View has core concepts relating to PDP, such as: material core, design core, manufacturing core, dimensional tolerance, geometry tolerance, etc. The concept core is modelled in OWL language with semantic rules in SWRL. The core concepts are specialized in Application View in Product Model and Manufacturing Model and enriched with the detailed information of the product that is being developed. More information can be added to this model by the constraints view and all information are semantically reconciled and interrelated through the semantic reconciliation view.

This concept was evaluated in a preliminary test case. The product is a polystyrene cup with thermal conservation properties. In the evaluation process the concept potential to support the information sharing between the conceptual designs and tooling design to avoid the shrinkage issues was analysed. The 3D model information was extracted and submitted to the IPDMS concept. More information was added through the constraints view. In the IPDMS, instances, context alignment, ontologies intersection and mapping concepts were established to create a product and manufacturing ontology model specialized with semantic rules to design the product tooling. The results demonstrate the potential of this concept to reduce the semantic obstacles during the information sharing across the PDP. To extend this research work it is necessary to explore more variables simultaneously and more phases of the PDP in order to analyse the potential of this concept in working and sharing information from multiple domains across different phases of PDP.

Acknowledgments. The authors would like to thank the Coordination of Improvement of Higher Education Personal – CAPES, under Science without Borders Program (Special Visiting Researcher) - Project 178/2012 and Pontifical Catholic University of Parana (PUCPR) for the financial support.

References

1. Pahl, G., Beitz, W.: Engineering Design: A Systematic Approach. Springer, Darmstadt (1996). 617 p
2. Rozenfeld, H., Forcellini, F.A., Amaral, D.C., Toledo, J.C., Silva, S.L., Alliprandini, D.H., Scalice, R.K.: Gestão de desenvolvimento de produtos: uma referência para a melhoria do processo. Saraiva, São Paulo (2006). 560 p
3. Szejka, A.L., Aubry, A., Panetto, H., Canciglieri Jr., O., Loures, E.R.: Towards a conceptual framework for requirements interoperability in complex systems engineering. In: Meersman, R., et al. (eds.) OTM 2014. LNCS, vol. 8842, pp. 229–240. Springer, Heidelberg (2014). doi:10.1007/978-3-662-45550-0_24
4. Szejka, A.L., Canciglieri Jr., O., Loures, E.R., Panetto, H., Aubry, A.: Requirements interoperability method to support integrated product development. In: 45th Computers and Industrial Engineering, vol. 147, pp. 1–8. Metz (2015)
5. Brunnermeier, S.B., Martin, S.A.: Interoperability costs in US automotive supply chain. Supply Chain Manag. Int. J. **7**(2), 71–82 (2002)
6. Barbau, R., Krima, S., Rachuri, S., Narayanan, A., Fiorentini, X., Foufou, S., Sriram, R.D.: OntoSTEP: enriching product model data using ontologies. Comput. Aided Des. **44**(6), 575–590 (2012)
7. Danjou, C., Le Duigou, J., Eynard, B.: Closed-loop manufacturing, a STEP-NC process for data feedback: a case study. In: Proceedings of the 48th CIRP Conference on Manufacturing Systems, Tokyo, vol. 41, pp. 852–857. Elsevier, Amsterdam (2016)
8. Demoly, F., Matsokis, A., Kiritsis, D., Gomes, S.: Mereotopological description of product-process information and knowledge for PLM. In: Rivest, L., Bouras, A., Louhichi, B. (eds.) PLM 2012. IAICT, vol. 388, pp. 70–84. Springer, Heidelberg (2012). doi:10.1007/978-3-642-35758-9_7
9. Liao, Y., Lezoche, M., Panetto, H., Boudjlida, N., Loures, E.R.: Semantic annotation for knowledge explicitation in a product lifecycle management context: a survey. Comput. Ind. **71**, 24–34 (2015)
10. BKCASE Editorial Board: The Guide to the Systems Engineering Body of Knowledge (SEBoK), v. 1.6. R.D. Adcock (EIC). The Trustees of the Stevens Institute of Technology, Hoboken, NJ. www.sebokwiki.org. Accessed 28 Mar 2016
11. Hameed, A., Preece, A., Sleeman, D.: Ontology reconciliation. In: Staab, S., Studer, R. (eds.) Handbook on Ontologies, pp. 231–250. Springer, Heidelberg (2004)
12. Penciuc, D., Durupt, A., Belkadi, F., Eynard, B., Rowson, H.: Towards a PLM interoperability for a collaborative design support system. Procedia CIRP **25**, 369–376 (2014)
13. Chungoora, N., Young, R.I.M., Gunendran, G., Palmer, C., Usman, Z., Anjum, N.A., Cutting-Decelle, A.-F., Harding, J.A., Case, K.: A model-driven ontology approach for manufacturing system interoperability and knowledge sharing. Comput. Ind. **64**(4), 392–401 (2013)
14. Canciglieri Jr., O., Young, R.I.M.: Information mapping across injection moulding design and manufacture domains. Int. J. Prod. Res. **48**(15), 4437–4462 (2010)

15. Yang, A., et al.: A multi-agent system to facilitate component-based process modeling and design. Comput. Chem. Eng. **32**(10), 2290–2305 (2008)
16. Noy, N.F., Rubin, D.L.: Translating the foundational model of anatomy into OWL. Web Semant. **6**(2), 133–136 (2008)
17. Gruber, T.R.: A translation approach to portable ontology specification. Knowl. Acquisition **5**(2), 199–220 (1993)
18. ISO (International Organization for Standardization). ISO 18629:2005: Industrial automation systems and integration - Process Specification Language (PSL), Geneva, CH (2005)
19. Gómez-Pérez, A., Fernández-López, M., Corcho, O.: Ontological Engineering: With Examples from the Areas of Knowledge Management, e-Commerce and the Semantic Web. Springer, London (2004)
20. Nagahanumaiah, K.S., Ravi, B.: Computer aided rapid tooling process selection and manufacturability evaluation for injection mold development. Comput. Ind. **59**(2/3), 262–276 (2008)
21. Kalfoglou, Y., Schorlemmer, M.: Ontology mapping: the state of the art. Knowl. Eng. Rev. **18**(1), 1–31 (2003)
22. Ehrig, M., Sure, Y.: Ontology mapping – an integrated approach. In: Bussler, C.J., Davies, J., Fensel, D., Studer, R. (eds.) ESWS 2004. LNCS, vol. 3053, pp. 76–91. Springer, Heidelberg (2004). doi:10.1007/978-3-540-25956-5_6
23. IEEE Standard Computer Dictionary: A Compilation of IEEE Standard Computer Glossaries. Institute of Electrical and Electronics Engineers (1990)
24. Web Ontology Language (OWL). http://www.w3.org/TR/owl-features/. Accessed 02 Apr 2016
25. SWRL - A Semantic Web Rule Language Combining OWL and RuleML. http://www.w3.org/Submission/SWRL/. Accessed 02 Apr 2016
26. Stumme, G., Maedche, A.: Ontology merging for federated ontologies on the semantic web. In: Proceedings of the International Workshop for Foundations of Models for Information Integration, pp. 413–418, Viterbo (2001)
27. Euzenat, J., Shvaiko, P.: Ontology Matching. Springer, London (2007)
28. ISO (International Organization for Standardization)/IEC (International Electrotechnical Commission). ISO/IEC 15288:2008: Systems and Software Engineering – System life Cycle Processes. Geneva, CH (2008)
29. Halpin, T.: Object-role modeling (ORM/NIAM). In: Bernus, P., Mertins, K., Schmidt, G. (eds.) International Handbooks on Information Systems, pp. 81–103. Springer, Berlin (2006)
30. Pan, W., Liu, D.: Mapping object role modeling into common logic interchange format. In: 3rd International Conference on Advanced Computer Theory and Engineering (ICACTE), vol. 2, pp. 104–109 (2010)
31. Mohan, M., Ansari, M.N.M., Shanks, R.A.: Review on the Effects of Process Parameters on Strength, Shrinkage, and Warpage of Injection Molding Plastic Component. Polymer-Plastics Technology and Engineering (just-accepted) (2006)

Lean Product Development and the Role of PLM

A Modular Approach for Lean Product Development (LPD) Based on System Engineering

Dao Yin(✉) and Xinguo Ming

Shanghai Institute of Producer Service Development,
Shanghai Research Center for Industrial Informatics,
Shanghai Key Lab of Advanced Manufacturing Environment,
Institute of Computer Integrated Manufacturing,
School of Mechanical Engineering, Shanghai Jiao Tong University,
800 Dong Chuan Road, Minhang District, Shanghai City,
People's Republic of China
yindao0909@126.com

Abstract. Metallurgical equipment belongs to the discrete manufacturing industry, in which large-scale equipment is common, and has feature of high level of customization, large variety, single and small batch. Under the model of design to order, R&D staff have to modify or redesign according to each order, leading to longer product development cycle and higher cost. This paper presents w-model of system engineering framework to solve the R&D cross sectoral collaborative problem. Top-down functional decomposition integrated with bottom-up component clustering is suggested by the author to form module for design knowledge reuse. In the end, this paper takes an illustrative example of lean metallurgical equipment development to demonstrate the feasibility and technical advantage of the approach.

Keywords: Lean product development · Product development value stream mapping · System engineering · Modular approach · Metallurgical equipment development

1 Introduction

Nowadays, the discrete manufacturing industry in China are facing product development problem, such as unclear R&D target, unclear personnel responsibility, unreasonable project planning, poor collaborative ability and so on. On the other hand, it is difficult to identify customer requirement which is more than ever and changes rapidly. Engineers have to design components with similar functions repeatedly. As a result, it calls for modular approach to eliminate unnecessary waste and reuse design knowledge. The poor cross-department collaboration and the lack of closed-loop feedback make it ineffective to meet customer needs. So it is necessary to consider the whole lifecycle of product development process in the view of system engineering [1].

Product development value stream mapping is a tool for process improvement, offering a visual way for people to observe the waste in the process more easily. The

R. Harik et al. (Eds.): PLM 2016, IFIP AICT 492, pp. 171–182, 2016.
DOI: 10.1007/978-3-319-54660-5_16

data, inventory state and other information in the information flow help to visualize the current state of the process and provide basic data for determining improvement goals [2].

Value stream mapping is the first step for lean product development. It helps to analyze the problem existing in product development and identify waste, working as a reference for development process reengineering implementation plan. Then the system engineering method helps to consider the relationship between different phases at each level, like design, manufacturing, assembly and maintenance. Modular approach is based on system engineering, because both modular decomposition and component clustering are related to levels. The aim of modular approach based on system engineering is to improve product development process and make the process lean [3].

2 Status Review for Lean Product Development (LPD)

Most scholars use concurrent engineering, Stage-Gate, IDEF models, ASME method, Fig role, Petri nets and other methods of production in the field of business process reengineering, only a few scholars have used value stream mapping method. Junfen [4] compared four kinds of methods. Based on her results, the author add value streaming mapping into the comparison. The scale is defined by four levels (poor, normal, good and excellent). For example, value stream mapping is easier for understanding than other method, we define the comprehensibility "excellent". So the comparison of approaches for LPD process reengineering is shown as the table below (Table 1).

Table 1. Comparison of approaches for Lean Product Development process reengineering

Attributes		Modeling method				
		Flowchart	Role behavior diagram	IDEF0	Petri net	Value stream mapping
Formalization	Comprehensibility	Good	Normal	Normal	Normal	Excellent
	Graphical representation	Good	Good	Good	Good	Good
	Computerization	Good	Normal	Normal	Normal	Normal
Completeness	Abstract mechanism	None	None	Exist	Exist	Exist
	Semantic rule	Poor	Poor	Exist	Exist	Exist
	Event trigger mechanism	Exist	None	None	Exist	Exist
Expression	Organization	none	Exist	Exist	Not good	Exist
	Function	Exist	Exist	Exist	Exist	Exist
	Data	Exist	None	None	None	Exist
	People	None	Exist	Exist	None	Exist
Extension	Cross functional process modeling	Support	No	Normal	Poor	Support
	Process simulation support	Not	Not	Not	Support	Support
	Dynamic modeling support	Not	Not	Not	Support	Support
	Assistant tool	Exist	None	Exist	None	None
	Business process reengineering support	Normal	Normal	Normal	Normal	Support

By comparison, Value Stream Mapping method can be seen in the superiority of the degree of formalization, completeness, modeling skills, model extension and other aspects. So in this paper, it is chosen for lean product development business process modeling analysis.

3 A System Engineering-Based Framework for LPD

3.1 Traditional V-Model of System Engineering

The pillars of traditional V-model of system engineering include systems thinking, concurrent engineering, teamwork, target-driven design, reusability, reliability, package and vehicle attribute focus. Figure 1 depicts the system using a diagram shaped like a “V”. As the requirements are cascaded, system, sub-system and component level requirements are defined. Once the final plan is established, the design and development of the vehicle is continued and verified up the right side of the “V” until the product is ready for launch [1]. But V-model of system engineering does not emphasize the point of product lifecycle. So that is why the author propose the concept of W-model of system engineering.

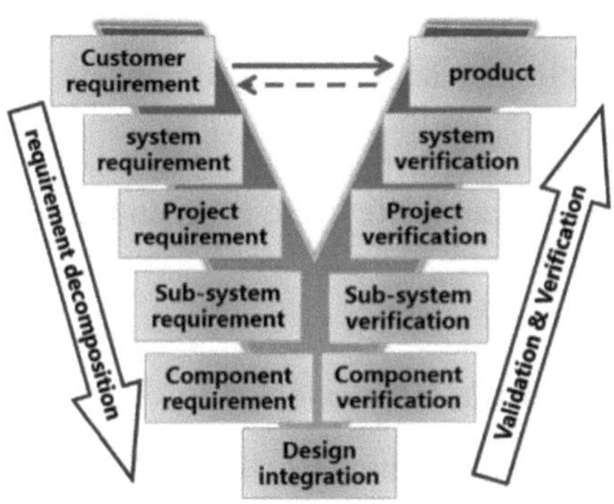

Fig. 1. V-model of system engineering

3.2 A New W-Model of System Engineering

The idea of W-model of system engineering is derived from the concept of DFX (Design for different requirements) and V-model of system engineering. From the top to the bottom, it is followed by the system level, subsystem level, component level and part level. From the left to the right, it is followed by the design phase, the manufacturing phase, assembly phase and maintenance phase (Fig. 2).

3.3 W-Model of System Engineering for LPD

On one hand, W-model of system engineering uses a cascade of targets through the vehicle. Along the cascade, system, sub-system, part, component level requirements are

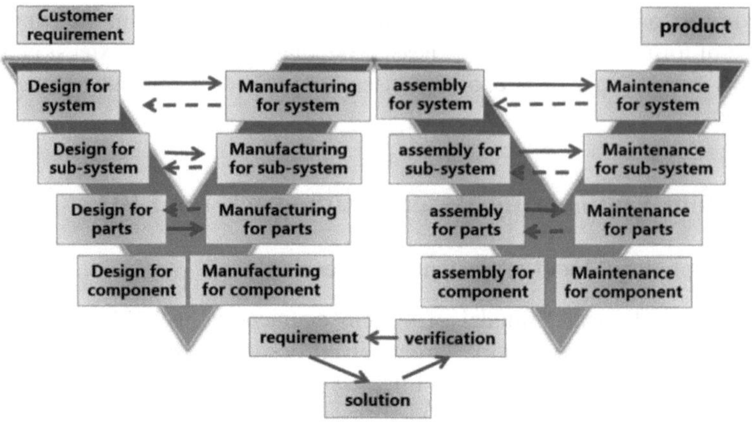

Fig. 2. W-model of system engineering

defined. On the other hand, W-model of system engineering uses the term "Design for X" to link customer requirements and quality criteria such as robustness, serviceability and others [5].

The purpose of DFM (Design for Manufacturing) is to minimize the overall component count and to optimize the remaining components so that the manufacturing costs to be reduced. DFA (Design for Assembly) focuses on the optimization of how product components can be moved, held, located and joint [6]. DFMA (Design for Maintenance) aims to lower overall life cycle costs and a product design that is optimized to its support processes.

3.4 Feasibility Analysis of the Framework

W-model of system engineering combine product lifecycle with system level form horizontal and vertical aspects. During the design phase, the designers need to consider the criteria and rules of manufacturing, assembly and maintenance, they will look some components as a module, which will help to reduce the number of components, simplify the process of assembly and improve the quality of repairing accordingly.

4 Modular Approach for Improvement in Lean Product Development

DFX is to minimize the overall component number, modular approach can reduce the number of components. Each level of W-model of system engineering calls for modular approach. And modular approach for different phases has different advantage. It can reduce design complexity for design, reduce manufacturing costs for manufacturing phase, improve the relative movement between one part and another for assembly and improve product maintainability for maintenance.

4.1 Module Decomposition

Module decomposition is determined by the requirement, principles, function, performance, structure, precision machining, assembly, cost, supply chain and other factors. Figure 3 shows module decomposition in accordance with function. Finally, module can be divided into five kinds, fundamental module, special module, auxiliary module, adaptive module and customized module. In this paper, functional decomposition and component clustering are integrated. Functional decomposition suits for conceptual design phase, while component clustering is mainly applied for engineering change phase.

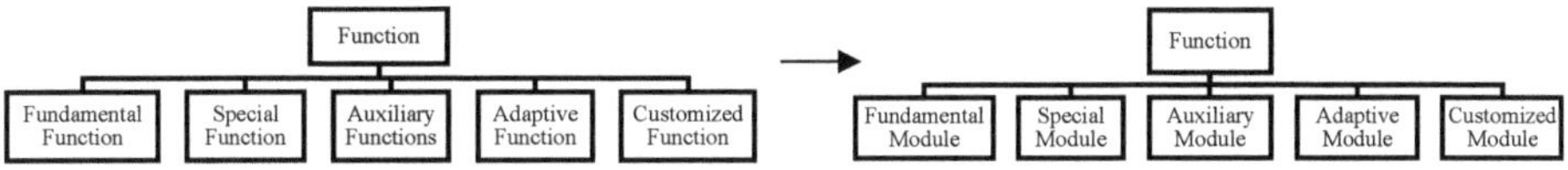

Fig. 3. The relationship between function decomposition and function module

4.2 Module Clustering

Module decomposition is top-down method, on the contrary, module clustering is bottom-up approach. Clustering analysis is based on the correlation of parts and components. The steps of clustering are shown in Fig. 4.

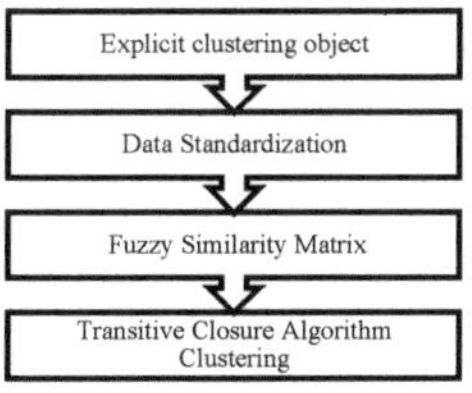

Fig. 4. Steps of fuzzy clustering analysis

Step 1 is to explicit clustering object. Imagine that the number of component is n, each component has m kinds of features. Finally, we get a n $\times$ m matrix.

$$X = \begin{bmatrix} x_{11} & x_{12} & \cdots & x_{1m} \\ x_{21} & x_{22} & \cdots & x_{2m} \\ \vdots & \vdots & \cdots & \vdots \\ x_{n1} & x_{n2} & \cdots & x_{nm} \end{bmatrix} \quad (1)$$

Step 2 is to standardize the data to avoid a large magnitude indicators highlight the neglect of magnitude smaller index. Each index is transferred into interval $[-1, 1]$.

$$x'_{ik} = \frac{x_{ik} - \frac{1}{n}\sum_{i=1}^{n} x_{ik}}{\sqrt{\frac{1}{n-1}\sum_{i=1}^{n}\left(x_{ik} - \frac{1}{n}\sum_{i=1}^{n} x_{ik}\right)^2}} (\mathrm{i} = 1, 2, \ldots, \mathrm{n}; \mathrm{k} = 1, 2, \ldots, \mathrm{m}) \tag{2}$$

$A = \min\{x'_{ik}\}$, $B = \max\{x'_{ik}\}$,

$$\mathrm{y}_{ik} = \frac{x'_{ik} - A}{B - A},\ 0 \leq \mathrm{y}_{ik} \leq 1 \tag{3}$$

Step 3 is to build up fuzzy similarity matrix $\tilde{R}$. $Y = [y_{ik}]_{n \times m}$, r_{ij} means the degree of similarity between y_i and y_j.

$$\tilde{R} = \begin{bmatrix} r_{11} & r_{12} & \cdots & r_{1n} \\ r_{21} & r_{22} & \cdots & r_{2n} \\ \vdots & \vdots & & \vdots \\ r_{n1} & r_{n2} & \cdots & r_{nm} \end{bmatrix} \tag{4}$$

Step 4 is to get the clustering result by using transitive closure algorithm clustering. According to transitive closure algorithm, there is min k to make $\tilde{R}^k$ a fuzzy equivalent matrix.

$$\mathrm{t}\left(\tilde{R}\right) = \tilde{R}^k = \underbrace{\tilde{R} \circ \tilde{R} \circ \cdots \circ \tilde{R}}_{k} \quad (\text{“}\circ\text{” means} (\wedge, \vee)) \tag{5}$$

4.3 Module Generation

The bigger the confidence level λ (λ is between 0 and 1) is, the bigger number of module and more sort of module, which is good for product modification. But this does harm to assembly. So, after the generation of module, there comes a multi-objective optimization model [7]. The constraints are design complexity A_D^Y, ease of manufacture A_F^Y, assembly complexity A_A^Y and ease of maintenance A_M^Y. Module size is defined as $\mathrm{a} = \frac{1}{\lambda}$. The bigger the size is, the smaller the number of module is.

$$A_D^Y = -\frac{1}{\mathrm{k}_a}\sum_{i=1}^{n} [d_i \ln d_i + (1 - d_i)\, ln(1 - d_i)] \tag{6}$$

K_{a} means module number corresponding with module size “a”. di stands for degree of certainty of the function i in design phase.

$$A_F^Y = -\frac{1}{\mathrm{k}_a}\sum_{i=1}^{n}\left[f_i \ln f_i + (1-f_i)\, ln(1-f_i)\right] \tag{7}$$

f_i stands for degree of certainty of the function i in manufacturing phase.

$$A_A^Y = -\frac{1}{\mathrm{a}}\sum_{j=1}^{k_a}\frac{n_t(j)}{n}\ln\frac{n_t(j)}{n} \tag{8}$$

n_t (j) stands for the number of function module of module j.

$$A_M^Y = -\frac{1}{\mathrm{k}_a}\sum_{i=1}^{n}\left[\eta_i \ln \eta_i + (1-\eta_i)\, ln(1-\eta_i)\right] \tag{9}$$

η_i stands for failure rate of module i. Finally, module clustering optimum solution depends on $B(Y)$

$$B(Y) = \min\{\tilde{A}_D^Y + \tilde{A}_F^Y + \tilde{A}_A^Y + \tilde{A}_M^Y\} \tag{10}$$

$$\tilde{A}_D^Y = \frac{A_D^Y}{\sum_{i=1}^{N} A_D^Y}, \tilde{A}_F^Y = \frac{A_F^Y}{\sum_{i=1}^{N} A_F^Y}, \tilde{A}_A^Y = \frac{A_A^Y}{\sum_{i=1}^{N} A_A^Y}, \tilde{A}_M^Y = \frac{A_M^Y}{\sum_{i=1}^{N} A_M^Y} \tag{11}$$

4.4 Technical Advantage of Modular Approach

Top-down module decomposition and bottom-up module clustering work together to avoid designing repeatedly, reduce waiting time, improve R&D efficiency and eliminate waste in product development. The multi-objective optimization process of module generation can avoid the impact of a single factor and improve the accuracy of the clustering results.

5 Illustrative Example of Lean Metallurgical Equipment Development

5.1 Current State of VSM for Metallurgical Equipment Development

Aluminum electrolytic multifunction machine is the key equipment for large-scale pre-baked anode aluminum electrolysis production. It can replace manual operations to complete the process of electrolytic crust, replacing the anode, the anode pit cleaning, feeding, and metering of aluminum, anode bus adapter, cell repair, lifting and other operations.

Pot tending machine consists of cart, tool cart, trolley car, hydraulic system, pneumatic system and electric control system. The product development can be divided into two parts from the aspect of structure, one is mechanical part and the other is electrical part. The product development process is shown in Fig. 5.

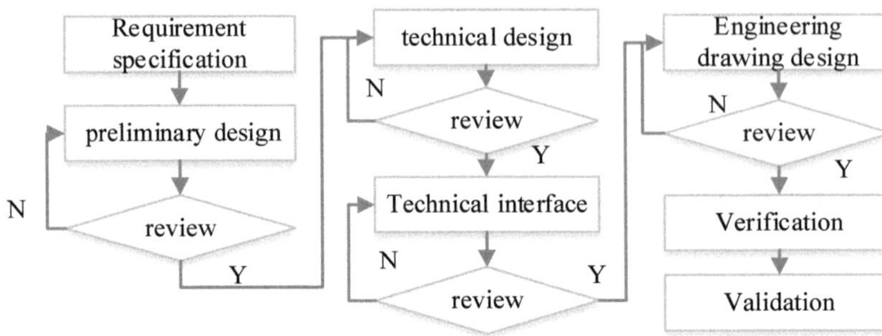

Fig. 5. The product development process of pot tending machine

Based on the product development process, with data and information being gathered, including process time, waiting time and talk time, the current state of value stream mapping of product development process of pot tending machine comes out as shown in Fig. 6 [8–11].

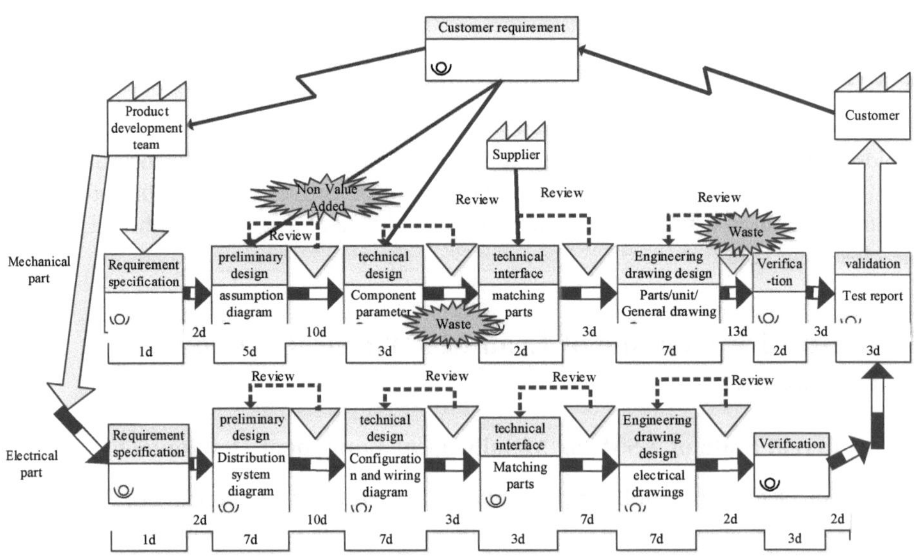

Fig. 6. The current state of value stream mapping of product development process of pot tending machine

5.2 Root Cause Analysis for Metallurgical Equipment Development

Figure 7 depicts eight kinds of waste in product development, including waiting, over process, over production, information defect, transmission, knowledge lost, moving and inventory. The cause of waste was analyzed via fishbone diagram. The root cause is the lack of systematic modular design methods, leading the product development target to be unclear, project planning unreasonable.

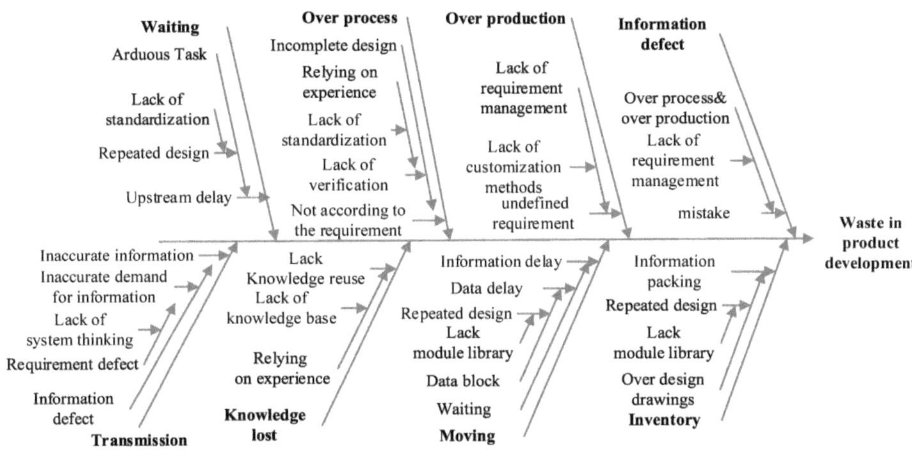

Fig. 7. Fishbone diagram of root cause analysis in product development waste

5.3 Improvements for Metallurgical Equipment Development

Crust breaker is an example of W-model of system engineering applied to improve the development. Crust breaker needs to ensure a certain angle, in order to make the fight against the hammer to hit the seam position. So oblique cylinder mounting and position should be considered in design phase. Further more, the influence of hydraulic cylinder piston rod length change in manufacturing phase, the interference of cylinder installation position after adjusting for connecting racks in assembly phase, the hammer blow strength and maintenance programs in maintenance phase should also be traded off in design phase. From the system engineering point of view, modular division of crust breaker is shown as below (Fig. 8).

As for modular approach, take tool cart as an example. The principle of function decomposition of tool cart module is similar to that of crust breaker depicted above. When engineering change occurs, modular clustering plays an important role. The Tool cart running device main components bill of material is shown in Table 2 as below.

According to Eqs. (1), (2), (3) and (4), components fuzzy matrix $\tilde{R}_{10\times 10}$ is shown in Table 3.

According to Eqs. (5)–(11), the clustering result is shown in Table 4.

From Table 4, the minimum value of B(Y) is 0.2023, so solution 2 is the optimum solution. The module generation result is four groups.

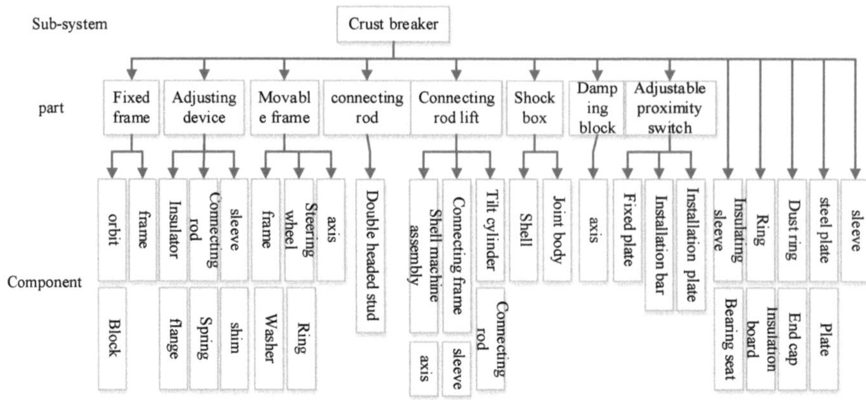

Fig. 8. Crust breaker modular hierarchy

Table 2. Tool cart running device main components bill of material

No.	Name	No.	Name	No.	Name
1	Active wheel group	5	Track brush	9	Ground wheel device
2	End beamI	6	End beamII	10	Beam
3	Driven wheel group	7	Upper horizontal wheel		
4	Track brush holder	8	Ground wheel bracket		

Table 3. Components fuzzy matrix table

	1	2	3	4	5	6	7	8	9	10
1	1	0.112	0.914	0.106	0.206	0.11	0.563	0.105	0.211	0.132
2	0.112	1	0.115	0.324	0.216	0.923	0.104	0.413	0.363	0.863
3	0.914	0.115	1	0.113	0.504	0.123	0.602	0.126	0.221	0.241
4	0.106	0.324	0.113	1	0.679	0.245	0.263	0.789	0.563	0.421
5	0.206	0.216	0.504	0.679	1	0.382	0.253	0.452	0.327	0.124
6	0.11	0.923	0.123	0.245	0.382	1	0.127	0.436	0.365	0.843
7	0.563	0.104	0.602	0.263	0.253	0.127	1	0.114	0.108	0.254
8	0.105	0.413	0.126	0.789	0.452	0.436	0.114	1	0.857	0.321
9	0.211	0.363	0.321	0.563	0.327	0.365	0.108	0.857	1	0.131
10	0.132	0.863	0.221	0.421	0.124	0.843	0.254	0.321	0.131	1

5.4 Future State of VSM for Metallurgical Equipment Development

Figure 6 shows where the waste and non-value added lie in. Then the root cause analysis in product development waste helps us find the key factors. By using W-model of system engineering framework for LPD and modular approach for improvement in Lean Product Development, the waste is reduce to a degree, as shown in Fig. 9.

Table 4. Clustering result

Solution	λ	Group division	Size	$B(Y)$
1	0.7	{1,3},{2,6,10},{8,9},4,5,7	6	0.2137
2	0.5	{1,3,7},{2,6,10},{4,5},{8,9}	4	0.2023
3	0.3	{1,3,7},{2,4,5,6,8,9,10}	2	0.2216

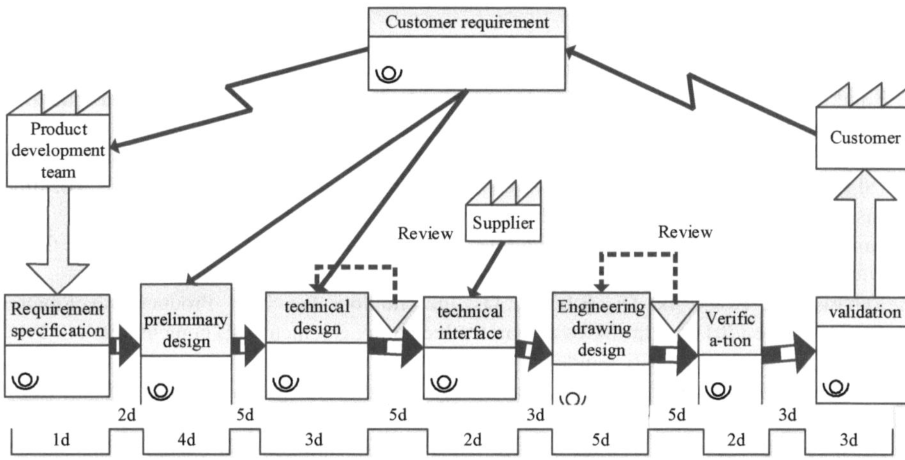

Fig. 9. The future state of value stream mapping of product development process of pot tending machine

5.5 Potential Industrial Benefits

W-model of system engineering can solve the problem about cross sectoral collaboration and shorten the waiting time in a rate of 29.5%.

Modular method based on top-down functional decomposition and the bottom-up modular clustering can improve the reusability of components and reduce development cost in a rate of 2%.

6 Conclusion and Future Perspectives

Product development is the lifeline of the development of an enterprise. Design process is not just the business of the R&D department personnel, but should be the enterprise participation. Waste should be eliminated in order to respond to customer needs rapidly, improve the design efficiency and save the cost of R&D. By describing the current status of development process, drawing the corresponding current value flow chart, the waste and non-value added links in the process are identified. W-model emphasizes the coordination of design, manufacturing, assembly and maintenance. Modular approach introduces the process of module partition, module clustering and module generation. The future perspectives are as below, Specific quantitative relationship between the levels of system, sub-system, component and parts needs deeper research. Modular configuration and product configuration are worth studying in the future, including configuration rules, configuration approach, configuration model and configuration processes.

References

1. Garza, L.A.: Integrating lean principles in automotive product development: breaking down barriers in culture and process. Master thesis, Massachusetts Institute of Technology (2005)
2. Tandon, S.: Process reengineering for the product development process at an analytical instrument manufacturer. Master thesis, Massachusetts Institute of Technology (2014)
3. Ansari, U.A.: Application of LEAN and BPR principles for software process improvement (SPI): a case study of a large software development organization. Master thesis, Blekinge Institute of Technology, Sweden (2014)
4. Junfen, Y.: Research on BPR modeling method and application. Master thesis, Ocean University of China (2009)
5. Zaharis, N., Kourtesis, D., Bibikas, D., Inzesiloglou, G.: New Product Development (NPD) Guide (2011). http://www.researchvalue.net/ipagreements/wp-content/uploads/2011/04/Binder_INTERVALUE_Guide.pdf
6. Eskilander, S.: Design for automatic assembly-a method for product design: DFA2. Kungl Tekniska Hogskolan (2011)
7. Meng, Z.: Research on key technologies in modular configuration design of mechanical products based on product family. Ph.D. thesis, National University of Defense Technology, China (2013)
8. GöRansson, G.: Value stream mapping in product development - adapting value stream mapping at Ascom wireless solutions. Master thesis, Chalmers University of Technology (2012)
9. Ranjan, A.: Process reengineering for new product introduction at an analytical instrument manufacturing firm. Master thesis, Massachusetts Institute of Technology (2014)
10. Tyagi, S., Choudhary, A., Cai, X., et al.: Value stream mapping to reduce the lead-time of a product development process. Int. J. Prod. Econ. **160**, 202–211 (2015)
11. Schwarck, A.M.H.: Improving the productivity of an R&D organization. Master thesis, Massachusetts Institute of Technology (2013)

Lean Product Development and the Role of PLM

Monica Rossi[1(✉)], Laura Cattaneo[1], Julien Le Duigou[2], Stéphane Fugier-Garrel[3], Sergio Terzi[1], and Benoît Eynard[2]

[1] Department of Management, Economics and Industrial Engineering, Politecnico di Milano, Piazza Leonardo da Vinci, 20133 Milan, Italy
{monica.rossi,laural.cattaneo,sergio.terzi}@polimi.it
[2] Department of Mechanical Systems Engineering, UMR CNRS 7337 Roberval, Sorbonne Universités, Université de Technologie de Compiègne, CS 60319, 60203 Compiègne Cedex, France
{julien.le-duigou,benoit.eynard}@utc.fr
[3] KLManagement, 30 rue Vincent Moris, 92240 Malakoff, France
sfugier-garrel@klmanagement.fr

Abstract. Lean Product Development (LPD) promises high product development success by strongly relying on knowledge. Though, despite many IT-based knowledge management tools exist to support and enable knowledge capture, use, formalization and reuse in product development, such as Product Lifecycle Management (PLM) systems, their use within the LPD context is either low or not discussed. This research aims at starting a debate on the role such technologies could have in LPD applications and product development success. The study involves two independent empirical research initiatives, one in France and one in Italy, and launches a discussion on the role of PLM in *customer value definition* in LPD initiatives.

Keywords: Lean Product Development · Product Lifecycle Management · Value definition · Industrial survey · Open questions

1 Introduction

Traditional product development experiences many problems such as mismanagement of tasks and activities, resources overload, frequent reworks and delays [1, 2]. Lean product development (LPD) proposes a consistent change in the traditional product development paradigm to entail such criticalities and today it is widely acknowledged that LPD represents one of the most critical and challenging area in the lean management field, affecting the success of the whole enterprise [3–7]. One of the main challenges comes from the nature of product development. While manufacturing deals with physical products, product development deals with untouchable flow of data, information and knowledge and this makes the development process uncertain, complex, and unpredictable [6, 7]. Moreover, work in progress in product development is mainly constituted of information and data stored in computers. Theoretically, Product Lifecycle Management (PLM) systems - that aim at providing the right data to the right

R. Harik et al. (Eds.): PLM 2016, IFIP AICT 492, pp. 183–192, 2016.
DOI: 10.1007/978-3-319-54660-5_17

person at the right time- have the potentialities to increase efficiency of product development process [8] and to emphasize the LPD intent of promoting effective and efficient knowledge management and learning. Though not many evidences exist yet about the enabling role of PLM to successful LPD applications and this research aims to encourage this debate. Starting from a background overview, the authors give some insights on the current understanding and challenges of both LPD and PLM.

The contribution to the debate comes through different levels. First of all the aim of the research is to understand the current level of diffusion of both LPD and PLM systems within industry. The authors conducted and compared two independent empirical researches run from 2012 to 2015 in Italy and France, involving a total of about 150 enterprises. Also the main challenges faced by companies when developing new products in today's market are mapped. The role of the use of PLM and LPD towards such problems is assessed, too. Finally, preliminary discussion on the role of PLM as enabler of the LPD process outcomes is proposed, that will hopefully stimulates further research, applications and debates.

2 Background

2.1 Lean Product Development

Lean Product Development is about creating value through a process that builds on knowledge and learning, enabled by an integrated system of people, processes, and technology [5–7]. The core of LPD, and its more paradoxical aspect, is the so-called *Second Toyota Paradox* of Set-Based Concurrent Engineering (SBCE) [9, 10]. SBCE bases on its three main principles of *exploration, communication* and *convergence. S*tarting from broad design space and driven by customer value, SBCE evaluates different alternatives that are progressively eliminated as soon as technical information becomes available. Main lessons from SBCE are to delay design decisions as much as possible and rely on proven knowledge, often represented in the form of trade-off curves [7, 10].

The attention posed to the system of people, process and technology [6] guarantees that different enterprise aspects are taken into considerations simultaneously to enable value creation. Visual management, Obeya, cross-functional team, design for-x techniques, people empowerment through training, just some of the several LPD practices that are leading Toyota, and many more, to successful stories. Though, given to the fairly new discipline and the uncertain nature of product development due to the abstraction and complexity of knowledge management and people empowerment, LPD still represents a true challenge for both practitioners and scholars.

2.2 Product Lifecycle Management

PLM is often seen as an extensive and comprehensive concept [11, 12], which defines the integration of different kind of activities that from a technical, organizational and managerial point of view are performed by engineering staff along the entire ideal lifecycle of industrial products, "from cradle to grave" [13].

However, in its practical essence, PLM defines the adoption of several software tools and platforms for supporting innovation and engineering processes [14]. According to the main business analysts, PLM is a leading global market of IT solutions, mainly segmented in two branches: (i) Authoring and Simulation tools and (ii) Collaborative Product Development platforms and environments. The first segment, includes virtual prototyping solutions (from CAD 3D and PDM, to Computational Flow Dynamic, etc.). The second branch develops collaborative functionalities supporting effective file sharing, document vaulting, work flow automation, team management, on distance working, etc. This last branch could help and support the LPD intent of promoting effective and efficient knowledge management and learning [15].

3 The Empirical Research

Two independent researches, both part of bigger research initiatives still running respectively in France and Italy, contribute to this study. Although independently designed, the studies investigate a large number of similar variables (in term of LPD practices, product development problems, and PLM adoption) that contribute to the same research objectives, and could hence be effectively compared, benchmarked and broadly discussed.

3.1 The French Investigation

The French study is the result of collaborative work between a French consultancy company KLManagement (KL), the French university Université de Technologie de Compiègne (UTC) and R&D managers of large French and foreign companies. This study, conducted in 2015, fits into the bigger on-going research within the platform KL-UTC to develop an innovative approach to manage R&D performances.

This specific study is taken via an online questionnaire that involved R&D Directors and CEOs from large groups operating in France and abroad. The surveyed companies come from various sectors, described in Table 1.

Table 1. The French sample

Sector	Number of enterprises
Automotive/aeronautical industry	10
Chemical and pharmaceutical industry	6
Agro-food	2
Business services	1
Others	5

3.2 The Italian Investigation

The Italian study have been conducted under the GeCo Observatory Initiative, a broader study started in 2012 at the School of Management, in Politecnico di Milano, and still on-going. The study considered in this paper analyzes the data collected for about a year across 2012 and 2013, through face-to-face interviews to over 100 companies.

Each interview involved a project manager, a technical director, and/or a team of engineers working in product development. An average of 2.5 h have been spent in each company for each interview, based on a semi-structured questionnaire. The sample in term of companies' size and sector is described in Tables 2 and 3, respectively.

Table 2. The Italian sample: *Size*

Size (number of employees)	N° of companies	Class	N° of companies
Micro (<10)	4	SMEs	38
Small (10 > employees < 50)	13		
Medium (50 > employees < 250)	21		
Big (250 > employees < 1000)	29	LARGE	65
Macro (>1000)	36		

Table 3. The Italian sample: *Sector*

Sector	Mechanics	Electrics	Electronics	Other
N° companies	44	27	18	14

4 Results and Discussion

This research investigates (i) the *problems* encountered in product development; (ii) the adoption of *LPD practices* and *PLM system*; and (iii) their mutual *correlations*. In the specific results are shown for the two separate studies (French and Italian) and then compared and discussed.

4.1 Problems in Product Development

Both researches identified - from literature and from discussions with experts- a list of common problems affecting product development, which could be classified in: *product quality not compliant with customers' expectations, too many and too late reworks, unneeded activities that generate delays, resources overload, management problems* (such as *unclear roles, inflexible resources, lack of resources*), *poor knowledge management,* and *others* (such as *high cost of projects, abandoned projects, loos of technical skills*). Problems are evaluated according to a Liker-type scale, where 1 means the problem never occurs, and 9 means the problem always occurs.

Problems in Product Development:
French Research. The main problem affecting the French sample is in term of *resources overload,* indeed companies declared they *find problems when managing projects without exceeding* or *because using non-planned resources*. Secondly, companies sometimes encounter *delays* problems, since *the Time To Market doesn't meet clients expectations, it is too long*. Also *projects errors/mistakes are reproduced, few lessons learned are undertaken and best practices are not formalized*, and *once defects are known or chronic, employees are not able to find solutions* determine a *poor*

knowledge management. Results on the problems in product development experienced by the French sample are summarized in Fig. 1.

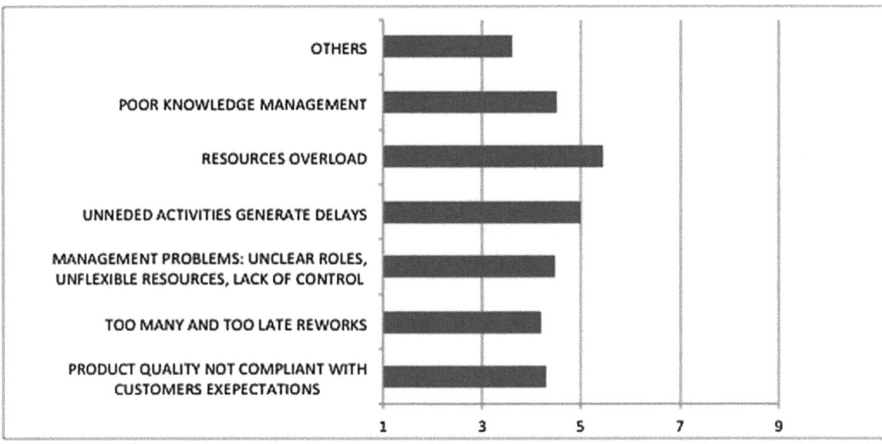

Fig. 1. Problems in product development: the French sample.

Problems in Product Development:
Italian Research. The main product development criticalities encountered in the Italian sample are in terms of *management problems*, happening when *in the development process the responsibilities are not well defined, as a result, the process is chaotic; the projects are very complex to be adequately managed and designers get lost in their activities;* and *the development process involves too many signatures and bureaucracy is a norm*. Secondly the *designers are overloaded and cannot keep up with the overload.* Also *designers often are asked to do many changes during the design process that frequently result in design reworks*. Data are in Fig. 2.

Fig. 2. Problems in product development: the Italian sample.

4.2 LPD Practice and PLM

LPD practices adopted within the companies belonging to the 2 samples and the use of PLM are investigated in this section. LPD Practices includes *design methods* (such as *Design for X, Variety Reduction Program*); *visual management* tools; *SBCE*; *standardization*; *quality function deployment* (*QFD*); *knowledge management methods*; *training and competencies development*; *multifunctionality* and *globalization of the project team*.

LPD Practice and PLM: French Research.
Each LPD practice, as well as PLM, where assessed in the French sample with a Boolean yes/no answer (companies could declare whether they use or not each of the LPD practice and PLM). Figure 3 shows the % of companies adopting the LPD practices and PLM. Most diffused LPD practices, used by more than 50% of companies are *visual planning and management, lean engineering* and *management competences enhancement.* A bit less then 50% of companies adopt PLM system.

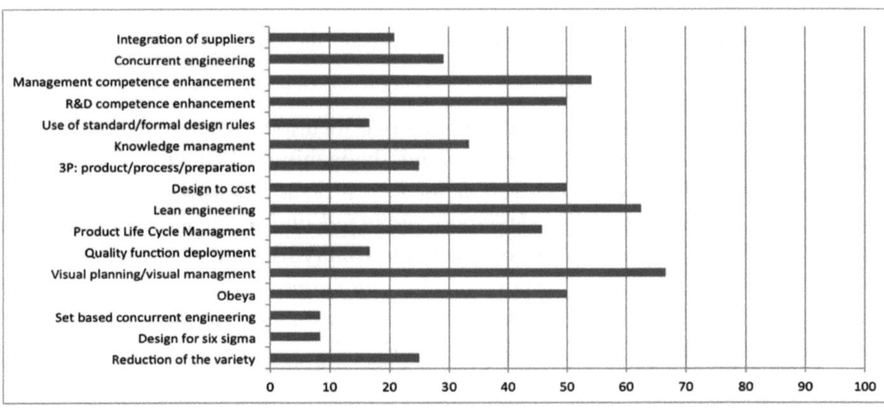

Fig. 3. Adoption of LPD practices and PLM: the French sample.

LPD Practice and PLM: Italian Research.
Within the Italian sample, the use of LPD practices and PLM has been assessed using a Likert-type 5 points scale, where 1 means *the practice is never used*, 9 stands for *always*. Figure 4 displays the diffusion of LPD practices and PLM within the sample. PLM is averagely used (more then 50%), as data and knowledge management system. In term of LPD practises it looks that companies are quite often adopting *SBCE*, in the specific for *evaluating more initial design alternatives*, *defining clear customer value*, and *highly relying on previous knowledge*. Other diffused LPD practices are the *use of standards and design* rules, and *concurrent engineering*.

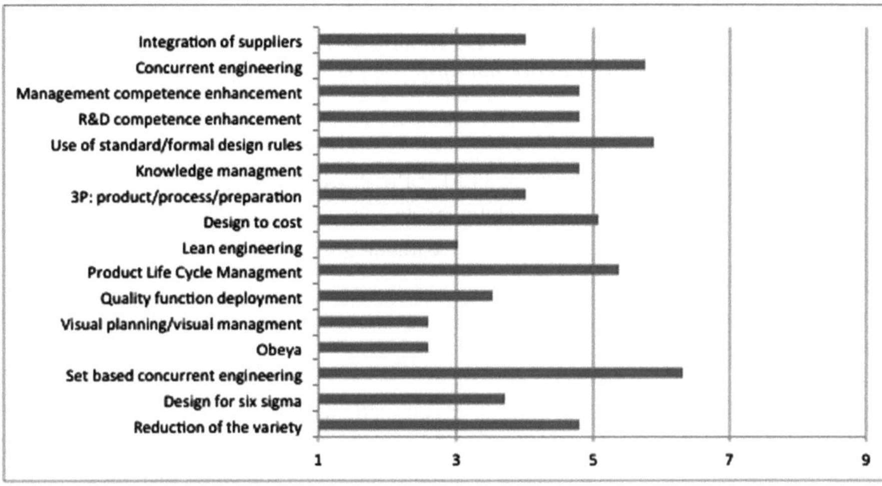

Fig. 4. Adoption of LPD practices and PLM: the Italian sample.

4.3 Correlations Between Problems, LPD Practices, PLM

This section analyses the correlations found between the use of practices (both PLM and LPD practices) and the existence of problems. Also it considers the correlations between the use of PLM and certain LPD practices, to give preliminary understanding on an eventual role of PLM as enabler of product development success (problems are used as a proxy of success) through LPD practices implementation.

Correlations Between Problems, LPD Practices, PLM: French Research.
Only few significant correlations have been found in the French research, maybe due to the small sample dimension. In the specific it looks like the most a company is able to embrace *SBCE*, the lower the *reworks problems* and *management problems* (*inflexible resources, lack of control*) (see Table 4).

Table 4. Significant correlations between PLM, LPD practices and problems: French sample. Rho symbol represents the Kendall correlation coefficient.

Variable 1	Variable 2	ρ
LPD practices vs problems		
SBCE	Too many and too late reworks	−0.23
	Management problems: unclear roles, unflexible resources, lack of control	−0.29

Correlations between Problems, LPD Practices, PLM: Italian Research.
Some significant correlations have been found in the Italian research. Particularly, lowest project *reworks* are linked to higher use of *SBCE* (in term of *final design choice, customer value definition,* and *knowledge from previous projects*) and higher use of

PLM. Higher use of *PLM* is enabling the ability of companies to implement *Modularization and Standardization* and *QFD*. Finally it is interesting to notice how the importance of proper *customer value definition* leads to a overall problems reduction (see Table 5).

Table 5. Significant correlations between PLM, LPD practices and problems: Italian sample. Rho symbol represents the Kendall correlation coefficient.

Variable 1	Variable 2	ρ
LPD practices vs problems		
SBCE (includes: *final design choice, Customer value definition, knowledge from previous projects*)	Too many and too late reworks	−0.24
Customer value definition	Too many and too late reworks	−0.41
	Management problems: unclear roles, unflexible resources, lack of control	−0.27
	Poor knowledge management	−0.28
	Duct quality not compliant with customers expectations	−0.18
PLM vs problems		
PLM	Too many and too late reworks	−0.17
PLM vs LPD practices		
PLM	Design method: modularization/standardization	0.25
PLM	QFD	0.27

5 Conclusions, Limitations and Future Work

This preliminary exploratory research indicates companies in France and Italy present commonalities in term of problems encountered in their product development, as well as adopted LPD practices. There is certain level of correlation between the use of some LPD practices and product development problems, in the specific *customer value definition* resulted to be the main driver for success.

Though a clear and extensive role of PLM as enabler of LPD practice usage and as directly linked to higher product development success (measured through product development problems) can't be strongly inferred. The use of PLM per se brings advantages in terms of reducing *reworks* – and this is not at all insignificant, given the weight reworks have in companies, together with *resources overload* and *poor management problems*- and, from the Italian sample, relations are showed between the use of *PLM* and *QFD* (actually very important in the customer value definition process) and *modularization and standardization* methods.

Some limitations apply to this research. First of all, the research wasn't initially designed to cover such a broader international scope and some misalignments between the two research streams apply. Though, even if designed separately the two researches have a high level of similarities that makes the analysis significant. More companies should be analysed, especially within the French context. Also, as typical in qualitative analysis, the subjectivity of the respondents is always a factor that lowers the results validity. This could be improved by increasing the number of companies within the samples. Also to extend the research towards other countries (either European or extra-European) could be beneficial.

This study moves the authors to stimulate the discussion towards this direction: *lean management states the importance of customer value above everything. Indeed better customer value definition enables product development success. Still problems remains, not all companies pay enough attention on proper customer value definition, and PLM is underused. Future debates should discuss the role of PLM as enabler of the customer value definition process (some initial results show its support in QFD and some design methods), and hence key for product development success.*

Acknowledgments. This work was partly funded by the European Commission through Manutelligence (GA_636951) Projects, as well as by the GeCo Observatory (http://www.osservatori.net/progettazione_plm). The authors wish to acknowledge their gratitude to all the partners for their contributions during the development of concepts presented in this paper. Moreover the authors want to express their gratitude to their partners in KLManagement (http://www.klmanagement.fr), who gave invaluable contribution to this research.

References

1. Rossi, M., Kerga, E., Taisch, M., Terzi, S.: Proposal of a method to systematically identify wastes in New Product Development Process. In: 2011 17th International Conference on Concurrent Enterprising (ICE), pp. 1–9. IEEE (2011)
2. Ballard, G.: Positive vs negative iteration in design. In: Proceedings of 8th Annual Conference of the International Group for Lean Construction, IGLC-6 (2000)
3. Womack, J.P., Jones, D.T., Roos, D.: The machine that changed the world. Rawson Associates, HarperCollins, New York (1990)
4. Womack, J.P., Jones, D.T.: Lean Thinking: Banish Waste and Create Wealth in Your Corporation. Simon & Schuster, New York (1996)
5. Ward, A.C.: Lean Product and Process Development. The Lean Enterprise Institute, Cambridge (2007)
6. Morgan, J.M., Liker, J.K.: The Toyota Product Development System. Productivity Press, New York (2006)
7. Rossi, M., Morgan, J.M., Shook, J.: Lean product and process development. In: Netland, T., Powell, D. (eds.) The Routledge Companion to Lean Management. Routledge, London (2016)
8. Bosch-Mauchand, M., Belkadi, F., Bricogne, M., Eynard, B.: Knowledge-based assessment of manufacturing process performance: integration of product lifecycle management and value-chain simulation approaches. Int. J. Comput. Integr. Manuf. **26**(5), 453–473 (2013)
9. Ward, A., Liker, J.K., Cristiano, J.J., Sobek, D.K.: The second Toyota paradox. How delaying decisions can make better cars faster. Sloan Manag. Rev. **35**, 43 (1995)
10. Sobek, D.K., Ward, A.C., Liker, J.K.: Toyota's principles of set-based concurrent engineering. Sloan Manag. Rev. **40**(2), 67–83 (1999)

11. Terzi, S., Panetto, H., Morel, G., Garetti, M.: A holonic metamodel for product traceability in product lifecycle management. Int. J. Prod. Lifecycle Manag. **2**(3), 253–289 (2007)
12. Terzi, S., Bouras, A., Dutta, D., Garetti, M., Kiritsis, D.: Product lifecycle management-from its history to its new role. Int. J. Prod. Lifecycle Manag. **4**(4), 360–389 (2010)
13. Grieves, M.: Product Lifecycle Management: Driving the Next Generation of Lean Thinking. McGraw Hill Professional, New York (2005)
14. Le Duigou, J., Bernard, A., Perry, N.: Framework for product lifecycle management integration in small and medium enterprises networks. Comput. Aided Des. Appl. **8**, 531–544 (2011)
15. Assouroko, I., Ducellier, G., Eynard, B., Boutinaud, P.: Knowledge management and reuse in collaborative product development – a semantic relationship management based approach. Int. J. Prod. Lifecycle Manag. **7**(1), 54–74 (2014)

PLM-Based Approach for Integration of Product Safety in Lean Development

Christophe Danjou[1(✉)], Julien Le Duigou[2], Magali Bosch[2], and Benoît Eynard[2]

[1] École de Technologie Supérieure, Universtié du Québec, Montréal, Canada
christophe.danjou@etsmtl.ca

[2] Department of Mechanical Systems Engineering, UMR UTC/CNRS 7337 Roberval, Sorbonne Universités, Université de Technologie de Compiègne, CS 60319, 60203 Compiègne Cedex, France
{julien.le-duigou,magali.bosch,benoit.eynard}@utc.fr

Abstract. First developed for manufacturing context of the Toyota Production System, the Lean approach has been extended to product development about 20 years ago. Lean Product Development approach emphasizes on a method to implement a flowing development process. However, some tasks require decision milestones that can interrupt this continuous process flow. The paper focuses on safety engineering, an aspect which requires decision milestones due to standardized validation processes. It proposes a specific way to integrate safety constraints into a continuous and flowing process of Lean Product Development. To perform the safety integration in Lean Product Development, the proposed method simultaneously addresses process improvement of both product development and safety control. The proposal is a five-step method addressing the whole product development process from the requirements engineering step to the validation of the product prototype. This method was tested on an industrial case study and implemented into PLM TeamCenter.

Keywords: Lean Product Development · Safety engineering · Integrated design · Collaborative engineering · Product Lifecycle Management

1 Introduction

Design, as defined by [1] is a complex and multifaceted phenomenon involving: collaboration of disciplinary product designers collaboration, a multitude of activities, procedures, related tools and knowledge, a variety of contexts and an organization.

Multi-disciplinary collaboration of product designers means that different point of views must be taken into account to achieve the best compromise for product development [2]. This considering the point of view as the vision and expertise of an expert involved in a design team [3]. Each expert brings his/her own specific knowledge and uses related tools to carry out his/her tasks within the design team (e.g. mechanical engineers use CAD system whereas safety engineers use FMEA tools for example). But they need to exchange information with the rest of the team in the collaboration purposes as enhanced in PLM approach.

R. Harik et al. (Eds.): PLM 2016, IFIP AICT 492, pp. 193–205, 2016.
DOI: 10.1007/978-3-319-54660-5_18

Safety is a combination of operational measures and design measures to prevent and mitigate accidents. The paper will focus only on the design aspect and how to integrate safety into product design and in particular into Lean Design, also known as Lean Product Development (LPD). This integration is especially difficult because safety process is made of predefined decision gates that interrupt the development process flow of the product [4], whereas LPD focuses on bringing new products faster and with less effort [5]. In the interest of reducing the time-to-market, safety may sometimes be reduced to its simplest form, leaving little traceability concerning the safety validation process [6]. As a response to the lack of safety traceability and with the interest of reducing lead time for product development, the paper will focus on a method to implement the "safety control" in LPD processes and PDM process management.

In the following section, a literature background is presented on the main concepts of LPD and on the safety integration in the development process. Section 3 details the proposed method for implementing safety in LPD. Section 4 presents the tools implemented and PDM architecture chosen in the case study, the results and barriers met during the implementation. In the last section the drawn conclusions and an overview of the future work are presented.

2 Literature Review and Analysis

2.1 Lean Product Development

Lean philosophy was first developed for manufacturing management by Shingo in the TPS - "Toyota Production System" [7]. This approach consists of both eliminating the manufacturing process' wastes (or Mudas) to reduce the process time, and improving the process efficiency. In Lean Manufacturing approach seven types of wastes can be identified: Over-production, unnecessary stock, inefficient transportation, unnecessary motion, waiting times, rejects and defects, and inappropriate processing [8].

Since the last century, the Lean philosophy has been enriched to cover new domains. Essentially improved by Womack and Jones, the Lean approach can now be applied to Lean Office, Lean Administration [9], and LPD [10]. The last approach aimed at improving the product development processes of companies by clarifying the added value of the process, identifying the wastes reducing the efficiency of this process and proposing tools to improve it.

2.1.1 The Value as an Indicator of the Flow

LPD consists in getting the most efficient and continuous process. In order to ensure the process efficiency, it is crucial that key indicators to be reached by this process are well identified [11]. The combination of those two aspects is classically called "Value". Once the value identified, the process can be drawn considering the new definition. Therefore, the value of the process flow must be clearly identified for a product development [12].

There exist various definitions of value, according to particular needs. The survey of value definitions does not reveal any definition of value that includes safety perspectives. Authors propose a value definition including safety as an extension of

Stanke's definition [13] where the term safety is added to complete the original version: *"Value is a system introduced at the right time and right price which delivers the best value in mission effectiveness, performance, affordability, safety and sustainability, and retains these advantages throughout its life"*. Stanke's definition has been chosen in this context since the whole Lifecycle is considered. Indeed for product development processes the safety has to be managed through the whole lifecycle from BOL to EOL.

2.1.2 The Wastes in Product Development Process

As explained in the previous section, value qualifies the process; therefore all the tasks not answering to the value requirements are considered as wastes. Hence two tasks categories can be identified: the added value tasks which have to be enhanced, the necessary non-added value and the non-added value tasks which have to be eliminated. Therefore once the value has been defined, it is possible to consider the wastes in order to eradicate them. The wastes in the PDP are different from those in manufacturing processes. Therefore, their relative activities are different thus their related actions with added values are not similar. This is why, in contrast to the seven wastes defined in Lean Manufacturing, [14] has identified six wastes for the PDP:

1. Wastes of resources
2. Waiting time
3. Information and knowledge waste
4. Missed opportunities and potential wastes
5. Motivation waste
6. Financial investment waste

In order to identify these wastes in the PDP, it will be necessary to clarify it using modelling tools like SIPOC (Supplier – Input – Process – Output - Customer), VSA (Value Stream Analysis), among others.

2.1.3 Tools to Maximize the Value of PDP

Several tools are available to make Lean processes by eliminating waste. Indeed, those tools help to clarify the process, identify its breakpoints, analyze those breakpoints and find solutions for making the PDP a Lean one. To create a Lean process it is essential to set up the framework and the possible actions and tools that can be deployed or used [5]. The section proposes a literature overview of the existing tools and methods and presents the chosen ones - applied in Sect. 4. Authors organize them along four main concepts: Philosophy, Modeling, Problem resolution method and Standardization.

Philosophy: There exists different kind of methodology to address improvement: Hoshin, X-Matrix, DMAIC… Developed by Motorola's engineers in the 1980's, the Lean Six-Sigma philosophy splits a project/process into five stages: Define, Measure, Analyze, Improve and Control (DMAIC) [15]. By following those stages, the project can be well-managed with a steering committee validating the transition between stages.

Modeling: To model a process, various strategies can be used: VSA, UML, BPMN… Value Stream Analysis regroups the tools for modeling processes as SIPOC/VOC (Voice of Customer) [16, 17] and Value Stream Mapping (VSM) [18]. The SIPOC method helps to identify relevant entities taking part in a global process. A meta-level process can be drawn with the SIPOC method. To complete this meta-process, the VOC method helps to identify the needs and thus to have a better knowledge of the concerned people [19]. The VSM allows the detailed modeling stage on the different flow, namely information and physical flows [20]. Once the new process has been designed, a RACI (Responsible – Accountable – Controller – Informed) analysis can help to specify and to verify the stakeholders' actions for each task [21]. This analysis determines the responsible person for each task, who is the one held accountable, who ensures that the task is carried out as expected and who must be informed of the task's performing.

Problem solving method: The problem solving can be realized by the following methods: Kaizen, 5-why questions, PDCA… Here the problem resolution can be done by a classic solving method using five 'why' questions, which helps to find the root cause of a problem. This solving tool can be coupled to the method developed by [22]. That method is based on five stages: problem definition, analysis of the current state, formulation of lean process strategies, creation of the future state and implementation, and continuous improvement. This method can be related to the Kaizen improvement, as the improvement actions are made step by step. In addition to the solving, a PDCA (Plan-Do-Check-Act) method can be used to follow the new implementation. Indeed, the PDCA method corresponds to the four implementation stages of planning the implementation, implementing it on a chosen task, checking the results and then propagating it to all of a company's processes.

Standardization: Knowledge integration is essential to improve the development flow. Using an existing and proven solution obviously helps to save time [23]. In the same way, the Genchi-Gembutsu method makes it possible to produce standard parts using parts which are already used in other company products. Analyzing the existing solutions enable designers to standardize the various technical solutions, thereby reducing the required investment. Collaborative technologies can be used in the same way to implement Lean processes [24]: Collaborative technology and Product Life-cycle Management (PLM) help companies to re-use existing solutions from one product to another by the use of historical information from their databases [25, 26].

In our proposal, the first step in LPD is to define the value. Next, the process must be drawn so that each waste will be clearly identified. Problem solving methods then help to improve the process. Finally, knowledge integration will complete the process by a standardization phase. However, these solutions do not take safety into account. The next section presents a literature review on safety, methods and working rules to define it in product development.

2.2 Safety in Product Development

2.2.1 Safety Definition

The section studies safety as one of the main added values for the development process. There exist a clear difference between security and safety: security is related to risks originating from malicious intent, independently of the nature of the related consequence, whereas safety addresses accidental dangers, i.e. without malicious intent, but with potential impacts on the system environment [27].

A dictionary defines "safety" as: "The condition of being safe, freedom from danger/risk/injury". For product development, safety could be defined as a contrivance or device designed to protect from risks or other events which are considered to be non-desirable. The definition relates the definition of safety given by the design department. In fact, designing a new product without any danger or risk is impossible. So why, safety product development can be defined as "the control of recognized hazards to achieve an acceptable level of risk". This can take the form of being protected from an event or from exposure to something that causes health risks.

2.2.2 Safety Process Management

There are many ways to ensure safety in product development. The first is normative safety. This kind of safety is fixed by standards, regulations or directives from national council or international communities. The CE marking [28] which gives directives for product safety is one example. It could be seen as a form of safety-certification milestones for decision meetings defined in the PDP. A gatekeeper makes a formal decision whether to continue or not the process. There exist specified requirement for documenting requirements of the decision at each decision milestone and an independent team carries out a review of this documentation to assess the proposed solution. The process progress will not be granted unless the project demonstrates a sufficient level of maturity as required for passing the specific decision milestone. A PDP based on these regulations must be kept up to date on the standards' evolution. Once the design of the product has been achieved, the regulation evolution is fixed. Therefore, a regulation watch is still necessary, until a design has been achieved.

A second way to ensure product safety requires all the reliability engineering studies. Reliability engineering is a sub-discipline within product development engineering which uses reliability rate to theoretically define the probability of failure. Therefore, in product safety it is imperative to have the best reliability on safety in devices or safety barriers. To determine this rate, some tools can be used: Fault Tree Diagrams and Failure Mode and Effect Analysis (FMEA). They both focus on a system approach as a set of sub-systems which are in interaction. The goal is to find the root causes of safety lack in order to determine a hypothesis on the failure risks. These hypotheses are ranked according to certain aspects: severity, probability of appearance and probability of detection, given the global hypotheses' risk level. The decision to create new safety barriers or to reinforce the consistency between safety barriers can then be made [29].

2.2.3 Safety Engineering

Product safety is mainly fixed during the design stage [30]. A well-designed product will have consistency considering safety aspects, whereas a lack of consistency will engage new studies once the product definition has been achieved and evolution will become hazardous. Therefore, it is crucial to clearly specify, at the early design stage, which safety aspects are required for a final product. Another objective for product safety is to have consistency between the safety choices made during the development stage. The more details are given in the requirements, the better the system will be in terms of safety, due to the consistency between the subsystems [31]. Consequently, the final product safety must be considered as a global system and not to each sub-system.

The following section proposes a method to address safety in the product development process while promoting the best-flowing development process. Indeed, consistency for the safety purpose could take extra time and create bottlenecks, which are unacceptable in LPD.

3 Proposed Approach for LPD and Safe Product

A number of methods for Lean efficiency have been put forward [32]. The proposal is to consider the safety and the PDP as two value streams: one on LPD aspects and the other in mean to enhance safety aspects. The proposal is based on a DMAIC approach. This method introduces a mean to achieve both objectives (Lean and safe) at the same time in the same study. To achieve those two aims with a DMAIC approach, the study must be divided into two parts to then determine the best match between a very safe product and the best lean process for product development. As shown in Fig. 1, the proposal sometimes split the stages into two tasks, whereas other stages allow treating both aspects in the same task. The product development process goes from the first specification of the product to its validation with the first good product, including the prototyping and validation.

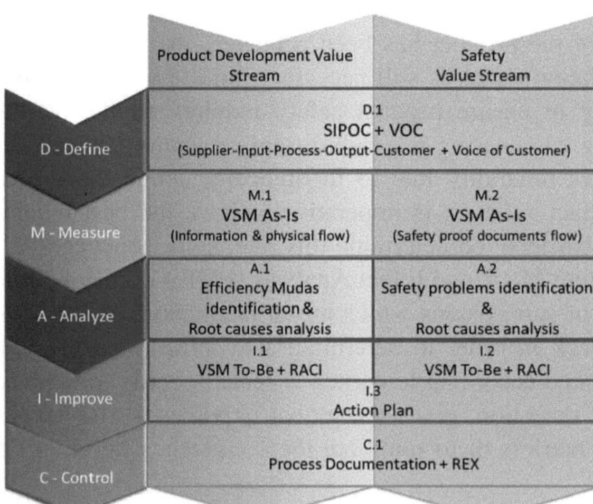

Fig. 1. DMAIC method for product development and safety value stream

For the "Define" stage (D), the method proposes to first draw up a macro process linking the different entities (SIPOC) in order to capture and to classify the roles of the process stakeholders. At this stage, the process is considered at a meta-level, and both product development and safety engineering aspects are included in this meta-process.

In the same way, the VOC method collects all the stakeholders' requests for the future process. The stakeholders' requests may contain ideas for improving the process efficiency and also the safety engineering process. Once the stakeholders interviews have been performed, all the requests can be processed in accordance with the thirteen principles of the Toyota Product Development process (Liker and Morgan [33]). In fact, the proposed classification of the thirteen principles in three categories helps the project leaders to identify if problems concern the skilled people (1), the tools and technology (2) or the process (3). The results of this study can be then compared to the new process in order to verify that all identified problems are treated.

In the "Measure" stage (M), the proposed method uses the VSM for mapping the process flow. This stage marks the first split between the respective value stream of product development and the safety engineering. The value stream of product development (M.1) focuses on the information flow between the different process tasks and between entities, and the material/physical flow between the entities (sub-assemblies, assemblies…). In parallel, the safety proof documents flow (M.2) has to be set on the VSM in order to maintain a focus on the safety flow breakpoints as well. These two value streams must be clearly identified on the VSM to introduce the analysis stage.

During the "Analyze" stage (A), the goal is to identify waste and breakpoints in the VSM. This stage is again split into two tasks. The first one (A.1) deals with the classic Mudas search in product development as seen in the literature survey in Sect. 2.1.2, identifying waste as resource wastes, waiting times, information and knowledge wastes, missed opportunities and potential wastes, motivation wastes, and financial investment wastes. Once the wastes have been identified, the next step is to find the root causes with a classic five-why method. This method helps to locate the root cause, reducing a problem to its simplest version. A solution can thus be found to each problem thanks to the break down, using Kaizen or other problem solving methods. Occurring in parallel to A.1, the other task (A.2) is the identification of safety problems. Literature does not propose wastes for safety engineering processes. The method proposal is to find wastes based on non-added value activities considering safety as the value for those aspects. Mostly, the safety wastes are similar to the wastes of PDP. According to the previous statement, seven safety Mudas are identified:

- Rework: consisting of all the tasks which need to be done again because the specifications have changed;
- Waiting time: consisting of the wait required for safety validation before beginning a new task;
- Unnecessary transfers: consisting of all the data exchanges for safety validation which are not addressed to the right person;
- Over-requirements: consisting of all the requirements which are not necessary for the final product safety;
- Uncompleted work: consisting of all the safety validation tasks which are in progress or that have been cancelled;
- Unsuitable information systems: consisting of dealing with knowledge problems and any lost information;
- Over-process: consisting of the actions which are not required by the process.

This identification aims at defining all the safety breakpoints and safety rework in the process, considering safety flow as the existence of safety proof documents. Similarly to the waste evaluation, a five-why method can be used to find the root causes of each breakpoint or rework on safety documents.

In the next stage, "Improve" (I), the goal is to specify the new process and to make an action plan to implement it. The specification of the new process (To-Be VSM) is again divided into several tasks. After finding a solution to each simple problem as a result of the "analyze stage", the new process has to take these solutions into account (I.1). In parallel to the new development process, the method proposes to create a dedicated process for safety engineering (I.2). While drawing these two processes, all the tasks have to be clearly defined: the inputs, the outputs and the role of the stakeholders. For this last point, the RACI tool can be used to specify who is Responsible and Accountable, who Controls and who is Informed. Once the two processes' tasks have been defined, the next step is to unify both action plans to implement the processes (I.3). Most of the actions are closely linked because the safety engineering process could be imposed on the new PDP. For the action plan a classic PDCA method able the leaders to follow the implementation.

Finally, the "Control" stage (C) addresses the process documentation with the company standards. Once the process has been implemented and the action plan performed, the process has to be controlled. This must be done to ensure that the results are conforming to the expectations and needs. Once the process has been implemented, a summary of the experience should be carried out, along with a promotion of the results within the company. This summary has two goals. The first is to promote this improved method throughout the company. This will allow the project/method to be deployed to the other PDP of the company. The second is to verify the process to ensure that it fulfilled the design objectives.

The purpose of this work is to develop a general method which will have to be customized to be in accordance with a company's standards and practices. A case study and the results of the method implementation are presented in the following section.

4 Case Study

4.1 Case Study Context

This section introduces a case study that specifies the context, the implementation with the five stages as proposed in Sect. 3, and an analysis of the obtained results. The case study came from the sector of aeronautics – space – defence. The R&D department concerned by study involves more than 150 peoples distributed on 3 locations and composed systems engineers, design engineers, simulation engineers, manufacturing engineers and quality engineers, technical and support staff. The duration of the study was of 6 months for the preliminary phase. The leading team of the study was composed of 10 peoples associating 2 project managers and the operational team for lean study.

Only the key information is revealed in this case study, due to the confidentiality agreement with the company where this method was applied. Therefore, the results and the schemas will have generic names.

The goal of this case study was to increase the safety level during the PDP while improving the PDP itself. It covers a PDP which counts eight different entities: requirements, designers, tests, final customer, manufacturing, quality, reliability engineering and the Health, Safety and Environment (HSE) group. The studied product is of a military nature and represents high safety risks for humans and for the company's infrastructure. This case study was to respond the standardization of the process into a PDM structure to make it Lean and safe.

4.2 Implementation

The proposed method, as detailed in Sect. 3, was structured in five stages. The first stage (D.1) helps to verify that all the entities involved in the PDP have been invited to join the project. To check each entity's role, each stakeholder was requested to draw their own macro process. Then a SIPOC and a VOC were carried out to launch the "measure" stage.

In the second stage, the stakeholders were asked to draw their specific processes with all their detailed tasks in order to define the value stream of the PDP and the safety engineering flow.

The third stage consists in identifying the Mudas as well as the PDP and the safety wastes, as mentioned in Sect. 3. These identifications helped to find solutions to the Mudas and to draw the new PDP. The identified Mudas were: resource wastes, waiting time, and information and knowledge waste. In the safety engineering process, five Mudas were identified: rework, waiting, over-specification, over-process, and unsuitable information systems.

In the "improve" stage, a new process was specified (Fig. 2). To define the new PDP and the new safety procedure, some tasks were modified and reorganized. To ensure the consistency of the new process, a RACI analysis was conducted for each task. The specification of new PDP was coupled to the action plan. Numerous proposed actions modified the way of thinking about the PDP. To implement the most efficient development process while integrating a safety view, decision milestones were introduced. These decision milestones verify the match between product specifications and the developed solutions. The new process development is described in Fig. 3. The new decision milestones are symbolized by the diamonds and represent a "go" or "no go" stage for management of safety aspects in the PDP.

To pass through these decision milestones, the safety specification is reviewed based on elements compiled by the safety procedures. The safety concept is introduced into the PDP through the safety folder. The safety folder first specifies the elements required to consider the product as safe at the end of the design. It is then enriched by the data collected during the PDP. The safety folder is divided into stages which are directly linked to the decision milestones of the PDP to secure the safety aspects. Hence, a tailored safety process can be drawn based on the safety folder evolution with the validation meetings.

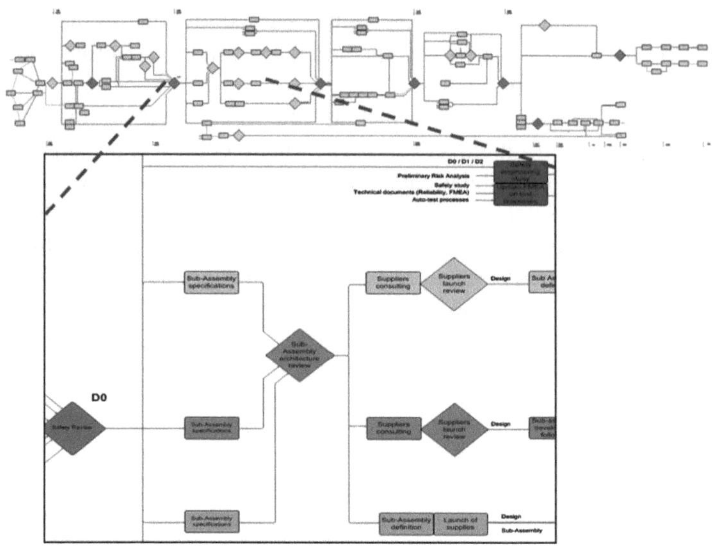

Fig. 2. VSM of the To-Be PDP after process improvements

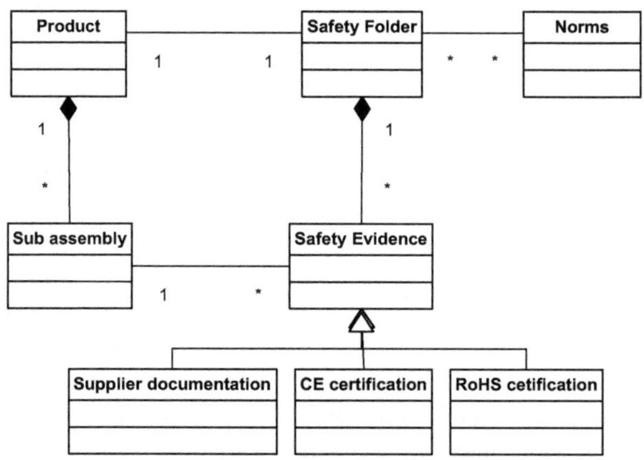

Fig. 3. UML class diagram of the TeamCenter architecture

The safety folder is over time enriched and several changes are addressed. This makes the folder management complicated. In order to manage this change, it was proposed use the data model and principles of a Product Data Management (PDM) system [34]. The company used the TeamCenter PLM system from Siemens. The architecture proposed by the authors is shown in Fig. 3. This architecture helps to locate all of the derived products, allowing re-using solutions and to manage the process change through the normative watch. The data model contains a document (standards) which summarizes all the normative versions used for the entire product. This will help the control of product change according the standardized view evolves.

Moreover, the use of this data model enables the value stream for the PDP by duplicating safety folders whenever needed and adding the safety design in the safety folder.

As seen above, the safety process is led by standardized rules, so standardized view is necessary, mandating its creation. To coordinate all this new elements, it was decided to introduce a new role as responsible for safety development in the company. This team member acts as the referent actor for all the safety questions. However, even though this person is the referent actor for all the safety aspects, the development process and safety folders are managed by the project leader.

5 Conclusion

This paper has detailed how to make a PDP more Lean and to simultaneously address safety aspects. To set the context, first, a review on classic LPD methods and implementation has been presented. Second, a survey on safety engineering and dependability studies has been drawn up.

Then a method integrating both antagonism aspects which are safety and Lean was proposed. Safety engineering increases process time and create bottlenecks if it is processed as a less important point. In splitting both aspects in two different tasks according to the DMAIC stages; the proposed method allows having safety integration in LPD. The superimposed safety process makes the safety value stream continuous.

In Sect. 4, the implementation results are presented. The obtained improvements on the PDP are described. Details on the new organizations with a safety referent are given. The proposed safety folder ensures safety to the final customer compiling all the safety data and documents through the product lifecycle. To enhance the safety traceability, new collaborative platform architecture has been proposed. So that it provides a way to improve the access to safety proof documents for the whole product lifecycle from the early concepts to product retailing. At least, the safety is integrated in the LPD process since its first stages of the project.

To summarize, the paper presents a way to integrate safety in Lean Process Development through PLM. By defining a new safety process independent of the development process, most of the bottlenecks have disappeared which allowed reading a Lean and safety based development process. This ensures a safe product for the final customer including all the safety procedures for the whole lifecycle.

References

1. Blessing, L.T., Chakrabarti, A.: DRM, a Design Research Methodology. Springer, London (2009)
2. Sohlenius, G.: Concurrent engineering. CIRP Ann. Technol. **41**, 645–655 (1992)
3. Brissaud, D., Tichkiewitch, S.: Product modems for Life_Cycle. CIRP Ann. Technol. **50**, 105–108 (2001)
4. Hale, A., Kirwan, B., Kjellén, U.: Safe by design: where are we now? Saf. Sci. **45**, 305–327 (2007). doi:10.1016/j.ssci.2006.08.007

5. Karlsonn, C., Ahlstrom, P.: The difficult path to lean product development. J. Prod. Innov. Manag. **13**, 283–295 (1996)
6. Hines, P., Francis, M., Found, P.: Towards lean product lifecycle management: a framework for new product development. J. Manuf. Technol. Manag. **17**, 866–887 (2006). doi:10.1108/17410380610688214
7. Shingo, S., Dilon, A.P.: Study of the Toyota Production System: From an Industrial Engineering Viewpoint. Productivity Press, New York (1989)
8. Womack, J.P., Jones, D.T., Roos, D.: The Machine That Changed the World. Rawson, New York (1990)
9. Mora, C.: The Complete Lean Enterprise: Value Stream Mapping for Administrative and Office Processes (2010). (Ed. by B. Keyte and D. Locher)
10. Liker, J.K., Morgan, J.M.: The Toyota way in services: the case of lean product development. Acad. Manag. Perspect. **20**, 5–20 (2006). doi:10.5465/AMP.2006.20591002
11. Al-Ashaab, A., Golob, M., Urrutia, U.A., et al.: Development and application of lean product development performance measurement tool. Int. J. Comput. Integr. Manuf. **29**, 1–13 (2016). doi:10.1080/0951192X.2015.1066858
12. Lindström, J., Löfstrand, M., Karlberg, M., Karlsson, L.: Functional product development: what information should be shared during the development process? Int. J. Prod. Dev. **16**, 95–111 (2012)
13. Stanke, A.: A framework for achieving lifecycle value in product development. Ph.D. thesis from Massachusetts Institute of Technology (2001)
14. Bauch, C.: Lean product development: making waste transparent. Ph.D. thesis from Massachusetts Institute of Technology (2004)
15. Breyfogle, F.W.: Implementing Six Sigma: Smarter Solutions Using Statistical Methods. Wiley, New York (2003)
16. George, M.L., George, M.: Lean Six Sigma for Service. McGraw-Hill, New York (2003)
17. Pyzdek, T.: The Six Sigma Handbook. McGraw-Hill Professional, New York (2003)
18. McManus, H.L.: Product Development Value Stream Mapping (PDVSM) Manual, pp. 1–15. Lean Aerospace Initiative, Cambridge (2005)
19. Chen, M., Lyu, J.: A lean six-sigma approach to touch panel quality improvement. Prod. Plan. Control **20**, 445–454 (2009). doi:10.1080/09537280902946343
20. McManus, H.L., Millard, R.L.: Value stream analysis and mapping for product development. In: Proceedings of 23rd ICAS Congress (2002)
21. Meran, R., Roenpage, O., Staudter, C.: Six Sigma. Springer, London (2006)
22. Nepal, B.P., Yadav, O.P., Solanki, R.: Improving the NPD process by applying lean principles: a case study. Eng. Manag. J. **23**, 52–68 (2011)
23. Brunel, S., Zolghadri, M., Girard, P.: Design products to learn and to use. Int. J. Prod. Dev. **13**, 84–94 (2011)
24. Le Duigou, J., Bernard, A., Perry, N.: Framework for product lifecycle management integration in small and medium enterprises networks. Comput. Aided Des. Appl. **8**, 531–544 (2011)
25. Montagna, F.: Decision-aiding tools in innovative product development contexts. Res. Eng. Des. **22**, 63–86 (2011). doi:10.1007/s00163-011-0103-z
26. Eynard, B., Yan, X.T.: Collaborative product development. Concurr. Eng. **16**, 5–7 (2008). ISSN 1063-293X
27. Piètre-Cambacédès, L., Bouissou, M.: Cross-fertilization between safety and security engineering. Reliab. Eng. Syst. Saf. **110**, 110–126 (2013). doi:10.1016/j.ress.2012.09.011
28. Council Directive 93/68/EEC: CE Marking, Directive 93/68/EEC. Off. J. L 220 (1993)
29. Baram, M.: Liability and its influence on designing for product and process safety. Saf. Sci. **45**, 11–30 (2007). doi:10.1016/j.ssci.2006.08.022

30. Dowlatshahi, S.: Material selection and product safety: theory versus practice. Int. J. Manag. Sci. **28**, 467–480 (2000). doi:10.1016/S0305-0483(99)00065-1
31. Lintala, M., Ovtcharov, J.: Enhancing system lifecycle processes by integrating functional safety information from practice into design requirements. Int. J. Adv. Robot. Syst. **10**, 1–14 (2013). doi:10.5772/56850
32. Welo, T.: On the application of lean principles in product development: a commentary on models and practices. Int. J. Prod. Dev. **13**, 316–343 (2011)
33. Liker, J.K., Morgan, J.M.: Lean product development as a system: a case study of body and stamping development at ford. Eng. Manag. J. **23**, 16–28 (2011)
34. Eynard, B., Gallet, T., Nowak, P., Roucoules, L.: UML based specifications of PDM product structure and workflow. Comput. Ind. **55**, 301–316 (2004). doi:10.1016/j.compind.2004.08.006

The Role of Manufacturing Execution Systems in Supporting Lean Manufacturing

Gianluca D'Antonio(✉), Joel Sauza Bedolla, Akmal Rustamov, Franco Lombardi, and Paolo Chiabert

Politecnico di Torino, Corso Duca degli Abruzzi 24, 10129 Turin, Italy
{gianluca.dantonio, joel.sauza, franco.lombardi, paolo.chiabert}@polito.it,
akmal.rustamov@studenti.polito.it

Abstract. In order to deal with global competition and increased customers expectation, companies must improve the efficiency of their manufacturing processes. Mainly, two approaches are available: the implementation of lean manufacturing practices and the deployment of information tools for data analysis. For a long time, these two strategies have been considered mutually exclusive; recently, it was understood that information concerning the manufacturing process is mandatory for the effective implementation of lean practices. This work aims at showing how Manufacturing Execution Systems (MES) can support the lean manufacturing paradigm into a medium size enterprise. The case study of a company in the supply chain of automotive components is presented to provide evidence about the role of MES and to highlight possible criticalities occurring during its implementation.

Keywords: Manufacturing Execution Systems · Lean manufacturing · Information tools

1 Introduction

Today enterprises are driven by a challenging market: on the one hand, companies have to deal with competitors spread all over the world, operating in a variety of different conditions. On the other hand, the expectation of customers is increasing: product with enhanced quality, innovative features and higher customization level must be delivered in shorter times and at a lower cost. Hence, to maintain and improve their competitive advantage, leading organizations in different industrial sectors need to improve process optimization and efficiency.

One of the initiatives that a company may undertake to improve its competitiveness is the implementation of *Lean Manufacturing* practices; this term has been first introduced by Womack [1] to describe the working philosophy deployed in Japanese companies, with particular concern for Toyota. The essence of this methodology is the elimination of waste and non-productive process, in order to focus on value added operations and produce high-quality products, at the customers demand pace, with little waste.

R. Harik et al. (Eds.): PLM 2016, IFIP AICT 492, pp. 206–214, 2016.
DOI: 10.1007/978-3-319-54660-5_19

Another approach is the deployment of automation and Information Technology (IT) tools, which allow to improve process planning and control, as well as to enhance the performance of each step of the manufacturing process. The landscape of the existing software classes and their purposes has been changing over the years, and is still evolving at a high pace. Today, beside the improvement of existing tools, huge efforts are made for the integration and the communication between different information tools and among systems deployed by different companies (for example, among firms belonging to the same supply chain).

For several years, Lean Manufacturing has been considered as opposed to the deployment of IT tools and their integration within and between firms [2, 3]. On one side, the philosophy of lean is "less is better": inventory, variability, material handling, options and choices must be reduced as much as possible to improve the performance of a company. Conversely, the philosophy of IT is "more is better": IT tools allow to better manage large amount of data, with increased flexibility, functions and features [2].

According to Ward and Zhou [2], the two classes of instruments are complementary both in the concept and in the application: IT tools can be considered a kind of higher-level planning system, while lean practices were related to shop-floor control and execution activities.

Nevertheless, in order to define improvement strategies and assess their impact, the collection and analysis of information is mandatory: the deployment of methodologies for Lean Manufacturing cannot exclude the use of IT tools. Hence, in the last years, IT instruments have been widely adapted, upgraded and expanded to deal with process monitoring and control activities.

The focus of this paper is on the role of Manufacturing Execution Systems (MES) – a class of IT tools – to support the implementation of Lean Manufacturing practices. The remainder of this paper is organized as follows: in Sect. 2 the Lean Manufacturing paradigm is introduced and some basic knowledge concerning MES is provided. In Sect. 3, the role of MES to support Lean Manufacturing is discussed. In Sect. 4, the case study of MES implementation into a medium size enterprise and the support in achieving Lean Manufacturing are presented. In Sect. 5, conclusive remarks and hints for future developments are discussed.

2 Background

2.1 Lean Manufacturing

Muda is a Japanese word meaning "waste": it is referred to any human activity that needs dedicated resources, but does not create value. Taiichi Ohno, a Toyota executive, introduced the concept of *muda* in manufacturing, to label all the activities that require resources to take place, but do not add value to the process or to the product [4]. In particular, he defined seven classes of waste that typically affect a manufacturing process. Namely: (i) Overproduction; (ii) Waiting; (iii) Transport; (iv) Extra processing; (v) Inventory; (vi) Motion; (vii) Defects.

These wastes do not add value to the product, hence customers are not willing to pay for them. Manufacturers have to become less wasteful in order to be more profitable and improve their competitiveness. A systemic method to eliminate *muda* is Lean Manufacturing [5]. It is an approach inspired by Japanese management methods, in particular by the Toyota Production System. The effectiveness of this approach led to interest among European and American companies. The first attempts in exporting Japanese production methods have been made in the 1970s [1]. At that time, the experience was not successful; according to the prevalent opinion, this was due to cultural differences and to the unique social context of Japan. Nonetheless, in the early 1990s, deeper empirical and theoretical research has been performed and the basis for the first definition of lean manufacturing has been provided [1, 6]. This approach is structured in the following 5 principles: (i) Specify value; (ii) Identify the Value Stream; (iii) Flow; (iv) Pull; (v) Perfection.

At the state of the art, the interaction between lean practices and information tools has not yet thoroughly studied. A research performed by Moyano-Fuentes et al. [7] showed that companies need to increase the degree of use of IT tools in order to implement lean manufacturing practices. Riezebos et al. [8] reviewed the role of IT in achieving lean production over three strategic topics: production control systems, computer aided production systems and maintenance processes. Powell et al. [9] analyzed ERP implementation processes and proposed a framework for ERP-based lean implementation, with particular concern for Small and Medium Enterprises (SMEs) [10].

2.2 Manufacturing Execution Systems

Manufacturing Execution Systems are IT tools commonly deployed in companies involved in traditional manufacturing. A MES enables information exchange between the organizational level, commonly supported by an Enterprise Resource Planning (ERP), and the control systems for the shop-floor, usually consisting in several, different, highly customized software applications [11]. A schematic of MES positioning in the framework of information tools supporting manufacturing is provided in Fig. 1.

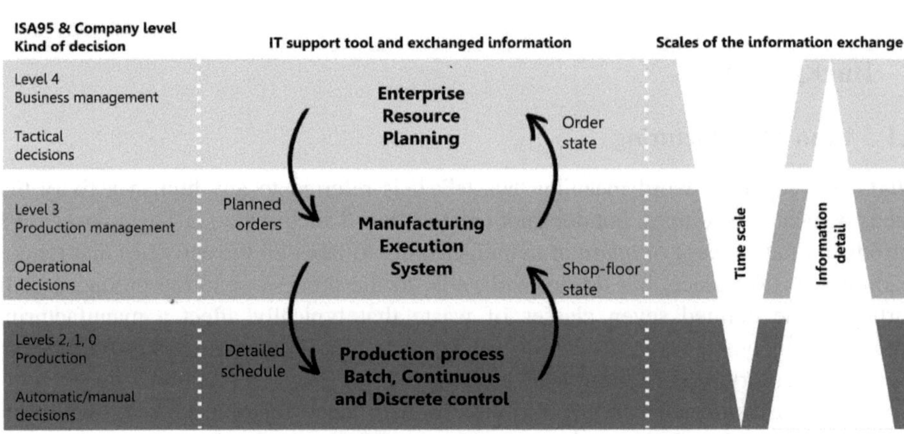

Fig. 1. Positioning of MES within an industrial framework.

The tasks in charge of a MES were proposed by Mesa International [12] in 1997, and then defined through the standards ISA95 [13] and IEC62264 [14]. A MES has two principal purposes. First, the system has to deal with the top-down data flow: the requirements and the necessities provided by the organizational level must be transformed into an optimal sequence planning meeting such targets. This sequence must be identified by best exploiting the available resources (such as staff, machines, materials, inventory) and taking into account the constraints of the process, such as processing and setup times, and workstations capacity.

The second aim of a MES is to manage the bottom-up data flow. Data concerning process performance and product quality can be gathered at the shop-floor level; the role of MES is to collect such data, analyze it through appropriate mathematical techniques, and extract a synthetic information to provide the business level with an exhaustive picture of the current state of the process. Possibly, the analysis should be performed in real-time, in order to make decisions to control the process with the necessary rapidity. Recently, the development of low-cost, small, easily available sensors led to a great diffusion of monitoring systems to assess product quality and process performance, and to support the improvement of production process.

MES were initially deployed in industries focused in the fields of chemistry and pharmaceutics; then, the spread of such systems increased, but for long time this tool has been considered useful only for large industries. In recent years, it was understood that the benefits provided by a MES can profitably support even smaller companies [15]. According to a recent survey [16], in Europe SMEs represent around the 99% of the enterprises; thus, the potential of MES application is very huge. However, in the implementation of a MES, SMEs and large companies have to face different issues. In Sect. 4, the attention will be focused on the SME perspective.

According to the last report of Markets and Markets [17], the MES turnover is expected to reach USD 12.6 Billion by 2020 at a CAGR[1] of 10.85% between 2015 and 2020. For a long period, Europe has been the main market for MES; nevertheless, in recent times the Asia Pacific region has superseded Europe as the biggest regional market. North and Latin America are, respectively, the 3rd and the 4th market [18]. The major players in the MES market include ABB Ltd. (Switzerland), Andea Solutions (Poland), Dassault Systemes SA (France), Emerson Electric Co. (US), General Electric Co. (US), Honeywell International Inc. (US), Rockwell Automation, Inc. (US), SAP AG (Germany), Schneider Electric SE (France), Siemens AG (Germany), and Werum IT Solutions GmbH (Germany).

3 MES Support to Lean Manufacturing

As stated in Sect. 1, for a long time the deployment of IT tools and the lean practices have been considered mutually exclusive. However, recently, the importance of deploying MES to support continuous improvement techniques has been shown. Cottyn [19] developed a framework for the integration of lean objectives into MES. He

[1] Compounded Average Growth Rate.

defined an automatic Value Stream Mapping (aVSM) methodology: the aVSM benefits from the information provided by the MES, since it is a rich source of information and historical data useful to define continuous improvement actions. On the other side, MES benefits from aVSM because it does not contain information concerning the value flow. The framework is validated through the case studies of a furniture firm and a food and beverage company.

A further recent work [20] aimed at the definition of a methodology for the development of MES-oriented tools to support the path towards Lean Manufacturing. It consists of three steps: (i) identification of the wastes to be eliminated; (ii) identification and description of all the components and resources involved in the process at stake; (iii) description of the analysis technique to be integrated into the MES (data source, mathematical algorithms, information to extracted). The methodology enabled to deal with both the top-down and the bottom-up data flows in charge of MES, and was applied to case studies in heterogeneous fields, such as subtractive and additive manufacturing processes, automated warehousing and automated transport of items through a manufacturing line. The research results provided evidence that the deployment of information-based techniques enables to develop adaptive strategies for waste reduction and achievement of lean manufacturing. The research also showed that an effectively implemented MES is, by itself, a lean tool: appropriate techniques must be implemented to transform the acquired data into the right amount of information, to be delivered at the right person, at the right time; ineffective tools lead to wastes such as useless effort in understanding data or oversized infrastructures for data transmission.

The findings presented in this and the previous Sections encourage the deployment of MES to improve the control of the process and to have a complete and updated picture of the manufacturing flow. In particular, MES can enable the identification of wastes and criticalities, and provide information to support decision aiming at overcoming such issued. The impact of SMEs in the European manufacturing has also been presented. Thus, in the following Section a MES implementation into a SME is presented: the aim of this case study is to show how this system can be implemented into a small size company, the implementation issues that may be faced and the support that it can provide in approaching lean manufacturing.

4 A Case Study in a SME

The mission of the industrial partner involved in this project is to design and produce interior components for buses, coaches and trains. Although it is a medium size enterprise, the company is composed of five subsidiaries, located in Europe, Middle East, Asia and America. Namely, the firm produces and assemblies lighting systems, handrails, ceiling panels, pillar coverings and luggage racks. Given this high variety of products, the company deploys a wide range of materials including HPL, plastics (PVC, ABS), metals (mainly aluminum), fiberglass, and textiles. The whole manufacturing process is composed of several operations such as cutting, bending, shaping, turning, milling, welding, assembly, surface coating, painting, and punching. Each product has its own manufacturing process. In this project, the Italian plant has been involved to test the implementation of a MES. This shop floor consists of 21 machines; among them, two are equipped with a PLC.

The Need for a MES. Before starting the project, data concerning the production were manually registered on paper sheets by shop-floor operators. Then, the same operators manually entered such data into the company's ERP. The information was used to evaluate performance indicators, such as machines utilization and overall process efficiency. Data concerning failures were collected into specific forms and managed without the support of ERP. This practice resulted in non-standardized data collection and imprecisions; further, in some cases data acquisition was missed. Although not efficient, this approach for data collection is still common for SMEs. Nonetheless, the lack of appropriate information tools may lead to issues such as missed, redundant, or discordant data. For these reasons, the industrial partner decided to introduce a MES into the company.

MES Implementation. The industrial partner had not yet installed any information systems in the shop-floor. Thus, to implement the MES two main issues have been dealt: (i) the acquisition of data; (ii) the infrastructure for data transmission to the central unit.

As stated, the shop-floor is composed of a heterogeneous variety of machines. Among them, only two are equipped with a PLC: so, data concerning work instructions, start and finish time, as well as the error codes related to possible failures are directly taken from the controller; the operator only has to log in the system before starting the operation. However, the majority of the machines is not equipped with a PLC and data must be manually entered. To support a profitable deployment of MES, manual machines have been equipped with a set of tablets connected with the central unit. Such devices are used as an interface between the operators and the MES.

Data transmission is performed through wireless connection: the installation of a cable network would have been more expensive and would have provided a lower flexibility.

MES Functionalities. Given the motivations leading to MES installation, the developed system aims at solving issues concerning the traceability of the performed operations.

From the shop-floor operators' perspective, the MES is a digital, standardized support to collect the information that was previously handled manually. Before starting an operation, the operator has to log in the system, by scanning a personal bar code or by entering his ID. Then, he must input the number corresponding to the production order at stake, as well as the work code. This step enables to extract the list of operations to be performed; the operator has to select the specific phase he is dealing with from a drop-down menu and the work instructions are shown. At this stage, all the data necessary to uniquely identify the operation have been introduced in the system. To begin working, the operator clicks a Start button: in this way, the system is aware that some resources are busy and cannot be allocated elsewhere. Similarly, when the operation is finished, a Stop button must be clicked. In the PLC-equipped machines, the last two steps are automatically performed. Data concerning the involved resources and the time took by the operation are saved for further analytics. The operator also has to input information concerning issues: a list of possible failures and quality defects is available to shorten the time spent in this task and to standardize the sent information. A free text field is also available for unexpected issues.

From the business level perspective, the interface of the MES enables to take snapshots of the shop-floor state at different time scales. First, the present utilization of the resources can be extracted at any time. Second, analytics concerning arbitrary time spans can be extracted: the average values for the utilization of the equipment, the overall efficiency of the process, the impact of defects and failures can be extracted. Further, the cost of processing a part or a lot can be evaluated. The traceability of the product through its manufacturing process enables to define a product passport [21], i.e. a document containing the whole chronology of the manufacturing steps experienced by each part.

The Support to Lean Manufacturing. The deployment of the presented MES enables to collect data concerning the events taking place at the shop-floor, the repartition of times, the utilization of the resources and the flow of items through the process. These data are collected through the interface provided to the operators; then, data analysis and aggregation are performed to support the decision making process at the business level. Such decisions must be aimed at the elimination of wastes, in order to focus the efforts on the operations that add value to the product and which a customer is willing to pay for. Given the classification of wastes provided in Sect. 2, the functionalities of the implemented MES enable to:

- Trace the impact of *Defects*: whenever a (semi-)finished item does not match the required quality level, the operator inputs an issue message into the MES. The analyses performed by the system enable to identify the classes of product or the operations mostly affected by defects. The tracking capability is an effective tool to support the identification of the ultimate reasons leading to poor product quality.
- Trace the impact of *Inventory* and *Waiting*: the capability of extracting the instant overview of the shop-floor enables to evaluate the number of items idle into the shop-floor. Inventory minimization is desirable, since idle parts require room to be stocked and represent money already spent which is not yet producing income. Waiting is the counterpart of inventory, since it represents the time that items spend without being processed or transported; this time is mainly due to not synchronized flows of materials. The information collected by the MES enables improved planning of operations and allocation of resources, aiming at minimizing waiting.
- Trace the impact of *Transport*. The chronology of the events experienced by the items enables to identify their path through the shop-floor. Thus, data collected over large time intervals can provide useful hints to re-arrange the layout of the plant, the position of the machines and the placement of warehouses in order to reduce the impact of transport: beside a time waste, transport is also a potential risk, since the items may be damaged.

5 Conclusions and Further Developments

In this work, the implementation of a MES into a medium size company has been presented. The work has been focused on the improvement of shop-floor data collection, aiming to enhance the quality of process knowledge and to support decision making processes. The system is still in a start-up phase: it has been successfully installed into the company, and beta test have been performed to ensure its correct deployment. The MES is now starting to be heavily used, hence a quantification of the advantages concerning will be available in the next months. The presented case study also represents a pilot test for the company, which consists of five plants spread in different geographical areas. The company aims at developing and setting a complete MES system into the Italian plant; after its validation and the evaluation of benefits, the MES will also be installed into the other plants.

The support that such system can provide to achieve Lean Manufacturing has been described in the previous Section. The current spread and the expected trends for MES diffusion in the next years have been presented in Sect. 2. Given these two concepts, it can be stated that in future a higher diffusion and support of information tools for setting up and tuning lean practices is expected.

However, the experience gathered through this case study showed that some criticalities may occur. A MES cannot be considered as a plug and play system: a robust system for data acquisition and transmission is necessary. The interaction between machines and MES can be managed by the PLC: the information collected during an operation can be sent to the system and stored. However, in the present case study, the majority of the machines was not equipped with a PLC. Thus, alternative ways to collect data had to be identified. The issue was tackled through the deployment of mobile devices, such as tablets: today, such devices provide a huge calculation capability at a low cost. The heterogeneous fleet of machines presented in this case study is not rare: the majority of companies all over the world can be classified as a small-medium enterprise. For this kind of companies, the turnover of machines occurs slowly, so a low-cost solution for the integration of information tools to trace the events occurring in the shop-floor and to improve process knowledge is desirable. In this case study, the cost necessary to develop the software, to equip the shop-floor with a wireless infrastructure for data transmission and to buy the mobile devices was in the order of 40k€.

References

1. Womack, J.P., Jones, D.T., Roos, D.: The Machine That Changed the World. Free Press, New York (1990)
2. Ward, P., Zhou, H.: Impact of information technology integration and lean/just-in-time practices on lead-time performance. Decis. Sci. **37**(2), 177–203 (2006). doi:10.1111/j.1540-5915.2006.00121.x
3. Powell, D., Binder, A., Arica, E.: MES support for lean production. In: Emmanouilidis, C., Taisch, M., Kiritsis, D. (eds.) Advances in Production Management Systems. Competitive Manufacturing for Innovative Products and Services: IFIP WG 5.7 International Conference, pp. 128–135 (2012). doi:10.1007/978-3-642-40361-3_17

4. Ohno, T.: Toyota Production System: Beyond Large-Scale Production, 1st edn. Productivity Press, New York (1988)
5. Womack, J.P., Jones, D.T.: Lean Thinking: Banish Waste and Create Wealth in Your Corporation, 2nd edn. Productivity Press, New York (2003)
6. Houy, T.: ICT and lean management: will they ever get along? Commun. Strateg. **59**, 53–75 (2005)
7. Moyano-Fuentes, J., Martines-Jurado, P.J., Maqueira-Marin, J.M., Bruque-Camara, S.: Impact of use of information technology on lean production adoption: evidence from the automotive industry. Int. J. Technol. Manag. **57**, 132–148 (2012). doi:10.1504/IJTM.2012.043955
8. Riezebos, J., Klingenberg, W., Hicks, C.: Lean production and information technology: connection or contradiction? Comput. Ind. **60**(4), 237–247 (2009). doi:10.1016/j.compind.2009.01.004
9. Powell, D., Alfnes, E., Strandhagen, E., Ola, J., Dreyer, H.: The concurrent application of lean production and ERP: towards an ERP-based lean implementation process. Comput. Ind. **64**(3), 324–335 (2013). doi:10.1016/j.compind.2012.12.002
10. Powell, D., Riezebos, J., Strandhagen, J.O.: Lean production and ERP systems in small- and medium-sized enterprises: ERP support for pull production. Int. J. Prod. Res. **51**(2), 395–409 (2013). doi:10.1080/00207543.2011.645954
11. Meyer, H., Fuchs, F., Thiesl, K.: Manufacturing Execution Systems (MES): Optimal Design, Planning, and Deployment, 1st edn. McGraw-Hill Professional, New York (2009)
12. MESA International: MES Functionalities & MRP to MES Data Flow Possibilities. White paper (1997)
13. ISA95: Enterprise - Control System Integration. Part 1: Models and Terminology (2000)
14. IEC62264: Enterprise-control system integration (2013)
15. Gaxiola, L., et al.: Proposal of holonic manufacturing execution systems based on web service technologies for Mexican SMEs. In: Mařík, V., McFarlane, D., Valckenaers, P. (eds.) Holonic and Multi-agent Systems for Manufacturing: 1st International Conference on Industrial Applications of Holonic and Multi-agent Systems, pp. 156–166 (2003). doi:10.1007/978-3-540-45185-3_15
16. European Commission: Statistics on small and medium-sized enterprises (2015). http://ec.europa.eu/eurostat/statistics-explained/index.php/Statistics_on_small_and_medium-sized_enterprises. Accessed 06 July 2016
17. Markets and Markets: Manufacturing Execution System Market by Deployment Type, Process Industry (Chemicals, Food & Beverages, Life Science, Oil & Gas, Power), Discrete Industry (Aerospace & Defense, Automotive, Medical Devices) and by Region - Global Forecast to 2020 (2015). http://www.marketsandmarkets.com/Market-Reports/manufacturing-execution-systems-mes-market-536.html. Accessed 06 July 2016
18. DKSH: Digitization and the market expansion services industry: driving Omni-channel growth. Fourth global market expansion services report (2014). http://www.rolandberger.asia/media/pdf/Roland_Berger_DKSH20140905.pdf. Accessed 06 July 2016
19. Cottyn, J.: Design of a lean manufacturing execution system framework. Ph.D. thesis, Gent University (2012)
20. D'Antonio, G.: Manufacturing execution systems for lean, adaptive production processes. Ph.D. thesis, Politecnico di Torino (2016). http://porto.polito.it/2641291/
21. European Resource Efficiency Platform: Manifesto & Policy recommendations (2012). http://ec.europa.eu/environment/resource_efficiency/documents/erep_manifesto_and_policy_recommendations_31-03-2014.pdf. Accessed 06 July 2016

PLM and Innovation

Virtual Twins as Integrative Components of Smart Products

Michael Abramovici, Jens Christian Göbel, and Philipp Savarino(✉)

Chair of Information Technology in Mechanical Engineering (ITM), Ruhr-University Bochum, Bochum, Germany
{michael.abramovici,jenschristian.goebel, philipp.savarino}@itm.rub.de

Abstract. Current ICT developments in the areas of micro-devices, hardware infrastructure as well as internet and software technologies lead to a change of the physical products we know today. Traditional products are becoming smarter every day. The product generation meeting these innovations is called "Smart Products". As a driver of the 4th industrial revolution these Smart Products will dominate most industrial sectors in the future. Product related data and the management of this data along the entire product lifecycle in the PLM context are becoming core components of these Smart Products. This is especially true for the tremendous amount of operational data generated by the Smart Products during their use phase. However, the management of Smart Products' data related to a magnitude of heterogeneous product models (virtual product twins) will be crucial for the persistence of industrial companies. This paper illustrates that the virtual product twins have to be considered as integral components of Smart Products by giving concrete examples for the application of various virtual and physical products in different lifecycle phases.

Keywords: PLM · Virtual twin · Smart Product

1 Introduction

Recent innovations in the fields of information and communication technologies (ICT) have a huge impact on physical products. These products affected mainly by the "Internet of Things" are called "Smart Products" [1]. Smart Products (SP) are Cyber-Physical Systems (CPS) defined as intelligent mechatronic products capable of communicating and interacting with other CPS by using different means such as internet or wireless LAN [2]. However, the central basis for Smart Products has to be seen in combinations of software (e.g. big data analytics) and hardware developments (smart devices) as well as communication infrastructure innovations (e.g. LTE). Furthermore, embedded micro-devices (e.g. micro-sensors) allow physical products to interact with their environment.

A survey from the academic society for product development (WiGeP) among more than 60 engineering managers from German industrial companies underlines the current transition from traditional physical products to network-based systems. More

R. Harik et al. (Eds.): PLM 2016, IFIP AICT 492, pp. 217–226, 2016.
DOI: 10.1007/978-3-319-54660-5_20

than 60% were already working on projects related to the 4th industrial revolution while only 3% haven't already taken first steps into action [3].

A main challenge concerning the management of SP-related data lies in the collection, integration and transformation into information in order to be valuable for an enterprise network. Due to the fact that Smart Products are intelligent and adaptive to their environment the management of the virtual product models become more and more important. The necessity of being able to predict the performance of a Smart Product or to manage for example product instances that are acting autonomously increases as the creation value doesn't end with the selling of the product [4].

This paper introduces a concept of virtual and physical product twins. It points out relevant product models such as CAD models and data like condition data of product components that build up the base for the virtual twins of a product. Based on these characteristics it will be shown by considering the example of a self-driving car that virtual product twins have to be regarded as integrative components of Smart Products. From this point necessary models and data that allow the creation of a virtual twin are analysed and systematized in a general way considering the whole product lifecycle.

2 From Traditional Products to Smart Products

The term "smart" is generally related to expressions such as clever, intelligent, agile, modern and intuitive. The characteristics of a Smart Product can be described considering components of a car (see Fig. 1) [5].

The process of becoming "smart" starts in this example with mechatronic systems, as they form a hybrid system consisting of a connected mechanic and electronic unit such as a car brake system. Intelligent mechatronic products evolve from mechatronic products. They are enhanced by a certain intelligence that allows them to adapt themselves according to their environmental awareness e.g. electronic stability control (ESC), which detects and reduces situational loss of traction. If intelligent mechatronic

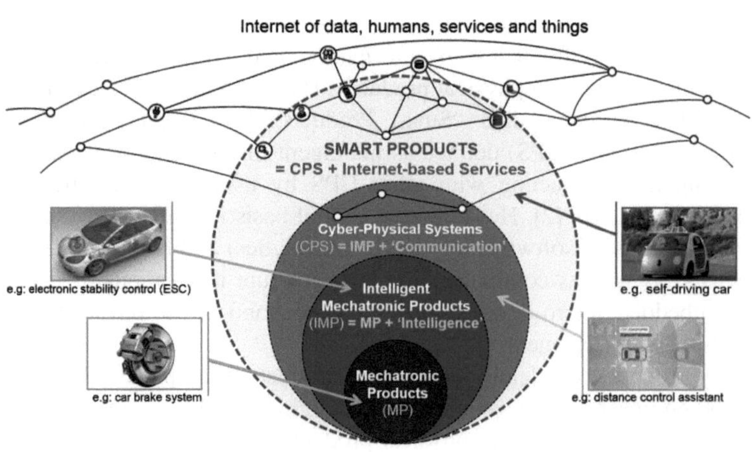

Fig. 1. Classification of products [6].

products are communicating with their environment and are acting accordingly they can be labelled as Cyber-Physical Systems (CPS). These CPS can be described with the help of a distance control assistant which is constantly in interaction with the car's environment in order to react situationally to the road behavior of other cars.

Lastly, CPS connected to the internet of data, humans, services and things (internet of everything) are called Smart Products. An example for such a Smart Product is a self-driving car, which combines all the above mentioned systems and is additionally connected to the Internet. The car is able to adapt and react accordingly to its environment and has therefore an awareness of its surrounding, e.g. by communicating with traffic lights while approaching an intersection. Nevertheless, it must be trackable where the exact position of the car is at any time as well as the car needs to know when the gas tank is below a certain level, react to temporary obstacles like construction yards or if the city introduces new one-way streets for example. This interaction between different kinds of data like environmental data or assignments, product models with all product-defining data and physical product data does not only apply to the phase of the car's lifecycle when it's actually driving on the street but has to be considered from the very beginning of the products' lifecycle until the end.

3 Virtual Twins of Smart Products

Originally the term "virtual twin" was introduced in NASA's technology roadmap "Modeling, Simulation, Information Technology & Processing". It was defined as an integrated multiphysics, multiscale simulation of a vehicle or system that uses the best available physical models and sensor updates to mirror the life of its corresponding flying twin [7, 8]. In other words, a virtual twin is a virtual copy of something physical modelled to behave realistically. Considering a Smart Product the virtual twin can be regarded as the notion where the data of each stage of the product lifecycle is transformed into information and is made seamlessly available to subsequent stages [9]. However, it is necessary to distinguish between a physical product lifecycle and a virtual product lifecycle as every physical phase of a products' lifecycle has a corresponding virtual lifecycle phase. In these lifecycle phases models and data can be found that can be located either in the virtual or the physical lifecycle of a product. For example, a geometric virtual product model during the product development phase matches with the physical prototype. The virtual production planning is linked to the physical act of production. During the product use phase, the virtual product use management assures the operation of the product and the virtual End-of-Life-Planning (EoL) is connected to the physical End-of-Life phase of the product lifecycle. Figure 2 shows dependencies between the physical product lifecycle and the virtual product lifecycle whose physical output, data and product models merge to a physical respectively a virtual twin. The physical twin can be considered as the physical output corresponding to the physical lifecycle phase e.g. a prototype or later the product. The virtual twin however is a mix of data and virtual models that build a copy of the physical twin.

As for the product development and the production phase the integration of models and data between the physical and the virtual product lifecycle has been addressed for

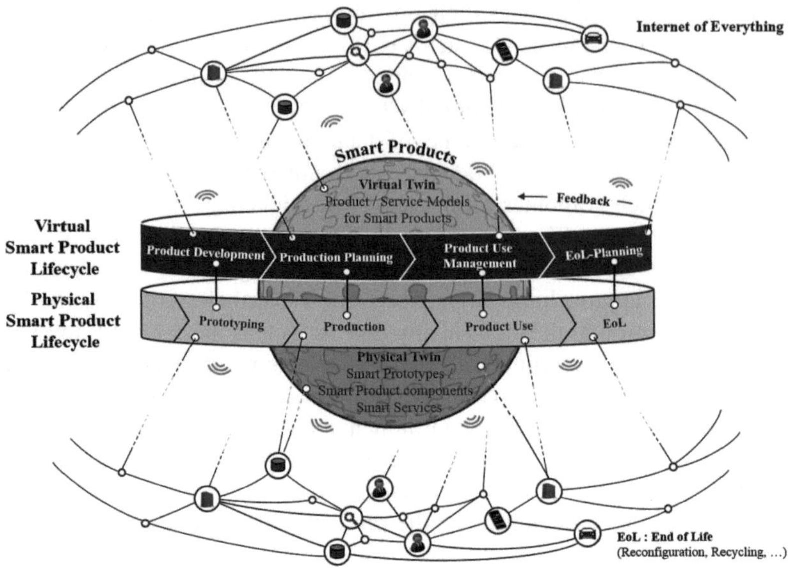

Fig. 2. Relations between the virtual and the physical smart product lifecycle.

many years and thus today is established in wide parts. In the product development phase for example functional important geometries of car engine components (e.g. cylinder heads) lie within tolerances of ±0.2 mm for casted shapes [10]. In general companies wait for the physical parts to become available in order to assemble a prototype and to inspect the quality as well as the build process. However, this can be time-consuming and costly if unsuspected errors occur despite using techniques like N-body simulation for example. Commercial solutions allow to predict the final quality of the design long before physical parts have to be manufactured. This can be realized for example by building a virtual twin in a CAD software with all the geometric information necessary (e.g. tolerances) and by linking this with a PLM-software where the product structure within the bill of materials (BOM) as well as a basic description of the build process is added. By simulating the build process of the assembly of many engine blocks possible interferences can be detected and solved by redesigning even before any prototype is manufactured [11].

During the production planning it is crucial to link the results of the product development phase with the manufacturing planning. Process plans for example that contain bills of materials can be updated in real time from the development phase. If e.g. the engines of the car were initially designed with cambelts but are now redesigned for reducing wearing parts by using cam chains this information can be passed directly from the designers to the manufactures. By establishing a new manufacturing operation the changed components can be assigned to it and a detailed production plan with time assignments to each individual step can be built [11]. Additional data from machines such as installation space or production speed as well as working plans, process plans, factory plans or product models like CAD data can provide a simulation of the production process to check productivity or most efficient manufacturing routes possible.

Finally, after the production plan for a product has been assigned the production can be executed. The virtual twin helps to surveil the performance of the production by assuring that resources are getting allocated to the adequate machines. This guarantees a flexible production or assists the quality control e.g. by comparing clearances from the development phase with the actually produced clearances by putting product model data in context with machine data.

After the product has been produced it reaches the product use phase. During this phase the use and enhancement of virtual product models increases with the "intelligence" of a product. Considering a Smart Product as described in chapter two as a CPS connected to the internet of data, humans and services the generated amount of data and the involved virtual models are manifold offering a huge spectrum of possibilities. A virtual twin of a Smart Product can for example support the physical product regarding its (predictive) maintenance or services. E.g. behavior models like safety or diagnosis systems or sensors at the Smart Product provide a dashboard with information such as the amount of fuel or the tire tread. Deducing from this data from different sources like physical product data (e.g. vehicle speed or load weight) and environmental data (e.g. road pavement or weather conditions) a virtual twin can react to situations in real time that could have led to dangerous situations based on low tire tread for example by activating assisting systems in a dangerous curve on a slippery road. Therefore, not only the above mentioned physical product and environment data in combination with the product models are crucial but also internet-connected services that make the car aware of the upcoming curve, such as a navigation app or the possibility to communicate with other cars for example. This however increases the need for the integrated management of the different product instances. This is due to the fact that every self-driving car has issues, such as the fuel or tire problems, that has to be monitored individually as all of the products are getting utilized differently. For example differs the distance covered by every car as well as the history regarding the amount of people transported, the type of roads used such as city streets or highways or the landscape the car has been driving through in regard to flat lands or mountainous areas. Product instance management is also affected by the individual maintenance history concerning the condition and functionality of the products' components but also regarding services or new business models like availability-orientated models, in which a customer has to rely on the availability of a car within a certain amount of time when he needs to use it. However to be able to manage each instance with a virtual twin data from the physical lifecycle such as the condition of car components (e.g. tire tread) or car behavior (e.g. speed) as well as data about the environment (e.g. weather) has to be matched with the corresponding product models such as the bills of materials, CAD data, software versions of e.g. assisting systems, material data, simulation data and diagnosis models and so on. This agglomeration of data can then manipulate the physical twin appropriate to the situation.

Lastly, the EoL-Planning of the virtual product lifecycle is connected with the EoL of the physical product with the help of their corresponding virtual and physical twin. One possible application is for example the reconfiguration of a Smart Product as the product itself or at least parts of it get either recycled or cater for a new or broader purpose. This can mean e.g. that software updates have to be executed where again data about the condition of the car (e.g. current software versions) has to be matched with environmental information (e.g. a navigation app where recently new built streets influence the traffic) and with instanced product model data. But also new operational purposes like using the car with a trailer for example or exchanging a component with a new one made from a different material can be simulated and its performance can be predicted.

A core question concerning the introduction of Smart Products is, which components of the virtual and which components of the physical lifecycle models and data have to be considered and how they have to be connected and integrated in order to get additional information in form of a virtual twin. Therefore, interdisciplinary (mechanics, electronics and informatics) models as well as physical product models and parts have to be combined to filter data that has to be transferred into context-specific information as for example the application of electronic stability control (ESC) in a car mentioned before.

This applies on the one hand to the virtual and physical product lifecycle phase of each lifecycle stage but on the other hand also to the seamless linking between the lifecycle stages. Figure 3 shows an overview of some important models and physical components that have to be considered and where their sources can be located.

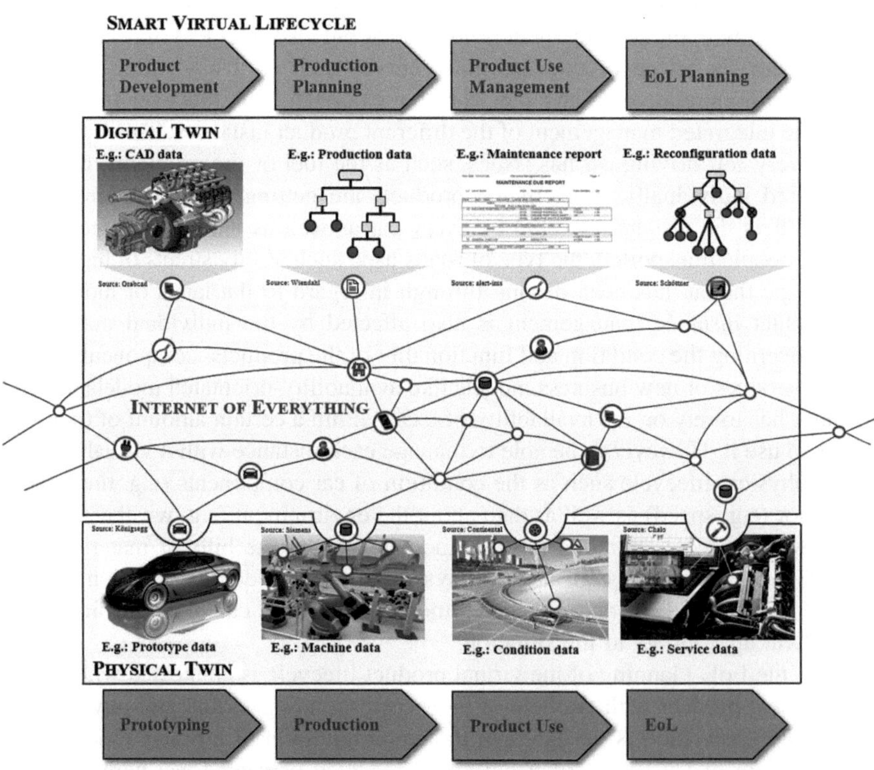

Fig. 3. Models and data exchanged between the lifecycle phases.

For the product development phase, the virtual product lifecycle includes for example CAD data, such as 3-D geometry models of parts and assemblies of the (self-driving) car. Further simulation data for e.g. finite element method to test the strength of connected components or kinematic properties is analyzed. Structural models about the product are handled in bills of materials. They include the basic assemblies of the product such as components implemented into the engine of the car. The physical product lifecycle at the development stage can contain the prototype with sensors that collect condition or test data, which can be part of the virtual twin. Prototypic realizations of the (self-driving) car can measure for example aerodynamic or tribological properties. This means all data from all the physical twins over the whole physical lifecycle gets collected, e.g. by sensors, and transferred into a cloud that belongs to the virtual twin. At the development stage for example a prototype with sensors can collect condition or test data. Prototypic realizations of the (self-driving) car can measure aerodynamic or tribological properties. This allows a real time mapping with data from the virtual lifecycle phase such as simulation data. By densifying all these data e.g. crash test data can be used to scale and simulate crashes with different environmental characteristics such as impact speed or angle.

During the production phase virtual data necessary for the virtual twin are e.g. process or production data for the time management of different sections of the car-production process. This includes the planning of materials as well as using CAD models to simulate a production environment with workspaces or NC-data to program machines in order to work according to the production plans. Also bills of materials with information about the stages of production are depicted in the virtual data of the production phase. The physical product lifecycle has information about production related data like the quantity of output or quality of produced components for example. The geometry of the car can be measured if they lie within tolerance ranges or measurement data can be collected if the produced parts fulfil the assigned job. Condition data such as information about the status of machines or even the product can help to assign and to bring autonomously material to machines in the sense of a self-optimizing factory so that capacities are exploited in the most efficient way.

Regarding the use phase on the virtual lifecycle phase for example software like firmware or apps with different versions need to be considered. These can refer to electronic assistant systems such as lane departure warning systems (LDW) for example, which means that the car is using simulation models itself while driving. Apps with map-systems for cities or assignments for the self-driving car as well as reconfiguration data to extend or change the purpose of the car are crucial data in this phase. Bills of materials are also part of this phase as they display service parts that had to be changed such as the cambelt for example. Simulation data based on feedback processes from the product can be used to simulate different scenarios, e.g. analyze if the self-driving car is able to drive a road with a certain gradient while being loaded with 65% of the permissible weight. Therefore, information about the condition of components, which are available with the help of sensors, are necessary. This data has to be densified collectively from and analyzed individually for every car so that each situation can be evaluated and solved independently. This includes also information concerning the environment of the car such as traffic signs or weather conditions in order to react in real time according to context.

The virtual lifecycle data during the EoL-phase focuses mainly on the question how to proceed with the car after it has fulfilled its primary purpose. This concerns reconfiguration data regarding different possibilities to use the car or at least parts of it. Therefore, material data about the condition of components has to be evaluated whether they can still be used in a different way. Again reconfiguration data is of importance in order to trace any new parts that have been built in during the use phase just as in the example of the exchanged cambelt above. If however no other purpose for the components can be found recycling data from the scrapping process can be collected in order to gain information for future actions. The physical counterpart to these data has to be collected by sensors from every instance as condition data. This is crucial for the tracing of replaced parts in every car for example.

Regarding the described physical and virtual lifecycles it became apparent that during the first two lifecycle stages (product development phase and production phase) the virtual lifecycle phase seems to be the dominant data source for the virtual twin to provide a benefit. Mainly CAD data as well simulation data or BOM suffice to make first assumptions about the behavior of a prototype. The same during the production phase where the product efficiency can be estimated with the virtual twin before one physical geometry has been produced. This however shifts during the last two lifecycle stages as condition data of components as well as environmental data are of high importance in order to actually influence the physical product with the help of simulation or behavior predictions by the virtual twin.

It becomes also obvious that some models and data can be found in more than one phase, such as CAD data and BOM as well as the stated importance of condition data during the product use phase or the EoL phase. This applies though for different kinds of models or physical lifecycle data depending on the product and what kind of information should be obtained with the help of the virtual twin. If these data und product models can be classified or systematized in a more detailed way, it might be possible to predict the degree of autonomy of a Smart Product or what kind of statements and with which certainty can be expected by the virtual twin.

4 Current Research Approaches Towards Virtual Twin Concepts

Most existing research activities in the area of lifecycle integration focus on different engineering methods that aim at the provision of an infrastructure, e.g. feedback management systems, to support either the seamless integration of different lifecycle phases or the integration of the virtual and physical product data in a certain lifecycle phase.

Eigner et al. developed a System Lifecycle Management (SysLM) as an engineering backbone for the description of complex product systems in the context of Smart Products. This approach offers an exchange of information among different disciplines such as mechanics, electronics and informatics for the whole lifecycle and integrates the management of services [12]. A cross-discipline specification technique for the system design was also introduced by Iwanek et al. in order to solve the discipline-spanning problems evolving from Smart Products regarding mechanic, electronic and informatics components [13]. Another approach in order to combine mechanical, electrical and software engineering along the lifecycle was introduced by Gausemeier et al. [14]. Durão et al. introduced an integrated component data model based on Unified Modeling Language (UML) to create a connected environment in manufacturing based on Cyber-Physical Production Systems (CPPS) where CPPS and Smart Products can store and exchange data throughout the entire lifecycle [15]. This approach aims specifically at breaking the isolated consideration of the virtual and physical lifecycle by introducing a concept for an integrated data model. A seamless introduction of the whole physical lifecycle phases was approached with the help of a Product Ontology (ONTO-PDM) [16]. This aims at facilitating the interoperation of all application software that share information during the different phases of the physical lifecycle.

An approach to support the integration within a lifecycle phase was introduced by Kubler et al. with a methodology for the management of product instances by using RFID technology [17]. An ontology-driven approach for sustainable product development in combination with decision making was also introduced by Stark and Pförtner. The ontology (OBISO) was validated on material decisions during the engineering process of a pedelec and follows the goal to provide a better usage of feedback information [18].

However, these approaches tend to focus only on one problem as they aim at integrating data either along the lifecycle phases or the virtual and physical product data within a lifecycle phase. A comprehensive consideration using both virtual and physical product twins and the identification of necessary product models or physical product data is missing today.

5 Conclusion

Every industrial product will have to face the impacts of the 4th industrial revolution in one way or the other. Physical products are getting smarter than ever due to their ability to communicate with their environment. This produces a huge amount of models and data that are connected to the Smart Product along its lifecycle and that need to be systemized and integrated in-between themselves. The virtual twin can be considered as a virtual reflection of a Smart Product. It integrates the management and analysis of these virtual models and data with data from the physical Smart Product and allows the simulation of scenarios based upon the aggregated information.

This paper pointed out the characteristics of Smart Products evolving from recent ICT innovations. Deriving from that point the concept of a virtual and a physical lifecycle was introduced by explaining the connection between every single lifecycle phase with the help of a self-driving car as an example for a Smart Product. It was shown that virtual twins can be regarded as the virtual copies of physical products along the entire lifecycle. Afterwards, models and data from the virtual and physical lifecycle were assigned to each lifecycle phase. It became obvious that some models and data were found in every stage so that the management of them can be seen as a crucial factor for the creation of a virtual twin. In future works a more detailed analysis of the impact of different models or product data might lead to a tendency of what features of a virtual twin can be realized, for example with the help of a maturity model.

References

1. Kagermann, H., Wahlster, W., Helbig, J.: Deutschlands Zukunft als Produktionsstandort sichern. Umsetzungsempfehlungen für das Zukunftsprojekt Industrie 4.0, Frankfurt/Main (2013)
2. Abramovici, M.: Smart products. In: Lapierriére, L., Reinhart, G. (eds.) CIRP Encyclopedia of Production Engineering, pp. 1–5. Springer, Heidelberg (2014)
3. Abramovici, M., Gebus, P.: Engineering of smart products and services: results of an Acatech industry expert study In: Proceedings ProSTEP iViP Symposium, Stuttgart, 20–21 April 2016, ProSTEP iViP Verein, Darmstadt (2016)
4. Schweitzer, E., Aurich, J.C.: Continuous improvement of industrial product-service systems. CIRP J. Manuf. Sci. Technol. **3**(2), 158–164 (2010)
5. Abramovici, M., Göbel, J.C., Neges, M.: Smart engineering as enabler for the 4th industrial revolution. In: Fathi, M. (ed.) Integrated Systems: Innovations and Applications, pp. 163–170. Springer International Publishing, Cham (2015)
6. Abramovici, M., Star, R. (eds.): Smart Product Engineering. Springer, Heidelberg (2013)
7. NASA Technology Roadmap, Modeling, Simulation, Information Technology & Processing Roadmap Technology Area 11 (2010)
8. NASA Technology Roadmap, Modeling, Simulation, Information Technology & Processing Roadmap Technology Area 11 (2012)
9. Rosen, R., von Wichert, G., Lo, G., Bettenhausen, K.D.: About the importance of autonomy and digital twins for the future of manufacturing. IFAC-PapersOnLine **48**(3), 567–572 (2015)
10. Fuchslocher, G.: ACTech: mehr Genauigkeit bei Gussteilen, Automobil-Produktion (2015)
11. Frankel, A.: Siemens PLM: Realized Products - The Real Value of the Digital Twin, (2015)
12. Eigner, M., Muggeo, C., Apostolov, H., Schäfer, P.: Kern des System Lifecycle Management: Im Kontext von Industrial Internet mit Industrie 4.0 und Internet der Dinge und Dienste, ZWF 2016 (01-02/2016) 63–68 (2016)
13. Iwanek, P., Gausemeier, J., Bansmann, M., Dumitrescu, R.: Integration of intelligent features by model-based systems engineering. In: Proceedings of 18th ISERD International Conference, Tokyo, Japan, November 2015
14. Gausemeier, J., Rammig, F.J., Schäfer, W. (eds.): Design Methodology for Intelligent Technical Systems: Develop Intelligent Technical Systems of the Future. Springer, Heidelberg (2014)
15. Durão, L.F., Eichhorn, H., Anderl, R., Schützer, K., de Senzi Zancul, E.: Integrated component data model based on UML for smart components lifecycle management: a conceptual approach. In: 12th IFIP International Conference on Product Lifecycle Management, Doha, Katar, 18–21 October 2015
16. Panetto, H., Dassisti, M., Tursi, A.: ONTO-PDM: product-driven ONTOlogy for product data management interoperability within manufacturing process environment. Adv. Eng. Informat. **26**(2), 334–348 (2012)
17. Kubler, S., Derigent, W., Främling, K., Thomas, A., Rondeau, É.: Enhanced product lifecycle information management using "communicating materials". Comput.-Aided Des. **59**, 192–200 (2015)
18. Stark, R., Pförtner, A.: Integrating ontology into PLM-tools to improve sustainable product development. CIRP Annals - Manufacturing Technology **64**(1), 157–160 (2015)

Linking Modular Product Structure to Suppliers' Selection Through PLM Approach: A Frugal Innovation Perspective

Farouk Belkadi[1(✉)], Ravi Kumar Gupta[1], Ekaterini Vlachou[2], Alain Bernard[1], and Dimitris Mourtis[2]

[1] Ecole Centrale de Nantes – IRCCyN – UMR CNRS 6597, 1 rue de la Noë, Nantes 44300, France
Farouk.belkadi@irccyn.ec-nantes.fr

[2] Laboratory for Manufacturing Systems and Automation (LMS), Department of Mechanical Engineering and Aeronautics, University of Patras, Rio Patras 26504, Greece

Abstract. To maintain market share rates, frugal innovation is a main solution for competitive enterprises to meet the customer's needs in different regional markets. The co-evolution of product and production network aims to manage local production sites of the OEM and several collaborative relations between OEM and supplier companies for better management of the project resources in the regional market. Supplier selection and evaluation are among the main factors to be resolved at the earlier stage to guarantee successful results from any OEM-Supplier collaboration. This paper discusses the potential of using a modular-based approach as a kernel methodology to support the co-evolution of product structure and production network definition, especially in the case of supplier selection for frugal innovation perspective. The application of PLM approach to manage interconnected data describing the co-evolution of the product structure and production network is also discussed.

Keywords: PLM · Co-evolution · Modular · Supplier selection · Frugal innovation

1 Introduction

In context of hard competitiveness and economic pressures, companies need to reach new markets (i.e. both emerging and mature market) by further sharpening their strategic focus on what customers really need. For this, frugal innovation theory is introduced to explain new market trends and to propose new solutions supporting these evolutions [1]. For Tiwari and Herstatt [2], frugal innovation refers to innovative products and services that "seek to minimize the use of material and financial resources in the complete value chain (from development to disposal) with the objective of reducing the cost of ownership while fulfilling or even exceeding certain pre-defined criteria of acceptable quality standards".

This theory results new category of products named "frugal" as an aggregation of the following attributes: **Functional** to answer the exact customer need by focusing on

R. Harik et al. (Eds.): PLM 2016, IFIP AICT 492, pp. 227–237, 2016.
DOI: 10.1007/978-3-319-54660-5_21

key product features; **Robust** with integration of recent technologies and facilities of maintenance high life duration; **User-friendly** through a simple and easy to use functions and interfaces; **Growing** through large production volumes enabling economies of scale; **Affordable** by offering to customer good "value for his money" through adaptable prices according to their socio-economic context; and **Local** to propose products mainly tailored to local requirements but also built using some production facilities (i.e. suppliers) and components from the targeted market [3].

To develop such kind of products, companies should adopt a customer-driven design process and an optimal co-evolution of the production strategy to reduce manufacturing and logistic costs, taking in consideration the capabilities, constraints and resources available in the targeted market. The design strategy respecting frugal attributes can be conducted through a set of following design actions:

- Design new specific modules or modifying the features of existing ones,
- Reuse existing solutions developed by the company in previous projects,
- Use standard modules developed by external suppliers for several products.

The co-evolution of the production network to support the adaptation of an existing product to a new market implies new changes on the production process or on suppliers to cope with new modification in the product structure (it can be the change of one module or modification of some module features). In parallel, the modification of the product structure can be a consequence of using a new module (or technology) proposed by a supplier in the local market which results in the co-evolution of the product structure with the production strategy [4]. The big challenge is then to have an efficient collaboration between the OEM company and all its suppliers.

The co-evolution of the production system should be extended to the production network level that aims to create several collaborative relations between the OEM (Original Equipment Manufacturer) and suppliers' companies for better management of their distinctive skills and resources in the whole production process [5]. Thus, Supplier selection and evaluation are among the main factors to be resolved at the earlier stage to guarantee successful results from any OEM-Supplier collaboration [6].

As per our study, an emerging market's needs can be solved by adapting an existing product and production which are well stablished in westerned and European markets to fulfil regional customer's requirements (new market) especially when the customer belongs to emerging markets (e.g. India, Africa and China). This adaptation of the existing product to emerging market is researched using frugal innovation. Few companies adopted the frugal innovation for the above aspects, but took long time to launch their product in the markets.

The research in ProRegio [7] is to fill these gaps. One part in this research is suppliers' selection respecting the requirements from regional markets and also company's policies.

In this context, this paper discusses the potential of using a modular-based approach as a kernel methodology to support the co-evolution of product structure and production network definition, especially in the case of supplier selection in context of frugal innovation. This approach is mainly suitable for design strategies based on the use of standard modules or the reuse of existing solutions (with possible adaptation). A smart algorithm is used to generate and evaluate the alternative supplier networks.

2 PLM Approach for Supplier Selection

2.1 Frugal Innovation and Suppliers' Selection

With respect to the frugal innovation principle, the global modular-based approach should handle the easier interpretation of customer requirements and the identification of only concerned modules to be considered for the customization process [8, 9].

The concept of module represents a physical or conceptual grouping of product components to form a consistent unit that can be easily identified and replaced in one product architecture in order to increase product variety and flexible adaptability [10].

In the proposed frugal innovation process (Fig. 1), the designer can propose several alternatives of product modules with specific features to cope with a set of customer requirements. These features concern technical characteristics used for the engineering perspective as well as useful inputs for building the related production network. Each module is identified with all possible production capabilities or suppliers able to provide it with the desired characteristics. The selection of the best alternatives of production systems or suppliers is fulfilled by taking in consideration of different facilities and constraints in the local market to build the global production network. Then the selection of the best module solutions can be obtained as a consequence of selecting the related production systems or suppliers.

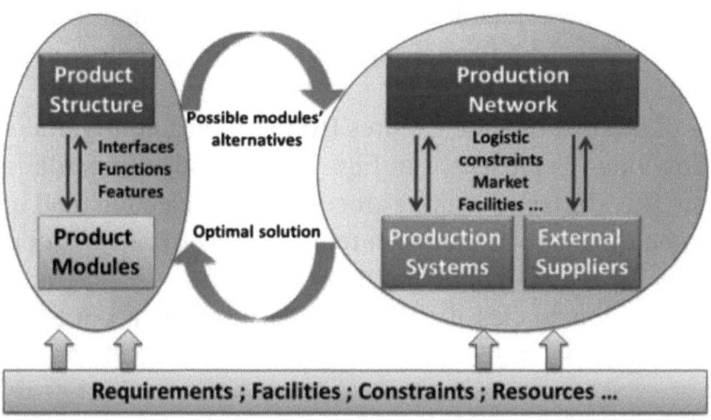

Fig. 1. Co-definition of product structure and production network

Production system refers to technological elements (machines and tools), organizational behavior and managing resources within OEM whereas supplier refers to external supplier of product modules and related supports. A supplier can be local or international based on local requirements and product modules characteristics.

By fixing the different production systems and suppliers (for final assembly and for the production of modules), the structure of the production network is defined as a combination of the selected items. The expected behavior of the network is obtained by the definition of the global planning and all collaborative processes supporting information and material exchange among these production systems and suppliers. Thus, the assembly process of the whole product structure is obtained according to the global production planning at network level.

Several collaborative relations between the OEM and suppliers are identified in the literature based on the level of integration of the supplier in the final project of the OEM [11]. At the low levels, suppliers are assimilated to simple executors of detailed specifications from the OEM. In more collaboration level, the supplier is more involved in the development project and participates to the definition of the product architecture (1st rank suppliers).

This nature of collaboration can provide serious advantages for the deployment of frugal innovation strategy in new markets. In this case the OEM will exploit some interesting and innovative solutions proposed by suppliers to design new frugal product or to adapt an existing one to one specific market. By this, the development process will follow a concurrent path in which the selection of the best product modules can be obtained from the identification of the best suppliers respecting the frugal requirements. Supplier selection strategy contributes principally to the improvement of "Robust", "Affordable" and "Local" attributes since it gives the possibility to the company to: use new solution that can enhance the product quality respecting the target market standard, moderate the cost by selling from competitive suppliers, especially when those ones are coming from the target market.

The concept of product module can be used to connect the product structure to different outputs of the suppliers involved in the related production network. Thus, using product module features combined with additional information from the final assembly process planning and logistic constraints in the local market can give interesting requirements for the evaluation of KPIs (Key performance indicators) useful to get an impartial assessment of potential suppliers' capacities before considering them in the production network.

The mapping of product module features (from product configuration view) to KPIs (suppliers selection view) is presented in Fig. 2. The product modules are the products of the suppliers. The decision making for supplier selection and product module selection is based on the mapping between requirements (product module features) and real values of KPIs for the suppliers and their products.

The role of mapping is to classify all available suppliers according to the matching level between their KPI values (representing real assessment) and product features

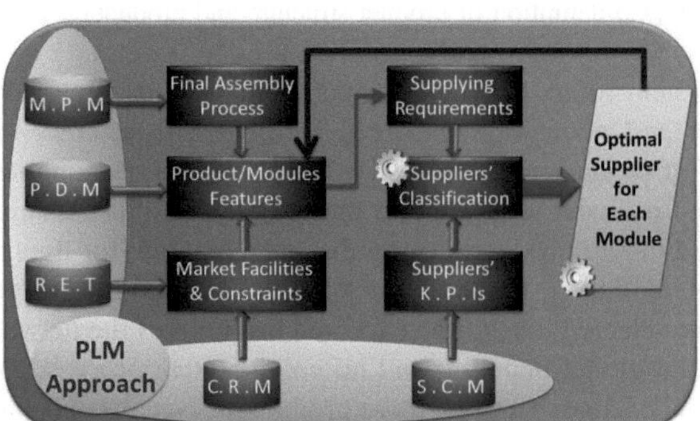

Fig. 2. Global PLM approach for supplier selection

(representing requirements). Some time, when there are limited possibilities of suppliers to cover the requested module, the mapping table can be used to adapt, if necessary, some product features according to the capacities of the related supplier.

The PLM approach can support the concurrent design process of frugal products and the supplier network through a smart management of product modules and related suppliers alternatives for several product configurations addressed to various markets. This is ensured through an optimal integration, storage and connection of numerous data coming from several applications, including suppliers' selection tools. Indeed, the implementation of PLM approach results from the integration between heterogeneous IT systems such as ERP (Enterprise Resource Planning), PDM (Product Data Management), SCM (Supply Chain management), etc. [12].

In the proposal, the supplier selection process is achieved based on several data stored on different business tools. This data is identified and managed in the PLM system as specific features connected to different product modules alternatives. Each module is analyzed to generate supplying requirements. The final decision is the identification of optimal "Modules-Suppliers" combination as fragment co-definition of best product structure and supplier network with respect to frugal attributes.

2.2 Product Features for Supplier Selection

To illustrate the proposed principle of solution for the use of modularity for supplier selection problem, an example of concurrent design process of frugal product and identification of possible suppliers for each module is presented in Fig. 3. This scenario deals with the case of adapting existing product architecture to a new market based on the capabilities of existing suppliers in the targeted market.

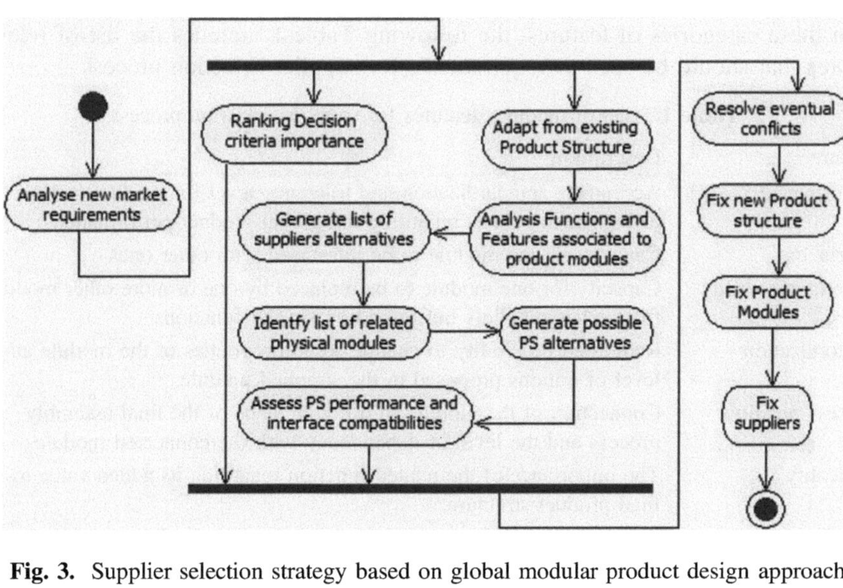

Fig. 3. Supplier selection strategy based on global modular product design approach

The process starts by the analysis of new market requirements (including specific customer requirements) and then search for existing product structures covering these needs. The analysis of modules functions and features as requirements is used to generate list of possible suppliers. The list of suppliers' alternatives will provide list of possible module alternatives matching with the same functions of the originally design product. Then several alternatives of product structures from the original one (developed in older projects) can be obtained as combination of the product modules proposed by the selected suppliers.

The performance assessment of each alternative will help to fix the best product structure and consequently the best product modules replacing the original ones. In final the list of supplier is fixed as those providing the selected modules.

To perform these decision making processes, additional categories of information should be embedded in the product module concept. The definition of product module through features is to connect different views of the product design and development.

Product module features are defined to translate the regional customer requirements to product design and connect the product design to production planning and supplier network design. The product modules' features are defined to address three categories objectives as inputs for frugal decision making problems regarding the objectives of the global modular product design approach:

- Analyzing customer/market requirements and linking product modules to requested functions in specific product architecture.
- Defining modules' parameters and its interfaces to support the design of new product (and related alternatives) as a consistent combination of product modules.
- Responding to production strategy (production system and network definition) through a consistent connection of modules to optimal production capabilities.

These three categories of features are used to identify requirements for supplying properties and production planning as well as to refine the selection of product module. From these categories of features, the following Table 1 includes the list of relevant features that should be used as requirements for supplier selection process.

Table 1. List of modules features for supplier selection process

Feature	Description
Performance	Acceptable standardization and tolerance level for product module performance values, regarding the global product performance.
Interfacing	Capacity to one module to be interfaced with other ones
Interchange-ability	Capacity for one module to be replaced by one or more other modules from other suppliers but providing similar functions.
Customization	Requested possibility to change some proprieties of the module and level of options proposed in the supplied module.
Process position	Connection of the module to different steps of the final assembly process and the level of dependency with the connected modules
Criticality	The importance of the related function regarding its added value to the final product structure.
Supplying tolerance	Level of request on the supplier in terms of cost, delivery time and confidence level as a consequence of the previous modules' features.

Figure 4 illustrates an example of using product module features (green color rectangle) to analyze product life cycle and generate additional Supplying Tolerance Features (inner blue color rectangle), to be considered as requirements for decision criteria for the selection of best suppliers for frugal innovation issue. These supplying decision criteria and/or related KIPs can be used for production network design.

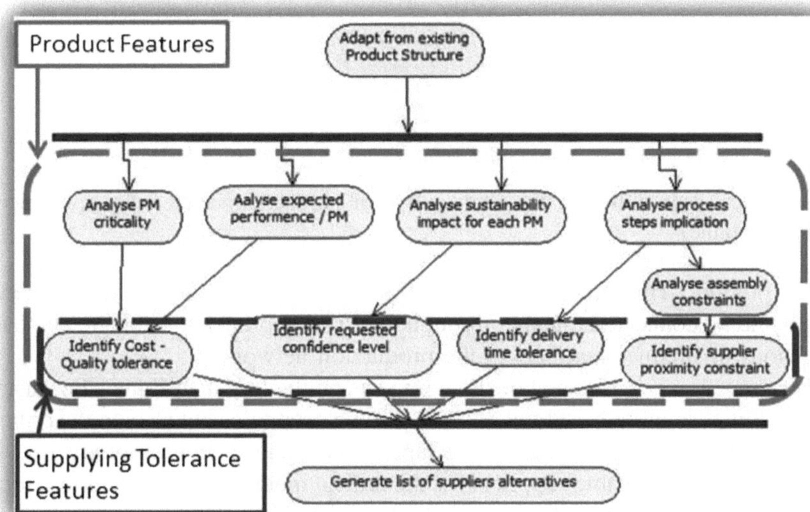

Fig. 4. Product module features as requirements for supplying decision criteria (Color figure online)

Through the application of the concurrent design of product structure and suppliers' network, conflict can appear from contradictions on results based on analysis of product module features on one side and supplying requirements on the other side, for example a module can have high performance but real risk on delivery time regarding the supplier capacities, especially if the module is requested earlier in the production process. This will imply important delays on the final assembly process of the product. Affordable and growing attributes are seriously affected.

Figure 5 illustrates such kind of conflicts between product modules "as designed" (inner blue color rectangle) and real modules "as produced by suppliers" (inner green color rectangle). It is shown that the product module "PM1" has product module feature "Criticality" value as "High". PM1.1 is the "Best" implementation and PM1.2 is the "Worst" one according to the related suppliers KPIs. However, PM1.1 presents a low level of interfacing with the PM 2.1 that is the only possible implementation of PM2. The conflict is that if the best product module with high criticality (PM1.1) is selected then supplying of other product module (PM2) is not possible.

There are two possibilities to resolve this type of situations either (i) Select the modules to be supplied as per the requested module features and redesign (or reselect new supplier) the product modules which are not possible to be supplied by any existing supplier, or (ii) Relax features' values for the conflicted product module in the

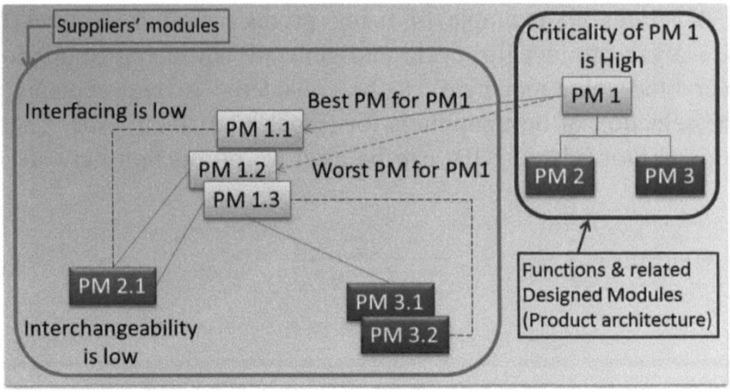

Fig. 5. Conflicts possibilities on the co-definition of product structure and supplier network (Color figure online)

requested product. Thus, product module features and KPIs for production network design should be connected together through the PLM approach to evaluate all possible combinations of product-suppliers in the production network.

This connection provides real positive impacts on the frugal attributes. For instance, deciding optimal supplier based not only on its own properties but also on the criticality of the related modules allows managers adapting the balance between product cost and quality by favoring reputable suppliers for the critical modules (high function criticality requesting high quality) even the price is high, and obtaining the less critical modules (less added value for the target market) from low cost suppliers.

3 Supplier Selection and Network Design Method

The supplier selection and network design method should be capable of generating alternative combinations of product-suppliers and evaluate their performance based on multiple and conflicting criteria based on the constrains-suggestions provided by the design during the generation of the different product structures. One of the main challenges during the supplier's selection and the supplier networks design is to select the optimum supplier based on their suitability and their availability. Therefore, the proposed work proposes a smart search algorithm capable of subset of total number of alternative manufacturing network configurations by utilizing three adjustable parameters [13]. The three control parameters that are utilized are the maximum number of alternatives (MNA) which controls the breadth of the search, the decision horizon (DH) which controls the depth of the search, and the sampling rate (SR) which guides the search towards the high quality branches of the tree of alternatives [14]. The optimum values of these factors will be obtained through a statistical Design of Experiments (SDoE) [15].

The main inputs of the proposed algorithm are the various product features generated by the product configuration and the pre-filtered list of suppliers based on their compatibility and their suitability, as well the bill of processes to produce the product modules and in general the final product. The decision-making procedure following by the supplier selection and networks design algorithm is based on resource-task assignment decisions. Considering that, in order to produce a part/module of the product a task should be performed by a resource and the resource belongs to a plant or to a supplier. In case of suppliers the task is directly connected with the supplier.

The main steps of the proposed algorithm the formalization of the alternatives, the criteria determination to satisfy the objectives, the definition of the criteria weights, the calculation of the criteria values and last is the selection of the optimum alternative based on their performance (Fig. 6) [14, 16].

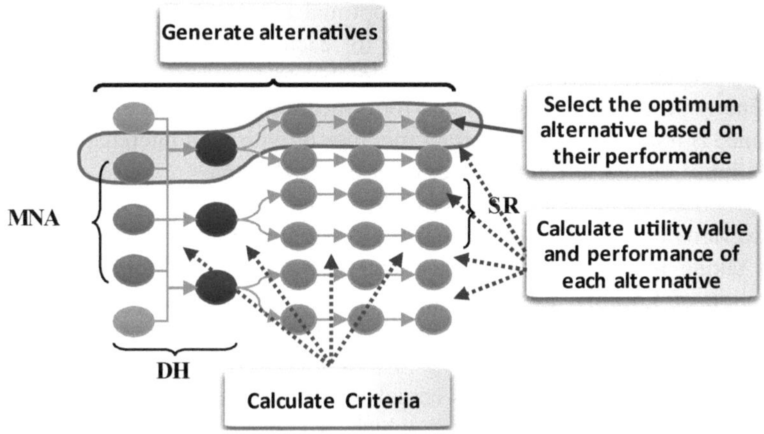

Fig. 6. Supplier selection and network design Algorithm-Smart search algorithm

Multiple and conflicting criteria are considered and are calculated by the smart search algorithm and during the decision making procedure. Production and Transportation Cost, Quality, Lead time, total Energy Consumption, CO2 emissions are among the main criteria considered [17].

To address the need of frugal innovation in the context of the supplier's selection method also the locality of the suppliers is considered as main criterion. Locality shows how close to the targeted market is the supplier. This will contribute to enhance the affordable and local attributes by reducing logistics costs and using existing standards in the target market since the providers are coming from the same market. Moreover, through the consideration of Locality, as criterion, local suppliers can be considered, increasing the market share of local markets.

The total network performance is calculated by measuring defined KPIs. In that stage, also the suggested KPIs, from the product configuration stage, are considered. The final results of the selected network are sending back to the PLM tool in order to fix the different modules of the product and finalize the design of the product.

4 Conclusion

The co-evaluation of product structure, production systems, and production network has been introduced as a key factor for the success of an enterprise in emerging markets to answer local needs by optimal utilization of local and global capabilities, constraints and resources. Global modular approach has been used to support the design and development of frugal product. The application of module concept for frugal innovation perspectives showed the need to re-think the definition of the product model and its integration in future generation of PLM systems. New features should be considered to represent requirements of production from frugal product side and to connect product design to production and supplying strategies.

Considering product features as decision criteria for supplier selection strategy will contribute to enhance the product frugal attributes, especially affordable, robust and local attributes. This is given through an optimal balance between cost, quality and delivery time requests, assessed separately for each product module according to its criticality in the target market, impact on the global performance and implication on the final assembly process. The logic is that for critical modules, strong trust on suppliers' performance is required. Less important modules or with high interchangeability allow more flexibility on the selection strategy for cost reduction.

The proposed methodology can provide a great advantage to companies that are moving towards frugal innovation concept by providing local, low-cost and affordable products taking into account local customer's requirements. Moreover, through the consideration of Locality, as criterion, during the proposed supplier's selection and networks design tool, local suppliers can be considered, increasing the market share of local markets.

This paper focuses on the conceptual solution instead of presenting the final implementation for industrial use case which is under development. The developed methodology is well appreciated by industrial partners as well as academic partners.

Acknowledgments. The presented results were conducted within the project "ProRegio" entitled "customer-driven design of product-services and production networks to adapt to regional market requirements". This project has received funding from the European Union's Horizon 2020 program under grant agreement no. 636966. The authors would like to thank the industrial partners involved in this research.

References

1. Zeschky, M., Widenmayer, B., Gassmann, O.: Frugal innovation in emerging markets: the case of mettler toledo. Res. Technol. Manag. **54**(4), 38–45 (2011)
2. Tiwari, R., Herstatt, C.: Frugal innovation: a global networks' perspective. Swiss J. Bus. Res. Pract. **3**, 245–274 (2012)
3. Berger, R.: Frugal Products: Study Results. Roland Berger Strategy Consultants, Stuttgart (2013). http://www.rolandberger.com/media/pdf/Roland_Berger_Frugal_products_20130212.pdf
4. Arndt, T., Hochdörffer, J., Moser, E., Peters, S., Lanza, G.: Customer-driven planning and control of global production networks - balancing standardisation and regionalisation. In: 18th Cambridge Int. Manufacturing Symposium, (UK), 24–25 September, pp. 60–74 (2015)
5. Hochdörffer, J., Arndt, T., Bürgin, J., Moser, E., Scherb, M., Lanza, G.: Evaluation of global manufacturing networks - a matter of perspective. In: 19th Cambridge International Manufacturing Symposium, Cambridge (UK), 24–25 September, pp. 327–339 (2015)

6. Cheraghi, S.H., Dadashzadeh, M., Subramanian, M.: Critical success factors for supplier selection: an update. J. Appl. Bus. Res. **20**(2), 91–108 (2004)
7. http://www.h2020-proregio.eu/
8. Du, X., Tseng, M.M., Jiao, J.: Product families for mass customization: understanding the architecture. In: Tseng, M.M., Piller, F.T. (eds.) The Customer Centric Enterprise, pp. 123–161. Springer, Berlin (2003)
9. Mourtzis, D., Doukas, M.: The evolution of manufacturing systems: from craftsmanship to the era of customization. In: Modrak, V., Semanco, P. (eds.) Design and Management of Lean Production Systems. IGI Global, Chapter 1 (2014)
10. Jiao, J.R., Simpson, T.W., Siddique, Z.: Product family design and platform-based product development: state-of-the-art review. J. Intell. Manufact. **18**, 5–29 (2007)
11. Calvi, R., Le Dain, M., Harbi, S., Bonottoo, V.: How to manage early supplier involvement (ESI) into the new product development process (NPDP): several lessons from a French study. In: 10th International Annual IPSERA Conference, Jönköping, Sweden (2001)
12. Bosch-Mauchand, M., Belkadi, F., Bricogne, M., Eynard, B.: Knowledge based assessment of manufacturing process performance: integration of product lifecycle management and value chain simulation approaches. Int. J. Comput. Integr. Manufact. **26**(5), 453–473 (2013)
13. Chryssolouris, G.: Manufacturing Systems: Theory and Practice, 2nd edn. Springer-Verlag, New York (2006)
14. Mourtzis, D., Doukas, M., Psarommatis, F.: A multi-criteria evaluation of centralized and decentralized production networks in a highly customer-driven environment. CIRP Ann. – Manufact. Technol. **61**(1), 427–430 (2012)
15. Phadke, M.S.: Quality Engineering Using Robust Design. Prentice Hall, Englewood Cliffs (1989)
16. Mourtzis, D., Doukas, M., Psarommatis, F.: Design and operation of manufacturing networks for mass customisation. CIRP Ann. – Manufact. Technol. **62**, 467–470 (2013)
17. Mourtzis, D., Doukas, M., Psarommatis, F.: A toolbox for the design, planning and operation of manufacturing networks in a mass customisation environment. J. Manufact. Syst. **36**, 274–286 (2015)

PLM in the Food Industry: An Explorative Empirical Research in the Italian Market

Claudia Pinna(✉), Marco Taisch, and Sergio Terzi

Politecnico di Milano, Department of Management, Economics and Industrial, Engineering Piazza Leonardo da Vinci, 20133 Milan, Italy
{claudia.pinna,marco.taisch,sergio.terzi}@polimi.it

Abstract. The Food and Beverage (F&B) industry has a unique role in all countries' economies because it is essential to people lives. In this paper, the focus will be on the Italian food industry, one of the main food producer. This study will present the first results of a wider research that has as main aim to understand how PLM is adopted in the food industry, its limits and its challenges. Indeed, the first results show the level of knowledge of PLM systems in this sector, both from the literature and from the market point of view. Furthermore, the paper shows the results of a preliminary empirical research, made through several case studies, on the role of PLM in the product development process of the food industry.

Keywords: New Product Development (NPD) · Product Lifecycle Management (PLM) · Food industry · New Food Development (NFD) · PLM for the food industry

1 Introduction: The Importance of the Food Sector

The Food and Bevereage (F&B) industry has a unique role in all countries' economies because it is essential to people lives. The industry works at various levels of society: there may be families that grow crops and so be self-sufficient, communities producing home-processed goods, local companies transforming crops from families for local markets, and international corporation globally delivering products across the globe. In this scenario, billions of people transform and sell food. [1] The food sector in Europe is the largest manufacturing sector in terms of value added, turnover and employment. It was also the second greatest sector for production between 2008 and 2013. In this paper, Italian food companies will be the boundaries of the analysis because the food industry is a pillar for the economy of this country. Indeed, this sector represents the second sector by revenue after the engineering industry. Companies in F&B industry face many challenges in managing their products and competing in the industry. According to Oracle [2], Siemens [3] and Kalypso [4], the F&B industry has to contend with different challenges, most of which are referred to: (i) *Retail consolidation*, (ii) *Ineffective innovation*, (iii) *Increasing regulatory requirements and unclear regulations*, (iv) *Empowered consumers*, (v) *Increasingly complex global supply chains*, (vi) *Sustainability*, (vii) *Time to Market*. Most of these challenges make reference to the need for change in the vision of the food product, from the company point of view. In

R. Harik et al. (Eds.): PLM 2016, IFIP AICT 492, pp. 238–247, 2016.
DOI: 10.1007/978-3-319-54660-5_22

order to remain competitive in the market, companies operating in this sector must be able to respond promptly to the continuous market and legislation changes. For these reasons, this paper focuses on the specific phase of the New Product Development (NPD) in the food sector, being the one with the highest relevance and that would mainly help this sector to deal with these challenges. This paper starts from a literature review about the level of knowledge of PLM in the food industry (Sect. 2). In this session, the vendors of PLM of the food industry are identified, mapping the main software categories offered by each vendor. Then, in Sect. 3, the results of an empirical research conducted among some of the main Italian food companies are reported. Finally, Sect. 4 concludes the paper, presenting some thoughts and future researches.

2 PLM and the Food Industry

All the challenges above mentioned can be well faced using methodologies and tools that allow keeping information consistent and together, make teams work globally, facilitate new product ideas, product portfolio, allow the simplification of packaging and recipe specifications, managing manufacturing planning and supply chain information. In fact, an integrated product lifecycle management (PLM) solution can streamline and improve the fundamental processes that influence the development, launch and ongoing management of products. Such solutions make it possible for food and beverage companies to accelerate innovation, increase profits from product introductions, reduce risks, and ultimately drive competitive advantage [2].

2.1 Literature Analysis: The Level of Knowledge of PLM in the Food Industry

This paper aims to discuss the first steps and results related to a wider research. Regarding the first phase of the research, it concerns to analyse the level of knowledge of PLM systems in the food sector from the literature point of view. It was decided to begin the literature analysis starting from those journals that have a higher rating. Regarding data sources for the review, chosen key words have been applied (product lifecycle management, computer aided, information system) to retrieve the articles of interest in the category “Food Science”, which resulted in 61 academic journals. In this elaborate will be treated the first results, characterized by the “product lifecycle management” keyword. Starting from this point, it has been collected 49 articles and, after a careful screening, only 20 studies remained in the final selection of articles. Analysing the results of this first search, the fact that, in the first search, on over 61 journals only 49 articles were found and only 20 were considered as interesting could mean a lack level of knowledge of the PLM system in the field analysed. There are in the literature several contributions dealing with themes related to the different phases of the product life cycle (according to Kiritsis [5], the product lifecycle can be defined by three main phases: Beginning of Life, Middle of Life and End of Life), analysed separately, and how the concepts or meanings of each phase have been evolved over time but it is never cited the PLM term. It is also true that the term “product lifecycle management" is a very broad topic. [6, 7] Indeed, considering the entire life cycle of the product, the PLM term is not often used as a unique term but it is more common to find other terms that indicate one of its specific phase, a specific method or the software names used in the different stages. In conclusion it could be said that the level of knowledge of the PLM systems is still low in the food sector from the literature point of view but there are different needs in the food sector that could be addressing through the implementation of the PLM systems.

2.2 PLM Vendors of the Food Industry

A very important phase of a PLM project is the implementation phase of these systems into the company. In this stage, the choice of PLM software is fundamental in order to get all the benefits from the implemented solution. Therefore, making an assessment of PLM vendors is a good strategy that leads to understand which solution fits better for each specific company. Given the importance of the decision, it is important to have an overview of the main PLM vendors on the market operating in food sector. According to Gartner [8], the major PLM vendors operating in food sector, in terms of market share and offered solutions, are: Dassault Systèmes [9], Infor [10], Oracle [11], SAP [12], Selerant [13], Siemens [14] and Trace One [15]. In 2012 Gartner rated 23 categories of PLM functionality for these seven vendors. These features were then evaluated on the basis of the more fundamental PLM needs of process manufacturers, giving origin to 9 software categories. [8] According to Gartner [16], it is possible to give some definitions of these categories:

(i) *CAD design management* includes software in support to design data management;
(ii) *CAD for packaging design* refers to software for packaging design, with for example tools designed for packaging professionals for structural design, product development, virtual prototyping and manufacturing;
(iii) *Formula and recipe management* includes software for formula or recipe calculation and validation for process manufacturers;
(iv) *Label and artwork management* refers to software that helps manufacturers develop labels and artwork for different markets that conform to market preferences and regulations;
(v) *PLM team collaboration* supports tools to collaboration among team members, enabling the facilitation, automation, and control of the entire development process;
(vi) *Product portfolio and program management* supports the continuous cultivation of product sets by prioritizing and managing product development and retirements;
(vii) *Report specific to the industry* supports tools for monitoring and developing report for specific industry sector;
(viii) *Product specifications* technology captures the descriptions and quantities of ingredients, materials and other content, including process information needed to produce, package and ship a product;
(ix) *Regulatory compliance* supports tools that enabling companies to identify what regulations, policies and obligations are applicable to them.

The Table 1, inspired by Gartner [8], shows the Software Categories offered by each of these vendors.

Table 1. Software categories offered by main PLM vendors operating in the food sector [9–15]

Software category/vendor	Dassault systèmes	Infor	Oracle	SAP	Selerant	Siemens	Trace one
CAD design management	x		x	x		x	
CAD for packaging design	x					x	
Formula and recipe management	x	x	x	x	x	x	x
Label management	x	x	x	x	x	x	x
PLM team collaboration	x	x	x	x	x	x	x
Product portfolio and program management	x	x	x	x	x	x	x
Report specific to the industry	x	x	x	x	x	x	x
Regulatory compliance	x	x	x	x	x	x	x
Specifications management	x	x	x	x	x	x	x

There are also other vendors in the PLM market which offer specific solutions for the food industry. In the Table 2 are shown the PLM categories offered by these other PLM vendors to the food industry.

Table 2. Software categories offered by other PLM vendors operating in food sector [17–23]

Software category/vendor	Sopheon	beCPG	Aras	Technia transcat	Parallaksis	LASCOM	Advanced software designs
CAD design management							
CAD for packaging design							
Formula and recipe management		x		x	x	x	x
Label management		x		x	x	x	x
PLM team collaboration	x			x			
Product portfolio and program management	x	x	x	x		x	x
Report specific to the industry		x	x	x	x		x
Regulatory compliance	x	x		x	x	x	
Specifications management		x	x	x	x	x	

3 A Preliminary Empirical Research

In order to better understand how the use of PLM systems could enhance the performances related to the different phases of the NPD in food industry, it is necessary to know how these processes happen. Given the absence of this information in the scientific literature it was decided to obtain them through an empirical research, interviewing some of the main Italian food companies. It has therefore developed a questionnaire consisting of 11 open questions. These questions are also related to the actors participating in this process, the kind of performances considered important for the food NPD, and the forces (internal and external) that lead to the decision to develop a new product and how long lasts this process (from concept to the launch stages). The questionnaire was designed to be subjected to those business functions that deal directly the innovation and the development of the new product, and thus the functions engaged in R&D and Marketing areas and then submitted in the form of interview to 10 different Italian large companies operating in food industry. Interviews were registered and answers were coded in a standard format, aligning terminology and concepts. In order to describe the product development process, 5 different "macro phases" have been defined, assigning a cardinality from 0 to 5 depending on the assigned sequentially. Moreover, each of these "macro phases" are characterized by various activities, which can change depending on the interviewed company. After these previous and necessary data adjustment, it was possible to analyse the clean data, obtaining the following result:

The Table 3 summarize the main questionnaire results listing the phases that characterize the food new product development, obtained through the company interviews. As can be inferred from this table, to each macro phase corresponds one or more activities that need to be developed in order to skip to the next macro phase. In fact, from the results of the interviews it is also possible to deduce that a NPD process, in food industry, is a process characterized by different macro phases, in turn characterized by more activities, which are carried out in a sequential manner. Thanks to the interviews analysis it can also be said that, compared to the sample studied, the companies operating in the food sector use the Stage and Gate model in order to organize the NPD process (Fig. 1).

Table 3. New product development main activities in food industry

Macro phase	Activities		
0	Planning	Concept generation	
1	Idea internal feasibility	Recipe development	Recipe internal feasibility
2	Prototyping	Product internal feasibility	Product external feasibility
3	Industrialization		
4	Production rump-up		

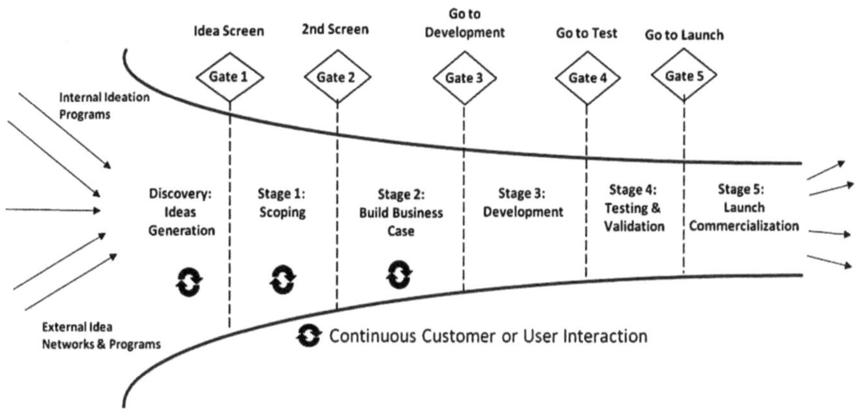

Fig. 1. A typical stage-gate process [24]

The elaborations of the questionnaire responses showed also other important results. First of all, the analysis of the questionnaire shows that the internal and external forces that push a food company to develop a new product are related to: (i) the customers (with their always changing needs), (ii) the marketing staff of the company (following their market analysis), (iii) the sales staff of the company and (iv) the regulatory compliance (refers to the country where the company sells or want to sell their products). In addition, these analyses also showed that the food NPD process is a collaborative process, characterized by the collaboration of most business functions that cooperate to each other. In particular, the results indicate that the business functions that mainly contribute to the food NPD process are: Research and Development, Marketing, Production, Quality and Engineering. In the questionnaire, two different categories of new product are taken into account, mainly related to the level of novelty of the product. Therefore, it will be referred to "radically new products" (not existing before in the company) and "improved products" (already existing in the company and incrementally improved over the time). These results disclose that (on average) 18 months are needed for the development of radically new products while 12 months for those that have to be improved. Other results are related to the factors that are considered fundamental for the new recipe development. In fact, when a food company decides to create a new recipe there are some factors that influence and that have to be taken into consideration in the NPD process. These important factors, listed in order of importance, are: quality, cost, customer satisfaction and Time to Market (TTM). The definition of these important factors have been previously defined, in order to support the person interviewed. Regarding the definition of quality, according to Grunert [25], it can be said that a product is a quality product "*only when producers can translate consumer wishes into physical product characteristics, and only when consumers can then infer desired qualities from the way the product has been built.*" The cost instead refers to the total cost to be incurred for the NPD (considering all the resources necessary for this process realisation). According to Kotler [26], "*customer satisfaction (or dissatisfaction) can be defined as the customer's perception of a product's qualities matching (or failing) their preconceived expectations*" while the Time to Market (TTM) is defined as "*time elapsed from the beginning of the planning horizon until the firm releases the new product for sale in the market*" [27]. In addition, the analysis of the questionnaire shows that most of the companies interviewed are not familiar with the main methodologies generally used along the NPD phase. According to Terzi there are a lot of methodologies that should be used in the PLM framework according to the different needs of the various phases of product lifecycle [28]. The main aim of this section of the questionnaire is to understand the level of use and of knowledge of the different methodologies in the NPD phase. In particular these methodologies are: theory for inventing problem solving (TRIZ) [29], quality function deployment QFD [30], value analysis and engineering VA&E [31], design to cost and target cost

Table 4. How systems fulfil PLM requirements in food industry

Software categories	IT systems			
Name	No	PDM/PLM	ERP	Other systems
CAD design management	60% do not use any system to support these categories	Software categories not very requested for food companies (20%)	ERP is not used there (0%)	Some companies use ad hoc systems to support the packaging design
CAD for packaging design				
Formula and recipe management	Only 20% of companies do not use any system to support these functionalities	These functionalities are the most used in food companies in a PLM system (40%)	Only 20% use ERP in Formula and recipe managementERP is not used in Label and management(0%)	Many companies rely on ad hoc systems (40%)
Label management				
PLM team collaboration	40% of the interviewed companies do not implement these categories in any system	These functionalities are the most used in food companies in a PLM system (40%)	ERP is not used there (0%)	Only 20% of companies uses ad hoc systems for these functionalities
Product portfolio and program management				
Report specific to the industry	40% of the interviewed companies do not implement these categories in any system	For reporting, companies still rely on internal instruments, not to PLM (20%)	Only 20% use ERP there	40% of companies use ad hoc systems also for specific reporting
Regulatory compliance	40% of the interviewed companies do not implement these categories in any system	No company supports this category in plm system (0%)	ERP is not used there (0%)	Companies prefer ad hoc solutions for experimented in their business (60%)
Specifications management	All companies use a system to manage the product specifications (100%)	Only 20% of companies use this categories supported in a PLM system	Only 20% use ERP there	Companies prefer ad hoc solutions for experimented in their business (60%)

management DTC/TCM [32], robust design and modular design [33], variety reduction program VRP [34] and risk analysis [35]. Going to the specific results, 60% of companies surveyed do not know any of these methods while some of them use QFD (10%), Risk Analysis (20%) and TRIZ (10%). Furthermore, 60% of these companies use methodologies ad hoc to support the NPD phase. The interviews also show that only 10% of the surveyed companies use PLM systems to support this phase. It is also important to note that the sample represents 10% of the total sample (large Italian food industries). The last question of the questionnaire refers instead to knowledge management. This question is fundamental because allowed to comprehend how the knowledge is managed in food companies, this is important, in fact the knowledge management is a key factor in the new product development and in the implementation of a PLM project. In order to implement KM, it is necessary to be able to manage several sub-processes that nowadays can be easily supported by the different software categories in various systems. In fact, those software categories can be implemented within system of different nature (e.g. PDM, ERP, PLM…). In the Table 4 are summarized the results obtained from the last question of the questionnaire showing the level of support of these categories, set out above, on information systems.

As shown in the Table 4, most companies use ad hoc systems to support these categories or do not support them at all. Moreover, there are few companies that use PLM systems to support some of these software categories. Starting from these last results, understanding the reason why most of these food companies are not familiar with the methodologies and why they are reluctant to the use of the PLM systems for NPD could be a further step of this research.

4 Conclusions and Further Research

As previously mentioned, according to the first analysis, the topic of PLM in the food sector is not yet widely covered from the literature point of view. Nevertheless, the market offers several PLM solutions for this industry. Indeed, there are many vendors of PLM solutions that offer dedicated and customized solutions for the food industry. As previous said, this industry is an ever-changing industry, which needs in continuous improvements and to be able to meet several challenges. The use of the PLM system could help to meet these challenges and to improve the NPD processes. The analysis of the interviews highlights that the NPD activities in food industry follow a clear process, with well-defined and sequential phases, with different control gates, from the concept generation to the launch stage. Furthermore, the knowledge of these phases and of the relevant performances will support the next steps of this research, consisting in a development of a model that will allow to figure out if the use of PLM solutions can improve the NPD performances. This model could be used by the food company to enabling them to: (i) assess their situation as-is compared to the performances identified, (ii) make benchmarking with other food companies, (iii) understand the areas in which they are weak and in which they must improve and (iv) understand the areas where they are likely to improve.

Acknowledgements. This work has been funded by the Italian project SMART MANUFACTURING 2020 – CTN01_ 00163_216744 – Cluster: CFI Fabbrica Intelligente.

References

1. Pfitzer, M., Krishnaswamy, R.: The Role of the Food & Beverage Sector in Expanding Economic Opportunity, p. 44 (2007)
2. Oracle, Product Lifecycle Management in the Food and Beverage Industry an White Paper, February 2008
3. Siemens, Siemens PLM Software for food and beverage White Paper (2011)
4. Kalypso, PLM Vivo : Rapid Deployment PLM for Food & Beverage White Paper, p. 12 (2010)
5. Kiritsis, D., Bufardi, A., Xirouchakis, P.: Research issues on product lifecycle management and information tracking using smart embedded systems. Adv. Eng. Informatics **17**(3–4), 189–202 (2003)
6. Schuh, G., Rozenfeld, H., Assmus, D., Zancul, E.: Process oriented framework to support PLM implementation. Comput. Ind. **59**(2–3), 210–218 (2008)
7. Ameri, F., Dutta, D.: Product lifecycle management: Closing the knowledge loops. Comput. Aided. Des. Appl. **2**(5), 577–590 (2005)
8. Findings, K.: A Guide to PLM Providers for Formulated Packaged Goods Industries, p. 27 (2012)
9. Dassault Systèmes. http://www.3ds.com/it
10. Infor. http://www.infor.com/industries/food-beverage/
11. Oracle. http://www.oracle.com/it/index.html
12. SAP. http://go.sap.com/italy/index.html
13. Selerant. http://www.selerant.com/corp/
14. Siemens. https://www.plm.automation.siemens.com/it_it/
15. Trace One. http://www.traceone.com/en/
16. Halpern, M., Jacobson, S.F., Franzosa, R., Suleski, J.: Hype Cycle for Process Manufacturing and PLM, 2015 (2015)
17. Technia Transcat. http://www.techniatranscat.com/techniatranscat
18. Sopheon. https://www.sopheon.com/
19. Parallaksis. http://www.parallaksis.com/
20. Lascom. http://www.lascom.com/
21. beCPG. http://www.becpg.net/
22. Aras. http://www.aras.com/
23. Advanced Software Designs. http://www.asdsoftware.com/
24. Edgett, S.J.: Idea - to - Launch (Stage - Gate®) Model : An Overview, pp. 1–5 (2015)
25. Grunert, K.G.: Food quality and safety: Consumer perception and demand. Eur. Rev. Agric. Econ. **32**(3), 369–391 (2005)
26. Kotler, P.H.C.P., Keller, K.L., Sivaramakrushnan, S.: Marketing Management 14th Canadian ed. Pearson Education (2013)
27. Carrillo, J.E., Franza, R.M.: Investing in product development and production capabilities: the crucial linkage between time-to-market and ramp-up time. Eur. J. Oper. Res. **171**(2), 536–556 (2006)
28. Garetti, M., Terzi, S., Bertacci, N., Brianza, M.: Organisational change and knowledge management in PLM implementation. Int. J. Prod. Lifecycle Manag. **1**(1), 43 (2005)

29. Altshuller, G.S.: The Art of Inventing (And Suddenly the Inventor Appeared). Technical Innovation Center, Worcester (1994)
30. Akao, Y.: QFD: Quality Function Deployment - Integrating Customer Requirements into Product Design. Taylor & Francis, Routledge (2004)
31. Kaufman, J.J.: Value Engineering for the Practitioner. North Carolina State University Press, NC (1990)
32. Michaels, J.V., Wood, W.P.: Design to Cost. Wiley, New Jersey (1989)
33. Jiao, J., Tseng, M.M.: Fundamental issues regarding developing product family architecture for mass customization. Integr. Manuf. Syst. **11**(7), 469–483 (2000)
34. Koudate, A.: Il management della progettazione (2003). ISEDI (Translated from Japanese to Italian by R. Manisera and R. Giovannuzzi)
35. Stein, J., Massey, A., Schwartz, S.: Fundamentals of Risk Analysis and Risk Management (1996)

GIS-Oriented Lifecycle Management for Sustainability

Kiyan Vadoudi(✉), Florian Bratec, and Nadège Troussier

ICD, HETIC Department, CREIDD, Université de Technologie de Troyes, UMR 6281, CNRS, Troyes, France
kiyan.vadoudi@utt.fr

Abstract. Studying a product's environmental impact on an interacted territory's environmental status before and after design can increase decision makers' accuracy when considering design for sustainability. Spatial representation of environmental information using Geographic Information Systems (GIS) is an approach to analyzing environmental status. This paper proposes a new data model to integrate geospatial data with product related data through environmental impacts over the whole lifecycle. This model uses coupling of GIS and PLM by ontology building. This new data model offers the possibility of enhancing sustainable products and obtaining more relevant results due to higher site specificity.

Keywords: Product lifecycle management · Geographical information system · Life cycle assessment · Ontology · Regionalization

1 Introduction

Product lifecycle management (PLM) is defined as the integrated management of product related information through the entire product lifecycle [1]. Recently, some studies on general capabilities of PLM to improve sustainability paradigm have been presented [2, 3], but the subject is still not solved completely. PLM for Design for Sustainability (DfS) involves several challenges and one of these is the lack of information for decision makers. Integration of software tools like Life Cycle Assessment (LCA) in support of DfS could be a solution. In the LCA framework [4], Life Cycle Inventory (LCI) consists of a model of the product system, its location (the technosphere and ecosphere) and a quantification of elementary flows. Then Life Cycle Impact Assessment (LCIA) looks at the fate of the substances and at the potential impacts of the intervention between the product system and the ecosphere [5]. Technological and environmental aspects are not independent and a change in the environmental setting implicitly needs a change in the technology used. As the characteristics and environmental status of ecospheres differ territorially, design characteristics and specifications of technologies need to be modified and adopted based on these differences, but we lack knowledge of how these features really would change design choices. Implementation of this approach in product and system design will require geospatial information about related ecosphere(s), but current models of product design do not include the support for geographical information.

R. Harik et al. (Eds.): PLM 2016, IFIP AICT 492, pp. 248–258, 2016.
DOI: 10.1007/978-3-319-54660-5_23

This paper aims at answering this problem by modeling the link between territory and PLM/LCA using a GIS/PLM/LCA framework. Firstly, it proposes a new product data model consisting of product data, environmental data, such as LCI, and geographical data about the environmental status of territory. This proposed model provides new design information for decision makers. Then, we discuss a case study: how this new information could change decisions in order to design for sustainability. Finally, we conclude with future works.

2 State of the Art on Tools to Support Design for Sustainability

Nowadays, sustainable development becomes more and more complex and knowledge intensive, requiring additional supports and assistance, especially in the early design stages. The intelligent use of existing digital databases like PLM could help to solve the problem. PLM enables the comparison, evaluation and optimization of the different product requirements, linking production information to design through the entire lifecycle. To succeed in the mission of supporting PLM, applications need reliable, complete and efficient data models to be able to filter, structure, integrate, control and channel flows of information.

In 2002 Fenves proposed the core product model (CPM) to support the full range of product lifecycle management (PLM) [6]. Gujarathi et al. [7] developed a common data model (CDM) containing all required parametric information for both CAD modeling and CAE analysis for CAD/CAE parametric integration. Recently Utpal et al. [8] developed an Integrated Product Information Model (IPIM) based on CPM in the context of sustainable design and manufacturing. Although MML, CPM, CDM and IPIM are used to extract and model the knowledge applied in technological systems, none of them are able to create a data list that can be used for sustainable design, especially from environmental aspect.

Since LCA have been developed to support DfS [9], but seems difficult to apply it in the early stages of design, because most of the existing tools based on LCA do not focus on design and they are set for a strategic management or a retrospective analysis of existing products. A real LCA can only be correctly used for a completely defined product where data about lifecycle are available and accurate. Regionalization is used as a solution to improve the accuracy of life cycle assessment (LCA) results and make it more relevant for decision makers. There has been a growing body of regionalized LCA research, and in particular many regionalized LCA models coupled with Geographical Information System (GIS) have been developed for agricultural products [10–13]. However, insufficient attention has been paid to industrial products, in terms of their regionalized life cycle inventory (LCI), the study of the related geographic location and status of environmental impacts before and after proposed design for each step of lifecycle. GIS has been used by several authors to integrate spatial differentiation in LCA, not only for the calculation of regionalized characterization factors but also for creating site-specific inventories and matching each of these [13, 14]. GIS, by accessing different sources of information (biological resources, pollution sources and affected areas, land cover and use, water availability and quality and energy sources and use), enables the use of a set of simple operations such as overlay, classification, interpolation and aggregation of spatial information [10] that could generate useful information for decision makers in support of DfS. In the next section a data model is proposed, which integrates GIS with environmental inventory (LCI) and product (CPM) data models.

3 Proposed Data Model (PEG)

This proposed conceptual model (Fig. 1) contains three sub data models, namely, product (P), environment impact (E) and geography (G).

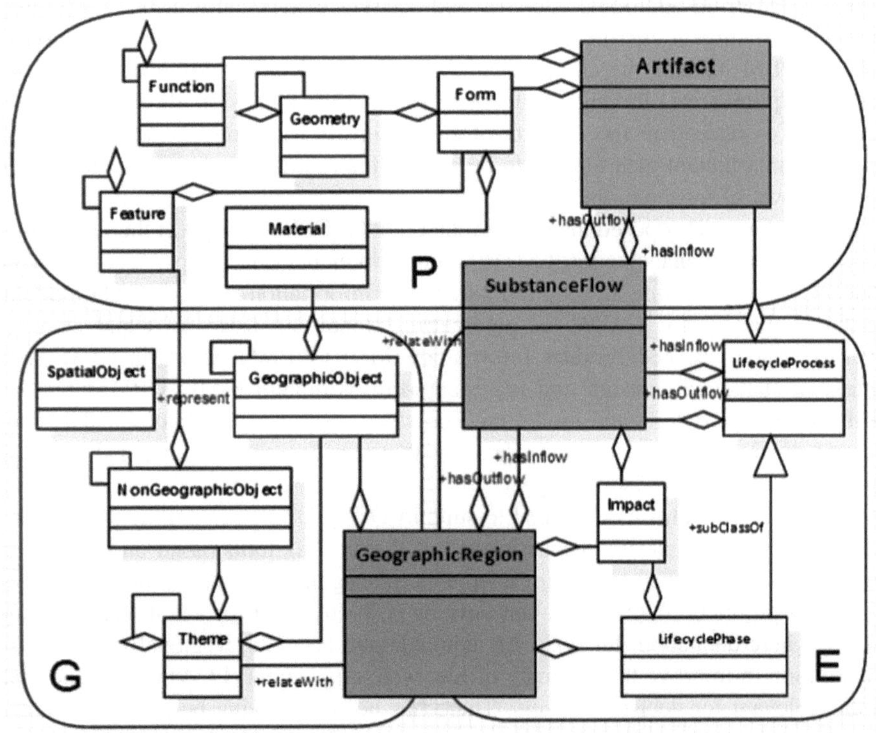

Fig. 1. PEG data model

'Artifact' is the main class of category (P), shown in grey. This class has relationships with category (E) through LifecycleProcess and SubstanceFlow classes. SubstanceFlow class, shown in red, is the main class of category (E) and a link between Artifact and GeographicRegion classes. Each one of these subsections are described in more detail below.

3.1 Product Data Model (P)

Data models and ontologies have been built to represent various engineering fields and product lifecycle stages in different categories. The knowledge models and ontologies focus on the product [6, 15–19], on the process [20–22], on the product-process [23–25] and etc. In the models on product category, many researchers based their works on NIST's core product model (CPM) because it is a base-level product model: generic, simple, open, non-proprietary, extensible and independent of any specific product development. Moreover, CPM capable of capturing engineering context commonly shared in product development activities, this makes it capable of supporting the full range of product lifecycle management (PLM) [26]. We will base category (P) on combining the advantages of CPM with our proposed goal of designing a manufactured product: Form, Geometry, Function, Material, Feature and Artifact classes are selected due to their strong relation with geographical and environment features.

3.2 Environmental Impact Data Model (E)

The first LCA ontology project was designed under Project CASCADE [27]. Bertin et al. [28] presented a semantic approach to LCA knowledge in 2012 which it is applied to energy environmental impact data management. In 2015 Yingzhong et al. [5] proposed an LCA-oriented semantic concept model for the product life cycle by dividing the environmental space of the product into technosphere and ecosphere. And recently Akkharawoot et al. [29] described a collaborative approach to ontology development for data qualification for life cycle assessment by taking into consideration the Life Cycle Inventory (LCI) and Data Quality Indicator (DQI). Part (E) of our model is based on a modified version of the model by Yingzhong et al. [5] due to its concentration on lifecycle view. In this semantic concept model, three top-level classes are defined: Product_Lifecycle class; Lifecycle_Process class and Substance_flow class. Substance_flow Class as a base of flow ontology is divided into three subclasses: Elementary_Flows class; Product_Flows class and Waste_Flows class. Elementary flows as the basis for calculating environmental impacts of a product life cycle can be classified into two further subclasses: Resources and Emissions classes.

3.3 Geography Data Model (G)

Geographical database modeling has been followed by different conceptual data models such as GeoOOA [30], Geo-ER [31], Geo-OMT [32], MADS [33] and GeoFrame [34]. Another study was carried out by Pedersen and Tryfona [35], who present a formal definition of a data model for a Geographical Data Warehouse (GDW) at the conceptual level. More recently, Malinowski and Zimanyi [36] presented a GDW data model based on the MADS model, which is, in turn, an object-based entity-relationship approach. Zghal et al. [53] propose a meta model based on the UML class diagram which addresses spatial dimensions, spatial hierarchies and spatial measures. From the mentioned data models, GeoFrame [34] is selected as (G) due to its ability to include pattern analysis which facilitates use of geographical data for designers from different backgrounds with little knowledge of software development methods. In this framework there are three main classes: Geographic_Region; Theme; Nongeographic_Object. Theme defines during conceptual design which can lead to the implementation of several layers. Geographic_Object class is a generalization for all classes of the domain that are perceived in the object view. The attributes defined in the class are mapped as rational table field. Geographic_Region Class can be defined by physical characteristics, human characteristics, and functional characteristics.

PEG model could provide the following information: (1) mapping the environmental impacts of designed product on interacted territory, defining specified design parameters like the materials (The materials thus chosen must be analyzed to satisfy the design form, overall production feasibility and especially the environmental impacts); (2) finding patterns for environmental impacts by comparing different maps which help to predict the environmental status of territory; (3) taking into account environmental condition of territory in product and system design which could lead to have changes in design specifications.

4 Case Study

The lifecycle of a flashlight, which is a simple manufacturing product, is provided to illustrate the new kind information supported by proposed model (Fig. 1). A simple flashlight consists of two main components: Body and head. The head contains the cap, lamp, lamp holder, lens and reflector, which is connected to the body including tail cap, spring, connector, on/off switch, brass slide and plastic shell which holds the battery. Using BOM information and the manufacturing process planning of the product, a manufacturing process tree can be obtained, combining the specific information of the materials used to make the parts, and the manufacturing unit process information. Because of the page limitation for submission processes of the conference, lifecycle is limited to manufacturing and end of life (EOL) processes (LifecycleProcess, LifecyclePhase) of plastic shell (Artifact & GeographiObject). The manufacturing phase of the plastic shell consists of manufacturing unit processes (gate to gate), which converts the polypropylene material by an injection process into a final shell product and the EOL consist collection and recycling process of plastic and also electrical parts (battery and lamp). For LCA study of this case, SO2 (SubstanceFlow & GeographiObject) is the only emission studied and included as GIS data. Champagne Ardenne in France (GeographicRegion) is considered as the geographical region where all up-stream process of electricity (SubstanceFlow & NonGeographiObject) and material productions (SubstanceFlow, Material, LifecyclePhase & GeographiObject) are located.

Elementary flow data as part of substance flow related to the manufacturing and EOL of this part is collected and used to create the flow instances. The other flows are sets of continuous production processes to produce materials and energy (cradle to grave), including polypropylene production, electricity production, etc. LCI data about the amount of SO2 emission for production processes is obtained from open source software OpenLCA [37] and ELCD database [38]. For example, the injection process consumes electricity so the power consumption can be defined as the reference flow and

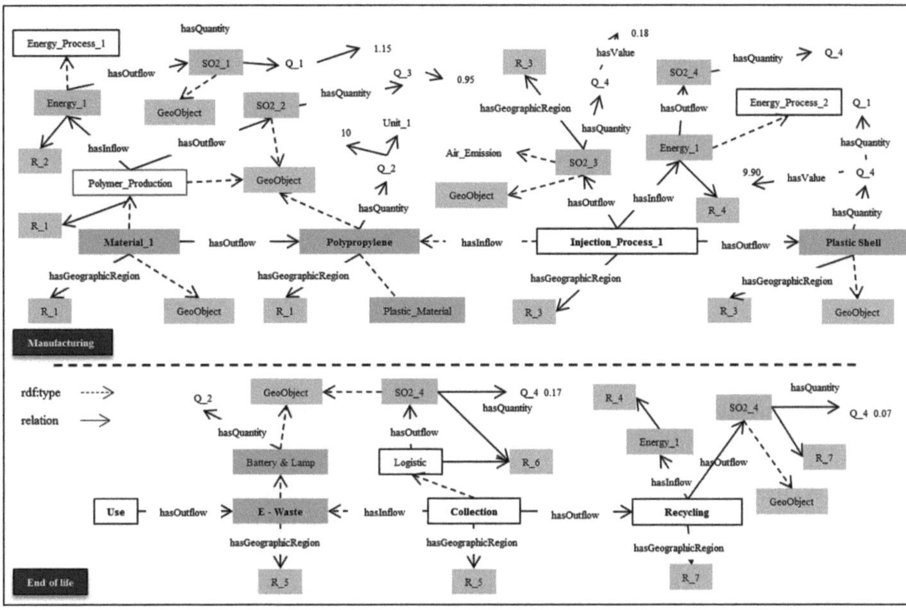

Fig. 2. Illustration of proposed data model for plastic shell production and end of life processes

input into the LCI database to obtain the environmental impact of all upstream processes of the electricity supply production. Figure 2 illustrates a semantic presentation for the part of the data model mentioned to tag the process instances, the flow instances and geographic regions instances. For example, the first node is polypropylene material, result of the "Polymer_Production" shown as class "Material_1". The geographical production location of the polymer is in Champagne Ardenne, referenced as "R_1" class which could be presented as a geographical object on the map as a part of up-stream process. Moreover, this class could also be named as the elementary flow/polymer producer/raw material/etc. layers. Polymer production needs electrical energy ("Energt_1" class) produced in another geographical location of same region ("class R_2"). "Injection_process_1" is part of the manufacturing process, and "SO2_3" is an instance of the Air_Emission class and its substance name is SO2, which is an instance of "GeoObject" enters entered geographic region R_3.

There are two approaches [39] to collecting E-wastes in France; individuals deliver e-waste to collection points inside cities and the second approach involves producers or individuals using out-of-town recovery centers. The first approach is selected as EOL process for this case study. Batteries and lamps ("E-waste class") is the result of outflow from use stage which has inflow to collection points (R_5). After collection, there is logistic process to deliver wastes into recycling centers (R_7).

Figure 3 presents SO2 emission for different geographical locations as GIS data layers. Map1, Map2 and Map3 are divided maps of each activity's impact and Total map is the SO2 emission of the total manufacturing process with its logistics etc.

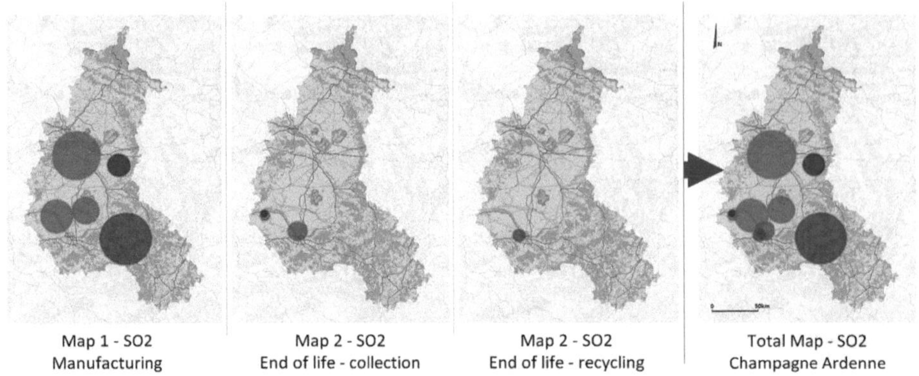

Fig. 3. SO2 emissions in different geographical location of manufacturing and EOL processes

In LCA, there are several data formats to describe environmental information. The most common among these are EcoSpold1, EcoSpold2 and ILCD and are based on the extended markup language XML [40]. In GIS there are two different approaches to represent geospatial information. The first approach is raster-based and uses formats derived from web-design (GeoTIFF, IMG, JPEG2000, etc.) [41]. The second approach is vector-based and is more commonly used today. Many formats can link information with coordinates using vectors, and the most popular are the GPS exchange format (GPX), the keyhole markup language (KML) and the geography markup language (GML) [42].

Considering the multiple existing formats to describe environmental and geospatial information, there are many ways to combine the data. However, there is still no format that allows data from LCA and data from GIS to be stored in the same file. To create the maps shown in Fig. 3, a PostgreSQL database was chosen to store the data and to make it available with the same system of language requests (SQL). On one hand, the ILCD format (based on XML) had to be covered in a relational data model to be included as SQL data tables. On the other hand, the PostgreSQL structure allowed us to link the LCA data with geospatial information: coordinates and geometrical objects (points in this case but it could also admit lines and polygons). The resulting data model, coupled to the JavaScript library OpenLayers permitted the LCA results to be displayed on a base map form MapQuest.

5 Discussion and Conclusion

The above analysis and results show that the proposed model and its semantic representation by case study can represent the interactions between the product and its territory and the quantized impacts on the environment and consumption for the resources within a product life cycle. Flow instances can be determined and presented as specific geographical features by different GIS data layers. Access to GIS layers can

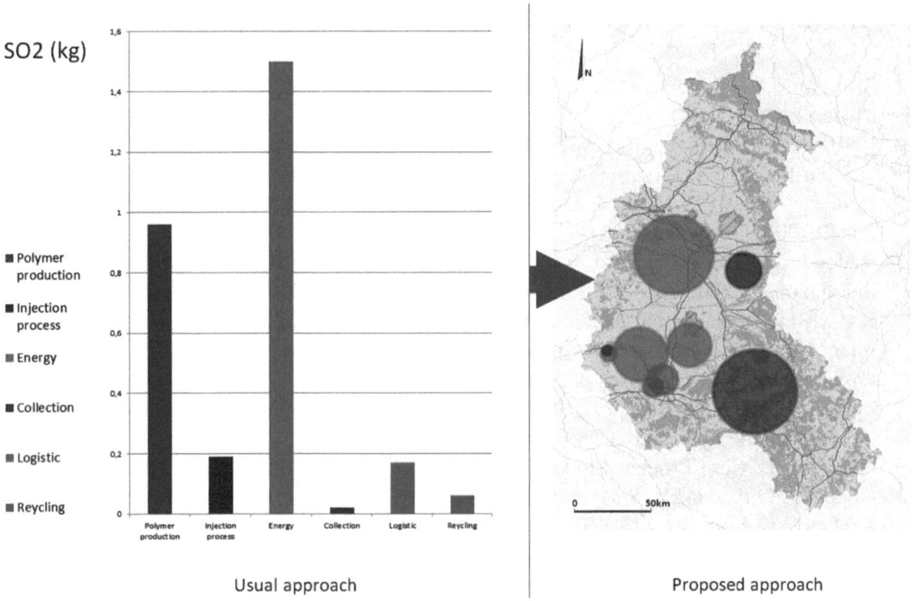

Fig. 4. Usual and proposed approach presentation on SO2 emission

help product designers to analysis the environmental impacts before and after design, which may change design characteristics and product specifications based on the environmental status of each territory. Using the proposed model, it will be possible to include geographical characteristics for environmental impact assessment and provide them to designers helping them to identify which product characteristics and specifications are the source of an impact in order to lead to better design for sustainability solutions Finally, as shown in Fig. 4, this approach can solve the problem of LCA which is not applicable in the early stages of design.

Tackling the challenge of design for sustainability requires an integrated and systematic approach in order to understand the relation, for a specific territory, between designed products and their subsequent impact on the environment. The methodology presented in this paper is an attempt to provide such an approach by proposing a model linking product information and the impact on interacted territory based on a PEG system. Using different geographical data layers, this model can provide valuable information for decision makers. For instance, in the case study presented, SO2 emission is defined as a data layer illustrated on a map, which could be combined and compared with other data layers to predict future changes. In order to know if it is really applicable and of interest to decision makers, we have to: (1) complete case studies with other flows and geographical data layers in terms of substance flows under consideration; (2) put it into practice and evaluate the interest for decision makers and sustainability in design situations with students and professionals.

References

1. Saaksvuori, A., Immonen, A.: Product lifecycle Management. Springer Science & Business Media, Berlin (2008)
2. Vadoudi, K., Allais, R., Reyes, T., Troussier, N.: Sustainable product lifecycle management and territoriality: new structure for PLM. In: Fukuda, S., Bernard, A., Gurumoorthy, B., Bouras, A. (eds.) PLM 2014. IAICT, vol. 442, pp. 475–484. Springer, Heidelberg (2014). doi:10.1007/978-3-662-45937-9_47
3. Vadoudi, K., Troussier, N.: A sustainable product model. In: DS 80-10 Proceedings of 20th International Conference on Engineering Design (ICED 2015), Design Information and Knowledge Management Milan, vol. 10, Italy, 27–30 July 2015 (2015)
4. International Standardization Organization ISO 14040: Environmental Management-Life Cycle Assessment-Principles and Framework (1997)
5. Zhang, Y., Luo, X., Buis, J.J., Sutherland, J.W.: LCA-oriented semantic representation for the product life cycle. J. Clean. Prod. **86**, 146–162 (2015)
6. Fenves, S.J.: Core Product Model for Representing Design Information. CiteSeer (2001)
7. Gujarathi, G.P., Ma, Y.-S.: Parametric CAD/CAE integration using a common data model. J. Manufact. Syst. **30**, 118–132 (2011)
8. Roy, U., Sarigecili, M.I.: Information models for processing product lifecycle functionalities and interfaces for sustainable manufacturing. J. Comput. Inf. Sci. Eng. **16**, 11005 (2016)
9. Samuel-Fitwi, B., Wuertz, S., Schroeder, J.P., Schulz, C.: Sustainability assessment tools to support aquaculture development. J. Clean. Prod. **32**, 183–192 (2012)
10. Rodríguez, C., Ciroth, A., Srocka, M.: The importance of regionalized LCIA in agricultural LCA—new software implementation and case study. In: Proceedings of 9th International Conference on Life Cycle Assess Agri-Food Sector, San Francisco, pp. 1120–1128 (2014)
11. Mutel, C.L., Hellweg, S.: Regionalized life cycle assessment: computational methodology and application to inventory databases. Environ. Sci. Technol. **43**, 5797–5803 (2009)
12. Bartl, K., Verones, F., Hellweg, S.: Life cycle assessment based evaluation of regional impacts from agricultural production at the Peruvian coast. Environ. Sci. Technol. **46**, 9872–9880 (2012)
13. Mutel, C.L., Pfister, S., Hellweg, S.: GIS-based regionalized life cycle assessment: how big is small enough? Methodology and case study of electricity generation. Environ. Sci. Technol. **46**, 1096–1103 (2012)
14. Brentrup, F., Küsters, J., Kuhlmann, H., Lammel, J.: Environmental impact assessment of agricultural production systems using the life cycle assessment methodology. Eur. J. Agron. **20**, 247–264 (2004)
15. Barbau, R., Krima, S., Rachuri, S., Narayanan, A., Fiorentini, X., Foufou, S., Sriram, R.D.: OntoSTEP: enriching product model data using ontologies. Comput.-Aided Des. **44**, 575–590 (2012)
16. Fiorentini, X., Gambino, I., Liang, V., Foufou, S., Rachuri, S., Bock, C., Mahesh, M.: Towards an ontology for open assembly model. In: International Conference on Product Lifecycle Management, Milan, Italy (2007)
17. Tursi, A., Panetto, H., Morel, G., Dassisti, M.: Ontological approach for products-centric information system interoperability in networked manufacturing enterprises. Ann. Rev. Control **33**, 238–245 (2009)
18. Rachuri, S., Baysal, M., Roy, U., Foufou, S., Bock, C., Fenves, S., Subrahmanian, E., Lyons, K., Sriram, R.: Information models for product representation: core and assembly models. Int. J. Prod. Dev. **2**, 207–235 (2005)

19. Gruhier, E., Demoly, F., Dutartre, O., Abboudi, S., Gomes, S.: A formal ontology-based spatiotemporal mereotopology for integrated product design and assembly sequence planning. Adv. Eng. Inform. **29**, 495–512 (2015)
20. Chang, X.: Ontology Development and Utilization in Product Design (2008)
21. Fortin, C., Huet, G.: Manufacturing Process Management: iterative synchronisation of engineering data with manufacturing realities. Int. J. Prod. Dev. **4**, 280–295 (2007)
22. Lee, J., Jeong, Y.: User-centric knowledge representations based on ontology for AEC design collaboration. Comput. Des. **44**, 735–748 (2012)
23. Demoly, F., Monticolo, D., Eynard, B., Rivest, L., Gomes, S.: Multiple viewpoint modelling framework enabling integrated product–process design. Int. J. Interact. Des. Manuf. **4**, 269–280 (2010)
24. Kim, K.-Y., Manley, D.G., Yang, H.: Ontology-based assembly design and information sharing for collaborative product development. Comput. Des. **38**, 1233–1250 (2006)
25. Panetto, H., Dassisti, M., Tursi, A.: ONTO-PDM: product-driven ONTOlogy for product data management interoperability within manufacturing process environment. Adv. Eng. Inform. **26**, 334–348 (2012)
26. Sudarsan, R., Fenves, S.J., Sriram, R.D., Wang, F.: A product information modeling framework for product lifecycle management. Comput. Des. **37**, 1399–1411 (2005)
27. Cappellaro, F., Masoni, P., Moreno, A., Scalbi, S.: CASCADE. In: The 16th Internationale Conference: Informatics for Environment Protection, pp. 490–493 (2002)
28. Bertin, B., Scuturici, V.-M., Risler, E., Pinon, J.-M.: A semantic approach to life cycle assessment applied on energy environmental impact data management. In: Proceedings of the 2012 Joint EDBT/ICDT Workshops, pp. 87–94. ACM (2012)
29. Takhom, A., Ikeda, M., Suntisrivaraporn, B., Supnithi, T., Hintemann, R., Fichter, K., Denward, M., De Jong, A., Olsen, R., Jakobi, T.: Toward collaborative LCA ontology development: a scenario-based recommender system (2015)
30. Kosters, G., Pagel, B.-U., Six, H.-W.: GIS-application development with GeoOOA. Int. J. Geogr. Inf. Sci. **11**, 307–335 (1997)
31. Hadzilacos, T., Tryfona, N.: An extended entity-relationship model for geographic applications. Acm Sigmod Rec. **26**, 24–29 (1997)
32. Borges, K.A.V.: Geographic data modeling–an extension of the OMT model for geographic applications. Esc. do Gov. MG/FJP, Belo Horizonte (1997)
33. Parent, C., Spaccapietra, S., Zimanyi, E., Donini, P., Plazanet, C., Vangenot, C.: Modeling spatial data in the MADS conceptual model. In: Proceedings of the 8th International Symposium on Spatial Data Handling, SDH 1998 (1998)
34. Iochpe, C.: Specifying analysis patterns for geographic databases on the basis of a conceptual framework. In: Proceedings of the 7th ACM International Symposium on Advances in Geographic Information Systems, pp. 7–13. ACM (1999)
35. Pedersen, T.B., Tryfona, N.: Pre-aggregation in spatial data warehouses. In: Jensen, C.S., Schneider, M., Seeger, B., Tsotras, V.J. (eds.) SSTD 2001. LNCS, vol. 2121, pp. 460–478. Springer, Heidelberg (2001). doi:10.1007/3-540-47724-1_24
36. Malinowski, E., Zimányi, E.: Representing spatiality in a conceptual multidimensional model. In: Proceedings of the 12th Annual ACM International Workshop on Geographic Information Systems, pp. 12–22. ACM (2004)
37. GreenDeltaTC GmbH, Berlin: openLCA Framework – Modular Open Source Software for Sustainability Assessment – version 1 (2008). http://www.openlca.org
38. European Commission, Joint Research Centre: ILCD Handbook: General Guide for Life Cycle Assessment: Detailed Guidance. Publications Office of the European Union, Luxembourg (2010)

39. Vadoudi, K., Kim, J., Laratte, B., Lee, S.-J., Troussier, N.: E-waste management and resources recovery in France. Waste Manag. Res **33**(10), 919–929 (2015)
40. Weidema, B.P., Bauer, C., Hischier, R., Mutel, C., Nemecek, T., Reinhard, J., Vadenbo, C.O., Wernet, G.: Overview and methodology: data quality guideline for the ecoinvent database version 3. Swiss Centre for Life Cycle Inventories (2013)
41. Selamat, M.H., Othman, M.S., Shamsuddin, N.H.M., Zukepli, N.I.M., Hassan, A.F.: A review on open source architecture in geographical information systems. In: 2012 International Conference on Computer & Information Science (ICCIS), pp. 962–966. IEEE (2012)
42. Bivand, R.S., Pebesma, E., Gómez-Rubio, V.: Spatial Data Import and Export. Springer, Heidelberg (2013)

PLM Tools

Automatic Assembly Design for Engineering-to-Order Products Based on Multiple Models and Assembly Features

Iraklis Chatziparasidis[1,2] and Nickolas S. Sapidis[2(✉)]

[1] Research and Development Department, Kleemann Hellas SA, Kilkis Industrial Area, P.O. Box 25, 61100 Kilkis, Greece
ihatz@kleemann.gr
http://www.kleemannlifts.com/
[2] Department of Mechanical Engineering, University of Western Macedonia, 50132 Kozani, Greece
nsapidis@uowm.gr,
http://mech.uowm.gr/index.php/staff/317

Abstract. When it comes to Engineering-To-Order (ETO) products, neither the exact number nor the form of the components in them can be predefined. Thus, existing assembly models and generative design techniques are not adequate to support development of design automation tools for ETO products. ETO companies usually use custom libraries with past case designs that are adjusted to a customer's requirements. This method is not cost effective and it is prone to human errors. In this work, we present the *Automatic Assembly Synthesis Model* (*AASM*), connecting a Knowledge Based Engineering (KBE) system and a CAD system to automate routine design tasks for ETO mechanical products.

Keywords: Automatic synthesis · Assembly features · Assembly model

1 Introduction

Today, in the context of a globalized market, customers have high demands for products that are tailored to their individual needs and are offered at a price that is very close to that of mass-produced products. Engineering-To-Order (ETO) companies offer to their clients products that are tailored to their needs. These companies are forced to reduce costs and lead time to gain an advantage over the competition. A major cost factor for ETO companies is the time required for the product to be designed and engineered, and for manufacturing drawings to be published and launched to the shop floor. In most cases, these companies have a number of premade 3D models (and the corresponding manufacturing drawings) and modify them to adjust the dimensions, the function and/or the aesthetics of the product to the customer requirements. Unfortunately, this method is prone to human errors, and these errors may create extra remanufacturing costs. An ETO company would gain a significant advantage by using a tool that would create automatically 3D assembly models for its products. Today, CAD systems can be used to partially automate some routine design operations when these are combined with

R. Harik et al. (Eds.): PLM 2016, IFIP AICT 492, pp. 261–274, 2016.
DOI: 10.1007/978-3-319-54660-5_24

generative modeling methodologies [1, 2]. However, this kind of tools can be used only in situations where all component configurations in the final product are known. Often this is not true, as many ETO companies prefer more flexible approaches to product configuration, employing, e.g., Knowledge Based Engineering (KBE) systems or Rule Based Management Systems (RBMS). These systems can be employed to effectively capture knowledge by storing technical guidelines, relations, facts [3], "best practices", and even a company's commercial and business rules. However, on the side of CAD systems a major limitation remains: it is extremely difficult to have pre-defined 3D assembly models matching all possible product configurations implied by a KBE system. Thus, this research proposes development of a routine-design automation tool that will create any 3D assembly model from scratch by synthesizing appropriate components. Since existing assembly modeling methods are not well suited for design automation procedures, we present, in this work, the *Automatic Assembly Synthesis Model (AASM)*, a method to link a KBE system and a CAD system.

2 Literature Review

2.1 Assembly Models and Assembly Features

According to Demoly et al. [4], Assembly Modeling deals with the definition of an informational product model including all product components and the related relationship information. In [5], we present an extensive review of the related research of the last 15 years, making clear that current assembly models are not adequate for automating assembly procedures. Existing assembly models, like the OAM [6], the AREP [7], the FGT [8], or those discussed in [9, 10], do not present a method to support transfer of product configuration information, from a KBE or RBS system to a CAD system, in a way that would facilitate automatic assembly synthesis. Thus, we focus, in this paper, on exactly presenting an assembly model and methodology appropriate for automatic assembly synthesis for ETO products.

In feature-based product modeling, the Assembly Feature (AF) is an important concept describing relationships and interaction regions between parts, however, currently there is no unified definition for it [11]. In [9], an AF is defined as an information carrier for assembly-specific information. In [8], an AF is defined as a pair of geometry features restricted by a specific assembly constraint. According to [12], an AF represents a region of a component that is of interest in the assembly context. In [6], an AF specifies relationships in a pair of assembled components. In [13], an AF is defined as an association between two form features which are on different parts. In [14], an AF is defined as a generic "solution" referring to two groups of parts that need to be related by a relationship to solve a design problem. In [15], mating features are defined as those features that comprise mating relations between parts to be assembled. In [16, 17], a method that simplifies complex products to achieve a virtual assembly modeling process in real time is presented. Here, form features are defined as generic shapes useful in computer-aided design applications, and assembly features are the connections between form features. In [7], an AF is defined as a property of an Assembly Unit (AU) providing assembly related information. An AU can be a sub-assembly, a component or an envelope. Envelopes are volumes within which parts and sub-assemblies are to be designed. In [18], the following concepts are presented: (a) Design Spaces, which are simplified objects defining the area that will be occupied by each component when the detail design phase will be completed. (b) Constraints, which describe, in an algebraic manner, the kinematic relationships between design spaces. (c) Interface Features, which are geometric entities that are used as connection interfaces between Constraints and Design Spaces. (d) Layout Components: These are produced by combinations of Design Spaces with Interface Features. (e) Connection Features: These are detailed form features that are designed by the designer and aim to implement the corresponding Interface Features. This methodology has as a priority to ensure the kinematic functionality of the assembly before proceeding to the detailed geometric design of individual components. Xu et al. [11] present the concept of Interaction Features Pair (IFP) describing how components interact with each other at the assembly creation stage. In [19], the authors propose a Feature-based design method, that focuses on modeling complex relations among features. Four kinds of features are proposed: (a) Conceptual Features, (b) Assembly Features (AFs), (c) Component Basic Features, and d) Component Detail Features. Ma et al. [20–22] introduce the concept of Associative Features which are features that cannot be represented using conventional features. An example is the cooling channels in a mold, which are represented as CAD solids called “cooling solids”. Thus, cooling channels are easily created by applying the solid-modeling subtract operator on the cooling solids and the initial mold. Dixon [23] presents a system that automatically identifies AFs. First, the user teaches the system interactively by examples of AFs. These AFs are then used as “standards” by the system to identify AFs in assembly models that are saved in a neutral format (e.g., STEP). Kim et al. [24] introduce a formalism and associated tools to capture joining relations in assemblies. In this work, a Mating Feature is defined as a set of component geometric-entities used to assemble parts. In [25], the use of assembly features in standard parts (e.g. bolts, nuts etc.) is proposed. In [26], Connection Features are functional relationships representing the internal degrees of freedom that the corresponding form features must have, to implement a specific connection type. In [27], a system for supporting rapid assembly modeling of standard parts is presented. The system is based on the concept of Typical Assembly Feature (TAF), defined as a geometric element of a component which can constrain and orient this component in an assembly. Singh and Bettig [28] have presented the concept of “assembly ports” as a method to embed assembly information into the part model in order to automate the process of applying mating constraints. An assembly port is defined to be a group of one or more low-level geometric entities, such as faces, edges, or centerlines, that undergo mating constraints in order to join parts in a CAD assembly. In [29, 30], the authors propose a framework method to integrate assembly modeling and simulation based on Assembly Feature Pairs. An Assembly Feature Pair consists of form-feature pairs containing information on assembly behaviors.

2.2 "Half" Assembly Constraints

Most contemporary CAD systems have tools implementing the concept of "half" assembly constraints, e.g., in *PTC Creo* they are called *Component Interfaces* [31], in *Autodesk Inventor* they are called *iMates* [32], etc. These tools allow the designer to store assembly constraints, in advance, in each component, during the design phase. These tools aim to cut down the time a user spends to assemble components. However, mere use of these tools alone cannot fully automate assembly synthesis, because of the lack of any information about the requested assembly's structure. In the present *AASM* model the concept of "half" constraints has been integrated as a fundamental block into the concept of *Assembly Feature (AF)*. By integrating the concept of "half" constraints, in the form of the *Semi-Constraint* object, into the AASM model, we provide a framework that can fully automate the assembly synthesis procedure. This way, 3D part models, that have not been designed together in an assembly, can be automatically connected if they contain compatible AFs.

3 The Automatic Assembly Synthesis Model (AASM)

The design automation procedure, proposed here, is based on the use of "generative part models" which generate the part instances that compose the desired 3D assembly. A generative part model differs from a single geometric part-model. While a geometric part model has fixed dimensions and features, the generative part model is a generic representation of the part and it is used to create instances with varying form and dimensions. Generative part models also contain special form features that are used as connection ports, named *Assembly Features* (*AFs*).

The *Automatic Assembly Synthesis Model (AASM)* includes two major components: The *Schematic Assembly Model (SAM)* and the *Intermediate Assembly Model (IAM);* see Fig. 1. The *Schematic Assembly Model* is a preliminary model that converts the structural rules, that are stored within a KBE system (e.g., in an IF…THEN…ELSE form), into an object-oriented assembly-structure form that functions as a configuration rule guiding the automatic assembly synthesis procedure. The SAM contains information on the structure of the desired 3D assembly and the connection types that must be applied on corresponding components. The SAM does not contain detailed information regarding how these connections will be implemented at the 3D geometry level in the CAD system. The IAM is an augmented implementation of the SAM. The IAM is based on the SAM regarding assembly structure information but it does also contain

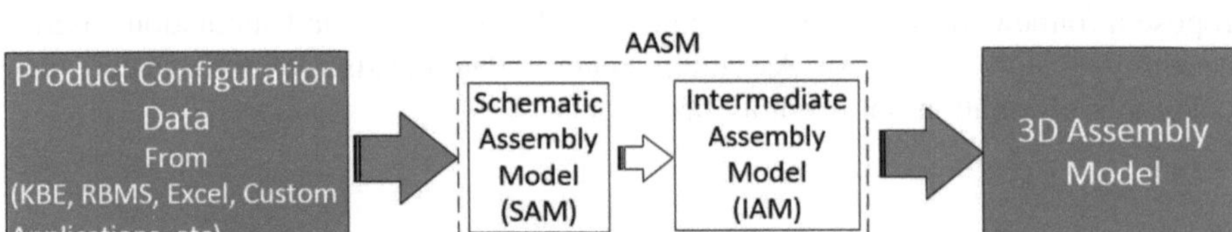

Fig. 1. AASM model

detailed information specifying which *Assembly Features* of each component must be used for the 3D assembly to be created.

In short, the SAM describes the assembly that the KBE system requires and the IAM represents the corresponding 3D assembly model that the CAD system will create. The separation between initial description and final implementation is one of the major attributes of AASM making it adequate for automatic synthesis of complex assemblies with significant variation in their configurations. Dividing AASM into two sub-models (SAM and IAM) results also into an increased flexibility, when it comes to implementation of a Design Automation tool for large teams of designers.

3.1 Assembly Feature (AF): A New Definition for the Automatic Assembly Synthesis Model

In this work, *Assembly Feature* is a graphical formation of the 3D component model that functions as a connection port allowing parts with compatible *Assembly Features* to be automatically connected. AFs are created by the designer during the design of each generative part model and are represented in an object-oriented manner within the AASM. An *Assembly Feature* is composed of graphical entities, which can be either B-Rep entities (like: vertices, edges or faces) or datum graphical objects (like: points, axes or planes) or a combination of these. These graphical entities will be matched, using specific assembly constraints, with the corresponding entities of the associated AF. Matching of these entities is achieved through embedded information in the form of attributes within the B-Rep model. Each of the entities forming an AF also includes a number of *Assembly Feature Attribute Pairs (AFAP)*; see Fig. 2. Each AFAP contains a reference to its parent graphical entity and to the type of a *Semi-Constraint* that must be used. Entities with compatible AFAPs are automatically matched via a matching algorithm. Compatible AFAPs are considered these that contain references to graphical entities of the same type and identical Semi-Constraint types. A *Semi-Constraint* is a special type of assembly constraint. *Semi-Constraints* are a way to define assembly constraints and assign them to the part model before assembling it into an assembly.

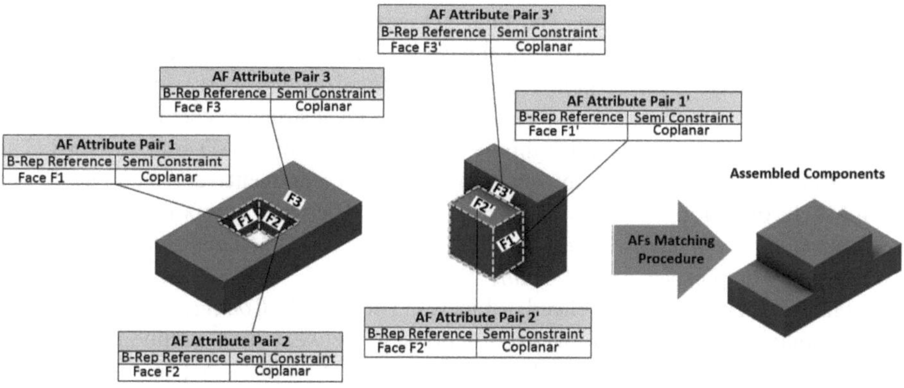

Fig. 2. Assembly features and assembly features attribute pairs

A *Semi-Constraint* is the “half” of an assembly constraint and is added to each of the corresponding components independently. Two *Semi-Constraints* have to be combined to form a complete assembly constraint. A *Semi-Constraint* is a label stored as attribute within the corresponding part of the B-Rep model. It is the CAD system that implements these labels by changing the position and orientation of the components. In most contemporary CAD systems, each part model and each assembly model has its own coordinate system. The position of a component within an assembly is specified by matching the position and the orientation of the component’s coordinate system relatively to the coordinate system of the assembly. The definition and/or the change of position of a component within an assembly are controlled by *Transformation Matrices*. Every movement or rotation of a part is translated into transformation of these matrices so that they define the new position and orientation of the part.

Three are the types of AFs used here: *Form Assembly Features (FAFs), Skeleton Assembly Features (SAFs) and Composite Assembly Features (CAFs). Form Assembly Features (FAF)* are these AFs that totally coincide with a corresponding form feature. *Skeleton Assembly Features (SAF)* are *Assembly Features* formed by auxiliary geometric entities like *Planes, Axes and Points*. SAFs can be used to represent a connection between parts when adequate FAFs are not present. *Composite Assembly Features* are used when the corresponding form feature that will be used as connection port does not provide all the necessary B-Rep entities to implement the connection. In these situations, auxiliary entities are used to complete the geometric description of the connection. The scope of most AFs is limited only at part level, meaning that these AFs are used only to connect the related part to other parts. However, there are cases where an AF that belongs to a specific component must function also as *Assembly Feature* of a newly-formed sub-assembly, to allow this sub-assembly to be connected with other components, forming another assembly. For these reason, all types of AFs can be declared to be *External Assembly Features*.

3.2 AASM: The Schematic Assembly Model (SAM)

The SAM consists of the *SAM Structure* object and the *SAM Connection Rules Collection* object (Fig. 3). The *SAM Structure* is a tree-based hierarchical structure object, resulting from the KBE system. The final 3D assembly model, that will be automatically synthesized, has to comply with the *SAM Structure*. This is the substantial difference between the *SAM Structure* object, presented in this work, and the previous approaches in the literature where tree-based hierarchical structures are used to describe the structure of an assembly after this is constructed by the CAD user [33–36]. The *SAM Structure* contains only information on what components are included in the assembly. Information about the connection relations between components is stored in the *SAM Connection Rules Collection*. Each row of the *SAM Connection Rules Collection* (Fig. 3) represents a *SAM Connection Rule*. The “:” symbol is used to represent the relation between the related objects. The *SAM Connection Rule* is an object-oriented representation of the relationship between two components linked together with a kinematic relationship called “*Kinematic Pair”*. A component can be either a part or an assembly. The *SAM Component* is the base class for the *SAM Part*

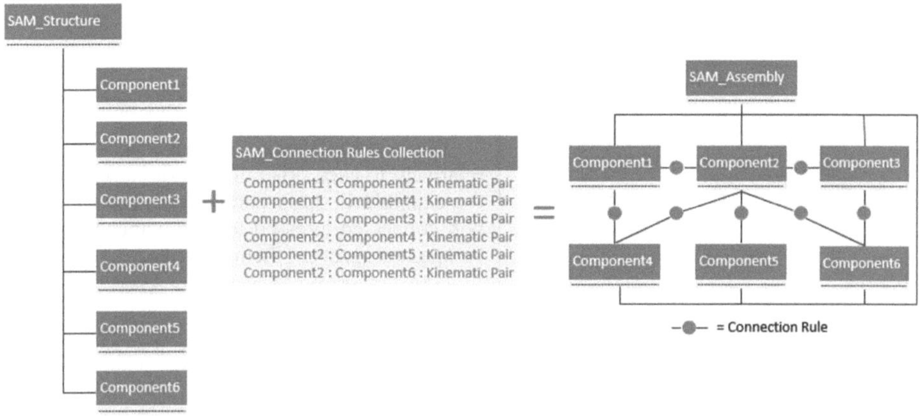

Fig. 3. The schematic assembly model consists of the SAM_structure and the SAM_connection rules collection

and *SAM Assembly* objects that derive from it. The *SAM Part* object represents a component that cannot be decomposed into components and the *SAM Assembly* object represents an assembly or a sub-assembly. Each *SAM Component* child instance object has member variables, numerical or boolean, named as *Attributes*, that control the form and the dimensions of the corresponding generative part model instance.

Chen et al. [33, 37] propose six kinematic pair types: *Prismatic Pair*, *Revolute Pair*, *Screw Pair*, *Cylindrical Pair*, *Spherical Pair* and *Planar Pair*. Demoly et al. [4] propose ten kinematic pairs: *Rigid*, *Revolute*, *Prismatic*, *Screw*, *Cylindrical*, *Spherical, Planar, Point-contact, Line-contact and Curve-contact*. Finally Csabai et al. [18] propose fourteen kinematic relations: *Distance*, *Spherical*, *In-plane*, *In-line*, *On-cylinder*, *Mate*, *Align*, *Cylindrical*, *Co-directional*, *Revolute*, *Prismatic*, *Universal*, *Screw* and *Rigid*. In this work, the role of the *SAM Kinematic Pairs* differs significantly from previous approaches. A *SAM Kinematic Pair* provides a description of the relative motion existing between two components. A *SAM Kinematic Pair* does not contain information on how this kinematic relationship can be implemented in the 3D assembly model. This kind of information is provided by the IAM, which will de described in Sect. 3.3. In this work, the AASM uses seven *SAM Kinematic Pairs*: *Rigid*, *Prismatic*, *Spherical*, *Cylindrical*, *Contact*, *Angular* and *Insert* (Table 1). The *Rigid*, *Prismatic*, *Spherical* and *Cylindrical* kinematic pairs are adopted from [4, 18, 33]. The *Contact* kinematic pair is added instead of a *Planar* since it can better describe the contact between planar and cylindrical faces. The *Insert* kinematic pair is added because it can better describe bolted connections and bearing-shaft type relations. Finally, the *Angular* kinematic pair is added to represent very common situations of angular relationships in mechanical assemblies like hinge-type connections.

By dividing the SAM into two parts (*SAM Structure* and *SAM Connection Rules Collection*) the model is better suited for cases where the same components with different connection rules can produce different valid assemblies.

Table 1. Kinematic pairs

Kinematic Pair		*Description*
	Rigid	Two components cannot be moved relatively to each other. These situations occur for example if these components are welded, bolt connected, pressed to fit together or other components prevent them to move.
	Prismatic	One component can slide relatively to another.
	Cylindrical	A cylindrical component (e.g. a shaft) is placed coaxially on cylindrical features (e.g. sliding bearings) of another component.
	Angular	"Hinge" type connection between two components.
	Insert	One component is inserted into hole/socket features of the second component e.g. a bolt inserted into a hole.
	Spherical	Two components share a virtually common centre.
	Contact	Two components are in contact at a line. This connection type is usually combined with other connection types. It could be used to indicate contact between two planar surfaces, or between two cylindrical surfaces, or between a planar and a cylindrical surface.

3.3 AASM: The Intermediate Assembly Model (IAM)

The *Intermediate Assembly Model (IAM)* fills the informational gap between SAM and the implemented 3D-CAD assembly model. IAM contains all the information on how components can be connected. IAM is created in four steps: During the first step, the initial structure of the IAM, based on the SAM, is created. For each *SAM Component* a corresponding *IAM Component* is created, and for each *SAM Connection Rule* an *IAM Components Association* object is created. An *IAM Component* is the base object for the *IAM Assembly* and *IAM Part* objects which are derived from it. An *IAM Assembly* object represents either a 3D sub-assembly that is part of a larger assembly (sub-assembly) or the final 3D assembly. An *IAM Part* object represents a component that cannot be further decomposed into components. Each instance of the *IAM Part* class includes a member function that is connected with the corresponding generative part model. During the second step, this member function generates all the corresponding 3D part model instances, but the IAM does not yet contain the information on how these part models should be connected to form a 3D assembly. This information is obtained during the third step (Fig. 4) where the *IAM Component Associations* objects, created at the first step, are completed with information on the AFs that will be used to form the corresponding connections in the 3D assembly.

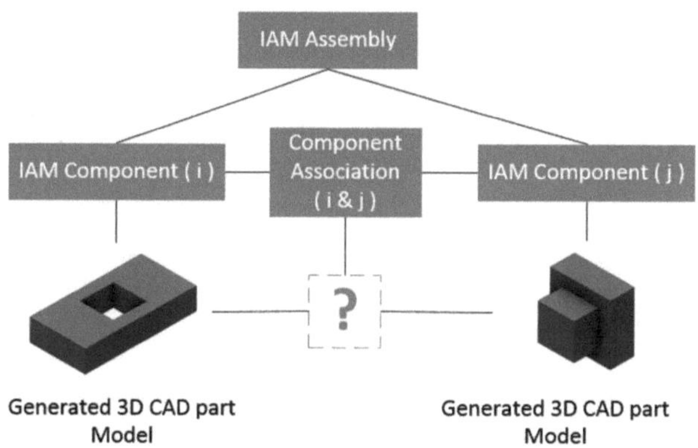

Fig. 4. Step 2: generation of 3D part models

During the third step, all 3D part models, created at the second step, are scanned and pairs of compatible AFs are associated through an *Assembly Feature Association* object *(AFA)*. For each compatible AF pair found, a new AFA object is created. The created AFAs are then associated with the corresponding *IAM Component Association* objects. An AFA object contains references to each of the associated *Assembly Features* and to a number of *Assembly Feature Attribute Pair Associations (AFAPA)*. An AFAPA is formed by two matched *Assembly Feature Attribute Pairs (AFAP)* (Fig. 5). This step completes construction of IAM (Fig. 6).

During the fourth step, *Component Association* objects (created in Step 1) are checked for compatibility to the corresponding *SAM Connection Rules*. Compatibility between a *SAM Connection Rule* and a *Component Association* object is confirmed through the compatibility between the *SAM Kinematic Pairs* and the *Assembly Feature Attribute Pairs* that implement them.

In Table 2, we present *SAM Kinematic Pairs* and AFAPs that implement them. Besides compatibility checks, connectability checks should also take place [28]. Connectability refers to the ability of two parts to become connected without the occurrence of "solid-solid interference". For connectability checks, an algorithm, based on CAD tools for interference and collision detection, is used.

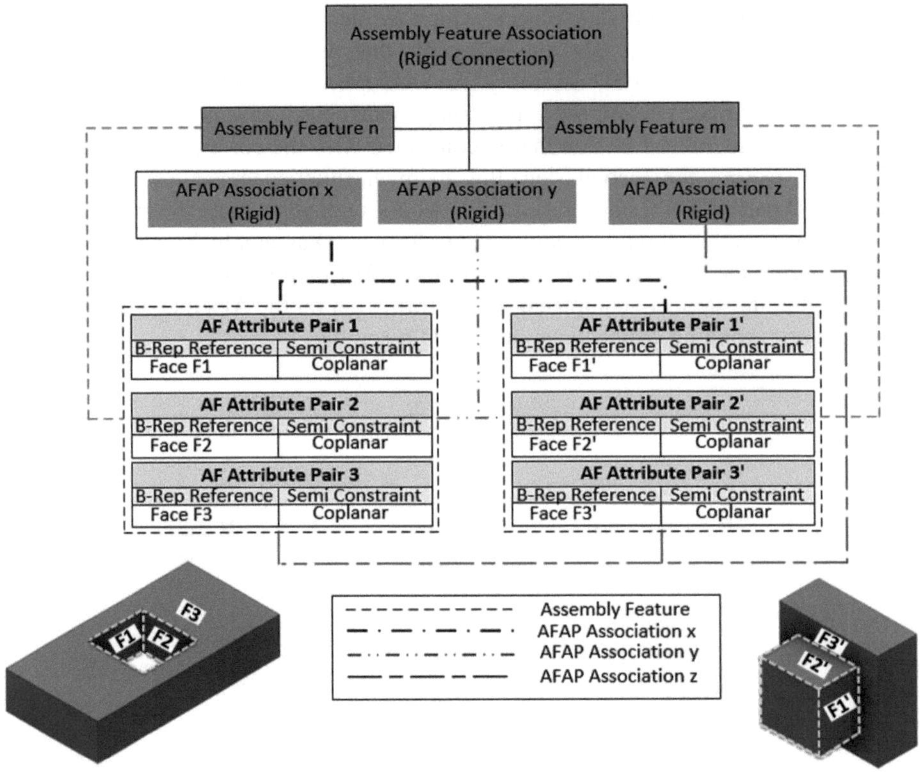

Fig. 5. AF association

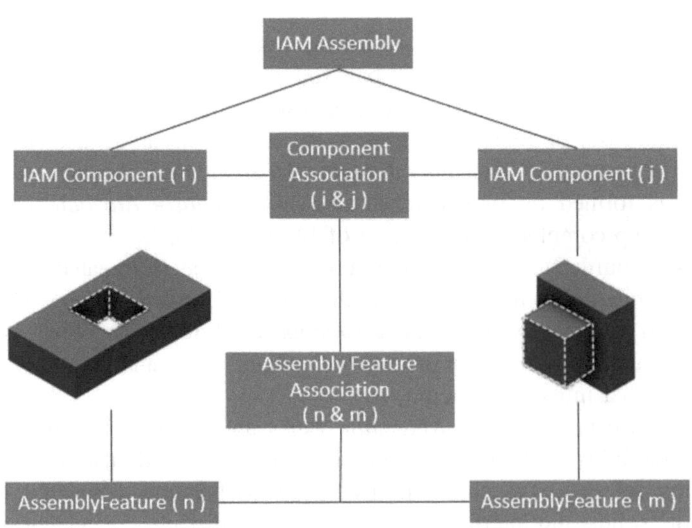

Fig. 6. Step 3: AF association

Table 2. Kinematic pairs and implementations using AFAPs

Kinematic Pair		***Assembly Feature Attribute Pairs Implementation***
	***Rigid***	Any combination of *AFAPs* that remove all the degrees of freedom between two components, e.g: • three "Plane : Coplanar" AFAPs. • or two "Plane : Coplanar" plus one "Plane : Align" AFAPs. • or one "Plane : Coplanar" plus two "Plane : Align" AFAPs. • or three "Edge : Align" AFAPs , etc.
	***Prismatic***	Any combination of *AFAPs* that allows only one-directional linear movement, e.g.: • two "Plane : Coplanar" AFAPs. • or two " Edge : Align" AFAPs. • or a combination of the above two.
	***Cylindrical***	An "Axis : Align" *AFAP.*
	***Angular***	A combination of: • one "Axis : Align" AFAP plus one "Surface : Angle" AFAP. • or one "Edge : Align" AFAP plus one "Surface : Angle" AFAP.
	***Insert***	Any combination of *AFAPs* that leaves only one rotational degree of freedom remaining, e.g.: • one "Plane : Coplanar" and one "Axis : Align" AFAPs. • or one "Plane : Align" and one "Axis : Align" AFAPs.
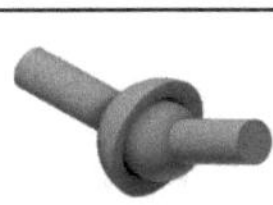	***Spherical***	All linear movement degrees of freedom are removed, all rotational degrees of freedom remaining: • one "Point : Coincidence" AFAP.
	***Contact***	A "Surface : Tangent" *AFAP.*

4 Implementation of the Automatic Assembly Synthesis Model

To test the effectiveness of the AASM, this has been implemented in a software system automating the synthesis of elevator-car 3D assembly models. This system includes four major components: (a) a commercial Rule Based System (IBM's ILOG),

(b) a commercial database system (Microsoft SQL Server), (c) a commercial 3D CAD system (Autodesk Inventor) and (d) the present Automatic Assembly Synthesis Model (AASM), developed as a CAD add-in, named as *CabinsKBE*, materializing this design automation workflow: [a] The customer's order is passed as input to the Rule Based System (RBS). [b] The RBS produces a detailed description for the elevator car, which is stored in the database. [c] The CAD system, extended with the *CabinsKBE* add-in, retrieves the stored configuration from the database, creates the corresponding SAM and IAM, generates all required 3D parts and, finally, synthesizes them into the 3D assembly.

CabinsKBE has managed to successfully assemble various types of elevator cars. Figure 7A presents an example of a panoramic-car assembly model synthesized by the present software. For this model, *CabinsKBE* created: 30 *SAM* and *IAM Component* instances, 69 *SAM Connection Rules* and *IAM Components* Associations, and 138 *AF*s. Figure 7B presents an example of a goods passenger car. For this assembly the AASM software created: 20 *SAM* and *IAM Component* instances, 23 *SAM Connection Rules* and *IAM Components* Associations, and 42 AFs. In both cases, all components were generated and then synthesized, into the desired assembly, by *CabinsKBE* in a fully automatic mode.

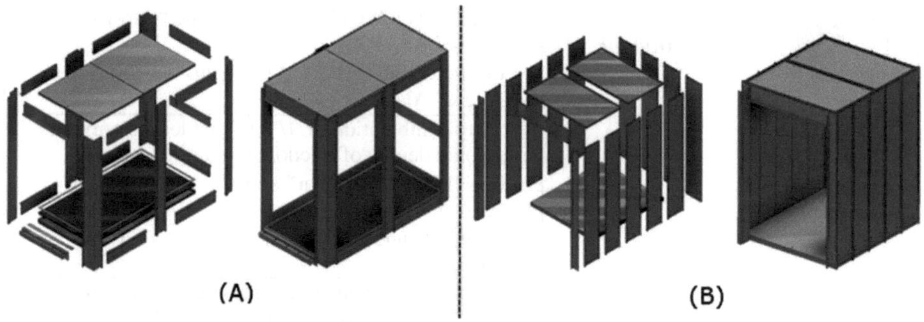

Fig. 7. A panoramic car (A) and a passenger elevator car (B) automatically synthesized using CabinsKBE.

5 Discussion - Conclusions

When it comes to Engineering-To-Order (ETO) products (e.g., products for which neither the number nor the form of components can be standardized), existing CAD tools and automation methodologies are not capable to support full automation of routine design procedures. The *Automatic Assembly Synthesis Model (AASM),* described above, has been shown adequate to: fill the communication gap between KBE (and/or Rules Based Systems [RBS]) and CAD systems, support automatic assembly synthesis, and construct valid 3D assembly models. The substantial features of AASM are its dual structure and the use of *Assembly Features* as they are redefined here. The dual structure of AASM makes it adequate to represent (a) the configuration structure implied by a KBE or a RBS system and (b) the specific assembly implementing this configuration. The effectiveness of the AASM model has been tested in a design automation system developed for elevator cars. The implemented system, at Kleemann Hellas SA, decreased significantly the time spent to process each car order. For example, the design time for a panoramic elevator car was reduced from six hours, when generative techniques and pre-designed assembly models are used, to fifteen minutes with the implemented AASM (*CabinsKBE*) software. Other benefits were that costs caused by human errors were eliminated and lead times for product delivery were significantly reduced.

Acknowledgments. This work was supported by Kleemann Hellas SA (http://www.kleemannlifts.com/).

References

1. Krish, S.: A practical generative design method. CAD Comput. Aided Des. **43**, 88–100 (2011)
2. Skarka, W.: Application of MOKA methodology in generative model creation using CATIA. Eng. Appl. Artif. Intell. **20**, 677–690 (2007)
3. Amadori, K., Tarkian, M., Ölvander, J., Krus, P.: Flexible and robust CAD models for design automation. Adv. Eng. Inf. **26**, 180–195 (2012)
4. Demoly, F., Toussaint, L., Eynard, B., Kiritsis, D., Gomes, S.: Geometric skeleton computation enabling concurrent product engineering and assembly sequence planning. Comput.-Aided Des. **43**, 1654–1673 (2011)
5. Chatziparasidis, I., Sapidis, N.S.: Automatic assembly synthesis based on multiple models and assembly features. Technical report, Department of Mechanical Engineering, UOWM (2016)
6. Rachuri, S., Han, Y.H., Feng, S.C., Roy, U., Wang, F., Sriram, R., et al.: Object-oriented representation of electro-mechanical assemblies using UML. NIST IR, vol. 7057 (2003)
7. Shyamsundar, N., Gadh, R.: Internet-based collaborative product design with assembly features and virtual design spaces. Comput.-Aided Des. **33**, 637–651 (2001)
8. Qi, F.: A online retrieving method for product functional and structural information based FGT model. WSEAS Trans. Comput. **8**, 1749–1759 (2009)
9. van Holland, W., Bronsvoort, W.F.: Assembly features in modeling and planning. Robot. Comput.-Integr. Manuf. **16**, 277–294 (2000)
10. Brunetti, G., Golob, B.: A feature-based approach towards an integrated product model including conceptual design information. Comput.-Aided Des. **32**, 877–887 (2000)
11. Xu, Z., Zhang, J., Li, Y., Jiang, S., Sun, Y.: Product modeling framework based on interaction feature pair. Comput.-Aided Des. **45**, 1591–1603 (2013)
12. Sugimura, N.: JNC proposal of STEP assembly model for products (2000)
13. Shah, J.J., Rogers, M.T.: Assembly modeling as an extension of feature-based design. Res. Eng. Des. **5**, 218–237 (1993)
14. Deneux, D.: Introduction to assembly features: an illustrated synthesis methodology. J. Intell. Manuf. **10**, 29–39 (1999)
15. Chang, C.-F., Perng, D.-B.: Assembly-part automatic positioning using high-level entities of mating features. Comput. Integr. Manuf. Syst. **10**, 205–215 (1997)

16. Xiao, H., Cheng, H., YU, J., Li, Y.: Dynamic assembly simplification for virtual assembly process of complex product. Assembly Autom. **34**, 1–15 (2014)
17. Yu, J.F., Xiao, H., Zhang, J., Cheng, H., Xin, B.: CAD model simplification for assembly field. Int. J. Adv. Manuf. Technol. **68**, 2335–2347 (2013)
18. Csabai, A., Stroud, I., Xirouchakis, P.C.: Container spaces and functional features for top-down 3D layout design. CAD Comput. Aided Des. **34**, 1011–1035 (2002)
19. Yin, C.G., Ma, Y.S.: Parametric feature constraint modeling and mapping in product development. Adv. Eng. Inf. **26**, 539–552 (2012)
20. Ma, Y.S., Britton, G.A., Tor, S.B., Jin, L.Y.: Associative assembly design features: concept, implementation and application. Int. J. Adv. Manuf. Technol. **32**, 434–444 (2007)
21. Ma, Y.S., Tong, T.: Associative feature modeling for concurrent engineering integration. Comput. Ind. **51**, 51–71 (2003)
22. Ma, Y., Britton, G.A., Tor, S.B., Jin, L., Chen, G., Tang, S., et al.: Design of a feature-object-based mechanical assembly library. Comput.-Aided Des. Appl. **1**, 397–403 (2004)
23. Dixon, A., Shah, J.J.: Assembly feature tutor and recognition algorithms based on mating face pairs. Comput.-Aided Des. Appl. **7**, 319–333 (2010)
24. Kim, K.-Y., Wang, Y., Muogboh, O.S., Nnaji, B.O.: Design formalism for collaborative assembly design. CAD Comput. Aided Des. **36**, 849–871 (2004)
25. Du, B., Wang, X., Feng, Y., Yu, D., Xu, G.: Intelligent assembly technology based on standard parts feature of CATIA. Mod. Appl. Sci. **8**, 49–55 (2014)
26. Noort, A., Hoek, G.F.M., Bronsvoort, W.F.: Integrating part and assembly modelling. Comput.-Aided Des. **34**, 899–912 (2002)
27. Li, G.D., Zhou, L.S., An, L.L., Ji, J.F., Tan, C.B., Wang, Z.G.: A system for supporting rapid assembly modeling of mechanical products via components with typical assembly features. Int. J. Adv. Manuf. Technol. **46**, 785–800 (2010)
28. Singh, P., Bettig, B.: Port-compatibility and connectability based assembly design. J. Comput. Inf. Sci. Eng. **4**, 197–205 (2004)
29. Zhang, J., Xu, Z., Li, Y., Jiang, S.: Framework for the integration of assembly modeling and simulation based on assembly feature pair. Int. J. Adv. Manuf. Technol. **78**, 765–780 (2014)
30. Sun, Y.L., Li, Y., Zhang, J., Xu, Z.J.: An automatic product assembly method based on assembly feature pair. Adv. Mater. Res. **655–657**, 1697–1701 (2013)
31. Toogood, R.: Creo Parametric 3.0 Advanced Tutorial: SDC Publications, Berkeley (2015)
32. Banach, D., Jones, T., Kalameja, A.: Autodesk Inventor 2010 Essentials Plus. Cengage Learning, Boston (2009)
33. Chen, X., Gao, S., Yang, Y., Zhang, S.: Multi-level assembly model for top-down design of mechanical products. Comput. Aided Des. **44**, 1033–1048 (2012)
34. Lee, K., Gossard, D.: A hierarchical data structure for representing assemblies: part 1. Comput.-Aided Des. **17**, 15–19 (1985)
35. Zeid, I.: CAD/CAM Theory and Practice, vol. 6. McGraw-Hill, New York (1991)
36. Lee, K.: Principles of CAD/CAM/CAE Systems. Addison-Wesley, Boston (1999)
37. Chen, X., Gao, S., Guo, S., Bai, J.: A flexible assembly retrieval approach for model reuse. Comput.-Aided Des. **44**, 554–574 (2012)

SDM Framework as a Support for Decision-Making Traceability in Design of Experiments Process

Farouk Belkadi[1(✉)], Luca Dall'Olio[2], Gilles Besombes[3], and Alain Bernard[1]

[1] Ecole Centrale de Nantes – IRCCyN – UMR CNRS 6597, 1 rue de la Noë, 44300 Nantes, France
farouk.belkadi@irccyn.ec-nantes.fr
[2] ALNEOS, 196 rue Houdan, 92330 Sceaux, France
[3] VALEO – Pôle systèmes thermiques centre R&D, La Verrière, France

Abstract. During the design of experiments process several simulations and experimentations are performed to evaluate all design solutions' alternatives. Technical meetings toke place regularly with the aim to select the product parameters and their values range to be considered in each simulation as well as the resolution methods and algorithms. One of the major problems concerns the lack of traceability and connections between all these design decisions and simulation results along the design process. A Simulation Data Management framework is proposed in this paper as a solution to resolve such kind of problems. This will enhance the final performance of the design of experiment process by reducing time of resolution and ensuring consistency of all simulation parameters, decisions and results.

Keywords: SDM · Design of experiments · Traceability

1 Introduction

Nowadays, products are more and more complex composed by huge quantity of components and embedding large variety of technologies. The development process of such products requires the interactions of many actors, working on different elements of the design project and focusing on the same sub-system with different points of view (mechanical, electrical, FEM, etc.).

Engineering activities take central place in the development process and has become more and more challenging, requiring different tools and methods. Numerical simulation is one of the important stages of the engineering process to validate design decisions and to assess product performance along each step of its lifecycle [1]. Designs of Experiments (DoE) methods are often used to monitor the simulation process. To shorten the simulation process, two approaches were identified: (1) the DoE process execution duration reduction and (2) the DoE preparation process shortening by managing and reusing simulation data.

R. Harik et al. (Eds.): PLM 2016, IFIP AICT 492, pp. 275–285, 2016.
DOI: 10.1007/978-3-319-54660-5_25

During these processes, product parameters, relations between these parameters, business constraints and rules, are allocated to interdependent sub-systems and considered on several computing algorithms with different objectives. Some parameters' values are resulted from the combination of other parameters, inputs of these simulation algorithms. This complexity requires one or more collaboration processes in order to help designers and decision-makers to converge their partial results into final and consistent result [2].

Due to these reasons, keeping the history of the design activity presents a great interest for the design project team and contributes significantly to shorten the process time and optimize the quality of the results. Traceability is usually associated with the activity of capturing, structuring and exploiting all information about the product, its parameters, states' evolutions, decisions and activities around this product, connected resources, tools, events, and the organization of these elements during the project [3].

Traceability is not an easier task because it needs the implication of several actors who are source of heterogeneous knowledge, generally implicit and difficult to formalize. The second reason is that asking individuals to keep formal trace of their activities in addition to realize these activities implies a significant cognitive workload, which can be a brake to such initiative.

In this context, it would be useful if designers could be encouraged to use the collaborative tools, enhanced by innovative technologies to keep a systematic record of the details of their activities and their corresponding situation.

In this context, one of the main challenges of the Simulation Data Management for Design of Experiment (SDM4DOE) project is to develop open-source simulation platform dedicated to DoE applications. This platform aims to support faster and efficient DoE processes, for complex numerical models, while ensuring traceability of generated data and providing a decision-aid system for DoE preparation.

This paper introduces concepts and specification to manage DoE process data. The DoE process characteristics are firstly described to highlight the need of traceability and data management in such complex process. The DoE data models developed to solve this issue is presented in the third section. The last section gives an overview of the SDM platform focusing on the traceability and data management functions.

2 Data Management and Traceability in DoE Process

2.1 Design of Experiment Process

A DoE is a set of experiments defined to assess the numerical model for different configurations of the product. A DoE is defined by its type (distribution of experiments in the design-space), the number and type of its factors (model parameters) and associated levels. A DoE process may have different objectives (exploration, product optimization, sensitivity analysis, etc.) and submitted to different constraints (e.g. computational budget). The computational cost of a DoE is the cost of the numerical model calculation multiplied by the number of experiments. Thus, an optimal strategy is to choose the most efficient DoE and to use a method for reducing the computational cost of each run.

The DoE process is based on the simulation process, which consists of three main steps [4] (Fig. 1). First, a parameterized numerical model of the studied system is created. Corresponding outputs (design parameters) are obtained by a specific solver and analyzed during the post-processing step, for model checking and product validation.

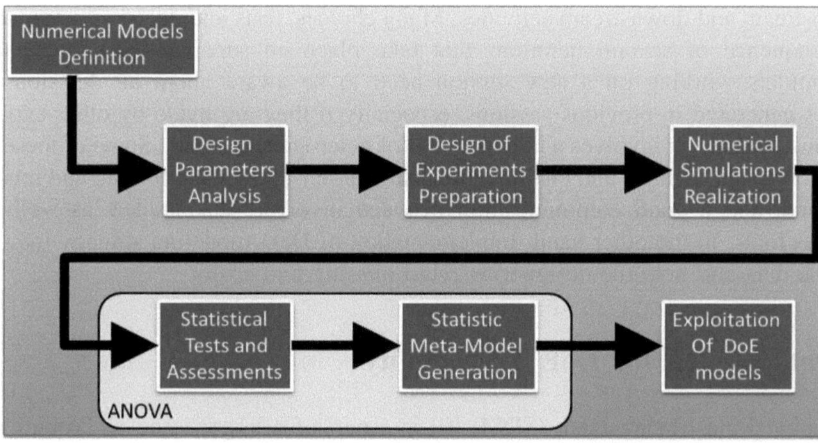

Fig. 1. Design of experiment process

After the definition and the validation of the numerical model [5], the available factors must be analyzed and selected to reduce the DoE cost, by a sensitivity analysis in the preparation step before starting simulations. Only most influent factors are kept, according to a specific output. To analyze accurately these influences, a meta-model (or surrogate model) is created in the last step from DoE results and statistical methods, as ANOVA. The meta-model can be reused to replace the numerical model for other studies in order to save time and cost.

All of these steps may generate a large amount of heterogeneous data and could be very expensive and time-consuming. An efficient DoE should minimize the number of runs and optimize the space-covering of the runs, according to the DoE objective (exploration, product optimization…).

2.2 Need of Traceability

Several types of DoE are available for numerical simulation [6] depending on its properties (space-filling, uniformity, etc.), objectives (exploration, optimization, etc.) and constraints (computational budget, output linearity properties, etc.). DoE type selection can be a long and difficult operation [7], needing assistance through the classification of all DoE types, simulation methods and used meta-models. Meta-models are used to replace a costly numerical model by a function faster to be assessed, for a specific output. The complexity and variety of meta-models depend on the DoE type and the business domain [8]. Although large quantities of methods and meta-models exist and some classification initiatives are already started, the need of robust tools to assist the hard task of identification of the best DoE methods and meta-models still a critical aspect to improve the design process.

In addition, the DoE process is a collaborative process in which several experts from different fields with different roles are involved. The effect of DoE results on the global product development process implies many interactions between DoE Process and upstream and downstream activities. Many choices, tests and decisions are made as a consequence of several iterations that take place on separate working sessions. Stakeholders working on a new session need to be aware about all decisions and choices generated in previous sessions, especially if they are made by other experts.

Thus, a DoE run involves a large amount of heterogeneous data. Some of these data needs to be standardized and classified to ensure easier knowledge finding and reuse on one hand, and a good communication between involved stakeholders as well used business tools, in the other hand. Implementation of Data modeling strategy may lead to reuse data and help the designer to avoid missing and errors.

3 Data Models for DoE Traceability

Simulation Data Management (SDM) [9] is a part of a larger issue of Product Data Management (PDM). PDM provides methods and tools to support the structuring, storage in shared repositories, management and sharing of product-related data and processes for its processing. More recently, SDM issues are associated with the new Product Lifecycle Management approaches (PLM) [10]. This covers technical data management systems of the product (PDM), the design support tools (CAD/CAE), manufacturing support tools (CAM) and other ERP applications [11]. Numerical DoE is a concrete example of the use cases of SDM tools. The realization of a DoE is based on the combined use of a set of design tools, simulation, computation, statistical processing and control of the computing process.

3.1 DoE Concepts Classification

In the context of the SDM4DOE project, a first study was realized to map and classify all data involved in a DoE process. The global organization of main data types are classified in the following items:

- The package "Design of Experiments": this first category of data aims to describe the main properties of DoE: objectives, the type, the nature of the studied phenomenon, etc.
- The package "Traceability and Administration" is used to link the DoE folder with its administrative and operational environment. This connection is done by several concepts such as: the reference of the project, the product and/or component associated with the DoE, the stakeholders involved in the working sessions, the timing of these working sessions with related decisions, etc.

- The package "Parameters" is the central node of the DoE data model. Through this concept the different types of parameters (factors) are classified according to their nature, their input/output status in the different steps of the DoE process and the possible intervals of variation of their value. The concept of "parameter" is used to define other specific properties but also to provide a common semantic for the codification of parameters' name. These concepts will allow communication between involved enterprise business platforms and with the SDM platform.
- The package "Business Models" is used to manage in a uniform way all types and versions of business models involved in a DoE process to facilitate their sharing. It also links parameters to business models. It mainly involves CAD models, FEM and meta-model data.
- The package "Storage-Representation" provides important information to SDM for data location identification for extraction and exploitation. Because of their heterogeneity and diversity of their sources, data are stored in different places and in different formats (databases, header files, etc.) according to their nature.
- The package "Simulation-Computing" lists all types of simulation scripts and possible methods of analysis in a DoE process according to a given problem in a specific domain. It also links these types of processing with concerned parameters.
- The package «Resources» completes the definition of processing by proposing a classification of all software and methodologies supporting the computations. This will allow SDM users to quickly define the various steps of the DoE. The concept of "computational cost" allows a better characterization of the various alternatives of computations to facilitate the selection of the DoE execution mode.

3.2 Traceability of Administrative Data

The traceability of administrative and decision making justification is made around the concept of DoE folder. Figure 2 illustrates the main concepts required for the representation of all administrative data for traceability issues. The concept of "DoE folder" is the classifier of all DoE realizations according to one alternative solution of the product (or component) and one physical analysis. Each DoE realization consists on the concrete selection of parameters and their value intervals, but also the execution of all simulations required by the selected physical analysis.

The DoE folder is associated to a specific project and it is the space of interaction of several experts. Each expert takes one or more roles in the DoE process. These roles can be changed during the real physical meetings. These meetings are represented by the class "working session", in which one or more DoE Folders and/or realization might be occurred.

For traceability and future reuse perspective, the different decisions taken during concrete realization are stored in the related class. The total computing costs of different realizations is described in the DoE folder as an indicator for future choice of simulation methods and scripts in similar situations.

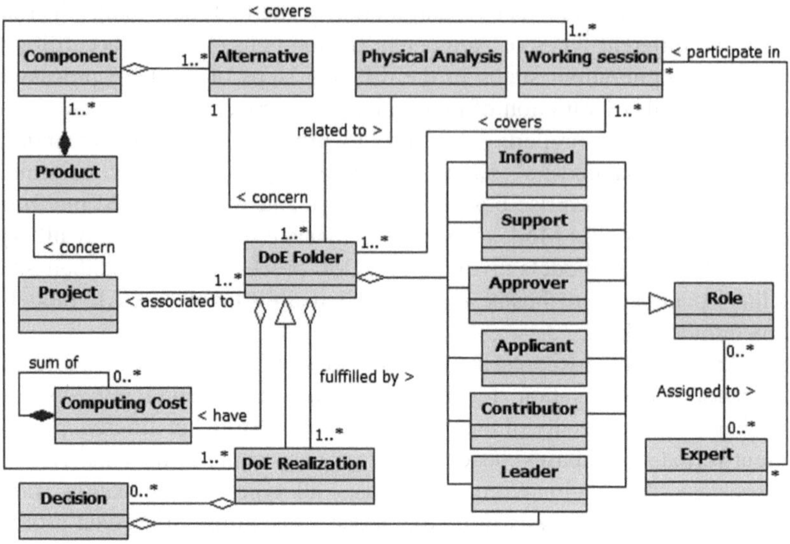

Fig. 2. The DoE folder

3.3 Traceability of Technical Data of the DoE

The main stage of DoE folder definition consists on the selection of parameters from the business model (FEM file). Then, the concrete realization of the DoE will start by the definition of variables inputs as instances of a sub set of the selected parameter (Fig. 3). The value variation of these instances could be obtained through fixed number, a mathematical formula or other random sampling generated by the Sampler module of Uranie software. The DoE realization result is obtained as a set of instances after a set of simulations and mathematical treatments (optimization, Anova, etc.).

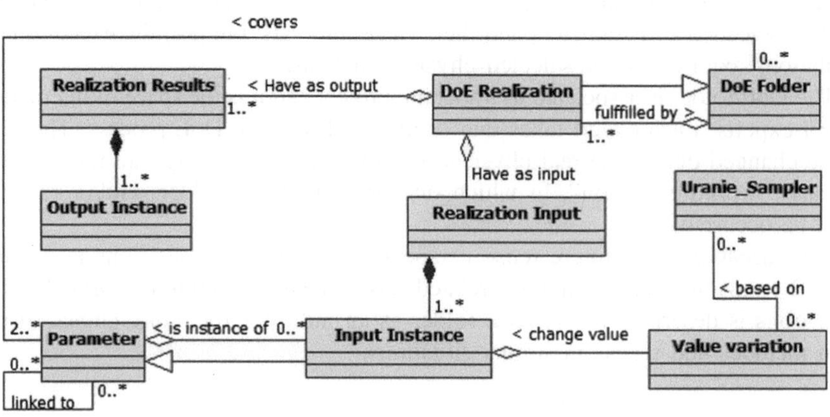

Fig. 3. Traceability of technical data

4 Models Implementation in the SDM Framework

To implement a DoE data management system, open-source software architecture is being developed in the SDM4DOE project. This architecture is developed as a SaaS web service, based on several open-source solutions. This section gives an overview of the developed platform focusing on the main data management functionalities.

4.1 Functional Architecture

As it is shown in the Fig. 4, the SDM platform supporting collaborative DoE process provides users a set of processing rules and management facilities of administrative and technical data during a work session. This is fulfilled via a web-based interface connected at to a cloud solution and provided from a web-server. It also allows viewing and navigating the previous PEN traceability data. To achieve processing features, the Uranie open-source software integration is launched in a computing cluster at the end-back layer. The kernel of the SDM framework is the shared workspace which makes connection between the web server and the company' computing cluster and includes several functionalities of data sharing and reporting.

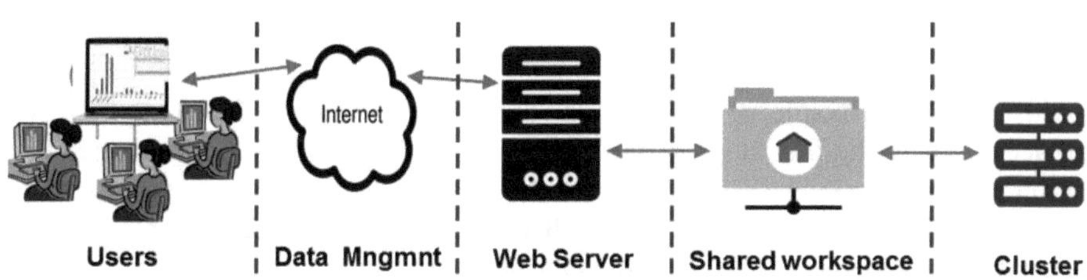

Fig. 4. Global architecture of the SDM framework

The computation chain of a DoE in the company's computing cluster is supervised by post-processing software Salomé. These services include the simulation software Code_Aster, in which acceleration methods of computations will be implemented.

Several functionalities are offered by the SDM framework to support the DoE process. The main interactions to fulfil these functionalities are summarized in the UML use case diagram bellow (Fig. 5). According to this diagram, the user can create new DoE folder and several realizations of this folder. At any moment he can edit the properties of an existing DoE folder and create new folder as an adaptation of existing one. This will help time saving and data messing especially when creating new version or variant of existing products (i.e. component).

Finding and Reuse functionalities are particularly appreciate when the user is searching for the optimal list of parameters and simulation method he should consider for his current problem. Knowledge base repository is used to support this functionality [12]. To perform a DoE realization, the connection of the workspace to different computing clusters allows users to verify availability and status of different cluster in

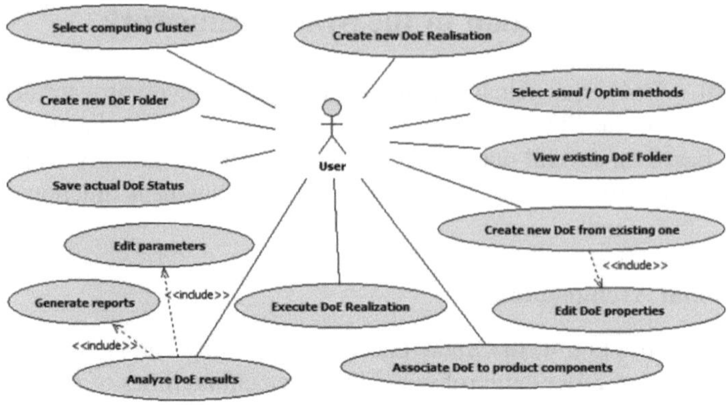

Fig. 5. Main interactions with the SDM framework

order to select the most suitable regarding to the complexity of the planned simulations. To analyze the results, two possibilities are offered: generating different reports with predefined set of information, and dynamic interface on which the user can observe the output of the meta-model for each combination of parameter values.

4.2 SDM GUIs Overview

To illustrate the principle of functioning, this section presents few Graphical User Interfaces used in the first steps of the DoE process. The starting point is already the creation of new working session (Fig. 6) that groups heterogeneous experts to take decisions about the current DoE. This will prepare the DoE execution by the identification of the available clusters and the clarification of the DoE objectives, the role of each participant and the concerned product components.

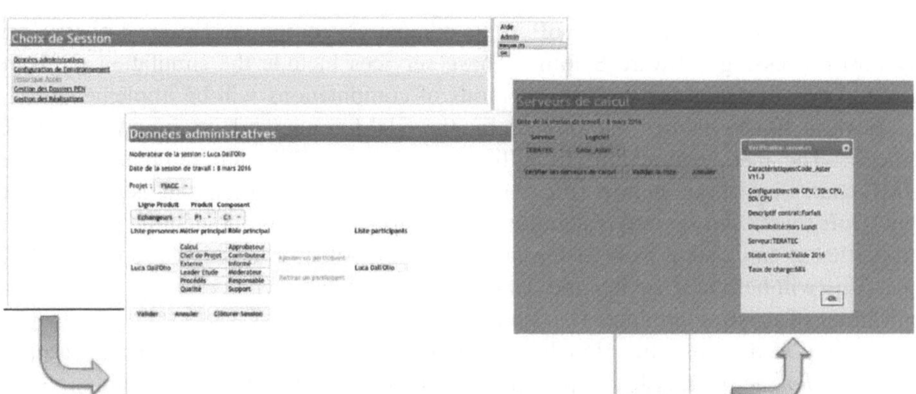

Fig. 6. SDM GUIs: New DoE working session

After fixing the administrative data, useful to handle decisions and results traceability, the user can decide to create a new DoE Folder, open existing one, create new DoE realization or view the results of last one and send execution order to the selected cluster. The manipulation of DoE folders and realizations implies the manipulation of related parameters, displayed in a separate window with default values (Fig. 7).

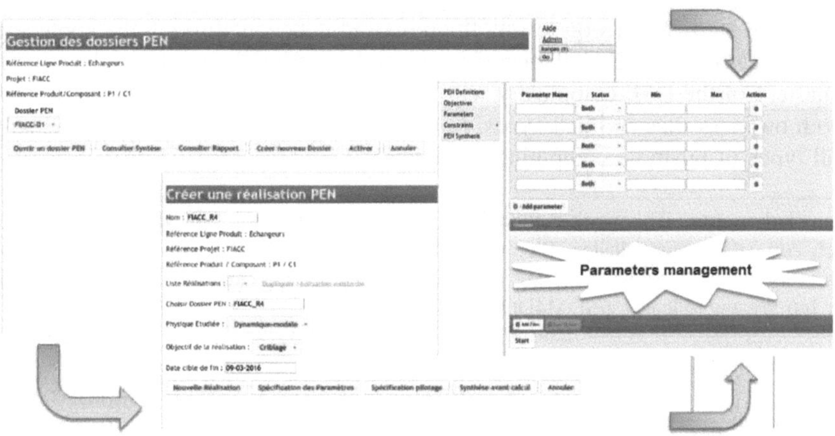

Fig. 7. SDM GUIs: DoE folder and instance

At any time, the user can edit the synthesis of the current DoE folder, all related realization as well the status of all launched simulations. Automatic workflow notifies the end of simulation. Then the user can request the results, which he can view and navigate on a separate window (Fig. 8). If the result is validated, it can be stored to be reused in future projects.

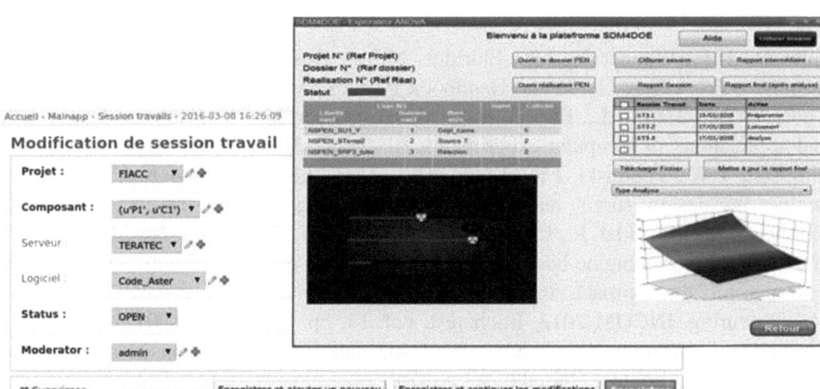

Fig. 8. SDM GUIs: edition of DoE synthesis and results

5 Conclusion

The first results of the SDM4DOE project show that existing SDM tools are not adapted to the heterogeneous nature of the DoE process data. Indeed, the optimization of a DoE process is based on the effective management of technical data, administrative data and also data related to the traceability of decisions. At this moment, a set of concepts has been proposed and is being refined and validate.

The next step consists on testing the proposed concepts through the application of the first version of the SDM platform in realistic industrial use cases. On the other hand, the mastery of the DoE complexity will be based on a standard codification proposal, on both business files and data types, to ensure the integration of SDM4DOE solution for all types of business computing platforms.

Acknowledgments. This work is funded by the French FUI project SDM4DOE and labeled by French competitiveness clusters SYSTEMATIC and ID4CAR. We also thank all consortium partners for their contribution during the development of ideas and concepts proposed in this paper http://www.id4car.org/SDM4DOE.html.

References

1. Bernard, A., Chenouard, R.: Multi-physics simulation for product-service performance assessment. In: 6th CIRP Conference on Industrial Product-Service Systems, vol. 16, Windsor, Ontario, Canada, pp. 21–25 (2014). http://dx.doi.org/10.1016/j.procir.2014.03.002
2. Kleiner, S., Anderl, R., Gräb, R.: A collaborative design system for product data integration. J. Eng. Des. **14**(4), 421–428 (2003)
3. Brand, S.C.: A process data warehouse for tracing and reuse of engineering design process. In: The Second International Conference on Innovations in Information Technology, ICIIT 2005, Dubaï (2005)
4. Charles, S.: Gestion intégrée de données CAO et EF. Contribution à la liaison entre conception mécanique et calcul de structures, Ph.D. thesis, Univ. Technologie de Troyes (2005)
5. Giles Jr., H.F., Wagner Jr., J.R., Eldridge, M.M.I: Design of Experiments, Extrusion: The Definitive Processing Guide and Handbook Plastics Design Library, pp. 291–308 (2014)
6. Chen, V.C.P., Tsui, K.L., Barton, R.R., Meckesheimer, M.: A review on design, modeling and applications of computer experiments. IIE Trans. **38**(4), 273–291 (2006)
7. Simpson, T.W., Peplinski, J.D., Koch, P.N., Allen, J.K.: Metamodels for computer-based engineering design: survey and recommendations. Eng. Comput. **17**(2), 129–150 (2001)
8. Castric, S., Denis-Vidal, L., Cherfi, Z., Blanchard, G.J., Boudaoud, N.: Modeling pollutant emissions of diesel engine based on kriging models: a comparison between geostatistic and Gaussian process approach. In: 14th IFAC Symposium on Information Control Problems in Manufacturing, INCOM 2012, Bucharest, vol. 14, pp. 1708–1715 (2012)
9. Charles, S., Ducellier, G., Eynard, B.: CAD and FEA integration in a simulation data management environment based on a knowledge based system. TMCE, Ljubljana, pp. 1719–1730 (2006)

10. Assouroko, I., Ducellier, G., Belkadi, F., Eynard, B., Boutinaud, P.: Improvement of engineering design and numerical simulation data exchange based on requirements deployment: a conceptual framework. In: 7th International Conference on Product Lifecycle Management, Bremen, Germany, pp. 487–497 (2010)
11. Bosch-Mauchand, M., Belkadi, F., Bricogne, M., Eynard, B.: Knowledge based assessment of manufacturing process performance: integration of product lifecycle management and value chain simulation approaches. Int. J. Comput. Integr. Manuf. **26**(5), 453–473 (2013)
12. Blondet, G., Belkadi, F., Le Duigou, J., Boudaoud, N.: Towards a knowledge based framework for numerical design of experiment optimization and management. Comput.-Aided Des. Appl. **13**(6), 872–884 (2016)

Interoperability Improvement in a Collaborative Dynamic Manufacturing Network

Emna Moones[1,2(✉)], El Mouloudi Dafaoui[2], El Mhamedi Abderrahman[2], Nicolas Figay[3], and Ali Koudri[1]

[1] Technological Research Institute SystemX, Palaiseau, France
{emna.moones, ali.koudri}@irt-systemx.fr
[2] Laboratoire Quartz EA 7393 IUT de Montreuil – Université Paris 8, 140 rue de la Nouvelle France, 93100 Montreuil, France
{e.dafaoui, a.elmhamedi}@iut.univ-paris8.fr
[3] Airbus Group Innovations, 12 rue Pasteur, 92150 Suresnes, France
nicolas.figay@airbus.com

Abstract. Today, more than ever, enterprise interoperability is a key factor of successful collaboration and exchange of information. It was identified as a critical need that has to be taken into account through the whole life cycle of the manufactured product and an essential property for development and growth. This is particularly significant when it comes to collaborative enterprise networks, like Dynamic Manufacturing Network (DMN), where a distinct group of partners is connected in a chain-like model and where cooperation is crucial to achieve a specific goal. Dealing with interoperability issues in a collaborative DMN, we have to mention the importance of product data and process standards implementation as interoperability enablers. This work seeks to contribute to the improvement of enterprise interoperability along the manufacturing phase of the product in a collaborative DMN. It illustrates the collaboration between the business planning level and the manufacturing level with the implementation of PLM (Product Lifecycle Management) standards. Our added value is to follow a multi-level approach based on the use of standards in a DMN. The proposed approach is highlighted by a manufacturing case study.

Keywords: Collaboration · DMN · PLM · Interoperability · Mediator · Standards · Multi-level approach

1 Introduction

The advent of digital technologies has led to stronger competitiveness and demand of products with lower cost, high quality and short delay of production in the industry. In response to this increasing competitiveness and higher demands in terms of services, most of governments are pushing initiatives to foster collaboration among industrial partners and with academic partners in order to push innovation and creation of more added values. This requires setting up new organizations with new business models along with suitable methodologies. One way to achieve more efficient collaborations

R. Harik et al. (Eds.): PLM 2016, IFIP AICT 492, pp. 286–295, 2016.
DOI: 10.1007/978-3-319-54660-5_26

today is to rely on an adaptive platform supporting relevant business rules and models. Such a platform shall provide services allowing the sharing of the right information in the right time and location for the right people. But, the lack of interoperability between Information Systems (IS) is increasingly becoming an issue in the collaboration and co-operation of enterprises. In this paper, we consider the use of open standards as key enablers for providing the required interoperability among the stakeholders involved in the collaboration. The use of open standards defines a common way to exchange data elements with shared syntax and semantics. Open standards ensure consistent management of data beyond technologies and allow harmonization of disparate information shared within the collaboration. There are numerous standards covering data exchange for various domains: ISO STEP[1] standard for the exchange of product model data, ISA-95[2] for the integration of enterprise and control systems, XML Process Definition Language (XPDL)[3] for exchanging business process definitions between different workflow products. Standard exchange and representations of data is not enough to ensure collaboration between organizations and emergence of innovative ideas. In order to improve the collaboration, we need to take into account industrial practices and life cycle issues: versioning, configuration, bug tracking, change requests, and so on. In the end, we need a support for a more holistic approach covering the whole life cycle of the product, from the initial idea to its realization, maintenance and withdrawal. Such an approach is covered by the PLM. Indeed, PLM represents a holistic approach for managing the different phases of the product along with the management of processes as well as physical and logical resources. It allows to support the exchange and the synchronization of information through the different phases of the product's life cycle in order to speed up its development or to improve its quality. The question that arises here is the following: how can we establish and improve the synchronization of information considering the heterogeneity of skills, tools and data when several stakeholders are involved in the collaboration. The Standard and Interoperability PLM (SIP)[4] project investigates this issue and aims to make collaboration more effective. For this purpose, one of the main objectives of this project is to specify a "test bed" to validate implementations of PLM standards, particularly in the context of a DMN. This paper presents results from the SIP project regarding the manufacturing phase. Those results are illustrated on an industrial case study aiming to improve interoperability between the business planning level, supported by Enterprise Resource Planning (ERP), and the manufacturing operations level, supported by Manufacturing Execution System (MES). In this use case, interoperability between ERP and MES tools is achieved thanks to the integration of the ISA-95 standard. This paper is structured as follow: Sect. 2 highlights our motivations, Sect. 3 presents the related works, Sect. 4 covers the proposed approach, and Sect. 5 presents the industrial case that illustrate our proposition. Finally Sect. 6 discusses our proposition and gives some hints for future works.

---

[1] http://www.steptools.com/library/standard/.

[2] https://www.isa.org/isa95/.

[3] http://www.xpdl.org/.

[4] http://www.irt-systemx.fr/systemx-lance-le-projet-sip-standards-interoperabilite-plm/.

2 Motivations

In order to enhance their competitiveness, companies no longer take ownership of all the assets and processes needed in delivering value to the customer. Instead, they focus on their core competencies and partnerships with companies possessing complementary strengths [1]. This has led to the rise of distributed and flexible manufacturing networks. However, the lack of an agile and responsive management methodology of such structures has hindered them from reaching their full potential. Today, the novel concept of DMN stands out as a cutting-edge solution in this quest, carrying a wide set of assets aiming to drive manufacturing organisations into the new global economy [2]. DMN is defined as a collection of independent companies, possessing complementary strengths and integrated with streamlined material, information, and financial flows that work together to meet market demands [1]. In this context, we need to deal with the issues of information integration and data shared across distributed heterogeneous application systems. For this purpose, we need to build up a high quality information integration platform. Indeed, one of the biggest current research challenges in networked manufacturing is to implement consistently the exchange and sharing of data. One way to improve collaboration in DMN is to improve interoperability, relying on the use of open standards. Ensuring effective and secured collaboration requires preparing and constructing operational interoperability [3]. According to [4], interoperability is defined as "the existence of different actors and systems which realise a collaborative action and the ability to communicate own data for actors which can be similar or radically different and to use these data". Some European research projects, such as ATHENA [5], have dealt with interoperability issues and have led to specifications and implementations of interoperability frameworks. These solutions present some weaknesses, for instance, the Athena Interoperability Framework (AIF) is insufficient for establishing operational interoperability at an acceptable price within a DMN. Moreover, open standards are not considered (e.g. ASD SSG[5] standards), and many interoperability brakes were not addressed, including testability of interoperability which is addressed by SIP approach [6]. Besides, interoperability remains today a real challenge for enterprises, and some brakes have been identified following the proposed solutions. In this context, our work addresses interoperability issues by suggesting a global approach which aims to deal with several interoperability levels using standards implementation in the whole life cycle of the product. Our goal is to contribute on proposing a solution for interoperability between ERP Information System and MES Information System. The following section presents some related works to our proposition.

3 State of the Art

Nowadays ERP systems have become predominant in medium and large companies [7]. They consist of series of integrated modules dedicated to the management of customers, suppliers and human resources, as well as the management of manufacturing. The goal

[5] ASD SSG: ePLM Interoperability, http://www.asd-ssg.org/ (2014).

of an ERP [8] is to support the unification of different departments of the company. To achieve this goal, an ERP relies on an application system. Information managed by an ERP can be used at different levels and for different purposes, e.g. the services of directions production, the customer relations or finance. ERP allows collaborative works between different services of an enterprise thanks to the use of a common interface to communicate and share data. Besides, MES systems are defined by [9] as a set of software and hardware components for the management and optimization of production activities from the launch of the order to the obtainment of the final product. The MES system is responsible for the production plan; it guides, initiates, responds and reports functionalities of the factory in real time. We can notice that these two systems have complementary functions. Some enterprise experiences [10] report that ERP and MES systems are fundamental and shall collaborate together. Indeed, ERP gives a global vision about the manufacturing of the product while MES monitors its production in real time. ERP and MES systems exchange and share information during the manufacturing process. It is therefore important to ensure the quality of collaboration between these two systems. To this end, a common standard for data exchange shall be elected and the ISA-95 standard seems to bridge the gap between ERP and MES systems. Collaboration between ERP and MES requires the use of a mediator ensuring the exchange of information. Indeed, several works have addressed the interoperability issue between IS. The result of those works is that interoperability remains a complex issue. According to [11–13] there are three levels of interoperability: conceptual, technological and organizational. Conceptual interoperability deals with the syntactic and semantic compatibilities when exchanging information. Technological interoperability refers to the use of computers or Information and Communication Technologies (ICT) to communicate and exchange information. Finally, organizational interoperability deals with the standard definition of responsibilities and authorities. These three levels are well addressed by the literature. For instance, the authors in [14] propose an holonic approach modeling the manufacturing process of a product. The holonic model is compared with two other standard models: the Unified Enterprise Modeling language (UEML) [15] for the business level supported by an ERP system and the ISA-95 [16] language for the manufacturing level supported by an MES system. The authors of this contribution propose a mapping of several semantics concepts between these two approaches. Contribution in [14] deals with the semantic interoperability between ERP and MES systems. This semantic interoperability issue is also addressed in [17]. This contribution provides a study on the impact of interoperability on the transition between the design and the manufacturing phases of the product. In particular, this contribution considers the value of the interoperability between Product Data Management (PDM), ERP and MES. The proposed approach is based on the use of ontologies related to STEP and ISA-95 standards. In [18], authors address the semantic barriers of the interoperability in achieved works as resulted to the semantic alignment between the ISA standard and the SCOR model [19]. In [20], the authors focus on the collaboration between ERP and MES systems. To solve the related issue, their works relies on a model driven approach to support the manufacturing process through models transformations. There are several works aiming to provide solutions to ensure interoperability at both semantic and technical levels. For example [21] proposed a modeling approach based on the STEP standard to deal with the consistent transition between design and manufacturing phases supported by PDM and ERP systems. In the case of point-to-point interoperability, a convertor has to be provided each time a new system is included in the network. Doing so, the number of convertors can increase quickly as the number of partners increases [21]. One way to deal with this complexity is to use a mediator when several partners shall collaborate together. For instance, authors in [22] use a mediator as a software module to exploit encoded knowledge about some sets or subsets of data. This mediator aims to provide relevant information to be consumed by higher layers of applications. The concept of mediators is introduced in [23], and is defined as a component enabling location of information and the solving of schematic and semantic conflicts. The SIP project has implemented a mediator platform as a service simplifying the use and the implementation of PLM standards. The work presented in this paper is one of the results of the SIP project, which relies on the use of PLM standards to deal with interoperability issues in the manufacturing phase between ERP and MES systems. Compared to the related works introduced before that address the interoperability only at semantic and technical levels, we propose to consider the interoperability issue from an holistic perspective, taking into account all interoperability levels. Our approach implements the ISA-95 standard which is the standard of integration between ERP and MES systems. Table 1, summarizes our position according to existing approaches.

Table 1. Position according to the state of the art.

Approaches	TI	SI	OI	MDA	Onto	ISA	STEP	NS	II	ERP/MES	Others
[14]	N	Y	N	Y	N	Y	N	N	N	Y	N
[17]	Y	Y	N	N	Y	Y	Y	N	N	Y	Y
[18]	N	Y	N	Y	Y	Y	N	N	N	N	Y
[20]	Y	N	N	Y	N	N	N	N	N	Y	N
[21]	Y	Y	N	N	N	N	Y	N	N	N	Y
Our approach	Y	Y	Y	Y	N	Y	N	N	Y	Y	N

TI: Technical Interoperability, SI: Semantic Interoperability, OI: Organizational Interoperability, Onto: Ontologies, NS: No Standard, II: Interoperability Improvement N: No, Y: YES.

In the following sections, we will explain the proposed approach illustrated by a case study in order to improve interoperability between business and manufacturing levels.

4 Proposed Approach

As mentioned in the previous section, point-to-point integration does not represent an adequate solution to foster collaboration between industrial partners. There is an imperative need to provide interoperability between these organizations supported by widely adopted standards. Consequently, the SIP methodology aims at validating implementation of a set of coherent PLM standards. One of the main objectives of the SIP project is to provide an innovative interoperability framework (shown in Fig. 1)

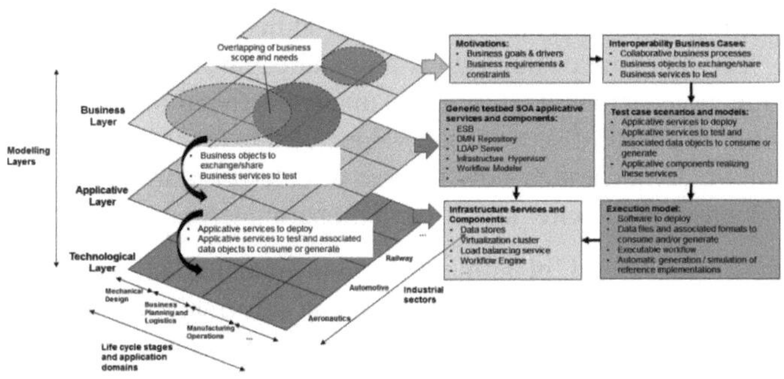

Fig. 1. Conceptual levels of archimate modeling

based on a model-driven methodology. The main outcome of this framework is the development of "test beds" to assess the implementation of PLM standards. This framework conforms to the TOGAF standard and its implementation relies on the Archi tool which supports the Archimate language [16]. In this way, we propose a multi-level approach as mediators using different tools adopted by the SIP methodology Fig. 1.

Figure 1 illustrates our approach to improve interoperability between ERP and MES systems following the different levels of interoperability and different layers of representation using a top-down way. To deal with the different interoperability issues presented in the previous section, in Fig. 2, we map the discussed interoperability levels with layers of the Archi framework. This multi-level approach allows us to address all interoperability brakes mentioned in the related work. The first step of our approach is to model the collaborative business scenario supported by both ERP and MES systems, and covered by the ISA-95 standard. The second step of the approach is to model the application including business functions. The last step consists in modeling the technical layer supporting the exchange of information, mainly through the use of XML technologies. Those steps are detailed in the following paragraphs.

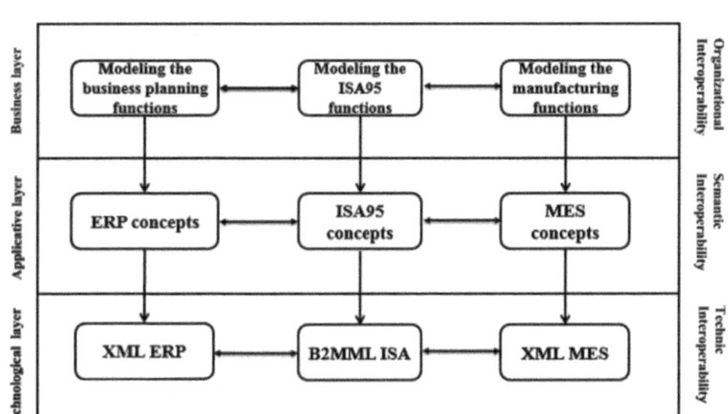

Fig. 2. Position relative to interoperability and framework levels

First Step. The organizational interoperability is addressed thanks to the use of an MDA methodology. The outcome of this step is a model capturing the functions of business planning, the functions of manufacturing and finally the functions providing a support for ISA-95 standard. We have discussed the values of this level in a previous work [16]. Indeed, in [16] we demonstrated how the use of enterprise architecture modeling languages could contribute to better specify and prepare interoperability business cases.

Second Step. Business and planning functions modeled in the previous step are refined in this step. At the end, business planning information shall be accessible for both ERP and MES solutions. This layer deals with semantic interoperability between ERP and MES systems. ERP and MES concepts are captured by meta-models and common concepts are compared in order to provide support for their semantic alignment. These meta-models are then instantiated to provide concrete data capturing production schedule and Manufacturing Bill of Material (MBOM). These models are then compared to ISA95 models conformant to the "Part2" of the standard in order to measure the gap between the ERP and the MES systems.

Third Step. The technical interoperability is supported by a connector playing the role of a mediator. It covers XML data extracted from the ERP solution to the standardized XML format of ISA-95 which is the Manufacturing Markup Language (B2MML). The structure of the connector is illustrated in Fig. 3. It relies on an Extensible Stylesheet Language Transformation (XSLT) to specify the transformation rules. B2MML is an XML implementation of the ISA-95 standard providing a common XML data structure to be exchanged by ERP and MES vendors. The specification of the B2MML schema in XSD complies the ISA-95 standard.

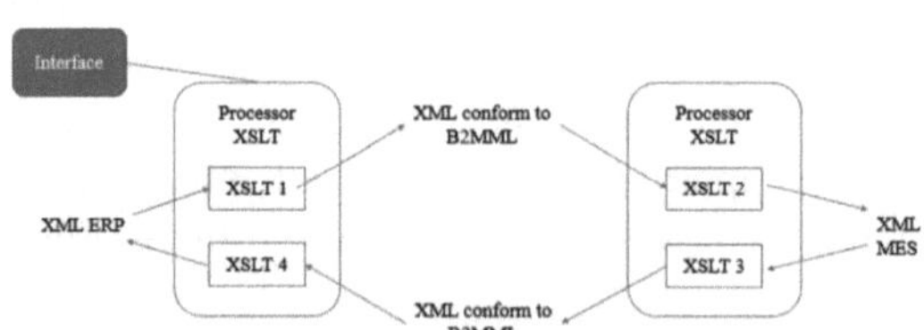

Fig. 3. Structure of XML/B2MML connector.

The added value of our connector consists in a more global integrated approach between business and manufacturing aspects. This connector is available on the SIP platform and can be used to test the consistency of ISA-95 standard implementations.

5 Case Study

DEKENZ[6] is a French company specialized in the development, the fabrication and the marketing of pens. The objective of this approach is to provide to universities a very concrete application. The production of every pieces and their integration is performed

[6] DEKENZ website: http://pm.flamant.free.fr/dekenz/?p=accueil.

by students at "La Halle Technologique" of the "IUT Montreuil"[7]. In [16], we dealt with the modeling of the ERP-MES data integration scenario of the DEKENZ case study. For this paper, we emphasize the exchange of MBOMs from the ERP system to the MES system. In order to do so, we convert the information extracted from the ERP to the ISA95 standard. For this purpose, we use the ODOO[8] ERP solution, which is a suite of open core enterprise management applications supporting billing, accounting, manufacturing, purchasing, warehouse management and project management. Practically, we start by extracting the XML file describing the MBOM from ODOO solution and we convert it to the B2MML format (Fig. 4).

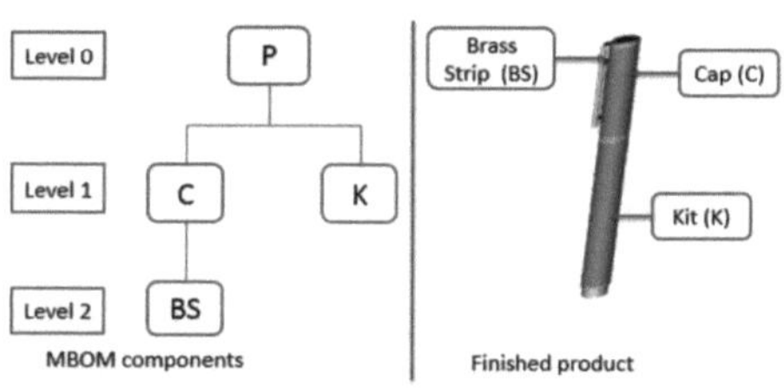

Fig. 4. Simplified DEKENZ MBOM

The resulting MBOM is composed of three levels: at the highest level (level 0) describes the Pen (P) composed by a Kit (K) and a Cap (C) in level 1. A Brass Strip (BS) is a component of the Cap at the lowest level. We capture this information in the MBOM file. We extract then the MBOM into an XML file conformant to the ERP data model. The next step is to convert the extracted information into the B2MML standard. The mapping between the concepts expressed XML ODOO ERP and the standardized B2MML format is presented in Table 2. The limit of this approach is that the mapping is performed manually by linking the concepts according to their semantic meaning.

Table 2. Correspondence between XML ODOO MBOM and B2MML ISA-95 MBOM.

XML ODOO	B2MML ISA95
Bill of material	Product definition
External ID	ID
Article name	Description
Range name	Equipment specification
Range charging post name	Equipment specification description
Line BOM article name	Material specification
Valid from	Duration
Valid until	Duration
Quantity article	Quantity

[7] IUT Montreuil website: http://www.iut.univ-paris8.fr/.

[8] https://www.odoo.com/fr_FR/.

This work has been developed through an internship, and is reported with more details in [24], and a first connector converting the XML information extracted from the ERP solution into the B2MML format according to the standard ISA-95 has been provided (Fig. 5).

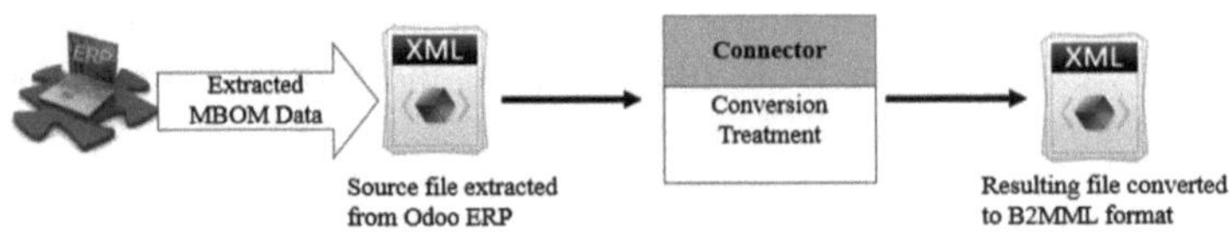

Fig. 5. Global architecture of the connector

6 Conclusion and Future Works

Enterprise applications need to be interoperable in order to achieve a seamless business integration across organizational boundaries in a DMN. This paper summarizes our approach to deal with interoperability issues between ERP and MES in a DMN. Our added value is to support a multi-levels approach based on the use of standards in a DMN. In addition to existing approaches, we support the technological level of interoperability. The approach is illustrated by a case study on an application from DEKENZ. Through our experimentation, we were able to simulate the collaboration. We have used the SIP "test bed" facilities to demonstrate the interest of using models to prepare, build, verify and validate enterprise interoperability. In future works, we will address the applicative and business level to enhance the proposed framework with functionalities like the simulation of the dynamic inclusion or exclusion of enterprises in the network. As manufacturing and engineering organizations become more and more globalized, the capability of simulating and monitoring accurately the operation of dynamic alliances at a very early stage becomes increasingly important. Our future research will investigate an innovative approach to assess enterprise interoperability in a DMN context.

Acknowledgments. This research work has been carried out under the leadership of the Technological Research Institute SystemX, and therefore granted with public funds within the scope of the French Program "Investissements d'avenir".

References

1. Viswanadham, N., Gaonkar, R.S.: Partner selection and synchronized planning in dynamic manufacturing networks. IEEE Trans. Robot. Autom. **19**, 117–130 (2003)
2. Markaki, O., Panopoulos, D., Kokkinakos, P., Koussouris, S.: Towards adopting dynamic manufacturing networks for future manufacturing: benefits and risks of the IMAGINE DMN end-toend management methodology. In: Workshop on Enabling Technologies: Infrastructure for Collaborative Enterprises WET ICE IEEE (2013)

3. Morris, E., Levine, L., Meyers, C., Place, P., Plakosh, D.: System of Systems Interoperability (SOSI): Final report (No. CMU/SEI-2004-TR-004). Carnegie-Mellon University Pittsburgh PA Software Engineering Institute (2004)
4. Daclin, N., Chen, D., Vallespir, B.: Développement de l' interopérabilité des applications de gestion industrielles: concepts de base et définitions. Presented at the (2005)
5. ATHENA: Interoperability Framework v2.0 - NEHTA. Interoperability Framew. v2.0 (2007)
6. Figay, N.: Interoperability of Technical Enterprise Application (2009)
7. Grabot, B., Mayére, A., Bazet, I.: ERP Systems and Organisational Change: A Socio-Technical Insight (2008)
8. Michael Tarn, J., David, C., Yen, M.B.: Exploring the rationales for ERP and SCM integration. Industr. Manag. Data Syst. **102**, 26–34 (2002)
9. Barkmeyer, E., Denno, P., Feng, S., Jones, A., Wallace, E.: NIST Response to MES Request for Information, pp. 1–24 (1999)
10. Origin, A.: La convergence entre MES et ERP favorise le partage des indices de performances, pp. 17–18 (2009)
11. Chen, D.: Enterprise Interoperability Framework. EMOI_INTEROP (2006)
12. Johan, U., David Chen, P.J.: Barriers to Enterprise Interoperability Presented at the (2009)
13. EIF: White Paper European Interoperability Framework, p. 40 (2004)
14. Baïna, S.: Interoperabilite dirigee par les modeles: Une Approche Orientée Produit pour l'interopérabilité des systèmes d'entreprise, p. 204 (2006)
15. Vallespir, B., Braesch, C., Chapurlat, V., Crestani, D.: L'Intégration en Modélisation d' Entreprise: Les chemin d'UEML. Presented at the (2003)
16. Moones, E., Vosgien, T., Kermad, L., Dafaoui, E.M., Mhamedi, A.El, Figay, N.: PLM standards modelling for enterprise interoperability: a manufacturing case study for ERP and MES systems integration based on ISA-95. In: 6th International IFIP Working Conference on Enterprise Interoperability (IWEI 2015) (2015). http://iwei2015.mines-ales.fr/#sthash.28fjHInQ.dpuf
17. Tursi, A., Nancy, I., Tursi, A.: Ontology-based approach for product-driven interoperability of enterprise production systems (2009)
18. Sakka, O., Boucher, X., Goepp-thiebaud, V., Maret, P.: Alignement sémantique entre référentiels d' entreprise - Application aux systèmes d' ex écution de la fabrication (MES) (2012)
19. Version, S.: Supply-Chain Operations Make Deliver Return Supply-Chain Operations Reference-Model
20. Auzelle, J.: d' un syst`eme d' information en entreprise centr´e sur le produit Thèse Docteur de l' Université Henri Poincaré, Nancy I (2009)
21. Paviot, T.: Méthodologie de résolution des problèmes d' interopérabilité dans le domaine du Product Lifecycle Management (2010)
22. Wiederhold, G.: Mediators in the architecture of future information systems. IEEE Comput. **25**, 38–49 (1992)
23. Jouanot, F.: Un modèle sémantique pour l' interopérabilité de systèmes d' information
24. Ben Salah, M.: Etude de l'interopérabilité technique dans le PLM: Application à un cas d'échange ERP/MES (2015)

Lathe Machining in the Era of Industry 4.0: Remanufactured Lathe with Integrated Measurement System for CNC Generation of the Rolling Surfaces for Railway Wheels

Ionuţ Ghionea[1(✉)], Adrian Ghionea[1], Daniela Cioboată[2], and Saša Ćuković[3]

[1] Faculty of Engineering and Management of Technological Systems, University Politehnica of Bucharest, Bucharest, Romania
ionut76@hotmail.com, adrianghionea@yahoo.com

[2] The National Institute of Research and Development in Mechatronics and Measurement Technique, Bucharest, Romania
cioboatadoina@yahoo.com

[3] Faculty of Engineering, University of Kragujevac, Kragujevac, Serbia
cukovic@kg.ac.rs

Abstract. Many projects and researches in the field of remanufacturing of specialized lathes are presented in the specialized literature. In the process of design for remanufacturing, a great number of solutions contain different aspects and data important to consider. The paper presents important stages of theoretical and applied research regarding the modernization of a conventional lathe with two working units by adaptation of four driving chains for CNC advance/positioning movements and improvements of translation couplings, adaptation of CNC equipment for driving and measuring simultaneous both wheels mounted on axle. The reducing of geometrical errors of the running profile is very important in reshaping the worn wheelsets. The lathe remanufacturing process involves the restoration of functional requirements and measurement of the geometric precision. The CNC capabilities of the remanufactured lathe require a database of parametric representation of profiles and rolling surfaces using CAD techniques according to international standards.

Keywords: Railway wheel profile · CNC lathe remanufacturing · Rolling surface reshaping · Wheelset

1 Introduction

Future industry relies on new design concepts and methods, data acquisition, processing, visualization, automation and manufacturing technologies [1]. Industry 4.0, a term coined by the German Government, is to undertake the challenges in integrating technologies like Cyber-Physical Systems, the Internet of Things, and the Internet of Services to advance improvements in industry as shown in Fig. 1. One of the main identified challenges is lack of adequate skill-sets and human resources to expedite the march towards industrial 4.0.

R. Harik et al. (Eds.): PLM 2016, IFIP AICT 492, pp. 296–308, 2016.
DOI: 10.1007/978-3-319-54660-5_27

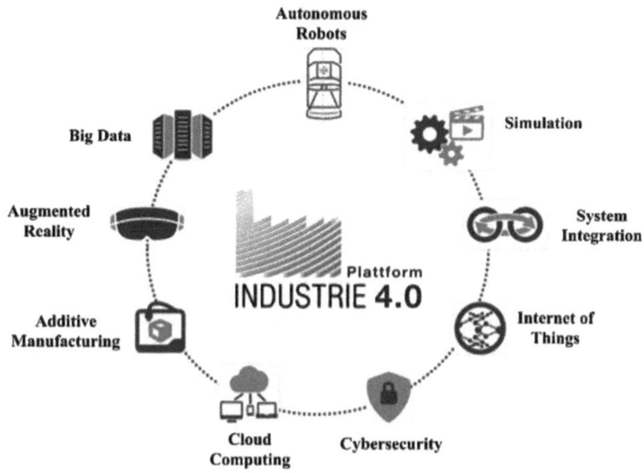

Fig. 1. Primary technologies of the new industrial paradigm – Industry 4.0

The lathes for processing the wheels and wheelsets of the railway vehicles are diversified and modernized in accordance with the requirements of railway transport standards and norms in the field. During the operation of the railway vehicle, the contact surfaces between the wheels and rail become worn [2]. This wear lead to changes in wheel and rail profile, contact surface and, consequently, to instability in the movement of vehicles. Therefore, the maintenance and repair of the rolling stock are important for traffic safety and passenger comfort [3, 4].

The wheelsets are the most loaded components of railway vehicles. They are subject of a continuous process of wearing according to difficult running conditions: non-uniform loads, alteration of rail and wheel profile, temperature variations, curved paths, sudden changes of speed, breakings, etc. In the moment that the wheels reach a critical level of wear, they must be reshaped or replaced, when the material to be removed by cutting exceeds a certain limit. Using wheels with appropriate profile reduce the risk of derailment and minimizes the dynamic interaction between the vehicle and the track, reducing noise, vibration and wear [5]. The researches in the domain of rail transport focus on increasing the reliability of the rolling stock and traffic safety, operating costs reduction, improvements of the manufacturing technologies, control, maintenance management, reduction of noise and wear in operation [6].

The main requirement of this approach is the profile processing and maintaining the contact surfaces of wheels and rails within geometric and functional parameters. Profiling and re-profiling of wheels are performed by technological processes on specialized lathes. Due to the high cost for acquisition of such a modern new machine tool, the manufacturers often have an option for the remanufacturing [7] of an existing machine tool. Thus, there is a need for development and implementation of an automated equipment for simulation, manufacturing and measuring of wheels running profile, both static and dynamic by adding driving, command and measurement systems. The remanufacturing costs are soon recovered by increasing the productivity and profiling/re-profiling accuracy. Also, the life of the lathe is highly increased.

2 Initial Setup: Structure of the Technological System

The analyzed technological system is composed of: a Polish machine tool UBC 150 RAFAMET lathe [8], modern measurement equipment, certain turning tools [9, 10] for this type of machine tool, CNC equipment, clamping devices, etc. A representation of the remanufactured lathe as it will be in the end of the project is done in Fig. 2 using a scheme of rotational and translational couplings that ensure the generation and auxiliary trajectories. The lathe processes the rolling surfaces of the wheelset in a single clamping, having two working units. Each one of these units has in its structure two radial sledges, a longitudinal sledge and a transversal sledge [11].

The two working units WU1 and WU2 have identical structures and driving systems. Their role, from the point of view of generating the running surfaces of the wheelset (WS), consist of movement B11, B12 and C1 for unit WU1, respectively, B21, B22 and C2 for unit WU2. Involving of wheelset in a cutting movement A (n_c) at both ends of the axle is ensured by two electric motors ME1, respectively ME2. The main spindles MS1 and MS2 using the clamping and fixing devices CD1, respectively

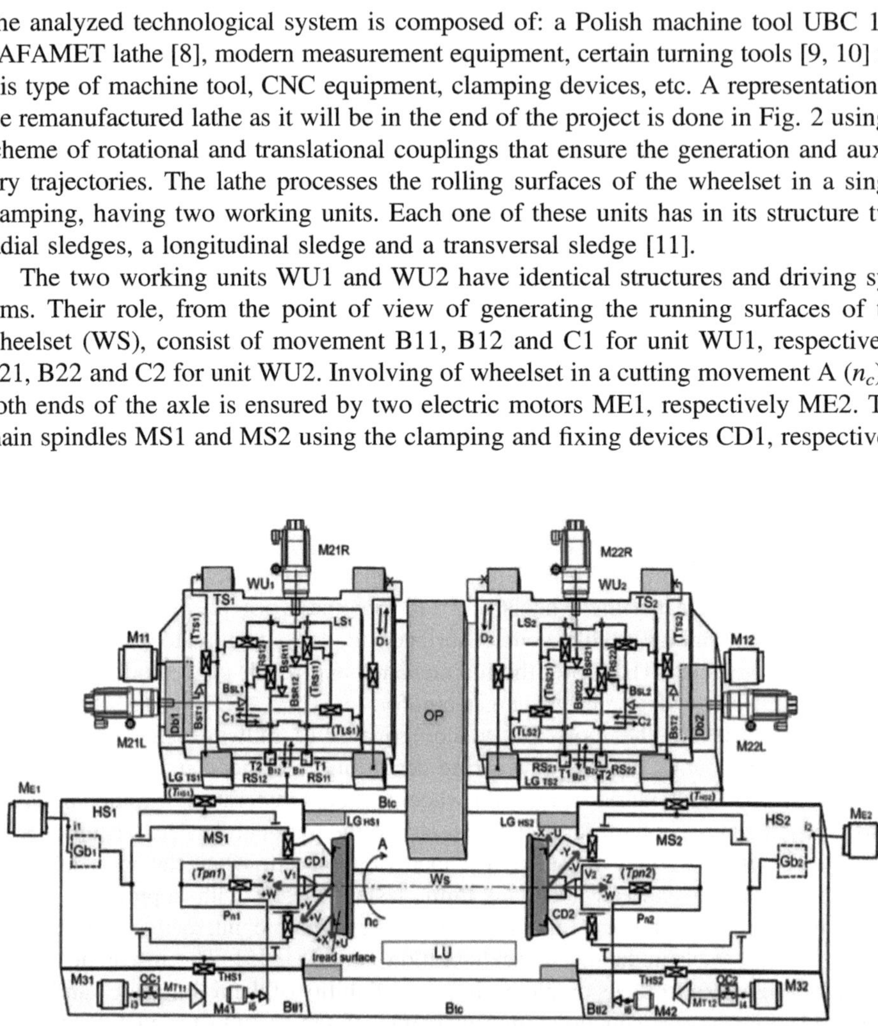

Fig. 2. Structure of the UB 150 RAFAMET lathe: A – main cutting motion, B1, B2 – advance radial motions and positioning, Bg – bearing, Bs – ball screws (L-longitudinal, T-transversal, R-radial), Btc – central bed, Btl – lateral beds, C1, C2 – advance longitudinal motions and positioning, CD – clamping devices, D1, D2 - transversal positioning, Db - distribution box, Gb – gearboxes, HS – headstocks, i - transmission ratios, LG – linear guides, LS1, LS2 – longitudinal sledges, LU - loading and unloading system of the wheelset, M11, M12 – advance and positioning electric drives with continuous adjustment, M21, M22 – synchronous servomotors (longitudinal L and radial R), M31, M32 – headstocks positioning electric drives, M41, M42 – pinolas positioning electric drives, ME11, ME12 – main electric drives, MS - main spindle, MT11, MT21 – nut screw mechanisms, OC – overload coupling, OP – operating platform, Pn – pinolas, RS11, RS12, RS21, RS22 – radial sledges, T1, T2 – tools, (TLS1), (TLS2) – translational couplings, TS1, TS2 – transversal sledges, (T), (R) – motion joints, Ws – wheelset, WU – working units.

CD2, provides driving rotational movement of the axle. The positioning movement is performed and controlled by CNC equipment on +Z and −Z directions, to determine the reference position depending on which they will be performed the movements for simultaneous processing of running profiles.

Figure 3 presents a simplified representation of the radial sledges RS' flow, of the longitudinal sledges LS and of the transversal sledges TS movements. There are indicated the electric motors M11, M21 for working unit WU1 and motors M12, M22 for working unit WU2 (see Fig. 2) [11]. Those movements (B11, B12, and C1) are performed with the feed rate v_{fn} for processing for positioning and with speed v_r for positioning. These movements are received from the motors M21, respectively M22. The D1 movement is achieved by motor M11 at the speed v_r and it is simultaneous with the D2 movement achieved by motor M12.

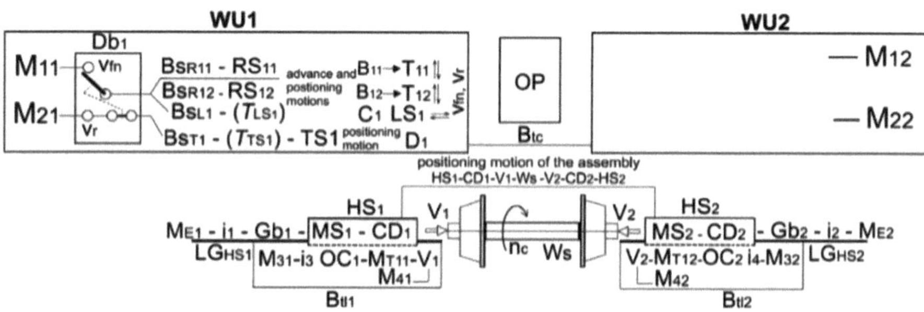

Fig. 3. The flow of the machining and positioning movements.

3 Requirements for Measuring Running Surfaces of the Wheels

In the Interoperability Technical Specifications relating to the "rolling stock" subsystem, developed according to the Directive 2008/57/CE, there are established the parameters of the wheel profiles. Running tread of the railway vehicles wheels is regulated by the normative covered by national and international rules [12]. The currently used profile of train wheels is composed of several spline segments, with fillet regions having well-defined geometry, forming a continuous curve at any point (Fig. 4). Since the form of the rolling profile is conditioned by form and inclination of the rails and because these parameters may vary from one country to another, each National Railway Administration has implemented or adopted a profile that satisfies the specific conditions of operating on its own railway network.

In Romania was created the profile S-78 [13], standardized for passenger and freight wagons fitted with UIC normalized flange.

Whatever form they have, profiles of the train wheels are defined by nine constructive areas. The UIC 510-2 [12] standard presents the main parameters that are defining the wheel profile: flange height, flange thickness, width of rim-tire, diameter of running tread, angle of external surface of flange.

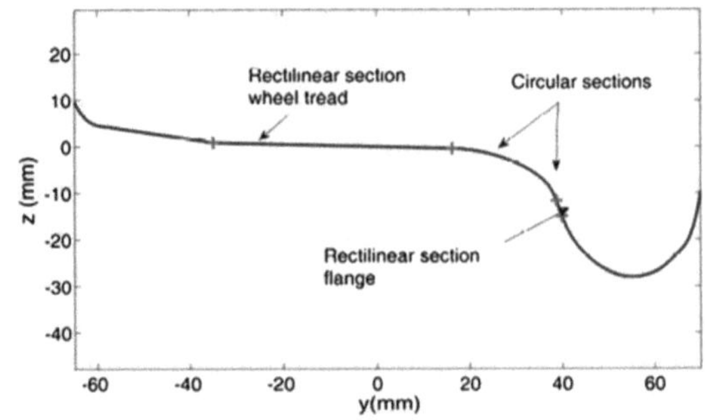

Fig. 4. Usual wheel profile geometry.

The designed shape of a wheel is represented by wheel profile drawing. The requirements to draw the wheel profile are described below and they are based on several parameters *Sd*, *Sh* and *qR* [1], which are represented in Fig. 5, where: *Sd* - flange thickness, *Sh* - flange height, *qR* - flange slope quota, *D* - running tread diameter, *ΔD* - deviation of this diameter, *L1* – top of flange, *L2* – total width of the profile, *L3* – running profile height. Usually, for the railway wheels, the most used values of the parameters are *L1* = 2 mm, *L2* = 70 mm, and *L3* = 10 mm. For tramways or light rail systems, these parameters may have different values.

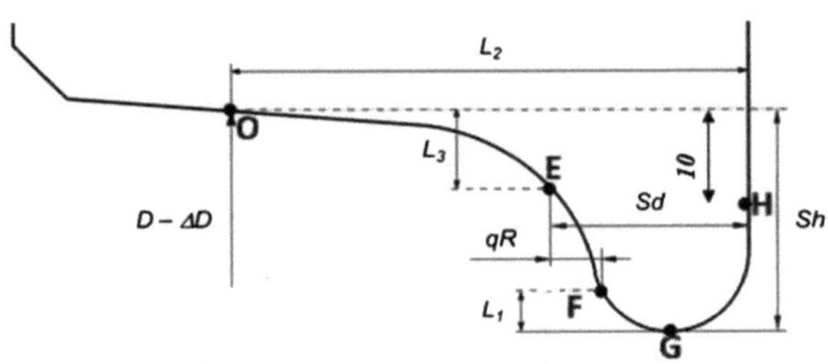

Fig. 5. Wheel profile standard values.

The flange thickness *Sd* is very important as it limits the lateral clearance of wheelset with respect to the track, which influences the vehicle stability and prevents it from derailment. The flange slope quota *qR* is also an important parameter because if it is too small, the wheel flange will be almost vertical, which implies that the transitions and the flange contacts will occur abruptly causing high contact forces that damage both wheel and rail. All these parameters can be measured and controlled using mechanical and optical instruments [14].

Wheel profile measurement must be made before re-profiling, to determine the wear and after processing, to determine the wheel conformity with specifications. Wheel profile measurement before and after re-profiling are still done on a large scale by manual methods. Manual measuring methods are more likely to generate errors and the operator may not be aware of them. The conventional systems are not capable of determining the correct position of a wheel profile to be obtained by re-profiling if the wheel is too worn, especially along its wheel rim and wheel flange, especially when the worn wheel flange extends almost perpendicularly to the wheel rim.

Based on these criteria adaptation of measurement systems on the CNC lathe [15] has the following advantages:

- Allows measurement of the profiles of both wheels on the axle mounted on the machine tool before and after processing, in the same coordinate system as the turning system;
- Enables processing of measured data (before re-profiling) for choosing the optimal profile for both wheels of one axle to be obtained by removing the minimum quantity of material;
- Allows the measured data to be live recorded in order to create a database for rolling stock traceability and follow up the stocks. These data can be also statistically processed to improve the CNC re-profiling;
- Increases accuracy and measurement speed.

The modern measurement instruments are adapted to be mounted on the lathe with two tools posts integrated with CNC controller, each tool post comprising longitudinal sledge movable in Z-axes direction and radial sledge movable in X-axes direction.

To achieve precision measurements, the machine tool shall have high accuracy tool positioning, drive and control system, least vibration and noise level, because the measurement systems are placed on the same radial sledges as the tools [14]. Probing of the wheel profile is done with two measuring systems (Fig. 6), positioned on the radial sledges numerically controlled of the two working units.

The measuring cycle for determining the dimensional and geometric characteristics of the wheel profile is shown in Fig. 7. The measurement is carried out on radial and axial directions. The measurement results are processed, displayed and transformed in functions by the CNC equipment.

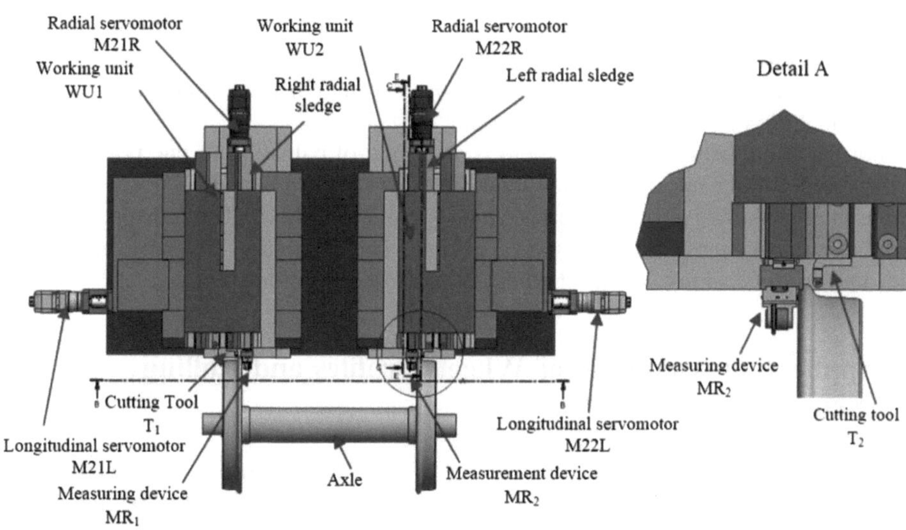

Fig. 6. Measuring system integrated on the same sledges with the tools.

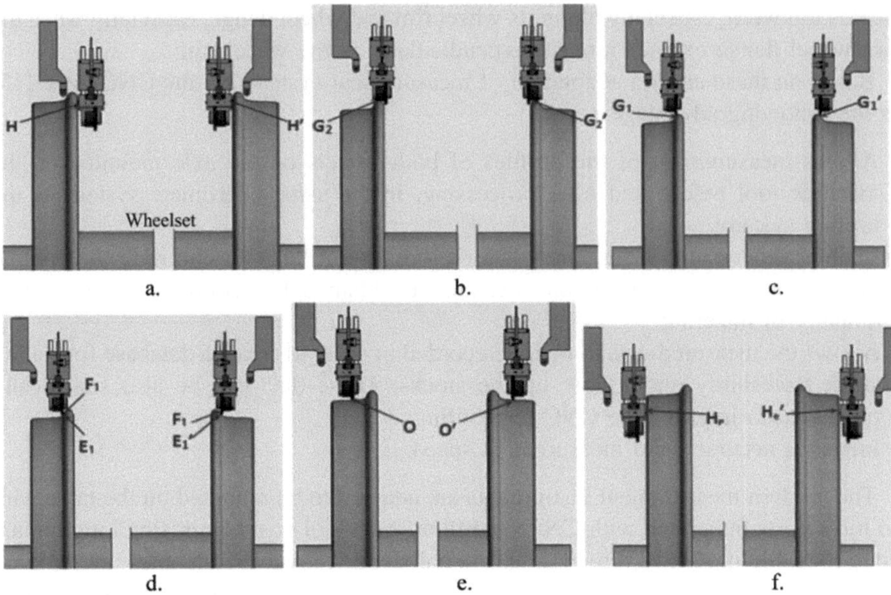

Fig. 7. Wheel profile measurement cycle: a. Internal frontal surface of wheel probing (points H and H′), b. Probing the top of the flange (G_2, $G_2^{'}$), c. Probing the start point of the fillet of external flange surface (G_1, $G_1^{'}$), d. Probing points delimiting external surface of the flange (F_1, E_1, $F_1^{'}$, $E_1^{'}$), e. Probing the running diameter (O, O′), f. Probing the external surface of the rim (H_e, $H_e^{'}$).

The measurement cycle begins with the palpation/probing of a point on the inner front surface of the wheel (H point in Fig. 5) for determining the position of the profile with respect to the coordinate system of the machine tool. Then, the axle is rotated at low speed for determining the runout of the internal surface of the wheel. The measurement is made simultaneously for both wheels on the axle.

Maximum positive deviations determine the starting position of the cutting tools on longitudinal direction for profiles processing (Fig. 7).

For the equipment calibration, there is a method of palpating of one point on each of the wheel rolling surface, on the radial direction (points G2 and G2') and of a point on the internal frontal surface of each wheel (points H and H'). The transducers of the two measuring systems are set to the zero value. The calibration is done using an axle with known dimensions (standard wheelset, not used in traffic).

4 Application: Database of Wheels Profiles and Rolling Surfaces

For the CNC programming and machining of the wheels profiles it is necessary to create a digital database of templates with different profiles versions for the majority of the railway vehicles in traffic.

Each profile is defined by a set of complex equations which define a certain rolling zone, in contact with the rail at some point. The parameterization of the profiles [16] in a database is done using CATIA v5 program that leads to an increased flexibility in creating the machining program.

It is also possible to introduce certain correction parameters of the profiles that deviate over the allowable limits from the standard shape and facilitate the automated measurement and control of the rolling surface. The digitization of rail wheel profiles also allows to choose the optimal reshaping profile so the machine tool removes a minimum amount of material.

The old, metallic templates are partially or totally replaced by this database with profiles to increase the machining precision and productivity.

The UIC/ERRI profiles (Fig. 8) of the wheels are ruled by SR EN 13715 + A1-2011 [17]. The most used profiles are: the profile UIC/ERRI for wheels with diameter D = 1000 mm and d = 760 mm, having the flange height h = 28 mm, UIC/ERRI D = 760 mm, d = 630 mm, h = 30 mm and UIC/ERRI D = 630 mm, d = 330 mm, h = 32 mm. These profiles have many points in common in certain zones, being drawn by the same equations.

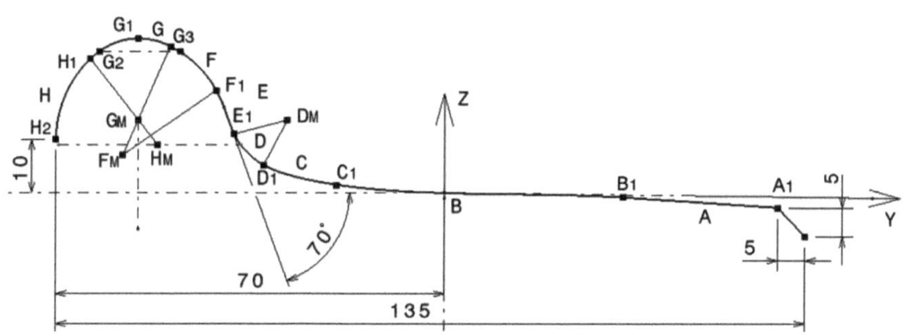

Fig. 8. General UIC/ERRI wheel profile

Following the standard UIC 510-2 [12], for each profile, the database contains a table with 263 pairs of points, having an increment of 0,5 mm on the horizontal Y axis. The respective coordinates on the vertical Z axis are given by the each formula corresponding to A…H zones. In the standard there are some check points on the profile, measured after a reshaping process. The profile may undergo some changes as a result of the shaping/reshaping on the lathe machine tool, but it must comply with the recommendations of the limit deviations specified in UIC norms and standards.

Also, on the profile there are marked the limit points delimiting its main zones and whose coordinates are used in the generation of the correct profile (A1, A2, .. H1, H2). Drawing and checking the profile is done using the parametric Eqs. (1)–(8).

As an example on how the database was created, we present by comparison two UIC/ERRI profiles for wheels with diameters ranging between D = 1000 mm and d = 760 mm and the flange height of 28 mm (first profile) with the UIC/ERRI D = 630 mm, d = 330 mm and h = 32 mm (second profile).

The quotas, in mm, on Z-axis of YOZ coordinate system for each zone, denoted A, B, …, H, are defined by the following equations:

$$\mathit{Zone\ A}:\ z = 1,364323640 - 0,066666667 \cdot y; \tag{1}$$

$$\mathit{Zone\ B}:\ z = 0 - 3,358537058 \cdot 10^{-2} \cdot y + 1,565681624 \cdot 10^{-3} \cdot y^2 - 2,810427944 \cdot 10^{-5} \cdot y^3 + 5,844240864 \cdot 10^{-8} \cdot y^4 - 1,562379023 \cdot 10^{-8} \cdot y^5 + 5,309217349 \cdot 10^{-15} \cdot y^6 - 5,957839843 \cdot 10^{-12} \cdot y^7 + 2,646656573 \cdot 10^{-13} \cdot y^8; \tag{2}$$

$$\mathit{Zone\ C}:\ z = -4,320221063 \cdot 10^{+3} - 1,038384026 \cdot 10^{+3} \cdot y - 1,065501873 \cdot 10^{+2} \cdot y^2 - 6,051367875 \cdot 10^{0} \cdot y^3 - 2,054332446 \cdot 10^{-1} \cdot y^4 - 4,169739389 \cdot 10^{-3} \cdot y^5 - 4,687195829 \cdot 10^{-5} y^6 - 2,252755540 \cdot 10^{-7} \cdot y^7; \tag{3}$$

$$\mathit{Zone\ D}:\ z = +16,446 - \sqrt{13^2 - (y + 26,210665)^2}; \tag{4}$$

$$\mathit{Zone\ E}:\ z = +93,576\,667\,419 - 2,747\,477\,419 \cdot y; \tag{5}$$

$$\mathit{Zone\ F}:\ z = +8,834924130 + \sqrt{20^2 - (y + 58,558\,326\,413)^2};\ \text{first profile} \tag{6}$$

$$z = +12,568005262 + \sqrt{23^2 - (y + 63,109590233)^2};\ \text{second profile} \tag{6'}$$

$$\mathit{Zone\ G}:\ z = +16 + \sqrt{12^2 - (y + 55)^2};\ \text{first profile} \tag{7}$$

$$y = +20 + \sqrt{12^2 - (x + 55)^2};\ \text{second profile} \tag{7'}$$

$$\mathit{Zone\ H}:\ z = +9,519259302 + \sqrt{20,5^2 - (y + 49,5)^2};\ \text{first profile} \tag{8}$$

$$y = +13,519259302 + \sqrt{20,5^2 - (x + 49,5)^2};\ \text{second profile} \tag{8'}$$

As shown in the equations presented above, the A -> E zones are identical. These equations were determined by theoretical and experimental studies.

In order to check the profiles, there are established the validity zones through the points A (from y = +60 to +32,158), B (y = +32,15796 to −26), C (y = −26 to −35), D (y = −35 to −38,4267), E (y = −38,4267 to −39,7645), F (y = −39,7645 to −49,6625), G (y = −49,66251 to −62,7647), H (y = −62,764705 to −70), in mm for the first profile. For the second profile, the coordinates are: A (y = +60 to +32,15796), B (y = +32,15796 to −26), C (y = −26 to −35), D (y = −35 to −38,426669071), E (y = −38,426669071 to −41,496659950), F (y = −41,496659950 to −46,153174292), G (y = −46,153174292 to −62,764705882), H (y = −62,764705882 to −70), in mm.

The curves centers coordinates are: DM (y = −26,211, z = +16,45), FM (y = −58,558, z = +8,835), GM (y = −55, z = +16), HM (y = −49,5, z = +9,52), in mm for the first profile and DM (y = −26,210665, z = 16,446), FM (y = −63,109590233, z = 12,568005260), GM (y = −55, z = 20), HM (y = −49,5, y = 13,519259302), in mm for the second profile.

It can be observed that many coordinates are identical for the two profiles, leading to an easier CNC programming and a more flexible database [17].

The values that are mapping the profile have a very good accuracy up to nine decimal places, their compliance is important, being determined by satisfying the kinematic and dynamic conditions. All these data are stored in the database to be used in the CNC machining process and in the measurement and control phases.

The coordinates of all points on each profile were created using the Eqs. (1) to (8) in the Microsoft Excel program. A part of the table, with several pairs of coordinates, is shown in Table 1. It can be observed the increment of 0,5 mm on the Y axis and the respective calculated values on the Z axis applying the formula in the *f(x)* field.

Table 1. Coordinates of points (pairs) defining the profile.

B10 | *fx* | =1,36432364-0,0666666667*A10

A B C D E F G H I J K L

1	y	z	13	54,5	-2,26901	25	48,5	-1,86901	37	42,5	-1,46901	49	36,5	-1,06901
2	60	-2,63568	14	54	-2,23568	26	48	-1,83568	38	42	-1,43568	50	36	-1,03568
3	59,5	-2,60234	15	53,5	-2,20234	27	47,5	-1,80234	39	41,5	-1,40234	51	35,5	-1,00234
4	59	-2,56901	16	53	-2,16901	28	47	-1,76901	40	41	-1,36901	52	35	-0,96901
5	58,5	-2,53568	17	52,5	-2,13568	29	46,5	-1,73568	41	40,5	-1,33568	53	34,5	-0,93568
6	58	-2,50234	18	52	-2,10234	30	46	-1,70234	42	40	-1,30234	54	34	-0,90234
7	57,5	-2,46901	19	51,5	-2,06901	31	45,5	-1,66901	43	39,5	-1,26901	55	33,5	-0,86901
8	57	-2,43568	20	51	-2,03568	32	45	-1,63568	44	39	-1,23568	56	33	-0,83568
9	56,5	-2,40234	21	50,5	-2,00234	33	44,5	-1,60234	45	38,5	-1,20234	57	32,5	-0,80234
10	56	-2,36901	22	50	-1,96901	34	44	-1,56901	46	38	-1,16901	58	32	-0,76901
11	55,5	-2,33568	23	49,5	-1,93568	35	43,5	-1,53568	47	37,5	-1,13568	59	31,5	-0,73471
12	55	-2,30234	24	49	-1,90234	36	43	-1,50234	48	37	-1,10234	60	31	-0,70353

These parametric values, in pairs, are inserted into CATIA v5 program. Due to the complexity and accuracy of the wheel profile and shape, it is used the Generative Shape Design (GSD) module and a file GSD_PointSplineLoftFromExcel.xls. The file also contains a few code lines to run a Macro.

If the coordinate values are correctly determined and sequenced in the Excel file, as a result of running the Macro in the Sketcher module, these points are inserted and connected by a spline curve. This is, in fact, the complex curve that establishes the profile to be followed for machining, as trajectory of the cutting tool edge tip through simultaneous movements on the two numerically controlled axes (see also Fig. 2).

The representation of the rolling surface of the wheel is possible by the profile rotation around the axis of the axle, located at the coordinate z = 450 mm (for the first profile) related to the point B in Fig. 8. This point B is located on the profile in the median plane of the running tread.

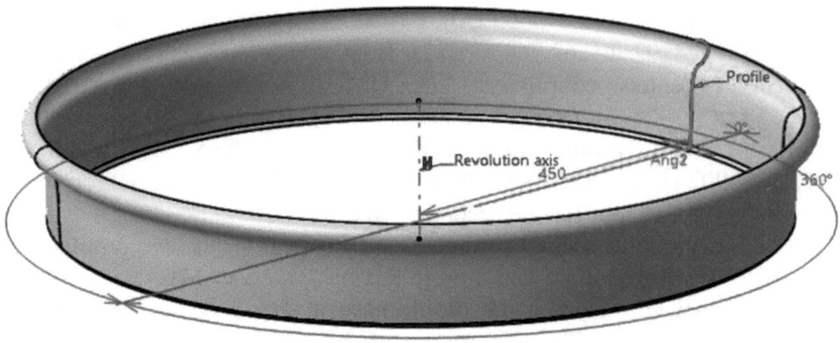

Fig. 9. Wheel surface obtained based on the parametrically drawn profile

The profile and surface are continuous and correct represented in Fig. 9. There is no need to model the other elements of the wheel, the simulation of the shaping/reshaping machining and the creation of the CNC code are possible based on this surface.

On the generated profile, created by points, but also on the obtained rolling surface, it is possible to apply different techniques to verify the precision of the drawing. These 263 pair of points are enough for an accurate resolution of the profile and surface. If a better precision is necessary, it can be achieved by decreasing the increment between the points on Y-axis, appropriately increasing their number.

The rolling surface thus established turns into solid using the Part Design module of CATIA v5 program. With this parametric surface (for each profile in the database) it is possible to perform the turning process simulation and develop the CNC program [18]. The complete modeling of the wheel and axle is certainly possible and even necessary in order to conduct complementary simulations to determine the mass, center of gravity position for various analyses (forces, stresses, temperature variations etc.) by the Finite Element Method.

5 Conclusions

The paper analyses the importance of the profile shape and the rolling surface quality of the railway vehicle wheels in accordance with the European and Romanian standards.

The parametric drawing methodology of the wheel profile shown in this paper aims to improve the shaping/reshaping by the cutting process of the rail wheels in order to improve the operating behavior of the wheel-rail coupling.

Following the modeling stages of the rolling surface and CAM simulation ones until obtaining CNC code, it is ensured the creation of a database with complex information on the profile shape, recommendations of the working parameters depending on the tools and on the chosen machine tool.

The creation of this database contributes to the modernization of RAFAMET UBC 150 lathe in accordance with the terms of the research contract and represents an important stage which will lead to an increased number of orders received by the beneficiary partner, but also as a working model for other users with manufacturing activities in the field.

The paper proposes, also, a complex structure of a measuring mechatronic system to be used in the profile evaluation after the processing on the lathe, versus the theoretic drawn profile. Implementing the profile measurement systems on CNC machine tools allows increasing the efficiency, quality, capability and accuracy of wheelsets profiling/re-profiling. Standard routines built into modern CNC controls simplify the integration of measuring cycles into machining operations.

Acknowledgments. The technological system is developed under Partnerships in Priority Areas Program - PNII supported by MEN-UEFISCDI, in the project PN II-PT-PCCA-2013-4-1681 – "*Mechatronic system for measuring the wheel profile of the rail transport vehicles, in order to optimize the reshaping on CNC machine tools and increase the traffic safety*" [19].

References

1. Industry 4.0, Digitalization for productivity and growth (2015). http://www.satisfactory-project.eu/wp-content/uploads/2015/10/EC-Industry-4.0-Digitalisation-for-productivity-and-growth.pdf. Accessed 19 September 2015
2. Shevtsov, I.Y.: Wheel/rail interface optimization. Technische Universiteit Delft, Netherland (2008)
3. Mazilu, T., Dumitriu, M.: Technology of railway rolling stock manufacture and repair. Matrix Rom Publishing House, Bucharest (2013)
4. Sebeşan, I., Ene, M.O.: Method of static determination of the safety against overturning of the road – rail machines. Sci. Bull. Univ. Politeh. Buchar. Ser. D **77**(1), 51–60 (2015). ISSN 1454-2358
5. Okagata, Y.: Design technologies for railway wheels and future prospects. Nippon Steel & Sumitomo Metal Technical report, No. 105 (2013)
6. Sebeşan, I.: Railway Vehicles Dynamics. Matrix Rom Publishing house, Bucharest (2011)
7. Hasan, F., Jain, P.K., Kumar, D.: Performance Issues in Reconfigurable Manufacturing System. DAAAM International Scientific Book, vol. 13, pp. 295–310. DAAAM International, Vienna (2014)
8. Technical instructions for function of the lathe UBC 150, Rafamet-Kuzina Raciborsc, Poland (1978)
9. Railway turning, re-turning and new wheel turning. Application Guide, Sandvik Coromant (2014)
10. Machining solutions for railroad car wheels re-turning. Catalogue ISCAR (2012)
11. Ghionea, A., Ghionea, I., Cioboata, D., Savu, M.: Preliminary considerations regarding modernization of the driving, CNC control and measurement systems of a lathe model UBC 150 RAFAMET. In: Proceedings of the IMC 2013 International Multidisciplinary Conference, North University of Baia Mare România – University College of Nyiregyhaza Hungary, pp. 65–72. Bessenyei Publishing House (2015)
12. UIC 510-2 Trailing stock: wheels and wheelsets. Condition concerning the use of wheels of various diameters, 4th edn (2004)
13. SR EN 13715 + A1:2011 Romanian standard, Railway applications - Wheelsets and bogies - Wheels – Tread profile (2011)

14. Cioboata, D., Abalaru, A., Stanciu, D., Logofatu, C., Ghionea, I., Szekely, S.: Technological system for profiling/re-profiling railway wheel sets. Rom. Rev. Precis. Mech. Opt. Mechatron. **47**, 79–85 (2015)
15. Kief, H.B., Roschiwal, H.A.: CNC-Handbuch. Carl Hanser Verlag GmbH & Co. KG, Germany (2013). doi:10.3139/9783446437180
16. Ghionea, I., Cioboată, D., Ghionea, A., Cuković, S.: Applicative CAD/CAM methodology for parameterization the rolling surface of railway wheels. Sci. Bull. Univ. Politeh. Buchar. Ser. D **77**(4), 151–164 (2015). ISSN1454-2358
17. Sandu, C., Ghionea, A., Ghionea, I., Cioboată, D.: Contributions to optimization of part program in processing and measurement phases of wheelset running profile. J. Proc. Manuf. Syst. 10(4), 165–170 (2015). Published by Romanian Academy Publishing House, Bucharest. http://www.icmas.eu/. ISSN 2067-9238
18. Anania, F.D., Bîşu, C., Zapciu, M., Pena, A.: Advanced parameterization of CAD-CAM process for machining rail wheels on a lathes. Proc. Manuf. Syst. **10**(4), 189–194 (2015)
19. Wheelreshaping project site (2016). http://www.catia.ro/wheel/wheelreshaping.html

Design of Handle Elevators and ATR Spectrum of Material Manufactured by Stereolithography

Diana-Irinel Băilă[1(✉)], Ionuţ-Gabriel Ghionea[1], Oana-Catalina Mocioiu[2], Saša Ćuković[3], Mihaela-Elena Ulmeanu[1], Cristian-Ioan Tarbă[1], and Livia-Veronica Lazăr[1]

[1] University POLITEHNICA of Bucharest, Bucharest, Romania
baila_d@yahoo.com, mihaela.lupeanu@yahoo.com, ticris@gmail.com, livia_veronica_lazar@yahoo.com, ionut76@hotmail.com,
[2] "Ilie Murgulescu" Institute of Physical Chemistry of Romanian Academy, Bucharest, Romania
oana.mocioiu@yahoo.com
[3] Faculty of Engineering, University of Kragujevac, Kragujevac, Serbia
cukovic@kg.ac.rs

Abstract. In medicine, the surgical instruments are realized using a variety of stainless steel, such as curved elevators. The quality and the price of surgical instruments differ in function of the manufacturing processes and the material used. This paper, presents a prototype of elevator, manufactured using two types of additive manufacturing process Direct Metal Laser Sintering – DMLS process for beaks and stereolithography process for the handles. The handle was made by means of stereolithography with the printer PROJET 1500, using a plastic material D638. The design and the quality obtained for the prototype of elevator is better, thanks to the material used and to the manufacturing process. The prototype of handle manufactured by stereolithography using the UV rays presents very good mechanical resistance and allows to be sterilized. For the handle of the elevator prototype there was performed a FEM analysis to identify stress locations and displacements. In this paper, was realized a Attenuated Total Reflection (ATR) analysis on the plastic material D638 to be examined directly in the solid state without further preparation.

Keywords: Handle of elevator design · Finite element methods · Stereolithography process · ATR spectrum

1 Introduction

In medicine, the surgery instruments are necessary to examine, manipulate, restore, and remove. The elevator is composed by: handle, shank and beak.

The difference between the elevators and forceps is linked to the force applied in the handle. The force of the elevator is applied between the tooth and the bone, so the force is not transmitted to the jaw. Elevators exert less directional force on the tooth, so this is unlikely to fracture. Warwick James elevators present a slim shaft and a beak

R. Harik et al. (Eds.): PLM 2016, IFIP AICT 492, pp. 309–318, 2016.
DOI: 10.1007/978-3-319-54660-5_28

with a rounded end. The beak may be in line with the shaft or curved to one side. This elevator is manufactured in sets of three: straight, as well as left and right curved.

In the dentistry domain, a variety of surgical instruments are used, made of Fe-Cr or Cu-Zn alloys. These alloys present good corrosion resistance and mechanical properties, a high degree of cleaning glass like and allow to be sterilized. Actually, both the turn and lift of the handle are cast in one piece [1–6].

For this paper's, dental elevator, the beak was designed by DMLS using Co-Cr alloy powders and the handle by stereolithography using a plastic material D638. The design and complex characteristics of the handle elevator are very important for medicines to be practical and comfortable to be used for extraction and for different surgical interventions [7–13].

The Film Transfer Imaging technology is used to allow parts to be built quicker than with other additive manufacturing technologies. The thin film of photopolymer is solidified using UV rays. The process is repeated, the entire part being build layer by layer. The parts can be built quickly, accurately and with a high resolution [14]. Due to photopolymer characteristic, for the final handle of the elevator prototype it was chosen the D638 VisiJet® FTI-Ivory material, with visible benefits. This material presents good yield strength and allows producing durable plastic prototype models with excellent, high resolution, details that were enough for functional testing [15].

DMLS manufacturing is a primary subject. Frequently, the alloys and metals used in DMLS process for surgical instruments are titanium, Ti6Al4 V, Co-Cr alloy, stainless steel 316L, zirconium, tantalum, gold and platinum [11–13]. Actually, a lot of polymers are accepted in the dentistry domain to be used for medical instrument or implant manufacturing [16–19].

The parts obtained via this technology have good mechanical properties, good corrosion resistance and do not need other rectification processes. All materials sintered by DMLS present a porous structure that influences the mechanical and corrosion behavior [15]. The mechanical simulation achieved on the elevator's handle shows very good mechanical properties. The handle was made following the literature recommendations [20].

In many biomedical engineering design problems, accurate prediction of the biomaterial mechanical response is essential in the development of many prostheses and medical devices [11–19]. In this process, structural analysis is a critical step in the prediction of fatigue limits and potential failure modalities. Practically, all the simulation methods are essential since experimental methods often require the creation of expensive, time-intensive prototypes and evaluations [1].

Further, many experimental parameters cannot be directly measured, but can only be computed. Moreover, analytical approaches can only provide a complete solution for simple geometries and loading conditions. Taken as a whole, most biomaterials defy simple material models. Therefore, numerical approches such as the Finite Element Method (FEM) or the Boundary Element Method (BEM) are most suitable for biomechanics problems [1].

FEM (Finite Element Method) represents the most popular numerical technique to perform stress and strain analysis. In this paper, was used FEM to determine the stress and displacements values for the handle curved elevators, realized from plastic material D638, by Stereolithography process [20, 21].

Attenuated total reflection (ATR) is a sampling technique used in conjunction with infrared spectroscopy which enables samples to be examined directly in the solid or liquid state without further preparation [22–24].

Infrared (IR) spectroscopy by ATR is applicable to the same chemical or biological systems as the transmission method. One advantage of ATR-IR over transmission-IR, is the limited path length into the sample [22–24].

FT-IR spectroscopy's strength is the structural identification of functional groups like for instance C = O, C-H or N-H. Furthermore, most substances exhibit a characteristic spectrum and can be identified by this similar to the human fingerprint [25, 26].

2 Experimental Work

The beak, the handles and the experimental samples are designed in SolidWorks and saved as .STL file. The beaks are sintered using Phenix Systems machine type PXS & PXM Dental, fiber laser (P = 50 W, λ = 1070 nm) and Phenix Dental as machine software.

The handles are manufactured by stereolithography using an ultraviolet PROJET 1500, 3D printer System. Net build volume of PROJET 1500 is 171 $\times$ 228 $\times$ 203 mm, with a minimal layer thickness of 102 μm and a vertical build speed of 12,7 mm/h.

The material used is a plastic material D638 with the following characteristics: density (liquid) at 30°C = 1,08 [g/cm3], tensile strength = 41630 [MPa], tensile modulus = 800–1200 [MPa], elongation at break = 41308 [%], flexural strength = 23–34 [MPa], flexural modulus = 750–1100 [MPa], impact strength = 16 [J/m], heat deflection temperature = 52 [°C], hardness, shore D = 77–80, glass transition = 82 [°C], ph at 1:1 in water = 6–7, insoluble in H_2O at 20°C, vapour pressure at 20°C < 2 [Pa].

The material was delivered in liquid state in 2 kg cartridges. The photopolymer composition is: isobornyl acrylate (15–25%), tricyclodecane dimethanol diacrylate (34–50%), urethane acrylate oligomers (30–40%).

Under normal conditions the photopolymer is usually stable but exposure to heat, sunlight and UV light was avoided when manipulated for 3D printing. While preparing the print, it was taken a special care about evacuating the gas from the printing area, as it could include CO_2, CO, NO_x and smoke and there were realized and implemented work safety measures.

The simulations by FEM were performed on a computer with processor Intel Core i7-4702MQ 2.2 GHz and 16 GB RAM, operating system Windows 8.1 Pro 64-bit. On the active part of the beak it was applied a distributed force of 20 N.

In FEM, a real structure is remplaced by a discrete model obtained by subdivision into a number of finite elements. The discretized model is composed of appropriatly shaped elements defined by a series of interconnected points known as nodes. The continuum problem with infinite degrees of freedom can thus be reduced to a discrete problem with finite degrees of freedom, and solved computationally with a series of simultaneous algebraic equations. In the ordinary formulation, the displacement field within each finite element is strictly related to nodal displacement by shape functions that can be derived from the interpolation of nodal displacements [1].

The structure of materials was investigated by FT-IR Spectroscopy with a Nicolet 6700 apparatus in 400–4000 cm^{-1} domain; with sensibility of 4 cm^{-1}. The device used for recording was an ATR with diamond crystal. The measurements were made directly on stereolithographyated material.

3 Results and Discussions

3.1 Handle Elevator Designed by Stereolithography Manufacturing Using Liquid Photopolymer

The beaks, the shanks and the experimental samples were designed in Solid Works and saved as STL file. The beak and the experimental samples were printed using the STL files generated by SolidWorks *sldprt files [21].

The 3D print process was performed by stereolithography with ultraviolet rays and using the PJP3P software, as in Fig. 1. An elevator handle has 36 g and the weight of support is just 3.3 g, so the lost material is very small.

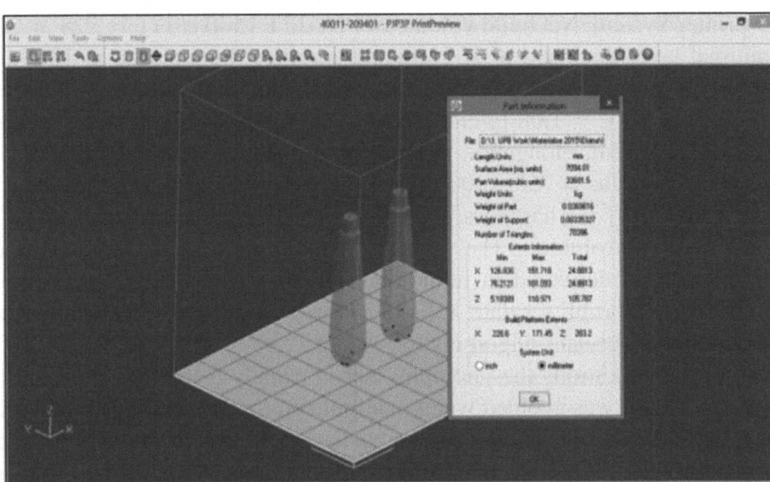

Fig. 1. Orientation and positioning of the handles prototypes on the build platform

The main manufacturing stages of handles prototypes and for experimental samples were as follows: 1. preparation, orientation and positioning of the *STL files; 2. 3D printing; 3. post-processing of the handles including cutting of the supports, washing and treatment with isopropyl alcohol and UV curing.

The elevator handle prototypes were obtained following the stages presented in Table 1. In Fig. 2 there are presented two elevator handle prototypes obtained by stereolithography with ultraviolet rays on PROJET 1500 machine. The handle and the beaks were assembled, the first by threading and other by pressing.

Table 1. Specific stages for the stereolithography technology using PROJET 1500 machine

Stages	Stereoliography technology
1. Preparation, orientation and position of the *STL files	Print job layout using the PJP3P software
2. 3D Printing	Machine preparation 3D printing process Component cooling
3. Post-processing	Part removal Part cleaning using isopropilic alcohol Removal of support structures Sanding of support witness marks Part UV curing in UV furnace for 30 min

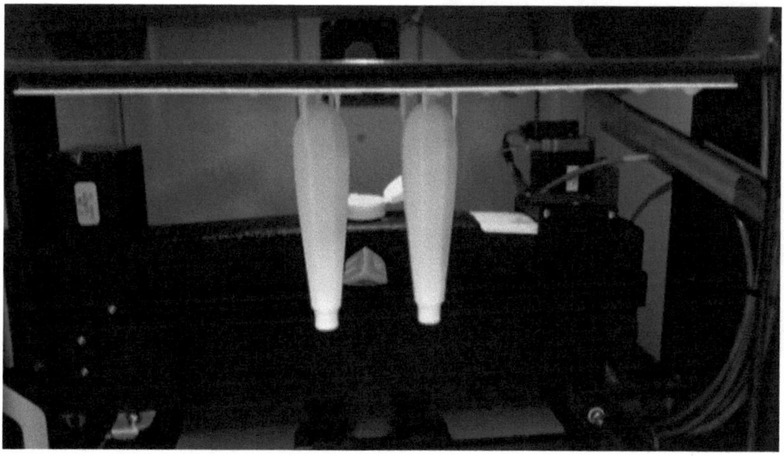

Fig. 2. Elevator handle prototypes obtained by stereolithography technology on PROJET 1500

The elevators with cylindrical shanks have a better mechanical resistance and a better assembly between beak and the handle. Both curved elevator prototypes can be used successfully in dentistry surgery.

3.2 Mechanical Simulations for Handle Elevator Prototype

For the considered elevator assembly, there was imposed a sintered material Co-Cr alloy by the Direct Metal Laser Sintering method and, also a plastic material D638 obtained by stereolithography method with ultraviolet rays.

The force of 20 N is applied to the beak part of the assembly. This beak is in contact with the muscles and bones of the patient. On the active part of the beak results a pressure of 4.7×10^5 N/m^2.

The elevator's handle is a model created by stereolithography, and its material has a yield strength of 2.2×10^7 N/m^2, Young modulus of 1.2×10^9 N/m^2, density of 1080 kg/m^3.

In order to analyze the elevator assembly through a FEM analysis, a mesh of points and elements is defined in CATIA v5, with a high precision for the handle (size = 0.8 mm, sag = 0.8 mm, Parabolic type).

As a result, after the simulations, in the assembly beak-handle was identified a maximum stress of 1.09×10^8 N/m^2, presented in Fig. 3.

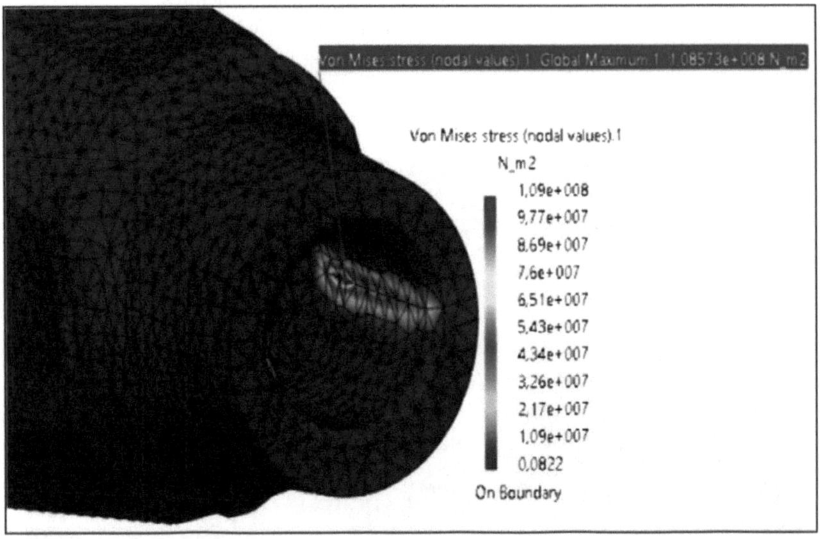

Fig. 3. Stress distribution in the handle

As a remark, after the FEM analysis, the resulting stress value in the handle is greater than the plastic material D638 yield strength.

This difference may lead to unacceptable displacements, even at tearing of the handle in the assembly area, in the case of hardly surgical interventions use conditions. For the easy surgical interventions, the handles can be use safetly. Thus, for the handle, it is recommended to choose another plastic material having a yield strength greater than 1.09×10^8 N/m^2. Considering also the safety factor, an usual steel material with an yield strength of 2.5×10^8 N/m^2 may be applied as well.

After applying the distributed force, the elevator assembly is elastically deformed and the maximum displacement area is located in the beak's end edge, with the value of 1.28 mm.

The FEM results obtained in this study have an error percent of 7.2% for the beak and of 9.1% for the handle, acceptable values for this type of assembly. The average time for each FEM simulation was about 1 h and there were used 268637 nodes and 176216 finite elements arranged on all the components of the elevator with 805911 degrees of freedom, the meshing of this assembly being high.

Resuming of the calculation steps was performed by some iterations, required to achieve the objectives imposed by the authors regarding the low error percentage.

The plastic handle can be a prototype and reference for future researches, but it can't be used for hardly surgical interventions, everyday situations and applications. By 3D modeling and printing several variants of handles and beaks may be produced using plastic and metal materials.

3.3 Infrared Spectroscopy

In the Fig. 4, it is presented the infrared spectrum of the material manufactured by stereolithography. The bands in 3200–4000 cm^{-1} are assigned to the vibrations of O-H bonds in alcohols.

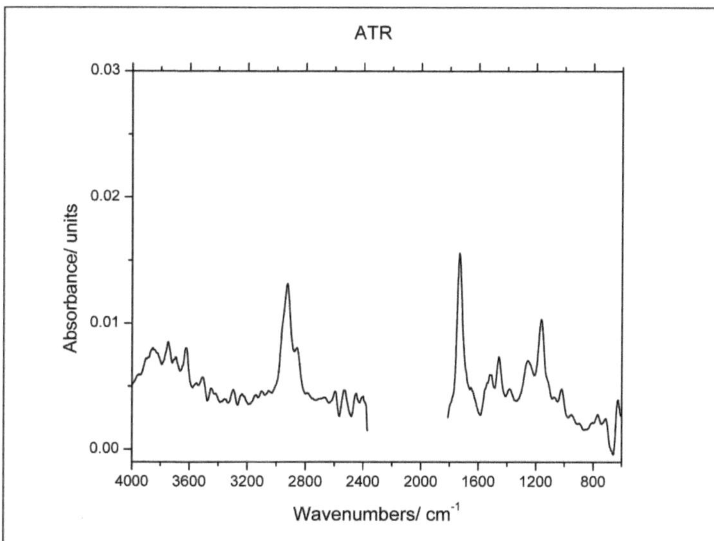

Fig. 4. ATR spectrum of material manufactured by stereolithography

The broad band presented at 2925 cm^{-1} with a shoulder at 2854 cm^{-1} are characteristic to the overlapping of the asymmetric and symmetric stretching bands of C-H bonds in CH_2 and CH groups. The band at 1455 cm^{-1} can be attributed to scissoring motions of $-CH_2-$ groups. The bands in 1250–1420 cm^{-1} range are assigned to scissoring and twisting motions of C-H bonds in -CH-OH group. The main band at 1734 cm^{-1} with a shoulder at 1650 cm^{-1} are characteristic to the asymmetric and symmetric stretching of C=O bonds in ketone. The vibrations corresponding to C-O-C bonds lead to two bands at 1069 and 1163 cm^{-1}. The band at 1026 cm^{-1} is assigned to stretching of (C-OH); while the band at 955 cm^{-1} is assigned to stretching of (C-O) bonds.

4 Conclusion

In this paper there were manufactured by stereolithography, two handle elevator prototypes. The beaks of elevators were previously made [21] by DMLS process, using Co-Cr alloy powder and a PXS & PXM Dental machine.

The plastic handles of elevators were made by stereolithography process with an ultraviolet PROJET 1500, 3D printer System. The FEM analysis show that the beaks of elevators, grace of the material used and of DMLS manufacturing process, can be used to remove the ligaments from tooth. The force of 20 N used for FEM analysis is greater that the force necessary for removal of ligaments.

The plastic handles, present a smaller rigidity, the resulting stress value of 1.09×10^8 N/m^2 is greater than the plastic material D638 yield strength 2.2×10^7 N/m^2. This means that for the handle of elevator, it is recommended to use a steel material with an yield strength of 2.5×10^8 N/m^2. The elevator prototypes obtained by rapid prototyping technologies (DMLS and stereolithography) are one of the first steps concerning the manufacturing of medical prototypes.

Many substances can be characterized, identified and also quantified. One of the strengths of IR spectroscopy is its ability as an analytical technique to obtain spectra from a very wide range of solids, liquids and gases. The material D638 made part from acrylics class and present excellent photo polymerization characteristics.

In the future, by Rapid Prototyping Technologies, various medical implants, artificial skin or various body parts will be able to be created.

Acknowledgements.
1. The work of D.I. Băilă and I.G. Ghionea is supported by the Sectorial Operational Programme Human Resources Development (SOP HRD), financed from the European Social Fund and the Romanian Government, under the contract number POSDRU/159/1.5/S/138963 – PERFORM.

2. The work of M.E. Ulmeanu has been funded by the Sectoral Operational Programme Human Resources Development 2007–2013 of the Ministry of European Funds through the Financial Agreement POSDRU/159/1.5/S/132397.

3. The work of C.I. Tarbă was partially supported by the strategic grant POSDRU/159/1.5/S/137070 (2014) of the Ministry of National Education, Romania, co-financed by the European Social Fund – Investing in People, within the Sectorial Operational Programme Human Resources Development 2007–2013.

References

1. Buddy, D.R., Hoffman, S., Schoen, F., Lemons, J.: Biomaterials Science, An Introduction to Materials in Medicine. Academic Press, San Diego (2013)
2. Silver, F.H., David, L.: Biomaterials Science and Biocompatibility. Springer, Berlin (1999)
3. Joon, B.P., Bronzi, J.D.: Biomaterials, Principles and Applications. CRC Press, London (1999)
4. Vida-Simiti, I.: Technological Properties in Powders Metallurgy. Enciclopedic Publishing House, Bucharest (1999)

5. Von Recum, A.F.: Handbook of Biomaterials-Evaluation, 2nd edn. Francis & Taylor Publishing House, London (1999)
6. Chu, C.L., Chung, C.Y., Lin, P.H., Wang, S.D.: Fabrication of porous NiTi shape memory alloy for hard tissue implants by combustion synthesis. Mater. Sci. Eng. A **366**, 114–119 (2004). doi:10.1088/1748-6041/6/4/045010
7. Nie, F.L., Wang, S.G., Wang, Y.B., Wei, S.C., Zang, Y.F.: Comparative study on corrosion resistance and in vitro biocompatibility of bulk nanocrystalline and microcrystalline biomedical 304 stainless steel. Dent. Mater. **27**, 677–683 (2011). doi:10.1016/j.dental.2011.03.009
8. Tang, Y.C., Katsuma, S., Fujimoto, S., Hiromoto, S.: Electrochemical study of type 304 and 316L stainless steels in simulated body fluids and cell cultures. Acta Biomater. **2**, 709–715 (2006)
9. Hryniewicz, T., Rokosz, K., Filippi, M.: Biomaterial studies on AISI 316L stainless steel after magnetoelectropolishing. Mater. J. **2**, 129–145 (2009). doi:10.3390/ma2010129
10. Berce, P., Bâlc, N., Caizer, N.C., Păcurar, R., Radu, A.S., Brătean, S., Fodorean, I.: Additive Manufacturing Technologies and Theirs Applications. Publishing House of the Romanian Academy, Bucharest (2014)
11. Băilă, D.I., Mocioiu, O.C., Zaharia, C., Trusca, R., Surdu, A., Bunea, M.: In vitro behavior of sintered compacts of Co-Cr doped with hydroxyapatite for biomedical implants. J. Optoelectron. Adv. Mater. **17**(7–8), 1210–1218 (2015). wos:000359967600047
12. Băilă, D.I., Mocioiu, O.C., Zaharia, C., Trusca, R., Surdu, A., Bunea, M.: Bioactivity of Co-Cr alloy samples sintered by DMLS process and coated with hydroxyapatite obtained by sol-gel method. Rev. Roum. Chim. **60**(9), 921–930 (2015). (IF 2014 = 0,311), wos:000366442600010
13. Băilă, D.I.: Researches concerning the phenomena at the interface for the sintered compacts of titan-hydroxyapatite. Adv. Mater. Res. **856**, 164–168 (2013). Indexed by Elsevier, ISSN 1022-6680, wos: 000336337600030
14. Ulmeanu, M., Doicin, C., Băilă, D., Rennie, A., Neagu, C., Laha, S.: Comparative evaluation of optimum additive manufacturing technology to fabricate bespoke medical prototypes of composite materials. Jurnalul de Materiale Plastice **52**(3), 416–422 (2015). WOS: 000362382300032
15. 3D Systems, Phenix Systems Materials. http://www.phenix-systems.com/en/materials. Accessed 15 Oct 2014
16. Chua, C.C., Leong, K.F., Lim, C.S.: Rapid Prototyping: Principles and Applications. World Scientific, Tokyo (2010)
17. Hunt, J.A., Callaghan, J.T., Sutcliffe, C.J., Morgan, R.H., Halford, B., Black, R.A.: The design and production of Co–Cr alloy implants with controlled surface topography by CAD–CAM method and their effects on osseointegration. Biomater. J. **26**, 5890–5897 (2005). doi:10.1634/stemcells.2005-0205
18. Independent dental supplies, Warwick James Curved Elevator. http://www.independentdental.co.nz/itemdetails/Ids-Warwick-James-Elevator/1566.aspx. Accessed 18 Sept 2014
19. Boutrand, J.P.: Biocompatibility and Performance of Medical Devices. Woodhead Publishing Series in Biomaterials, London (2012)
20. Komiyama, O., Lobbezoo, F., De Laat, A., Iida, T., Kitagawa, T., Murakami, H., Kato, T., Kawara, M.: Clinical management of implant prostheses in patient with bruxism. Int. J. Biomater. **2012**, 1–6 (2012). doi:10.1155/2012/369063
21. Băilă, D., Doicin, C., Cotruţ, C., Ulmeanu, M., Ghionea, I., Tarbă, C.: Sintering the beaks of the elevator manufactured by direct metal laser sintering (DMLS) process from Co-Cr alloy. J. Metalurgija Croatia **55**(4), 663–666 (2016). ISSN 0543-5846, eISSN: 1334-2576
22. https://en.wikipedia.org/wiki/Attenuated_total_reflectance

23. Harrick, N.J.: Internal Reflection Spectroscopy, p. 342. Wiley, Hoboken (1967). ISBN 978-0-470-35250-2
24. Kazarian, S.G., Chan, K.L.A.: Applications of ATR-FTIR spectroscopic imaging to biomedical samples. Biochim. et Biophys. Acta (BBA) – Biomembranes, **1758**(7), 858–867 (2006). doi:10.1016/j.bbamem.2006.02.011
25. https://www.bruker.com/fileadmin/user_upload/8-PDF-Docs/OpticalSpectrospcopy/FT-IR/ALPHA/AN/AN79_ATR-Basics_EN.pdf
26. http://www.utsc.utoronto.ca/~traceslab/ATR_FTIR.pdf

Establishing Semantic Equivalences in Aircraft Ontology to Enable Semantic Interoperability

B. Damayanthi Jesudas(✉) and B. Gurumoorthy

Product Lifecycle Management Lab,
Centre for Product Design and Manufacturing,
Indian Institute of Science, Bangalore, India
{damayanthi, bgm}@cpdm.iisc.ernet.in

Abstract. In the use of ontologies to address semantic interoperability problems in PLM, either a lexicon or a list of synonyms of the terms in the domain are used to establish semantic mapping. This paper proposes a methodology to establish semantic equivalence of concepts with those in a given ontology based on some textual information about the new concept. This approach involves the classification of the information input into a structure form using natural language processing tools. Aircraft ontology available in literature, is taken as reference domain ontology for this purpose. Text input about the concept is parsed and the parts of speech (POS) tags are analyzed to obtain a structured representation. The structure is then compared to that in the domain ontology to decide if the input concept is part of the reference ontology and if so the concept it is equivalent to is identified. Results from an implementation of this procedure are shown and further work discussed.

Keywords: Product Lifecycle Management (PLM) · Semantic interoperability · Aircraft ontology · A320 aircraft · POS tagging

1 Introduction

Product Lifecycle Management (PLM) "is a systematic, controlled method for managing and developing industrially manufactured products and related information. The core of PLM (product lifecycle management) is the creation, preservation and storage of data relating to the company's products and activities" [1]. "A major requirement for efficient PLM is the traceability of the product which is the acquirement of information along the product's lifecycle about the product" [2]. The information and knowledge resources used during the product development process emerge from different application domains like design, manufacturing, support, production, services, so on and these are developed by experts from the respective domains. Multiple source vendors, contract manufacturers, distribution, and sales partners also add importance to the product by using existing information [3]. "Especially knowledge that is produced from different expert domains is not comprehensible for everybody, though the access to knowledge from these expert domains by others from outside the expert domain is inevitable" [4]. One common problem in acquiring knowledge is the use of terms that are particular to the group or the expert responsible

R. Harik et al. (Eds.): PLM 2016, IFIP AICT 492, pp. 319–328, 2016.
DOI: 10.1007/978-3-319-54660-5_29

for the knowledge. This lack of shared vocabulary across users is referred to as the semantic interoperability problem [5].

Semantic interoperability refers to "the ability of different organizations to understand the exchanged data in a similar way" [6]. Semantic interoperability problem arises due to semantic heterogeneity, which occurs whenever two contexts do not share the same interpretation of information [7]. The causes of semantic heterogeneity [8] are,

1. Decentralized content generation. Geographically and functionally distributed teams are involved in the development process [9, 10], and the teams use different ways of representing product data.
2. Multiple perspectives (conceptualizations) of the reality. Each individual has different interpretations as they have different backgrounds and expertise. For example, 'afterburner' is also termed as 'reheater' in an aircraft and 'reheater' is also termed as 'superheater' in Energy/Power plants.
3. Ambiguity, inconsistency and vagueness. This happens because of the usage of different terminologies. For example, the part combustion chamber may appear in documents as blast chamber, combustion chamber, firing chamber or combustor [11].

The above mentioned are the main causes of semantic heterogeneity which leads to semantic interoperability problems. Thus, it is evident that different information resources/applications may use different terminologies for the same entity. Even when applications use the same terminology, they often associate different semantics with the terms or represent different parts/systems [11]. Also, "semantics associated with a term in different applications are different" [12]. Thus, it is difficult to achieve semantic interoperability by merely sharing terminologies, as semantic interoperability requires explicit definition of specifying the semantics of the terminologies. This lack of explicit definition of the semantics hinders the information retrieval process.

Ontologies are used to address semantic interoperability as these provide better understanding and processing of information in the form of concepts and relations associated between them. These are used for knowledge representation, as they specify the knowledge in a well-defined and unambiguous manner. The useful features of ontologies are, to share common understanding of the information among different application systems and to reuse the existing domain knowledge. "Ontologies support interoperability by enabling the specification of semantics-preserving mappings between the terminologies of different applications. "If 'term' in Application A and 'term' in Application B have logically equivalent definitions, then the mapping of these two terms preserves their semantics" [12].

This paper addresses the issue of mapping concepts to a given domain ontology. The result of mapping could be that the concept exists in the given ontology in which case semantic equivalence (important for addressing semantic interoperability) is established. The other two options are that the concept belongs to the ontology but is not present in it. In this case the ontology gets automatically populated. The last case is that the concept does not belong to the domain of the ontology. Traditionally the first case of establishing semantic equivalence has been achieved with keyword search with the aid of a lexicon or through the use of synonyms. These approaches do not solve the problem as lexicon may not be complete to provide meanings to all terminologies. For example, terminologies like 'combustion turbine' an equivalent of 'gas turbine', 'combustor' equivalent of 'combustion chamber' etc., are not found in WordNet. Therefore, it is proposed to give some text as information about the concept and from this unstructured data, structured information is obtained that can then be compared with the domain ontology. This aids to analyse, compare and process the information easily. Here, mapping is between the user's input and the domain ontology. For this purpose, example aircraft ontology [13] is taken as reference ontology. The text given by the user as input to query the ontology is parsed using Stanford dependency parser [14] for assigning parts of speech tags to each word in the text as noun, verb, adjective, etc. This is analysed to construct a structured representation. Then semantic equivalence is established between user's input and ontology and semantic information from text is extracted.

2 State of the Art

Ontologies are being used for a long time to support semantic interoperability as these define the domain knowledge explicitly. Ciocoiu et al. [12] gave an overview of the use of ontologies to facilitate interoperability among manufacturing process applications. It is indicated that interoperability is affected by the context in which it is viewed, different representations of the same information, using different concepts and terminology for the same terms in different contexts to mean different things. In the manufacturing scenario, the problem is that each of the teams will be using different software applications to represent and reason about the products and processes from their particular perspectives.

Stoimenov et al. [15] presented architecture for semantic heterogeneity of geographic information based on ontologies. A semantic mediator called GeoNis is provided as a solution, which is a framework for interoperability of GIS applications.

Bittner et al. [16] explained the use of ontologies in facilitating interoperability between software systems used in computer aided design, architecture engineering and construction, and geographic information processing. Orgun et al. [17] discussed the various approaches to providing interoperability to multiple heterogeneous ontologies, which is still primarily a semi-automated process.

Zhan et al. [18] proposed an ontology-based method for discovery and retrieval of geographic information to overcome shortage of approaches based on keywords. A top level ontology is used to find relevant concepts. Besides, implementation for this should be developed. Felic et al. [4] presented an approach for process-oriented semantic management that allows management and sharing of knowledge across the product lifecycle. Knowledge links are introduced between knowledge base extensions for knowledge to be understandable between experts, which are a way to achieve semantic interoperability. It is from the perspective of process chain rather than product model. Creating and establishing knowledge links for collaborators of different domains is yet to be worked on.

From the above literature it is evident that a lot of study has been done on the use of ontologies in addressing semantic interoperability. Also, proposals are made in using ontologies as semantic mediators to address semantic interoperability, implementation of which however has not been reported. Ontologies are also employed in document retrieval using semantic similarity measures. In most cases, a top level/local ontology is used for aiding the semantics. Semantic interoperability between ontologies is addresses through ontology mappings. It is proposed that two data types are semantically equivalent if they have the same defining attributes and operations and the same set of constraints on those attributes and operations [17]. Unlike the approaches discussed above, this work classifies a concept with respect to a given ontology without using similarity measures.

3 Methodology

In the use of ontologies to address semantic interoperability the difficulty is, the use of a lexicon corresponding to the domain or a list of synonyms for each concept in the ontology, that assist in mapping for similar meaning terms. Both approaches, development of lexicon specific to a domain or identification of synonyms for each concept are very cumbersome and completeness of either the lexicon or the list of synonyms can never be guaranteed. An alternate approach is proposed in this paper, which uses NLP techniques for classifying a concept with respect to a given ontology. It is proposed to take some textual information about the concept as input. The user input text is parsed and the parts of speech (POS) tags are analyzed to obtain a structured representation that is then compared with the domain ontology. There are three outcomes of the classification. They are:

1. The concept is similar to a concept in the ontology. In this case semantic equivalence between the two is recorded.
2. The structured form in which the input concept is captured is similar to the structure for concepts in the ontology but the concept is not similar to any concept in the ontology. In this case the concept is added as a new concept to the ontology.
3. The structured form in which the input concept is captured is different from the structure for concepts in the ontology.

The methodology developed is shown in Fig. 1. The input text is parsed for (POS) Parts-Of-Speech tagging using available natural language processing tools.

From the POS tagged texts, determiners, prepositions, conjunctions, verb forms etc., are filtered. As the ontology has parts and parameters, verb forms are also filtered. POS tags that falls under different types of nouns, adjectives that describe the nouns and cardinal numbers are considered. The words in the text that are tagged are then analyzed to identify a structured representation for the concept described by the text.

Firstly, the extracted information is searched for similar concepts in the ontology. As some terms appear in more than one concept structure, all terms that appear in a particular concept structure are considered for establishing equivalence. That is, aircraft has engine, fuselage etc., and engine is connected to fin, fuselage and wing. So, fuselage appears both in aircraft attributes as well in engine attributes with a different relation. Primarily in this work all terms appearing in a single concept structure are considered. And the above stated existence of terms in multiple concept structures is another issue which is to be addressed. The first condition is, if the concept is present in

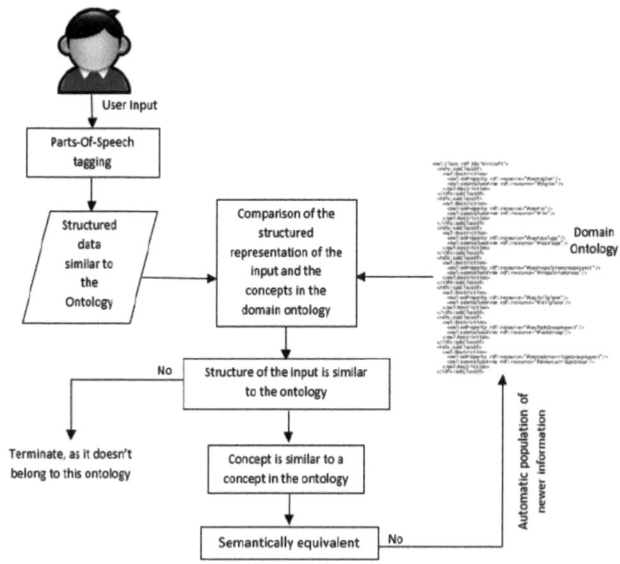

Fig. 1. Methodology developed for addressing semantic interoperability for a given domain ontology.

the ontology then the attributes corresponding to the concept are checked and if they are same, equivalence is established. The second condition is, if concept is not present in the ontology, then also the attributes are checked and if the attributes are similar for a particular concept, then equivalence is established between them.

The flow chart for algorithm for mapping the obtained structure of information and ontology is shown in Fig. 2.

4 Preliminary Results and Discussion

The proposed methodology has been implemented. The domain ontology used is, an aircraft ontology available in the public domain [13]. This is built using NeOn Methodology, with four first level basic classes, "Aircraft", "AircraftSubComponent", "AircraftAspect", "AircraftParameter". Figure 3 shows part of the aircraft ontology. The procedure for obtaining a structure for the input concept and comparison with the domain ontology has been implemented in C# on a Windows platform. Input text that describe concepts is taken from information available on the A320 aircraft online [19–21]. Some inputs are given generally with A320 data to test the system. First, the input text was chosen such that they contained terminologies related to aircraft domain like 'aircraft', 'engine', 'fin', 'thrust', 'cabin'. These were used as seed words which aid in obtaining the structure. Type of inputs with examples for the three subcases of the first case, semantically equivalent information is provided.

For an example text, 'A320 aircraft is powered by CFM56 engine with a single-aisle fuselage', the POS tagged text is 'A320/NNP aircraft/NN is/VBZ

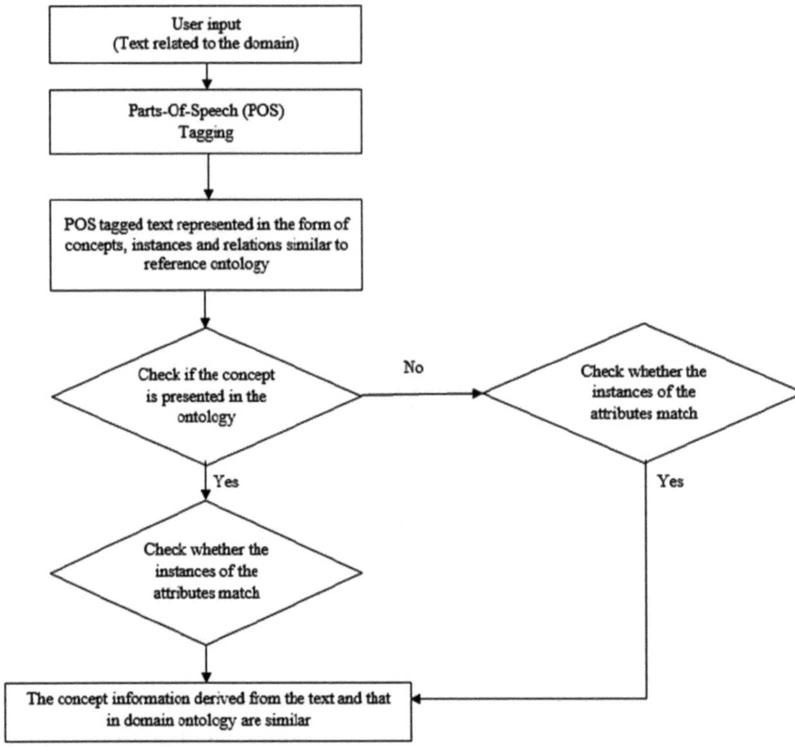

Fig. 2. Flow chart for the algorithm for mapping

```
- <owl:Class rdf:ID="Aircraft">
  - <rdfs:subClassOf>
    - <owl:Restriction>
        <owl:onProperty rdf:resource="#hasEngine"/>
        <owl:someValuesFrom rdf:resource="#Engine"/>
      </owl:Restriction>
    </rdfs:subClassOf>
  - <rdfs:subClassOf>
    - <owl:Restriction>
        <owl:onProperty rdf:resource="#hasFin"/>
        <owl:someValuesFrom rdf:resource="#Fin"/>
      </owl:Restriction>
    </rdfs:subClassOf>
  - <rdfs:subClassOf>
    - <owl:Restriction>
        <owl:onProperty rdf:resource="#hasFuselage"/>
        <owl:someValuesFrom rdf:resource="#Fuselage"/>
      </owl:Restriction>
    </rdfs:subClassOf>
  - <rdfs:subClassOf>
    - <owl:Restriction>
        <owl:onProperty rdf:resource="#hasPropulsionGroupAspect"/>
        <owl:someValuesFrom rdf:resource="#PropulsionGroup"/>
      </owl:Restriction>
    </rdfs:subClassOf>
```

Fig. 3. Example aircraft ontology [13].

powered/VBN by/IN CFM56/CD engine/NN with/IN a/DT single-aisle/JJ fuselage/NN'. /. From the tagged text, noun (NN), proper noun (NNP), cardinal number (CD), adjective (JJ) are considered and verb forms (VBZ, VBN), preposition (IN), determiner (DT) are filtered, which ends up in useful information. From the above tagged text, the content that is of interest is (A320/NNP aircraft/NN), (CFM56/CD engine/NN) and (single-aisle/JJ fuselage/NN). It is evident that the terminologies 'aircraft', 'engine' and 'fuselage' help in information extraction from input text. The aircraft, noun (NN) is identified by the proper noun (NNP), A320. The 'engine' by cardinal number (CD) 'CFM56' and 'fuselage' by the adjective (JJ) 'single-aisle'. The information is extracted using C# and the extracted representation for this is shown in Fig. 4.

A320 aircraft is powered by CFM56 engine with a single-aisle fuselage.

Aircraft	-	A320
Engine	-	CFM56
Fuselage	-	single-aisle

Fig. 4. Extracted representation for a given input

Next, input text that did not contain any keywords from the reference ontology was considered. For example, in the text 'CFM56 has a bypass ratio 6:1, generating 150 KN thrust', the term 'engine' is not stated for 'CFM56'. The POS tagged for this text is, 'CFM56/NNP has/VBZ a/DT bypass/NN ratio/NN 6:1/CD ,/, generating/VBG 150/CD kN/NN thrust/NN'./. The extracted representation for this is shown in Fig. 5. Here based on comparison with the domain ontology, the CFM56 is labeled as an instance of concept Engine.

CFM56 has a bypass ratio 6:1, generating 150 KN of thrust.

CFM56		
Bypass ratio	-	6:1
Thrust	-	150KN

Fig. 5. Extracted representation for a given input

Figure 6 shows part of the domain ontology and Fig. 7 shows indication of established equivalence. The text provided by user is explicit, meaning it is clearly stated that A320 is a type of aircraft. It is clearly shown in the ontology, that the top

```
- <owl:Class rdf:ID="A320">
  - <rdfs:subClassOf>
    - <owl:Restriction>
        <owl:onProperty rdf:resource="#hasEngine"/>
        <owl:hasValue rdf:resource="#CFM56"/>
      </owl:Restriction>
    </rdfs:subClassOf>
  - <rdfs:subClassOf>
    - <owl:Restriction>
        <owl:onProperty rdf:resource="#hasFuselage"/>
        <owl:hasValue rdf:resource="#single-aisle"/>
      </owl:Restriction>
    </rdfs:subClassOf>
</owl:Class>
```

Fig. 6. Part of domain ontology with A320 aircraft data

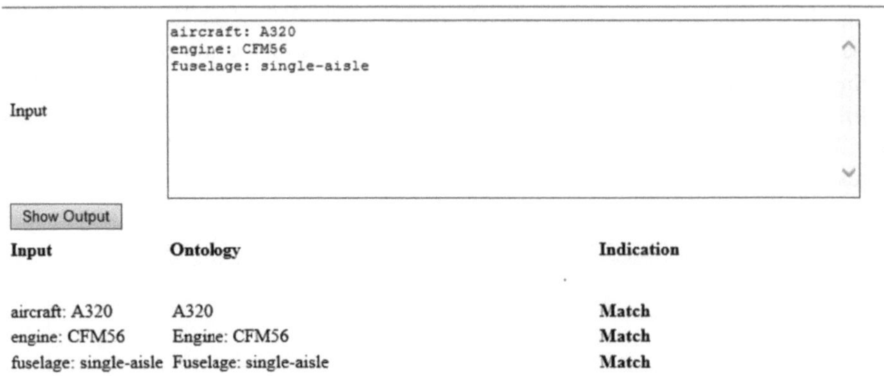

Fig. 7. Establishing semantic equivalence for user input and domain ontology

level concept doesn't contain the seed word. In this case, the value of the seed word plays pivotal role and it is used for mapping. Since, all attributes are matching it is indicated as 'match'.

Figure 8 shows the other case, wherein the top level concept doesn't match but the entire attributes match. This information is considered similar and is indicated to the user. In this case, it is evident that user has given similar word in different form and the similarity in the values of the attributes help in resolving this problem. As there are numerical values describing aircraft parameters, mapping is based on their equivalence. Also, the extracted information contains terms whereas the information in the ontology contains 'relation' plus the term like 'has' engine. While mapping the relations are replaced with only terminologies.

Also, the text given as input should be grammatically correct, as it is parsed for parts of speech tagging with a standard parser. Grammatical errors may cause inappropriate tagging by the parser because of the misplacement of parts of speech which leads to inappropriate mapping. Therefore, it is advisable to give well-formed text as input, which can be interpreted correctly.

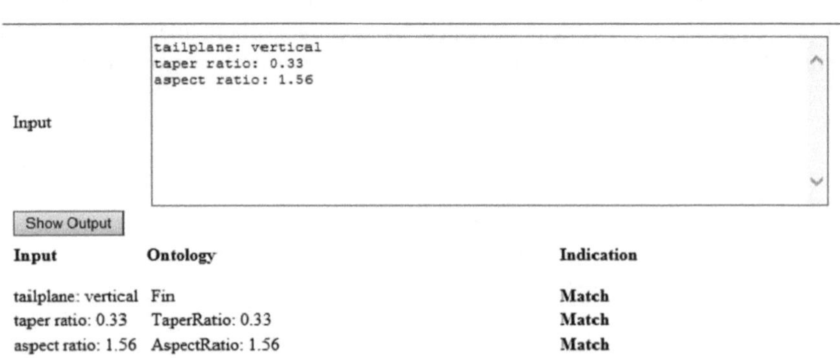

Fig. 8. Establishing semantic equivalence for second case of user input and domain ontology

5 Conclusions

The use of ontologies in supporting semantic interoperability has problems owing to the problem of different semantics for terminologies. Even, the use of a lexicon or a list of terms doesn't assist in mapping as they don't provide meanings to all terminologies. An alternate approach is proposed in this paper for classifying a concept with respect to a given ontology. It is proposed to take some textual information about the concept as input. The user's input is parsed using Stanford online dependency parser and the parts of speech (POS) tagged text is analysed for extracting information similar to that of the reference ontology. Available aircraft ontology is taken as reference ontology. Text on 'Airbus A320' aircraft is used as input. Three issues that occur while mapping the extracted information from the input text to the reference ontology are identified. They are semantically equivalent information, information that doesn't exist in the ontology and information that doesn't belong to the ontology. In this work, the first case has been addressed. The second and third cases are to be addressed and work is ongoing for the same.

References

1. Saaksvuori, A., Immonen, A.: Product Lifecycle Management. Springer, Berlin Heidelberg (2004)
2. Matsokis, A., Kiritsis, D.: An ontology-based approach for product lifecycle management. J. Comput. Ind. **61**(8), 787–797 (2010)
3. Dutta, D., Wolowicz, J.P.: An introduction to product lifecycle management (PLM). In: 12th ISPE International Conference on Concurrent Engineering: Research and Applications. Fort Worth/Dallas, TX, USA (2005)
4. Felic, A., Konig-Ries, B., Klein, M.: Process-oriented semantic knowledge management in product lifecycle management. Procedia CIRP **25**, 361–368 (2014). In: 8th International Conference on Digital Enterprise Technology
5. Jesudas, D.B., Gurumoorthy, B.: Natural language processing (NLP) driven ontology modeling to address semantic interoperability in information retrieval. In: 5th International Conference on Product Lifecycle Modelling, Simulation and Synthesis, Hyderabad (2015)
6. Sharma, S., Goyal, S.B., Shandliya, R., Samadhiya, D.: Towards XML interoperability. In: Wyld, D., Zizka, J., Nagamalai, D. (eds.) Advances in Computer Science, Engineering & Applications. Advances in Intelligent and Soft Computing, vol. 166, pp. 1035–1043. Springer, Heidelberg (2012)
7. Mao, M.: Ontology mapping: towards semantic interoperability in distributed and heterogeneous environments. Ph.D. thesis, University of Pittsburgh (2008)
8. Freitas, A.: Coping with data variety in the big data era: the semantic computing approach, Insight Centre for data analytics, Rio big data meetup. http://www.slideshare.net/andrenfreitas/coping-with-data-variety-in-the-big-data-era-the-semantic-computing-approach. Accessed 24 Nov 2015
9. Boeing. http://787updates.newairplane.com/787-Suppliers/World-Class-Supplier-Quality. Accessed 24 Nov 2015
10. Boeing homepage. http://787updates.newairplane.com/787-Suppliers/World-Class-Supplier-Quality. Accessed 24 Nov 2015

11. Gupta, R.K., Gurumoorthy, B.: Shape-function-relationship (SFR) framework for semantic interoperability of product model. In: International Conference on Product Lifecycle Management, PLM 2009, Bath (2009)
12. Ciocoiu, M., Gruninger, M., Nau, D.: Ontologies for integrating engineering applications. J. Comput. Inf. Sci. Eng. **1**, 12–22 (2001). American Society of Mechanical Engineers, New York
13. Aircraft-Ontology. https://github.com/astbhltum/Aircraft-Ontology. Accessed 28 Jan 2016
14. Stanford dependency parser online. http://nlp.stanford.edu:8080/parser/. Accessed 2 Feb 2016
15. Stoimenov, L., Stanimirovic, A., Djordjevic-Kajan, S.: Semantic interoperability using multiple ontologies. In: Proceedings 8th AGILE Conference on GIScience, Estoril, Portugal, pp. 261–270 (2005)
16. Bittner, T., Donnelly, M., Smith, B.: Ontology and semantic interoperability. J. Large-scale 3D Data Integr.: Chall. Oppor. 139–160 (2005)
17. Orgun, B., Dras, M., Nayak, A., James, G.: Approaches for semantic interoperability between domain ontologies. J. Expert Syst. **25**, 179–196 (2008)
18. Zhan, Q., Zhang, X., Li, D.: Ontology-based semantic description model for discovery and retrieval of geo-spatial information. In: The International Archives of the Photogrammetry, Remote Sensing and Spatial Information Sciences, vol. 32 (2008)
19. A320. http://www.airbus.com/aircraftfamilies/passengeraircraft/a320family/a320/. Accessed 02 Feb 2016
20. A320. http://www.airbus.com/aircraftfamilies/passengeraircraft/a320family/a320/performance/. Accessed 02 Feb 2016
21. CFM56. https://en.wikipedia.org/wiki/CFM_International_CFM56. Accessed 02 Feb 2016

Cloud Computing and PLM Tools

Integration of Mobile Device Features in Product Data Management Systems

Jens Michael Hopf(✉)

Institute for Information Management in Engineering (IMI),
Karlsruhe Institute of Technology (KIT), Karlsruhe, Germany
michael.hopf@partner.kit.edu

Abstract. Mobile devices have evolved rapidly in recent years and have become an everyday commodity. The young mobile PLM market is still in its infancy. At present, companies have covered their business processes with stationary workstations while mobile business applications have limited relevance and have been used to a limited extent. Companies can cover their overall business processes more time-efficiently and cost-effectively when they integrate mobile users in workflows. Mobile device features have the potential to significantly support the product development process through interactive user interactions and make them more effective. Moreover, entirely new workflows can be defined and established by considering mobile situations in business processes, which were excluded from the outset in the stationary context. This paper presents a novel approach for the usage of mobile device features in PDM systems to enhance user experience through novel interaction methods.

Keywords: PDM · Mobile device feature · Architecture · Product development

1 Introduction

The number of product variation on the world-wide market has increased significantly over the last few decades that consumers can easily find a broad range and assortment of goods [1, 2]. Nowadays, customers have better access to information resources related to consumer products than 20 years ago. Detailed product features, competitive market exchange, and consumers who share their experiences with others are no longer obstacles. Compared to earlier years, this results have been changed in several significant ways. The consumer behavior has been less continuous and unstable than before. Consumer behavior has been changed in such a way that customers increasingly expect a product experience. It is equally important for the consumer to be able to identify with the product, because it is not only a product, but also offers valuable experiences. Through this shift, partly as a result of an improved market transparency, the power of the consumer has been expanded, so that companies must respond more to customer needs and thereby being found difficult to build a loyal consumer base who tends to switch faster the product and therefore the manufacturer. In order to ensure customer loyalty, on the one hand the company must have a high level of innovation capability to place new ground-breaking products and solutions with unique

R. Harik et al. (Eds.): PLM 2016, IFIP AICT 492, pp. 331–340, 2016.
DOI: 10.1007/978-3-319-54660-5_30

characteristics on the market and on the other hand it is essential to offer new products to the global market in even shorter intervals. A high pace of innovation and the constant shortening development cycles of products have become major challenges for companies and their employees. Whereas previously decisions were made only in the late phases of the product life cycle, this has been postponed due to cost savings, shorten the product development, and production in an earlier phase of the design and construction process [3]. Employees must be assisted by their company in their task to provide a permanent access to appropriate information over the entire product life cycle at the suitable time in the right place and in the appropriate form where they are needed [4]. The quantity of information is not important, but rather a purposeful provision of information for the respective mobile context of the person to fulfill and support them in their tasks. However, this implies a deeper connection between the different stages of a product life cycle having a huge impact on other stages. To achieve this for PDM activities in mobile situations, totally new approaches for collaboration and interaction must be innovated and developed with the support of the all product lifecycle stages. An improved collaboration with the appropriate stages could be achieved if a better supply and contribution of information takes place. When a timely and up to date data supply is established quickly, the areas can start to plan more effectively the next steps, which shorten the follow-up process and the product quality. In this context, the importance of information quality in PLM must be taken into account and is discussed from a production process perspective [5]. This paper presents a novel approach of mobile device feature (MDF) usage for PDM systems as well as identifies and discusses MDF pattern. Different integration approaches for MDFs are presented and discussed with related limitations. This paper is organized as follows: Sect. 2 analyzes and evaluates currently used MDF techniques within the PDM field. Sections 3 and 4 present the methodical approach considered for the MDF integration as well as differentiate the terms for this work. Section 5 identifies MDF pattern whereas Sect. 6 presents and discusses the integration approaches. Sections 7 and 8 presents an industrial use case and discusses the limitations. Finally, in Sect. 9, conclusions and suggestions for further research are formulated.

2 Related Work

In the field of Knowledge Management, research about user's context and presentation of content in the mobile environment has been performed as determined in [6, 7] as well as proposed knowledge framework in [8]. Nevertheless, both approaches are limited to the semantic collaboration and content presentation. An approach for the integration of powerful hardware features in a generic way is still missing and is presented in this work. Methods focusing only on different types of mobile applications have their limitations. The implementation of business applications designed for various mobile operating systems is very time-consuming and expensive, thus it is difficult to develop such application as well as implement process changes in a short time interval. Today, those native business applications have to be individually designed and implemented for each mobile operating system and for each business process. Moreover, the diversity of platform specific user interfaces was examined in [9]. The usability across all platforms for operational purposes on the basis of native applications is difficult. In a business environment it is important to access company-specific functions and processes using a unified way. Different user interfaces would negatively affect the productivity of the mobile user when they change the device platform. This point of view is supported by a survey performed by Page in 2013 that users ask about apps more than they ask about the device specification [10]. Another aspect is the delivery of native business applications, because it is unusual to distribute company specific and internal software through application distribution platforms such as *Google Play* or *Apple's App Store* which are primarily designed for end-consumers. PDM applications are generally made for a selected circle of people who participate in the product lifecycle. Native business applications on mobile devices are characterized by a wide variety of platforms, and also by limitation of simultaneous updates on all mobile devices at the same time. Web applications would solve the problem of updating, because they are browser-based largely executed on the server side, but they provide only limited access to hardware features. So far, it can be hard to combine the respective advantages of native business apps and web apps together for PDM, i.e. to model and manage various business processes centrally and to create dynamically new business processes considering mobile features. The classic mobile support for employees can be realized especially in areas where value added related tasks need to be provided in an environment characterized by mobility [11]. In addition, opportunities exist to increase the capability and efficacy through the integration between physical objects in the real world and business information systems [11] to cover existing PLM workflows for mobile users. The overarching objective was already defined at a general and abstract level for the Internet of Things in order to provide additional information for the realities and to minimize information gaps [12]. In the field of CMMS[1], there are already approaches of a web-based communications between mobile devices and maintenance systems. Such approach is described in [13] as a multi-tier architecture, which is based on CMMS and DSS[2] web services. This paper has simulated a corrupt bearing, which sensor data was read from the machine and stored for data acquisition as well as signal analysis in the database. Mobile users remotely access the results through the middleware layer. In this context, a bridge between the field of PLM and CMMS/SLM[3] would be beneficial.

3 Methodical Approach

Firstly, it is essential to identify and delimit the different contexts of MDF usage and subsequently understand their interactions and relationships. The contexts *Users*, *Software*, and *Business* could be identified (see Fig. 1).

[1] Computerized Maintenance Management System (CMMS) describes the logical support of maintenance procedures for products and product-related components.

[2] Decision Support System (DSS) describes a software-based system for operational and strategic decision-making.

[3] Service Lifecycle Management (SLM) deals with the lifecycle administration and control for product service activities.

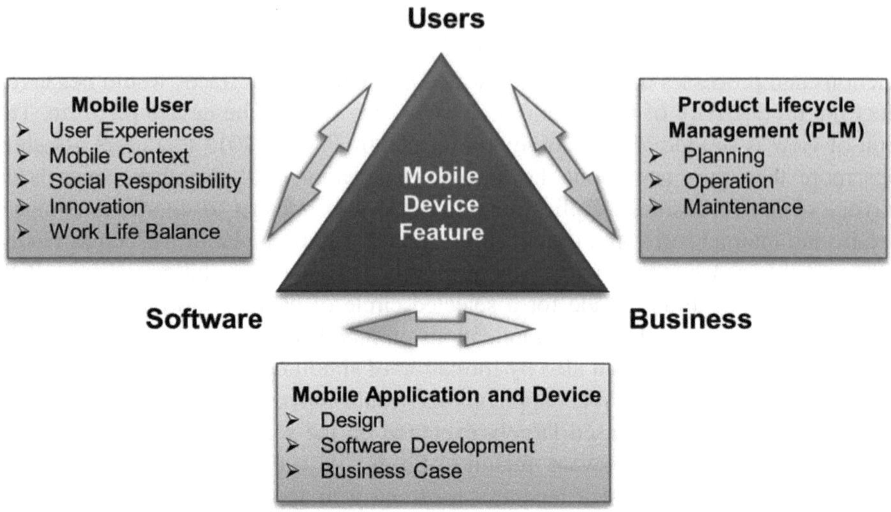

Fig. 1. Contexts of mobile device features

Firstly, the *User* context focus on mobile users who interact in a mobile context. This context can be divided into three sub-areas. The *technical level* describes the challenges of the user dealing with mobile devices. The main focus is set on the user who has developed a corresponding behavior due to the technical circumstances. The *social level* represents the acceptance of the mobile user to communicate because of the technical capabilities of a device. Finally, the personal needs of the mobile user are investigated on the *human level* in order to achieve a high user acceptance of the mobile device. Secondly, the context of *Software* has to deal with the technical integration part which has a wide range of mobile operating systems and MDFs. Mobile applications are dependent on the particular mobile platform, so that the development requires enormous efforts to ensure a consistent user experience across all mobile platforms. The variety of mobile platform and device types represent the wide spectrum of mobile technologies which satisfy different uses depending on the context and can be used at various locations. Finally, the *Business* context is dealing with different PDM providers with partly proprietary components. Traditional worker's desk of engineers participating in the lifecycle, has mainly a local workstation in the office. This workstation is used to handle all engineering tasks and decisions from a single point. Once an engineer leaves the workspace, a contribution of new information is no longer possible and all important product data are limited accessible if it has not been printed or noted. Therefore, product information can only be consumed unless it has been selected before. Any new generated information which is related to the lifecycle can only be transferred to the PDM backbone when the engineer returns to the workplace. Here, new knowledge could be lost when information has been only communicated verbally between the persons or written down on a piece of paper. In addition, new updates will be reported back to the lifecycle after a time delay. Other persons involved in the lifecycle could access the updated status only after a certain time. Incorrect product information can cause in such situations additional costs for the company and delays in the lifecycle. Such impacts could have a negative effect on the competitiveness of the company. In a study published by the Institute of Mechanical Engineering (ITM) at the Ruhr University Bochum in cooperation with IBM was identified as the primary potential benefits in the product lifecycle, the increase of the process efficiency through faster data distribution, data access, data search as well as less repeated re-entry of the same data [14]. Such situations of missing or invalid product information can be avoided by mobile solutions and also improve the productivity of the business because new updates are immediately available for other persons involved in the product lifecycle.

4 Mobile Device Features

Currently there is not clear understanding what MDF stands for. MDFs represent capabilities and services of a mobile device in order to generate added value for the user. For example, using the smartphone camera to scan the barcode of a book to query additional information about author. Conventional mobile phones offer only basic functionalities like phone to each-other and save contacts on a SIM card, while feature phones provide advanced capabilities such as camera and web browser. However, feature phones do not provide the width range of capabilities as smartphones. Smartphones are considered as high-end devices because the higher purchase price compared to low-end feature phones warrant additional hardware feature and thus better hardware equipment. In addition, feature phones are mainly provided with a restricted manufacturer-specific proprietary firmware. However, smartphones provide a mobile platform with an extensive API that allows the provision of own mobile applications. In addition, the API integration to access hardware-specific features of the mobile platform is more efficient. Initially, a clear distinction and definition for the terms hardware feature, software feature and Mobile Feature are carried out. A hardware feature represents a hardware-specific technical capability which is not supplied by the mobile platform, but managed and controlled. For example, a camera consisting of a lens, image sensor and other components. A software feature is an ability that is completely provided by logical software-based components. This type of capability does not require hardware specific characteristics, such as a pocket calculator or a file manager. At work, a mobile feature is seen as an abstract element, which is derived and composed from hardware-specific and software-based capabilities. However, it is not necessarily required for a mobile feature to be derived from both types of capability. Table 1 illustrates this aspect.

Table 1. Mobile device feature examples.

Example no.	Mobile feature	=	Software feature	+	Hardware feature
1	Object identification	=	Object recognition	+	Camera
2	Person localization	=	Personal identification	+	GPS
3	Language assistant	=	Speech recognition	+	Microphone
4	Authenticator	=	Fingerprint recognition	+	Fingerprint sensor

5 Mobile Device Feature Pattern

PDM concepts cover a variety of application scenarios differing from the respective industry and individual customer requirements. Customers describe abstractly formulated user stories about what functions and features the software is supposed to provide. The user story must be described in an adequate level of detail to derive the corresponding use cases, requirements, and finally to identify patterns. Subsequently, the patterns are described and assigned into various categories. From the variety of application scenarios, eight primary groups were derived and abstracted (see Fig. 2). These abstracted application scenarios cover most of typical scenarios from the PDM domain and can contribute added value to the mobile PDM sector. The groups are composed mainly by activities (verbs) that express an action or a state of an object. Accordingly, objects can be *observed*, *identified*, *analyzed*, *located*, *examined* as well as objects can *collaborate* and information over objects can be *contributed*. However, the grouping can also be organized from the feature perspective and therefore a distinction into three groups takes place: (1) a feature interacts with the user independent from foreign components, (2) a feature works within a dependent component (e.g. workflow) as well as (3) a feature works independently and automatically from other components without user interactions. The classification by object activity appears to be more suitable.

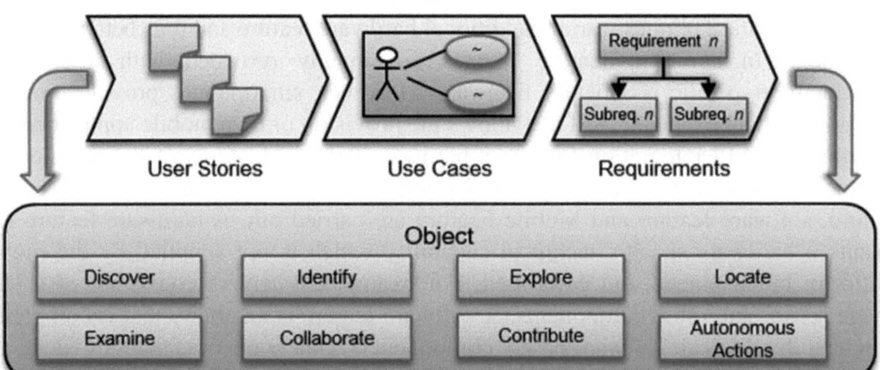

Fig. 2. Groups of MDF pattern

6 Mobile Device Feature Integration Approach

The MDF integration can be accomplished by different options (see Fig. 3). The first option describes the direct integration of mobile features in the PDM system. In this case, the mobile device features are called directly. The control and management of the mobile devices and associated features for all device classes takes place directly in the PDM system. However, this integration type is problematical in two respects. On the one hand the core competence of the PDM is the provision of product development data across all product lifecycle phases and not the control and administration of MDFs

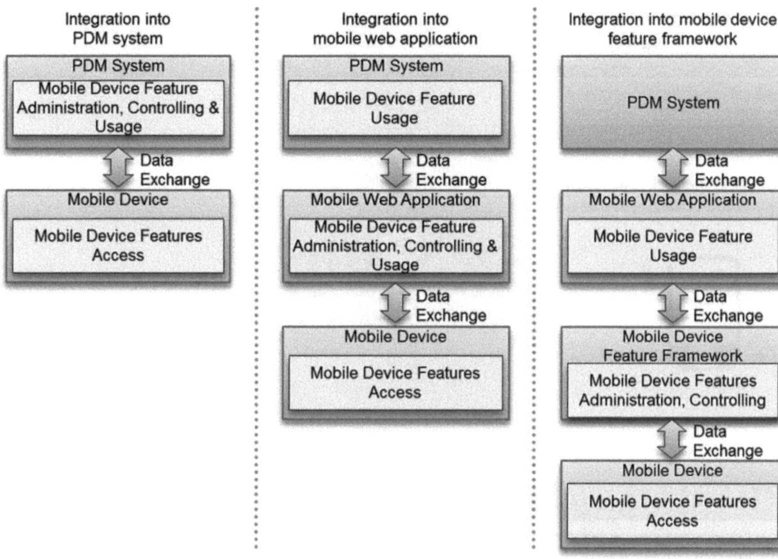

Fig. 3. PDM integration options for mobile device features

for all mobile device classes, and on the other hand, rapid technological leaps in mobile ICT sector represent an enormous challenge for PDM manufacturers. The second option pursues the notion of an outsourced control and management competence into the mobile web application. This option prevents potential problems with configurations and customizations of the PDM system. However, the basic problem with this method is that all mobile web applications possess these competencies of MDF control and no overall coordination of various feature-enabled mobile web applications exist. Furthermore, additional expenses arise for the feature logic development and maintenance in the web application. The third option favored a framework for the integration of MDFs. The competences of the framework include administrative tasks of the feature control, assignment and provision the MDFs for various mobile web applications and PDM modules.

7 Industrial Use Case

This paper has applied the presented approach by a case study of developing a web-based mobile application to query the PDM data of an 'Issue' object and using MDFs to perform object-related tasks (see Fig. 4). Based on the patterns, the mobile user can perform various object interactions such as *View*, *Navigate*, *Capture*, *Localize*, and *Identify* through the MDF support. Conventional input devices (e.g. soft keyboard of the mobile device) are no longer compulsory to interact with digital objects in the PDM world. All context-related interactions with the object are performed for the current user context. The interaction is not limited to a specific object types, but can be used for all objects in the PDM system and other software systems.

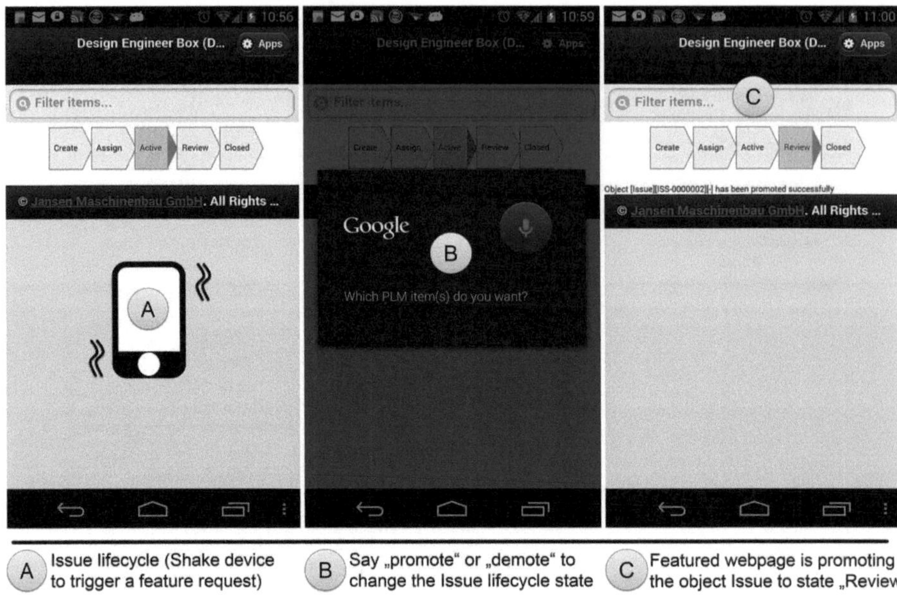

Fig. 4. Interaction with PDM objects using acceleration sensor and voice recognition as MDFs

8 Limitations

The MDF usage in PLM provides not only benefits, but also have some limitations:

1 The technological progress requires a continuous reconsideration of MDFs. Serious changes can be observed particularly in the mobile sector, because new device classes are pushed in the market in short time intervals and new technological standards are being set. Mobile platforms are strongly affected because the support is completely discontinued after a few years. The missing technological adaptation of implemented software to new technologies would ultimately lead to unsupported configurations in newer software versions as well as incompatibilities may result in various infrastructure components. However, the business logic would not be affected, because the business logic is isolated from the mobile devices and operates independently.

2 The social interactions can take an influence on the social relationship of people. The nature of the social interactions and its impact on the social relationship may have country or region-specific reasons. Thereby, social aspects addresses the privacy, user context, and cultural needs which plays another important role for the user acceptance of MDFs. The behavior of the mobile user is deeply rooted into the culture and linked to social aspects. Cultural aspects are often not sufficiently taken into account in mobile software. The perception of cultural backgrounds is complex, because the patterns differ in a high degree from culture to culture. Thereby, the privacy of every culture is more or less pronounced. Cultural aspects are

comprehensive and diverse. Therefore, a more detailed and country-specific research that captures the relevant cultural aspects are required.

3 The MDF usage also places demands on mobile networks such as network reliability, system availability, standardization, costs for transport of mobile data, and communication encryption. Most of the developed country fulfill the demand but there is a gap particularly in rural regions and developing countries.

9 Conclusions and Future Works

This paper has presented an approach for the integration of MDFs in PDM systems to close the gap in the interaction of objects between the real objects and digital PDM objects. The suggested approach provides significant advantages for mobile users in the interaction with PDM information but also other software systems such as ERP and CMMS. For many years, PDM-related tasks have been performed exclusively on stationary workstations. By introducing new classes of mobile devices, the mobile revolution began ultimately, which led that long-established patterns of thought and behavior were broken and existing processes have been accordingly revised or completely redefined. Existing processes have been accordingly revised or completely redefined. This meant that mobile situations could be considered now and will not be excluded from the outset anymore. The mobile revolution has initiated a change that defines new standards in the communication and interaction between people in various industrial fields. MDFs are insufficiently used for industrial purposes. However, the market demands that companies of various industrial sectors increase steadily the innovativeness and the efficiency of processes and operations so that products in a wide variety can be pushed in the market in ever shorter development cycles. Companies that do not bow to the market conditions lose competitiveness and will quickly fall behind. In order to prevent this case, free space for creativity and innovation must be given to employees. Since most creative ideas and inspirations arise spontaneously and are first discussed by the employees in the collective, MDFs support the employee in the media communication and interaction in mobile situations. In addition, data is collected mainly through manual input forms that have not been optimized for mobile applications. Furthermore, user-specific contexts are neither perceived nor taken into account in the application. MDFs assist users in this situation in the data acquisition and consummation over all stages of the product lifecycle through innovative data interactions and context-sensitive information. The specific problem lies in a missing generic possibility to integrate features for PDM systems. The fact that the majority of mobile PDM applications have been implemented proprietary and natively, a unified and cross-system look ahead approach was missing to solve this problem. Therefore, it was necessary to develop an approach that takes into account the various aspects of the mobile feature integration from a generic perspective. Only such an innovative and holistic approach provides the possibility to integrate mobile features for all phases of the product lifecycle and to avoid isolated solutions in form of individual native implementation in context of mobile PDM applications.

References

1. Kinkel, S.: Anforderungen an die Fertigungstechnik von morgen. Wie verändern sich Variantenzahlen, Losgrößen, Materialeinsatz, Genauigkeitsanforderungen und Produktlebenszyklen tatsächlich? Mitteilung aus der Produktionsinnovationserhebung, Fraunhofer Institut System und Innovationsforschung, Karlsruhe (2005)
2. Holweg, M., Pil, F.K.: The Second Century. Reconnecting Customer and Value Chain Through Build-to-Order: Moving Beyond Mass and Lean Production in the Auto Industry. MIT Press, Cambridge (2004)
3. Eigner, M., Stelzer, R.: Product Lifecycle Management. Ein Leitfaden für Product Development und Life Cycle Management, 2nd edn. Springer, Berlin (2009)
4. Sendler, U.: Das PLM-Kompendium. Referenzbuch des Produkt-Lebenszyklus-Managements. Springer, Berlin (2009)
5. Wuest, T., Wellsandt, S., Thoben, K.-D.: Information quality in PLM: a production process perspective. In: Bouras, A., Eynard, B., Foufou, S., Thoben, K.-D. (eds.) PLM 2015. IAICT, vol. 467, pp. 826–834. Springer, Heidelberg (2016). doi:10.1007/978-3-319-33111-9_75
6. Antoniou, G., Grobelnik, M., Simperl, E., Parsia, B., Plexousakis, D., Leenheer, P., Pan, J.: The Semantic Web: Research and Applications. LNCS. Springer, Heidelberg (2011)
7. Balfanz, D., Grimm, M., Tazari, M.-R.: A reference architecture for mobile knowledge management. In: Davies, N., Kirste, T., Schumann, H. (eds.) Mobile Computing and Ambient Intelligence: The Challenge of Multimedia. Dagstuhl, Germany (2005)
8. Zammit, J.P., Gao, J., Evans, R.: A framework to capture and share knowledge using storytelling and video sharing in global product development. In: Bouras, A., Eynard, B., Foufou, S., Thoben, K.-D. (eds.) PLM 2015. IAICT, vol. 467, pp. 259–268. Springer, Heidelberg (2016). doi:10.1007/978-3-319-33111-9_24
9. Larysz, J., Němec, M., Fasuga, R.: User interfaces and usability issues form mobile applications. In: Snasel, V., Platos, J., El-Qawasmeh, E. (eds.) ICDIPC 2011. CCIS, vol. 189, pp. 29–43. Springer, Heidelberg (2011). doi:10.1007/978-3-642-22410-2_3
10. Page, T.: Use of mobile device apps in product design. Int. J. Green Comput. **4**(1), 18–34 (2013)
11. Hess, T., Figge, S., Hanekop, H., Hochstatter, I., Hogrefe, D., Kaspar, C., et al.: Technische Möglichkeiten und Akzeptanz mobiler Anwendungen. Eine interdisziplinäre Betrachtung. Wirtschaftsinformatik **47**, 6–16 (2005)
12. Fleisch, E.: Das Internet der Dinge. Ubiquitous Computing und RFID in der Praxis. Springer, Berlin (2005)
13. Campos, J., Jantunen, E., Prakash, O.: A web and mobile device architecture for mobile e-maintenance. Int. J. Adv. Manuf. Technol. **45**(1), 71–80 (2009)
14. Abramovici, M.: Benefits of PLM in der Automobilindustrie. Ergebnisse einer Benchmark-Studie. Hg. v. Ruhr-Universität Bochum. Maschinenbauinformatik (ITM). Bochum (2009). http://www.mesago.de/. Accessed 01 July 2013

Implementation of Machining on the Cloud: A Case Study in PLM Environment

Saurav Bhatt[1,3](✉), Frédéric Segonds[2], Nicolas Maranzana[2], Améziane Aoussat[2], Vincent Frerebeau[3], and Damien Chasset[3]

[1] Delhi College of Engineering, Delhi, India
saurav_dce373@yahoo.co.in
[2] Arts et Métiers, Paris Tech, LCPI, 151 Boulevard de l'Hôpital, 75013 Paris, France
[3] Dassault Systemes, 10 Rue Marcel Dassault, 78140 Velizy Villacoublay, France

Abstract. This paper focuses on the implementation of cloud solutions in the field of machining which is encompassed by the much larger field of manufacturing. Machining is the process of material removal to transform raw materials into final desired shape while manufacturing is the creation and assembly of components and finished products for sale. With the advent of new technologies, a lot of advancements have been made in the field of machining in the last few decades. We are seeing an explosive growth in the field of information technology and the world is more connected than ever before. The current scenario calls for manufacturers to change the way they perform operations by using cloud services rather than installing and customizing the softwares within their own organizations. This paper examines the intersection of the fields of machining and cloud computing to propose solutions for revolutionizing the way machining is done. After performing tests that involve machining simulations and creation of a collaborative working space to exchange data, we can conclude that it is completely feasible to perform machining operations on cloud. The findings of this study give an insight into the adoption of cloud technology in the machining field and provides useful information to industry professionals wishing to implement cloud solutions in their businesses and to scientists wishing to undertake work in this field.

Keywords: Machining · Cloud · PLM

1 Introduction

With the advent of new technologies, researchers and industry professionals constantly strive to look for new ways to innovate in the field of design and manufacturing. It has become a challenge to meet the dynamics of today's marketplace in the manufacturing field as the product development processes are geographically spread out. With the developments in the field of Information Technology (IT), efforts are now directed towards making advancements in the field of design and manufacturing by using IT tools and PLM concepts. We have noticed that cloud computing has brought a

R. Harik et al. (Eds.): PLM 2016, IFIP AICT 492, pp. 341–355, 2016.
DOI: 10.1007/978-3-319-54660-5_31

revolution in the field of information technology sector due to its distributed network access, flexibility, availability on demand and pay per use services. The potential advantages of applying cloud computing technology in the field of machining is coming into picture and a research work for implementing the cloud technology in IT field is needed. The idea of performing machining on cloud is still in its infancy but the industries are striving an effort to move to cloud rather than using the traditional ways as soon as possible. The organisation of the research paper is done in the following way: we first shed light on the concept of cloud computing and manufacturing, the developments that have taken place in the machining processes, the collaborative and distributed manufacturing on cloud and industry of future. After this, we have demonstrated that machining on cloud is feasible through our tests and finally, the conclusions and the future work to be performed are highlighted.

2 Literature Review

2.1 Cloud Computing

The word *cloud computing* came into existence in the year 2007 but the concept behind cloud computing find its roots in the 1960s [1]. National Institute of Standards and Technology (an industrial standard), defines the cloud computing as: "Cloud computing is a model for enabling ubiquitous, convenient, on-demand network access to a shared pool of configurable computing resources (e.g., networks, servers, storage, applications, and services) that can be rapidly provisioned and released with minimal management effort or service provider interaction" [2]. Cloud computing is derived from concepts like virtualization, service oriented architecture and software as a service and is defined as providing computing resources (i.e. software and hardware) to individuals and businesses on demand over the internet on a pay per use basis. Cloud computing is made up of three key elements: Large scale data centres hosted on remote servers, Services (software and hardware resources provided over the internet), Low cost computers and other web-enabled devices like laptops, smartphones, etc. Cloud computing is an innovation and has got different meanings when seen from different perspectives. According to the technical perspective, cloud computing has evolved a lot from simple machines used for calculation to utility, grid and finally cloud computing. From the business viewpoint, cloud computing is a breakthrough which is changing the way the information technology resources are deployed and is creating new business models.

There are principally three types of clouds: Public, Private and Hybrid cloud [3].

In a Public cloud, access to resources is provided over a public network by companies that own and operate them. There is no need to purchase hardware, software or any supporting infrastructure and resources can be accessed from anywhere over internet.

Private cloud, on the other hand, is operated solely for a single organization and it provides highly automated management and control of resources. It is managed internally or by a third party and is preferred by classic IT as in private cloud there isn't a real change in governance.

Hybrid cloud combines features of both public and private cloud and allows to keep critical applications and technical data on private cloud and less sensitive data on public cloud.

Apart from different types of clouds, there are three types of cloud computing services, namely, Infrastructure as a Service (IaaS), Platform as a Service (PaaS) and Software as a Service (SaaS) [4].

In SaaS, a pre-made application, along with any required software, operating system, hardware and network is provided. Applications run on distant computers on the cloud and the users connect to them through internet/web-browser. There is no need to purchase, install, update or maintain the software.

In PaaS, an operating system, hardware and network are provided and the customer installs or develops the softwares and applications. Thus, PaaS provides an environment based on cloud to deliver web based applications.

Lastly, in IaaS, only the hardware and network are provided and the customer installs or develops the operating systems, software and applications. So, computing resources including networking, storage, servers and data centre space are provided on a pay per use basis. The Fig. 1 below gives a clear and concise view of how different components of the system are managed for different types of cloud computing services. The benefits of cloud services include massive reduction in capital expenditure, getting away with the complexity of operating computers and networks and performing more efficient computing by centralized data storage, processing and bandwidth.

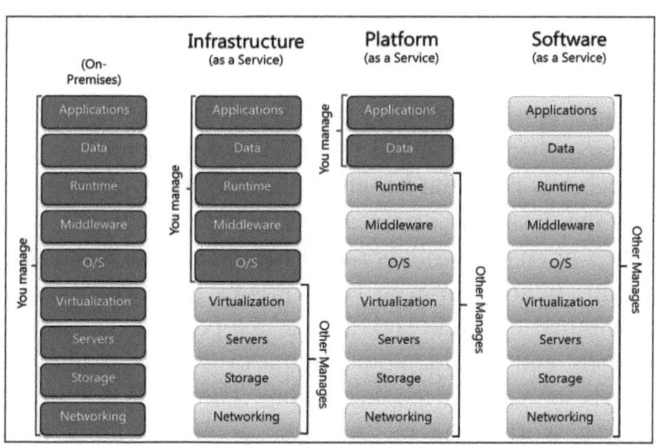

Fig. 1. Cloud services types [5]

Thus by using cloud services, we can transfer the responsibility of running hardware and software within the organization to the internet. The Table 1 below highlights some of the research work done in the field of cloud computing.

Table 1. Research work performed in the field of cloud computing

Author	Subject of discussion
Bayramusta and Nasir [6]	Evolution of cloud computing and the benefits and challenges related to cloud computing adoption
Ratten [7]	Proposition of the use of social cognitive theory in continuous use intention of cloud computing services
Kim [8]	Discussion on the adoption of cloud computing services and the associated technical issues
Buyya et al. [9]	Proposition of an architecture for creating cloud with market oriented resource allocation by leveraging technologies like Virtual Machines
Abadi [10]	Examination of the limitations and opportunities of deploying data management on the emerging cloud platforms

2.2 Manufacturing on Cloud

This paper deals with the concept of machining on cloud but considerable amount of work can be found on the much larger domain i.e. Manufacturing on Cloud. Cloud Manufacturing is a customer-centric manufacturing model that exploits on-demand access to a shared collection of diversified and distributed manufacturing resources to form temporary, reconfigurable production lines which enhance efficiency, reduce product lifecycle costs, and allow optimal resource loading in response to variable demand based customer generated tasks [11]. Cloud manufacturing is a concept that is entirely based on the concept of cloud computing. Li et al. [12] first used the term cloud manufacturing in the year 2010. Besides Li et al., Zhang et al. [13], Wu et al. [14], Schaefer et al. [15] and many others have also proposed definitions of cloud manufacturing.

The idea of providing manufacturing services on the internet was in fact developed a long time ago. Researchers envisaged the propagation of internet technologies in the production process and its potential benefits to significantly change the environment of industrial firms in the last few decades and many web based systems have been developed since then to sustain collaborative activities in different lifecycle phases of product development. Internet or web technologies have been continuously used to integrate these distributed lifecycle activities of the product development into a global integrated environment and considerable amount of work is available that explores the concept of using web services for manufacturing. The Table 2 below provides a list of some of the research work done on the concept of providing manufacturing as a service.

Cloud based services have the ability to provide new methods of innovation, engineering design, and manufacturing that were not possible in the past. The concepts of mass collaboration, distributed design, and distributed manufacturing propelled by the Internet are now actually realizable for the next generation of product design and manufacturing. The Table 3 below highlights some of the research work performed in the field of Collaborative Design and Distributed Manufacturing.

Table 2. Research work performed on the subject "Manufacturing as a Service"

Author	Subject of discussion
Goldhar et al. [16]	Future implications of computer integrated manufacturing
Rajagopalan et al. [17]	Implications of the internet for design and rapid manufacturing technologies
Erkes et al. [18]	Implementation of manufacturing services available over the internet
Tao [19]	Key advantages and challenges of implementing cloud manufacturing
Zhang [20]	Cloud manufacturing as a way to solve bottlenecks in the manufacturing field
Terrazas [21]	Cloud manufacturing as a service concept

Table 3. Research work performed on subject "Collaborative Design and Distributed Manufacturing"

Author	Subject of discussion
Valilai and Houshmand [46]	Development of an integrated and collaborative manufacturing platform to support a distributed manufacturing system using a service-oriented approach based on the cloud computing paradigm
Wang et al. [47]	Development of a cloud based manufacturing system to support ubiquitous manufacturing which provides a service pool that maintains physical facilities in terms of manufacturing services
Andreadis et al. [48]	Examination of the role of collaborative design in manufacturing in the era of cloud computing and proposal of a specific architecture with different servers for the implementation of a collaborative cloud based design system
Wu et al. [49]	Study on applications of cloud computing paradigm in product design and manufacturing and exploration of the potential of utilizing cloud computing for selected aspects of collaborative design, distributed manufacturing, collective innovation and virtualization

2.3 Machining Technology Developments

As mentioned earlier, manufacturing is a global term that encompasses machining and for our study, we have focussed on the machining domain only. In this section, an overview of the advancements made in the machining processes to realize innovative product concepts have been underlined. With the advancements of technology, machine tools have been used to produce desired work piece shapes by controlling relative movements of work piece and machine tool. The developments in NC systems have made it possible to machine sophisticated parts with high accuracy. There are numerous methods to perform machining and considerable amount of literature can be found on the methods that are available today. Considering the scope of this study, we have discussed the principal machining operations and highlighted the research work performed in these fields in the form of tables.

2.3.1 Turning

Turning is one of the most common metal cutting operation. In turning, a work piece is rotated about its axis while a single-point cutting tool is fed into it, thus, shearing away unwanted material and creating the desired part. Turning can occur on both external and internal surfaces to produce an axially-symmetrical contoured part [22]. During turning operation, a piece of relatively rigid material is rotated and a cutting tool is traversed along 1, 2, or 3 axes of motion to produce parts of precise diameters and depths. The turning processes are typically carried out on a lathe and can produce various desired shapes (Table 4).

Table 4. Research work performed on subject of turning

Author	Subject of discussion
Revel et al. [23]	Proposition of a high precision hard turning operation for finishing of AISI 52100 bearing components
Gok [24]	Development of a three-dimensional finite element model to calculate the process parameters for turning operations
Vijayaraghavan et al. [25]	Proposition of a finite element based data analytics approach for modelling turning process of Inconel 718 alloys
Jain et al. [26]	Proposition of a method for optimisation and evaluation of machining parameters for turning operation of Inconel-625
Brecher et al. [27]	Investigation of the optimal process parameters for parallel turning operations

2.3.2 Milling

Milling is the process of machining flat, curved, or irregular surfaces by feeding the workpiece against a rotating horizontal cutter containing a number of cutting edges. The milling machine basically consists of a motor driven spindle, which mounts and revolves the milling cutter, and a reciprocating adjustable worktable, which mounts and feeds the work piece [28]. The milling process removes material by performing many distinct and small cuts. This is accomplished by using a cutter with many teeth, spinning the cutter at high speed, or advancing the material through the cutter slowly. Mostly, a combination of these three approaches is used to remove material (Table 5).

Table 5. Research work performed on subject of milling

Author	Subject of discussion
Tsai et al. [29]	Exploration of the usage of milling process to mill thin walled conical and tubular work pieces
Budak [30]	Study of the analytical force and stability models to optimize the milling process and achieve improve part quality and productivity
Warghat and Deshmukh [31]	Optimization of the machining parameters for end milling operation
Owodunni and Pinder [32]	Sustainability improvement in milling operation through improved tool design and optimized process parameters
Garg et al. [33]	Modelling of a milling process by a complexity based evolutionary approach

2.3.3 Drilling

Drilling is the process of producing round holes in a solid material or enlarging existing holes by using multi-tooth cutting tools called drills or drill bits. Various cutting tools are available for drilling, but the most common is the twist drill [34]. Drilling is one of the most complex machining processes and the principal characteristic that distinguishes it from other machining operations is the combined cutting and extrusion of metal at the chisel edge in the center of the drill (Table 6).

Table 6. Research work performed on subject of drilling

Author	Subject of Discussion
Chatterjee et al. [35]	Investigation of the simulation and optimization of machining parameters in drilling of titanium alloys
Giasin et al. [36]	Experimental study on drilling of unidirectional GLARE fiber metal laminates
Perrona et al. [37]	Exploration of the possibility of drilling of high quality features in green powder metallurgy components
Biermann and Kirschner [38]	Experimental investigations on single lip deep hole drilling of super alloy-Inconel 718 with small diameters
Khashaba et al. [39]	Machinability analysis while drilling woven GFR/epoxy composites

2.3.4 CNC Machining

CNC (Computer Numeric Control) is a process that involves the use of computer to control the machine tools. The tools that can be controlled in this manner include lathes, mills, grinders etc. In CNC Machining, numeric control is used to control the machine tool. A customized computer program is written for an object and the machine is programmed using CNC machining language (called G-code) that controls all the features like feed rate, coordination, location and speed. It is possible to control exact position and velocity of the machine tool using CNC and it can be used to manufacture both metal and plastic parts [40] (Table 7).

Table 7. Research work performed on subject of CNC machining

Author	Subject of Discussion
Yang and Feng [41]	Research on multi-axis CNC programming for machining large hydraulic turbine blades
Safaieh et al. [42]	Proposition of a novel methodology for cross-technology interoperability in CNC machining
Newman et al. [43]	Study of the process planning for CNC machining to make it more energy efficient.
Zhu et al. [44]	Study on tool orientation and optimization for 3+2-axis CNC machining of sculptured surface
Soori et al. [45]	Investigation of the dimensional and geometrical errors of three-axis CNC milling machines in a virtual machining system

Research work highlighted in the tables above gives an idea that work is being continuously done in the field of machining. Today, industry professionals are facing challenges that didn't exist in the past. The world is going faster and is more connected than ever before which provides new opportunities and risks. The current situation demands for a change in the way machining is performed and cloud services provide a great opportunity to achieve it. The intersection of cloud computing and machining field can help in tackling problems like: how to accelerate time to market, how to optimize design and machining time, how to work together using a collaborative platform, how to increase resource utilization, how to instantly access machining solutions and how to reduce capital cost and complexity. This paper addresses the need for implementing cloud services in the field of machining in order to allow data exchange, designing, machining and simulation over geographically distributed network. In this study, by using a cloud based collaborative platform to exchange data and perform machining operations and simulation, we have shown that concept of performing machining on cloud is achievable and we are not far away from implementing these solutions in the real world.

2.4 Industry of Future: A Viable Platform for Deploying Machining on Cloud

French government's initiative "Industry of Future" [50] launched in 2015 answers to the shortcomings that are present at the moment by helping companies modernize their production base by using digital technologies. The objective today is not to provide best product or service but to propose solutions that bring products and services together. The aim is to form a more connected, more competitive industry that responds to the needs of the customers quickly. The principal challenges to achieve this goal are: Developing cutting edge technologies, Encouraging and enabling digital transformation throughout the ecosystem of mid-sized companies, Transformation of companies business models, Upskilling the industrial workforce and training the employees to be proficient in using the new technology and Developing a collaborative platform for sharing the data and information. The French industry of future has aimed to develop solutions for nine priority markets, namely, Smart food choices, Digital confidence, Smart devices, Data economy, Medicine of the future, Tomorrow's transport, Eco-mobility, Smart cities and New resources. For the purpose of our study, we consider it as a viable platform to perform machining on cloud for the industries wishing to digitize their ways of machining as one of the principal aims of the Industry of Future platform is to develop a network of regional platforms to enable the companies to pool and test new technologies and train their workforce to use these new tools. Using the regional platform, pilot projects can be launched to bring together industrial players in the process of launching or planning to launch a project to share best practices and develop a unified collaborative approach. The Industry of Future concept involves building collaborative R&D projects to fill existing gaps in today's technologies and is based on convergence of factories, connected objects, robotics, cyber security and other technology that parallel the Machining on Cloud concept of digitization of machining methods of small and medium enterprises via innovative and collaborative platforms. Moreover, the scope and governance of Industry of Future project is designed in a way so as to ensure a natural interface with the German Industry 4.0 platform that aims to revolutionize machining processes by merging of the internet and factories, thus, leading to tools and workstations communicating constantly via the internet and virtual networks. Industry of future like German Industry 4.0 is also based on total reorganization of the mode of production by using existing tools and placing greater reliance on collaboration over networks.

3 Machining on Cloud Using a Collaborative Platform

In the last few decades, numerous developments have taken place in the domain of machining-ranging from simple operations on a lathe machine to complex program based operations on CNC. Cloud computing is continuously revolutionizing the computer systems and is providing greater dynamism and flexibility to a variety of operations. Cloud computing has occupied a significant position in the IT industry and its implementation can be seen in different sectors and industries. Despite its omnipresence, cloud computing services haven't been used in machining field yet and a major technological shift can be brought by using cloud services for performing machining operations.

The way machining operations are performed today are quite efficient and a lot of advancements have been made over the years but they lack the ability to allow users (designers etc.), who are geographically spread out, to work in a collaborative environment, which can be made possible by cloud computing. Working collaboratively on a common platform on cloud will provide more agility and capability to work in real time, thereby, allowing exchange of data and information easily to drive profitability.

As discussed earlier, researchers have already explored the concept of collaborative design and manufacturing on cloud in the past. The work presented here focusses on machining domain and deals with the creation of a collaborative working framework on cloud to answer the problem of lack of a collaborative environment for users who are geographically spread out. Collaborative environment can be accessed on cloud to get data and perform simulations to visualize everything digitally before actually going into the production phase, thus, optimizing the overall process.

As a part of the study, we also performed both face to face interviews and filling of a survey form to take into account the perspective of manufacturing industries (particularly SMEs) and investigate what is preventing them from using cloud services for machining operations even though they are using it for other purposes. From the results of the survey, we found that the industries are quite familiar with the cloud computing technology and are willing to adopt new technology to save money but are hesitant in adopting it due to the following principal reasons: Lack of confidence in the successful implementation of cloud services, Concerns over data security and loss, Difficulty in learning and using Cloud Technology, Cloud service availability issues and the Cost of using cloud services. Through our study, we have tried to answer the concerns of the industry professionals by demonstrating that it is feasible to perform machining on cloud using a collaborative platform in a secure way.

3.1 Case Study: Implementation of Machining on Cloud at Dassault Systemes

In order to create a collaborative working space and perform machining simulations on cloud, we used 3DExperience platform (a platform used for performing CAD, PLM tasks) and DELMIA software (used for machining, simulation and operations) of Dassault Systemes. The test run was performed internally within the Dassault Systemes to demonstrate the successful implementation of cloud services for performing machining operations. The Table 8 below lists the technical specifications of the performed test.

Table 8. Technical specifications of the performed test

Technical specifications	
Platform	Windows 7 64-bit service pack 1
Browser	Internet explorer 11
Java	Version 8 update 51
Cloud service	3DS public cloud
Computing service	SaaS service on 3D experience platform
Machining software	DELMIA
Machining role	NC multi-axis milling programmer
Machining application	Multi-axis machining

In our study, we have considered an industrial collaboration scenario between an OEM (original equipment manufacturer) and a Supplier. OEM gives the order to the Supplier to make the part and Supplier provides the machined part to OEM based on the provided data. The data exchange between the OEM and Supplier is done by creating a Collaborative 3D Space. A collaborative workspace or shared workspace is an inter-connected environment in which all the users at dispersed locations can access and interact with each other. Appropriate licenses and roles are allotted for the creation and management of the collaborative space and both the OEM and the Supplier are put on the same tenant (a tenant is a group of users who share a common access with specific privileges to the software instance). Furthermore, the visibility of the space is set to private so that a person who is not a member of the collaborative space can't access the data. Firstly, the OEM creates the 3D space and 3D Part and provides the data to the Supplier (Fig. 2). In the scenario, the OEM can provide input as only a 3D

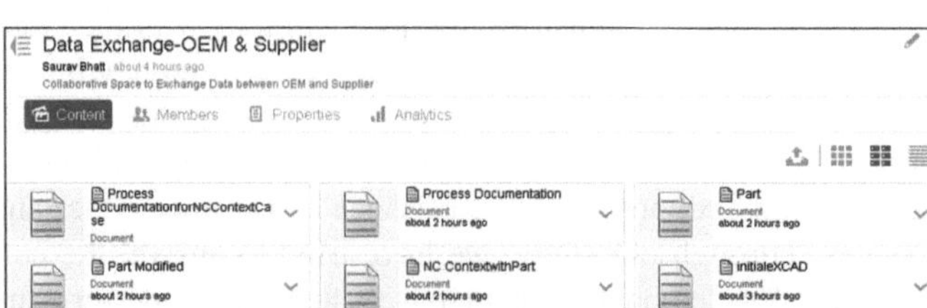

Fig. 2. Upload of data on the created collaborative 3D space by OEM

Part, Process documentation (process, tools list etc. in pdf/excel format), NC (machine, tools, setup in 3D format) context or a combination of these inputs (Fig. 3). After performing the allotted tasks, the Supplier provides the physical 3D part, NC (numeric control) code and 3D process as output to the OEM.

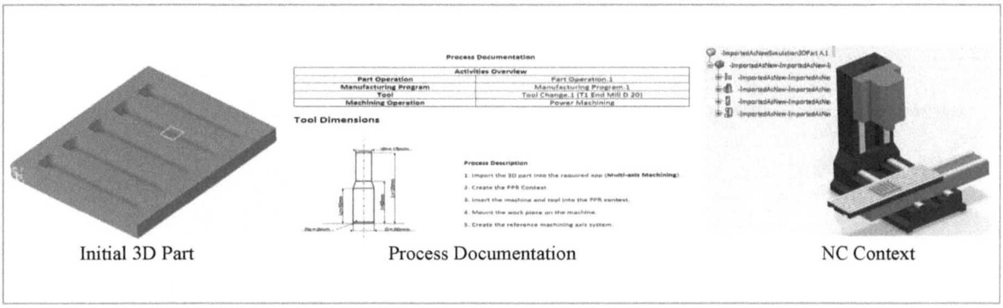

Fig. 3. Inputs provided by OEM to supplier

The process consists of importing the input 3D part in the platform and then creating a PPR context. A PPR context allows you to make a manufacturing context, which contains products, manufactured items, systems, operations, and resources. In order to define the PPR context, a mill tool assembly, a NC machine setup with reference axis systems are defined. The part is machined using a Power Machining operation and for that, all the required parameters like machining strategic and geometric parameters, feed rate, spindle speed etc. are carefully selected. After defining all the parameters, the tool path is computed and the simulation is performed to obtain the desired results (Fig. 4). In the process, we have created only one Power Machining operation for the sake of simplicity but it is possible to perform any required machining operation like drilling, turning etc.

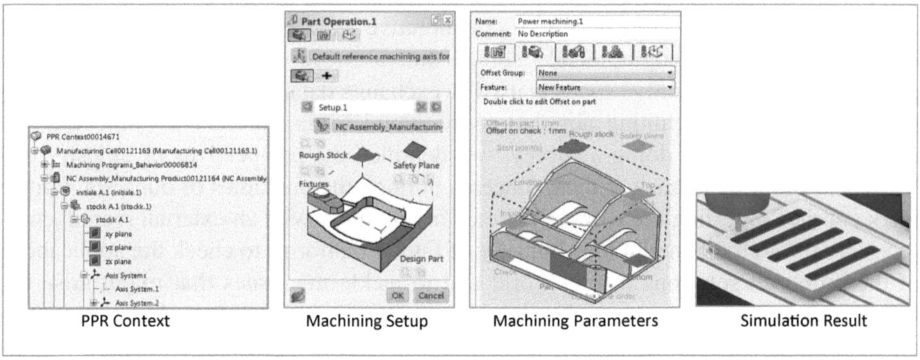

Fig. 4. Machining PPR context, parameters and simulation result

After performing the simulation and obtaining the final 3D process, the Supplier uploads the output data (Fig. 5) on the same collaborative space for the OEM (Fig. 6). The management of data (machines, tools etc.) during the entire process is done using the product lifecycle management tools of the software. The results obtained after the successful completion of our test demonstrates that it is completely feasible to work in a collaborative working environment and perform machining simulations on cloud.

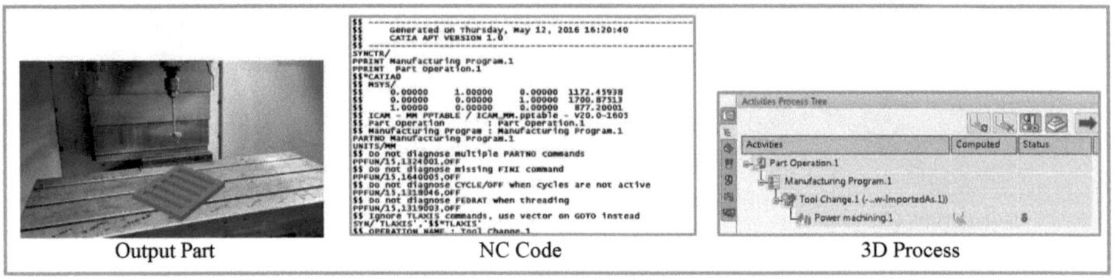

Fig. 5. Outputs provided by the supplier to OEM

Fig. 6. Upload of data on the created collaborative 3D space by supplier

4 Conclusions and Future Work

The concept of cloud computing has been around for some time but its implementation in the field of machining has not been explored yet. The work performed in this study examines the intersection of these two fields to provide industry professionals with cloud based solutions. The concept of collaborative work environment that allows the end users, who are geographically spread out, to work on a common platform is presented. The collaborative space is used to exchange data, make modifications in real time and perform machining simulations on cloud using different possible test scenarios. In addition, by doing a survey, we identified the perspectives of industry professionals and tried to answer their concerns through the outcomes of our tests. Further work consists of testing the work performed in this study with an external manufacturer (possibly through the medium of Industry of Future platform) to check the applicability of the proposed solutions in real world and to tackle the issues that might arise and make necessary improvements. Another improvement to this work could be creation of a dashboard to monitor the activity of an end user who is using machining applications on cloud and to measure the proper functioning of the proposed solutions. The findings of this study will be useful to the industry professionals wishing to perform machining operations on cloud by utilising a collaborative working platform.

References

1. Licklider, J.C.R.: Topics for discussion at the forthcoming meeting, memorandum for: members and affiliates of the intergalactic computer network. Advanced Research Projects Agency (1963). http://www.kurzweilai.net/memorandum-for-members-and-affiliates-of-the-intergalactic-computer-network
2. Mell, P., Grance, T.: The NIST definition of cloud computing. National Institute of Standards and Technology, U.S. Department of Commerce (2011). http://csrc.nist.gov/publications/nistpubs/800-145/SP800-145.pdf
3. Defining Cloud Computing Key Characteristics, Deployment and Delivery Types. http://tek-tips.nethawk.net/defining-cloud-computings-key-characteristics-deployment-and-delivery-types/
4. Introduction to Cloud Computing. https://www.priv.gc.ca/resource/fs-fi/02_05_d_51_cc_e.pdf
5. Types of Cloud Services. https://blogs.msdn.microsoft.com/wael/2011/01/19/types-of-cloud-services/
6. Bayramusta, M., Nasir, V.: A fad or future of IT? A comprehensive literature review on the cloud computing research. Int. J. Inf. Manag. **36**(4), 635–644 (2016)
7. Ratten, V.: Continuance use intention of cloud computing: innovativeness and creativity perspectives. J. Bus. Res. **69**(5), 1737–1740 (2016)
8. Kim, W.: Cloud computing: today and tomorrow. J. Object Technol. **8**(1), 65–72 (2009)
9. Buyya, R., Yeo, C., Venugopal, S., Broberg, J., Brandic, I.: Cloud computing and emerging IT platforms: vision, hype, and reality for delivering computing as the 5th utility. Future Gener. Comput. Syst. **25**, 599–616 (2009)
10. Abadi, D.: Data management in the cloud: limitations and opportunities. IEEE Data Eng. Bull. **32**(1, article 312), 3–12 (2009)
11. Wu, D.: Cloud manufacturing: strategic vision and state of art. J. Manuf. Syst. **32**(4), 564–579 (2013)
12. Li, B., Zhang, L., Wang, S.L., Tao, F., Cao, J.W., Jiang, X.D., Song, X., Chai, X.D.: Cloud manufacturing: anew service-oriented networked manufacturing model. Comput. Integr. Manuf. Syst. **16**(1), 1–7 (2010)
13. Zhang, L., Luo, Y., Tao, F., Li, B., Ren, L., Zhang, X., Guo, H., Cheng, Y., Hu, A., Liu, Y.: Cloud manufacturing: a new manufacturing paradigm. Enterp. Inf. Syst. **8**, 1–21 (2012)
14. Wu, D., Thames, J., Rosen, D., Schaefer, D.: Towards a cloud-based design and manufacturing paradigm: looking backward, looking forward. In: IDETC/CIE, pp. 1–14 (2012)
15. Schaefer, D., Thames, J., Wellman, R., Wu, D.: Distributed collaborative design and manufacturing the cloud-motivation, infrastructure, and education. American Society for Engineering Education, Annual Conference and Exposition (2012). https://www.asee.org/public/conferences/8/papers/3017/download
16. Goldhar, J.D., Jelinek, M.: Manufacturing as a service business: CIM in the 21st century. Comput. Ind. **14**, 225–245 (1990)
17. Rajagopalan, S., Pinilla, J., Losleben, P., Tian, Q., Gupta, S.: Integrated design and rapid manufacturing over the Internet. In: 1998 ASME Design and Computer Engineering Technical Conferences (DETC98/CIE-5519), Atlanta, GA (1998)
18. Erkes, J.W., Kenny, K., Lewis, J., Sarachan, B., Sobolewski, M., Sum, R.: Implementing shared manufacturing services on the World-Wide Web. Commun. ACM **39**(2), 34–45 (1996)
19. Tao, F.: Cloud manufacturing: a computing and service-oriented manufacturing model. Proc. Inst. Mech. Eng. Part B: J. Eng. Manuf. **225**, 1969–1976 (2011)

20. Zhang, L.: Cloud manufacturing: a new manufacturing paradigm. Enterp. Inf. Syst. **8**(2), 167–187 (2014)
21. Terrazas, G.: Cloud manufacturing: a proof of concept of manufacturing-as-a-service. http://www.cs.nott.ac.uk/~pszga/papers/cmpocmaas.pdf
22. Turning and Lathe Basics. http://manufacturing.stanford.edu/processes/Turning&LatheBasics.pdf
23. Revel, P., Jouini, N., Thoquenne, G., Lefebvre, F.: High precision hard turning of AISI 52100 bearing steel. Precis. Eng. **43**, 24–33 (2016)
24. Gok, P.: Development of three-dimensional finite element model to calculate the turning processing parameters in turning operations. Measurement **75**, 57–68 (2015)
25. Vijayaraghavana, V., Garga, A., Gaob, L., Vijayaraghavanc, R., Lud, G.: A finite element based data analytics approach for modeling turning process of Inconel 718 alloys. J. Clean. Prod. **137**, 1619–1627 (2016)
26. Jain, H., Tripathi, J., Bharilya, R., Jain, S., Kumar, A.: Optimisation and evaluation of machining parameters for turning operation of Inconel-625. Mater. Today: Proc. **2**(4–5), 2306–2313 (2015)
27. Brecher, C., Epple, A., Neus, S., Fey, M.: Optimal process parameters for parallel turning operations on shared cutting surfaces. Int. J. Mach. Tools Manuf. **95**, 13–19 (2015)
28. Milling Operations. http://www.longwood.edu/assets/chemphys/ch8.pdf
29. Tsai, M., Tsai, N., Yeh, C.: On milling of thin-wall conical and tubular workpieces. Mech. Syst. Signal Process. **72–73**, 395–408 (2016)
30. Budak, E.: Milling Process. http://www.sabanciuniv.edu/mdbf/mrl/PUBLICATIONS/diemold_46.pdf
31. Warghat, S., Deshmukh, T.: A review on optimization of machining parameters for end milling operation. Int. J. Eng. Res. Appl. (IJERA) (2015). ISSN 2248-9622
32. Owodunnia, O., Pinder, D.: Sustainability improvement in milling operation through improved tool design and optimized process parameters. Procedia CIRP **40**, 498–503 (2016)
33. Garg, A., Lam, J., Gao, L.: Energy conservation in manufacturing operations: modelling the milling process by a new complexity-based evolutionary approach. J. Clean. Prod. **108**(Part A), 34–45 (2015)
34. Drilling and Reaming. http://me.emu.edu.tr/me364/ME364_machining_drilling.pdf
35. Chatterjee, S., Mahapatra, S., Kumar, A.: Simulation and optimization of machining parameters in drilling of titanium alloys. Simul. Model. Pract. Theory **62**, 31–48 (2016)
36. Giasina, K., Soberanisb, S., Hodzica, A.: An experimental study on drilling of unidirectional GLARE fibre metal laminates. Compos. Struct. **133**, 794–808 (2015)
37. Perrona, E., Blaisa, C., Pelletier, S., Thomas, Y.: Drilling of high quality features in green powder metallurgy components. Mater. Sci. Eng., A **458**(1–2), 195–201 (2007)
38. Biermann, D., Kirschner, M.: Experimental investigations on single-lip deep hole drilling of super alloy Inconel 718 with small diameters. J. Manuf. Process. **20**(Part 1), 332–339 (2015)
39. Khashaba, U., Sonbaty, I., Selmy, A., Megahed, A.: Machinability analysis in drilling woven GFR/epoxy composites. Compos. Part A: Appl. Sci. Manuf. **41**(3), 391–400 (2010)
40. CNC Machining. http://www.thomasnet.com/about/cnc-machining-45330503.html
41. Yang, L., Feng, J.: Research on multi-axis CNC programming in machining large hydraulic turbine's blades based on UG. Procedia Eng. **24**, 768–772 (2011)
42. Safaieh, M., Nassehi, A., Newman, S.: A novel methodology for cross-technology interoperability in CNC machining. Robot. Comput.-Integr. Manuf. **29**(3), 79–87 (2013)
43. Newman, S., Nassehi, A., Asrai, R., Dhokia, V.: Energy efficient process planning for CNC machining. CIRP J. Manuf. Sci. Technol. **5**(2), 127–136 (2012)
44. Zhu, Y., Chen, Z., Ning, T., Xu, R.: Tool orientation optimization for 3+2-axis CNC machining of sculptured surface. Comput. Aided Des. **77**, 60–72 (2016)

45. Soori, M., Arezoo, B., Habibi, M.: Dimensional and geometrical errors of three-axis CNC milling machines in a virtual machining system. Comput. Aided Des. **45**(11), 1306–1313 (2013)
46. Valilai, O., Houshmand, M.: A collaborative and integrated platform to support distributed manufacturing system using a service-oriented approach based on cloud computing paradigm. Robot. Comput.-Integr. Manuf. **29**(1), 110–127 (2013)
47. Wang, X., Wang, L.: Ubiquitous manufacturing system based on cloud: a robotics application. Robot. Comput.-Integr. Manuf. **45**, 116–125 (2016)
48. Andreadis, G., Fourtounis, G., Bouzakis, K.: Collaborative design in the era of cloud computing. Adv. Eng. Softw. **81**, 66–72 (2015)
49. Wu, D., Thames, J., Rosen, D., Schaefer, D.: Enhancing the product realization process with cloud-based design and manufacturing systems. J. Comput. Inf. Sci. Eng. **13**, 041004 (2013)
50. Industry of Future. http://www.economie.gouv.fr/files/files/PDF/pk_industry-of-future.pdf

Cloud Based Meta Data Driven Product Model

Arun Kumar Singh[1,2(✉)], B. Gurumoorthy[2], and Latha Christie[1]

[1] Microwave Tube Research and Development Centre (DRDO), Bangalore 560013, India
arunsingh_aks@yahoo.com
[2] Centre for Product Design and Manufacturing, Indian Institute of Science, Bangalore 560012, India
bgm@cpdm.iisc.ernet.in

Abstract. Product model using Core Product Model (CPM) and its extension Open Assembly Model (OAM) has been implemented with cloud compatible open source technologies. Implementation focuses on data structure for capturing assembly hierarchy, part details, part features and feature associations. Super Constraint Tolerance Feature (SCTF) model has been used to extract information from STEP file. A case study on Cylinder cap assembly has been taken to showcase the data structure and classes. Entity Attribute Value (EAV) model has been used to manage and store the product metadata and product data. Parts and assemblies are defined as entities, product metadata as attributes and product data as values has been stored in separate tables. Methods to populate product model at different stages of design has also been discussed.

Keywords: Cloud · PLM · Core Product Model · Open Assembly Model

1 Introduction

Cloud compatible technologies are gaining popularity in recent times. Most of the traditional Product data models were developed keeping in mind single-user model based environment at single/multiple location installations. With the advent of the Internet more and more products are designed and manufactured globally in a distributed and collaborative environment. Cloud compatible platforms also enable to incorporate open source web technologies. Web based systems can be used to take advantage of social networking tools for knowledge capturing.

Product model should be able communicate with other systems in a plug and play manner by providing standard definitions for interfaces. For example system will be interoperable if Geometry is captured or translated using STEP from/to traditional CAD tools. Incorporation of already existing standards like STEP to define geometry will reduce efforts in system compatibilities and import/export of geometry data in/out of product model at different stages of product life. STEP is a mature and widely used standard for the exchange of product data. In practice, STEP tends to be invoked only late in the product development process, after all design decisions have been made and when the product is ready to be manufactured or assembled. Thus, STEP is used for the exchange of information that is the outcome of design activities, rather than for the

R. Harik et al. (Eds.): PLM 2016, IFIP AICT 492, pp. 356–364, 2016.
DOI: 10.1007/978-3-319-54660-5_32

information produced and used through the development of the design. STEP provides no support for design evolution, for the early phases of design when descriptive information is sparse.

The product model presented here may be seen as the precursor for STEP in the lifecycle of a product, capturing all the information relevant to the ongoing design process until the product design is firmed up, approved and committed to manufacturing.

2 Product Models

2.1 Core Product Model (CPM)

National Institute of Standards and Technology (NIST) proposed Core Product Model (CPM) to cater issues of interoperability and having a product model, which can cater needs of Product Lifecycle Management (PLM) from conceptual design stage to end of product life. The objective of the NIST CPM [1] was to provide a base-level product model that is: not tied to any vendor software; open; non-proprietary; simple; generic; expandable; independent of any one product development process; and capable of capturing the engineering context that is most commonly shared in product development activities. CPM focuses on artifact representation including function, form, behavior and material, physical and functional decompositions, and relationships among these concepts. The model is heavily influenced by the Entity-Relationship data model [2].

The model consists of two sets of classes, called object and relationship. The two sets of classes are equivalent to the Unified Modeling Language (UML) terms of class and association class, respectively. CPM supported the notions of form, function, and behavior.

2.2 Open Assembly Model (OAM)

An object-oriented definition of an assembly model called the Open Assembly Model (OAM) is explored, which is as an extension to the CPM. The assembly model represents the function, form, and behavior of the assembly and defines both a system level conceptual model and associated hierarchical relationships. [3] The schema incorporates information about assembly relationships and component composition; the representation of the former is by the class **AssemblyAssociation**, and the model of the latter uses part-of relationships. The class **AssemblyAssociation** represents the component assembly relationship of an assembly. It is the aggregation of one or more **ArtifactAssociation**.

An **Assembly** is a composition of its subassemblies and parts. A **Part** is the lowest level component. Each assembly component (whether a sub-assembly or part) is made up of one or more features, represented in the model by **OAMFeature**. The **Assembly** and **Part** classes are sub-classes of the CPM **Artifact** class and **OAMFeature** is a subclass of the CPM **Feature** class. In CPM, **Geometry** and **Material** aggregate into **Form**. **Form** and **Function** aggregate into CPM **Feature** class.

The class **AssemblyFeatureAssociation** represents the association between mating assembly features through which relevant artifacts are associated. The class **ArtifactAssociation** is the aggregation of **AssemblyFeatureAssociation**.

3 Cloud Computing

Cloud-based Product model refers to a service-oriented networked product development model in which service consumers are enabled to configure, select, and utilize customized product realization resources and services ranging from CAE software to reconfigurable manufacturing systems. This is accomplished through a synergetic integration of the four key cloud computing service models: Infrastructure-as-a-Service (IaaS), Platform-as-a-Service (PaaS), Hardware-as-a-Service (HaaS), and Software-as-a-Service (SaaS) [4].

Cloud-based Product model refers to a networked design model that leverages cloud computing, service-oriented architecture (SOA), Web 2.0 (e.g., social networking tools), and semantic web technologies to support cloud-based engineering design services in distributed and collaborative environments [5].

The key issue in improving design communication is the extent to which design engineers fully understand a complex design process, in particular, design tasks that need to be finished or identification of individuals from whom specific information can be accessed. In traditional collaborative design systems, communication can be seen as a one-way process with a linear sequence of design. Because of the use of social media in cloud based system, design communication can be improved through multiple information channels (e.g., social networking tools and product review tools) in which information flow can take place in multiple directions [5]. In traditional systems, computer-aided application tools are standalone systems and are designed for single user without communicating and collaborating with others [6]. In Cloud based system, engineering design requires more communication and collaboration within and across organizations on the modeling, analysis, and optimization of a design.

Designers can access manufacturing information like process sheets, inspection reports, issues associated in manufacturing product components and all the related information of a product while designing new products or modifying the existing products. Manufacturing personnel can communicate with the designer and all the communication data can be associated with the product form (artefact attribute) and can be saved for future references.

4 Attribute Sets (Meta Data) Driven Product Model

A cloud based/compatible data structure of CPM/OAM has been created, which can be used by designers to capture, store and retrieve product data. In early stages of product development when detailed geometry information is not available, it becomes difficult to associate function and behavior information to the product. There can be scenario where product is to be designed from sketch and scenario, where some reference/existing product was designed in the same environment, is available and only needs to be modified for better performance, cost reduction or new added features. Product model should be able to adapt and work in both the situations and provide methods which can be used to capture, store and retrieve design rational, assembly and tolerance information from the conceptual design stage up to the timeline where designer deals with the function and performance of product.

In situations where reference product is available and products only need feature modifications, old product design repository should be able to create new instances of whole project either with class structure skeleton model (without form, function, behavior data) or with full product history including data. A data driven attribute repository has been proposed which can be a platform to add new features for existing product designs. This repository can act as base model to define artefact. Any artefact definition would need attributes to define the form, function or behavior. Artefact may have one set of attributes for form (Geometry and topology) and others to define artefact's function and behavior. Data driven approach is adopted having EAV (Entity Attribute Value) model to capture the product information. Flow chart for attribute set creation and selection has been shown in Fig. 1.

Semantic development is fully domain driven approach and it cannot be pre-built in Product model, which will make it domain specific product model. Main focus for developing the product Meta data in form of attribute set comes on designer. In multi domain design scenario, designers from different domain expertise can prepare their respective domain attribute sets, which in turn forms a collective attribute set definition.

Geometry_Meta_Data class has been inherited from CPM's geometry class. Geomtery_Meta_data contains variables to define attribute sets, attributes name and types. It contains functions *AddAttribute(), AddDataToAttribue(),* and *ShowAttributeData()* to store/retrieve attribute sets and attribute data to database. *AssemblyFeature* and *CompositeFeature*, which are inherited from OAM's Feature class, have been further extended to AssemblyFeature_Meta_data and CompositeFeature_Meta_data. Class structure and its functions are shown in Fig. 2. These methods

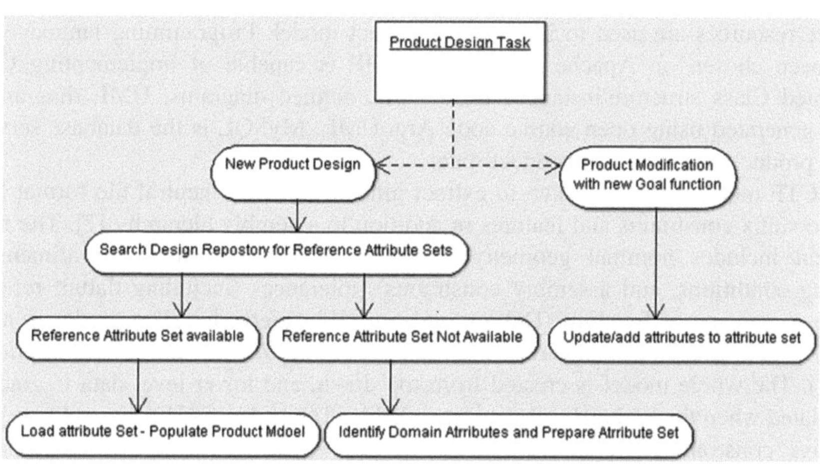

Fig. 1. Flow chart for preparation of product model attribute set (Meta data)

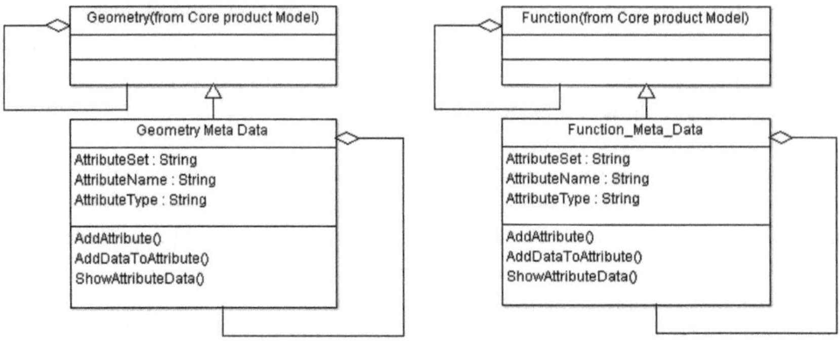

Fig. 2. Extended geometry and function class having methods for attribute sets and data holders

include functionality to make a connection to database and run required database queries like INSERT/UPDATE/SELECT or DELETE.

In Entity Attribute Value (EAV) model Entity definitions, attribute definitions and attribute values are stored in separate tables of database. This makes attribute set (meta-data) definition flexible as entities and attributes can be added or deleted on the fly whenever need arises. The product model need not be changed for addition or deletion of domain specific attributes. Product model, Meta Data and product data exists separately. Product models can grow from conceptual design level having very few entities and attributes into fully developed attribute set at the advanced stages of Product Design.

5 Implementation

5.1 Programming Platform and Data Structure

Meta-Data Driven Product model is implemented on Cloud compatible platform. Open source resources are used to implement product model. Programming language PHP has been chosen on Apache web server. PHP is capable of implementing Object Oriented Class structure/instances from UML defined diagrams. UML diagram has been generated using open source code ArgoUML. MySQL is the database server to store product metadata and product data.

SCTF model has been taken to extract information from neutral file format STEP and to suffix constraints and features in addition to assembly hierarchy [7]. The model content includes nominal geometry (features), constraints (including dimensions, mating conditions, and assembly constraints), tolerances (including datum reference frames), degrees of freedom (DOFs), and assembly hierarchy. The model is named *Super-Constraint-Tolerance-Feature-Graph-Based Model (or the SCTF Model for short)*. The whole model is created from top down, and lower level data is gradually populated when the higher-level data is available. The order is “The general tree, parts, features, constraints, tolerances, DOFs”.

5.2 MySQL Table Structure for Assembly Hierarchy

The first step to implement data structure for SCTF is assembly hierarchy definition. Assembly hierarchy is implemented using General Tree. Data Structure for general tree needs definition of Tree node class and general tree class. General tree node needs data member variable (data) and three pointers – its parent, its child and its siblings. Classes need to be defined to traverse, modify and retrieve data from the general tree.

General tree represents a hierarchical data. MySQL is a relational database. Tables of relational database are not hierarchical (like XML), but are simply a flat list. Hierarchical data has a parent-child relationship that is not naturally represented in relational database table. Hierarchical data is a collection of data, where each item has a single parent and zero or more children (With the exception of the root item, which has no parent). There are two models for dealing with hierarchical data in relational database management systems (RDBMS) – adjacency list model and the nested set model.

5.2.1 Adjacency List Model

In the adjacency list model, each item in the table contains a pointer to its parent. The topmost element has a null value for its parent. The adjacency list model has the advantage of being simple.

5.2.2 Nested Set Model

In the nested set model, we can look at hierarchy in new way, not as nodes and lines but as nested containers. Hierarchy is still maintained, as parents envelop their children. These can be represented in a table through left and right values to represent the nesting of nodes. We start numbering at the leftmost side of the outer node (Main assembly) and continue to the right. This approach is called *modified preorder tree traversal algorithm*. The full tree can be retrieved through the use of *a self-join* query that links parents with nodes on the basis that a node's left value will always appear between its parent's left and right values. Functions for finding all the leaf nodes, retrieving a single path, finding the depth of nodes, depth of a sub-tree, finding the immediate subordinate of a node, adding new nodes, deleting nodes are easy to implement compared to adjacency list model.

Next Layer of SCTF Graph consists CTF graph, which is a nested *doubly-linked list* data structures. At the first layer, it is a *list* of "parts" contained in the assembly/subassembly node. At the second layer, each "part" is composed of a *list* of geometric "features". At the third layer, each geometric "feature" contains its basic geometric data, a *list* of geometric constraints, a *list* of tolerances, a *list* of DoFs, and a *list* of associated points.

6 Case Study - Cylinder Cap Assembly

A cylinder-cap assembly has been taken to implement product model. 3D modeling software SolidWorks is used to model the assembly. A STEP translated model has been taken. Assembly consisting of 4 unique parts (subartifacts) namely cylinder, cap, key and bolts, is shown in Fig. 3.

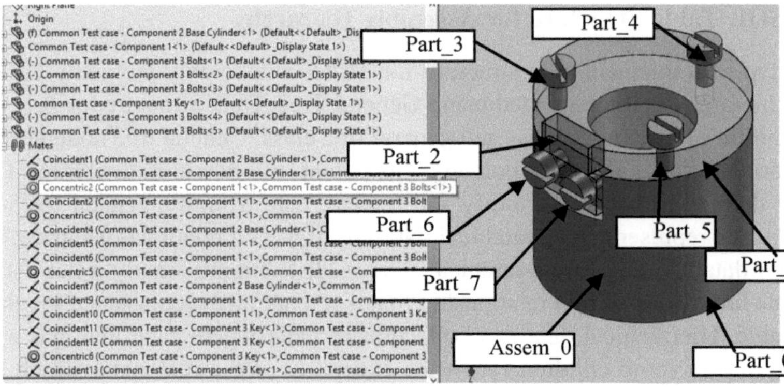

Fig. 3. Cylinder cap assembly with part details and constraints (AssemblyFeatureAssociations)

Assembly hierarchy is implemented using nested set model shown in Table 1. Nested set model makes it easy to query the parts contained in an assembly. Like any part which is having its Comp_left and Comp_right values in-between 1 and 18 will be a part of Assem_0.

ArtifactEntities in Table 2 is listing all the assemblies and parts associated with Cylinder Cap Assembly. In CPM, to store artifact data information instance has been mentioned which can hold the values of Properties. EAV (Entity Attribute Value) model is used to store these values. For example Table 3 is defining the ArtefactFeature Entities. Table 4 is holding attributes for these entities and Table 5 contains the attribute values (Product Specific data). Tables 3 and 4 are containing the Meta data for product, whereas the real product data is in Table 5. When designing a new Cylinder Cap Assembly (Conceptual), it can be started with the Meta data i.e. entities and attributes. These tables can be built based on the information available with the designer at different stages of Product Lifecycle. Designers have flexibility to add new form or function feature attributes.

Table 1. Nested set model table for assembly hierarchy

Artefact_id	Artefact_name	Comp_left	Comp_right
1	Assem_0	1	18
2	Part_0	2	3
3	Part_1	4	5
4	Part_2	6	7
5	Part_3	8	9
6	Part_4	10	11
7	Part_5	12	13
8	Part_6	14	15
9	Part_7	16	17

Table 2. ArtefactEntities

Artefact_id	Artefact_name	Artefact_Type (Part/Assembly)	Artefact_Label
1	Assem_0	Assembly	Cylinder cap assembly
2	Part_0	Part	Cylinder
3	Part_1	Part	Cap
4	Part_2	Part	Key
5	Part_3	Part	Bolt_0
6	Part_4	Part	Bolt_1
7	Part_5	Part	Bolt_2
8	Part_6	Part	Bolt_3
9	Part_7	Part	Bolt_4

Table 3. ArtefactFeature_entity

ArtefactFeature_id	Artefact_id	ArtefactFeature_name	ArtefactFeature_type
1	2	Centre_hole	Hole
2	2	Fastening_hole_0	Tapped hole
3	2	Fastening_hole_1	Tapped hole
4	2	Fastening_hole_2	Tapped hole
5	2	Fastening_hole_3	Tapped hole
6	2	Fastening_hole_4	Tapped hole
7	5	Threaded_bolt_0	Threaded pin
8	6	Threaded_bolt_1	Threaded pin

Table 4. ArtefactFeature_attributes (For Fastening_hole_1)

ArtefactFeature_attribute_id	ArtefactFeature_id	ArtefactFeature_attribute_name
1	3	Centre
2	3	Axis
3	3	Radius
4	3	Height
5	3	thread_size

Table 5. ArtefactFeature_value (For Fastening_hole_1)

ArtefactFeature_value_id	ArtefactFeature_Attribute_id	ArtefactFeature_value
1	1	22.6873
2	2	0,0,1
3	3	5
4	4	15
5	5	M5

The AssemblyFeatureAssociation information is shown in Table 6. It lists Part feature's association with other part's feature. These can be implemented by doubly linked list.

Table 6. AssemblyFeatureAssociation

ArtefactFeature_id1	ArtefactFeature_id2	Association
3	7	LocationConstraint_concentric
4	8	LocationConstraint_concentric
9	13	LocationConstraint_coincident
10	14	LocationConstraint_coincident

7 Conclusion

The data structure has been created using CPM and its extension OAM. STEP File containing geometric data is used to extract the assembly hierarchy and part details. Case Study implementation shows that CPM /OAM can be implemented using open source cloud compatible technologies. Data structure containing Meta data and Product data for assembly hierarchies, parts, features and its associations (Constraints) has been implemented and demonstrated in Cylinder Cap assembly case study. The subsequent steps to SCTF graph are data structure for tolerances and artefact feature's DOFs, which can assist in Assembly planning and Goal based Tolerances allocation.

References

1. Fenves, S.J., Foufou, S., Bock, C., Sriram, R.D.: CPM2: a core model for product data. J. Comput. Inf. Sci. Eng. **8**(1), 014501-6 (2008). ASME
2. Foufou, S., Fenves, S.J., Bock, C., Sudarsan, R., Sriram, R.: A core product model for PLM with an illustrative XML implementation. In: Proceedings of the PLM International Conference on Product Lifecycle Management, Lyon, France, July 2005, pp. 21–32. Inderscience Publishers (2005)
3. Rachuri, S., Han, Y.-H., Foufou, S., Feng, S.C., Roy, U., Wang, F., Sriram, R.D., Lyons, K.W.: A model for capturing product assembly information. J. Comput. Inf. Sci. Eng. **6**(1), 11–21 (2006)
4. Wu, D., Rosen, D.W., Schaefer, D.: Cloud-based design and manufacturing: status and promise. In: Schaefer, D. (ed.) Cloud-based Design and Manufacturing: A Service-Oriented Product Development Paradigm for the 21st Century, p. 282. Springer, London (2014)
5. Wu, D., Schaefer, D., Rosen, D.W.: Cloud-based design and manufacturing systems: a social network analysis. In: International Conference on Engineering Design (ICED 2013), Seoul, Korea (2013)
6. Red, E., French, D., Jensen, G., Walker, S.S., Madsen, P.: Emerging design methods and tools in collaborative product development. J. Comput. Inf. Sci. Eng. **13**(3), 031001 (2013)
7. Shen, Z., Shah, J., Davidson, J.: Analysis neutral data structure for GD&T. J. Intell. Manuf. **19**(4), 455–472 (2008)

Knowledge-Based Application of Liaison for Variant Design

Shantanu Kumar Das(✉) and Abinash Kumar Swain

Department of Mechanical and Industrial Engineering,
Indian Institute of Technology, Roorkee, India
shantanuds0206@gmail.com,
Shantanu.abinash@springernature.com,
swainfme@iitr.ac.in

Abstract. This paper proposes the use of liaison to develop a knowledge based system for variant design application to assist and guide designers at earlier stage of product development. A knowledge based framework has been proposed to support the joining process selection during variant design, where liaison act as an interface. Various liaison knowledge is represented in a complete and systematic manner. These liaison knowledge includes various geometric and non-geometric information. A user interface has been developed. A query engine is built and used to enable reasoning the joining process based on the requirement of a variant product. An industrial case study of two variants of automobile front bumper is provided in order to illustrate and validate the proposed knowledge based framework.

Keywords: Variant design · Liaison · Ontology · Knowledge based framework

1 Introduction

Diversified customer requirement and growing competition in the global market demands manufacturer to provide an increased variety of product. In order to fulfill this increased demand of higher variety of products [1] in the shortest possible time with lower tooling cost, industries are under tremendous pressure in current times. In addition, manufacturers are providing great efforts to shorten the product development cycle to enable new models or variants of an existing product to be brought out more quickly, more often and with lower tooling costs. The use of a higher variety of product led to the development of complex manufacturing and assembly system. As a result the new design or variant design calls for a major change in the assembly process or sequence where possible, which is very much expensive to handle. In particular, in the context of variants, it is important that changes in the design either avoid or minimize the need to change or modify the assembly line. For variant design, the changes in the design refer the change in existing component's dimension, change in material type, or form of the component. In order to address the above change there are changes in the assembly joint or liaison. In this paper, liaison is defined as a structured collection of various geometric and non-geometric information of parts in an assembly that is associated with one or more assembly process. As design is a knowledge intensive

R. Harik et al. (Eds.): PLM 2016, IFIP AICT 492, pp. 365–374, 2016.
DOI: 10.1007/978-3-319-54660-5_33

work which takes 20% of the designer's time in searching and analyzing various past information [2], it is required to develop a knowledge based framework which can capture, store, share and reuse the knowledge across various domains. In this paper, a knowledge based framework using liaison is developed in order to reduce product development life cycle for the variant design. Various geometric attributes of assembly components are considered along with some non-geometric attributes for systematic representation various design knowledge. This systematic representation of various knowledge is required in order to maintain various knowledge in proper format so that it can be interpreted and retrieved easily by a computer system.

Various authors represented liaison for collaborative product development [3], assembly sequence planning [4], concurrent evolution of product model with the process model [5] and maintaining associativity between product model and process model [5]. Another important field is a variant design where liaisons are required for concurrent evolution of design of product family and the corresponding assembly system. The prime motivation for this interest is to reduce the design and manufacturing cycle time by identifying the infeasibility and inconsistency in the existing assembly process in the early stages of product variant design. In order to address above, a knowledge based framework developed for selection of assembly joining process for variant design application at the early stage of product development. This knowledge base is providing the required information for joining process selection during the variant design.

The rest of the paper is structured as follows. Section 2 discusses various literatures related to the proposed work. A knowledge based framework developed in Sect. 3 for joining process selection which includes representation of liaison, selection of liaison knowledge for variant design. In Sect. 4 an industrial case study of two variants of automobile front bumper is provided in order to illustrate and validate the proposed knowledge based framework. The paper concludes with the discussion of the contributions and its various future applications.

2 State of the Art

In this section various literatures related to liaison to support variant design and knowledge based application of liaison are reviewed.

2.1 Liaison Used for Variant Design

In the recent decades, variant design has attracted more researchers. Many literatures related to liaison based variant design are discussed in this section. Luh et al. [6] stored hierarchical component interaction information in a QDSM (quantified design structure matrix) and defined it as a liaison, which is applied for variant design solution in a product family. Bryan et al. [7] combined precedence diagram of all product variants of a product family and defined this information as liaison. Further, these information are used for the calculation of assembly time for each instance of base modules and differentiating modules in a product family of office chairs. ElMaraghy and AlGeddawy

[8] addressed about a product variant design model which satisfy various customer's needs in a market. Further, different dependency matrices and liaison graphs are extracted along with the component's architectural constraints in order to identify the best modular product family design. AlGeddawy and ElMaraghy [9] differentiated various products into variants in a product family based on commonality and differentiation between parts and component for the development of a reactive platform design model. Based on various attributes like materials for various components, possible modularity, possible integration, moving components, etc., different liaison graphs have been developed to identify the adjacency of component and to assist in the cladistics analysis to develop a reactive platform design.

2.2 Knowledge Based Application of Liaison

In this section, various literatures restraining to the knowledge based application of many liaison information are discussed. L'Eglise et al. [10] developed a multicriteria decision aid method which helps the designer to choose the suitable joining process for each electro-mechanical product at the early stage of product realization. Various attributes like joint geometry, joint properties, production, materials and process have been included in the knowledge base for the development of a multicriteria decision aid method. Zha et al. [11] developed a knowledge based framework by considering functional, hierarchical relationship between the assembly components for assembly orientated design and assembly sequence planning. Kim et al. [12] introduced assembly design formalism which captured the knowledge related to assembly joining relationship comprising of joint features, mating feature, assembly engineering relation, spatial relationship specification and assembly features which is enhanced using ontologies for collaborative assembly information sharing framework by using OWL & SWRL. Lohse et al. [13] considered different liaisons (i.e. contact liaison, form fit liaison, tight fit liaison, screw fit liaison) in order to develop a product and assembly process domain ontology framework for deciding various assembling operations. Zha and Sriram [14] presented a knowledge based framework which captures, represents and manages product family design knowledge and helps in product variant assessment.

Kim et al. [3] developed a knowledge based framework in which various knowledge related to joining process like riveting, adhesive bonding, fastener, welding, metal stitching, soldering, brazing, spot welding, etc. are described in mereotopological manner. This mathematical description and the Semantic Web Rule Language (SWRL) helps in representing the difference of similar looking joints and also helps in defining the assembly design terms and their correlations. Further, it is used for collaborative assembly design where various knowledge related to joining process is captured using ontology and retrieved, shared & reused across different environment. Demoly et al. [15] developed a mathematical description of product relationship based on mereotopology at different abstraction levels in order to have a greater understanding of product definition and assembly and they have presented the description by ontological implementation using OWL DL and SWRL. Mas et al. [16] proposed a knowledge based application for aircraft assembly line design using assembly joint and its process information along with some jigs, tools and human resource knowledge. However this knowledge based system only considered the assembly process information of liaison without considering other aspects of knowledge related to design, production and functional requirement for selection of liaison and its possible joining processes.

In summary most of the representations of liaison available in the literature have only considered the mating and the hierarchical relationship in an assembly without considering the actual process required for mating. Further, research related to non-geometric liaison information associated with variant design are scarce in the literature. Hence based on the extensive literature review, it is concluded that the various knowledge based system available in the literature are not capable to provide a clear picture for use the liaison for variant design applications at the early stages of product realization.

3 Knowledge Based Framework for Selection of Joining Process

A knowledge based framework for the selection of joining process in variant design is shown in Fig. 1. It consist of five basic units: customer requirement for variant product, user interface, knowledge base, multiple criteria decision making & query engine.

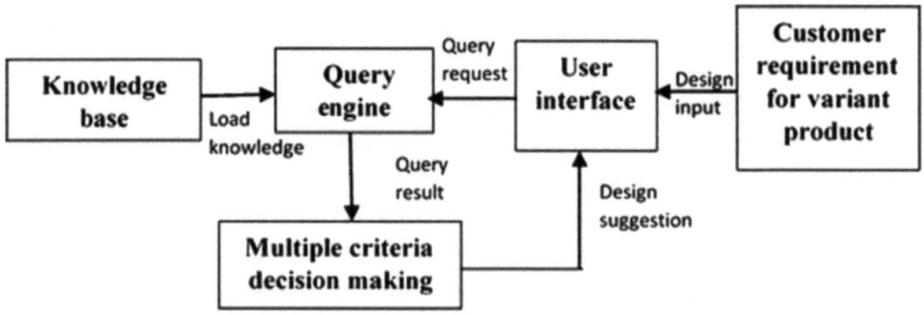

Fig. 1. Knowledge based framework for selection of joining process in variant design

Various steps for creating the knowledge based system are defined below in detail.

Customer Requirement for Variant Product: Based on the customer requirement like reducing the cost of the product or making the product to be lightweight, the designer has to change material type, joint design type etc. These design inputs are submitted to the user interface module and changed according to the requirement for variant product.

User Interface: The user interface module provides an interface for selection of various design knowledge based on the requirement for a variant product. These design knowledge is submitted to a query engine for reasoning about the process. The query results are collected in the multiple criteria decision making module. The designer takes expert advice and if there is any change in the design knowledge, then it is submitted to the user interface module.

Knowledge Base: In the knowledge base module various geometric and non-geometric design knowledge are represented in a complete and systematic manner. When a query is fired by the designer, these knowledge is loaded into the query engine and help in retrieving the joining process.

Multiple Criteria Decision Making: The query results from the query engine are collected in a multiple criteria decision making module and the designer takes the expert advice for analyzing the results. If there is any design suggestion, then it is submitted to the user interface module for further reasoning purpose.

Query Engine: When a query is fired from the user interface module, the query engine loaded requires knowledge to be retrieved from the knowledge base module. By the use of this knowledge, it enables reasoning about the joining process and also transfers the query result to the multiple criteria decision making module.

Due to variant design, following types of changes are observed, which need to be tackled for the development of knowledge based system for selection of joining process.

Due to change in the form of component the joint design type is changed as shown in Fig. 2(a). The change in the component modifies the joint design type due to the rigidness of material. If one of the component is plastic in nature, then it can be assembled by the cylindrical snap-fit joint as shown in Fig. 2(b). When the material of a component changes, then there is a change in liaison type because of the rigidness of material it can't be assembled by cylindrical snap-fit joint. It can be fixed by some other joints like screwed joint or welded joint as shown in Fig. 2(c). Due to the dimension

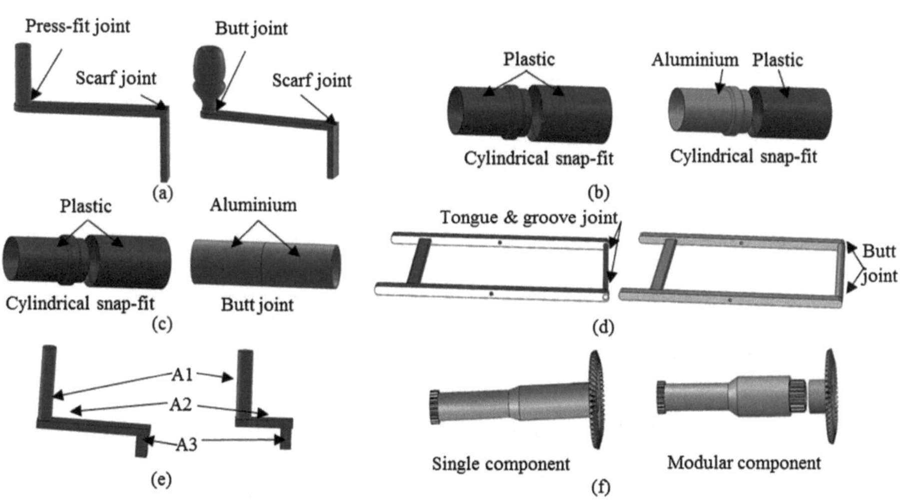

Fig. 2. (a) Change in joint design type (b) change in material without change in joint design type (c) change in material with change in joint design type (d) change in component's dimension with change in joint design type (e) change in component's dimension without change in joint design type (f) change in product architecture

constraint, the joint design type is changed by modifying the diameter of the component as shown in Fig. 2(d). This is an example of scalable variant design where the length of the A2 component changes without change in liaison type as shown in Fig. 2 (e). The bevel gear having single component is converted into a modular architecture in order to change the material for reducing the weight of the shaft of the part without losing the strength of the teeth. This is a variant design for a lighter product by changing the design from integral to the modular architecture as shown in Fig. 2(f).

3.1 Development of Liaison Knowledge Based System Using Ontology

In this paper various geometric attributes and non-geometric attributes of liaison are represented using Protégé 3.3.5 [17] which is an open-source ontology framework for building knowledge based acquisition tool developed at Stanford University. Various liaison attributes and their values of root gap, material type, thickness, production rate, loading mode, strength, surface finish etc. are stored for development of a knowledge database as shown in Fig. 3. Also, various interrelationships between the joining process and different liaison attributes are made for the development of knowledge based system. Earlier Swain et al. [5] extracted various joint designs like lap, butt, etc. and used these for process selection by considering only the geometric attributes of liaison. In this paper various geometric attributes along with non-geometric attributes are considered for selection of joining process based on the requirement for a variant product.

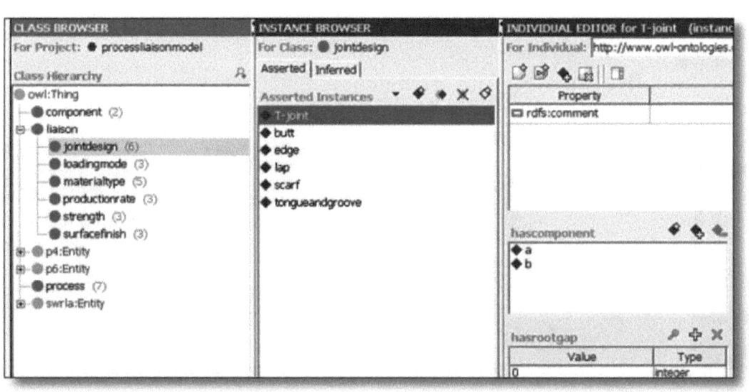

Fig. 3. An instance of assembly joint design and its process parameters

A user interface has been developed and is shown in Fig. 4. The designers have to scrutinize various liaison knowledge for the selection of the process according to the design, functional and production requirement of a variant product. For example, when the joint design type is changed from butt to tongue and groove to fulfill the customer requirement, then designer changes the values of "hasjointdesign" attributes in the user interface and reasons about the joining process using the query engine. In this way the

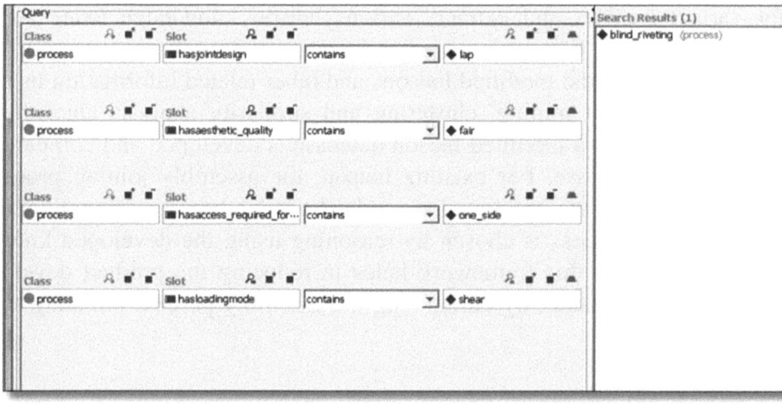

Fig. 4. A user interface for the selection of attributes in joining process selection

designer can change various values of attributes according to the need of the design and can retrieve the joining process using query engine.

A variant design application of developed knowledge based system is defined in a framework as represented in Fig. 5. In this framework, designer first develops the CAD

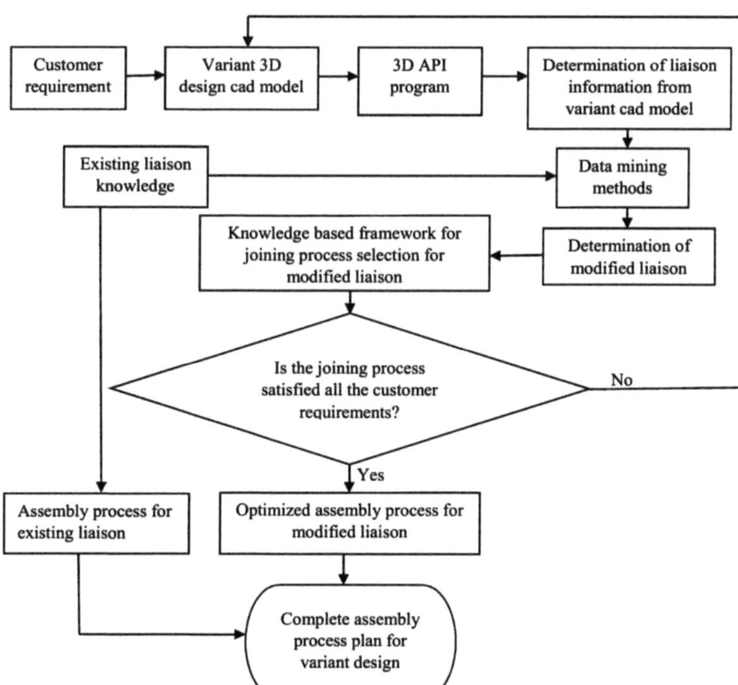

Fig. 5. A framework for variant design application

model for variant product and extracts various liaison knowledge using API programming. This variant liaison knowledge is compared with the existing liaison database for determining the modified liaisons and other related information using data mining methods like text mining, clustering and similarity analysis algorithms etc. Hence, using this process a modified liaison database is developed and compared with the existing liaison database. For existing liaison, the assembly joining process has been already available in the previous liaison database. In the case of modified liaison the assembly joining process is chosen by reasoning using the developed knowledge based framework. Hence this framework helps in reducing the product development life cycle of a variant product by eliminating the assembly process planning time for existing liaison.

4 Industrial Case Study

An industrial case study of two variants of front bumper in automobile are used as example to illustrate and validate the above knowledge based framework. In this paper, two front bumpers from Toyota and Mitsubishi [18] are taken as a variant product for the validation of the proposed framework. In the variant design of bumper, joint design types between components are changed due to the change in form of components or mixing and matching of components. There is a chance of changing the assembly joining process and needs proper verification for obtaining the modified liaison and its joining process.

In the Mitsubishi-triton-front-bumper there are 4 types of joint designs namely lap joint, tongue & groove joint, corner joint and press-fit joint. The lap joint is present between components namely Frontsideface-3ton(A) and Bumper link 3ton-1(C), and Frontsideface-3ton(A) and Bumper link 3ton-2(D). There are 3 tongue and groove joints which are present between components namely Fog lamp bracket3ton-1(B) and Fog lamp triton-1(E), Fog lamp bracket3ton-2(F) and Fog lamp triton-2(H), and Grill hilux-1(I) and Frontsideface-3ton(A). The corner joint is available between the components namely Fog lamp bracket3ton-1(B) and Frontsideface-3ton(A), Fog lamp bracket3ton-2(F) and Frontsideface-3ton(A), and Bracket roller-1(G) and Frontsideface-3ton(A). There are two press-fit joints present between components namely Fog lamp bracket3ton-1(B) & Fog lamp triton-1(E), and Fog lamp bracket3ton-2(F) & Fog lamp triton-2(H). In the Toyota-fj-cruiser-front-bumper there are 4 types of joint designs namely lap joint, tongue and groove joint, corner joint and press-fit joint. The lap joint is present between components namely Frontsideface-3ton (A) and Bumper link 3ton-1(C), Frontsideface-3ton(A) and Bumper link 3ton-2(D), Bracket roller-1(G) and Frontsideface-3ton(A), Fog lamp bracket3ton-2(F) and Fog lamp triton-2(H), and Fog lamp bracket3ton-1(B) and Fog lamp triton-1(E). There is one tongue & groove joint which is present between components namely Grill hilux-1 (I) and Frontsideface-3ton(A). The corner joint is available between components namely Fog lamp bracket3ton-1(B) and Frontsideface-3ton(A), and Fog lamp bracket3ton-2(F) and Frontsideface-3ton(A). There are 2 press-fit joints present between components namely Fog lamp bracket3ton-1(B) and Fog lamp triton-1(E), and Fog lamp bracket3ton-2(F) and Fog lamp triton-2(H).

Due to the variant design there is a change in the form of assembly components as shown in Figs. 6 and 7. Due to this, there is a change in the assembly joint design (modified liaison) available between the assembly components and its joining process. At this stage, the knowledge based framework of liaison will helps in deciding the suitable joining process for a particular joint design by optimizing the several attributes during the selection of processes.

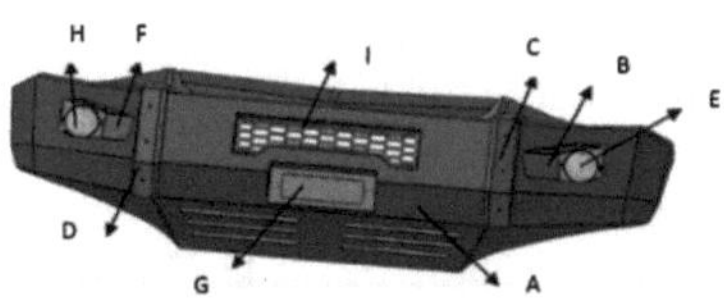

Fig. 6. Mitsubishi-triton-front-bumper

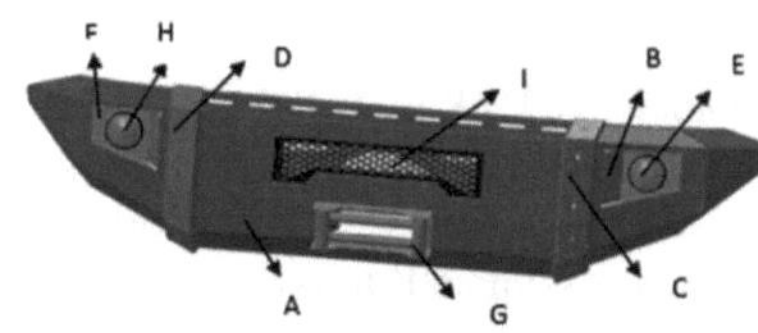

Fig. 7. Toyota-fj-cruiser-front-bumper

In this industrial case study, the modified liaison found between components of two variants of the front bumper are shown in Table 1. Due to this change in liaisons, there will be a change in the assembly joining process. This can be tackled by the above knowledge based framework by changing the value of required attributes in the user interface according to the requirement of a variant product. Also, by submitting these values to the query engine and executing this will generate a suitable joining process which reduce the process planning time of modified liaison. So this knowledge based framework will help in reducing the product development life cycle time for a variant product.

Table 1. Change in liaisons during variant design

Involved components		Existing liaisons	Modified liaisons
Bracket roller-1(G)	Frontsideface-3ton (A)	Corner-joint	Lap joint
Fog lamp bracket3ton-2(F)	Fog lamp triton-2 (H)	2-tongue and groove joint,1 press fit	1-press-fit & 4-lap-joint

5 Conclusion and Future Work

In this paper, a knowledge based framework of liaison is developed for the selection of suitable joining process for variant design application. In the knowledge based system various geometric attributes and non-geometric attributes of liaison are represented systematically using ontology. A user interface is developed and a query reasoning engine is implemented for retrieving the suitable processes according to the requirements for a variant product. An industrial case study of two variants of automobile front bumper are used in order to illustrate and validate the proposed knowledge based framework. The knowledge based framework can be extended to resolve the challenges related to the concurrent evolution of product family and its assembly system.

References

1. ElMaraghy, H., Schuh, G., ElMaraghy, W., Piller, F., Schönsleben, P., Tseng, M., Bernard, A.: Product variety management. CIRP Ann.-Manuf. Technol. **62**(2), 629–652 (2013)
2. Lowe, A., McMahon, C., Culley, S.: Information access, storage and use by engineering designers, part 1. J. Inst. Eng. Des. **30**(2), 30–32 (2004)
3. Kim, K.Y., Yang, H., Kim, D.W.: Mereotopological assembly joint information representation for collaborative product design. Robot. Comput.-Integr. Manuf. **24**(6), 744–754 (2008)
4. Mathew, A.T., Rao, C.S.P.: A novel method of using API to generate liaison relationships from an assembly. J. Softw. Eng. Appl. **3**(02), 167 (2010)
5. Swain, A.K., Sen, D., Gurumoorthy, B.: Extended liaison as an interface between product and process model in assembly. Robot. Comput.-Integr. Manuf. **30**(5), 527–545 (2014)
6. Luh, D.B., Ko, Y.T., Ma, C.H.: A structural matrix-based modelling for designing product variety. J. Eng. Des. **22**(1), 1–29 (2011)
7. Bryan, A., Wang, H., Abell, J.: Concurrent design of product families and reconfigurable assembly systems. J. Mech. Des. **135**(5), 051001 (2013)
8. ElMaraghy, H., AlGeddawy, T.: New dependency model and biological analogy for integrating product design for variety with market requirements. J. Eng. Des. **23**(10–11), 722–745 (2012)
9. AlGeddawy, T., ElMaraghy, H.: Reactive design methodology for product family platforms, modularity and parts integration. CIRP J. Manuf. Sci. Technol. **6**(1), 34–43 (2013)
10. L'Eglise, T., De Lit, P., Fouda, P.: A multicriteria decision-aid system for joining process selection. In: 2001 Proceedings of the IEEE International Symposium on Assembly and Task Planning, pp. 324–329. IEEE (2001)
11. Zha, X.F., Lim, S.Y., Fok, S.C.: Integrated knowledge-based assembly sequence planning. Int. J. Adv. Manuf. Technol. **14**(1), 50–64 (1998)
12. Kim, K.Y., Wang, Y., Muogboh, O.S., Nnaji, B.O.: Design formalism for collaborative assembly design. Comput.-Aided Des. **36**(9), 849–871 (2004)
13. Lohse, N., Hirani, H., Ratchev, S., Turitto, M.: An ontology for the definition and validation of assembly processes for evolvable assembly systems. In: 2005 The 6th IEEE International Symposium on Assembly and Task Planning: From Nano to Macro Assembly and Manufacturing, (ISATP 2005), pp. 242–247. IEEE, July 2005
14. Zha, X.F., Sriram, R.D.: Platform-based product design and development: a knowledge-intensive support approach. Knowl.-Based Syst. **19**(7), 524–543 (2006)
15. Demoly, F., Matsokis, A., Kiritsis, D.: A mereotopological product relationship description approach for assembly oriented design. Robot. Comput.-Integr. Manuf. **28**(6), 681–693 (2012)
16. Mas, F., Ríos, J., Gómez, A., Hernández, J.C.: Knowledge-based application to define aircraft final assembly lines at the industrialisation conceptual design phase. Int. J. Comput. Integr. Manuf. **29**(6), 677–691 (2016)
17. 3.3.5 Protégé. http://protege.stanford.edu/download/protege/old-releases/Protege%203.x/3.3.1/
18. http://www.grabcad.com

Traceability and Performance

Traceability in Product Supply Chain: A Global Model

Dharmendra K. Mishra[1(✉)], Aicha Sekhari[1], Sebastien Henry[2], and Yacine Ouzrout[1]

[1] DISP Laboratory, University Lyon 2 Lumiere, Lyon, France
{dharmendra-kumar.mishra,aicha.sekhari}@univ-lyon2.fr, Sebastien.henry@univ-lyon1.fr
[2] DISP Laboratory, University Claude Bernard Lyon 1, Lyon, France
yacine.ouzrout@univ-lyon2.fr

Abstract. Products undergo through various processes in their lifecycle from production till use across the complex supply chain. Multiple actors are involved in these processes, generating ample amount of data. All the actors must share these data to make supply chain agile, effective and efficient to enhance the production control process. A traceability system companies use to trace these data. The current traceability system company use, is based on one step up and one step down principle, that is, immediate neighbouring actors share the information among themselves. No all the actors in supply chain share information among themselves which prevents collaboration. But, all these information are needed across the supply chain to enhance the quality of the product. In this work, we propose a global model for traceability to enhance the collaboration among every actors in supply chain with sharing of all the required information. Based on the model, we propose our data model.

Keywords: Traceability · Product supply chain · Global traceability · Modelling

1 Introduction

Products move from various points in supply chain before reaching to the end users. There are multiple actors in the supply chain having multiple roles and objectives. For example, the manufacturers may be buyer of one product and it may be the seller of some other products. Similarly, a supplier may be supplying more than one products manufactured by multiple manufacturers to more than one manufacturers. This results the supply chain management, a complex process. The actors generate much information at every point in supply chain from production till use of the product. These information are needed for the manufacturers to enhance quality control process. There are many examples of hazards happened in the food products. Mad cow disease, horse meat scandal are a few among them. The food and pharmaceutical products are directly related with people's health. A minor contamination with such products causes a big hazards to people. Companies need to recall the product from market after such contamination. They must pay attention to each and every process involved from

R. Harik et al. (Eds.): PLM 2016, IFIP AICT 492, pp. 377–384, 2016.
DOI: 10.1007/978-3-319-54660-5_34

production till use of the product. They need to know the cause of contamination. They must focus to enhance the processes involved from production till delivery of the products to end users to prevent such happenings in the future. There are some other issues like brand protection, reducing the time to go to market, the companies must focus so as to compete in the market. To achieve all these issues, the actors must need information associated at each point in the supply chain.

As described in the above paragraph, companies are facing with lot many of similar challenges. A timely extraction of information generated at each point is essential for them to cope with the above stated challenges they are facing with. Traceability is a method the companies have been using since a long to trace these data in the supply chain. It is the process of tracking the location of the product in downstream and tracing the process involved during various phases of product development in upstream. As per APICS (American Production and Inventory Control society), traceability is registering and tracking of parts, process and materials used in production by a lot or serial number [1]. In another definition given by GS1 (Global Standards), an organization working in the field of developing various standard, traceability is the ability to follow or study out in detail, or step by step, the history of a certain activity or a process [2].

Enhancing the product quality, delivering the product on right time in the market, fighting product counterfeiting to protect the brand are the key challenges companies must have to cope with. A proper trace and track mechanism is quite helpful and essential to cope with these challenges. There are many actors in supply chain separated around the globe having multiple roles and objectives, make the modern day supply chain: a complex system. Tracing all the information at each point is still a challenge. Many works are found in literature in this area. The authors implement traceability system in pharmaceutical supply chain using RFID (Radio Frequency Identification), EPC global (Electronic Product Code) and ebXML (Electronic business using eXtensible Markup language) [3]. I. Charfeddine et al. proposed an intelligent framework for traceability of containerized goods based on multi agent system and semantic web technology [4]. A traceability system to trace the data is developed in vegetable supply chain [5]. The authors use 2D barcode to identify the product's data from cultivating to marketing and use web based technology to extract these information [5]. In another work, a system is developed to track the information related with beef slaughter till packaging in the beef supply chain [6]. A traceability system is developed and implemented in frozen shrimp products and verified and validated to evaluate the system's performance [7]. In another work, need of traceability system is studied to ensure the food safety [8]. In their work, R. Badia, P. Mishra et al. identify the advancement in technology in the recent traceability system which tracks the information from farm to fork through smart phone [9]. A tracefood framework is developed to exchange the information among actors to solving the proprietary nature of the internal system [10]. But, none of the work guarantee to implement the global traceability system exchanging the information among every actors in global supply chain. In modern traceability system, the actors manage internal traceability using ERP (Enterprise Resource Planning), MES (Manufacturing Execution System) etc. These systems are linked with immediate neighbouring actors. In other word, we can say that output produced by an actor is not linked with input of all the actors. This is a key challenge of modern day supply chain network, which creates a barrier of tracing the cause, when some problem occurs at any point in the network. The purpose of this work is to develop a model to enhance the collaboration among every actors by sharing the traceability data.

The rest of this paper is organized as follow. Section 2 describes the research problem and objectives, A bi-graph model to represent sharing information is described in Sect. 3, proposed data model is described in Sect. 4 and finally Sect. 5 concludes the work.

2 Research Problem and Objective

As discussed in Sect. 2, SCM (Supply Chain Management) is a complex process. There are multiple actors having multiple roles and objectives. They are separated at multiple points around the globe. Large amount of data is generated at each point through these actors in entire life cycle of the product. The actors must share these data among themselves to make product visible across the supply chain to make it agile and transparent. At one point, among these data, some are very crucial and sensitive, while all the actors are not known to each other in the global supply chain on the other, cause them not to share all these data. But the collaboration must be needed by sharing all the necessary information to address the issues discussed in Sect. 2. This work aims to address the issue formulating a research question: how to make collaboration among multiple stakeholders across global supply chain?

3 Bi-Graph Model for the Global Supply Chain

To show the collaboration among multiple stakeholders, we adopt bi-graph model proposed by [11]. But, we consider all the stakeholders in global supply chain in contrast to few. In graph theory, bi-graph (Short form of bipartite graph) is a graph, whose vertices are divided into two disjoint independent sets U and V of which there is an edge from every vertices in U to that of in V, such that $U \cup V$ = All the vertices in the set and $U \cap V = \varphi$ that is null. There are two entities in the supply chain process: Actors and the Products. There exist a multiple relationship between these two entities [11]. Bi-graph has strong ability of reasoning and logic that attracts researcher from academia and industries to use it [11].

Bi-graph is a strong tool that can be used to show these relationship. It is used to model many complex network, modern coding theory etc. [11]. In this work, it helps to show the various relationship among the entities, which is used to trace the required information at every point through an algorithm, as our future work.

We consider a main manufacturing company M1 producing the product by taking sub products, raw materials etc. supplied by more than one suppliers. Figure 1 shows supply chain process of the various actors.

The symbol M, S, D, and C stands for manufacturer, supplier, distributer and customer respectively. More than one suppliers supply the product to main manufacturer (M1) manufactured by more than one manufacturers (M2 to Mn). The main manufacturer after its internal process (producing, packaging, etc.) produces the main

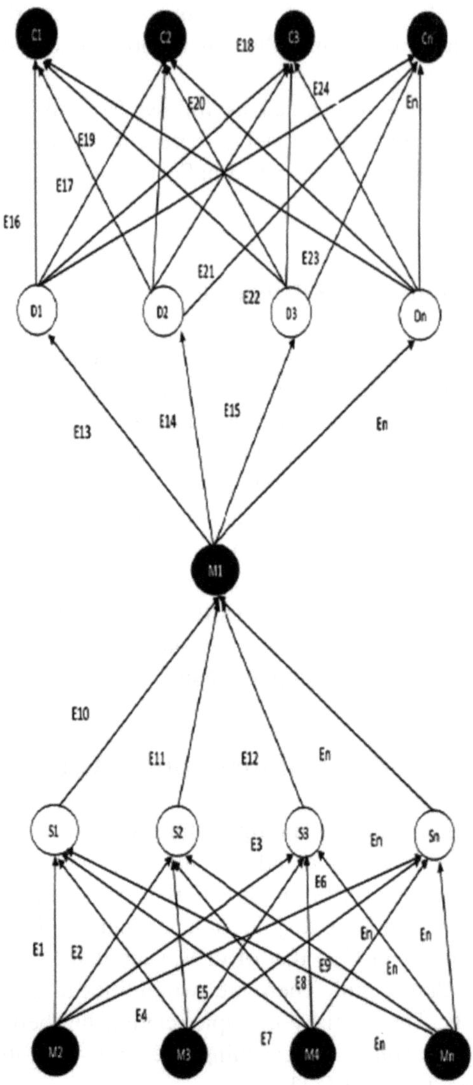

Fig. 1. Supply chain process

product and sends them to various customers through various distributers. The customer may be a retailer, a wholesaler or an end user. The relationship is shown by various edges from E1, E2….En.

We model this scenario using the bi-graph technique as shown in Fig. 2. Let us consider G (A, B, E) be a bi-graph where A = A1, A2…..An represents the actors (Manufacturer, Supplier, Distributer and Customer) shown in dark circle. B = B1, B2…..Bn represents the sub-products, raw materials or finished product shown in white circle. E = E1, E2……En represents the edges connecting the two vertices. The edges

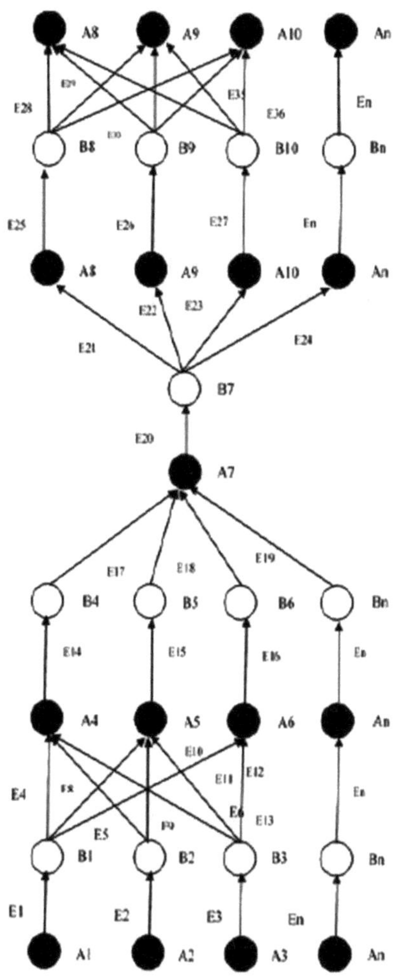

Fig. 2. Bi-graph model of supply chain process

represents the relationship between two vertices sets. The relationship is one to one, one to many, many to one and many to many.

The model is applicable to any product manufacturing company. It is necessary to identify the specific point through which the product undergoes. This depends on the type of industry. For example, if we consider a food industry, the product moves from farm to the manufacturer to the distributer or transporter and finally to the end users. Actors produce information through internal process at all of these points. For example, at farm, the farmers do the cultivation, maintains the soil information, bow seeds etc. Similarly, the manufacturer maintains the supplier's information, processing information of raw materials, packaging information etc. It is also necessary to identify the type of the products. The product may be semi-finished or the final one.

The traceability system stores all these information produced by actors at each link that is traceable if needed. In the next section, we explain the data model we developed to show the types of data generated by the actors and the relationship between them.

4 Data Model

The information sharing and management requires the logical representation of data produced by each actors. Figure 3 shows the data model we propose. It is assumed that there is one main manufacturer who manufactures the final product by assembling or processing the semi-finished products supplied by more than one suppliers. Suppliers in turn supply the semi-finished products manufactured by more than one manufacturers. There are more than one distributer delivering the finished product to many customers. We consider each actors of supply chain and address the issue of complexity. Some

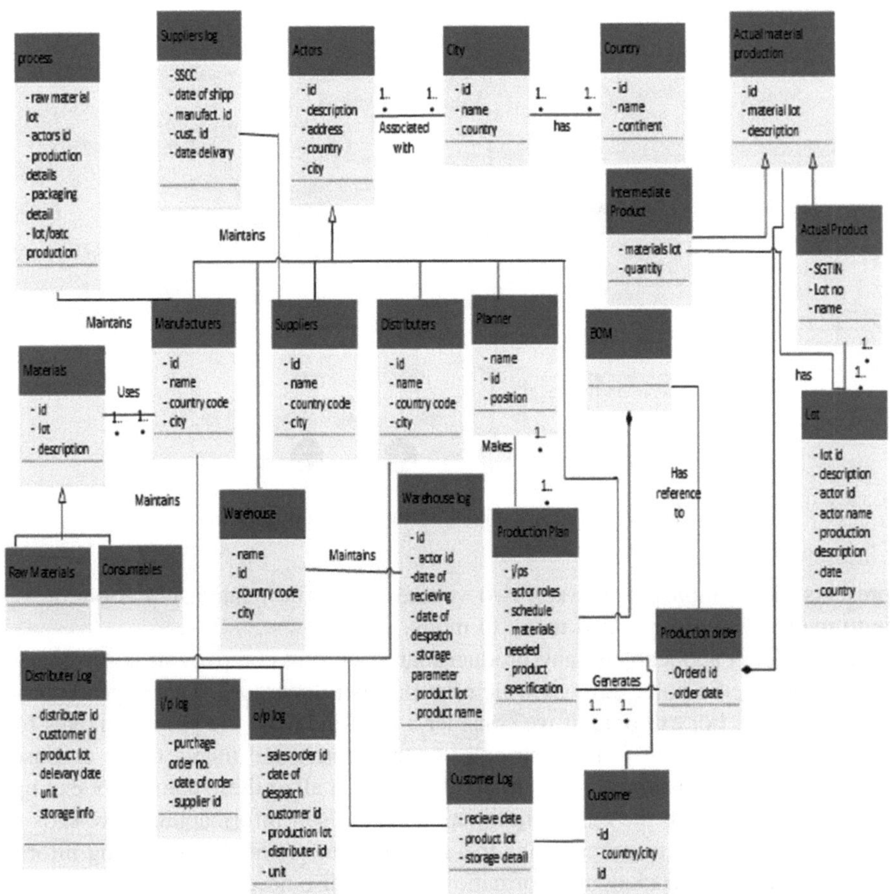

Fig. 3. Data model

works related with data models are found in literature. Thierno et al. develop a data model to handle unitary traceability based on IEC 62264 and GS1 global standard [12].

The authors aims to represent the internal traceability data to find the root cause and facilitate data exchange. In another work, a data model is proposed to support the traceability process in the food supply chain [13]. Similarly, M. khabbaji et al. propose data model to manage the lot traceability on the basis of make order [14]. The model is said to support to control the material flow in all quality and production process. Some other works [14, 15], develop internal traceability data model in terms of materials and process data registration. We propose to address the global traceability data model tracing each data at each point from production till the use of the product. It starts with company planner who makes the production plan based on which the order is generated. The production plan also contains the BOM of the product. Each actors are assigned with unique identification number. The actors are linked with city and country to show the geographic distribution. The country and city has unique identification code which act as the foreign key for all the actors. All the actors maintain its own log storing all the necessary information. The manufacturers maintains i/p log that contains date of order, order id and supplier id to show on which date it receives the semi-finished product and which supplier is responsible to supply that product. It also maintains o/p log and processing information. The output log contains the sales order and customer information with distributer id. The processing data contains how the products are manufactured, the actors involved in packaging, warehousing etc. The supplier, warehouse and distributer also maintain their own log having the information like date of delivery, date of receiving, storage information, SSCC (Serial Shipping Container Code), customer's information, product lot etc. The product lot has relation with all the actor with reference to country id to track the location of the product with lot id, description, actors involved etc.

The final product contains SGTIN (Serialized Global Trade Item Number), lot number and name of the product having the relation with lot, intermediate product and actual material production.

The data model shown in Fig. 3 has all the traceable data and their relationship. These data are traced putting lot-id as keyword through a novel algorithm as our future work and implemented in a user friendly web based system based on cloud. We use EPC global network as a standard and use case for the validation.

5 Conclusion

The product's safety in the global supply chain is still a challenge. Companies need to enhance the product's quality and make it safer to prevent some sort of problem across the chain. To achieve this, a global traceability system is needed to trace all the required information. But, the actors don't share all the information among themselves. All the actors are not well known to each other. They produce various sensitive information which they do not share in the network, which prevents the collaboration among them. In this paper, we propose a bi-graph model to show the relationship among all the stakeholders. Based on this model, we propose a data model to show types of data generated at each point and link between them. The model reduces the supply chain complexity by increasing the collaboration among every actors.

References

1. Alfaro, J.A., Rabade, L.A.: Traceability as a strategic tool to improve inventory management: a case study in the food industry. Int. J. Prod. Econ. **118**, 104–110 (2009)
2. The GS1 Traceability standard: What you need to know, GS1 (2007)
3. Barchetti, U., Bucciero, A., et al.: Impact of RFID, EPC and B2B on traceability management of the pharmaceutical supply chain. Department of Innovation Engineering, University of Salento, Italy
4. Charfeddine, I., Mounir, B., et al.: Intelligent framework for traceability of containerized goods. IEEE (2011)
5. Qiao, S., Wei, W., et al.: Research on vegetable supply chain traceability model on two dimensional barcode. In: International Symposium on Computational Intelligence and Design (2013)
6. Feng, J., Fu, Z., et al.: Development and evaluation on a RFID based traceability system for cattle/beef quality safety in China. J. Food Control **31**, 314–325 (2013)
7. Djatha, T., Ginantaka, A.: An analysis and design of frozen shrimp traceability system based on digital business ecosystem. IEEE (2014)
8. Aung, M.M., Chang, Y.S.: Traceability in a food supply chain: safety and quality perspectives. Food Control **39**, 172–184 (2014)
9. Badia, R., Mishra, P., et al.: Food traceability: new trends and recent advances, a review. Food Control **57**, 393–401 (2015)
10. Stordy, J., Thakur, M., Olsen, P.: The tracefood framework-principles and guidelines for implementing traceability in food value chains. J. Food Eng. **115**, 41–48 (2013)
11. Li, X., Liu, X., et al.: Bigraph-based modeling and tracing for the food chain system. In: IEEE International Conference on Information Science and Cloud Computing Companion (2013)
12. Diallo, T.M.L., Henry, S., Ouzrout, Y.: Using unitary traceability for an optimal product recall. In: Grabot, B., Vallespir, B., Gomes, S., Bouras, A., Kiritsis, D. (eds.) APMS 2014. IAICT, vol. 438, pp. 159–166. Springer, Heidelberg (2014). doi:10.1007/978-3-662-44739-0_20
13. Pizzuti, T., Mirabelli, G.: The global track & trace system for food: general framework and functioning principles. J. Food Eng. **159**, 16–35 (2015)
14. Khabbazi, M.R., Ismail, N., Ismail, Y.: Data modelling of traceability information for manufacturing control system. IEEE (2009)
15. Jansen-Vullers, M.H., Van Drop, C.A., et al.: Managing traceability information in manufacture. Int. J. Manag. **23**, 395–413 (2003)

Processing and Visual Analyze of Heterogeneous and Multidimensional Data in Biomedical PLM Context

Marianne Allanic[1(✉)], Pierre-Yves Hervé[2], Alexandre Durupt[3], Marc Joliot[2], Philippe Boutinaud[1], and Benoit Eynard[3]

[1] CADESIS Company, Courbevoie, France
{mallanic,pboutinaud}@cadesis.com
[2] Université de Bordeaux, GIN, IMN, UMR 5293 CNRS CEA, Bordeaux, France
{pierre-yves.herve,marc.joliot}@u-bordeaux.fr
[3] Sorbonne Université, Université de Technologie de Compiègne (UTC), UMR 7337, Compiègne, France
{alexandre.durupt,benoit.eynard}@utc.fr

Abstract. The emergence of PLM for biomedical imaging lifecycle management highlights the needs for management and analysis of heterogeneous, complex and multidimensional data in PLM systems. Data provenance in biomedical imaging domain is complex, notably provenance of processing data, and to ensure full traceability in a purpose of reuse, processing operations must be integrated to PLM systems and processing provenance must be easily analyzable by users. The DIMP (Data Integrated Management and Processing) method was designed for this objective: it allows user to launch easily processing chains from PLM systems and ensures a full management of provenance. The MDG (Multidimensional Dynamic Graph) representation is introduced to formalize complex provenance and data relationships. JGEX (Json Graph EXchange) file format and NeuroGraphViewer web graph visualization client have been developed to facilitate the analysis of MDG. An application of the DIMP method to the study of functional brain connectivity through MDG analysis encourages further work on analysis of complex relationships in PLM systems.

Keywords: Heterogeneous data · Multidimensional data · Graph · Processing integration · Biomedical · PLM (Product Lifecycle Management)

1 Introduction

The application of Product Lifecycle Management (PLM) concepts to the management of biomedical imaging study lifecycle [3] raises new challenges for the PLM community. Biomedical imaging data are heterogeneous (nature, type and source), due to the natural interdisciplinary of the domain. The lifecycle of a biomedical imaging study is composed of four stages: (1) study specifications, (2) raw data, (3) derived data and (4) published data. The high cost of data (both acquisition and processing) and the need

R. Harik et al. (Eds.): PLM 2016, IFIP AICT 492, pp. 385–398, 2016.
DOI: 10.1007/978-3-319-54660-5_35

for reproducibility make data reuse and sharing a necessity [15]. Therefore, keeping data provenance throughout stages of study is a strong concern for the community.

Data processing in biomedical imaging domain is complex: many steps of registration (temporal, spatial) and reconciliation are required to get readable images, and even more steps to analyze them. Obviously, biomedical PLM users cannot set up processing provenance by hand, neither analyze it at a glance in the system in order to reuse data (raw, derived and processing steps). The paper addresses these last issues, by proposing a method for integrated processing management in PLM systems and a way of representing complex relationships so they can be easily analyzed.

Section 2 introduces existing approaches for the processing and analyze of complex relationships and heterogeneous data, from biomedical imaging domain and PLM points of views. Section 3 presents the Data Integrated Management and Processing (DIMP) method, which ensures full provenance of processing data. Section 4 presents the Multidimensional Dynamic Graph (MDG) representation in order to analyze provenance and complex data in biomedical imaging domain. In Sect. 5, an application of the DIMP method to the study of functional brain connectivity through MDG analysis is developed. To end with, the results are discussed in Sect. 6.

2 Approaches for Processing and Analyze of Complex Relationships and Heterogeneous Data

First, data processing is introduced both for biomedical imaging and PLM domains. Second, representation of complex relationships with graphs is discussed. To end with, a synthesis of existing approaches towards our concern is proposed.

2.1 Data Processing

Data processing is the operation of transforming data through algorithms, which results in simplified, combined or formatted data. In order to be able to understand how data were obtained and how to reproduce exactly a processing chain, keeping data provenance is unavoidable.

2.1.1 Processing of Biomedical Imaging Data

Provenance is crucial in biomedical imaging domain [13]: cohorts get bigger and bigger, data acquisitions are expensive and results must be reproducible – both for scientific cross validation and longitudinal studies. As images processing is very complex (dependencies, loops, multi-inputs…), the community of biomedical imaging developed pipeline tools that handle workflows and calls to required libraries, notably LONI pipeline [8], Nipype [9] and PSOM [6]. Figure 1 shows as a graph a Nipype workflow to compute raw images as a graph in Tulip visualization software. Processing steps are complex and the chain is difficult to understand at a glance, which implies using interactive visualization tools.

More and more data repositories in biomedical imaging propose integrated features to launch workflows, however no one offers provenance management of derived data

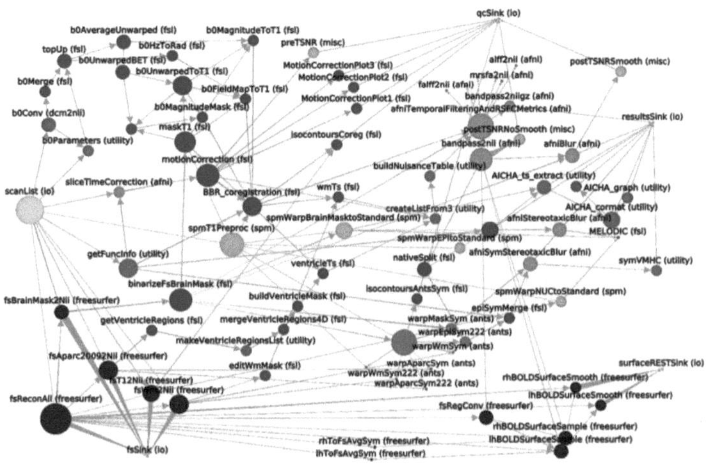

Fig. 1. Graph representation of a Nipype workflow, visualized in Tulip software. processing units are linked by input data flows. colors represent software applications. (Color figure online)

once the computation is done. Processing provenance have been described by two major models: process-oriented model [17], that suits to frameworks, and data-oriented model [16], that suits better for sharing data between laboratories.

2.1.2 Data Processing in PLM Systems

Data processing integration was not an initial concern in PLM systems. However, simulation lifecycle management has become very valuable to manufacturing companies, as simulation predicts the behavior of a system without performing a physical experiment, which saves time and costs. A simulation process is composed of three steps, as defined by [2]: (1) modelling, (2) solving and (3) post-processing. At each of these steps, choices are made: input Computer-Aided Design (CAD) model, parameters, hypotheses and Computer-Aided Engineering (CAE) tool to use. As these steps are, most of the time, embedded in CAE systems, the traceability of simulation processing is not fully covered in PLM systems.

2.2 Graph Analyze of Complex Relationships

Data dependencies can become complex when it deals with the modelling of systems and processes, whatever their nature – physical, biological or software. One way to analyze these complex relationships is to visualize them with graphs. A graph G is commonly defined as a set of vertices V and a set of edges E, such as (where u and v are any vertices of the graph):

$$G = (V, E) \; with \; E \subseteq \{(u, v) | u, v \in V, u \neq v\}. \tag{1}$$

Table 1 present the definitions of the main types of graphs used to represent heterogeneous data with complex relationships, depending on data characteristics.

Table 1. Definitions of the main types of complex graphs.

Graph type	Definition
Multivariate M	Graph with n attributes A are added to vertices and edges, such as (for vertices, similar for edges): $A = \{A_1, \ldots, A_n\} = (a_{ij})(j = 1\ldots\|V\|; i = 1\ldots n)$ with A_i a column of the table of attributes and $a_u = (a_{u1}, \ldots, a_{un})$ describes all attribute values of node u [11]
Compound C	$C = (G, T)$ is composed of $G = (V, E_G)$ and a tree $T = (V, E_T, r)$, where r is the root vertex, sharing a set of edges, such as $\forall e = (v_1, v_2) \in E_G$, $v_1 \notin path_T(r, v_2)$ and $v_2 \notin path_T(r, v_1)$. Vertices sharing a parent in T belong to the same group and vertices linked to the same parent in G share a generic relationships [1]
Dynamic Γ	Sequence of graphs $\Gamma = (G_1, G_2, \ldots, G_n)$ where $G_i = (V_i, E_i)$ are static graphs whose subscript refers to a time point $\tau = (t_1, t_2, \ldots, t_n)$ [5]

Multivariate graphs allow to take data attributes into account during analysis. The types of graphs can be combined, by example a multivariate dynamic graph.

2.2.1 Graph Analysis in Biomedical Domain

Graphs are used a lot in biomedical domain, to analyze proteins, genes, brain organization, etc. and also processing workflows (see Sect. 2.1.1). Data to be represented by graphs are multivariate (characteristics of brain regions, proteins, algorithms…), dynamic (evolution of brain organization through ageing, evolution of genes combinations, longitudinal studies…), multidimensional (comparison of subjects and groups of subjects in a cohort depending on their characteristics, comparison of families of proteins, comparison of processing chains…). However, graph analysis (both algorithmic and visual) in these domains is at its beginning, as it is for instance in neuroimaging [10].

2.2.2 Relationships Analysis in PLM Systems

PLM systems manage heterogeneous data (concepts, file formats, metadata…), complex relationships (dependencies) and multidimensional data (BOMs, versioning…). Limits of current PLM interfaces to analyze complex relationships have already been highlighted [4]: no features allow users to check relationships consistence, to browse efficiently relationships, to analyze dependencies or to detect patterns.

2.3 Synthesis of Presented Approaches

Data processing workflows in biomedical imaging domain are very complex, so processing should be integrated to be able to manage full provenance in PLM systems. Therefore, a first concern of the paper is to address the integration of processing chains in PLM systems, from workflow launch to the management of resulting data.

Graphs are a good representation for complex relationships. Provenance data and biomedical data in general are multivariate, dynamic and multidimensional. However, current graph types cannot represent all these types of data combined. A second concern in the paper is to propose a suitable graph representation to enable multidimensional dynamic graph analysis.

3 Data Integrated Management and Processing (DIMP)

In a context of biomedical PLM (Biomedical imaging Lifecycle Management – BiLM), data is traced at every step of study: from study specifications to published results. In imaging domain, processing chains to obtain useful derived data are complex (multi-inputs, dependencies, loops). To ensure full traceability, the *Data Integrated Management and Processing* (DIMP) method propose to integrate processing tasks to the PLM system: users launch workflows from PLM interface and resulting data are automatically uploaded and linked to inputs, definitions and parameters data. First an extension of the BMI-LM data model for biomedical PLM is presented: it allows to reuse easily processing chains on new data. Second, the stages of the DIMP method are described.

3.1 Workflow Input (WFI): Definition of the Integrated Processing

The BioMedical Imaging – Lifecycle Management (BMI-LM, see details in [3]) data model is composed of generic objects representing concepts associated with specific classes based on domain ontologies. The nineteen generic concepts (see Table 2 below) are divided in three categories:

1. *Definition objects*: they described how *result objects* were obtained and they can be reused from one study to another. They are part of the provenance strategy.
2. *Result objects*: they store data of the study, raw and derived, in shape of datasets (files) and metadata. They belong to a specified study.
3. *Ambivalent objects*: depending on the context, these objects can be used as a *definition object* or a *result object.* They are part of the provenance strategy.

Basically, to launch a processing, users must define: (1) data to compute, (2) algorithms to apply, (3) values of algorithmic parameters. In biomedical imaging domain, a major concern is the reproducibility of results, both on same data and on new data: in longitudinal imaging studies, subjects are having imaging exams regularly on a long period of time (two to ten years), and exactly the same processing chains must be applied to data can be compared.

To meet this objective, a generic object is added to the BMI-LM data model: *WorkFlow Input* (WFI). Its role is to gather all the definition objects needed to launch a processing chain: the processing chain itself (object: *Processing Definition*), processing parameters (object: *Processing Parameters*) and the definition of input data (objects: *Data Unit Definition, Processing Unit Definition*). These last data are crucial: they allow the PLM system to query the right data, at any moment, for the subjects selected by the user. Figure 2 shows how using WFI is particularly valuable to reproduce same processing chain several time on new data (acquisitions on the fly, longitudinal studies, new studies).

Table 2. Generic objects of the BMI-LM data model according to study stages and categories.

Study stages	Definition objects	Result objects	Ambivalent objects
1.Specifications		Study	
2.Raw data	Subject	StudySubject	
	Exam Definition	Exam Result	
	Acquisition Definition	Acquisition Result	
	Data Unit Definition	Data Unit Result	
	Acquisition Device		
3.Derived data	Processing Definition	Processing Result	Reference Data
	Processing Unit Definition	Processing Unit Result	Subject Group
	Processing Parameter		
	Software Tool		
4.Published results			Bibliography Reference

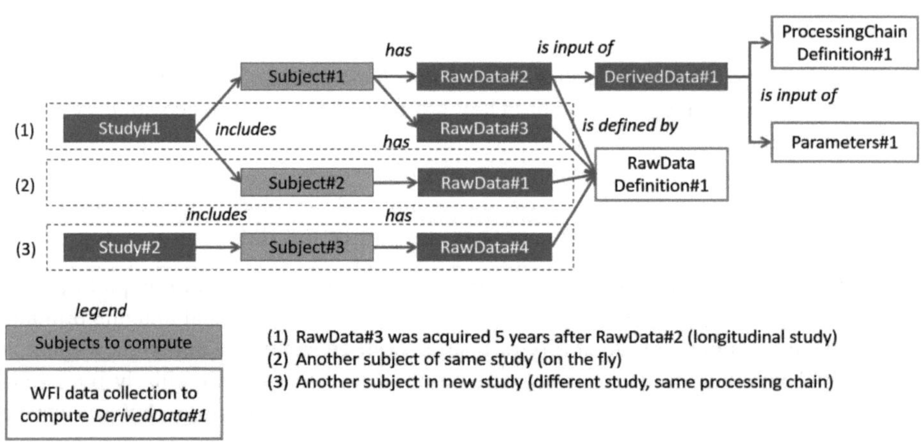

Fig. 2. Diagram showing interest of WFI for three use cases in a simplified representation of data management in PLM systems with BMI-LM concepts. Definition of input data (raw data in the figure, but it could be derived data), definition of processing chain and parameters are collected in WFI by users. When a processing chain has to be computed again on new data, WFI is reused and the targeted subjects are given to the system to query corresponding input data. For use case (1), appropriate raw data is found by excluding data that has already been computed with the processing chain and parameters of the WFI.

3.2 Stages of Integrated Processing in PLM

The main objective of Data Integrated Management and Processing (DIMP) method is to ensure quality provenance of derived data by reducing manual operations from users: data resulting from processing chains are automatically linked to input data, definition of processing chain and parameters. The DIMP method is defined by the following stages:

Initialization

1. (user) build or identify WFI
2. (user) launch integrated processing workflow
   - select WFI
   - select subjects

Workflow execution

3. (PLM system) query input data
4. (PLM system) export in working folder
   - input data
   - definition of the processing chain
   - parameters of the processing chain
5. (pipeline script stored in the definition of the processing chain) execute processing operations locally or on computing grid

Traceability operations

6. (PLM system) upload resulting data
   - create corresponding *result objects*
   - link *result objects* to input data, and *definition objects* (definition of the processing chain and parameters)
7. (user) receive an email: data are ready

4 Multidimensional Dynamic Graph (MDG) Analysis

Section 2.2 highlighted that existing types of graphs are not suitable to represent multivariate data evolving through several dimensions. This section presents a new way of representing and analyzing complex relationships between heterogeneous data. First, a new type of graphs, *Multidimensional Dynamic Graphs* (MDG), is introduced. Second, a file format, *JGEX*, and a web graph visualization client, *NeuroGraphViewer*, are introduced: they were developed to fit the characteristics of MDGs and allows their storage and analysis.

4.1 Multidimensional Dynamic Graphs (MDG) to Analyze Complex Provenance

A *Multidimensional Dynamic Graph* (MDG) Γ is defined by a sequence of graphs:

$$\Gamma = (G_1, G_2, \ldots, G_n). \quad (2)$$

where $G_i = (V_i, E_i)$ are static graphs, called *configurations*, whose subscript refers to a *dimensional* moment $M = (m_1, m_2, \ldots, m_n)$: every dimensional moment represents a snapshot of the MDG. Attributes may be associated to every element of the MDG (vertices and edges) and the graph itself. These attributes may evolve according to the dimensions. An element of a dimension is called a *condition*. An illustration of a MDG is given in the Fig. 3 below to help reader's understanding.

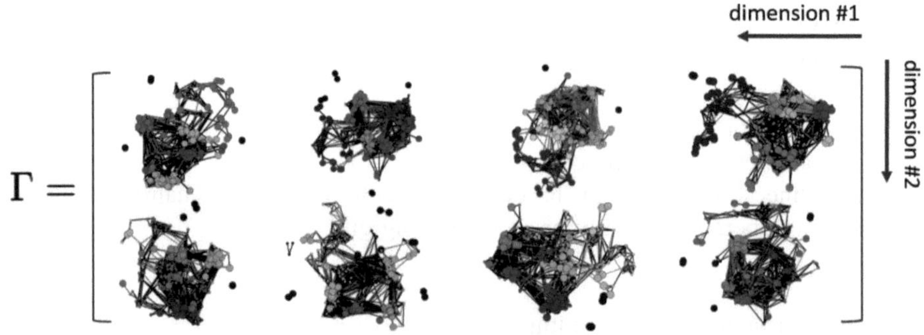

Fig. 3. The multidimensional dynamic graph Γ is composed in height configurations, according to conditions of dimensions: four conditions for dimension #1 and two conditions for dimension #2.

The MDG allows multivariate data, as well as complex and compound relationships that evolve according to many dimensions.

4.2 Json Graph Exchange (JGEX) Format to Store MDG Data

Many graph formats are available; in order to choose a suitable one for MDGs, eleven of them (most commonly used and referred) were tested according to the following characteristics – all required to store MDGs: weighted graphs, attributes on elements of the graph, visualization attributes, default value on an attribute, hierarchical graphs, dynamic graphs, multidimensional dynamic graphs, many graphs, attributes on graphs, groups of nodes and references across graphs.

The result of the comparison in presented in Table 3. No format is currently able to store MDG characteristics. GEXF (Graph Exchange Format) can be extended and is only missing multidimensional dynamic graphs and references across graphs, however XML language is quite wordy which implies heavier files. Therefore, there is a strong need to create a new file format to store MDGs.

Table 3. Comparison of the characteristics of existing graph format.

	Weighted graphs	Attributes	Visualisation attributes	Default value of an attribute	Hierarchical graphs	Dynamic graphs	Multidimen-sional dynamic	Many graphs	Attributes on graphs	Groups of nodes	References across graphs
CSV	■										
DL Ucinet	■	■									
DOT Graphviz	■		■								
GDF	■	■	■	■							
GEXF	■	■	■	■	■	■		■	■	■	
GML	■	■	■								
GraphML	■	■	■	■	■	■			■		
NET Pajek	■	■									
TLP Tulip	■	■	■	■	■						
VNA Netdraw	■	■									
DGS	■	■									

Json Graph Exchange (JGEX) format has been designed to support the exchange of dynamic multidimensional data between programs and applications. JGEX format is an extension of JSON format, and its schema can be found online[1]. The main structure of a JGEX file is composed of some metadata, a list of graphs and a list of definitions of attributes. Any defined attribute can be a dimension, and any attribute can vary along a dimension, which allows infinite possibilities.

4.3 NeuroGraphViewer Web Client

Besides topological analysis, interactive visual analysis is useful to understand complexity: it plays the role of an external cognitive support [12]. However, existing graph viewers do not allow browsing of multidimensional dynamic data. NeuroGraphViewer is web client developed for BIOMIST project (see Sect. 5.1) that responds to MDG requirements, its last stable version is available online[2].

Distinctive features of NeuroGraphViewer are (1) the management of filters and display parameters as specific graphs, which allows them to be exported and imported easily, and (2) the possibility to connect to Teamcenter PLM system (edited by Siemens Industry Software), in order to query the database and visually browse and analyze data relationships. Other main features are (3) browsing through dimensions of MDGs and through multi-views display, (4) import and export of JGEX files (including filters and display parameters) as well as other graph formats (TLP, GEXF) and CSV so that any user can build a graph without learning specific formats, and (5) the connection

[1] http://www.swocloud.net/redmine/projects/biomist-public/wiki/En-jgex.

[2] http://212.83.190.113/.

to a selection of graph analysis libraries to perform topology and layout algorithms, in particular some algorithms were developed to fit MDG analysis.

5 Application: Management and Analyze of Neuroimaging Data in Teamcenter PLM Center

This section presents an application of the DIMP method to the study of functional brain connectivity through MDG analysis, in the context of BIOMIST project.

5.1 Use Case: Study of Functional Brain Connectivity with Biomedical PLM

Functional brain connectivity studies aim at improving understanding of brain organization and how brain regions are working together, with Magnetic Resonance Imaging (MRI) techniques. Subjects' brains are segmented in regions, and the connectivity of each pair of regions is measured, which can be represented by graphs (vertices are regions and connectivity values are edges). Subjects' characteristics (sex, handedness, psychology, genetics…) affect brain organization, therefore MDG are used to represent brain connectivity according to many dimensions.

The proposed use case covers all phases of a study: from study specification and raw data to derived data analysis and publication of results. The stages of the uses case are presented in Fig. 4.

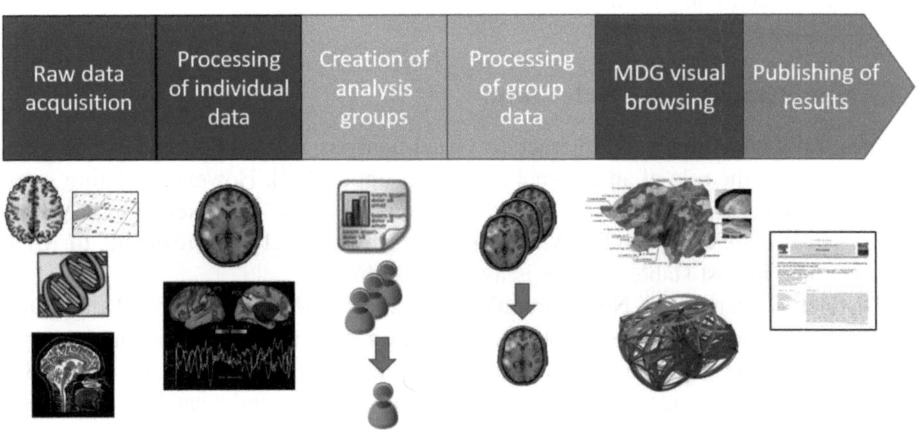

Fig. 4. Stages of the use case

5.2 Application to the BIL&GIN Dataset

The BIL&GIN dataset [14] has been created by the GIN research group to study hemispheric specialization from cognitive, behavioral, genetic and functional points of view. 45% of the 453 subjects in the dataset are left-handed, which is a bigger proportion than average stated in population.

The dataset is managed for the BIOMIST project [7] in Teamcenter 10 PLM system (edited by Siemens Industry Software) with the BMI-LM data model. A domain classification has been designed based on existing neuroimaging ontologies, and it was implemented in Teamcenter module of classification. Confidentiality and Protected Health Information (PHI) are managed thanks to regular access management and to the project structure (one project is one study) available in the software.

The use case is applied, processing data are computed with DIMP method and final MDG data is stored in JGEX format and analyzed with NeuroGraphViewer web client. DIMP method is implemented with Nipype pipeline tool that drives processing workflows on local computing grids.

Figure 5 presents results obtained with the DIMP method on the BIL&GIN dataset: the complete processing chain is traced in the PLM system, including data inputs, processing definition and processing parameters. MDG of brain connectivity are processed in JGEX format and can be analyzed in NeuroGraphViewer web client.

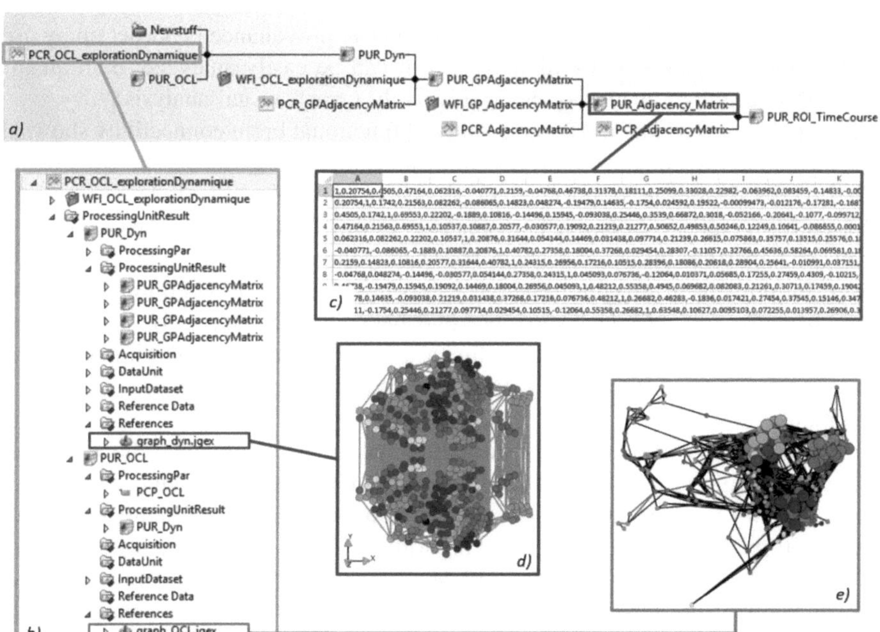

Fig. 5. View of some data resulting from the application of DIMP method to the BIL&GIN dataset in Teamcenter PLM system. (a) Processing chain from an individual adjacency matrix to the final MDG to study functional brain connectivity. (b) Data and relationships of the final layout processing of the MDG: data inputs (adjacency matrices of the 4 groups), processing definition, processing parameters, final JGEX dataset. (c) Adjacency matrix of an individual. (d) and (e) Visualization of the MDG in NeuroGraphViewer web client, respectively with a 2D-anatomical layout and a OCL-force layout.

NeuroGraphViewer also allows to query objects from Teamcenter. In the interface of the web client, users may analyze queried relationships with available libraries of algorithms, apply filters and adjust the layout in an interactive way. The graph created from Teamcenter objects and relationships can be saved in JGEX format for further analyses.

A video showing the whole steps of the use case, from individual raw data to dynamic graphs of subjects' groups, in Teamcenter and in NeuroGraphViewer is available online at the web site of BIOMIST project (http://biomist.fr).

6 Conclusion and Discussion

The work presented addresses integrated processing management and analysis of complex relationships in biomedical PLM systems. The DIMP method ensures a complete and integrated provenance of processing data in PLM systems. MDG representation allows to formalize heterogeneous data and complex (dynamic and multi-dimensional) relationships. A new file format, JGEX, allows to store and to exchange MDG data in PLM systems and with NeuroGraphViewer web client.

The combination of these methods and tools constitutes an efficient way to manage quality derived data with full processing provenance: provenance is not set up by users, which prevents mistakes and omissions, and it can be easily analyzed, both quantitatively (graph topology analysis) and qualitatively (graph visual analysis).

The application of this work to the study of functional brain connectivity shows that biomedical imaging domain would benefit from using PLM systems. The work done on the BIL&GIN dataset in Teamcenter PLM system is understandable by users external to the study – thanks to a complete provenance –, which means that derived data can be reused, and that the processing chain that was computed can be applied to another dataset. In biomedical imaging research – and in particular in neuroimaging –, correlations between subjects' characteristics and behavior are looked for, which implies that data are analyzed through many dimensions. By enabling multidimensional representation of data, MDGs open promising perspectives for finding patterns and correlations.

However, graph drawing and information visualization domains have started to focus on dynamic graphs very recently (the last ten years) and there are still some aspects that have not been addressed, no speaking of MDGs. So future work should focus on proposing topology and layout algorithms for MDG analysis, which would be useful both for provenance analysis in PLM systems and biological networks analysis.

Even if this work was developed for biomedical imaging study management, there is nothing preventing manufacturing industry from benefiting of it. First, the DIMP method could be used to enhance simulation lifecycle management. Second, relationships between the different BOMs of a product (requirements, eBOM, mBOM…) are complex and MDG representation could be of great interest for understanding impacts of a change in the requirements, to check for consistency through BOMs or to analyze the evolutions of configurations of a product.

Acknowledgments. The work presented in the paper is conducted within the ANR (Agence Nationale de la Recherche)-funded project BIOMIST (no. ANR-13-CORD-0007) for thematic axis no. 2 of the Contint 2013 Call for Proposal: from content to knowledge and big data. This study also benefitted from ABACI, a project that is supported by a public grant from the French Agence Nationale de la Recherche within the context of the Investments for the Future Program, referenced ANR-10-LABX-57 and named TRAIL. The authors would like to thank Thierry Brial, Nicolas Boulic and Arthur Grioche from Cadesis, and Pierre-Yves Hervé from the GIN, who supported technically their work.

References

1. Abello, J., Kobourov, Stephen, G., Yusufov, R.: Visualizing large graphs with compound-fisheye views and treemaps. In: Pach, J. (ed.) GD 2004. LNCS, vol. 3383, pp. 431–441. Springer, Heidelberg (2005). doi:10.1007/978-3-540-31843-9_44
2. Adams, V.A.: Designer's Guide to Simulation with Finite Element Analysis. NAFEMS, Knutsford (2008)
3. Allanic, M., Durupt, A., Joliot, M., Eynard, B., Boutinaud, P.: Towards a data model for PLM application in Bio-Medical Imaging. In: Horvath, I., Rusak, Z. (eds.) Proceedings of TMCE 2014, 19–23 May 2014, pp. 365–376. Organizing Committee of TMCE 2014, Budapest, Hungary (2014)
4. Allanic, M., Brial, T., Durupt, A., Joliot, M., Boutinaud, P., Eynard, B.: Towards an enhancement of relationships browsing in mature PLM systems. In: Fukuda, S., Bernard, A., Gurumoorthy, B., Bouras, A. (eds.) PLM 2014. IAICT, vol. 442, pp. 345–354. Springer, Heidelberg (2014). doi:10.1007/978-3-662-45937-9_34
5. Beck, F., Burch, M., Diehl, S., Weiskopf, D.: The state of the art in visualizing dynamic graphs. In: 2014 9th-13th InfoVis Conference EuroVis STAR (2014)
6. Bellec, P., Lavoie-Courchesne, S., Dickinson, P., Lerch, J., Zijdenbos, A., Evans, A.C.: The pipeline system for Octave and Matlab (PSOM): a lightweight scripting framework and execution engine for scientific workflows. Front. Neuroinf. **6**, 7 (2012)
7. BIOMIST. http://biomist.fr. Accessed 04 Jan 2016
8. Dinov, I.D., Van Horn, J.D., Lozev, K.M., Magsipoc, R., Petrosyan, P., Liu, Z., Toga, A.W.: Efficient, distributed and interactive neuroimaging data analysis using the LONI pipeline. Front. Neuroinf. **3**, 22 (2009)
9. Gorgolewski, K., Burns, C.D., Madison, C., Clark, D., Halchenko, Y.O., Waskom, M.L., Ghosh, S.S.: Nipype: a flexible, lightweight and extensible neuroimaging data processing framework in python. Front. Neuroinf. **5**, 13 (2011)
10. Hutchison, R.M., Womelsdorf, T., Allen, E.A., Bandettini, P.A., Calhoun, V.D., Corbetta, M., Penna, D., Stefania, D., Jeff, H., Glover, G.H., Gonzalez-Castillo, J., et al.: Dynamic functional connectivity: promise, issues, and interpretations. Neuroimage **80**, 360–378 (2013)
11. Jusufi, I.: Multivariate networks: visualization and interaction techniques. Ph.D thesis (2013)
12. Keller, T., Tergan, S.-O.: Visualizing knowledge and information: an introduction. In: Tergan, S.-O., Keller, T. (eds.) Knowledge and Information Visualization. LNCS, vol. 3426, pp. 1–23. Springer, Heidelberg (2005). doi:10.1007/11510154_1
13. MacKenzie-Graham, A.J., Van Horn, J.D., Woods, R.P., Crawford, K.L., Toga, A.W.: Provenance in neuroimaging. NeuroImage **42**(1), 178–195 (2008)

14. Mazoyer, B., Mellet, E., Perchey, G., Zago, L., Crivello, F., Jobard, G., Delcroix, N., Vigneau, M., Leroux, G., Petit, L., et al.: BIL&GIN: a neuroimaging, cognitive, behavioral, and genetic database for the study of human brain lateralization. NeuroImage **124**, 1225–1231 (2015)
15. Poline, J.-B., Breeze, J.L, Ghosh, S., Gorgolewski, K., Halchenko, Y.O, Hanke, M., Haselgrove, C., Helmer, K.G, Keator, D.B, Marcus, D.S, Poldrack, R.A, Schwartz, Y.,
16. Simmhan, Y.L., Plale, B., Gannon, D.: A survey of data provenance in e-science. ACM Sigmod Rec. **34**(3), 31–36 (2005)
17. Zhao, J., Goble, C., Stevens, R., Bechhofer, S.: Semantically linking and browsing provenance logs for e-science. In: Bouzeghoub, M., Goble, C., Kashyap, V., Spaccapietra, S. (eds.) ICSNW 2004. LNCS, vol. 3226, pp. 158–176. Springer, Heidelberg (2004). doi:10.1007/978-3-540-30145-5_10

Product Development and PLM Performance Measures: A Multiple-Case Study in the Fashion Industry

Elisa d'Avolio(✉), Romeo Bandinelli, and Rinaldo Rinaldi

Department of Industrial Engineering, University of Florence, Florence, Italy
{elisa.davolio, romeo.bandinelli, rinaldo.rinaldi}@unifi.it

Abstract. Performance measurement represents one of the key lever to increase business competitiveness. Fashion companies are characterized by the centrality of products, so development and engineering should be monitored and controlled through proper performance measures. The goal of the entire study is to discuss how performance measurement is able to address and sustain the product development process within the fashion supply chain, considering also the involvement of PLM. A case study analysis has been conducted to select and validate the main measures related to product development and PLM.

Keywords: Performance measurement · Product development process · Product Lifecycle Management · PLM · Fashion industry

1 Introduction

The importance of performance measurement was first acknowledged a long time ago but, as the years have gone by, Supply Chain (SC) complexity has taken over. The aim of the present study is to highlight the importance of performance monitoring with a special focus on the product development process.

Performance measurement is a cross department practice, which should support and control the overall set of processes within the SC: product development (PD) is just one of them, but it becomes strategic for particular industries as in the Fashion business environment.

The product and its progress are key features for a fashion company that is trying to compete on quality and time-to-market.

From concept to production, the leading role is played by products: each season several items are proposed; depending on the market segment that the company choose to satisfy, the number of new products compared to the "carry over" may vary. Lots of collection, departments and people are involved so that measuring performance is a strategic imperative.

Nevertheless, the growing amount of information related to the product is triggering the importance of proper Information and Communication Technologies (ICTs) supporting PD. The Product Lifecycle Management (PLM), well known in the manufacturing industry from almost two decades, is spreading also in the fashion industry. An

R. Harik et al. (Eds.): PLM 2016, IFIP AICT 492, pp. 399–410, 2016.
DOI: 10.1007/978-3-319-54660-5_36

inner circle of PLM vendors is proposing ad hoc solutions: they are fitting the requirements of fashion companies, more and more complex in terms of data management.

Performance measurement is also including PLM on its evaluations, as a system that has to be reliable in order to allow users to develop collections and that is producing measurable benefits.

The goal of the entire study is to discuss how performance measurement is able to address and sustain the PD process within the fashion SC, considering also the involvement of PLM.

A case study analysis has been performed to compare literature review results, mostly related to the manufacturing industry, with empirical evidences.

The paper is organized as follows: the second section describes the main literature about PD Key Performance Indicators (KPIs); in the third section, the methodology is presented and in the fourth section the main results are analyzed. The paper concludes with several remarks and future challenges.

2 Literature Review

Performance measurement is a largely debated topic within scientific literature, since the 90's, but the number of papers which deal with PD, as a specific process within SC, is just a small subset. The latter becomes smaller and smaller as the focus shifts to the fashion industry.

In order to study the large number of performance measures available, researchers have categorized them. A framework has been proposed for performance measurement based on three main components to manufacturing SC success: resources, output and flexibility [1]. Another classification based on the main SC performance measures distinguishes between innovativeness, information accuracy and timeliness [2]. Other approaches include SC management models [3, 4] or Balanced Scorecard for SC management evaluation [5]. Just a little part of the analyzed literature [6–8] is focused on the fashion industry: the authors analyze particular measures, mostly related to Marketing and Retail needs or to sustainability issues.

The topic of PD performance measures is still underexplored in literature. PD activity is intrinsically intangible, non-routine, uncertain and organizationally complex. These special characteristics combine to make PD performance measurement especially challenging.

According to [9], a given performance measure is characterized by the combination of four aspects: its managerial purpose, object of interest, measurement forms and linkages with other metrics. The dimensions and elements of these four characteristics make up a formative framework defining the space of conceivable PD metrics.

More industry-specific papers [10, 11] describe how PD can be better controlled for manufacturing and high tech companies. A research [10] has led to the development of the performance measurement for product development (PMPD) methodology to guide managers in the use of performance measures to improve decision-making during the PD process.

According to [11] several PD tools and techniques (for example, DOE, FMEA/DFMEA, and supplier involvement) have a significant effect on the overall performance of PD and on a number of performance indicators, but their utilization is not especially high.

The Information Technology (IT) business value refers to the organizational performance impacts of IT, including productivity enhancement, profitability improvement, cost reduction, competitive advantage, inventory reduction, and other measures of performance [12]. The effect of investments in Enterprise Systems (ES) on long-run stock price and profitability performance have been reported by [13]: the authors highlight the improvements in profitability by adopters of ERP systems.

[14] propose a solution, based on the key performance indicator (KPI) method, for evaluating the benefits introduced by the adoption of a PLM tool in a manufacturing company. The study sheds some light on the need to identify a set of significant indicators that could synthesize the company behavior.

The literature analysis has not allowed the authors to gather information about PD and PLM performance measures in the fashion industry. In order to reach the goal of the present study and to fill the literature gap, several case studies have been conducted.

3 Research Approach

The research has been inspired by several projects carried out in fashion companies that are recognizing the importance of performance measurement and its role in the PD process.

The starting point has been a literature review, that has allowed the authors to learn from other studies and compare metrics and viewpoints about KPIs classifications.

Consequently, the research has focused on two main areas: PD KPIs and PLM KPIs; the first one is more process-oriented and the second one more IT-oriented, but both are strictly linked to product development.

Given the different approaches to performance measurement and involvement of information technologies, two parallel case studies have been conducted.

Case study has been chosen to investigate the choices in terms of approach to performance management in Italian fashion companies. This methodology is adopted to gain a more in-depth understanding of the dynamics present within single settings [15]. In order to increase confidence in the findings, multiple-case sampling has been used [16].

For the first area of interest, i.e. PD KPIs, a questionnaire has been designed and administrated to six fashion companies, as shown in Table 1. The sample has been classified basing on:

- The activities conducted in-house or outsourced: it is a driver of the importance that the business assigns to several tasks.
- The main product represents the core business and reveals the companies' critical success factors (CSFs): quality seems to be more strategic for leather goods and timing for ready-to-wear (RTW).
- The companies' sizes in terms of stock keeping units (SKUs)
- The market segment the companies belong to

Table 1. Case studies conducted for PD KPIs

Cases	In-house activities	Main product	N° SKU	Market segment
Case 1	All	Leather goods	>1000	Luxury
Case 2	Distribution, product development	Ready-to-wear	>1000	Diffusion
Case 3	Distribution, retail, product development	Ready-to-wear	500–1000	Diffusion
Case 4	All but production	Outerwear	100	Diffusion
Case 5	All	Leather goods	>1000	Prêt-à-porter
Case 6	All	Made to measure	>1000	Luxury

The firms are international brands with at least a business unit in Italy. The half part of the sample is composed of big high fashion (luxury) companies, producing leather goods (shoes, bags, accessories) or made to measure garments. While, other three companies are medium lines selling ready to wear (pants, skirts, sweaters, dresses) and outerwear (jackets, trench, winter coats). The authors have decided to involve companies paying huge attention to the PD process, which is always conducted in-house. The interviewees were Managers of the finance, product development and production departments.

For the second area of interest, i.e. PLM KPIs, only IT and Data Managers have been involved because of their higher knowledge about enterprise systems, configurations and interfaces. This analysis required a more detailed study, given the lack of literature researches and the complexity of the topic.

Two big high fashion companies, representing internationally iconic brands and selling mainly leather goods, participated to this second stage of the research (Table 2). They manage in-house the great part of the business processes and have implemented the same fashion-specific PLM solution, which is properly integrated with other systems.

Table 2. Case studies conducted for PLM KPIs

Cases	In-house activities	Main product	N° SKU	Market segment	PLM implementation
Case 1	All	Leather goods	>1000	Luxury	Since 3 years
Case 2	All but production	Leather goods	>1000	Luxury	Since 2 years

In Figs. 1 and 2 the different methodologies have been represented. The research that has led to the acknowledgement of PD KPIs and performance measurement approach has been a validation of already known, but more industry-specific, performance measures.

Instead, the research that has led to the acknowledgement of PLM KPIs has been introduced by a generic examination of PLM KPIs but the biggest contribution has come from meetings dedicated to IT issues.

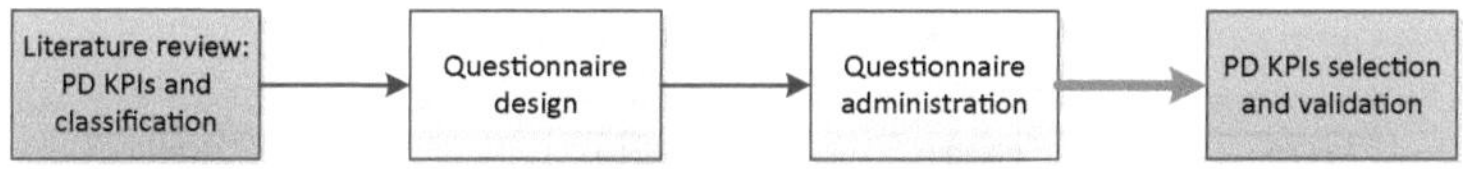

Fig. 1. Methodology adopted for PD KPIs

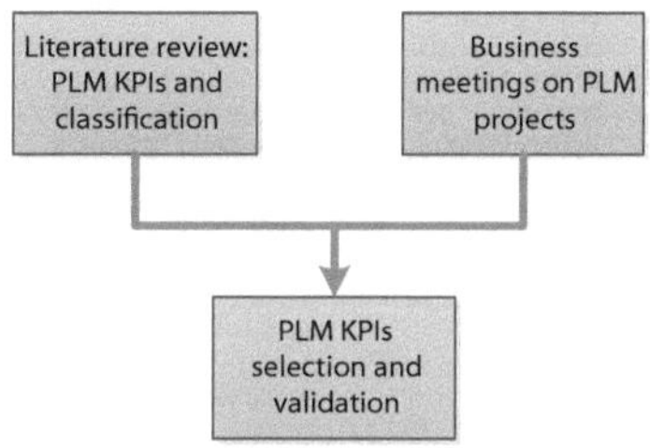

Fig. 2. Methodology adopted for PLM KPIs

4 Discussion

In order to investigate about PD performance measures in the fashion industry, a "draft" list of KPIs has been identified from the literature review. The interviewees were asked to examine this list and to specify the degree of importance of the indicator, according to a 1–4 scale (1 = Not important; 2 = Low importance; 3 = Important; 4 = Very important).

Moreover, interviewees detailed for each measure the typology of ICT tool (e.g. PDM, PLM, Business Intelligence, ERP) adopted in order to store and monitor KPIs.

In Table 3 the validated list of PD KPIs is detailed and classified basing on resource, cost and time measures. The last column of the table, counts the number of cases adopting each KPI: resource and cost KPIs are the most adopted by the companies interviewed, in particular prototype and sample annual costs and HR employment in different departments.

Each case study described in Table 1, has its own way to manage those KPIs.

The first case is a high fashion company that prefers to monitor production KPIs more than PD ones. Just few PD measures are controlled and they have a low importance. PLM is still not implemented, but a PDM provides the information to manage KPIs.

The second case is a RTW company that pays huge attention to PD, also for time KPIs. A Business Intelligence solution is able to trace data about performance measures, but the firm is not ready to a full PLM implementation.

The third case is a RTW diffusion company that controls other SC KPIs and has a holistic approach to performance measurement. It monitors all the KPIs listed in Table 3 and is using a PDM solution.

The fourth case is an outerwear company that is not measuring lots of KPIs among the PD measures: it prefers to monitor just cost KPIs, so it has a financial approach to performance measurement. These are controlled through a Business Intelligence solution.

Table 3. Classification of PD KPIs

KPI ID	KPI classification	PD KPIs	Description	KPIs adoption (0-6 cases)
PD-1	Resource	Human resources (FTE) - Design	Average number of HR employed in the Design Department	4
PD-2	Resource	Human resources (FTE) - Product Development	Average number of HR employed in the PD Department	5
PD-3	Resource	Human resources (FTE) - Modelling	Average number of HR employed in the Modeling Department	5
PD-4	Resource	Human resources (FTE) - Prototyping	Average number of HR employed in the Prototyping Department	5
PD-5	Resource	Number of fabrics (FW)	Average number of fabrics adopted during the fall-winter season	3
PD-6	Resource	Number of fabrics (SS)	Average number of fabrics adopted during the spring-summer season	3
PD-7	Resource	Number of colors (FW)	Average number of colors developed during the fall-winter season	3
PD-8	Resource	Number of colors (SS)	Average number of colors developed during the spring-summer season	3
PD-9	Resource	Number of planned models (briefing)	Average number of models planned during the briefing	3
PD-10	Resource	Number of final models (briefing)	Average number of actual models calculated during the briefing	4
PD-11	Resource	Product typology (% carry over and new models)	Percentage of carry over and new products within a season	3
PD-12	Cost	Prototypes annual cost	Average annual cost to produce prototypes	6
PD-13	Cost	Samples annual cost	Average annual cost to produce samples	6
PD-14	Cost	Prototype Cost/Production Cost	Ratio between the average prototype cost and the average production cost	3
PD-15	Cost	Sample Cost/Production Cost	Ratio between the average sample cost and the average production cost	2
PD-16	Cost	Fitting costs/ Production cost	Ratio between the average fitting cost and the average production cost	1
PD-17	Time	Compliance with Marketing Brief	Ratio between the average number of models planned and the average number of actual models calculated during the briefing	3
PD-18	Time	Compliance with the product engineering schedule (FW)	Ratio between the actual time and the planned time to engineer products during the fall-winter season	2
PD-19	Time	Compliance with the product engineering schedule (SS)	Ratio between the actual time and the planned time to engineer products during the spring-summer season	2
PD-20	Time	Number of fitting sessions (FW)	Average number of fitting session during the fall-winter season	1
PD-21	Time	Number of fitting sessions (SS)	Average number of fitting session during the spring-summer season	1

The fifth and the sixth cases have in common the strategic goal to sell premium quality products: leather goods (fifth case) and ties, scarves and made-to-measure garments for men (sixth case). PD is definitely their core business, so they measure many of the listed KPIs, more than measures related to other SC processes (sourcing, production, distribution, etc.). They strongly believe in handcrafted tradition and are still not able to innovate through PLM solutions.

This first step of the research has been particularly interesting because interviewees have validated the list of performance measures and acknowledged the importance of proper tools supporting PD management.

Coming to the second part of this research, i.e. investigating PLM performance measures in the fashion industry, the main results are listed in the Tables 4, 5, 6, 7, and 8.

Table 4. PLM time KPIs

KPI ID	PLM KPIs	Description	Process
PLM-1	Time to create/copy a style/material	Average time to create a new style/material or a carry over	Data management
PLM-2	Time to create a new BOM	Average time to create a new BOM	Data management
PLM-3	Time to create/copy a new BOM item	Average time to create a new BOM item	Data management
PLM-4	Time to create a color library	Average time to create a seasonal color library	Data management
PLM-5	Time to issue a supplier request	Average time to send to suppliers a technical sheet containing information for product prototyping/sampling	Data management
PLM-6	Time to massively issue supplier requests	Average time to send to suppliers more technical sheets containing information for products prototyping/sampling	Data management
PLM-7	Time to load aggregated information in table views	Average time required to display information related to more styles in a table view	Data management
PLM-8	Processing time for costs calculations	Average elapsed processing time to execute an expression related to cost calculation	Data management
PLM-9	Time to print a table view	Average time to print the information contained in a table view	Printing
PLM-10	Time to print a set of BOMs	Average time to print the information contained in a (BOM)	Printing
PLM-11	Time to print Data Packages	Average time to generate and print a Data Package containing more sheets	Printing
PLM-12	Time to export the report of BOM items to ERP	Average time to run the scheduled export batch containing information about styles and the related materials	Import/Export configuration
PLM-13	Time to export the report of supplier quotes to ERP	Average time to run the scheduled export batch containing information about styles and the related quotes	Import/Export configuration
PLM-14	Time to import style/material/suppliers codes from PDM	Average time to run the scheduled import job containing information about styles/materials/suppliers	Import/Export configuration
PLM-15	Time to download reports imported in PLM	Average time to download a single report imported into PLM	Import/Export configuration

Table 5. PLM cost KPIs

KPI ID	PLM KPIs	Description	Process
PLM-16	Number of PLM incidents (monthly)	Average number of system issues noticed by users	Data management
PLM-17	Cost to implement a custom configuration	Average cost to implement medium-high configuration based on business requirements	Data configuration
PLM-18	Data searching time	Refers to the capability of the user interface to be simple and friendly	Data management
PLM-19	Cost to upgrade release version	Average cost to upgrade the system to the new release	Data configuration

Table 6. PLM quality KPIs

KPI ID	PLM KPIs	Description	Process
PLM-20	Number of seasonal data to be exported to ERP	Average number of data exportable to ERP related to a season (including several collections and styles)	Import/Export configuration
PLM-21	Frequency of master data export to ERP	Average frequency of master data export from PLM to ERP	Import/Export configuration
PLM-22	Loop monitoring & controlling	Availability of a tool to control and remove potential loops	Data configuration
PLM-23	PLM system scalability	Refers to the PLM capability to increase its performance to accommodate the resources growth	Data configuration
PLM-24	Information tracking	Refers to the PLM capability to allow product information traceability and history	Data configuration

Table 7. PLM flexibility KPIs

KPI ID	PLM KPIs	Description	Process
PLM-25	Number of user profiles	Average number of users configurable in PLM	Data configuration
PLM-26	PLM footprint in the fashion company	Percentage of business processes supported by PLM	Data management
PLM-27	PLM system flexibility	Refers to the PLM ability to adapt to possible or future changes in business requirements	Data configuration

Table 8. PLM infrastructure KPIs

KPI ID	PLM KPIs	Description	Process
PLM-28	Number of upgraded releases per two-year period	Number of releases provided by the PLM vendor	Data configuration
PLM-29	Business compliance to PLM software requirements	Considers client system requirements	Data configuration
PLM-30	Business compliance to PLM hardware requirements	Considers database and application server hardware configuration	Data configuration
PLM-31	Number of OOTB Business Objects	Average number of Business Objects implemented out-of-the-box in PLM	Data configuration

KPIs have been assessed basing on:

- a performance measure classification: time, cost, quality, flexibility and infrastructure KPIs. The majority of PLM KPIs are time-based measure because one of the main challenges in PLM implementation is the reduction of time-to-market and time to develop products.
- a process classification: data management, data configuration, printing, import/export configuration. PLM solutions allow to manage data from the user interface (create styles, colors, materials. etc.) or to configure data in proper settings (define templates, attributes, behaviors on copy, validation rules, etc.).

Other IT solutions and layers could be interfaced to PLM, as printing layers, ERP, MRP and PDM. When PLM is the master data for PD, an import/export job scheduling is available through stored procedures or proper tables.

During business meetings, the following KPIs have been identified and validated, explaining the general meaning and the background.

Time measures are mainly related to actions taken by users in day-by-day data management, developing styles and materials. The latter two represent the core business objects (BOs) for a fashion PLM solutions. Users usually manage properties within single BOs or aggregated information in table views, including data of more departments (shoes, bags, accessories, etc.) and more collections. One of the key features of a flexible PLM is the opportunity to introduce expressions calculating costs or ensuring data validation: the elapsed processing time may vary depending on the number of objects involved and on the complexity of the expression. Users also need to export data from PLM and to send it to suppliers: data packages, bill of materials (BOMs), quotes reports have to be printed in pdf files. The performances of the printing process have been also included because sending product information to factories is fundamental for companies which outsource production, as long as printing massive data (e.g. all the BOMs by collection) may take long times. Export batches are the protagonists of data exchange with business enterprise tools. They are scheduled through proper jobs and have to be as fast as possible to ensure data updates and real time collaboration. Other information are imported in PLM, as material codes, and their availability is also remarkable.

Cost measures refers to issues noticed by users, that could be bugs or simple needs for training, requiring an application maintenance service. Costs related to the upgraded release and to an additional customization should be taken into account.

Quality measures represent authentic drivers to select a business specific PLM, given the enterprise architecture structure. The number of aggregated data to be exported to ERP and the frequency of export are strictly dependent on the business environment needs: from four times to once in a day, a company should need to export all the information of more than two seasons.

Flexibility measures could refer to the capability of PLM to support the majority of business processes linked to products. When agile deployment is feasible, the PLM vendor is also able to introduce proper changes to the present configuration and this is a measure of flexibility too.

Finally, infrastructure measures could be seen from the business viewpoint or from the PLM vendor perspective. In the first case, the business needs to understand if it is compliant to PLM system requirements and hardware configuration. In the second case, the PLM has to guarantee an adequate number of out of the box (OOTB) business objects and several upgrades, at least for bug fixing reasons.

The case studies related to PLM performance measures are particularly meaningful because through the listed KPIs it is possible to finalize an all-embracing PLM assessment and, in detail, to:

- compare different PLM solutions
- compare different versions of the same PLM solution
- compare the data management before/after PLM
- compare different configurations of the same PLM solution (in different companies).

While time KPIs are more industry specific, the remaining are more generic performance measures that could be monitored in any PLM project.

This analysis about PLM performance measures differs from the one related to PD KPIs because an evaluation of the measures within the case studies is still missing. Nevertheless, the companies interviewed have demonstrated how strategic business alignment, process-based PLM design and reduction of customizations are critical success factors for fashion firms implementing a PLM solution.

One of the main improvements consists in changing the way to work and PLM enables this change. To better perform, a company has to focus on process enhancement and then on system change, avoiding to customize the solution to support old processes.

Software customizations entail an effort in terms of costs and time; PLM is also more expensive to maintain and less flexible for future integrations. Choosing OOTB configuration is one the right ways to improve the overall set of PLM performances.

5 Conclusions and Future Work

This research has the objective to underline the importance of PD performance measures for fashion companies. A preliminary literature review has introduced the authors to KPIs analysis and classification, concerning both PD process and PLM. A lack of studies in the fashion industry has been noticed and a case study analysis has been performed.

The authors have tried to provide a comprehensive view of the measures related to product lifecycle, starting from process to data management. PD KPIs has been validated with each company interviewed and a qualitative estimation of the measures has demonstrated the chosen approach to performance measurement.

PLM KPIs has been identified through a more complex and deep analysis with process owners and ICT managers. This analysis represents a preliminary stage to evaluate PLM performance within fashion companies, through proper industry-specific KPIs.

The interviews have allowed the authors to describe in a qualitative manner the best way to perform PD process and PLM implementation. Future researches will be conducted to achieve a quantitative assessment of PD and PLM measures, in order to ensure generalizability of results.

References

1. Beamon, B.M.: Measuring supply chain performance. Int. J. Oper. Prod. Manage. **19**, 275–292 (1999)
2. Cai, J., et al.: Improving supply chain performance management: a systematic approach to analyze iterative KPI accomplishment. Decis. Support Syst. **46**, 512–521 (2008). Elsevier B.V.
3. Gunasekaran, A., et al.: A framework for supply chain performance measurement. Int. J. Prod. Econ. **87**, 333–347 (2004)
4. Sheperd, C., Gunter, H.: Measuring supply chain performance: current research and future directions. Int. J. Prod. Perform. Manage. **55**, 242–258 (2004)
5. Bhagwat, R., Sharma, M.K.: Performance measurement of supply chain management: a balance scorecard approach. Comput. Ind. Eng. **53**, 43–62 (2007)
6. Mattila, H., et al.: Retail performance measures for seasonal fashion. J. Fash. Mark. Manage. **6**(4), 340–351 (2002)
7. Moore, M., Fairhurst, A.: Markerting capabilities and firm performance in fashion retailing. J. Fash. Mark. Manage. **7**(4), 386–397 (2003)
8. de Brito, M.P., et al.: Towards a sustainable fashion retail supply chain in Europe: organisation and performance. Int. J. Prod. Econ. **114**, 534–553 (2008)
9. Tatikonda, M.V.: Product development performance measurement. In: Handbook of New Product Development Management, p. 199 (2008)
10. Driva, H., Pawar, K.S., Menon, U.: Measuring product development performance in manufacturing organisations. Int. J. Prod. Econ. **63**, 147–159 (2000)
11. Tsu-Ming, Y., Pai, F.-Y., Yang, C.-C.: Performance improvement in new product development with effective tools and techniques adoption for high-tech industries. Qual. Quant. **44**, 131–152 (2010)

12. Melville, N., Kraemer, K., Gurbaxani, V.: Review: information technology and organizational performance: an integrative model of IT business value. MIS Q. **28**, 283–322 (2004)
13. Hendricks, K.B., Singhal, V.R., Stratman, J.K.: The impact of enterprise systems on corporate performance: a study of ERP, SCM, and CRM system implementations. J. Oper. Manage. **25**, 65–82 (2007)
14. Alemanni, M., et al.: Key performance indicators for PLM benefits evaluation: the Alcatel Alenia Space case study. Comput. Ind. **59**, 833–841 (2008)
15. Yin, R.K.: Case Study Research: Design and Methods. Sage Publication, Beverly Hills (1984)
16. Miles, M., Huberman, A.M.: Qualitative Data Analysis. Sage Publications, Beverly Hills (1984)

Mobile Manipulator Performance Measurement Towards Manufacturing Assembly Tasks

Roger Bostelman[1,2(✉)], Sebti Foufou[3], Steve Legowik[4], and Tsai Hong Hong[1]

[1] National Institute of Standards and Technology, Gaithersburg, MD 20899, USA
roger.bostelman@nist.gov
[2] Le2i, University of Burgundy, BP 47870, 21078 Dijon, France
[3] CSE Department College of Engineering, Qatar University, P.O. Box 2713, Doha, Qatar
[4] Robotic Research, LLC, Gaithersburg, MD 20878, USA

Abstract. Mobile manipulator performance measurement research is relatively minimal as compared to that of robot arms. Measurement methods, such as optical tracking systems, are useful for measuring the performance of mobile manipulators, although at a much higher relative cost as compared to artifacts. The concept of using test artifacts demonstrates to potential manufacturers and users of mobile manipulator systems that relatively low cost performance measurement methods exist. This paper discusses the concept of reconfigurable mobile manipulator artifacts that were designed and built. An artifact was then used through experimentation to measure the performance of a mobile manipulator to demonstrate the feasibility of the test method. Experimental results show a promising test method to measure the performance of mobile manipulators that are to be used for manufacturing assembly tasks, where at least the mobile manipulator tested has the capability to perform assembly to 1 mm positional accuracy or greater.

Keywords: Mobile manipulator · Performance measurement · ASTM F45 · Artifacts · Ground truth

1 Introduction

Mobile robots and mobile manipulators have been popular research topics [1–5]. But, in general mobile manipulators have been further investigated recently and are now becoming commercial tools for industrial use [6–8]. In research, considerations have focused on the coordination of movements of the robot and the base since redundant degrees-of-freedom (DoF) exist by adding the moving base. An example mobile manipulator consists of a six DoF robot arm (manipulator) mounted onboard a wheeled base (e.g., automatic guided vehicle (AGV) or mobile robot) with two translational and one rotational DoF in the horizontal plane for a total of nine DoF [9]. Some mobile manipulators have more or fewer DoF and may also be equipped with vertical axis motion control of the robot arm base.

R. Harik et al. (Eds.): PLM 2016, IFIP AICT 492, pp. 411–420, 2016.
DOI: 10.1007/978-3-319-54660-5_37

As with robot arm or AGV performance, it is important for manufacturers and users of mobile manipulators to implement performance measurements to understand their system capabilities for appropriate application. For example, a user may wish to apply a mobile manipulator to assemble an engine having relatively high tolerances and associated costs as compared to inserting relatively low tolerance and cost rivets into sheet metal covers.

Measurements of the performances of mobile manipulators performing standard tasks (poses and motions) are non-existent except for simply ensuring that the task has been more or less completed. Robot performance measurements may include path comparison and path drawing, Cartesian and polar coordinate measuring, triangulation, optical tracking, inertial measuring, as well as the difference in position and orientation, or pose, of mainly the end of arm tooling from the commanded robot pose. Ground truth measurement using motion tracking systems of various techniques provides relatively accurate robot joint, segment, or tool point position information such that comparisons can be made to the commanded pose. Summarizing review of robot, mobile robot, and mobile manipulator performance measurement research shows this as being relatively new to the research community [10].

A survey of research on performance measurement of mobile manipulators [10] was published by the National Institute of Standards and Technology (NIST) as basis for research in the Robotic Systems for Smart Manufacturing (RSSM) Program [11]. The Program develops and deploys advances in measurement science that enhance U. S. innovation and industrial competitiveness by improving robotic system performance and other aspects to achieve dynamic production for assembly-centric manufacturing. Recently, NIST has been measuring performance of mobile manipulators using both a motion tracking system and artifacts designed at NIST. The artifacts can provide an inexpensive, yet low uncertainty method for manufacturers and users to measure the performance of mobile manipulators.

Performance standards, such as ASTM F45 [12], can also benefit from the use of low cost, high accuracy artifacts to develop generic test methods so that manufacturers and users perform similar and comparative tests. Specifically, ASTM F45.02 Docking and Navigation subcommittee is developing work item WK50379 [13] on docking unmanned ground vehicles and their onboard equipment, such as manipulators. In this work, the use of artifacts is being considered as ground truth for mobile manipulator performance measurement.

This paper discusses the design and use of the NIST artifacts, called reconfigurable mobile manipulator artifacts (RMMAs), in measuring mobile manipulator performance. The concept of using artifacts and programmed algorithms to control the manipulator are discussed. An experiment demonstrating feasibility and experimental results is then discussed followed by conclusions that suggest follow-on measurements.

2 Performance Measurement Using Artifacts

The concept includes positioning a mobile manipulator next to an artifact as well as positioning and orienting the end of arm tool (EOAT) attached to the manipulator at specific locations above an artifact to digitally detect fiducials with known uncertainty. The performance evaluation criteria include the:

- Time to register the mobile manipulator to the artifact
- Time to move from the registration points to the assembly points
- Repeatability after registration
- Number of search steps equating to the initial distance from registration/assembly points
- Detection of reflectors with varying diameters

Artifacts, called reconfigurable mobile manipulator artifacts (RMMAs), were designed at NIST to include square, circle, triangle, straight and curved lines, and sinusoidal geometric patterns of tapped holes drilled into machined plates with tolerance of ±0.025 mm. The static and index artifact, RMMA-1, is shown in Fig. 1(a) beside a mobile manipulator. A dynamic RMMA, RMMA-2, is shown in Fig. 1(b). Static means a stopped vehicle with the only onboard manipulator moving to detect fiducials. Index means the mobile vehicle moves from one static location to another where the manipulator cannot physically reach all patterns from one stopped location. Dynamic means both a continuously moving vehicle and onboard manipulator to detect fiducials. Figure 1(c) shows a 457.2 mm square pattern of four reflector fiducials located at the square corners of RMMA-1 and Fig. 1(d) shows a close-up of the reflector inside the square tube reflector housing (which also supports a collimator to be explained later).

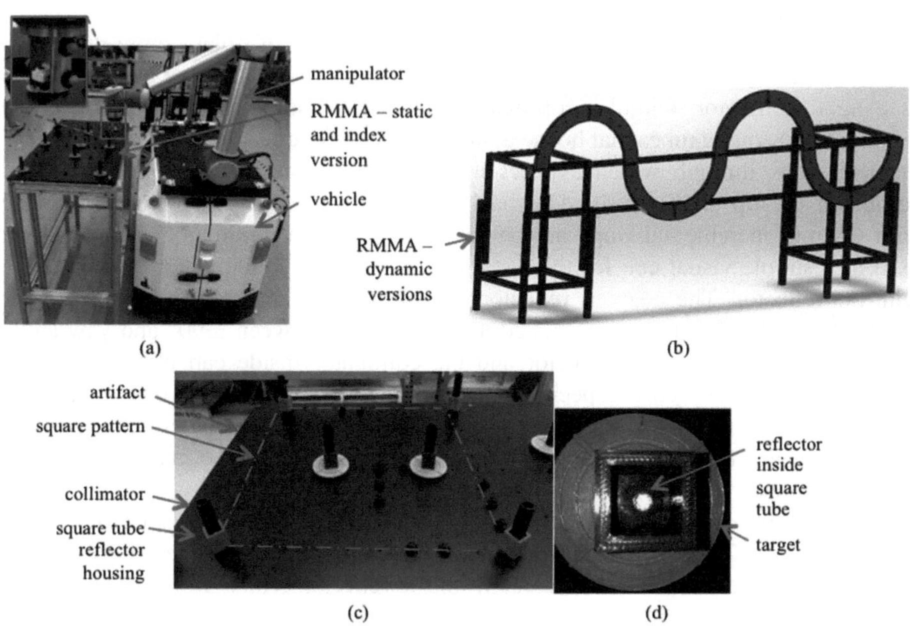

Fig. 1. Reconfigurable mobile manipulator artifacts (RMMAs) showing (a) static and index version (RMMA-1) and (b) dynamic version (RMMA-2). (c) Static and index version square pattern of reflectors and (d) close-up, top view of an illuminated reflector inside the square tube. The inset in (a) shows the retroreflective laser sensor used to detect reflectors.

Both RMMAs can be in a horizontal (as tested in this research), vertical, or other orientation, at short-to-tall heights, and even configured overhead as would be typical of assembly in manufacturing facilities for an unlimited set of performance measurement possibilities. The EOAT was a retroreflective laser sensor (RLS) that emits light to a reflector and is detected by the RLS. A camera, with a light source, could instead be used as the detection sensor, especially with a larger diameter reflector or other spot. For the RLS/reflector concept, no camera software algorithm was required as the RLS connected directly into one of the manipulator digital inputs. The reflectors can have specific diameters depending upon the required uncertainty for their location. The manipulator[1] used has manufacturer's specified repeatability of 0.1 mm [14] and the AGV navigation sensor has manufacturer's specified resolution of 1 mm [15]. No information is provided by the AGV manufacturers to specify the vehicle performance such as position accuracy. As published in [16], 6.3 mm diameter reflectors were used to test mobile manipulator uncertainty as an initial concept feasibility test.

For our tests, detector-to-reflector distance parallel to the laser axis was approximately 127 mm where the minimum and maximum detection distances are 100 mm and 10 m respectively. The distance would be representative of a programmed waypoint above and in-line with the next manipulator task point aligned to grip or insert a part or perform another task. The desired uncertainty may be, for example, a part insertion alignment tolerance required for a manufacturing assembly process. Moving along this grip/insertion line, parallel to the laser, at the aligned pose to the task point, also provides some knowledge of insertion performance (i.e., if the task point is continuously detected along the grip/insertion line).

Each adapter, to be screwed into the various patterns of holes, supports a background target, a circular reflector, a square tube reflector housing, and a cylinder used as a light collimator. Circular collimators are inserted into three dimensional (3D) printed (blue) square tubes that house a micro reflector, a reflector cover with a specific diameter hole, through which exposes the reflector, on top of the reflector and the collimator on top of the cover. Flat background targets, measuring 7.6 cm diameter with 6.4 mm incremental rings are perpendicular to each collimator and sometimes used as a simple visual cue for the test director when the manipulator does not align with the reflector. The adapter, reflector, housing, target, and collimator can be perpendicular to the flat surface or rotated to pitch angles between ±90° and yaw angles between 0° and 360°. The reflector and the collimator inside can be any diameter, dependent upon the sensor specification and the desired measurement uncertainty. Experiments for this paper utilized 1 mm through 6.3 mm diameter reflector cover holes where the 1 mm diameter hole was used for registering the manipulator to the reflector center.

Without the collimator, as shown in Fig. 1(c), the reflector can be detected at approximately ±20° to the vertical axis. For the collimators used, the reflector can be detected at a maximum 3.2 mm radius from the reflector center. It can be detected at

[1] Disclaimer: Commercial equipment and materials are identified in order to adequately specify certain procedures. In no case does such identification imply recommendation or endorsement by the National Institute of Standards and Technology, nor does it imply that the materials or equipment identified are necessarily the best available for the purpose.

approximately ±7° to the vertical axis when using a 12.7 mm inside-diameter collimator. Collimators could be made with even smaller inside-diameters to force more perpendicular manipulator tool point axis pose to the reflector.

The RLS, shown in Fig. 1(a), shows the sensor mounted in-line and perpendicular to the manipulator tool point. Initial alignment to the reflector can occur using one of several methods briefed in [16]. For our experiments, we aligned the RLS using the manipulator jog mode from the teach pendant until the laser detected the two registration reflectors for both the circle and square reflector patterns. Therefore, we could read directly from the teach pendant the end-effector coordinates to return to during our experiment.

An optical tracking measurement system was initially used as ground truth [17] for comparison to the use of artifacts and to measure all system components simultaneously for test method development. The ground truth system has static positional accuracy of 0.02 mm, however costs approximately 20 times the cost of the artifact concept. Figure 2 shows a snapshot of the optical tracking system markers used as fiducials and positioned on the square pattern of collimators. The tracking system measured the performance of the vehicle, manipulator, and artifact within the same system of reference. In this paper, the focus is to discuss the comparison between only the manipulator and artifact as a low cost, relatively high accuracy measurement method. The potential for artifacts being made using three dimensional (3D) printing could lower the cost further by an order of magnitude, or 200 times, as demonstrated through machining costs of the RMMAs and the 3D printing of parts used with the artifact.

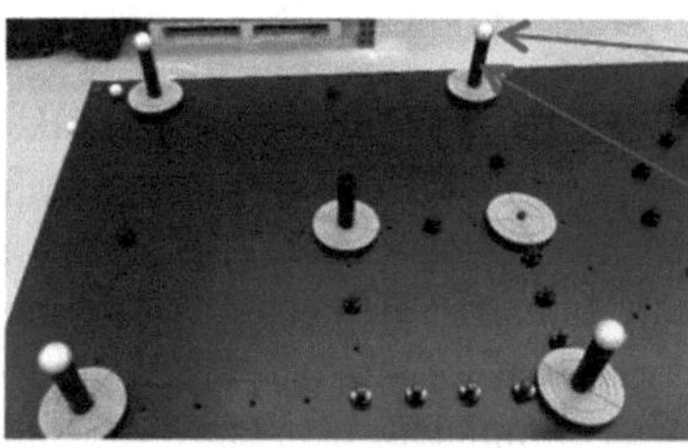

(a)

Fig. 2. RMMA with optical tracking system markers on each collimator. Markers are also shown in Fig. 1(a) attached to the retroreflective laser sensor held by the manipulator.

3 Experiments

The experiment consisted of moving the AGV from a home position away from the RMMA-1. The AGV control program moved the AGV to the first location where its position and orientation or pose was pre-determined by the AGV control program. AGV orientation angles were programmed to be at 45° with respect to the RMMA-1. Upon completion of the pattern detection for a location, the AGV moved to the second location and pose, and so forth until six locations were completed. The AGV completed the test by returning to the home position.

A modified registration method for registering the mobile manipulator to the RMMA was recently developed that uses the components shown in Fig. 3, including a 3D printed aperture housing, collimator, micro-reflector, and a camera iris aperture. The aperture allows the opening to the reflector to not only be any size, but to also

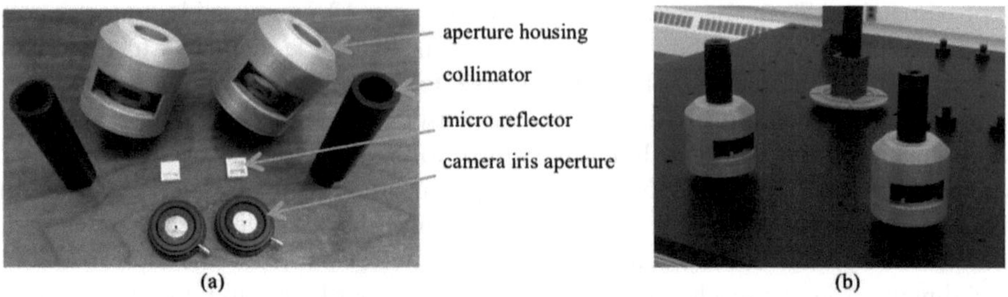

Fig. 3. (a) Components used for registration and (b) registration fiducial mechanism attached to the RMMA.

center the opening. This ensures that the two registration fiducials are centered on the reflector even when using a much larger reflector for all other fiducials. The smallest aperture opening used was 1 mm diameter while all other fiducials were 3.2 mm or 6.3 mm diameter. The RLS did not return a 'detect' at a smaller diameter than 1 mm diameter aperture setting.

A circular search pattern was used in previous tests [16] to register the manipulator to the first reflector. Once the first fiducial was acquired, it was possible for a registration skew to occur as only the edge of the pattern may have been detected and the opposite side of the second fiducial used for registration could cause an incorrect performance measurement of the mobile manipulator. The circular search began with a step increment chosen to be approximately half of the diameter of the fiducial being tested. For example, an initial step size of 3.1 mm was chosen for a 6.3 mm fiducial to be detected. However, after the initial circle of steps was completed, the step moved to the next larger 3.1 mm circle step radius (e.g., from 3.1 mm to 6.2 mm radius from the start location) and at the same step arc angle (e.g., 15°) causing much larger steps to occur as the circle pattern grew. Instead, a square pattern was tested for the research described in this paper that kept the same step size throughout the entire search. An example of the square step pattern is shown in Fig. 4 where the search begins away from the reflector at the chosen start point (yellow arrow dotted end) and each step moves along the small white or gray arrows until the RLS detects the reflector with the red arrow step.

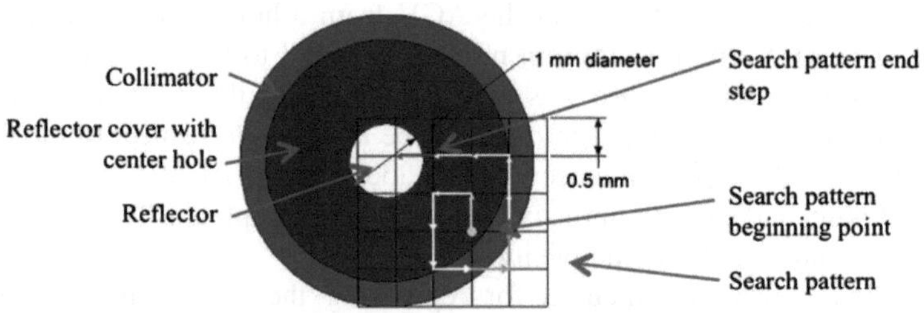

Fig. 4. Example square step search pattern drawing. The pattern begins with the yellow arrow dotted end and ends when the reflector is detected with the red arrow search step. (Color figure online)

The Mobile Manipulator program controlled the manipulator during the tests. It interfaced with the AGV directly to obtain the current AGV position and orientation, and it interfaced with the AGV control program (Transport Structure) running on the Order Manager application to coordinate the motion of the arm with the motion of the AGV. The AGV control program signaled the Mobile Manipulator program when it arrived at one of the stop or test locations. The AGV control program also sent the identification number of the test location. The Mobile Manipulator program read the current AGV pose and used it to compute the initial search location of the two registration reflectors in the target pattern (circle or square). Additional patterns could also have been used in the Mobile Manipulator program.

The manipulator was first moved from a stowed location over the body of the AGV to a staging location directly in front of the AGV. The manipulator was then moved from the staging location to the first of the two registration reflectors. The staging location was chosen so that the manipulator could make a straight line motion from the staging location to a registration reflector located in front of, or to either side of, the AGV without colliding with its shoulder joint. After moving to the first registration reflector, the manipulator performed a square spiral search to determine the exact location of the reflector. When it determined the location of the first registration reflector, the program repeated the process with the second registration reflector. When the locations of the two registration reflectors were determined, the program had sufficient information to compute the locations of the other fiducials in the square or circular patterns. The initial search was not counted as a performance criteria since the mobile manipulator could use various types of registration techniques, such as: physical contact using a touch probe [18], cameras detecting fiducials [19], or laser interferometry, theodolites, and coordinate measuring arms [20]. However, for comparison to repeatability, the initial registration number of iterations count was logged and included in results.

Once the locations of all reflectors in the pattern were computed, the manipulator cycled through them a set number of times – 32 times for each pattern in this experiment. At each reflector, the RLS checked to see if the manipulator was aligned with the reflector.

When the test was completed, the manipulator was moved to the staging location and then the stow location. When the manipulator was back in the stow location, the Mobile Manipulator program signaled to the AGV control program that it was clear to move.

The positions of the index fiducials for the targets were recorded prior to performing the repeatability tests. The AGV was first moved to a location where it could reach both of the index fiducials. The current location and orientation of the AGV was recorded. The arm was repositioned manually until the sensor detected alignment with each of the index fiducials, and the manipulator position was recorded. This information, along with the manipulator base position relative to the vehicle's coordinate system, allowed the correct manipulator coordinates for the index fiducials to be calculated for an arbitrary AGV location. This allowed the AGV to approach the target/work area from any direction and to compensate for variation in the AGV's stopping pose.

The calibration of the manipulator base location involved recording the position of one or more fiducials from a variety of locations. Both the AGV location and the manipulator coordinates of the fiducials were recorded. This data was processed using an iterative, non-linear model to find the best value of the base position and orientation

4 Results

The mobile manipulator performance measurement results using the RMMA-1 included only the detection of reflectors for each pattern and after initial registration. By comparison, the initial number of search steps used to register the manipulator at the first reflector was recorded. Results are shown in Table 1. The repeatability performance measurement process began once the mobile manipulator was registered to the artifact after initial registration and moving through the square or circle pattern one time and with the AGV statically positioned at a pattern. Measurements of 'detect' or '1' were logged for each RMMA-1 reflector location. If a search was required to find the fiducial after registration, the measurement at that reflector was counted as a 'no detect' and the number of search steps was recorded.

Table 1 shows: the consecutive position number and programmed AGV position, the AGV pose angle (heading), the circle or square pattern being detected, the total number of reflectors to detect for 32 pattern iterations after the registration pattern, the reflector diameters for each pattern (rounded to whole numbers), the number of reflectors detected and detection percentage, and the initial number of search steps needed to register to the first reflector after the AGV stopped. The AGV stop points programmed are shown in Fig. 5. The lines leading to the stop points indicate the AGV orientation.

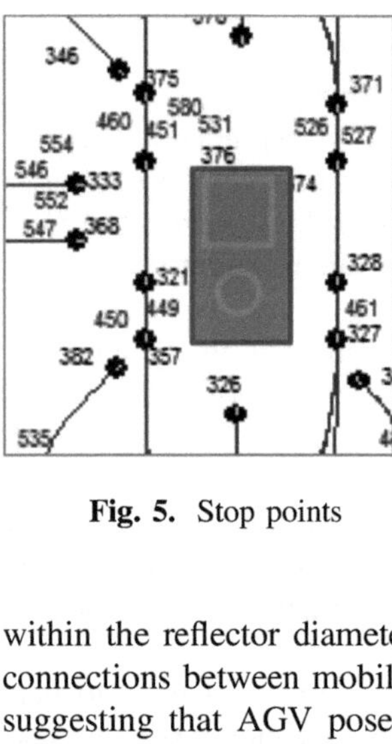

Fig. 5. Stop points

The table shows very high repeatability results at 97% or above as shown in the "% detected" column of the table. The results demonstrate a good test procedure for determining repeatability of a mobile manipulator to register to and access assembly points within the reflector diameters chosen. Further tests are required to understand direct connections between mobile manipulator performance and system pose, for example, suggesting that AGV pose at 0° provides higher performance than at other angles. Results here do not show this since position 6 included the AGV being at 90° and yet, was repeatable to 100%. Several additional tests are envisioned as well, such as: repeatability of the same pattern followed by the other pattern, both from different AGV poses; using the 1 mm registration reflectors for all patterns followed by the same size reflectors for all, such as 3 mm; and using 1 mm diameter reflectors for all points within each pattern to provide a possible detection limit.

Table 1. Test results of the mobile manipulator accessing the RMMA from various stop points (see Fig. 4) and various AGV poses. The gray rectangle in the center of the stop points map shows the approximate RMMA square and circle pattern locations.

Position number	AGV position	Pose angle, deg	Pattern	Number of reflectors to detect	Reflecter diameter sizes	Number reflectors detected	% detected	Initial number of search steps to register to fiducial #1
1	326	90	Circle	192	1 mm, 6 mm	188	98%	561
2	346	315	Square	128	3 mm	124	97%	613
3	368	0	Circle	192	1 mm, 6 mm	192	100%	181
4	333	0	Square	128	3 mm	128	100%	73
5	382	45	Circle	192	1 mm, 6 mm	191	99%	377
6	328	90	Square	128	3 mm	128	100%	1921

5 Conclusion and Future Work

As discovered in a NIST survey of mobile manipulator research [10], performance measurement of these systems is minimal as compared to robot arms. Measurement methods, such as using optical tracking systems, are useful methods for measuring mobile manipulator performance, although at a much higher cost. The use of known artifacts, called reconfigurable mobile manipulator artifacts, to measure the performance of mobile manipulators is being researched at NIST to demonstrate the feasibility of the test method. The concept of using artifacts demonstrates to potential manufacturers and users of mobile manipulator systems that relatively low cost performance measurement methods exist. Artifacts, such as the RMMA-1 and in the future, RMMA-2, allow an unlimited number of performance measurement configurations. The measurement of mobile manipulator repeatability and accuracy for very low resolution tasks (e.g., positioning bags of product) through very high resolution tasks (e.g., assembly of parts for manufacturing) is achievable through the use of RMMAs. Static and index tests have been completed using this method and have proven feasible. Experimental results show a promising test method to measure performance of mobile manipulators that are to be used for manufacturing assembly tasks, where at least the mobile manipulator tested has the capability to perform assembly to 1 mm positional accuracy or greater. Future test method developments should not only include dynamic mobile manipulator performance measurements, but also include the suggested tests in the results section. Additionally, rapid registration techniques, finer retroreflective laser sensors allowing smaller diameters, and in turn, physically providing peg-in-hole measurements with variable peg and hole chamfers, are expected to provide even higher performance measurements towards assembly applications of mobile manipulators.

References

1. Shneier, M., Bostelman, R.: Literature Review of Mobile Robots for Manufacturing, NIST Internal report #8022 (2014)
2. Katz, D., Horrell, E., Yang, Y., Burns, B., Buckley, T., Grishkan, A., Zhylkovskyy, V., Brock, O., Learned-Miller, E.: The UMass mobile manipulator UMan: an experimental platform for autonomous mobile manipulation. In: Workshop on Manipulation in Human Environments, at Robotics: Science and Systems (2006)
3. Hamner, B., Koterba, S., Shi, J., Simmons, R., Singh, S.: An autonomous mobile manipulator for assembly tasks. Autonomous Robot **28**, 131–149 (2010). doi:10.1007/s10514-009-9142-y
4. Djebrani, S., Benali, A., Abdessemed, F.: Modeling and control of an omnidirectional mobile manipulator. Int. J. Appl. Math. Comput. Sci. **22**(3), 601–616 (2012). doi:10.2478/v10006-012-0046-1
5. Vannoy, J., Xiao, J.: Real-time Adaptive Motion Planning (RAMP) of mobile manipulators in dynamic environments with unforeseen changes. IEEE Trans. Robot. (5), 1199–1212 (2008)
6. Motoman, Y.: MH80 robot unloading trucks - from Wynright Corporation. http://www.youtube.com/watch?v=8wngL0BnF_4. Accessed 18 June 2013
7. Guizzo, E.: Meka Robotics, Announces Mobile Manipulator with Kinect and ROS. http://spectrum.ieee.org/automaton/robotics/humanoids/meka-robotics-announces-mobile-manipulator-with-kinect-and-ros. Accessed 16 Feb 2011
8. Green, T.: KUKA Falls First, Buys Swisslog for $335 M. Who's Next? Robot. Bus. Rev. (2014)
9. Miksch, W., Schroeder, D.: Performance-functional based controller design for a mobile manipulator. In: Proceedings IEEE International Conference on Robotics and Automation, 12–14 May 1992
10. Bostelman, R., Hong, T., Marvel, J.: Survey of research for performance measurement of mobile manipulators. J. Natl. Inst. Stand. Technol. (2016, inpress)
11. Robotic Systems for Smart Manufacturing Program. National Institute of Standards and Technology (2016). http://www.nist.gov/el/isd/ms/rssm.cfm
12. ASTM F45 Committee on Driverless Automatic Industrial Vehicles (2016). www.astm.org
13. ASTM F45.02 Docking and Navigation subcommittee, work item WK50379. (2016) www.astm.org
14. Universal Robots A/S-UR10 User Manual, Version 3.0 (rev. 15167) (2014)
15. SICK 2D Laser Scanners. https://www.sick.com/media/pdf/1/41/841/dataSheet_LMS100-10000_1041113_en.pdf
16. Bostelman, R., Hong, T., Marvel, J.: Performance measurement of mobile manipulators. In: SPIE 2015, Baltimore, MD, April 2015
17. Bostelman, R., Falco, J., Shah, M., Hong, T.H.: Dynamic metrology performance measurement of a six degree-of-freedom tracking system used in smart manufacturing In: ASTM International Autonomous Industrial Vehicles: From the Laboratory to the Factory Floor (2016)
18. MasterCal (2005). http://www.americanrobot.com/products_mastercal.html
19. Atcheson, C.B., Heide, F., Heidrich, W.: CALTag: high precision fiducial markers for camera calibration. In: Vision Modeling and Visualization (2010)
20. Mauricio, J., Motta, S.T.: Robot calibration: modeling measurement and applications. In: Huat, L.K. (ed.) Industrial Robotics: Programming, Simulation, and Applications. InTech, Rijeka (2006). ISBN 3-86611-286-6

Building Information Modeling

Building Lifecycle Management System for Enhanced Closed Loop Collaboration

Sylvain Kubler[1(✉)], Andrea Buda[2], Jérémy Robert[1], Kary Främling[2], and Yves Le Traon[1]

[1] Interdisciplinary Centre for Security Reliability and Trust, University of Luxembourg, 2721 Luxembourg, Luxembourg
{sylvain.kubler,jeremy.robert,yves.letraon}@uni.lu
[2] Department of Computer Science, Aalto, School of Science, P.O. Box 15500, 00076 Espoo, Finland
{andrea.buda,kary.framling}@aalto.fi

Abstract. In the past few years, the architecture, engineering and construction (AEC) industry has carried out efforts to develop BIM (Building Information Modelling) facilitating tools and standards for enhanced collaborative working and information sharing. Lessons learnt from other industries and tools such as PLM (Product Lifecycle Management) – *established tool in manufacturing to manage the engineering change process* – revealed interesting potential to manage more efficiently the building design and construction processes. Nonetheless, one of the remaining challenges consists in closing the information loop between multiple building lifecycle phases, e.g. by capturing information from middle-of-life processes (i.e., use and maintenance) to re-use it in end-of-life processes (e.g., to guide disposal decision making). Our research addresses this lack of closed-loop system in the AEC industry by proposing an open and interoperable Web-based building lifecycle management system. This paper gives *(i)* an overview of the requirement engineering process that has been set up to integrate efforts, standards and directives of both the AEC and PLM industries, and *(ii)* first proofs-of-concept of our system implemented on two distinct campus.

Keywords: Product Lifecycle Management · Internet of Things · Building lifecycle management · Interoperability · Quality Function Deployment

1 Introduction

Building Information Modeling (BIM) is not a new concept, but rather one that is playing an increasingly larger role in the architecture, engineering and construction (AEC) industry. From design to construction, the concept of BIM has been a feature across many industries for nearly 30 years [18]. It remains a strong and important player in the field because of its ability to allow designers to go beyond representing the physical space of a new or retrofitted building to the intrinsic properties of the structure as well. BIM is not just about the design of new buildings, it also plans for years of use. This is because designing, scheduling, constructing and evaluating a building is done in the BIM model long before any construction actually takes place. Although it is true

R. Harik et al. (Eds.): PLM 2016, IFIP AICT 492, pp. 423–432, 2016.
DOI: 10.1007/978-3-319-54660-5_38

that the future of the construction industry is digital and that BIM facilitating tools and standards (e.g., IFC) will foster long-term facility management, there are still technological and managerial challenges ahead [5]. The nature of these challenges depend on the building lifecycle, which is generally defined as a three-phase process [8]: *(i) Beginning-of-Life (BoL)* including design, manufacture and construction of the building; *(ii) Middle-of-Life (MoL)* including its use and maintenance; and *(iii) End-of-Life (EoL)* including its disposal and recycling. Our research puts special emphasis on post construction challenges.

One of the major challenges after the delivery of the building (i.e., when starting MoL) lies in the difficulty to close the information loop between all phases of the building lifecycle. For example, due to the lack of system integration and other factors such as the non-maturity of the IoT (Internet of Things), it is not that easy to collect, capitalize, and share information/knowledge acquired from MoL (e.g., during use and maintenance activities) with other building lifecycle stakeholders, and *vice-versa* [12]. This is all the more important since such information could result in enhanced decision-making in BoL (e.g., to improve the next generation of buildings and boost the innovation process by capturing new business and user needs), or in EoL (e.g., to guide decision-making about the reuse of components by having information related to the building use conditions). The establishment of such a closed-loop information/collaboration structure throughout the asset lifecycle is not only facing the AEC industry but other sectors, too, e.g., manufacturing where concepts such as *Closed-loop PLM*[1] [13, 14] emerged over the last decade.

Given the above, the contribution of our work is twofold: *(i)* design/develop an open & interoperable building management system that integrates efforts, outcomes (technologies, standards…) and directives of both the AEC industry and adjacent sectors such as Closed-loop PLM and IoT; *(ii)* set up an effective and evolutive requirement engineering framework for ensuring successful system component development. Sections 2 and 3 deal respectively with these two contributions, Sect. 4 presents proofs-of-concept of our system, conclusion follows.

2 When BIM Meets Closed-Loop PLM

The differences between BIM and PLM chiefly surround their capacity for technical and organizational integration. However, they both share a number of similarities relative to their approach to data sharing and project management activities [14]. Although there is only a few documented efforts of implementing PLM in AEC companies, the challenges that follow on from these shared characteristics may provide fertile grounds for sharing lessons learned. Section 2.1 focuses on BIM throughout the building lifecycle, while giving insights into current Closed-loop PLM research and practices. Against this background, Sect. 2.2 discusses the importance of having accurate requirements to transfer those practices to the AEC/BIM industry, and how this can be achieved using an evolutive requirement engineering framework (Fig. 1).

---

[1] This concept is also referred to as CL2M: http://cl2m.com.

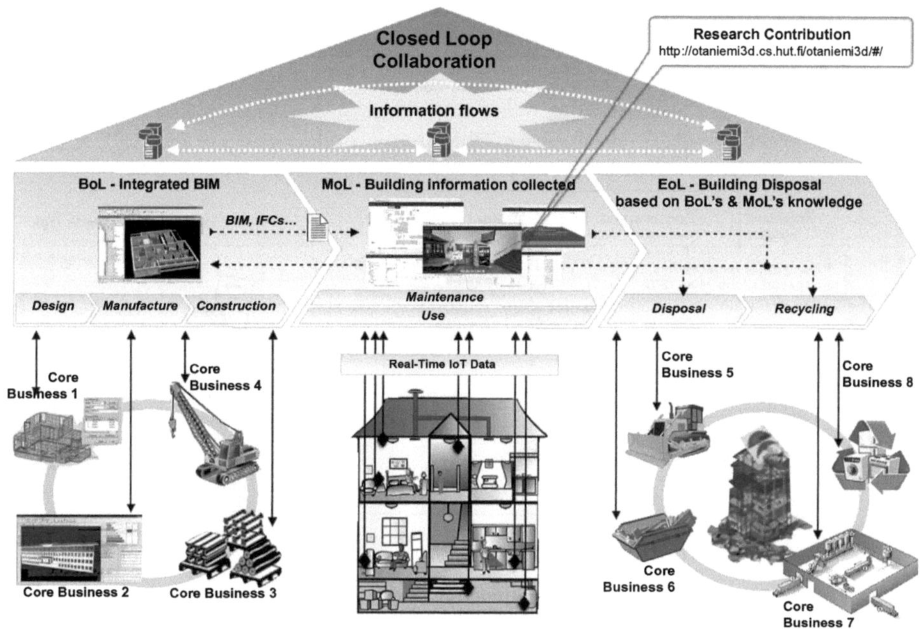

Fig. 1. Building lifecycle management system combining BIM & adjacent sectors' efforts

2.1 Whole Lifecycle Approach

Managing vast amounts of disparate information throughout an asset lifecycle (car, airplane, building…) is an enormous challenge for organizations, particularly in terms of enforcement and compliance. Information governance enforces desirable behavior in the creation, use, archiving, and deletion of corporate information. By closing the loop, rules and policies are defined, policies are managed and enforced, authorized records are accessed when and as needed, and metrics are available to audit the current rules and policies. All this provides a way to continuously assess and update the process for optimum results.

Unlike this vision has been widely explored in PLM, it has only been in the last 5 to 7 years that an increasing focus on the application of BIM throughout the whole building lifecycle has emerged, and the significance of business process integration been acknowledged [14]. BIM servers are now being developed to provide a large integrated data- and knowledge-base that can be leveraged not only in design and engineering, but also in construction operations (BoL), facilities maintenance (MoL), and disposal activities (EoL) [8]. Such a building lifecycle's vision is depicted in Fig. 2, where research efforts are increasingly focused on "closing the loop" to foster collaborative processes, shared resources and decision-making [2]. Although some challenges remains to be addressed in BoL, the major challenge in the context of 'closed-loop' information starts from the delivery of the building, where BIM and other BoL models fall into oblivion. This means that all the knowledge generated in BoL is not, or at least cannot easily be re-used in MoL and EoL, while some reports highlight

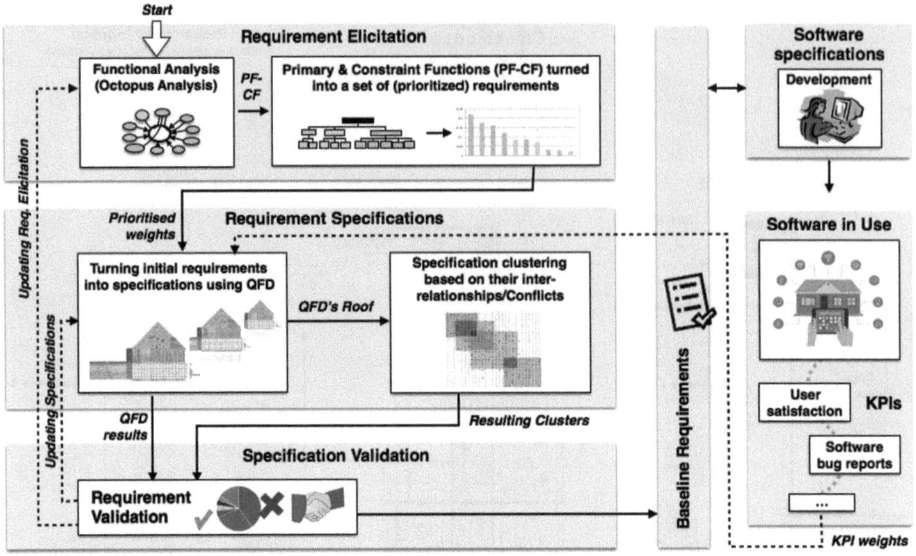

Fig. 2. Evolutive requirement engineering framework for system development

substantial profits that could accrue from such information loops [13]; for example, Barlish and Sullivan highlight the fact that 85% of the lifecycle cost of a facility occurs after construction is completed [4] and, in this respect, that using BIM-related information in downstream processes could help to save money.

As mentioned above, the concept of closed-loop PLM (or CL2M) has developed theories and tools to enable closing the information loop between multiple lifecycle phases [11, 15]. This concept emerged from the PROMISE EU FP6 project, where real-life industrial applications required the collection and management of product instance-level information for many domains involving heavy and personal vehicles, household equipment, *etc.* Information such as sensor readings, alarms, assembly, disassembly, shipping event, and other information related to the entire product lifecycle needed to be exchanged between products and systems of different organizations. Based on the needs of those applications, requirements for data exchange were identified and, as no existing standards could be identified that would fulfill those requirements without extensive modification, new messaging interfaces were proposed (see e.g. [11]). Those specifications have since then been further developed by the IoT WG of The Open Group and implemented by several EU project consortia (e.g., LinkedDesign FP7, bIoTope H2020[2]). Recently, The Open Group published those specifications as two distinct – *but complementary* – standards, namely the Open Messaging Interface (O-MI) and Open Data Format (O-DF) standards [11].

Our research work and contribution originate from this state-of-the-art with the specific aim of developing a user-friendly building lifecycle management system

[2] http://biotope-h2020.eu/.

relying on open and interoperable standards like O-MI/O-DF. To this end, it is of the utmost importance to select and/or set up an effective and evolutive requirement engineering framework for the development of successful system components, especially in new and cross-domain contexts, as is the case in our study (combination of standards/directives from the AEC/BIM and Closed-loop PLM & IoT sectors). The next section briefly discusses such a requirement engineering framework.

2.2 Requirement Engineering Framework

Accurate requirements provide the foundation for successful product development. Three main steps can be identified in requirements engineering [16]:

1 *Requirements inception:* start the process (business need, market opportunity…);
2 *Requirements management*: to capture new needs/contexts over time.

In our context, customer needs must be transferred into product and process requirements without necessarily developing all possible technical characteristics, but only the ones that fulfil the needs for efficient closed-loop information and collaboration in a building's lifecycle context. Let us add that the production activity is supposed to be traceable back at least indirectly to customer requirements.

Given this, our research work develops an hybrid framework based on the synthesis of well established techniques from software engineering and management theory and tools [9]. An overview of this hybrid engineering framework is provided in Fig. 2, which combines (i) a functional analysis (using the Octopus diagram); (ii) a requirement prioritization technique (using AHP – Analytic Hierarchy Process) [18]; (iii) a method that transforms prioritized requirements into quantitative parameters/specifications (using QFD – Quality Function Deployment) [7]; and (iv) a spectral algorithm method for clustering specification conflicts identified through the QFD matrices [3]. These phases are followed up by the software development phase, as well as the definition of KPIs (key performance indicators) to assess whether the system is free of defects, meets the user needs that may evolve over time, and so on. In the context of smart buildings, similar approaches for the development of smart home components was followed, e.g. Durrett et al. [10] used QFD to effectively satisfy customers' needs as part of an integrated smart home environment. Popescu et al. [17] used QFD combined with AHP to identify a set of functions of lighting, heating, security, furniture, *etc.*, that could have a critical contribution to the independent living capacity of people with special needs, if receiving smart abilities. However, none of these frameworks and analyses consider needs related to the whole building lifecycle, along with the imperative to enable closed-loop information and collaboration among distinct lifecycle stakeholders.

As a consequence, an appropriate hybrid engineering framework that enables to integrate such needs, and appropriate technology enablers from the AEC and PLM industries, is defined and proposed in this study, as will be discussed in Sect. 3.

3 A Hybrid Engineering Framework for Development of Building Lifecycle Management System Components

As previously stated, and depicted in Fig. 2, our framework starts with a functional analysis using the Octopus diagram that identifies the Primary Functions (denoted PF) as well as the Constraint Functions (CF) between the system to be developed and its environment (e.g., actors, directives, services, etc.). Figure 3 provides insight into the Octopus diagram related to our building lifecycle management system, where the different PF and CF functions are further described in Table 2. Based on these PF and CF functions, high-level requirements are formulated in the form of a hierarchy representing distinct categories (e.g., CF2, CF3 and CF5 falls within the scope of "Building lifecycle"-related requirements, etc.). Due to space limitation, the final requirement hierarchy is not presented in this paper, but a first insight into the categories are illustrated through the Octopus's color code in Fig. 3.

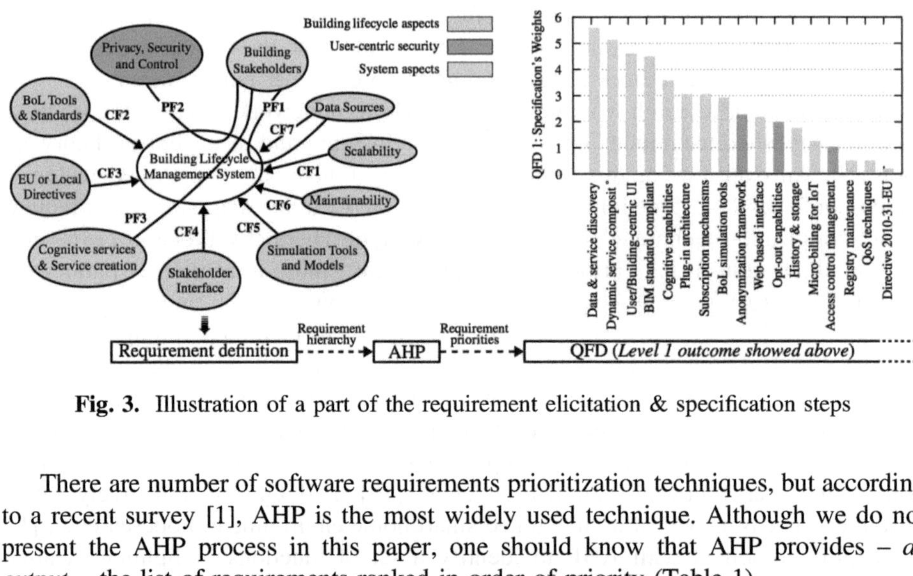

Fig. 3. Illustration of a part of the requirement elicitation & specification steps

There are number of software requirements prioritization techniques, but according to a recent survey [1], AHP is the most widely used technique. Although we do not present the AHP process in this paper, one should know that AHP provides – *as output* – the list of requirements ranked in order of priority (Table 1).

Such a requirement ranking, associated with the priority weights, are used as input of the QFD. QFD is both a requirement definition and conceptual design tool that systematically documents customer needs, benchmarks, competitors, and other aspects, and then transforms the list of prioritized requirements into design specifications. The QFD methodology flow involves four basic phases that occur over the course of the product development process. During each phase one or more matrices are generated (*cf.* block in Fig. 2 entitled *"Turning initial requirements into specifications using QFD"*), where the specifications (including their respective weight) resulting from the QFD matrix of phase n feed the matrix of phase n + 1. Figure 3 provides insight into the specifications resulting from the first QFD matrix, which all bring first

Table 1. Primary & Constraint Functions (PF-CF) formalized through the octopus diagram

PF/CF	Description
PF1	Enable building stakeholders to easily access and manage various types of data sources (internal or external to the building) according to their role (e.g., maintainers have different information needs than inhabitants).
PF2	Comply with building stakeholders' expectations in terms of Security & Privacy (e.g., some information must be displayed or hidden to a specific category of stakeholders).
PF3	Enable stakeholders to easily create new services based on the integrated data sources and a portfolio of "processing blocks" (including diagnosis, maintenance prediction, event-detection, storage…)
CF1	Ensure the system's scalability (e.g., to dependably integrate new data sources and/or creating new services);
CF2	Make it possible the integration of AEC solutions/standards such as BIM (e.g., IFC, Cobie…);
CF3	Comply with directives affordable plus-energy or nearly zero energy buildings (e.g., Directive 2010-31-EU);
CF4	Provide users with open/ubiquitous GUIs that enable to take into account live stakeholder's preferences, both intuitively and explicitly (e.g., inhabitants habits, preferences, maintainer's needs…);
CF5	Enable live (MoL) simulations based on models made available from BoL (e.g., to identify whether the energy or thermal building's behavior has drifted from initial BoL simulation models);
CF6	Facilitate maintenance of the building lifecycle management system/software in a holistic manner (e.g., reporting of sensor failures to the building manager, of software bugs to developers…);
CF7	Enable interoperability and openness among information systems from the whole building lifecycle;

technological or scientific enablers to fulfil one or more requirements. For example, Fig. 3 shows that the two most important enablers with respect to our initial requirements are *(i) Data & service discovery:* to enable any building stakeholder to discover and access, when and as needed, information sources and associated knowledge; *(ii) Dynamic service composition:* to enable building end-users to create their own services using a portfolio of "processing blocks" (including diagnosis, maintenance prediction, event-detection, storage…).

As highlighted in our requirement engineering flow (see Fig. 2), a spectral method for clustering conflicts that arise from the QFD matrices' roof[3] is further applied, followed up respectively by a validation phase of the specifications and the development of the software components. To guarantee that our system remains competitive over the short and long term, specific Key Performance Indicators (KPIs) are defined to assess in a quantitative manner several aspects such as the software bugs, the user satisfaction and new needs, *etc.* Although not presented in this paper, it is important to note that these KPI metrics continuously feed the QFD matrices (see Fig. 2), thus helping to produce new releases of the system/software with added or rectified features.

4 Proof-of-Concept – Building Lifecycle Management System

The first releases of our building lifecycle management software have been supplied[4], enabling any developer to deploy and instantiate it in his/her own environment/buildings. Two proofs of concept of such an instantiation are today available online, namely at Aalto Smart Campus[5] and Sophia Antipolis Smart Campus[6].

[3] The QFD roof emphasis whether two specifications positively or negatively impact on each other.

[4] https://github.com/AaltoAsia/Otaniemi3D.

[5] http://otaniemi3d.cs.hut.fi/otaniemi3d/.

[6] http://sparks-vm26.i3s.unice.fr:8080/html/webclient/index.html.

Figure 4 provides screenshots of the web-based dashboard that any building end-user/stakeholder can access and use as they see fit. First, stakeholders are able to discover (in a city or region) all the buildings that are compliant with our system, or more specifically compliant with the IoT standards used for data exchange (i.e., O-MI/O-DF in our case). The discovery can be achieved both in a visual manner (Google Map, as shown with the dashboard view denoted by 1 in Fig. 4) or automated manner (using the RESTful discovery mechanism supported by O-MI, see e.g. [12]). From this stage, the stakeholder can access both the Floor/2D model (see arrow denoted by 2) as well as the 3D model of the building (see arrow denoted by 3). Those views have been directly generated using – *as input* – the integrated BIM/IFC file, which is now able to be enriched with live sensor data, e.g. the room "Cafeteria" collects Co2, Humidity, Occupancy and Temperature sensor data. Along with this 2D/3D views, another view – *a 360°'s picture of the room (see arrow denoted by* 4*)* – is supported wherein there is a twofold benefit (i) a building manager can notify the system that a new smart-connected object has been added, but also where it has been added in the room (e.g., a new smart coffee machine), but can also and foremost link the virtual sensor with the real-life information sources (i.e., physical sensors in this example); (ii) any end-user can see where the information source is located, which is a key contextual information that can be further used when developing additional services that rely on or use this information (e.g., if a sensor is located above an oven, the developer can identify it, integrate it to his/her knowledge, and handle it as needed).

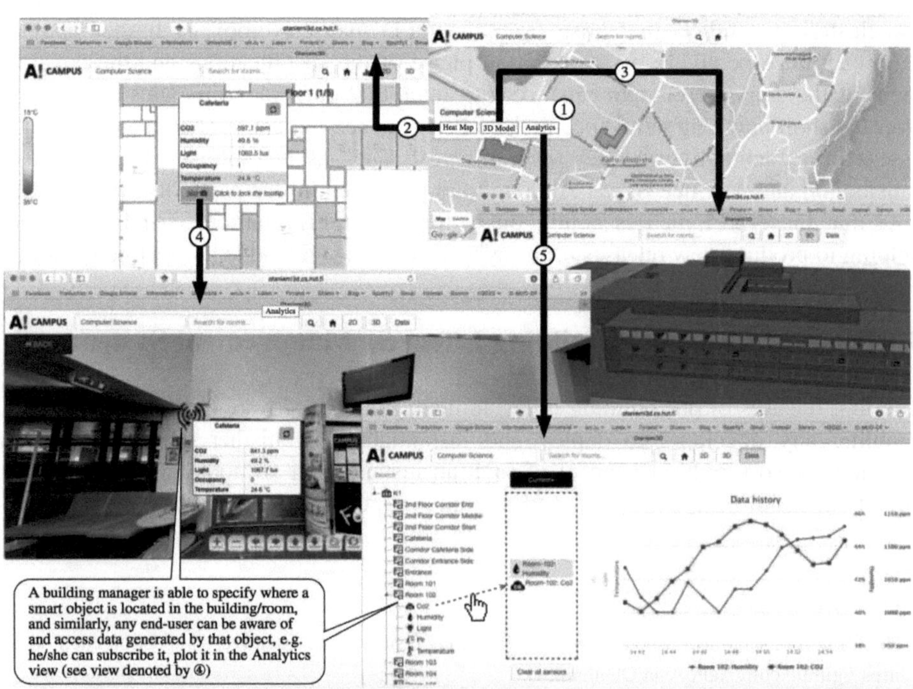

Fig. 4. Screenshots of the current building lifecycle management system (Aalto Smart Campus)

Finally, our system provides initial Analytics' services (see arrow denoted by 5) such as basic plotting of sensor data over a certain period of time regarding one or a group of rooms, but also more complex/cognitive services like the prediction of specific events (energy, failures, *etc.*).

As a final step, we sum up in Table 2 the set of features – *based upon the specifications resulting from the QFD matrix Level 1 (see Fig. 3)* – that have been fulfilled in the first release of our building lifecycle management software (see column denoted "Today's System features" in Table 2), but also the ones that will be addressed through the H2020 bIoTope project and that will be integrated later on (next releases). It can be observed that, in this first software/system release, the specifications having received the highest priorities with respect to the initial requirements (note that the specifications in Table 2 are listed in order of priority).

Table 2. Current vs. Future building lifecycle management system features

	QFD Level 1 Specifications	Today's System features	Future features to be developed in the framework of the bIoTope H2020 project
1	Data & service discovery	▲ *(supported by O-MI/O-DF standards)*	▲ *(more advanced/intelligent discovery services)*
2	Dynamic service composition	▲ *(first widgets – screenshot ① in Fig. 4)*	▲ *(a more friendly UI & additional widgets)*
3	User/Building-centric UI	▲ *(see screenshots in Fig. 4)*	▲ *(context-aware UI: location or role-dependent)*
4	BIM standard compliant	▲ *(IFC files used as input of our system)*	✗
5	Cognitive capabilities	✗	● *(Autonomous reasoning capabilities)*
6	Plug-in architecture	▲ *(requires user interaction)*	▲ *(new agents specific to building environments)*
7	Subscription mechanisms	● *(supported by O-MI/O-DF standards)*	✗
8	BoL simulation tools	✗	✗
9	Anonymization framework	✗	● *(relying on k-anonymity & blurring techniques)*
10	Web-based interface	● *(see screenshots in Fig. 4)*	✗
11	History & storage	▲ *(basic database storage)*	▲ *(new Big Data related capabilities)*
12	Micro-billing for IoT	✗	● *(digital currency + data quality frameworks)*
13	Access control management	✗	● *(using XACML or similar standards)*
14	Registry maintenance	● *(basic log recording)*	✗
15	QoS techniques	✗	● *(using e.g. Software-Defined Network)*
16	Directive 2010-31-EU	✗	✗

LEGEND: ● *Feature fulfilled;* ▲ *Feature partly fulfilled;* ✗ *Feature not fulfilled*

5 Conclusion

It is still challenging to close the information loop between multiple building lifecycle phases (e.g., by capturing information and knowledge from MoL for re-using it in BoL and/or EoL processes), which opens up opportunities for enhanced decision-making and cost saving (e.g., in facilities management). Our research addresses this lack of closed-loop system by developing an open, interoperable and integrated Web-based building lifecycle management system that integrates efforts, directives and technological enablers from both the AEC and PLM/IoT. This paper gives insight into the requirement engineering framework that has been set up for the development of system components, as well as the first proofs-of-concept of the system implementation (running on two distinct campus).

Acknowledgements. The research leading to this publication is supported by the National Research Fund Luxembourg (grant 9095399) and the EU's H2020 Programme (grant 688203).

References

1. Achimugu, P., Selamat, A., Ibrahim, R., Mahrin, M.: A systematic literature review of software requirements prioritization research. Inf. Softw. Technol. **56**(6), 568–585 (2014)
2. Aram, S., Eastman, C.: Integration of PLM solutions and BIM systems for the AEC industry. In: Proceedings of 30th International Symposium of Automation and Robotics in Construction and Mining, Montréal, pp. 1046–1055 (2013)
3. Atkins, J.E., Boman, E.G., Hendrickson, B.: A spectral algorithm for serialization and the consecutive ones problem. J. Comput. SIAM **28**, 297–310 (1998)
4. Barlish, K., Sullivan, K.: How to measure the benefits of BIM – a case study approach. Autom. Constr. **24**, 149–159 (2012)
5. Azhar, S., Khalfan, M., Maqsood, T.: Building information modeling (BIM): now and beyond. Constr. Econ. Build. **12**(4), 15–28 (2015)
6. Becerik-Gerber, B., Jazizadeh, F., Li, N., Calis, G.: Application areas and data requirements for BIM-enabled facilities management. J. Constr. Eng. Manag. **138**(3), 431–442 (2011)
7. Chan, L.K., Wu, M.L.: Quality function deployment: a literature review. Eur. J. Oper. Res. **143**(3), 463–497 (2002)
8. Dave, B., Kubler, S., Främling, K., Koskela, L.: Opportunities for enhanced lean construction management using internet of things standards. Autom. Constr. **61**, 86–97 (2016)
9. De Gea, J.M.C., Nicolas, J., Aleman, J.L.F., Toval, A., Ebert, C., Vizcaìno, A.: Requirements engineering tools: capabilities, survey and assessment. Inf. Softw. Technol. **54**(10), 1142–1157 (2012)
10. Durrett, J.R., Burnell, L.J., Priest, J.W.: A hybrid analysis and architectural design method for development of smart home components. IEEE Wirel. Commun. **9**(6), 85–91 (2002)
11. Främling, K., Holmström, J., Loukkola, J., Nyman, J., Kaustell, A.: Sustainable PLM through intelligent products. Eng. Appl. Artif. Intell. **26**(2), 789–799 (2013)
12. Främling, K., Kubler, S., Buda, A.: Universal messaging standards for the IoT from a lifecycle management perspective. IEEE Internet Things J. **1**(4), 319–327 (2014)
13. Jupp, J.R., Singh, V.: Similar concepts, distinct solutions, common problems: learning from PLM and BIM deployment. In: Fukuda, S., Bernard, A., Gurumoorthy, B., Bouras, A. (eds.) PLM 2014. IAICT, vol. 442, pp. 31–40. Springer, Heidelberg (2014). doi:10.1007/978-3-662-45937-9_4
14. Kiritsis, D.: Closed-loop PLM for intelligent products in the era of the internet of things. Comput.-Aided Des. **43**(5), 479–501 (2011)
15. Laplante, P.A.: Requirements Engineering for Software and Systems. CRC Press, Boca Raton (2013)
16. Popescu, D., Popescu, S., Bacali, L., Dragomir, M.: Home "smartness"-helping people with special needs live independently. In: International Conference of Management Knowledge and Learning and Technology Innovation and Industrial Management, Romania (2015)
17. Saaty, T.L.: The Analytic Hierarchy Process. McGraw-Hill, New York (1980)
18. Succar, B.: Building information modelling framework: a research and delivery foundation for industry stakeholders. Autom. Constr. **18**(3), 357–375 (2009)

BIM Ecosystem Research: What, Why and How? Framing the Directions for a Holistic View of BIM

Vishal Singh(✉)

Department of Civil Engineering, Aalto University, Espoo, Finland
Vishal.Singh@Aalto.fi

Abstract. This paper presents theoretical arguments for BIM ecosystem research, based on concepts of coevolution and emergence in a complex network of constituent elements: products, processes, people, technology and policies. Broader trends such as Internet of Things, data analytics, and digital manufacturing are increasingly becoming integral to BIM systems. Consequently BIM research is evolving along multiple pathways. Therefore, there is need for methodologies and approaches to analyze BIM ecosystem. Three types of ecosystem analyses are proposed: (1) BIM-Ecosystem Retrospective Analysis (BIM-ERA), to understand the ecosystem's constituents and their dependencies, based on facts and history, (2) BIM-Ecosystem Feasibility analysis (BIM-EFA), to be able to use the knowledge of the constituents and their dependencies to assess whether an intended intervention in a given ecosystem is feasible or not, and (3) BIM-Ecosystem Impact Analysis (BIM-EIA), to be able to conduct what-if studies to assess the potential short-term and long-term impact of a potential action.

Keywords: BIM · Ecosystem · Coevolution · Impact analysis · Research methods

1 Introduction

Building Information Modelling (BIM) has gained global attention across the industry, academia and the policy makers. This is fueling rapid growth of the BIM ecosystem, which, following [1], has been defined as the network of interacting technologies, processes, policies and organizations that collectively determine the development and evolution of BIM related products and services [2]. For example, BIM adoption in the US grew from 17% in 2007 to a remarkable 70% in 2012 [3]. During the same period several new BIM products and services have emerged in the market, while government agencies across countries such as the UK have created national BIM guidelines and policies. In such a dynamically evolving BIM ecosystem there is limited understanding of how the BIM technologies, processes, policies and organizations are mutually coevolving. These developments have opened a new multi-disciplinary research frontier around BIM, with long term implications for theory, education and practice.

In the recent years, several streams of BIM research have emerged across specific issues such as BIM adoption, product data models and standards, facilities

R. Harik et al. (Eds.): PLM 2016, IFIP AICT 492, pp. 433–442, 2016.
DOI: 10.1007/978-3-319-54660-5_39

management, and collaboration [4]. However, the lack of systemic understanding of the BIM ecosystem is a critical knowledge gap that needs attention. First, since BIM is viewed as a collaborative approach, the potential benefits of BIM are contingent on how the technologies, processes, policies and the organizations fit together e.g. [5]. Second, a comprehensive understanding of the systemic challenges is critical to facilitating effective BIM strategy and execution. Third, the emerging BIM research discipline requires strategic insights and directions for future research.

Therefore, this position paper aims to highlight the need for a theoretical basis to understand the patterns and implications of the coevolution in BIM ecosystem at the micro (e.g. project and organization) and macro levels (e.g. industry and society). A better understanding of the BIM ecosystem will improve decision making and collective growth for various stakeholders who are directly or indirectly part of the BIM ecosystem. For example, at the macro level, what are opportunities and challenges for different stakeholders in the evolving BIM ecosystem? What role can the government agencies, policy makers and regulations play in fostering a BIM ecosystem that is conducive to economic, environmental and social welfare? At the micro level, what are the dependencies across emerging technologies, processes and organizations that we need to know for effective management and implementation of BIM-based projects? Similarly, how are the macro and micro levels of BIM ecosystem mutually related? And, how are the broader technological trends such as internet of things (IoT) and digital manufacturing likely to affect the BIM ecosystem?

In addition, there are several fundamental conceptual issues that need to be resolved. For example, how do we define the boundary of the BIM ecosystem? Which technologies, which roles, what processes, and what policies, direct or indirect, should be considered part of the BIM ecosystem and which need not? Or a more fundamental question is whether we at all need to define the boundary? What are the theoretical and conceptual implications of the chosen approach and how could that impact BIM research and development, as well as decision making in practice?

More recently, a systemic view of BIM is starting to emerge in the discussions such as BIM research frameworks e.g. [6], BIM execution plans e.g. [7], and maturity matrices e.g. [8]. Along with these, a comprehensive understanding of BIM ecosystem is required, especially from the viewpoint of co-evolutionary mechanisms and dependencies across different levels of granularity, micro to macro. An endeavour to understand the systemic change in construction is not new. Previous attempts at forming a systemic view of the development of construction IT have typically taken the form of industry forecasting, review articles, policy documents, strategy reports and roadmaps e.g. [9, 10]. Therefore, one of the key objectives of this paper is also to clarify how the proposed BIM ecosystem perspective is different to such approaches, and yet how the ecosystem perspective can also contribute to the development of maturity models, creating roadmaps and identifying strategic directions for research and practice.

2 BIM Ecosystem: What Should We Aim to Research and Why?

2.1 Identifying the Key Constituents of the BIM Ecosystem

The first steps is to identify the key constituents and categories, such that the key elements and their position in the ecosystem can be located. This iterative identification, mapping and clustering of the elements is a longitudinal process because the ecosystem continues to evolve. Such an effort will require a methodological approach, grounded in sound-theoretical and conceptual basis. An ontology to describe the BIM ecosystem is desirable. The ontological approach can build on related work in the literature. For example, [8] have described eight key components of a BIM maturity model, in the context of macro-level BIM adoption. A critical review of the different approaches to classifying and clustering the constituent elements of the BIM ecosystem is needed to assess their strengths and limitations. There is conspicuous absence of any methodological analysis or critical review of these classifications in the BIM literature. Critical questions need to be discussed and debated. For example, what are the structural characteristics of the ecosystem: is there a structural pattern at all? Is it hierarchical and/or nested and/or modular? What are the levels of details to consider? How do we ascertain the parity of the different concepts chosen for each level? etc.

2.2 Identifying Dependencies and Rules of Interaction Between the Elements

The dependencies between the constituent elements need to be identified [11, 12]. These dependencies influence the patters of emergence, which can be traced from the historical data, but at the same time these dependencies may influence the emergent patterns of the future. While mapping the dependencies between these elements, once again several aspects need to be considered. For example, which relationships are constant and which of these are variable? What are the factors influencing the variable relationships, for e.g., temporality, regionality, etc.? What are global and local variations in the dependencies? How can the dependencies be defined?

2.3 Developing Methodologies for BIM Ecosystem Analysis

Besides knowing the constituent elements of the BIM ecosystem, its structural characteristics, and the dependencies between the elements, we need methodologies to analyze the dynamic patterns of evolution - to understand how changes emanate and propagate through the ecosystem - to assess aspects such as stability, robustness and centrality of the ecosystem, as found in any complex network e.g. [13]. The methodological approaches can broadly focus on the following aspects:

BIM Ecosystem Retrospective Analysis (BIM-ERA). The retrospective analysis is based on the past, and hence, there are historical data, facts and experiences to build an understanding of the BIM ecosystem. While the future evolution may or may not be dependent of the past events, lessons learnt from the past, and dependencies and patterns observed in the past, may provide useful insights into the future trends.

BIM Ecosystem Feasibility Analysis (BIM-EFA). Once a mapping of the BIM ecosystem begins to emerge, it is desirable to be able to make informed decisions about potential actions that can be taken to bring about a desired change in the ecosystem. The feasibility analysis methods should allow assessing whether a potential action or solution is possible within the given ecosystem or not, that is, is the action or solution feasible? Constraints within the environment or dependencies with other potential actions or problems may render a solution non-feasible in the context. Such an assessment should also give insights into potential barriers to feasibility.

BIM Ecosystem Impact Analysis (BIM-EIA). An action or solution that is feasible may have varied short-term and long-term impact on the ecosystem, some of which may be desirable and some may not. Thus, it is not sufficient to analyze the feasibility, but it is equally important to analyze the impact of the action or solution. The concept of BIM-EIA is inspired by approaches such as Environmental Impact Assessment e.g. [14] commonly used in ecological domains, where systemic changes or likely change propagation and impact is thoroughly studied before a major action or solution is approved. This aspect has so far been entirely overlooked in the study of ICT or business ecosystems, both within and outside BIM research. Nonetheless, impact analysis should be considered for the following reasons:

Some actions or solutions may have high initial investment both in terms of cost, time and effort, which means they require systemic effort for implementation and execution over a longitudinal period of time. Such efforts can only be made occasionally. For example, in the context of BIM systems if an organization makes an investment to adopt new BIM applications across the teams, then the cost of the applications, training the staff, and beginning to use it effectively is a high investment decision. Once that has been committed to and reached mid or advanced stage, then moving to another set of applications across the teams in a short-term, even if they may be better than the chosen solution, will become extremely challenging.

Some actions or solutions may be irreversible in nature. For example, organizations may invest in building systemic processes and culture to support certain technologies and approaches. Once these actions and steps have been taken they cannot be undone, and more systemic effort will be required to replace them if they do not provide the intended outcomes, or worse, lead to undesirable outcomes.

While some actions or solutions may require one-off effort, other actions or solutions may require continuous effort over a longer period of time. It is important to assess whether continuous effort is sustainable or not.

In considering impact analysis, it is also important to define a benchmark to identify what is the alterative? That is, while it is important to assess what may be the impact of an action, it is also important to assess what will happen if the action is not taken? Is there an alternative action, and how does it compare? Contingent on the type of action or solution, the future course of actions such as flexibility, adaptability, scalability, etc. can be severely impacted.

3 How Is the Proposed BIM Ecosystem Approach Different?

This section briefly discusses how the proposed approach is different to the existing approaches in BIM research and practice from a systemic point of view:

Normative Models of BIM Research Versus Co-evolutionary View of BIM Ecosystem. Most of the current approaches to present a systemic view around BIM are descriptive and normative. Typically, these approaches outline sequential and linear stages and directions of BIM development [15]. For example, BIM-levels 0–3 have been defined, as progressive and sequential levels. While such clear definitions of the levels are useful in determining the maturity levels and creating a roadmap, it can be argued that such an approach fails to sufficiently account for emergent trends and directions of development within the context of BIM research. For example, parallel developments such as laser scanning, internet of things (IoT), etc. are being integrated into the BIM systems, but these cannot be directly straightjacketed into the current definitions of these pre-defined levels, which are limiting, and close-ended. In contrast, the ecosystem approach emphasizes a co-evolutionary view, whereby the constituent elements are mutually evolving. At the same time, it starts with a premise that the boundary of the ecosystem is fuzzy and ill-defined. Theoretically, the co-evolutionary nature and the fuzzy boundary of the ecosystem means that we do not yet understand the lifespan of the BIM ecosystem, and nor do we know where all, in which directions, and by how much, the BIM ecosystem could grow. Consequently, while assessing the maturity in BIM research is useful, the maturity models need to be revised every once in a while and the limitations of defining the maturity level at any given time need to be outlined, because the reference lifespan and scope of BIM research is inadequately understood.

The Concept BIM Ecosystem Impact Analysis or Any Equivalent Concept Does Not Exist. The existing approaches have (1) somewhat focused on understanding and mapping the constituent elements of what we describe as the BIM ecosystem, and the dependencies between them, i.e., kind of retrospective analysis, or (2) somewhat focused on understanding how to bring about a desired change within the context of the BIM ecosystem, i.e., kind of feasibility analysis. For example, developing mapping frameworks, maturity models, creating roadmaps, forecast models, etc. fall in this category, with the objective to try and understand what is out there, and what can be done in the future to reach a desired state. However, the concept of impact analysis has not been considered at all, and there has been no discussion on whether the short-term or long-term implications of decisions taken in the current context can be or should be evaluated upfront. The objective of such impact analysis is to reinforce and validate the suitability of the feasible actions and solutions in the larger social, economic and environmental context, as well as to prepare in advance to address likely unintended effects of an action or solution.

Some of the other key factors that we propose to consider while developing an understanding of the BIM ecosystem, and which need clarification include:

Distinguishing Between Deterministic, Predictive, and Exploratory Preparations. Developing models of a complex system with the view to try and understand likely future trends is often viewed with skepticism, because a number of forecast models and roadmaps have failed to make any meaningful contribution and they have been way off the mark. Therefore, it is important to clearly outline the purpose and expectations from a BIM ecosystem model. Rather than trying to build a deterministic or predictive model that can forecast how the BIM ecosystem will evolve, the BIM ecosystem research should allow exploration of various what-if scenarios that indicate numerous potential paths of evolution of the BIM ecosystem, given different conditions and emergent situations. It is expected that a what-if study will allow the ecosystem stakeholders to be better prepared for the likely scenarios than otherwise.

Multiplex Networks. The use of social network analysis and similar methods to understand the dynamics of construction sector is not new. Several aspects of construction sector, ranging from teams and project management to understanding the industry level interaction have been studied using the network approach. Nonetheless, given the complexity of network research and the challenges in mapping the network dependencies, the typical research is limited to one view of the network, whereas the actors within a given network may have different dependencies within the same network, or may be part of multiple networks at the same time, which all might influence their decisions and actions in any given network. This is typically overlooked because multiple networks are not juxtaposed and investigated at the same time. Therefore, the multiplex networks approach [16] needs to be considered in developing a comprehensive understanding of the BIM ecosystem.

BIM is Beyond Tools and Processes. Following considerable debate on whether BIM is merely a tool or a process, there is an increasing acceptance that BIM is a set of tools, process and policies. Nonetheless, if the research in BIM needs to be advanced it is desirable to look beyond this view as well. For example, the evolution of BIM has many similarities with Management Information Systems (MIS), where similar debates ensued for a while. Eventually MIS emerged as a formal discipline in itself with several notable theoretical perspectives associated with MIS research in areas such as cognition [17], media [18], social science [19], and behaviour [20]. In contrast, there has been limited theory building attempts in BIM research. Thus, it is argued that analogous to MIS we also need to view BIM as a discipline where fundamental theoretical contributions can be made both within and across multi-disciplinary boundaries.

4 Building a Comprehensive View of the BIM Ecosystem

This section reviews some of the complementary research methods and approaches that can be used to understand and analyze the BIM ecosystem.

Empirical Studies. Qualitative empirical research based on case studies, surveys, workshops, interviews and similar data collection techniques is the most dominant research method in current research on building a holistic view of BIM. Typically the findings are used to identify various (success) factors associated with BIM and how they impact adoption, maturity, etc. Many of these studies focus on micro-ecosystem, especially based on case projects and feedback from the actors involved in the project.

Other studies focused on macro-ecosystem tend to include workshops, surveys and focus groups to assess the status of BIM adoption, perception of actors and different stakeholders, role of standards, etc. However, barring a few notable articles, there is limited attempt to build a theory of BIM, and most articles report observations and findings without much articulation towards theory building.

Delphi Studies. Delphi methods are based on systemic engagement and interviews with a panel of experts. Interviews are conducted in multiple iterative rounds, separately with each member of the panel. It is expected that the expert opinions of the BIM ecosystem will converge with each round. The success of Delphi studies is contingent on how quality of the chosen panel and how representative the panel is of the various facets of the BIM ecosystem.

Literature Review. Literature review can be qualitative and subjective, which is typically the case, or they can be objective and quantitative, based on computational methods that can also analyze large data sets e.g. [4].

Data Mining and Analytics. With data mining and analytics, e.g. Big Data approach, it should be possible to conduct a comprehensive retrospective analysis, BIM-ERA, to assess and understand how the BIM ecosystem has evolved. The data-driven, fact-based findings can complement the views and opinions of experts about the evolution of BIM ecosystem, including those in Delphi Studies. The data analytics approach can be applied at both macro and micro levels. At macro levels, the trends and patterns can be studied at the industry level, while at the micro-level the large amount of data generated during a project or several projects can be analyzed to identify the patterns and dependencies at the project level. Furthermore, at the project level there is also a possibility now to mine all the BIM data generated during the project, and such as an analysis could also give insights into design decision making and associated dependencies.

Complex Systems and Networks. BIM ecosystems can be viewed as complex systems and networks. The complex systems approach has been applied by researchers in understanding construction projects as well the construction sector. The different related research methodologies can also be applied to the understanding of the BIM ecosystem. Some of relevant methodologies could include network analysis, mathematical and stochastic modeling, and simulations.

Simulation-Based What-if Studies. One of the objectives of trying to understand and build a theory of the BIM ecosystem is to be able to assess the patterns of evolution, and be able to conduct feasibility analysis as well as impact analysis. The challenges in conducting feasibility analysis and impact analysis is to be able trace the various dependencies and their consequences over a longitudinal chain. That is, an undesirable potential impact may be associated with a factor further down the value chain, and not necessarily easy to trace without a thorough analysis. As an analogy, a single move in a game of chess may be detrimental further down the game, but may not be obvious in the immediate few steps. The implications of this step is not independent of how the next few steps pan out, and how the opponent responds to the steps taken by the first player. These sequence of steps are typically non-deterministic, and hence, various possible paths of evolution are possible. Computational simulations based on probabilistic models provide a powerful method to conduct what-if studies, and these methods have been used successfully in various fields of complex systems research.

As discussed in this section, there are multiple research methods that can be used to study the BIM ecosystem, and the different methods can mutually complement and reinforce the understanding of the ecosystem, Fig. 1.

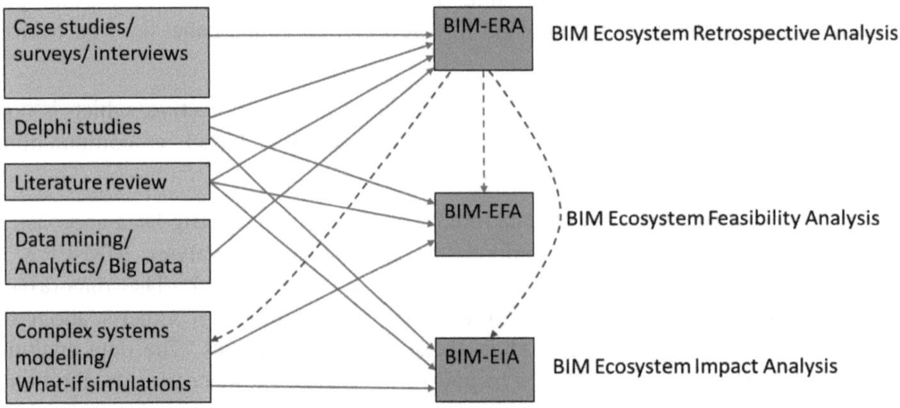

Fig. 1. Research methods applicable to different aspects of BIM ecosystem anaylsis

5 Conclusions

This paper argues the need for a BIM ecosystem perspective, based on the concepts of co-evolution and emergence. The paper argues that barring a handful of notable articles there has been limited effort at building a holistic and theoretical view of BIM research environment. Furthermore, the typical approach in developing a systemic view of BIM research and development has been descriptive or normative, giving guidelines and defining levels of maturity, with limited space to account for emergent factors. The paper argues that the normative models of BIM research are limiting because they assume closed boundaries and scope of BIM. In contrast, the broader socio-technical trends such as building automation systems, IoT, big data analytics, etc. are also finding their way into the mainstream BIM research and BIM systems. Consequently, discussions on maturity models and BIM levels appear hasty and misplaced until the BIM ecosystem boundaries are established with greater research rigour. Considering the co-evolutionary nature of the constituents of the BIM ecosystem, the definition of the BIM ecosystem boundary remains a challenging tasks.

Therefore, this research emphasizes the need for theoretical and methodological approaches to support BIM ecosystem analysis based on the underlying dependencies, patterns and mechanisms of co-evolution. Three different aspects of ecosystem analysis are differentiated (1) BIM-ERA that uses varied methods including qualitative studies, Delphi studies, literature review and big data analytics to review how the BIM ecosystem has evolved, based on the experience so far, (2) BIM-EFA that uses the understanding of the BIM ecosystem built from BIM-ERA, together with Delphi studies, literature review and what-if simulations based on complex systems modelling to assess the feasibility of desired actions in a given ecosystem, and (3) BIM-EIA that also uses the understanding of the BIM ecosystem built from BIM-ERA, together with Delphi studies, literature review and what-if simulations based on complex systems modelling to assess the short-term and long-term impact of a potential feasible action. One of key contributions of this paper is to highlight the need for a BIM-EIA framework, which has not been considered at all in the current BIM literature.

In addition, it must be noted that most of the current articles directed towards a holistic view of BIM research are based on expert opinions, theoretical arguments or other qualitative studies, but there is very little use of complementary methods such as complex systems modelling, what-if simulations or data analytics. It can be argued that the ability to compute emergent patterns of evolution and emergence over longitudinal patterns is limited in such qualitative approaches, while computational methods can be used to explore unlimited number of potential paths of evolution for extended periods of time, under varied what-if conditions. The usability of such computational models are dependent on how well we understand the underlying mechanisms and patterns in BIM ecosystem, and how well we are able to translate them into computational models where complex patterns emerge at global levels, based on well-established dependencies and rules of local interactions between constituent elements.

In summary, this paper argues the need for an ecosystem view of BIM research, based on diverse theoretical and methodological approaches. The paper is a first attempt at articulating the directions and approaches that are required to create such a systemic view, and this remains the primary limitation of the paper. Such an attempt requires collective debate, review and iterations, and one of the main purposes of this paper is exactly to initiate such a theoretical and methodological culture in BIM research.

References

1. Moore, J.F.: The Death of Competition Leadership and Strategy in the Age of Business Ecosystems. HarperBusiness, New York (1996). ISBN 0-88730-850-3
2. Gu, N., Singh, V., London, K.: BIM ecosystem: the coevolution of products, processes, and people. In: Kensek, K., Noble, D. (eds.) BIM in Current and Future Practice, pp. 197–211. (2014)
3. Bernstein, H.M. (ed.): The Business Value of BIM in North America: Multi-year Trend Analysis and User Ratings (2007–2012). McGraw-Hill, New York (2012). SmartMarket Report
4. Yalcinkaya, M., Singh, V.: Patterns and trends in building information modeling (BIM) research: a latent semantic analysis. Autom. Constr. **59**, 68–80 (2015)
5. Singh, V., Gu, N., Wang, X.: A theoretical framework for BIM-based multi-disciplinary collaboration platform. Autom. Constr. **20**, 134–144 (2011)
6. Succar, B.: Building information modelling framework: a research and delivery foundation for industry stakeholders. Autom. Constr. **18**(3), 357–375 (2009)

7. Messner, J., Anumba, C., Dubler, C., Goddman, S., Kasprzak, C., Kreider, R., Leicht, R., Saluja, C., Zikic, N.: BIM Project Execution Planning Guide. Penn State, State College (2010)
8. Succar, B., Kassem, M.: Macro-BIM adoption: conceptual structures. Autom. Constr. **57**, 64–79 (2015)
9. Rezgui, Y., Zarli, A.: Paving the way to the vision of digital construction: a strategic roadmap. J. Constr. Eng. Manag. **132**(7), 767–776 (2006)
10. Kim, C., Kim, H., Han, S.H., Kim, C., Kim, M.K., Park, S.H.: Developing a technology roadmap for construction R&D through interdisciplinary research efforts. Autom. Constr. **18** (3), 330–337 (2009)
11. Peters, D.P.C., Pielke, R.A., Bestelmeyer, B.T., Allen, C.D., Munson-McGee, S., Havstad, K.M.: Cross-scale interactions, nonlinearities, and forecasting catastrophic events. Proc. Natl. Acad. Sci. **101**(42), 15130–15135 (2004)
12. Rammel, C., Stagl, S., Wilfing, H.: Managing complex adaptive systems-a coevolutionary perspective on natural resource management. Ecol. Econ. **63**(1), 9–21 (2007)
13. Strogatz, S.H.: Exploring complex networks. Nature **410**, 268–276 (2011)
14. Stewart-Oaten, A., Murdoch, W.M., Parker, K.R.: Environmental impact assessment: pseudoreplication in time? Ecology **67**, 929–940 (1986)
15. BIS/Industry Working Group: Building Information Modelling (BIM) Working: Party Strategy Paper. Government Construction Client Group, London (2011)
16. Kim, J.Y., Goh, K.-I.: Coevolution and correlated multiplexity in multiplex networks. Phys. Rev. Lett. **111**, 058702 (2013)
17. Vessey, I., Galletta, D.: Cognitive fit: an empirical study of information acquisition. Inf. Syst. Res. **2**, 63–84 (1991)
18. Daft, R.L., Lengel, R.H.: Information richness a new approach to managerial behavior and organizational design. In: Cummings, L.L., Staw, B.M. (eds.) Research in Organizational Behavior, vol. 6, pp. 191–233. JAI Press, Homewood (1984)
19. Mumford, E.: Sociotechnical Systems Design: Evolving Theory and Practice. Manchester Business School, Manchester (1985)
20. Venkatesh, V., Morris, M.G., Davis, G.B., Davis, F.D.: User acceptance of information technology: toward a unified view. MIS Q. **27**(3), 425–478 (2003)

Comparing PLM and BIM from the Product Structure Standpoint

Conrad Boton[1(✉)], Louis Rivest[1], Daniel Forgues[1], and Julie Jupp[2]

[1] Ecole de Technologie Supérieure, Montréal, Canada
{conrad.boton, louis.rivest, daniel.forgues}@etsmtl.ca
[2] University of Technology Sydney, Ultimo, Australia

Abstract. The increasing use of Building Information Modelling (BIM) across the construction industry highlights the potential for a common endpoint with manufacturing industries. Previous research work has shown that it is possible to improve BIM with the features and the best practices from Product Lifecycle Management (PLM) approach. This article provides a comparison between the PLM and BIM approaches from the standpoint of the Product Structure (PS) and the Bill of Material (BOM). It discusses the need to explicit a structuring concept in the BIM approach in order be able to switch to an information-centric management approach in construction projects instead of the current activity-based approach.

Keywords: BIM · PLM · Product Structure · Bill of Material · BOM · Construction

1 Introduction

Considered to be refractory to information technology, the construction industry has suffered a great delay in terms of productivity compared to other industries such as aerospace and automotive. The sector is characterized by high fragmentation, heterogeneous project teams and a lack of interoperability. For decades, several studies have explored the role of information technology as an integrating element and enabler of productivity without much success until recently [1–3].

Yet with the rise of BIM [4], the industry seems at a crossroads. Indeed, BIM appears to have the potential to solve a number of persistent problems in the sector (interoperability, optimization of information flows, etc.) that will lead to improvements in productivity [2, 5]. While early studies focused on interoperability issues and other technological improvements, it appeared quite soon that the great value of BIM lay in collaboration and optimization of information flows throughout the project life cycle: unfortunately the source for most of the current limitations of the BIM approach. Recent research [6–8] suggests improving BIM based on best practices from PLM.

Jupp [6] recently studied the consequences of incomplete BIM implementation in construction projects. The results suggest that the PLM approach actually provides interesting features to solve many of the problems currently encountered in the BIM approach. Indeed, similarities exist between the current upheavals in construction and the changes observed in complex manufacturing industries a few years ago with the

R. Harik et al. (Eds.): PLM 2016, IFIP AICT 492, pp. 443–453, 2016.
DOI: 10.1007/978-3-319-54660-5_40

arrival of the PLM approach [7]. In addition, the philosophy and overall objectives of BIM are similar to the PLM approach.

Recent studies suggest that as a methodology, instead of evolving into a construction-dedicated PLM approach, that BIM and the structured product data stemming from its modelling processes be used to create an effective connection between the application of PLM and ERP systems to construction projects [9]. Holzer presents the Bill-Of-Materials (BOM) as the missing link between BIM and existing (and largely disconnected), feasibility, design, construction and operational processes [9].

The concept of the BOM is widely used in other industrial sectors, and the Product Structure is central to PLM systems. Moreover, "unlike product structures, a BOM cannot store a complete customized products family" [10] and "does not consider the product data that is associated with the technical objects" [10]. However, these two concepts are useful and practical in manufacturing industries to convey information throughout the entire lifecycle of a project.

Since the construction industry is comparable to the other discrete manufacturing industries, despite some notable differences, these concepts then appear to be very interesting directions with good potential in enabling an information-centric management approach in construction projects in the age of BIM.

We could reasonably argue that PLM systems would not be the same without a Product Structure to organize data. However, while the construction industry uses product breakdown structures, comparing PLM and BIM through the way product structure is defined and exploited could bring valuable insight on the differences between these sectors and the tools they use. Ultimately, this comparison could even provide a way to transpose some PLM successes to BIM. This article explores the concepts of BOM and Product Structure in the light of current BIM practices and provides a discussion on how PLM and BIM compare with respect to the notion of the Product Structure as conceived of in discrete manufacturing industries. It first introduces the background through the peculiarities or the construction industry and the related works. It then defines the different concepts and discusses how they can be seen as structuring concepts in the BIM approach.

2 Background

2.1 Particularities of the Construction Industry

It seems important, before going further, to present a comparison between the construction industry and other manufacturing industries. In a study by Green et al. [11] a comparison between the construction and aerospace industries provides an accurate representation of the differences of context between these industries. They identify two major elements to analyze these differences: the structural differences and the relationship with government. It is generally accepted that the construction sector is larger but still very fragmented and localized, while the aerospace industry has highly consolidated in recent decades due to considerable competitive pressure. In previous research on construction industry fragmentation, Howard et al. [1] distinguish vertical fragmentation from horizontal fragmentation. Vertical fragmentation concerns the fact that a construction project is divided into several more or less short phases. Horizontal fragmentation relates to the fact that multiple different specialist interactions occur during the same phase. The combination of vertical and horizontal fragmentation therefore gives rise to small specialist firms operating on small local markets.

If the last decades have seen the merger of several major players in the aerospace industry to form large blocks, mergers observed in construction remain comparatively low [11]. The structure of the construction industry can be illustrated by a large-based pyramid dominated by small firms. While the dominance in the aerospace industry is made by large companies with a much more widespread technological expertise throughout the supply chain. Competition between firms in construction is done more on cost than on technical expertise. In addition, the combination of technological requirements and the complex network of interdependences in aerospace is a significant barrier for new entrants, which is far from the case in construction [11]. The last structural difference identified by Green et al. [11] is related to the customer base that seems highly diversified in construction but very narrow in aerospace, which is characterized by long-term collaborative relationships between a small number of highly sophisticated clients.

Moreover, unlike aerospace, the construction sector is marked by high flexibility and a strong sense of "laissez-faire" that governments prefer to see as an advantage for the sector [11]. This need for flexibility was confirmed by Kubicki [12] who finds that it occupies a central place especially during the construction phase where mutual adjustment is important. A very recent study showed empirically that there is significant difference between the as-planned activities and the actually-performed activities [13]. In reality, the work processes are usually not documented and they are "voluntarily" informal. This makes traceability of accurate information very difficult.

Despite these differences, the two industries remain altogether comparable for many reasons. Patrick [14] highlights the fact that both try to manufacture a product using appropriate resources (materials, equipment, labor). The product is manufactured using a specific process, and its implementation takes place on a particular site. The quality/cost ratio is very important and there is a need for optimization.

2.2 Related Works

Based on an empirical research, Jupp [6] studied the consequences of incomplete implementation of BIM as is currently the case in most applications of the methodology. The study identifies three types of problems: process-based issues, technology-based issues and policy-based issues. The study then identifies the basic features of PLM in order to demonstrate that there are a range of established solutions that cover a large part of these problems. The results show that PLM can actually be an opportunity to expand existing applications of BIM. However the study also suggests that the transverse application of a BIM-PLM solution that is based on discrete manufacturing processes might lead to other types of problems due to the complexity of interfaces observed in construction projects. Indeed, the problems observed in the use of BIM in construction projects are often specific to the client and the project's principal requirements, while the PLM approach is based on generic features. Moreover, the complexity and the large uncertainties of the collaborative environment in the construction industry suggest great caution. In the same period, Aram and Eastman [8] proposed a discussion on the improvement of BIM with PLM functionalities. They noted that it should be necessary to modify and adapt many aspects of current PLM technology before being able to apply it in construction due to the major differences between the construction and the PLM's traditional target industries [8].

Jupp and Nepal [7] explored how BIM and PLM have impacted the professional practices in construction and manufacturing industries. For each industry, they explored the way BIM or PLM change the working practices through the new activities they come with, the new responsibilities and roles, the competencies needed and the relations in the supply chain. The study highlighted the unique characteristics of each industry and PLM and BIM contrasts. They concluded that the level of BIM maturity across the construction industry is improving, increasing the possibility to reach a "common endpoint with manufacturing industries". In the same spirit, Holzer [9] noted that the full potential of the BIM approach has reached a maturity at a level that is possible to consider its integration, through the definition of BOM, with PLM systems, and moreover with the production line. According to this research, the efforts undertaken in the past to link the manufacturing data with construction information in the frame of ERP systems have failed due to the use of 2D CAD that is not best suited for this purpose. With BIM, it is now possible to have the necessary information-centric project delivery approach. So it can be easier to integrate construction processes with product information.

In complement to these researches, many technology-centered works attempted to merge BIM and PLM capabilities into a single technological environment [15–17]. If the effectiveness of these solutions remains to be seen, they have the merit of showing that a sum of features cannot be the solution to issues unresolved in the adoption of PLM, nor of BIM.

3 Product Structure: The Missing Link in the BIM Approach?

3.1 What Is It?

Jansen-Vullers et al. [18] defined the Bill of Materials as "a list of components required for the production of a parent item". In the form of a network the BOM "goes-into relationships", and usually stores the number and type of relationships between component units necessary for the parent unit [19]. The structure of a BOM differs according to the production environment it is demanded by. Maull et al. [20] distinguish five different production environments (demanding different BOM structures) including make-to-stock, assemble-to-order, make-to-order, engineer-to-order, and selling capacity. In a make-to-stock environment, a BOM is prepared for each product and a percentage BOM regroups similar final products. In an assemble-to-order environment, modular BOMs are used because it is impractical to define a BOM for each product due to the large variety of products. In make-to-order environments, four different BOM types are used: a planning BOM for forecasting purposes (relationships between product families and components), a standard BOM (semi-finished products released from engineering), a reference BOM (kinds of the product), and an order BOM (used in the case of particular orders from customers). In engineer-to-order environments, because customers change their requirements throughout the life of the product, the BOM is developed gradually. BOMs usually begin in the design-engineering department but are found in the inventory control, procurement, shipping, marketing, manufacturing, field services, and even in the accounting department [21].

There should be no confusion with the Product Structure even if in colloquial language, a BOM is often referred to as a Product Structure [21]. According to Brière-Côté et al. [22], these two concepts are different despite their similarity. As a single-level part list, a BOM, is considered as a simple filtered Product Structure snapshot at some point during the life of the product development [10], and is not identical to a Product Structure [21], which is defined as "an organized hierarchical collection of technical objects that are linked via 'part-of' relationships" [10]. The Product Structure then "describes hierarchically, using items, how a product can be generated from assemblies, sub-assemblies, and components" [21]. Resulting from a logical breakdown technique with particular concerns, the Product Structure stores not only technical objects but also associated product data and customized product families in a dynamic way and according to different views (e.g., a structural view, filtered view, cognitive view) [10]. Figure 1 illustrates a structured view of as-specified, as-designed and as-planned technical objects, product data and customized product families. Eynard et al. [23] noted that all instantiated data are managed and stored in the Product Structure.

In PLM tools, these data are classified using metadata and appropriate links are established between the parts and related files through metadata configurable links [23].

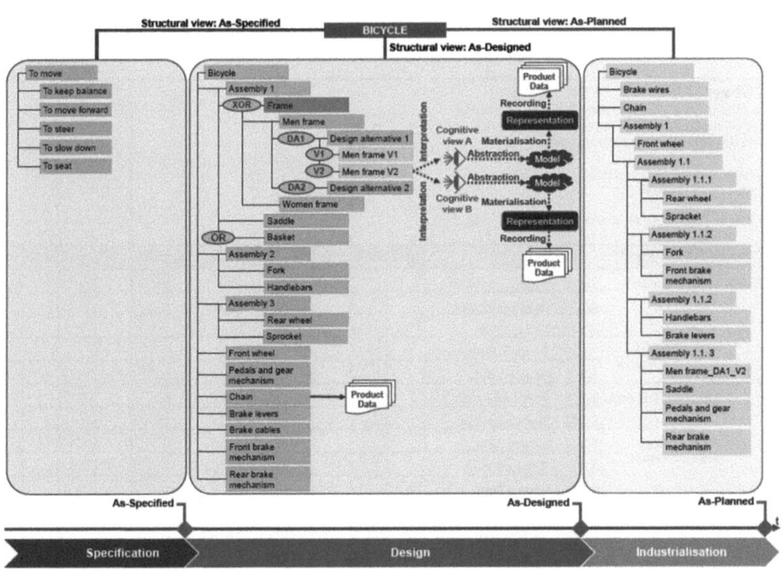

Fig. 1. Example of a multi-view product structure (Source [10])

In practice the Product Structure can encompass various data types. Trappey et al. [24] identified at least 10 major data types and functions including product definition, service parts support, material purchase planning, assembly sequence, order entry facility, resource analysis, pricing, cost analysis, manufacturing instruction, and engineering change control. For product design and manufacturing management purposes, PLM systems require, in addition to the product structure manager, a workflow engine which "according to the product structure, sends the right available data at the right time to the right user" [23]. This constitutes an important aspect in optimizing the information flow in the PLM approach.

3.2 The Need to Explicit a Product Structure Concept in the BIM Approach

To ensure that the appropriate information is contained within the model, current BIM practices suggest identifying the function of the model and specify the related information requirements prior to implementation so as to develop the model accordingly. Kreider and Messner defined a BIM use as "a method or strategy of applying Building Information Modeling during a facility's lifecycle to achieve one or more specific objectives" [25]. Twenty-five BIM uses have been identified (e.g., 3D coordination, design review, cost estimation, phase planning, site analysis, mechanical analysis, etc.) with various use frequencies and different impacts in the industry [26]. To define information requirements, a Model Element Table (MET) is used. The MET structure in construction is quite similar to the BOM in manufacture. It summarizes the list of the model elements but also "indicates the LOD [Level of Development] to which each Model Element Author (MEA) is required to develop the content of the Model Element at the conclusion of each phase of the Project" [27] (See Fig. 2). Thus despite their

§ 4.3 Model Element Table

Identify (1) the LOD required for each Model Element at the end of each phase, and (2) the Model Element Author (MEA) responsible for developing the Model Element to the LOD identified.

Insert abbreviations for each MEA identified in the table below, such as "A – Architect," or "C – Contractor."

NOTE: LODs must be adapted for the unique characteristics of each Project.

Model Elements Utilizing CSI UniFormat™				LOD	MEA	LOD	MEA	LOD	MEA	LOD	MEA	LOD	MEA	LOD	MEA	Note Number (See 4.4)
A SUBSTRUCTURE	A10 Foundations	A1010	Standard Foundations													
		A1020	Special Foundations													
		A1030	Slab on Grade													
	A20 Basement Construction	A2010	Basement Excavation													
		A2020	Basement Walls													
B SHELL	B10 Superstructure	B1010	Floor Construction													
		B1020	Roof Construction													
	B20 Exterior Enclosure	B2010	Exterior Walls													
		B2020	Exterior Windows													
		B2030	Exterior Doors													
	B30 Roofing	B3010	Roof Coverings													
		B3020	Roof Openings													
C INTERIORS	C10 Interior Construction	C1010	Partitions													

Fig. 2. Excerpt of a Model Element Table (MET) [27]

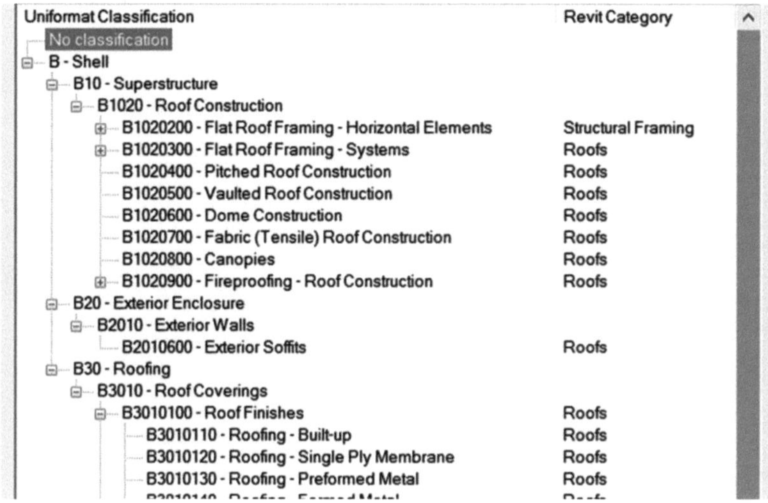

Fig. 3. Example list of model element hierarchies in Revit

similarity in terms of structure, unlike the BOM which is extracted from the model, the MET serves as base for the construction of the model.

The BIM model is then developed according to the requirements defined in the MET. In current BIM tools, it is possible to generate a model elements hierarchical list and many concepts are used that could be similar to Product Structure, including the Product Breakdown Structure (PBS) and the Model Element Breakdown (MEB).

According to Gijezen et al. [28], the PBS "divides the final object in physical systems, components, and elements". The PBS concept is well known in the BIM approach. For example, it plays an important role in 4D simulation where the model creation consists of linking it with the Work Breakdown Structure (WBS) from the schedule [29]. Moreover Gijezen et al. [28] showed how the PBS could be used to improve the clash detection process in 3D coordination. In BIM software, it is also known as the Model Element Breakdown (MEB), as described by Saluja [30], that can be used to create information exchange worksheets. Figure 3 shows an example of a model elements hierarchy list as presented in Autodesk Revit.

Some BIM software dedicated plugins (BOM to Excel[1], SysQue BOM[2], etc.) are emerging, suggesting that the way the MEB is managed in BIM tools seems insufficient to cover practitioners' needs. For instance, if it is possible to extract detailed "materials and quantities takeoffs" from current BIM software such as Revit, it seems not possible to manage the breakdown structure "according to different views" [19] in order to allow the different production environments to make different demands on the structure" [20]. For example, the construction schedule and cost estimate remain as two separate autonomous files in typical approaches to BIM [32].

---

1 http://www.hingepoint.com/products/bom-revit-app.

2 http://sysque.com/sysque-modules/sysque-bom.

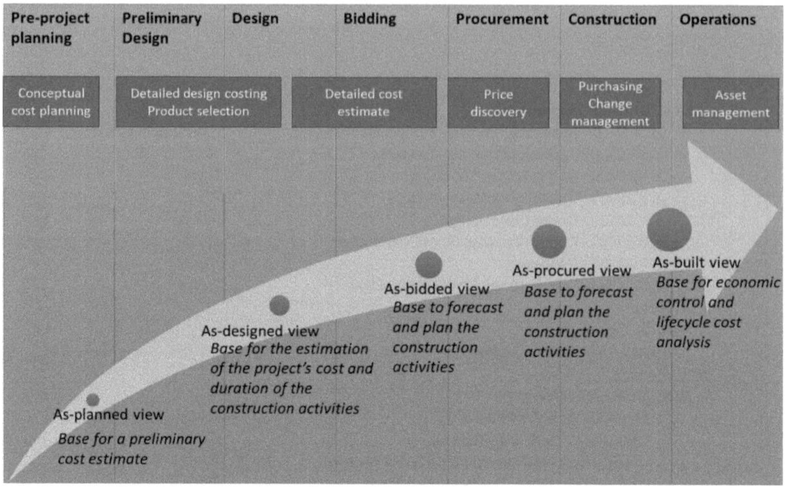

Fig. 4. Possible evolution of the product structure views for cost estimation BIM use

The approach taken by Trimble's Vico software does provide the ability for the building information model to become somewhat more integrated relative to the notion of a Product Structure in manufacturing. It achieves this by removing the need to link disparate schedules generated by what are typically separate and independent 3D, 4D and 5D models [32]. The integrated Vico model thus enables the definition of how long it will take to install the amount of materials being derived from the model. This approach reflects a manufacturing mindset as the unified schedule becomes a product of what and how much will be built and represents this in a particular order that has construction logic. Indeed, BIM use encompasses many processes (3D, 4D and 5D) that call for different views of the product structure. Moreover, in the framework of a specific BIM use (e.g. 3D coordination, cost estimation, phase planning, etc.) many sub-processes corresponding to different views are necessary throughout the project lifecycle. For example, based on the study conducted by Monteiro and Martins [31], Fig. 4 proposes the different views necessary for the various processes of Cost Estimation throughout the project lifecycle. The purposes of such views are also indicated.

4 Conclusion and Future Works

Several recent research works have addressed the improvement of BIM based on PLM's best practices. If these works are interesting milestones, a major limitation of current BIM practices lies in the fact that the perspective of construction project management is still activity-based rather than information-centric. To implement an information-centric perspective and fully capitalize the potential of BIM in order to optimize flows within the production line, it is necessary to define a structuring concept linking the BIM model, the BIM uses and the other information flows in the project. This paper proposed a discussion on why and how the Product Structure, well-known in manufacturing industries and less in construction, could be such missing link.

In current BIM approach, it is possible to make correspondences between some of the representations used (Model Element Table, Quantity Take-Off, Design Brief, Contract Program, etc.) and the BOM and the Product Structure in discrete manufacturing. However, and unlike what is seen in PLM, they are all disconnected and aren't linked with associated product data and customized product families. Then, the main gap in expliciting a Product Structure in the BIM tools concerns its integration within the model. That is to provide links and representations of this data for different BIM dimensions (3D, 4D and 5D) and BIM uses purposes. Moreover the model validation (even at the handover stages) is rarely undertaken and the quality of data beyond geometry is largely poor (even naming and layer conventions are often very poor throughout design stages) as the quality of data is not audited systematically and progressively. The discipline-based modelling process (architectural, structural, mechanical, electrical, hydraulic, fire, and site models) requires frequent federation processes that go beyond the typical design coordination reviews and extend into model quality audits.

Future works will deepen the comparison between how PLM and BIM tools allow product structure manipulation. The aim is to provide a factual and precise comparative approach which could eventually, according to the findings, lead to a cross pollination from the PLM approach to the BIM approach. Moreover it will be important to study how the IFC information model can efficiently be replaced at the heart of BIM practices in order to play the critical structuring backbone role.

References

1. Howard, H., Levitt, R., Paulson, B.C., Pohl, J.G., Tatum, C.B.: Computer integration: reducing fragmentation in AEC industry. J. Comput. Civ. Eng. **3**, 18–32 (1989)
2. Sacks, R., Barak, R.: Impact of three-dimensional parametric modeling of buildings on productivity in structural engineering practice. Autom. Constr. **17**, 439–449 (2008)
3. Arayici, Y., Coates, P., Koskela, L., Kagioglou, M., Usher, C., O'Reilly, K.: Technology adoption in the BIM implementation for lean architectural practice. Autom. Constr. **20**, 189–195 (2011)
4. Eastman, C., Teicholz, P., Sacks, R., Liston, K.: BIM Handbook: A Guide to Building Information Modeling for Owners, Managers, Engineers, and Contractors. Wiley, Hoboken (2008)
5. Eadie, R., Browne, M., Odeyinka, H., McKeown, C., McNiff, S.: BIM implementation throughout the UK construction project lifecycle: an analysis. Autom. Constr. **36**, 145–151 (2013)
6. Jupp, J.R.: Incomplete BIM implementation: exploring challenges and the role of product lifecycle management functions. In: Bernard, A., Rivest, L., Dutta, D. (eds.) PLM 2013. IAICT, vol. 409, pp. 630–640. Springer, Heidelberg (2013). doi:10.1007/978-3-642-41501-2_62
7. Jupp, J.R., Nepal, M.: BIM and PLM: comparing and learning from changes to professional practice across sectors. In: Fukuda, S., Bernard, A., Gurumoorthy, B., Bouras, A. (eds.) PLM 2014. IAICT, vol. 442, pp. 41–50. Springer, Heidelberg (2014). doi:10.1007/978-3-662-45937-9_5

8. Aram, S., Eastman, C.: Integration of PLM solutions and BIM systems for the AEC industry. In: Proceedings of 30th International Symposium of Automation and Robotics in Construction and Mining, Montreal, pp. 1046–1055 (2013)
9. Holzer, D.: Fostering the link from PLM to ERP via BIM. In: Fukuda, S., Bernard, A., Gurumoorthy, B., Bouras, A. (eds.) PLM 2014. IAICT, vol. 442, pp. 75–82. Springer, Heidelberg (2014). doi:10.1007/978-3-662-45937-9_8
10. Pinquié, R., Conception, L., Produits, D.: An illustrated glossary of ambiguous PLM terms used in discrete manufacturing. Int. J. Prod. Lifecycle Manag. **8**, 142–171 (2015)
11. Green, S.D., Fernie, S., Weller, S.: Making sense of supply chain management: a comparative study of aerospace and construction. Constr. Manag. Econ. **23**, 579–593 (2005)
12. Kubicki, S.: Assister la coordination flexible de l'activité de construction de bâtiments, Une approche par les modèles pour la proposition d'outils de visualisation du contexte de coopération (2006)
13. de Blois, M., Lizarralde, G., De Coninck, P.: Iterative project processes within temporary multi-organizations in construction: the self-, eco-, re-organizing projects. Proj. Manag. J. **47**, 27–44 (2016)
14. Patrick, C.: Construction Project Planning and Scheduling. Prentice Hall, Upper Saddle River (2003)
15. Reefman, R.J.B., van Nederveen, S.: A controlled integral product model (IPM®) in building and construction. In: CIB W78-W102 2011: International Conference (2011)
16. Lebègue, E., De Almeida, R., Pinon, L.: Lascom AEC BIM Edition, un couplage BIM IFC et PLM. In: BIM & Maquette numérique pour l'architecture et la construction, Eyrolles, pp. 107–114 (2014)
17. Popov, V.: BIM/PLM bentley platform. In: Conference on Digital Construction (2014)
18. Jansen-Vullers, M., van Dorp, C., Beulens, A.J.: Managing traceability information in manufacture. Int. J. Inf. Manag. **23**, 395–413 (2003)
19. Schuh, G., Rozenfeld, H., Assmus, D., Zancul, E.: Process oriented framework to support PLM implementation. Comput. Ind. **59**, 210–218 (2008)
20. Maull, R., Hughes, D., Bennett, J.: The role of the bill-of-materials as a CAD/CAPM interface and the key importance of engineering change control. Comput. Control Eng. J. **3**, 63 (1992)
21. Saaksvuori, A., Immonen, A.: Product Lifecycle Management. Springer, Berlin (2008)
22. Brière-Côté, A., Rivest, L., Desrochers, A.: Adaptive generic product structure modelling for design reuse in engineer-to-order products. Comput. Ind. **61**, 53–65 (2010)
23. Eynard, B., Gallet, T., Nowak, P., Roucoules, L.: UML based specifications of PDM product structure and workflow. Comput. Ind. **55**, 301–316 (2004)
24. Trappey, A.J.C., Peng, T.-K., Lin, H.-D.: An object-oriented bill of materials system for dynamic product management. J. Intell. Manuf. **7**, 365–371 (1996)
25. Kreider, R., Messner, J.: The Uses of BIM: Classifying and Selecting BIM Uses. Pennsylvania state University, University Park (2013)
26. Kreider, R., Messner, J., Dubler, C.: Determining the frequency and impact of applying BIM for different purposes on building projects. In: Proceedings of the 6th International Conference on Innovation in Architecture, Engineering and Construction (AEC), pp. 1–10 (2010)
27. American Institute of Architects: E202-2008 Building Information Modeling protocol exhibit (2008)
28. Gijezen, S., Hartmann, T., Buursema, N.: Organizing 3D building information models with the help of work breakdown structures to improve the clash detection process (2009)
29. Zhou, W., Heesom, D., Georgakis, P., Nwagboso, C., Feng, A.: An interactive approach to collaborative 4D construction planning. Electron. J. Inf. Technol. Constr. **14**, 30–47 (2009)

30. Saluja, C.: A process mapping procedure for planning building information modeling (BIM): execution on a building construction project, pp. 1–152 (2009)
31. Monteiro, A., Poças Martins, J.: A survey on modeling guidelines for quantity takeoff-oriented BIM-based design. Autom. Constr. **35**, 238–253 (2013)
32. Hardin, B., McCool, D.: BIM and Construction Management: Proven Tools, Methods, and Workflows, 2nd edn. Wiley, Hoboken (2015)

Big Data Analytics and Business Intelligence

On Applicability of Big Data Analytics in the Closed-Loop Product Lifecycle: Integration of CRISP-DM Standard

Elaheh Gholamzadeh Nabati[1(✉)] and Klaus-Dieter Thoben[2]

[1] International Graduate School for Dynamics in Logistics, University of Bremen, Bremen, Germany
nab@biba.uni-bremen.de

[2] BIBA - Bremer Institute für Produktion und Logistik GmbH, Bremen, Germany
tho@biba.uni-bremen.de

Abstract. The product use data can have an important role in closed-loop product lifecycle management (CL-PLM), where information feedbacks from the use data can contribute to improve the product design and performance. The product usage data can nowadays be collected easier than before, with the aid of sensors and technologies embedded in products. However, the collected data can have complex characteristics. They come from various sources, have different formats and high volume. In order to improve the product lifecycle processes with these data, discussing the use of data analysis in the product lifecycle is necessary. Analyzing the data with such characteristics has been also considered in the context of big data analytics. In this paper an approach for standardization of the process of usage data analysis based on a standard called Cross Industry Standard Process for Data Mining (CRISP-DM), is introduced and its potential integration in CL-PLM is investigated. The reference steps of analyzing usage data are identified. They cover the processes between data generation until feeding back the knowledge of use to the product design phase.

Keywords: Big data · Closed-loop product lifecycle · CRISP-DM · Product use data · Standardization

1 Introduction and Problem Description

Product lifecycle is referred to the different stages which product goes through during its life span. Usually these steps are seen from the time the concept of the product is developed until the retirement and recycling. These stages can be grouped into three phases. Beginning of the life (BOL), middle of the life (MOL) and end of the life (EOL). BOL includes product development and manufacturing. MOL starts when the product is put into operation and EOL refers to the activities of recycling and disposing [24, 27]. Closed-loop PLM focuses on enabling continues flow of information between different phases of the lifecycle [10]. Improving the information flows includes better use of product lifecycle data and enhancing the processes of the lifecycle with them. For example, improving the product development and design process with the product

R. Harik et al. (Eds.): PLM 2016, IFIP AICT 492, pp. 457–467, 2016.
DOI: 10.1007/978-3-319-54660-5_41

use data. In this regard, accurate understanding of product operating condition helps design engineers to find the cause of failures. Thus, it can increase the reliability of product [8].

In the CL-PLM with the help of intelligent products, the product use data can nowadays be collected easier than before. These products which are equipped with sensors and embedded technologies, can capture and transmit data when they are under operation. Yet, the modern use data has complex characteristics. These characteristics include the followings; they come from various sources and different formats. They are being produced with a high speed and their amount is larger than the use data gathered previously from the product. Therefore, in order to improve the product and the product lifecycle processes with these data, discussing the use of data analysis in the product lifecycle is necessary.

From the other hand, mentioned characteristics of modern use data, collected by smart products are similar to "Big data" characteristics. Big data is the data which has high volume, high speed of generation (veracity of generation) and consists of variety of source and formats [20]. In this paper, we discuss the product use data from the perspective of big data analytics. The big data analytics has not been discussed in the CL-PLM broadly so far. The aim of this study is to provide an overall view from the potential mechanism of using big data analysis in the CL-PLM. For this reason, we seek to find the reference processes. The information feedback flow from the use process to the design process is focused in this paper. The importance of this analysis is that currently, there is no instruction or standard processes which guide on how to find this information feedback and how to transform use data into useful information for this aim. Finding the reference steps in this case is very beneficial. Because it is independent from tool or technique of data capturing, analyzing and information feedback gaining. Moreover, most of the current practices in the field of PLM to model the information flows address the IT and computer science perspective. Little research has been done that focus on the processes.

Therefore, in this research we investigate the modification and integration of Cross Industry Standard Process for Data Mining (CRISP-DM), which is a well-known standard process for data analysis, in the CL-PLM. This is done based on the characteristics of usage data and information feedbacks between usage and design phase. This paper is organized as follows. Section 2 describes the state of the art. Section 3 explains the research approach for integrating the data analysis to the CL-PLM. Section 4 provides a brief discussion and in Sect. 5 the conclusion is presented.

2 Related Work

2.1 CL-PLM and Information Feedbacks to Improve Design

Traditionally, the product use data can be gathered mainly by methods such as questionnaire and interview from the customers or by analyzing the failures happened to the products from maintenance or warranty reports. This information is later applied to improve the design reliability. However, this kind of feedback generation takes long until it turns to actionable information for the designers [1]. Also, the designers should apply a lot of assumptions about the product's condition of the use. However, by development of the concept of CL-PLM, accessibility to usage data is increased. In addition, processing of these data and new methods of getting information feedbacks gained significant attention. One reason is that now it is possible to achieve a complete view of the product usage instead of only using the data from usage measurements [5].

Several researchers addressed the information feedback from the usage data in the CL-PLM by data analysis techniques. For example, [1] discussed the integration of data analysis methods in the production phase for manufacturing of steel. [13] considered the feedback generation from product use when data for several instances of the same product should be summarized and extracted. [13] used the Bayesian method as the technique to generate information feedbacks from usage data for the aim of improving the product design. [1] studied integration of usage data from the condition monitoring system to PLM systems. [16] made a similar research on the data of condition monitoring systems for a conveyor belt and proposed a methodology to integrate the results in BOL. From the literature it can be observed that data analysis plays an important role in transforming the usage data to relevant information feedbacks for the product design.

In order to gain better information feedbacks, it is important to identify the source and understand the characteristics of usage data [36]. This knowledge can help to find a suitable data analysis method for generating feedbacks. More description in this regard is provided in Sect. 2.2.

2.2 Product Usage Data and Its Characteristics

The usage data in the CL-PLM can be gathered by smart products. In this paper smart products are referred to consumer products which are equipped with sensors, RFID or embedded technologies. They can collect the information about their status and use condition [19, 31].

The sensors installed on the devices, can stream the data such the environmental condition, status of product and history of changes, type of the use and performance of product.

There are also other sources of product use data. The data which can be gathered from mobile applications, social media and websites. These type of data can show the user's opinions about the product or problems with the product.

All these data sources, have specific characteristics. They can be collected every few minutes. They are being generated very fast. For example, in the case of sensor data, the measurements can be done every few minutes. They have various formats and characteristics. For example, the sensor can be presented in log files or excel sheets, while the text data from maintenance reports is unstructured and cannot be presented well with the excel sheets. Moreover, usually they contain not only one measurement, but also a batch of data for every measurement interval. Therefore, when we consider the amount of the data and the speed of their generation we are exposed to a big amount of data. It can be said that the product use data has the characteristics of variety, velocity and volume (3V), similar to the characteristics in the context of big data analytics. More explanation is provided in Sect. 2.3.

2.3 Big Data Analytics to Support Getting Information Feedbacks from Usage Data

Big data is considered as *"high-volume, high-velocity and high-variety data that demand cost-effective, innovative forms of information processing for enhanced insight and decision making"* [20]. The data analytics is part of big data technology which aims to convert the data into useful information. These information has the potential to provide insight for the decision making. For example, in the maintenance it can help to find the failures before they happen. In spite of slight differences, the terms big data analytics, data mining and data analysis are used interchangeably in this paper.

Data analysis has been seen as a complementary service and not as a main module in the CL-PLM. However, regarding the importance of usage data and its potential to improve lifecycle activities, it is worthy that usage data be discussed and more investigated. One aspect which needs attention is to find a uniform and standard guideline for the use of big data analysis in the CL-PLM. Applying a standard can have several advantages for CL-PLM. For example, it can act as a guideline. So, it reduces the need for the high skilled people for analysis of data. Also it leads to time and cost saving. From the theoretical perspective, it offers stable model development for the problems in the lifecycle because it is a generic model and can be used apart from the tools and techniques used for modelling.

In the next section CRISP-DM as a standard for processes of data analytics and data science is explained. Additionally, its applicability to the CL-PLM is tested.

2.4 Crisp-DM

"Cross Industry Standard Process - for Data Mining" (CRISP-DM) is a data analysis process standard that describes commonly used approaches for performing analysis of data when the volume of the data is high. It is applicable in various industries. This standard was founded by SPSS in a cooperative project, where Daimler Chrysler, was also a shareholder [23]. Currently, this process model is supported by IBM. It is one of the most widely used standard by the data mining practitioners. This model consists of different levels of abstraction. Figure 1 shows the data mining methodology based on CRISP- DM processes and sequences. In this figure the high level processes are shown. The business understanding shows the requirements of the data analysis problem from business perspective. It emphasizes on understanding the goal of data analysis and recognizing the aspects of problem very well. The data understanding process includes the initial data collection and becoming familiar with the data, its variables and dimensions. The data preparation contains the filtering, aggregating, selecting the parameters and constructing a subset of data suitable for the analysis. The modelling phase different models are fitted to the data and the optimal values are found. The relevant models covered are the machine learning, data mining and statistical analysis. At the evaluation stage the goodness of the model and the outcome gained from it is assessed. At last, during the deployment phase the knowledge gained from the modeling is discussed with the user and applied to the problem in action [37].

The aim of selection of CRISP-DM is, that it can cover analysis of data when the data has high volumes. Therefore, it can be suitable for modelling the use data.

Fig. 1. CRISP-DM processes and cycle [23]

However, it does not take into account all the characteristics of product use data such as variety of sources and fast generation. For example, the data can come from the sensor also from the web. There are no instructions in the CRISP-DM for handling variety of formats specially the unstructured data. Moreover, it does not take the data veracity into account. Similar problems exist when it comes to data that are generated very fast for example by sensors. These aspects have not been considered in this standard. In the next section in order to leverage the limitations of the standard, we investigate current available big data analytics frameworks and suggest solutions.

3 Approach: Integrating the Data Analysis in the Closed-Loop Product Lifecycle

For covering the dimensions of use data which are not included in CRISP-DM, such as variety and veracity, we go through the current available big data analytics frameworks. Twenty-three papers with big data process frameworks from the state of the art of big data analytics were selected. The papers are either published by renowned research databases or are the technical report of companies, who are active in the field of big data. For example, [14, 30]. We determined the steps common between the frameworks. The steps regarding to conducting the analysis on data are investigated. Moreover, the steps of data analytics have been compared with the steps of CRISP-DM standard. Table 1 shows this comparison.

In Table 1, the frameworks are listed. They are compared with the CRISP-DM (column 2 to 7). Column 2 to 7 shows the phases of CRISP-DM, including business understanding, data understanding and etc. If the framework supports any of these phases, it is marked with 1. Otherwise, if the process is not considered in the framework it is marked with 0.

As mentioned before, the frameworks which cover the aspects of data variety and veracity were selected. Therefore, complementary processes exist in the framework,

Table 1. Assessment of big data analytics frameworks and comparison with CRISP-DM steps

Framework name	Business understand	Data understanding	Preparation	Modelling	Evaluation	Deployment	Other processes
(Big data consulting) [4]	1	1	0	1	1	0	Impact analysis, research best practices of big data
(Business Biro) [7]	1	1	0	1	0	1	Define big data architecture
(Loshin) [28]	1	1	0	0	0	0	
(Krishnan) [25]	0	1	1	1	0	0	Data acquisition, data storage, big data visualization
(Philip Chen and Zhang) [30]	0	0	1	1	0	0	Data storage, decision making, Big data visualization
(Reffat et al.) [32]	0	0	1	1	0	0	Data storage
(Dayal et al.) [11] a	0	1	1	1	0	0	Define big data architecture, data generation, Data warehousing (storage)
(Dayal et al.) b	1	0	0	1	1	1	Data flow integration
(Dayal et al.) c	0	0	1	1	1	0	Unstructured data modeling
(Assunção et al.) [3]	1	1	1	1	1	1	Data source, big data visualization
(Pääkkönen and Pakkala) [29]	0	1	1	1	1	1	Data generation, data management, data extraction (acquisition), storage
(Vera-baquero et al.) [35]	0	0	1	1	1	1	Control and monitor the results
(Lavalle) [26]	1	1	0	1	0	1	
(Ren and Zhao) [33]	0	1	1	1	0	1	Data acquisition, data storage, data management
(Gandomi and Haider) [20]	0	0	1	1	0	1	Data acquisition and record (storage), data management
(Zhan et al.) [38]	0	0	1	1	0	0	Data generation
(Catley et al.) [9]	1	1	1	1	0	1	
(Folorunso and Ogunde) [18]	0	0	0	1	1	1	Decision maker, BPR, new uses in process
(Fernández et al.) [17]	0	0	1	1	0	1	Data management, parallel computing, data storage
(Accenture) [2]	1	0	1	1	1	1	Matrices, insight validation, business review cycle
(Booz Allen Hamilton Inc.) [6]	0	1	1	1	0	1	Data acquisition
(Diamantoulakis et al.) [12]	0	0	1	1	0	0	Data source (generation), distributed processing
(Dutta and Bose) [14]	1	0	1	1	1	1	Data acquisition, data visualization, integration with IT systems
(Hackathorn) [21]	0	1	1	1	1	1	Automate and operationalized, data acquisition
(Hashem et al.) [22]	0	0	1	1	1	0	Data source, data visualization
Sum	9	12	19	24	11	15	

which is not included in the CRISP-DM phases. The complementary processes are presented in the last column of the table under the name “other processes”. At the end the frequency of observed processes is calculated.

Table 2 shows the steps of processing big data, from initial data generation to gaining the useful knowledge from the data and make it actionable. Also the frequency of their observation in the big data frameworks are reported. The steps are also relevant for product use data. These steps can be followed as a reference guide line. These steps are useful to pursue, particularly in the case a data analysis project conducted in the CL-PLM. In the following we explain more about each process.

Table 2. Frequency of observed processes. Results from 25 big data frameworks

Big data analysis steps	Frequency observed in the frameworks
Data generation	6
Data acquisition	6
Data storage	6
Business understanding	9
Data understanding	12
Data management	3
Parallel computing	2
Preparation	19
Modelling	20
Evaluation	11
Visualization	5
Deployment	15

The first process is data generation. It means first the data are produced by the smart devices. It can be in form of the measurements by the sensors, such as temperature, vibration or other parameters relevant to the functionality of the product or its condition of use. Afterwards, the data are acquired from the smart product and put in to the storage area or to the analytical system. The importance of data acquisition is, to find all the information about the product usage, some sources of data need to be automatically extracted from the internet. The new data acquisition procedures and tools has been developed in the recent years to fulfill this need.

Data storage process come afterwards. The data storage has not been considered as an independent and major process in CRISP-DM. A reason can be in the CRISP-DM only storage in form of relational databases has been considered. In other words, storage of structured data. However, the data which are relevant for product use are partly in form structured data. They are also in other formats. Such as unstructured (text) format. Therefore, the data storage in cases were data with 3V characteristics exist should be recognized as a main task. Therefore, it has a major role for CL-PLM regarding management of product use data.

One of the other processes which was not clearly discussed by CRISP-DM, but is very important relating to use data is data visualization. Visualization is one of the most effective ways to communicate the results of analysis (data behavior) with the users. Not only modelling the data matters but also how to represent is to the decision maker who wants to use it for getting the insight and making decisions based on these data.

Yet, to make the data analysis suitable for CL-PLM, only the data analysis steps are not sufficient. We need to identify the steps of using the knowledge and transform it to information feedbacks to the design. For achieving this goal, in the second part of the study, a similar approach is done to identify the processes after finding initial insight from data analysis models until transforming and using the information as information feedback to the product design. In this part, analysis of 18 other frameworks was done. They were selected from the literature of improving the product design by taking into account the field data and product use, for example [15, 34]. The processes are grouped to four steps (Table 3). Then the frequency of each process in the data analysis models has been calculated. The results of these analyses are presented in Table 3. The total frequency of observed process in the frameworks is reported in the second column of Table 3.

Table 3. Results from 18 product design feedback frameworks

Step of product design improvement	Frequency observed in the frameworks
Root cause analysis/tests/experience	6
Severity analysis	2
Identification of degradation mode	3
Decision support integration	5

As illustrated in Table 3, root-cause analysis process contains the methods for problem solving and transforming the insight gained from the usage data to the useful information for the designers. In this process, techniques such as Failure Mode and Effect Analysis (FMEA), Failure Tree Analysis (FTA), Failure Mode Effect and Criticality Analysis (FMECA), tests and experiments are included. In fact, these techniques are applied to the data after modeling by data analytical methods. Ranking and identifying the severity of the problem for design modification is an important step. However, in the literature cited in this survey was only observed two times as a main process. The degradation mode identification and modelling its function has also proposed by some authors. In the last process, some authors integrated the knowledge to the decision support system for giving feedback to the designers.

4 Discussion

This paper tried to make the first step of the standardization in CL-PLM for analysis of the usage data collected from the smart products and introduce how a solution in this respect could look like. In this respect, we reflect the applicability of CRISP-DM. Moreover, we investigated the standard processes of usage data analysis and information feedback to product design. Some issues which need attention are listed as follows.

The Scale of Data Analysis: In the CL-PLM we can model the information flows regarding one product item or class. The standard processes of the data analysis and feedback generation (Tables 2 and 3), can be the same for all these categories. However, based on the scale, the focus of main processes can vary. For example, in the case of item-level data analysis enabling the track and trace of the product matters. In the case of complex engineering products, it can be important to model the interaction between several constituted modules (parts) of the product with each other. As an instance, in the case of degradation analysis, the effect that one faulty part can make for the other parts near it. In the case of mass produced products, the advances in the field of IoT, summarizing the knowledge gained from analyzing the behavior of several products and connecting the products should be considered.

The Uncertainties of Mapping. Methodologies for analyzing the data from intelligent products is still under development. The best practices for analyzing the product use data in the CL-PLM are not still specified. Consequently, standardization of process for data analysis on use data in the CL-PLM is on its early phase. However, in this research first step is made in this regards. This was done through analyzing the relevant literature and suggesting a current applicable standard.

Open Issues. We need to have approaches to deal with increase of product usage data. Also there are considerations for the modeling in action. For example, the availability of complete data. Specifically, when the use condition is captured but not all the necessary data which affect the problem under study has been captured. Aspects of data analysis, for example the difficulties in data storage when the usage data volume is very high and need distributed storage or the use of cloud services, also analysis of unstructured data still need research.

5 Conclusion

In this research analyzing the product use data for improving the design activities was addressed from the view point of big data analytics. First, the characteristics of new sources of product use data was described. Afterwards, a relevant methodology called CRISP-DM, from the field of data science, was introduced to the CL-PLM and its integration discussed. The steps of data analysis to information feedback generation for the design was the outcome of this paper. These steps can be a guide for the ones who want to apply data analysis in CL-PLM. The future work includes further investigation of the applicability of CRISP-DM for other types of information feedbacks in the lifecycle. Such as, feedback from the use data to the production or to the end of life phase. In addition, the proposed standard processes should be tested with case studies.

Acknowledgment. This research is supported by the DAAD-GSSP (Deutsche Akademischer Austauschdienst) scholarship.

References

1. Abramovici, M., Fathi, M., Holland, A., Neubach, M.: Integration of product use information into PLM. In: Proceedings of the 15th CIRP International Conference on Life Cycle Engineering. The University of New South Wales, Sydney (2008)

2. Accenture: Analytics in Action: Breakthroughs and Barriers on the Journey to ROI, Technical report, Accenture (2013)
3. Assunção, M.D., et al.: Big data computing and clouds: trends and future directions. J. Parallel Distrib. Comput. **79**, 3–15 (2015)
4. Big data consulting (2012). https://bigdataconsulting.wordpress.com/consulting/
5. Bluenose (2016). http://www.bluenose.com/blog/6-ways-to-increase-revenue-with-product-usage-data
6. Booz Allen Hamilton Inc.: The Field Guide to Data Science. 2nd edn. Booz Allen Hamilton Inc, McLean (2013)
7. Business Biro (2014). http://www.businessbrio.com/big-data.html
8. Carlson, J., Murphy, R.: Reliability analysis of mobile robots. In: Proceedings of IEEE Robotics and Automation (ICRA 2003), pp. 274–281 (2003)
9. Catley, C., Smith, K., Mcgregor, C., Tracy, M.: Extending CRISP-DM to incorporate temporal data mining of multi- dimensional medical data streams: a neonatal intensive care unit case study. In: IEEE International Symposium on Computer-Based Medical Systems, pp. 1–5 (2009)
10. CL2 M (2008). http://promise-innovation.com/cl2m
11. Dayal, U., Castellanos, M., Simitsis, A., Wilkinson, K.: Data Integration Flows for Business Intelligence, pp. 1–11. ACM, Saint Petersburg (2009)
12. Diamantoulakis, P., Kapinas, V., Karagiannidis, G.: Big data analytics for dynamic energy management in smart grids. Big Data Anal. High-Perform. Comput. **2**(3), 94–101 (2015)
13. Dienst, S., Ansari-Ch, F., Holland, A., Fathi, M.: Necessity of using Dynamic Bayesian Networks for feedback analysis into product development. In: IEEE International Conference on Systems Man and Cybernetics, pp. 939–946 (2010)
14. Dutta, D., Bose, I.: Managing a big data project: the case of ramco cements limited. Int. J. Prod. Econ. **165**, 293–306 (2015)
15. Fathi, M., Holland, A.: Knowledge-based feedback integration to facilitate sustainable product innovation. In: IEEE conference on Emerging Technologies & Factory Automation, ETFA 2009, pp. 1–8. IEEE (2009)
16. Fathi, M., Holland, A., Abramovici, M. Neubach, M.: Advanced Condition Monitoring Services in Product Lifecycle Management, pp. 245–250. IEEE, Las Vegas (2007)
17. Fernández, A., et al.: Pattern recognition in Latin America in the "Big Data" era. Pattern Recogn. **48**(4), 1185–1196 (2014)
18. Folorunso, O., Ogunde, A.: Data mining as a technique for knowledge management in business process redesign. Electr. J. Knowl. Manag. **1**(2), 33–44 (2004)
19. Främling, K., Nyman, J.: Information architecture for intelligent products in the internet of things. In: Beyond Business Logistics proceedings of NOFOMA, pp. 224–229 (2008)
20. Gandomi, A., Haider, M.: Beyond the hype: big data concepts, methods, and analytics. Int. J. Inf. Manag. **35**, 137–144 (2015)
21. Hackathorn, R.: Evolution of Big Data Analytics: Experiences with Teradata Aster and Apache Hadoop. Bolder Technology Inc., Boulder (2013)
22. Hashem, I.A.T., et al.: The rise of "Big Data" on cloud computing: review and open research issues. Inf. Syst. **47**, 98–115 (2014)
23. IBM, Managing big data for smart grids and smart meters, Somers, IBM Corporation, New York (2012)
24. Kiritsis, D.: Closed-loop PLM for intelligent products in the era of the internet of things. CAD Comput. Aided Des. **43**(5), 479–501 (2011)
25. Krishnan, K.: Big Data Processing Architectures. In: Data Warehousing in the Age of Big Data, pp. 29–43. Morgan Kaufmann, Waltham (2013)

26. Lavalle, S., et al.: Analytics: the new path to value. In: MIT Sloan Management Review. IBM Corporation (2010)
27. Liu, W., Zeng, Y., Maletz, M. Brisson, D.: Product lifecycle management: a review. In: International Design Engineering Technical Conferences and Computers and Information in Engineering, San Diego, USA, pp. 1213–1225 (2009)
28. Loshin, D.: Business processes and information flow. In: Business Intelligence: the Savvy Manager's Guide, Newnes, pp. 77–90 (2012)
29. Pääkkönen, P., Pakkala, D.: Reference architecture and classification of technologies, products and services for big data systems. Big Data Res. **2**(4), 166–186 (2015)
30. Philip Chen, C., Zhang, C.-Y.: Data-intensive applications, challenges, techniques and technologies: a survey on big data. Inf. Sci. **275**, 314–347 (2014)
31. Ranasinghe, D., Harrison, M., Främling, K., McFarlane, D.: Enabling through life product-instance management: solutions and challenges. J. Netw. Comput. Appl. **34**, 1015–1031 (2011)
32. Reffat, R., Gero, J., Peng, W.: Using data mining on building maintenance during the building life cycle. In: Proceedings of the 38th Australian & New Zealand Architectural Science Association (ANZASCA) Conference, pp. 91–97. University of Tasmania (2006)
33. Ren, S., Zhao, X.: A predictive maintenance method for products based on big data analysis. In: International Conference on Materials Engineering and Information Technology Applications (MEITA 2015), pp. 385–390 (2015)
34. Shin, J.H., Kiritsis, D., Xirouchakis, P.: Design modification supporting method based on product usage data in closed-loop PLM. Int. J. Comput. Integr. Manuf. **28**(6), 551–568 (2015)
35. Vera-baquero, A., Colomo-palacios, R., Molloy, O.: Towards a process to guide big data based decision support systems for business processes. Procedia Technol. **16**, 11–21 (2014)
36. Wellsandt, S., Hribernik, K., Thoben, K.-D.: Sources and characteristics of information about product use. Procedia CIRP **36**, 242–247 (2015)
37. Yun, Z., Weihua, L., Yang, C.: Applying balanced scordcard strategic performance management to CRISP-DM. In: Information Science, Electronics and Electrical Engineering (ISEEE), pp. 2009–2014 (2014)
38. Zhan, J., et al.: BDGS: A scalable big data generator suite in big data benchmarking. In: Advancing Big Data Benchmarks, pp. 138–154 (2013)

Big Data Analytics as Input for Problem Definition and Idea Generation in Technological Design

Ma-Lorena Escandón-Quintanilla[1(✉)], Mickaël Gardoni[1,2], and Patrick Cohendet[3]

[1] Ecole de Technologie Supérieure, Montreal, Canada
ma-lorena.escandon-quintanilla.1@etsmtl.net,
[2] Institut National des Sciences Appliquées, Strasbourg, France
mickael.gardoni@etsmtl.ca
[3] HEC Montreal, Montreal, Canada
patrick.cohendet@hec.ca

Abstract. Big data analytics enables organizations to process massive amounts of data in shorter amounts of time and with more understanding than ever before. Many uses have been found to take advantage of this tools and techniques, especially for decision making. However, little applications have been found in the first stages of innovation, namely problem definition and idea generation. This paper discusses how big data analytics can be utilized in those stages. It includes an example of application in problem definition and proposes a case study implementation in a higher education setting for idea generation.

Keywords: Problem definition · Idea generation · Big data analytics · Innovation

1 Introduction

The current economy's fast-paced product development cycle has lead companies to decrease the time in all stages of new product development. Even before this change, companies spent proportionally little time in the idea generation process, compared to the time spent in technical development and testing. Little by little, companies are realizing the need for and the power of good ideas, thus requesting employees to dedicate more time and resources to the first stages of the new product development process, namely the identification of the opportunity or problem statement, information gathering, and the idea generation.

To create new ideas, the individual must form new combinations of knowledge he or she already possesses [1, 2]. However, it has been found that that participants will gravitate towards known solutions [3] and that popular ideas are constantly recombined [1]. To produce a radical result, the ideator needs to make highly varying ("wild") combinations [1]. It is necessary to find ways to promote wild combinations.

In previous literature, authors have discussed options to manage ideas in a product development process, designing collaboration platforms and software to facilitate the documentation and exchange of ideas. But with new information technologies, it is

R. Harik et al. (Eds.): PLM 2016, IFIP AICT 492, pp. 468–477, 2016.
DOI: 10.1007/978-3-319-54660-5_42

possible to benefit from the wealth of data we are able to collect and process. Data can enable organizations to find insights related to their processes, clients and market.

This article discusses the use of big data analytics for problem definition and idea generation. It includes a case where big data analytics was used to identify problems and a proposed use of readily available analytics tools to facilitate idea generation.

2 Idea Generation Sessions

Idea generation is the fundamental step of the innovation process and, more importantly, it "is central to engineering design" [4]. Participants from different domains or areas of expertise can work together during idea generation (ideation) sessions, to exchange and create knowledge, usually for a specific aim.

The purpose of ideation sessions is to set an environment and implement creativity techniques that will help participants produce, express and combine ideas. Another advantage of idea generation sessions is that the ideas of others sometimes trigger the creation of related or new ideas [5].

Ideation sessions are an interesting example to explore creativity support systems because of their unique characteristics: a defined purpose, limited time, multidisciplinary teams and willingness to create knowledge [6]. While there is not one generally agreed process for idea generation sessions, Shneiderman et al. [7] propose the following phases, found in recent literature and commonly accepted for new product development cycles (Fig. 1).

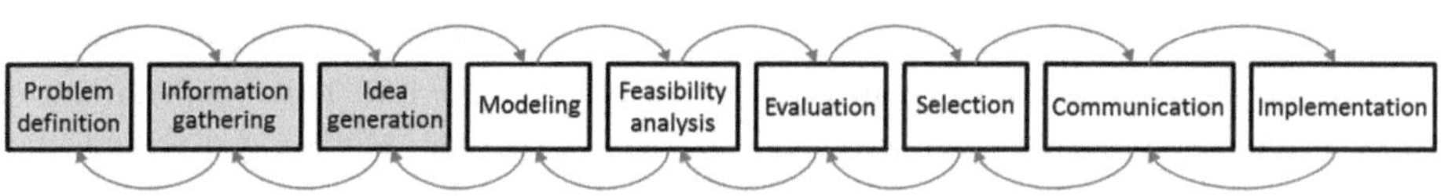

Fig. 1. Process for idea generation sessions in [7]

There are many areas of opportunity to improve for the process of idea generation: sharing more ideas, providing feedback and decreasing the time it takes for the team to develop ideas into concepts.

Based on the process for idea generation sessions by Shneiderman et al. [7] and the examples found on extant literature, we categorized the use of information and identified how big data analytics can be used tool to help teams. It can be used in four phases of the process: to identify areas of opportunity (need identification), as input for inspiration (information gathering), to identify unrelated ideas to combine in new concepts, and to obtain insight from a large amount of ideas from a crowdsourcing effort (evaluation). For this work, the focus lays on the first stages, highlighted in Fig. 1.

3 Big Data Analytics

People collaborate in many different ways, by sending emails with attachments, by sharing documents on the cloud, talking over the phone, exchanging messages. Information systems allow for those communications to occur, and to document the exchanges. All the data generated and collected in an organization is a source of untapped knowledge that can lead to inventive designs of new products and services if analyzed using powerful tools.

Big data is characterized not only by the speed of generation (velocity), but also the different types of data that must be analyzed (variety) and the massive amount of data being collected (volume) (Gartner's Laney, 2001, in [9]). To those characteristics, more recent authors have appended the dimensions of veracity [10], meaning how reliable information is, and value [10], which considers the impact the data can have on the organization when analyzed.

Big data analytics enables organizations to analyze their data in a way that was not possible before, by bringing together different sources of information and finding trends that are only visible with large amounts of data. This will make it easier to visualize the gaps in a domain [8]. The use of big data analytics will depend on the availability of the tools required to perform the analysis, and the characteristics (e.g. duration, number of participants, access to external sources of data) and aim of the idea generation session.

3.1 Problem Definition/Need Identification

Müller et al. [8] created a software to support the identification of unexplored research areas through data attributes and visualizations. They propose that information (data) can be used to guide researchers to new unexplored paths. They theorize that data can be examined iteratively for "divergent and convergent thinking" to generate new hypotheses [8].

In this same spirit, data from various sources can be collected and exploited to find areas of opportunity for an organization. It is possible to find new applications or markets for the products and services, or even expertise already possessed. For researchers, it can signal new areas to explore. For artists and creators, it can find previously unthinkable combinations. Figure 2 depicts the flow of information to use big data analytics for problem or need identification.

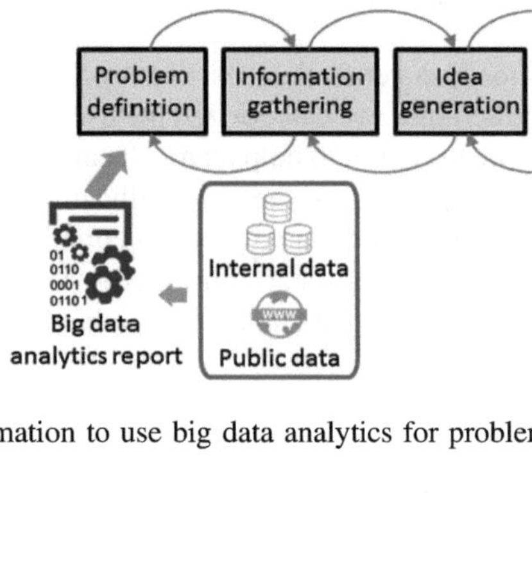

Fig. 2. Flow of information to use big data analytics for problem or need identification

3.2 Idea Generation

Information inputs can help bolster the creativity of participants to generate ideas given that "creative thinking involves a process of iterative activation of 'cues'" [11]; furthermore, the likelihood of creating new knowledge from recombination is greater as we increment the number of external inspirations (Cohen and Levinthal [9]). Several works discuss the use of information as input for creativity:

- In [11] to support music composers through cues and suggestions.
- In [12] to support brainstorming by recommending computer generated "ideas" (extractions from three databases).
- In [13] to support the generation of alternative ideas using data prompting.
- In [14] to complement the idea generation process by using aggregated data.

The examples listed demonstrate that there is an interest to enhance idea generation through the use of information. However the risk is that the material selected to form the knowledge base will already be biased towards a known solution. By using big data analytics, the information will reveal trends and connections that were previously unseen. This effect can potentially be amplified when extracting date from unrelated or complementary knowledge domains to promote new combinations.

Figure 3 depicts the flow of information to use big data analytics for problem or need identification.

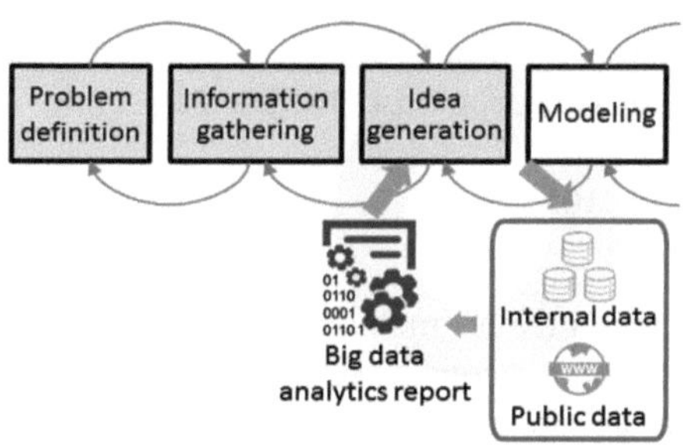

Fig. 3. Flow of information to use big data analytics as input

4 Application in a Higher Education Setting

Big data analytics in the context of a complete new product development process can be used as a support for participants to identify problems and generate ideas. To test this hypothesis, the authors designed three case studies to be performed sequentially. This will enable to study the impact of the use throughout the whole creative process. The three case studies will take place in several higher education environments:

- **Problem definition:** big data analytics will be used to define the challenges to be solved in subsequent activities. This case study has been completed and is presented in Sect. 4.1.

- **Information gathering:** the authors will build a knowledge base to be provided to participants of an innovation competition. This proposed case study is presented in Sect. 4.2.
- **Idea generation:** during a month-long intensive master course on innovation, the authors will provide students with access to big data analytics tools. This proposed case study is presented in Sect. 4.3.

Evaluation Criteria. The creative process is measured by different metrics depending on the authors, for example:

- Applicability of concepts [15]
- Complexity level of concepts [15]
- Detail of concepts [16]
- Novelty of concepts [4, 15, 16]
- Number of characters of a conclusion [17]
- Number of chats [17, 18]
- Number of comments [15]
- Number of ideas [4, 15, 16, 17, 19–22]
- Number of ideas evaluated [15]
- Number of ideas shared [19]
- Number of participants [18]
- Number of record cards/sticky notes [18, 23]
- Number of whiteboard events [23]
- Perceived team cohesiveness/effort [19]
- Quality of concepts/Ideas accepted [4, 16, 20, 22]
- Time [17–19, 23]
- Variety of concepts [4, 16]

Given that there is currently no method to objectively measure the quality of an idea, this criterion will not be considered. Other metrics, such as the number of characters in a description, do not seem relevant to assess the impact of big data analytics for problem definition, information gathering or idea generation. It is also assumed that the concepts will be applicable to the problem at hand. Consequently, the focus will be on these four metrics: comments (feedback from the participants), complexity, ideas shared, and variety of ideas (to be assessed by domain experts).

We believe that the use of big data analytics as input for creativity will provide participants with hints to novel associations that may result in ideas with greater complexity and varied from current or competing solutions We expect to obtain positive feedback from participants regarding the use of data as input for the session and as a support to merge concepts and find innovative solutions.

The following sections describe the application performed to support one of the organizations in finding the challenges to propose to an innovation competition, a proposal to apply big data analytics for information gathering for participants of the innovation competition, and the proposed approach to support idea generation for solution design during a summer school.

4.1 Problem Definition/Need Identification

In order to apply big data analytics for problem definition, the researchers worked with one of the organizations that will propose challenges for both the competition and the summer school. Their objective is to work with challenges related to river water quality and conservation. Since the problems to be solved were not defined, a creativity session was held to identify areas of opportunity.

The session took place on the 30th of March, 2016 at the *École de technologie supérieure* in Montreal. All the community was invited to participate through the weekly bulletin board, 18 participants were registered, and 15 attended the session.

Input Data. As discussed before, there is an enormous wealth of external and publicly available data that can be utilized. However, there is a difficulty in selecting relevant and valuable data, and cleaning the information to make it usable for the purpose. In this case, because the aim was to identify problems related to rivers, freshwater and water conservation which can potentially be solved by a technological solution or a data analysis solution, the data selected to be used as input are patents. Patents offer the advantage of having pre-defined sections, describing a problem and the solution. To perform the data analysis, patents from Patbase which include keywords such as "freshwater" and "data analysis" + "river" were extracted.

Work Session. It is important to set objectives and to provide participants with a sense of progress. To ensure the achievement of the purpose of the work session, a series of activities were planned for participants to follow (Table 1).

Table 1. Activities followed during the problem definition session

Activity	Time allocated
Welcome/Introduction to the topic	20 min
Group formation/Personal introduction	10 min
Identification of elements in the problem	30 min
Identify connections and relationships between elements	30 min
Identify key issues	30 min
Use of big data analytics (identification of new issues)	30 min
Presentation of issues identified	30 min

After a brief welcome and explanation of the purpose of the session, participants were first asked to identify all the elements of the problem (stakeholders, inputs, outputs). The second step was to relate all the elements and identify which cause problems. The boards pictured in Fig. 4 demonstrate the different approaches of teams to identify the elements of river issues. Each group of participants proceeded to identify key issues (examples can be seen in Fig. 5). The purpose of this activity was to clearly state the key issues.

For the following phase of the work session, the teams were provided with access to a big data analytics analysis tools pre-loaded with freshwater and river related patents. The software used to analyze the data is IPMetrix [24], from the company

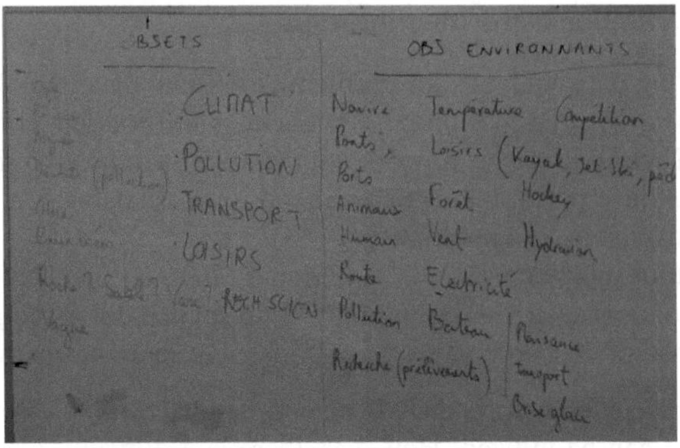

Fig. 4. Team list the elements of the issue

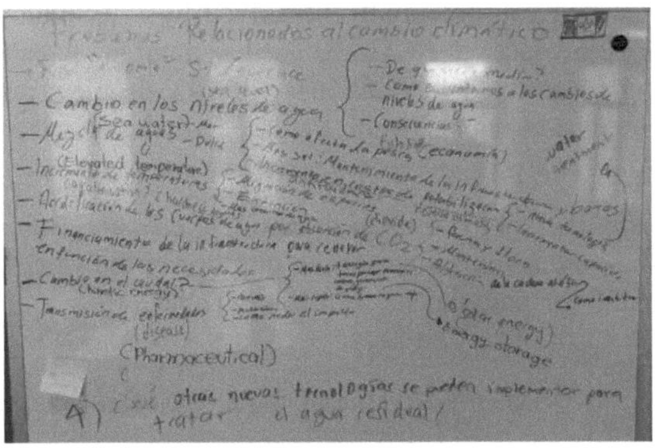

Fig. 5. Teams identify key issues

TecKnowMetrix, which provides semantic analysis and cartographies of the information. In this session, the purpose was to use big data analytics as an information input to trigger new relations. Participants had time to explore the different concepts in the visualizations and selected various concepts to combine with their previously identified issues. The objective was to provide participants with new concepts that could work as prompts to open new fields of possibility, by considering the materials, measures, technologies or concepts in the mapped domain.

Table 2 is a comparison of the results from each group of participants before and after the access to external data:

Table 2. Results of issues identified per group

Group	Number of participants	Issues identified originally	Issues identified with support	Total
1	5	5	3	8
2	6	3	1	4
3	4	5	2	7

Participants mentioned that they were able to identify links because of their previous knowledge, reinforcing the notion that the use of data as input can trigger the exploration of different directions.

4.2 Information Gathering

For the competition, a world-wide event called *"Les 24 heures de l'innovation"*, organizations propose a challenge, and participants have 24 h to work on a solution. At the end of the 24 h, the best solutions are awarded a prize. The competition takes place in over 40 sites in 20 countries around the world, at the same time. All students will be given access to information gathered to give them insights to the challenges proposed. The main site of the competition is the *École de technologie supérieure* in Montreal.

Measuring the Impact. The objective of providing participants with data is to improve the novelty and originality of the solutions proposed. To measure the effect, a comparison will be made in the evaluation grid scores for innovativeness given to the winning solutions from this edition (compared to previous editions).

4.3 Idea Generation

The next ground for experimentation will take place in the month of July, during the "ÉTS Internationals Summer School on innovation and technological design". In total, fifty engineering students will take part in the course, where they learn about the innovation process, creativity techniques, and work on a team project solving one of the challenges. The objective is to arrive to a functional prototype. Students will be placed in one of the 6 project teams. The teams will select one challenge to solve during the course, and will be guided by professors in the technical side and the creativity and innovation approach.

The students will have the possibility to implement different idea generation tools and techniques. For each, they will have a workshop where they will use the tool or technique and apply it to the problem they are trying to solve. The ultimate goal of providing participants with creative tools and techniques is to arrive to an original solution for the challenge (problem) to be solved.

Additional to the aforementioned tools and techniques, one course will be taught where they will learn to explore data to find hints for solutions.

Tracking the Results. Because students will employ different tools and techniques, we need to compare the results of the application of each. To do so, students will be required to carry an "idea journal". In this journal, each group must document the ideas generated during each workshop. Ideas can be documented using brain-maps, lists, drawings, sketches or photographs to represent the work achieved with the tool/technique.

5 Discussion and Conclusion

Solving problems and creating good ideas for new products, services and technologies are too important to rely only on human capacity to create and collaborate. Great inventions are built in the vast knowledge that was created before us. However, we live in an age where there is too much information for humans to absorb. There is a latent need to make sense of all the data generated every day. In this data therein lay clues for exciting combinations, hints to better solutions.

The purpose of using big data analytics in an idea generation context is precisely that of taking advantage of the wealth of knowledge available through the application of information technologies. The data by itself does not generate value, it is the participants making sense of it and making new connections which can create value.

This paper presented an example of how including data in a problem-identification process can spark new combinations to explore different directions. The next work is expected to provide insights into the use of big data analytics for idea generations with the purpose of designing novel solutions.

Acknowledgments. Ma-Lorena Escandón-Quintanilla would like to thank the Mexican National Council of Science and Technology (CONACYT) for her scholarship.

References

1. Fleming, L., Szigety, M.: Exploring the tail of creativity: an evolutionary model of breakthrough invention. Advances in Strategic Management, vol. 23, pp. 335–359 (2006)
2. Koestler, A.: The act of creation (1964)
3. Howard, T.J., Culley, S.J., Dekoninck, E.: Information as an input into the creative process. In: DS 36 Proceedings DESIGN 2006, the 9th International Design Conference, Dubrovnik, Croatia (2006)
4. Glier, M.W., Schmidt, S.R., Linsey, J.S., McAdams, D.A.: Distributed ideation: idea generation in distributed capstone engineering design teams. Int. J. Eng. Educ. **27**(6), 1281–1294 (2011)
5. Munemori, J., Yoshino, T., Yunokuchi, K.: A spiral-type idea generation method support system for sharing and reusing ideas among a group. In: Proceedings of the IEEE International Conference on Systems, Man and Cybernetics (2001)
6. Jiménez-Narvaez, L.M., Desrosiers, S., Gardoni, M.: Creative teamwork in quick and long term project development, 24 hours of innovation (2011)
7. Shneiderman, B., Fischer, G., Czerwinski, M., Resnick, M., Myers, B., Candy, L., Edmonds, E., Eisenberg, M., Giaccardi, E., Hewett, T., Jennings, P., Kules, B., Nakakoji, K., Nunamaker, J., Pausch, R., Selker, T., Sylvan, E., Terry, M.: Creativity support tools: report from a U.S. national science foundation sponsored workshop. Int. J. Hum.-Comput. Interact. **20**(2), 61–77 (2006)
8. Müller, L., Wetzel, T., Hobohm, H.C., Schrader, T.: Creativity support tools for data triggered hypothesis generation. In: KICSS, pp. 24–27, November 2012
9. Kabir, N., Carayannis, E.: Big data, tacit knowledge and organizational competitiveness. J. Intell. Stud. Bus. **3**, 54–62 (2013)
10. Koutroumpis, P., Leiponen, A.: Understanding the value of big data. In: IEEE Conference on Big Data. Sillicon Valley, CA, October 2013

11. Hamman, M.: Priming computer-assisted music composition through design of human/computer interaction. In: Mastorakis, N.E. (ed.) Mathematics and Computers in Modern Science - Acoustics and Music, Biology and Chemistry, Business and Economics, pp. 75–82. World Scientific Engineering Society (2000)
12. Shan, Z., Zhu, Y., Zhao, T.: Kaleidoscope: computer-assisted ideation through idea network exploration. CS 224W 2013 Project Final report. Department of Computer Science, Stanford University (2013)
13. Maccrimmon, K.R., Wagner, C.: The architecture of an information system for the support of alternative generation. J. Manage. Inf. Syst. **8**(3), 49–67 (1991)
14. Dove, G., Jones, S.: Using information visualization to support creativity in service design workshops. In: Proceedings of ServDes (2014)
15. Ardaiz-Villanueva, O., Nicuesa-Chacón, X., Brene-Artazcoz, O., De Acedo, S., Lizarraga, M.L., De Acedo, S., Baquedano, M.T.: Evaluation of computer tools for idea generation and team formation in project-based learning. Comput. Educ. **56**(3), 700–711 (2011)
16. Wodehouse, A., Ion, W.: Augmenting the 6-3-5 method with design information. Res. Eng. Des. **23**(1), 5–15 (2012)
17. Munemori, J., Nagasawa, Y.: GUNGEN: groupware for a new idea generation support system. Inf. Softw. Technol. **38**(3), 213–220 (1996)
18. Yuizono, T., Kayano, A., Shigenobu, T., Yoshino, T., Munemori, J.: Groupware for a new idea generation with the semantic chat conversation data. In: Khosla, R., Howlett, R.J., Jain, L.C. (eds.) KES 2005. LNCS (LNAI), vol. 3681, pp. 1044–1050. Springer, Heidelberg (2005). doi:10.1007/11552413_148
19. Graetz, K.A., Barlow, C.B., Proulx, N., Pape, L.J.: Facilitating idea generation in computer-supported teleconferences (1997)
20. Jung, J.H., Schneider, C., Valacich, J.: Enhancing the motivational affordance of information systems: the effects of real-time performance feedback and goal setting in group collaboration environments. Manage. Sci. **56**(4), 724–742 (2010)
21. Parjanen, S., Hennala, L., Konsti-Laakso, S.: Brokerage functions in a virtual idea generation platform: possibilities for collective creativity? Innov.: Manage. Policy Pract. **14**(3), 363–374 (2012)
22. Wang, H., Ohsawa, Y.: Data-driven innovation technologies for smarter business from innovators' market game to ichance creativity support system. In: Ohsawa, Y., Abe, A. (eds.) Advances in Chance Discovery, vol. 423, pp. 107–125. Springer, New York (2013)
23. Gumienny, R., Gericke, L., Wenzel, M., Meinel, C.: Supporting creative collaboration in globally distributed companies (2013)
24. IP Metrix Solution - TKM (2016). Tkm.fr. http://www.tkm.fr/en/ip-metrix-solution.php. Accessed 10 June 2016

Toward an Extensive Data Integration to Address Reverse Engineering Issues

Jonathan Dekhtiar[1(✉)], Alexandre Durupt[1], Matthieu Bricogne[1], Dimitris Kiritsis[2], Harvey Rowson[3], and Benoit Eynard[1]

[1] Department of Mechanical Systems Engineering, UMR UTC/CNRS 7337 Roberval CS 60319, Université de Technologie de Compiègne, 60203 Compiègne Cedex, France
contact@jonathandekhtiar.eu, jonathan.dekhtiar@utc.fr

[2] Swiss Federal Institute of Technology at Lausanne (EPFL), STI-IPR-LICP, 1015 Lausanne, Switzerland

[3] DeltaCAD, 795 Rue des Longues Raies, 60610 La Croix-Saint-Ouen, France

Abstract. Mechanical Reverse Engineering has been getting increasingly more attention from the industry. It aims rebuilding a broad Digital Mock Up (DMU) in order to redesign and/or remanufacture a product. Some of the reverse engineering challenges are to perform an efficient knowledge extraction out of the original product, and then to process the data it and consolidate them for further analysis. These data could be extracted from a vast number of different data as such as Manufacturing Data, Technical Reports, Design Data (e.g. CAD Files, technical drawings, etc.), Quality procedures, etc. Moreover, the amount of data stored by the companies' information system keep on rapidly growing. We propose to use data science in order to cope with the previous issues. This paper aims to detail the different possibilities offered by the data science field of expertize, more precisely in terms of machine learning, text mining and computer vision, but also to give a brief overview on the future works we will research. This paper position itself as a roadmap for our further proceedings.

Keywords: Reverse engineering · Knowledge Based Engineering · Data science · Machine learning · Deep learning · Computer vision

1 Introduction

Over the last decades, mechanical reverse engineering has been getting more and more interest from the industry, many industrial situations require to perform some reverse engineering process, such as remanufacturing a part which has been originally produced without any Computer-Aided Design (CAD) system. For instance, we could mention the need of remanufacturing a part of a Nuclear Power Plant which is likely to have been manufactured between 1960 and 1980 in France and thus it is unlikely that CAD software has been used to design most parts. Each situation requires a specific analysis. What are the different elements at our disposal? How reliable are they? Do we need to preprocess them? What do we aim to reverse engineer? How precisely do we

R. Harik et al. (Eds.): PLM 2016, IFIP AICT 492, pp. 478–487, 2016.
DOI: 10.1007/978-3-319-54660-5_43

need to perform these operations? Reverse Engineering is a wide field that could and should operate all along the product lifecycle. Let's have a closer look on how Reverse Engineering fit into a PLM approach.

2 PLM, a Product and DMU Centric Approach

Product Lifecycle Management (PLM) systems are, nowadays, widely used and a common response to cope with numerous mechanical engineering and manufacturing issues. They appear to be the main answer to many challenges induced by the ever-demanding market, the global competition, the inevitable growing customer needs and shortening products' and components' lifecycle.

Moreover, the concept of "*extended enterprise*" is becoming the norm, and thus companies are facing a rapid and massive increase in data exchanges, but also in collaborations between a vast amount of expertizes. This trend could be an obstacle if not well managed. PLM systems are thought and designed to address such problematic during the whole product lifecycle.

As this study partly focuses on data that could be found in such systems, we considered in this study this definition of PLM system: it is a "*collaborative backbone allowing people throughout extended enterprises to work together more efficiently*". It is "*a holistic business concept developed to manage a product and lifecycle including not only items, documents and BOM's, but also analysis results, test specifications, environmental component information, quality standard, engineering requirements, change orders, manufacturing procedures, product performance information, component suppliers, and so forth*" [1]. As a matter of fact, a PLM system is a *product-centric* approach used during the whole product lifecycle. Its different steps have been specified and described in the scientific literature [2], and could be schematized as follows (Fig. 1):

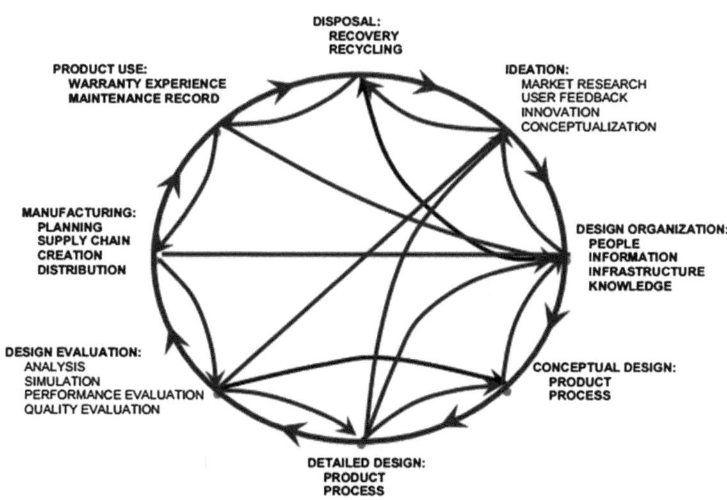

Fig. 1. PLM systems are used during the whole Product Lifecycle [2]

In our frame of research, the Digital Mock-Up (DMU) concept seems to have a prominent role. We will use this notion as a *numerical container* during the whole product lifecycle for every kind of product-related documents, files, technical reports, photos, videos, Bill of Materials (BOM), Computer-Aided Design (CAD) files, etc. We believe that expert knowledge could be extracted or deduced from all kinds of data, and therefore it seems essential to agree on an extensive definition of the DMU.

3 Related Works

3.1 Reverse Engineering, an Essential Part of the Product Lifecycle

Our approach aims knowledge integration from products and for the products. But also to enhance and speed up the design tasks carried out in an industrial manufacturing context. Reverse Engineering (RE) is precisely the field of expertize which focuses on such goals. But also on understanding the design intents and manufacturing processes [3]. In contrast with the RE process, we find Forward Engineering (FE) which is the traditional engineering workflow process (designing, manufacturing, maintaining, etc.) [4]. FE goes from high-level ideas and concepts to a manufactured part or product, contrary to RE, which goes from an analysis of the existing situation to higher-level.

So how could RE be part of the product lifecycle described by Subrahmanian et al. [2]? Here are a few examples, highlighted in the book written by Raja et al. [4].

- Conceptual Design and Detailed Design:
  - The original manufacturer doesn't exist any more or doesn't manufacture the part or product any more. However, the need is still here (e.g. long life parts in nuclear power plants).
  - There is no CAD model. It may never have existed, or have been lost. We need to re-engineer a complete CAD 3D model.
  - A company wants to speed-up its FE activities by using previous knowledge and experiences already inside the company's Information System (IS) (e.g. rapid-prototyping activities [5]).
  - Evolving a product for the purpose of improving some characteristics or to modify the product's specifications (e.g. reinforcing a part which is too easily damageable).
- Manufacturing:
  - Rapidly adapt the manufacturing resources (human, materials, machines, etc.)
  - Automate and systemize the quality check all along the manufacturing chain (e.g. comparing a *real* product to a *numeric* ideal version or to a *supposed perfect* previously produced part).
  - Speeding up CNC Code generation by using previous knowledge on each specific machine. [6]
- Disposal:
  - Recycling and dismantling process has been lost or has never produced. Nonetheless such documents could become mandatory by law depending on the country.

Out of this list, we can mention that it is not necessary to reverse engineer the whole DMU in each use-case. We can and we should focus on multiple levels of granularity. In some cases, we will need to reverse engineer the 3D CAD File. In other cases, it could be just the BOM or the documentation. And finally we could also have an industrial need which requires a combination of all the previous ones. To summarize, the use case determines which part of the DMU and how precisely we will need to reverse engineer.

3.2 Data Heterogeneity in Companies' Information Systems

In order to perform a broad and efficient a reverse engineering workflow, we need to gather, clean, sort, process and make sense of a large amount of data. As these data are highly related to some specific engineering expertise, they could be labelled *engineering data.*

These data could be found inside a vast variety of systems, such as PLM systems, Product Data Management (PDM) systems, Enterprise Resource Planning (ERP) systems, Knowledge Based Engineering (KBE) systems, Databases, etc.

They are, by nature, utterly heterogeneous. We mean that the data type and format vastly vary between the data. Here are some examples to illustrate our point (Table 1).

In addition to the heterogeneous aspect, companies are facing a rapidly growing amount of generated and stored data. Most manufacturing machines are now connected to the local network and operated by a computer. They produce manufacturing logs which can be stored in raw files, in databases or in systems such as ERPs (which basically run over databases). Emerging technologies such as NFC/RFID tend to produce even more data allowing advanced and complex tracking of every part during the whole product lifecycle. It is in this way that car manufacturers can gather a very large amount of data, during maintenance phase, about the product. Moreover, generalization of extended companies, extreme personalization and the recent emergence of the *Internet of Things* tend to reinforce this trend. All of these facts have led to an explosion in data amounts stored in Information Systems.

As seen previously, engineering data are, by nature, heterogeneous. Some are structured, others are raw files. And even if we only wanted to focus on the structured

Table 1. We propose four categories to classify the different data types and formats with a non-exhaustive list of data-sources.

Raw data *(no defined structure)*	1D data *(tabular data)*	Imagery data	
		2D data	3d Data
Quality procedures Technical reports Documentation	Databases BOMs *(if well formatted)* Assembly trees Basic characteristics *(colour, weight, etc.)* Manufacturing logs	Photos Plans X-Rays Screenshots	CAD File Exchange formats *(stl/step/iges)* Laser scans Tomography Point Clouds CMM

data, which is not our goal, the data's structure vastly varies. This great disparity implies that a specific method must be developed for each data type.

3.3 Available Solutions on the Market

Over the last decades, improvements on data acquisition techniques have permitted to elaborate complex methods to perform geometrical recognition and canonical form detection [7]. Mathematical and geometrical analysis has been previously performed in order to *clean* and fill holes in a 3D mesh obtained by laser-scan for instance [8]. Such advances could, of course, be the ground basis of RE oriented software. If we have a look to the available solutions on the market to answer the RE needs, we could find the well-known market leading solution GeoMagic Design X (formerly RapidForm XOR) developed by 3D systems. This software allows the user to generate CAD Models from 3D Scan Data (mesh or point clouds). Metris 3D developed similar software: Focus Reverse Engineering which basically offers the same features and possibilities. Unfortunately, they all produce a non-editable solid model or weakly feature-based 3D Model, and therefore perform little to no expertize knowledge integration. Even if, such approach could be compliant for the emerging 3D printing industry, it provides insufficient information to be a solid backbone for products redesign and remanufacturing.

3.4 Knowledge-Based Approaches in Reverse Engineering

Based on that observation, many research projects were launched aiming knowledge integration. In this sense, Knowledge-Based Engineering (KBE) appears to be the answer for capturing and reusing previous knowledge. These approaches gain meaning especially through a reverse engineering process. The main aspects of KBE could be summarized as follows: *knowledge*, *engineering* and *automation* [9]. One of the most-known methodologies is MOKA (Methodology and software tools Oriented to Knowledge-based engineering Applications) [10], an eight steps KBE lifecycle. We could also highlight the methodology KOMPRESSA (Knowledge-Oriented Methodology for the Planning and Rapid Engineering of Small-Scale Applications) [11] which focus on Small to Medium Enterprises. More specifically dedicated to the reverse engineering context, we could find the Knowledge Based Reverse Engineering (KBRE) [12] methodology developed for the project PHENIX. Nonetheless, none of these approaches gives an effective framework to perform knowledge extraction for a vast amount of heterogeneous data. Some initiatives try such as the METIS project [13–15] aims to solve such problematic. However, it appears that only a few data types have been covered and we might expect to find expertize knowledge in many more of them. Moreover, the proposed approach is mainly data-type specific and strongly relying on a domain expert to operate the different reverse engineering steps.

We propose to cope with this issue by using technologies and methods of the ***Data Science*** field of expertize. Let's have a closer look to the offered possibilities.

4 Prospective Approach

4.1 What Do We Mean by Data Science?

Data Science is the field of expertize which focus on *making sense of the data* in a very broad view. Analysing and understanding the data are two pillars of the methods. It aims to elaborate a model able to explain the data and make accurate predictions on new data. Prediction accuracy is measured by a set of statistical tools that we won't develop here. On the other hand, predictions mainly refer to classification tasks.

It is fundamental to point out that Data Science and more specifically Machine Learning (ML) techniques are not a solution for every type of problem. However, ML techniques can greatly help to solve problems that would be inconvenient to treat in a conventional way.

- The rules are hidden, or not very well known: Many human tasks require complex decision processes, the rules may vastly vary between each of us and we might not even be conscious of this process and why we made such a choice. For instance, a spam filter is a fully personalized program that learns, from your habits, which emails are spam. We could also mention some effortless tasks for a human being such as detecting a face. So much effortless, that sometimes our brain may mistakenly identify faces in nature (e.g. clouds, trees, etc.) or human-made objects. It's called Pareidolia. However, it is a tremendously difficult task for a computer to learn how to detect faces.
- Scaling is not humanly possible: It might be possible for a human to classify a few hundred emails a day and decide whether they are spam or ham (non-spam). This task may become cumbersome when you need to process millions of emails each day, as Google, Yahoo, Microsoft and other companies do. Nonetheless, ML techniques are pretty efficient to address such problems, moreover, many of them might become more accurate and efficient while working at large scales.

Both situations are very similar to the context of our study. And this is why we assume we could use data science and machine learning to improve state of the art results for the issues mentioned beforehand.

4.2 What Data Science and Machine Learning Techniques Could We Use to Address Some of the Aforesaid Issues?

There are two main types of machine learning techniques. The first is *Supervised Learning* (SL), it requires an access to the domain expertize knowledge during the model construction. The second is known as *Unsupervised Learning* (UL), contrary to the previous case, it doesn't use any kind of knowledge during the model construction. It is important to notice that there exists other types such as *weakly supervised learning* [16], *semi supervised learning* [17], *reinforcement learning* [18, 19], etc. However, we won't focus on these types of algorithm for a feasibility study, we still could come back to them afterwards once the validity of our approach has been proven.

To be brief, we expect, from a ML algorithm (supervised or not), to produce a statistical model able to sort out the data in different categories. One may distinguish two major steps in using a ML algorithm, the first one is called *training*, the model is fit to explain at best the *training data*. However, we need to be careful on many pitfalls such as over/under fitting in order to preserve a proper accuracy and generalizability of our model in order to explain new data. Once the model has been estimated sufficiently correct, it's ready to be used in production and deployed. Applications and softwares could be produced over it. (e.g. an accurate spam detection model allows to create a comfortable to use anti-spam solution). There also exist models that are able to handle regression problems, in this particular case, the output is no longer a category, but an equation that describes the relationship between two or more variables. Nevertheless, this type of output is out of the scope of this paper.

With SL, the number of categories is fixed by the expert. And a name is associated with each category. The expert needs to label every training data. In other words, the expert needs to give the expected output for each training data (e.g. We have available of 5000 emails to train a spam filter model, the expert needs to label each of the email whether it's spam or ham, but we could have done a 3 categories model: Spam/Ham/Important emails).

With UL, the number of categories depends on how many categories we want to have in our model, even if we don't really know exactly what they could be. We call these categories: *clusters*. The algorithm will then look for the best split to form X clusters, where X is the desired quantity of clusters. UL is especially useful when the expertize knowledge is hard to obtain or too expensive. UL helps to highlight the underlying structure of the data in finding similarities between data and forming groups with statistically similar data.

4.3 Text Mining–Raw Data Focused Approach

Let's imagine that we have 1,000,000 reports or bills produced during ten years of manufacturing activities in an aeronautical context. These documents come from every part of the company. They are all associated with one plane and only one. However, no tags are associated with these documents and I would like to retrieve every document related to thermic aspects. On the next day, we need, for a quality audit, to extract every quality procedure and report. It might be quite a tedious task to operate by hand. However, *Text Mining* (TM) is the subfield of ML which aims to address such problems. Given a few documents of each type (e.g. quality check, thermic, materials, design, financial, manufacturing, disposal, etc.), we could imagine a system trying to solve such an issue. If it is proven to work, it would not only work in the reverse engineering context but also in the forward engineering context. It would allow to display a filtered and context-based view of the DMU. Such issues have been highlighted in the European Project LinkedDesign [20, 21].

4.4 Computer Vision – 2D and 3D Data Focused Approach

We have seen we could use TM to classify, sort and filter textual documents. However, how could we classify, sort or filter imagery documents (e.g. photos, videos, plans, 3D scans, etc.) depending on the context or the desired expected output. A realistic industrial situation could be: we have 3D scanned a car engine, and we would like to reverse engineer the BOM in order to understand its functioning.

We propose to use another domain of data science known to address such problems: *Computer Vision* (CV). Basically CV aims to acquire, process, analyse describe, and understand at best the content of an imagery data [22–25]. Some of the typical tasks of CV are, for instance, object recognition (also called object classification), pose estimation, image segmentation, object tracking in image sequences. Messy backgrounds tend to make these tasks even more difficult (Figs. 2 and 3).

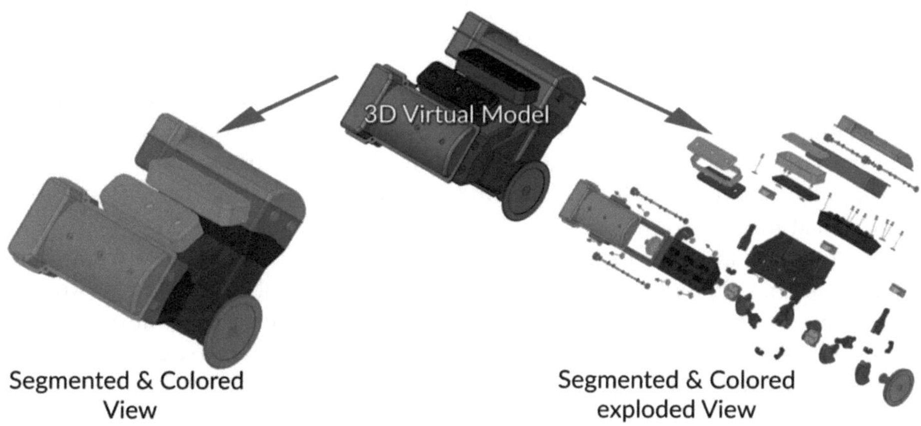

Fig. 2. Picture of the original 3D engine on the middle. On both sides the CV algorithm gives a theoretical output: a **segmented** and **classified** view of the assembly.

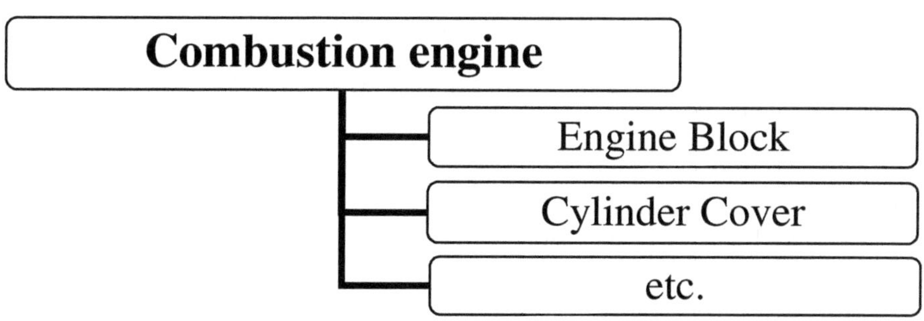

Fig. 3. The overall process could aim at producing a mechanical expertize oriented view based on the output given by the CV algorithm.

We also would like to use such technologies in order to measure and characterize the mechanical parts in imagery data (2D or 3D). Being able to describe each part in terms of physical properties (e.g. diameter, length, etc.) appears to us to be also a crucial and essential goal to achieve. We identified a few publications in the scientific literature that could help to answer such problematic [26, 27].

5 Conclusion

This contribution is a prospective approach aiming to summarize goals being pursued but also the challenges we would like to overcome. Massive and multi-source data is the tall order of tomorrow.

We believe that, beside the creation of new challenging issues for the manufacturing industry and the researchers, it could create new ways to solve and address classical engineering issues. And since knowledge and heterogeneous data integration is one of the main courses of action in reverse engineering to perform, such an approach takes on even more significance in a reverse engineering workflow.

It is for these reasons that given the limitations of typical Knowledge-Based Engineering approaches to perform a broad knowledge integration, but also bearing in mind the fast-growing amount of data stored inside the companies' information systems and the needs of reverse engineering, we are convinced of the revelance of a data-oriented methodology.

Our future works will focus to prove its effectiveness and will also try to build different metrics in order to compare the performance of the different working approaches. We hope and aspire to prove not only the revelance but also the effectiveness of a data-oriented approach to address issues related to reverse engineering and knowledge-based engineering.

References

1. Saaksvuori, A., Immonen, A.: Product Lifecycle Management. Springer, Heidelberg (2008)
2. Subrahmanian, E., Rachuri, S., Fenves, S.J., Foufou, S., Sriram, R.D.: Product lifecycle management support: a challenge in supporting product design and manufacturing in a networked economy. Int. J. Prod. Lifecycle Manag. **1**, 4–25 (2005)
3. Várady, T., Martin, R.R., Cox, J.: Reverse engineering of geometric models - an introduction. Comput.-Aided Des. **29**, 255–268 (1997)
4. Raja, V., Fernandes, K.J.: Reverse Engineering: An Industrial Perspective. Springer Science & Business Media, Berlin (2007)
5. Yan, X., Gu, P.: A review of rapid prototyping technologies and systems. Comput.-Aided Des. **28**, 307–318 (1996)
6. Danjou, C., Le Duigou, J., Eynard, B.: Closed-loop manufacturing, a STEP-NC process for data Feedback: a case study. Procedia CIRP **41**, 852–857 (2016)
7. Várady, T., Facello, M.A., Terék, Z.: Automatic extraction of surface structures in digital shape reconstruction. Comput.-Aided Des. **39**, 379–388 (2007)

8. Pernot, J.-P., Moraru, G., Véron, P.: Filling holes in meshes using a mechanical model to simulate the curvature variation minimization. Comput. Graph. **30**, 892–902 (2006)
9. Ammar-Khodja, S., Perry, N., Bernard, A.: Processing knowledge to support knowledge-based engineering systems specification. Concurr. Eng. **16**, 89–101 (2008)
10. Stokes, M.: Managing Engineering Knowledge: MOKA: Methodology for Knowledge Based Engineering Applications. ASME Press, New York (2001)
11. Lovett, P., Ingram, A., Bancroft, C.: Knowledge-based engineering for SMEs — a methodology. J. Mater. Process. Technol. **107**, 384–389 (2000)
12. Durupt, A., Remy, S., Ducellier, G., Bricogne, M.: KBRE: a proposition of a reverse engineering process by a KBE system. Int. J. Interact. Des. Manuf. (IJIDeM) **4**, 227–237 (2010)
13. Bruneau, M., Durupt, A., Roucoules, L., Pernot, J.-P., Rowson, H.: A methodology of reverse engineering for large assemblies products from heterogeneous data. In: Tools and Methods of Competitive Engineering (2014)
14. Bruneau, M., Durupt, A., Roucoules, L., Pernot, J.-P., Eynard, B.: Towards new processes to reverse engineering digital mock-ups from a set of heterogeneous data. In: INGEGRAPH - ADM - AIP - PRIMECA (2013)
15. Ouamer-Ali, M.-I., Laroche, F., Bernard, A., Remy, S.: Toward a methodological knowledge based approach for partial automation of reverse engineering. In: CIRP Design Conference, pp. 270–275 (2014)
16. Crandall, D.J., Huttenlocher, D.P.: Weakly supervised learning of part-based spatial models for visual object recognition. In: Leonardis, A., Bischof, H., Pinz, A. (eds.) ECCV 2006. LNCS, vol. 3951, pp. 16–29. Springer, Heidelberg (2006). doi:10.1007/11744023_2
17. Chapelle, O., Schlkopf, B., Zien, A.: Semi-Supervised Learnin. Springer Science+Business Media, Berlin (2010)
18. Kaelbling, L.P., Littman, M.L., Moore, A.W.: Reinforcement learning: a survey. J. Artif. Intell. Res. **4**, 237–285 (1996)
19. Sutton, R.S., Barto, A.G.: Reinforcement Learning: An Introduction. Springer Science+Business Media, Berlin (1998)
20. Nadoveza, D., Kiritsis, D.: Ontology-based approach for context modeling in enterprise applications. Comput. Ind. **65**, 1218–1231 (2014)
21. Nadoveza, D.: Towards Ontology-based Context Modeling for Manufacturing Applications (2014). http://infoscience.epfl.ch/record/203793
22. Klette, R.: Concise Computer Vision. Springer, London (2014)
23. Stockman, G., Shapiro, L.G.: Computer Vision, 1st edn. Prentice Hall PTR, Upper Saddle River (2001)
24. Morris, D.: Computer Vision and Image Processing. Palgrave Macmillan, Basingstoke (2003)
25. Jähne, B., Haußecker, H.: Computer Vision and Applications: A Guide for Students and Practitioners. Academic Press Inc., Cambridge (2000)
26. Lee, H., Kwon, H., Bency, A.J., Nothwang, W.D.: Fast Object Localization Using a CNN Feature Map Based Multi-Scale Search (2016)
27. Srivatsa, R.S., Babu, R.V.: Salient object detection via objectness measure. In: Image Processing (ICIP), pp. 4481 – 4485 (2015)

Information Gathering in Closed-Loop PLM Systems - Social Networks as Models for the Internet of Things?

Marco Lewandowski(✉) and Klaus-Dieter Thoben

BIBA – Bremer Institut für Produktion und Logistik Gmbh
at the University of Bremen, Bremen, Germany
{lew, tho}@biba.uni-bremen.de

Abstract. Different recent approaches from the Product Lifecycle Management (PLM) or Internet-of-Things (IoT) area describe a product-centric view on data and information which are collected by different stakeholders and systems along the lifecycle in order to enhance retrospective analytics, predictive analytics, business decisions, etc. The purpose of this paper is to investigate the basic principles of information sharing, communication and collaboration in traditional human-centric social networks and discuss whether these can be applied to data and information exchange in the PLM/IoT sector. With respect to the methodology applied to this investigation, recent communication mechanisms in social networks as well as in product-centric IoT platforms are systemized and abstracted. Based on the transformation of social network means for IoT, possible improvements of IoT platforms are discussed, resulting in demonstrations of possible PLM usage. In summery, the paper draws implications about the adoption of valuable Social Network means for product-centric usage.

Keywords: Closed-loop PLM · Social networks · Internet of Things · Data analytics · Social Internet of Things

1 Introduction

The innovation cycles of many products shorten due to different driving forces like customer demand, technical progress, new competitors with substitutive products, etc. Customers are no longer just a passive role in the product development process because they express their product and service experiences and opinions for instance in social networks. Furthermore, products more often contain electronics, so called product embedded information devices, that enable them to be smart and connected in the sense that data, commands and information can be shared and transmitted via internet. The ability of a product to connect to other things, humans or services via internet is reffered to as the Internet of Things (IoT, cp. [1–3]). Obviously, the growing number of data sources with a huge amount of product-centric information clarify that the digital revolution with a growing number of product-integrated information technology (IT) supports product and service innovations. Besides the customer demand for smart and connected products and services, IoT delivers advanced approaches to effectively enable productivity growth and innovation in research and development departments.

R. Harik et al. (Eds.): PLM 2016, IFIP AICT 492, pp. 488–497, 2016.
DOI: 10.1007/978-3-319-54660-5_44

At this, IoT also encourages that Product Lifecycle Management (PLM) is no longer just a software suite for managing data and processes in the design phase of products but a complete IT-supported concept for managing (perspectively individual) products along the complete lifecycle in all phases. This concept is sometimes referred to as closed-loop PLM [4–6]. Another perspective enhances the physical core product term with a virtual representative that holds product-related data and which is called Digital Twin or Product Avatar [7, 8]. Accordingly and in summary, enterprises face a growing number of requirements of different stakeholders along the life-cycle to access data of products, which implies the requirement to interact with this new generation of PLM systems.

The magnitude of different data sources and the continuously advancing technical progress complicate general standards on common data formats for product-related data, although attempts exist (e.g. [9]). The purpose of this paper is to investigate whether means of human-centric social networks, namely following entities, subscriptions to topics, (virtual) friendships, hashtags, etc. can be used to overcome the need for precisely defined data exchange formats and interfaces in collecting product-relevant data. At this, this paper should serve as a starting point to compare requirements of different sectors. The basic principles of information sharing, communication and collaboration might be applied to data and information exchange in the PLM/IoT sector meaning that relevant information independent from the source is gathered according to the individual stakeholder requirements and presented to human-beings. With the so-called Social Internet of Things (SIoT) the paradigm of information distribution via social network models has already been discussed (e.g. [10–12]), however the PLM perspective has not been explicitly considered so far.

The remainder of the paper is organized as follows. In Sect. 1 a brief literature review is given to provide background information on recent work about the SIoT and related aspects. With the state of practice also recent IoT platforms available on the market are characterized with respect to obstacles that could occur for future PLM systems. With respect to the methodology applied to this paper, Sect. 2 discusses general communication mechanisms in social networks and in IoT platforms and discusses improvements of IoT platforms by means of SIoT. The results are summed up in Sect. 3. Finally, Sect. 4 draws implications about Social Network means in the PLM software sector and points out possible future research.

1.1 Literature Review

IoT is a paradigm which describes that pervasive everyday objects will gain the ability to connect to the internet and to interact and cooperate with each other [3]. Due to the predicted number of devices that will likely connect to IoT – [13] estimates a potential economic impact of $2.7 to $6.4 trillion per year by 2025 and [14] a total number of 6.4 billion devices in 2016 – the provision of middleware functionality with protocols that support the exploitation of things-related services is the main issue for reliable IoT architectures [15, 16]. Among others, [10–12] therefore the introduction of the concept of social relationships between smart technical objects is referred to as the Social Internet of Things (SIoT).

The main challenges to overcome are:

- An IoT structure which is reliably and scalable in order to ensure network navigability [10, 15, 17]
- Creation and Exploitation of services through (social) service repositories [16]
- Transfer the use of models to study social networks in the IoT domain [10, 15]
- Guarantee a level of trustworthiness like friendships in (human) social networks [10, 15]

The different research works about SIoT address mainly technical issues by adopting means of (human) social networks. [18] proposes to use relationship means (friendships) of typical social networks to share the services of a thing. At this, [19] analyses the social relations between nodes in the internet of things. Further work is done on fundamental IoT architectures based on the model of scalable social networks [10, 15, 17]. At least the combination of traditional human (social) networks with technical IoT networks is investigated by [20–22].

While the general usage of social networks caught the interest of researchers worldwide (cp. e.g. [23–25]), a fundamental consideration about social network means in networks of technical items in the IoT is lacking.

With respect to the PLM software area, concepts for the acquisition of data along the lifecycle are broadly described (cp. e.g. [4, 6]) which could be referred to the topic IoT, anyhow, just few work can be found that addresses the aspect of social networks or SIoT. Considerations about the Product Avatar concept are closest to this idea (e.g. [26]). While the acquisition of product-related information in social networks is state of the art [27], this is not subject of this investigation. On the social-technical collaboration of smart things in the SIoT and the PLM sector, no contributions in the available literature can be found.

1.2 State of Practice

Besides considering the available research work on the topic of IoT and in particular SIoT, it is further important to illustrate the state of practice regarding this technologies. IoT is already successfully implemented in several industries by the help of IoT platform provider such as ThingWorx [28], Xivley [29] or Oracle [30], to name just a few. Also the leading cloud provider offer IoT solutions such as Microsoft [31], AWS [32] or IBM [33].

Recent IoT system approaches have typically in common, that the "smart" IoT devices are connected via a connectivity layer to a cloud based storage system [1, 34]. The connectivity layer offers standard interfaces such as RESTful WebAPIs, MQTT, OPC-UA, Web sockets, etc. The cloud storage system could be enhanced by further system functionality such as event processing, filtering, device management, predictive analytics, etc. External sources of data could be integrated into most systems and the connectivity layer further provides standard application interfaces for external applications, views, dashboards and similar. The general architecture of IoT systems is provided in the following Fig. 1.

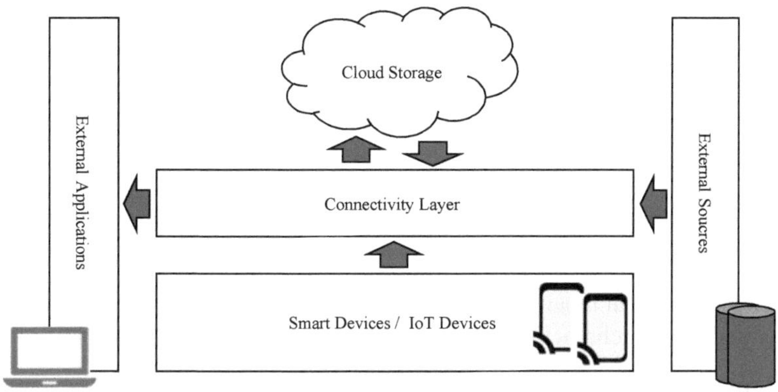

Fig. 1. General architecture of most available IoT systems

A special attention has to be paid to the Message Queuing Telemetry Transport (MQTT) standard, which is on the one hand standardized by ISO [35] and on the other hand already state of practice in several of the mentioned IoT platforms. MQTT offers a publish/subscribe model which is handled by an MQTT broker. That means that sensors (on smart devices) publish their values to a broker instance. Other devices or applications can subscribe to this data channel by addressing the MQTT broker interfaces so that data will be published along the chain to the final device or application [36]. The following Fig. 2 gives a brief overview about the concept.

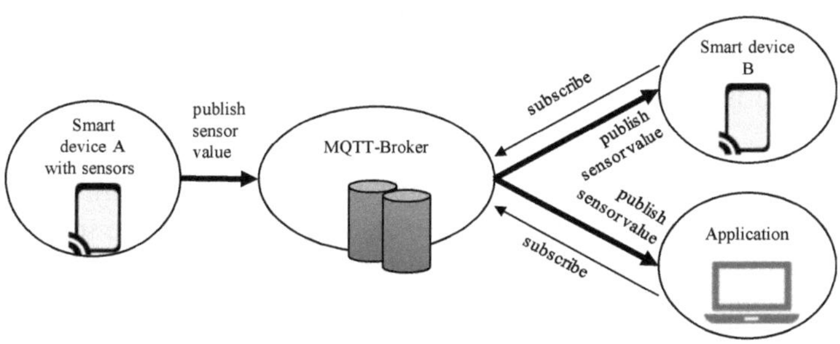

Fig. 2. MQTT publish/subscribe model (according to [36])

2 Method

Based on the argumentation above, the growing number of devices and the intended usage of more and more IoT related information and analysis in human-centric systems like PLM systems lead to the point, that means of (human) social networks could serve as interesting paradigms for communication and collaboration also in SIoT systems. To investigate the suitability of the different means, common known approaches are (a) briefly presented, (b) discussed in the context of IoT and PLM and (c) assessed against the main challenges of broad IoT usage in the following. The main challenges as stated in the previous Sect. 1.1 are (a) *Trustworthiness* by means of friendship-like structures between smart products, (b) *Service discovery* of data and information channels of smart products, and (c) *Interoperability* between different platforms.

2.1 Common Means for Communication and Collaboration in Social Networks

The following common means are taken from typical public and private social network platforms and briefly characterized against the above-mentioned criteria:

Friendships

Persons, organizations and further entities in traditional social networks are able to connect with each other on a platform by expressing so-called "friendships". Friendship implies a relation between the entities, essentially if the friendship has to be confirmed by the invited person. Other functions which are called "following" do not require confirmation. Implicitly friendships form networks of entities that share something together (like interests, same origin, often related to real life).

With respect to IoT, things can be seen entities so that adopting the tool of friendships could also implicitly map networks between devices. The logical relationship between a smart device might contain further smart components as "friends" but also the PLM application or another device. The obvious detriment is that "friendships" have to be classified by means of semantic description (e.g. component, same device, data consuming application, etc.).

Anyhow, the flat hierarchy in the description of networks by the example of friendships addresses explicitly the trustworthiness between smart objects in general as PLM application, for instance, might automatically get access to the components which are connected to them on the second and third level.

Hashtags

Hashtags are tools to describe a continuous text with meta-information. The term derives from the character hash (#) and from the word "to tag" in the sense of assigning a keyword. Hashtags are valuable tools to categorize text messages ad-hoc that means without predefining categories for the messages. At this, it is possible to have flat structures that assign messages to many different hashtags which are also relevant for SIoT. Within messages also the tag "@user" is common to indicate a particular receiver or stakeholder of the message. In consequence, consuming application like the PLM system can follow specific hashtags to get access to different smart objects that post messages under the particular hashtag. A further advantage is that new hashtags that derive from technical progress can easily be added implicitly. However, those categories are not defined in advance contradict to most of today's processes. Hashtags could address the *service discovery* aspect in SIoT.

Interest Subscriptions/Groups

In social networks users can express their interest in different topics (like movies, music, etc.), in general by subscribing to a topic (groups) or content provider. Most of these topics are represented by a particular stakeholder which acts as a content provider and accordingly distinguishes the concept from the hashtag concept. Anyhow, the interest subscription implies the agglomeration of entities with the same interest and again forms a layer of network relations. The messaging with interest groups is categorized in advance as it is dedicated to the particular channel. Anyway, using hashtags or sharing messages is not excluded and broadens the reach of the information in the network.

With respect to SIoT, the subscription could serve as a model for sharing the interest of smart objects for instance on same external information sources or services (e.g. a web service with weather data). From this point of view, the ability to subscribe to services addresses the *service discovery* aspect. Anyhow, the concept implies that each single entity has to initiate the subscription, which is comprehensible for human beings but might be challenging to implement it into smart devices. In the broad sense, the concept corresponds to the MQTT standard.

Sharing

In social networks, messages and information by users can be shared which means that an entity is providing the content of the message and the reference to the original author to its own network (friends, groups, etc.). The message has a broader reach and is in general shown on the different user timelines. The basic idea implies that "friends" might be interested essentially in topics and messages of friends which share the same interests.

From today's point of view, it is hardly conceivable that smart objects decide autonomously what might be of interest for other objects. Anyhow, research in the field might show that together with all available meta-information and network structures, this could be possible without predefined rulesets. More comprehensible is the use of this tool in PLM systems, which means that the user as part of the SIoT platform could share data and information as well as essentially already processed information in terms of analytics and forecasts. At this, sharing makes use of *trustworthiness* and could enable *service discovery* and *interoperability* and addresses humans and IoT devices in social-technical networks.

Timeline

The timeline is a functionality often offered to users in social networks as the landing page of the platform. The timeline shows (in chronological sequence) the top messages of entities, friends, interest, groups and similar. At this, the timeline offers the users of social networks, on the one hand, a restricted view on topics with the most likely importance for the consumer. On the other hand, it is the most relevant tool for broadening information in networks.

From the SIoT perspective, the timeline might remain a user interface element but again it could serve as a valuable tool to provide data, information and processed analysis to human actors in the SIoT for instance via PLM systems. At this, it definitely addresses the *service discovery* for humans in the resulting social-technical networks.

Voting (Like, Dislike)

Several social networks offer the possibility to like or dislike a message which accordingly expresses consent with the content or the opposite. The resulting number of likes and dislikes is a measure for importance and reach in social networks.

As a kind of performance indicator, the concept of voting can also be applied to SIoT, as smart objects might vote for services that do analysis or predictions within SIoT. Considering PLM systems with humans involved analysis, predictions, data and information of smart objects that might appear on user timelines can also be voted against importance. At this, voting could contribute to *service discovery* in SIoT.

Instant Messaging
Instant messaging (IM) is a tool which is used by users within social networks to send private messages. Although no real technical difference between IM and email can be found, IM is often preferred for short and informal communication. With respect to SIoT, IM equals a direct Device-2-Device communication. From the technical perspective, communication is not challenging but the depending intelligence by context-awareness of devices or even predefined rulesets are research challenges and require at least reliable *service discovery*.

2.2 Platform Interoperability Between Social Networks

For the sake of completeness, platform interoperability aspects between social networks will be most likely an obstacle for the penetration of IoT in the market. The problem is foreseeable as today's social networks and state-of-the-art IoT platforms are hardly interoperable. Within this paper, we figured out the following initial approaches of traditional social networks.

Share Buttons
Essentially websites and blogs make use of share buttons which offer the users in social networks the possibility to share content (as described before) directly from the particular website in different social networks. Partly it is also possible to "cross share" posts between different network platforms. For IoT and SIoT this aspect might be an example which can be adopted in the sense of sharing or "cross-posting" data channels to other SIoT platforms (even those that are not public but in-house).

Interoperable Clients
For social networks clients are available that can sum up information of different networks. Anyhow, this implies individual interfaces to every platform often with the problem that only subsets of the range of functions can be supported. The same challenge is present for IoT and SIoT which should not result in the unilateral connection of one particular PLM system with one IoT platform. Standards for data exchange might temporarily be helpful but will not avoid technical progress leading to the same problem again.

Social Media Management Software
For professionals in social networks (e.g. marketing agencies contracted by enterprises), social media management software exists that is able to serve different social media platforms from one tool. Implications of the interoperable clients apply here alike.

3 Results

From the comparisons of established social network means and challenges of (S)IoT, the following preliminary results include a summarized suitability assessment of social network means for mainly technical aspects of IoT and implications of the results for integration of IoT in PLM systems.

4 Discussion and Outlook

The key focus of PLM systems is the human being, in most cases engineers and industrial managers of technical products to be more precise. In addition to the systematic presentation of implications in Table 1, the investigation indicates, that the consequently resulting social-technical networks have to be considered where PLM software tools are in focus. I.e. users will have to deal with information from many devices in the IoT. At this, established social network functions can be considered and consolidated with the technical implications of managing huge amounts of smart devices, as a dynamic selection of relevant data and information is promised.

Table 1. Summarized suitability of social networks means

Social network aspect	Direct applicability for IOT	Direct applicability for PLM	Addresses SIoT challenge		
			Trust-worthiness	Service discovery	Inter-operability
Friendships	yes	yes	X		
Hashtags	yes	yes		X	
Interest subscriptions/groups	partly	yes		X	
Sharing	partly	yes	(needed)	X	X
Timeline	no	yes		X	
Voting (like, dislike)	partly	partly		X	
Instant messaging	challenging	yes		(needed)	
Share buttons	challenging	yes			X
Interoperable clients	As workaround	As workaround			X
Social media management software	As workaround	As workaround			X

Based on the first investigation in this paper, the authors will spend further effort in demonstrating the complete chain of integrating IoT data into PLM systems by means of social network functions enhancing the product avatar concept.

Acknowledgments. This work was partly supported by the project FALCON, which has received funding from the European Union's Horizon 2020 research and innovation programme under grant agreement No 636868.

References

1. Kang, Y., Han, M., Han, K., et al.: A study on the Internet of Things (IoT) applications. IJSEIA **9**(9), 117–126 (2015)
2. Gubbi, J., Buyya, R., Marusic, S., et al.: Internet of Things (IoT): a vision, architectural elements, and future directions. Future Gener. Comput. Syst. **29**(7), 1645–1660 (2013)
3. Atzori, L., Iera, A., Morabito, G.: The Internet of Things: a survey. Comput. Netw. **54**(15), 2787–2805 (2010)
4. Kiritsis, D.: Closed-loop PLM for intelligent products in the era of the Internet of Things. Comput.-Aided Des. **43**(5), 479–501 (2011)
5. Hadaya, P., Marchildon, P.: Understanding product lifecycle management and supporting systems. Ind. Manage. Data Syst. **112**(4), 559–583 (2012)
6. Shin, J., Kiritsis, D., Xirouchakis, P.: Design modification supporting method based on product usage data in closed-loop PLM. Int. J. Comput. Integr. Manuf. **28**(6), 551–568 (2014)
7. Wuest, T., Hribernik, K., Thoben, K.-D.: Can a product have a facebook? A new perspective on product avatars in product lifecycle management. In: Rivest, L., Bouras, A., Louhichi, B. (eds.) PLM 2012. IAICT, vol. 388, pp. 400–410. Springer, Heidelberg (2012). doi:10.1007/978-3-642-35758-9_36
8. Wuest, T., Hribernik, K., Thoben, K.: Digital representations of intelligent products: product avatar 2.0. In: Abramovici, M., Stark, R. (eds.) Smart product engineering: Proceedings of the 23rd CIRP Design Conference, pp. 675–684. Springer, Berlin (2013)
9. Denkena, B., Mörke, T., Krüger, M., et al.: Development and first applications of gentelligent components over their lifecycle. CIRP J. Manuf. Sci. Technol. **7**(2), 139–150 (2014)
10. Atzori, L., Iera, A., Morabito, G., et al.: The Social Internet of Things (SIoT) – when social networks meet the Internet of Things: concept, architecture and network characterization. Comput. Netw. **56**(16), 3594–3608 (2012)
11. Dutta, D., Tazivazvino, C., Das, S., et al.: Social Internet of Things (SIoT): transforming smart object to social object. In: NCMAC 2015 Conference Proceedings (2015)
12. Laboratory ARTS, University Mediterranea of Reggio Calabria Social Internet of Things (n. d. 2012). http://www.social-iot.org/. Accessed 13 Apr 2016
13. Manyika, J., Chui, M., Bughin, J., et al.: Disruptive Technologies: Advances that will Transform Life, Business, and the Global Economy. McKinsey Global Institute, San Francisco (2013)
14. van der Meulen, R.: Gartner Says 6.4 Billion Connected "Things" Will Be in Use in 2016, Up 30 Percent From 2015 (2015). http://www.gartner.com/newsroom/id/3165317. Accessed 14 Apr 2016
15. Atzori, L., Iera, A., Morabito, G.: SIoT: giving a social structure to the internet of things. IEEE Commun. Lett. **15**(11), 1193–1195 (2011)
16. Beltran, V., Ortiz, A.M., Hussein, D., et al.: A semantic service creation platform for social IoT. In: IEEE World Forum on Internet of Things (WF-IoT), pp. 283–286 (2014)
17. Ning, H., Wang, Z.: Future Internet of Things architecture: like mankind neural system or social organization framework? IEEE Commun. Lett. **15**(4), 461–463 (2011)
18. Guinard, D., Fischer, M., Trifa, V.: Sharing using social networks in a composable web of things. In: 8th IEEE International Conference on Pervasive Computing and Communications Workshops (PERCOM Workshops), pp. 702–707 (2010)

19. An, J., Gui, X., Zhang, W., et al.: Nodes social relations cognition for mobility-aware in the Internet of Things. In: 4th IEEE International Conference on Cyber, Physical and Social Computing (CPSCom), pp. 687–691 (2011)
20. Kranz, M., Roalter, L., Michahelles, F.: Things that twitter: social networks and the Internet of Things. In: What can the Internet of Things do for the Citizen (CIoT) Workshop at The Eighth International Conference on Pervasive Computing (Pervasive 2010) (2010)
21. Holmquist, L.E., Mattern, F., Schiele, B., et al.: Smart-its friends: a technique for users to easily establish connections between smart artefacts. In: Abowd, G.D., Brumitt, B., Shafer, S. (eds.) Ubiquitous Computing: International Conference Proceedings, pp. 116–122. Springer, Heidelberg (2001)
22. Treeline: How we used #Slack to control the Internet of Things (n.d. 2016). http://treelineinteractive.com/blog/using-slack-with-the-internet-of-things/. Accessed 14 Apr 2016
23. Bisgin, H., Agarwal, N., Xu, X.: Investigating homophily in online social networks. In: IEEE/ACM International Conference on Web Intelligence-Intelligent Agent Technology (WI-IAT), pp. 533–536 (2010)
24. Cheung, C.M., Chiu, P., Lee, M.K.: Online social networks: why do students use facebook? Comput. Hum. Behav. **27**(4), 1337–1343 (2011)
25. Heidemann, J., Klier, M., Probst, F.: Online social networks: a survey of a global phenomenon. Comput. Netw. **56**(18), 3866–3878 (2012)
26. Wuest, T., Hribernik, K., Thoben, K.: Accessing servitisation potential of PLM data by applying the product avatar concept. Prod. Plan. Control **26**(14–15), 1198–1218 (2015)
27. Kenly. A., Poston, B.: Social Media and Product Innovation: Early Adopters Reaping Benefits amidst Challenge and Uncertainty. Kalypso White paper (n.d.)
28. ThingWorx Foundation. http://www.thingworx.com/. Accessed 14 Apr 2016
29. Xivley. https://xively.com/. Accessed 14 Apr 2016
30. Oracle Internet of Things. https://www.oracle.com/solutions/internet-of-things/. Accessed 14 Apr 2016
31. Microsoft Azure IoT Suite. https://www.microsoft.com/en-gb/server-cloud/internet-of-things/azure-iot-suite.aspx. Accessed 14 Apr 2016
32. AWS IoT. https://aws.amazon.com/iot/. Accessed 14 Apr 2016
33. IBM Watson IoT Platform. https://www.ibm.com/marketplace/cloud/internet-of-things-cloud/us/en-us. Accessed 14 Apr 2016
34. Porter, M.E., Heppelmann, J.E.: How smart, connected products are transforming companies. Harv. Bus. Rev. **93**, 96–114 (2015)
35. ISO Information Technology – Message Queuing Telemetry Transport (MQTT) v3.1.1 35.100.70 (ISO/IEC 20922) (2016)
36. Götz, C.: MQTT: Protokoll für das Internet der Dinge: Einst für die Ölpipeline, nun offener Standard (2014). http://www.heise.de/developer/artikel/MQTT-Protokoll-fuer-das-Internet-der-Dinge-2168152.html. Accessed 29 Mar 2016

Information Lifecycle Management

Multi-party Interactive Visioneering Workshop for Smart Connected Products in Global Manufacturing Industry Considering PLM

Satoshi Goto[1,3,4](✉), Elio Trolio[2], Osamu Yoshie[3], and Kin'ya Tamaki[4]

[1] Business Transformation Management, PTC Japan Co. Ltd., Tokyo, Japan
sgoto@ptc.com
[2] IoT Strategy & Business Consulting, ThingWorx Inc., Raleigh, USA
elio.trolio@thingworx.com
[3] Graduate School of Information, Production and Systems, Waseda University, Tokyo, Japan
yoshie@waseda.jp
[4] Human Innovation Research Center, Aoyama Gakuin University, Tokyo, Japan
kinya.tamaki@gmail.com

Abstract. Currently, Internet of Things (IoT) is a dominant technology and a core mechanism for the third Information Technology (IT) revolution. Many benefits are expected to be enabled by implementing the IoT technologies through the product lifecycle management (PLM) process, such as remote monitoring of field service and predictive quality reliability engineering design in R&D. Smart connected products (SCPs) are forecast to produce tremendous business value. However, significant business challenges are associated with SCPs. Manufacturers have difficulty in rapidly launching IoT products in the market. This paper proposes a pragmatic visioneering workshop framework informed by real-world industry practices. The group facilitation for visioneering focuses on identifying the relation between the 26 practical IoT use cases through the PLM process. Moreover, the proposed workshop format will also enable the participants to engage in a discussion and interact with the framework through use case analysis.

Keywords: Internet of Things (IoT) · PLM process · Smart connected products (SCPs) · Multi-party interaction · Visioneering workshop facilitation

1 Introduction

Currently, Internet of Things (IoT) is a dominant technology and is called the third information technology (IT) revolution [7]. The IoT technology enables multiple opportunities and business values through the entire product life cycle management (PLM) process [12]. Remote monitoring of field service and predictive quality reliability engineering design in R&D. Smart factories are alone valuated as a \$3.7 trillion

R. Harik et al. (Eds.): PLM 2016, IFIP AICT 492, pp. 501–511, 2016.
DOI: 10.1007/978-3-319-54660-5_45

dollar industry and are forecast to produce tremendous business value [5]. It is estimated that 30 billion connected "things" will exist by 2020 [4].

Global discrete manufacturing companies such as automotive and high-tech electronics and industrial equipment manufacturers are currently facing significant IoT related business challenges. It is very difficult for these companies to rapidly launch IoT products in the market because of the new complexity derived from the addition of software applications and connectivity components. According to the results of IDC research, it was found that 66% of the discrete manufacturers pursue IoT initiatives and 40% of them are still at the pilot trial stage [4]. In addition, top-level executives are faced with new strategic challenges such as identifying new corporate models to accelerate the investment in R&D. Moreover, they are still struggling to get started. The PLM experts who are assigned the task of IoT promotion in such companies have various individual opinions and pursue different directions. This causes difficulties in choosing a single direction and achieving consensus regarding the development of smart connected products (SCPs). Therefore, companies spend more time in the planning stage of SCPs as compared to general products. In this new era of SCP development, the first critical step is to coordinate the early stages of the PLM process. Thus, a multi-party interactive consensus-building approach is very important; such an approach must be rapid.

This paper proposes a pragmatic visioneering workshop framework informed by real-world industry practices. The group facilitation of visioneering focuses on identifying the relation between the key issues and challenges in some of the 26 practical IoT use cases. It identifies how a company can plan an SCP solution and craft a high-level IoT value roadmap chart understanding each phase of the PLM process. This paper also proposes to incorporate a workshop format that will enable participants to engage in a discussion and interact with the framework through customer value chain analysis (CVCA) [3] referring to the IoT use cases as a guide during the group discussion session.

The paper is organized as follows: Sect. 2 briefly presents the 26 IoT use cases that are categorized through the entire product lifecycle stages. Section 3 proposes a framework of IoT visioneering workshop agenda. A case study of a workshop conducted by a leading global discrete manufacturer is discussed in Sect. 4. We discuss whether the visioneering framework was valuable to the participants in group facilitation in the SCP concept planning phase. Finally, in Sect. 5, it is concluded that the workshop provided a benefit of achieving consensus in a shorter time period than that expected by the participants. Moreover, an outlook on this study is also mentioned in the conclusion of this paper.

2 IoT Use Cases Throughout Product Lifecycle Stages

To overcome the stuck business situation described in Sect. 1, templates of the 26 IoT use cases have been developed [9–11]. These templates are used as a guide to help the stakeholders who seek to understand how to create a business value of SCP solutions in the early stage of product strategy planning. Each use case is defined as a typical IoT practice example that is experienced by hundreds of manufactures through the PLM

Table 1. IoT use cases aligned with PLM processes [11]

Category (a.k.a. PLM process)	IoT Use Case
(A) Marketing and sales	1. Customer insights and opportunities
	2. Flexible billing and pricing models
	3. New value added services
(B) Product development	4. Connected product usage analysis
	5. Connected product quality analysis
	6. Connected software management
(C) Operations and manufacturing	7. Asset and material tracking
	8. Connected operations intelligence
	9. Unified key performance indicators
	10. Real-time asset health monitoring
	11. Operations management improvements
(D) Service and support	12. Monitoring and diagnostics
	13. Remote service
	14. Automated service execution
	15. Condition-based predictive maintenance
	16. Connected service parts planning
(E) Information and operational technology	18. Flexible product and asset connectivity
	19. Identity and security management
	20. Scalable IoT operations management
	21. Seamless IoT data integration
	22. Automated analytics and actions
	23. Rapid IoT application development
(F) Customers	24. Usage and performance dashboard
	25. Customer self-service
	26. Product personalization

processes. The 26 use cases are also categorized by six key product lifecycle stages (Table 1) so that the use cases aligned with the PLM process can be recognized.

The contents of the above 26 use cases are mainly utilized at the proposed visioneering session during the group activity; the participants can clearly determine what they need to focus on for their IoT initiatives. One of the benefits is that it helps the group to quickly understand and easily choose key IoT initiatives in shorter discussion time, for example, in 15–20 min. A more specific description of this is provided in Sect. 3.

3 Design of IoT Visioneering Workshop

3.1 Background and Aim

This workshop is designed for product managers and lead engineers who are working at manufacturing companies. As a background, C-level executives assigned them to be as corporate led IoT product promotion members. However, the workshop members are not always available to work full-time on the assigned mission. Thus, an efficient and more productive approach is required that will enable consensus building over a shorter time. The members need to rapidly provide a single common SCP solution idea that contributes to the executives' strategic goals. This paper aims to provide a procedure for thinking through facilitated group visioneering approaches in such business situations.

3.2 Proposed Workshop Agenda and Timetable

Table 2 shows the proposed agenda for the visioneering workshop for multi-party participants invited from the various product and service development organizations in the company. The timetable is very compact, and an intensive configuration for such busy participants is a necessary and sufficient condition. The workshop is designed to be completed in a total of 5 h and is configured in 7 step-by-step sessions.

Table 2. Proposed agenda template for the visioneering workshop

Round#	Session agenda	Interval (min.)	Clock time (as sample)
1	Introduction/Agenda Review	15	13:00–13:15
2	IoT introduction & strategy overview	30	13:15–13:45
3	Global industry IoT case studies	45	13:45–14:30
	Break time	15	14:30–14:45
4	Group work for visioneering		
	Step 1. Identify stakeholders		
	Step 2. Select major IoT use cases	120	14:45–16:45
	Step 3. Narrow-down use cases		
	Step 4. Craft IoT value roadmap		
	Step 5. Set metrics for IoT business		
5	Group presentation	15	16:45–17:00
	Break time	15	17:00–17:15
6	IoT enablement	30	17:15–17:45
7	Wrap-up/Next steps Discussion	15	17:45–18:00
	Total	300	13:00–18:00

3.3 Preliminary Questionnaire

A preliminary questionnaire is an efficient approach for obtaining the participant's individual thoughts and insights in advance and is employed to facilitate the smooth running of the workshop. The following is the proposed format for the questionnaire comprising two parts.

Part 1: Ask for Business Strategies (Value Drivers) Part 1 of the questionnaire asks the questionee about Business Strategies and comprises 6 options (Fig. 1) called "Value Drivers" [9–11]. These 6 options are organized into two categories. Options 1–

3 are based on "Operational Effectiveness" and are aimed at helping to improve the optimization of the operational performance. Options 4–6 are for strategic differentiation. The idea of Part 1 is based on the competitive strategy framework developed by Professor Michael Porter [6, 7].

Part 2: Ask for Current States (Challenges)
Part 2 is focused on typical common business challenges (Fig. 1). Twenty options are given that comprehensively describe the end users' problems through the entire product lifecycle process with examples such as the slow pace of product innovation and expensive internal development process for SCP projects.

Questionnaire for IoT Visioneering Workshop

The Questionnaire consists of 2 parts - Business Strategies (Value Drivers) and Current State (Challenges). Firstly, plesase enter your contact information, and fill out the questionnaire to the best of your ability. Part 1 is relatively asking you based on *your future expectations*, Part 2 is based on *current business conditions*. Both are not for based on past. When complete, be sure to save to a unique file name ("File>Save As "Filename - your name" from Excel Menu) and return it to the activity sponsor via email. Thank you in advance for your participation in this important activity.

Contact Information

Name	
Title/Role	
Division	

Part 1 Business Strategies (Value Drivers)

Please enter the importance of the following Value Drivers (business strategies) to your company. This is a force ranking - assign values from 6 ("most important") to 1 ("least important") for each of the 6 items. *Don't enter same digit number to multiple cells.		Chose Importance from Pick List ↓↓
1	Optimize Operational Performance Combine real-time data from assets, enterprise systems, and people to increase operational efficiency of equipment, plants and logistics	
2	Improve Risk Management Improve ability to proactively identify and mitigate financial, safety, environmental, and regulatory compliance risk	
3	Reduce Product and Service Costs Implement proactive service, limit warranty costs and risks, and optimize service and product development processes	
4	Improve Customer Experience Make products smarter, easier to update, and more personalized to improve customer experience and value	
5	Differentiate Product and Service Offering Quickly deliver compelling, differentiated products and services that meet or anticipate customer demands	
6	Enable New Revenue Streams Maximize revenue opportunities and value capture from new services or new business models	

Part 2 Current State (Challenges)

The followings are typical challenges that company is facing as current state. Please review this list and rate the most important in your business environment as a force ranking from 5 - 1, where 5 is Most Important. You can select only 5 out of 20 items, others are keeping as blanks. *Don't enter same digit number to multiple cells.		Chose Importance from Pick List ↓↓
1	Slow pace of product and service innovation	
2	Inefficient identifying up-sell and cross-sell opportunities	
3	Inability to differentiate offering or enter new markets	
4	Losing market share to new or low cost competitors	
5	Inability to identify and manage the configuration of fielded products, systems, and assets	
6	Limited visibility into product performance, usage, environment, and quality	
7	Inability to aggregate, analyze, and visualize operational intelligence across systems, assets, and people	
8	Inability to quickly re-configure manufacturing systems and introduce new smart technologies	
9	Inability to get real-time correlated data from proprietary systems and heterogeneous equipment	
10	Difficult to incorporate data from existing business systems and external sources in IoT applications	
11	Poor capture and management of quality-related feedback causing repeated problems	
12	Difficult to track quality and identify root cause	
13	Inability to hire and retain skilled technical staff	
14	Rising service and warranty costs	
15	Poor product / equipment performance or unscheduled downtime	
16	Low service level agreement (SLA) compliance	
17	Increasing demand for new views into production / operation data	
18	Inability to securely connect products and manage and analyze data	
19	Internal development of IoT projects are slow and costly	
20	Existing IoT solutions unable to scale or meet new data requirements	

Fig. 1. Preliminary questionnaire (Part 1 and Part 2) https://jp.surveymonkey.com/r/XKQ9ZFV

Web-Based Assessment Tool The proposed preliminary questionnaire is also available as a Web-based system for the workshop participants so that they can respond to the questionnaire on the Web (https://jp.surveymonkey.com/r/XKQ9ZFV). The questionnaire must be submitted a couple of days prior to the date of the workshop. The option selection for Part 1 and Part 2 is very easy for the questionee, and it normally takes 15 min to complete each Part. The Web system is a freeware that everyone can use on the Web [13]. An Excel sheet is also available for the participants who cannot access the internet environment (Fig. 1).

3.4 Design of Group Facilitation for Visioneering Session

This workshop emphasizes intensive group work (round#4 in Table 2), wherein 4 or 5 people per group and 2 or 3 groups per workshop are reasonable. Moreover, 2 facilitators support all the group activities. During the group session, many debating situations are possible. In one case, each person has his own opinion and may try to push his own idea to others. In another roundtable, the group discussion would be very quiet and low-key; nobody tries to speak up and the participants are just watching each other until someone makes a comment. Either one of these two cases is not always ideal for building a consensus for a single direction. Furthermore, a difficulty in reaching the final goal of the group discussion outcome will be faced in both cases. Therefore, the following five pragmatic steps are proposed as an engineering facilitation methodology aiming to smoothly achieve a consensus for a single direction (Table 3).

Table 3. Five steps for group facilitation at a visioneering session

Step#	Group discussion topic
1	***Identify stakeholder***—utilizing Customer Value Chain Analysis (CVCA)
2	***Select Top 6 IoT Use Cases***—aligning with corporate Value Drivers
3	***Narrow-down the Use Cases***—selecting 3 out of 6 for to be more specific
4	***Craft IoT Value Roadmap***—positioning the Use Cases on the value maturity
5	***Set Metrics (KPIs)***—qualifying Business Goals

Step 1: Identify Stakeholders—utilizing Customer Value Chain Analysis (CVCA)
Using CVCA methodology [3], the group members are encouraged to discuss all the people and processes that impact or depend on the product or asset. First, this requires the group members to select a product or asset to focus the discussion on; the members will select and identify as many stakeholders as possible, such as internal/external and direct/indirect. The roles of the stakeholders should be specific. The discussed stakeholders should then be connected with a line. As a result, a CVCA diagram is drawn surrounding the selected product or asset. This task is aimed to help the members realize that there are many influencers and to expand the value of the product or asset connecting various stakeholders. For this step, 20 min is an appropriate amount of time.

Step 2: Select Top 6 IoT Use Cases—aligning with corporate Value Drivers
In the second step, the group members will review the 26 use case examples and select 6 use cases. This is to support their conclusion whether their selected product or asset will become worthwhile as a future SCP solution. In addition, they need to understand which of the selected use cases provide business impact for the specific Value Drivers (Business Strategies) based on the preliminary results of Part 1 of the questionnaire. For this step, 15 min is an appropriate amount of time.

Step 3: Narrow-down selected Use Cases—selecting 3 out of 6 for to be more specific
In the third step, the participants review and prioritize the above selected 6 use cases and select the top 3 use cases. Then, the members will discuss why these use cases were selected. Finally, they will unanimously agree on the most important use case for the first action on the future roadmap. For this step, 10 min is an appropriate amount of time.

Step 4: Craft IoT Value Roadmap—positioning the Use Cases on the value maturity
The members will use the selected top 3 use cases to consider the steps and value maturity. Considering the As-Is situation and examining the result of the preliminary questionnaire, they will create an IoT Value Roadmap to add a To-Be objective and goal for each step (Fig. 2). For this step, 45 min is an appropriate amount of time.

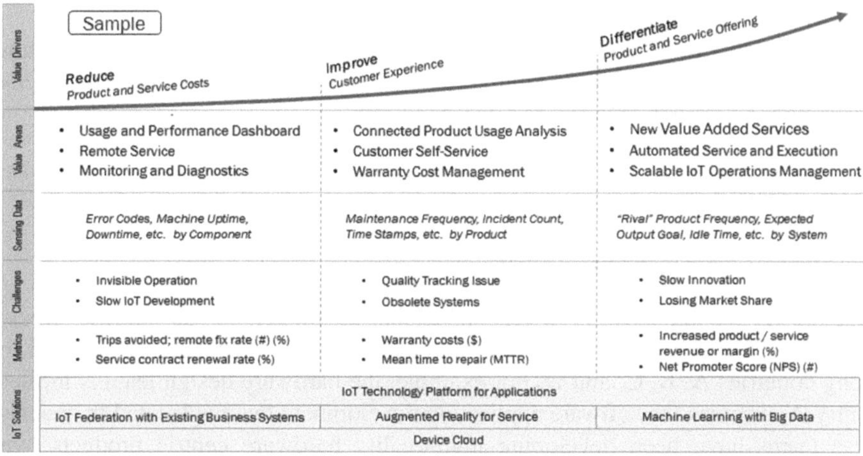

Fig. 2. Tailored IoT value roadmap with maturity curve (a Sample Template)

Step 5: Set Metrics (KPIs)—qualifying Business Goals During step 5, the group members will identify action items to move forward utilizing the use cases. In parallel, they discuss key metrics (KPIs) for each use case. KPI examples should be provided by the facilitator to the group members. The selected metrics would be significant indicators of whether the planned business transformation is correctly promoted with the SCP solutions that they would develop. Finally, they will draw one single page as a high-level IoT value roadmap putting all of the insights that they discovered through the steps 1–4. For example, how to better qualify selected use cases, from which use case should we begin, and what are the "quick wins" or "strategic values." For this step, 30 min is an appropriate amount of time.

3.5 Key Achievements of Visioneering Workshop

Through the visioneering session, the following are achieved as group work outcomes recognizing the group members' efforts.

All-Hands Intensive Group Presentation

Regarding the visioneering session, it is most important to recognize its group efforts. The participants intensively work together during the limited session time such as for 120 min. At the end of the group session, the group presentation time is required by the facilitator. The aim of this step is that all of the participants at the workshop are able to get a mutual understanding and compare with other group members' outcomes. The presentation time for each group is only 5 min. It should include the group CVCA diagram and the high-level SCP value roadmap discussed during the group work (Fig. 2). After the presentation time, the audience (other groups) must ask constructive questions to the presenter group (at least 2 questions). Thus, presentation time provides critical insights regarding the value propositions.

Tailored IoT Value Roadmap with Maturity Curve
At the end of the group discussion, a value roadmap is crafted as a one-page summary. Figure 1 is an example that is configured with Value Driver, Value Area, Sensing Information, Challenge, Metric, and IoT Solutions.

4 Case Study

4.1 Background and Opportunity

Company-X (as anonym) is a leading global manufacturer of specific precision instruments. Company-X's product development process is globally distributed, e.g., among countries A, B, C, and D. For example, the hardware design team is located in country A, whereas the software application development team is located in country B. These teams have been developing high-quality hardware centric products over a period of time, and the company has built a dominant position in the specific global market. The market is quite oligopolistic and has a high entry barrier because of the severe industry-specific regulations. Because the IoT technology is recently recognized as a disruptive innovation that can transform the existing product functionalities, the boundaries of the competition shift and expand from the exiting industry to a broader system of products. Moreover, there was a threat of a severe battle for Company-X. This was a new competitive era with not only the existing competitors but also with the newly entering cost-competitive emerging companies.

In such a new business transformation, the senior executive officer in charge of a global business unit in Company-X decided to start a "vision definition" for their future IoT-enabled SCP solutions. This required collaboration with the corporate product management team and the local development members who are distributed among the various countries. A critical challenge was how the differences of cultures and opinions among the members can be efficiently controlled to enable the formulation of a single and common future vision in a short time frame such as a half-day internal big meeting.

This was an opportunity for our study team to propose our developed visioneering workshop framework to the officer, supporting Company-X's vision-making initiative as an independent third party. It was a significant empirical study opportunity for us to examine whether the workshop framework can validate our study concept and its assumption.

4.2 Characteristic of Participants

The following distributed members were gathered at a single location in country A (Table 4). They came from four different regions around the world and their nationalities and mother tongues were different. To support mutual communication, a dedicated interpreter staff was assigned for translation between English and the local language of country A.

Table 4. Attendees list of the visioneering workshop at company-X

Group name	Participant (individual#)	Business title	Region (Work location)	Mother tongue
Group-A (w/global managers)	1	VP	Americas	*language-a*
	2	Director	EMEA	*language-b*
	3		Americas	*language-a*
	4			*language-a*
	5	General Mgr.	Asia-Oceania	*language-c*
	6		EMEA	*language-b*
	7	Manager	Asia-Oceania	*language-c*
Group-B (w/local managers)	8	General Mgr.	Asia-Oceania	*language-c*
	9			
	10			
	11			
Group-C (w/local engineers)	12	Manager	Asia-Oceania	*language-c*
	13	Sr. Engineer		
	14			
	15	Engineer		

4.3 Discussions

In this paper, we focus our discussion on the "Group Work for Visioneering" session for Round#4 in Table 2 based on the result for the actual case of Company-X. The developed group facilitation approach has comprehensively provided significant insights to the workshop group members. This allowed them to identify IoT values that they have never previously realized. The following three items were particularly significant discussion points.

Well-Balanced PLM Process as IoT Use Cases
The predefined IoT use case templates allowed the group members to provide well-balanced strategy planning workflow in IoT topics and discussions. Although most of the participants were basically from the "engineering department," they realized the value of selecting some of the IoT initiatives of the product manufacturing and field service processes that were not within their specialties. The initiatives they selected were also well-aligned with the corporate strategy. These potential values would not have been discovered without the use of such templates. In addition, the participants from the "*hardware*" design team recognized the importance of the value of "*software*" rather than hardware innovation. Another remarkable contribution by the facilitator was that the 26 use cases were prepared as "26 cards." This means that the group members enjoyed the group discussion time as if they were playing cards, which had a positive effect by relaxing the participants and enabling them to think about brand new ideas.

Doubling Productivity vs. Negative Business?
During the group work session, the facilitator was rigidly measuring the session time with a stopwatch. This brought about a remarkable increase in productivity. Moreover,

the predefined timetable was a quite a useful guide for the facilitator. In fact, there was a very positive endorsement from a lead participant in the workshop, *"Without such time management and use case templates, we could not complete on time. We would spend twice as much time as we actually did."* On the other hand, the rigid timing also identified some of the participants' mental stress due to the busyness forced by the facilitator. This should be a topic for improvement in a future study.

***Multi**-linguistic Party and Challenges on Remote facilitation*
Although each group (A, B, and C) comprised people with different backgrounds and cultures from overseas countries, no operationally fatal problems were identified during the group discussion time. All three groups achieved the final conclusions. However, we have to admit the contribution of the professional interpreter's savvy. Such multinational and multi-linguistic group activities are currently estimated to be increasing. We are still dependent on such a talent of the interpreter for better human communication for the solution of the problems involved in the discussion in such a diverse environment. Furthermore, in this case, another facilitator joined remotely through the Web from his base country. Currently, Web meeting applications such as WebEx on a smartphone are very convenient and cheaper than ever before. Thus, we actually applied a remote facilitation style during round#3 in Table 2. This had a negative influence because it was quite difficult for the remote facilitator to recognize the audiences' personal perceptions. Generally, it is very important to understand how a remote facilitator can be acceptable in such an unknown situation [2]. This should be improved in the workshop agenda design based on the previous literature and cross-disciplinary studies and research.

5 Conclusions and Future Work

We proposed a visioneering workshop approach utilizing the 26 IoT use cases through the PLM process. We have identified some significant values during the proposed group facilitation approach at a global manufacturing company focused on specifically planning an SCP concept as a part of IoT product solution suite. We also recognized that the proposed approach was acceptable for the workshop participants because they were able to achieve a common vision and consensus on a single SCP concept in a shorter time than they initially estimated. For the workshop participants, the largest contribution was made by the ability to use the comprehensive formatted 26 IoT use case examples. The participants clearly imagined future candidates of IoT solutions because the use cases were pragmatic business templates and were demonstrated in the actual industry environment.

On the other hand, we need to consider the remote facilitator's role at the requirement gathering phase described in the literature [2] as a possibility of virtual meeting space with ICT remote environment. As the next step, we are building on the research of previous studies in directions such as visual planning for virtual multi-site teams [1, 8]. Furthermore, we would like to investigate the effects of adopting innovative user experiences such as augmented reality. This would provide a supportive effect for the globally distributed participants as if they worked together in-person in the same workshop room.

References

1. Bertilsson, J., Wentzel, G.: Visual Planning. Coordination and Collaboration of Multi-site Teams in Product Development Organisations (2015)
2. Damian, D.E., et al.: An exploratory study of facilitation in distributed requirements engineering. Requirements Eng. **8**(1), 24–26 (2003)
3. Donaldson, K.M., Ishii, K., Sheppard, S.D.: Customer value chain analysis. Res. Eng. Des. **16**(4), 174–183 (2006)
4. IDC InfoBrief sponsored by PTC: Connected Products and Operation. Reshaping the Manufacturing and Operations Landscape (2015)
5. James, M.: The Internet of Things. Mapping the Value Beyond the Hype (2015)
6. Porter, M.E., Heppelmann, J.E.: How smart, connected products are transforming companies. Harvard Bus. Rev. **93**(10), 96–114 (2015)
7. Porter, M.E., Heppelmann, J.E.: How smart, connected products are transforming competition. Harvard Bus. Rev. **92**(11), 64–88 (2014)
8. Project Visit. http://www.projectvisit.org/. Accessed 1 Oct 2015
9. PTC Inc.: IoT Value Roadmap. http://www.ptc.com/File%20Library/IoT/IoT-Use-Case-eBook.pdf. Accessed 10 June 2016
10. PTC Community. https://www.ptcusercommunity.com/docs/DOC-8646. Accessed 19 Mar 2016
11. PTC Inc.: To Create Real Business Value You Need to Identify and Prioritize the Specific IoT Use Cases. http://www.ptc.com/internet-of-things/use-cases. Accessed 1 Mar 2016
12. Stark, J.: PLM and the IoT (#4): The Opportunities of the IoT. PLM Consultant and Owner, John Stark Associates. https://www.linkedin.com/pulse/plm-iot-4-opportunities-john-stark?trk=mp-reader-card. Accessed 11 Jan 2016
13. Survey Monkey. https://www.surveymonkey.com/mp/aboutus/. Accessed 9 Mar 2016

Understanding PLM System Concepts to Facilitate Its Implementation in SME: The Real Case Study of POULT

Laureline Plo[1,2], Vincent Robin[2(✉)], and Philippe Girard[2]

[1] Groupe POULT – Site de Montauban, Montauban, France
l.plo@groupe-poult.fr
[2] IMS Laboratory, University of Bordeaux, Talence, France
{vincent.robin,philippe.girard}@u-bordeaux.fr

Abstract. In 2012, our research team in partnership with LASCOM (a French PLM software editor) proposed models and an approach to help SMEs when they decide to deploy PLM systems [1, 2]. Our approach was to use formalism based on mind maps to promote exchanges between customer/users and PLM editor. Objective was to facilitate definition of elements that have to be defined, modeled, evaluated and implemented in a software solution to make deployment process more effective. Different real case studies emphasized that our approach have to evolve to be more "customer" centered. In this paper we present one of these real case studies which is in progress. This research collaboration concerns POULT, a manufacturer of biscuits which decided to deploy a PLM solution in few months. We describe the adopted approach to analyze the users' needs and draft the request for proposal which will be send to PLM editors.

Keywords: PLM concepts · Progressive "user" centered approach

1 Introduction

For SMEs, PLM system is a solution to manage all the processes and associated data generated by events and actions of various lifecycle agents (both human and software systems) and distributed along the product lifecycle phases, from the beginning to the end of life [3]. SMEs have some difficulties in the use of PLM systems and do not exploit their full potentiality and a big amount of information and knowledge is being lost or requires a higher human effort to be preserved [4, 5]. The main problems for SMEs in the exploitation of a PLM system are the lack of models to represent the product lifecycle [5] and the approach used by PLM editor to adapt and deploy their solutions for SME [1]. This approach is often iterative and incremental and based on models and prototypes (Fig. 1). It offers a bottom-up approach to analyze and model the decisional, functional and organizational structure of the customer but partially ensures consistency between the expectations/needs and the functional aspects of the PLM solution. Moreover, the number of iterations to define the users' expectations is too important and the capitalization of actors' feedback is not sufficiently taken into

R. Harik et al. (Eds.): PLM 2016, IFIP AICT 492, pp. 512–522, 2016.
DOI: 10.1007/978-3-319-54660-5_46

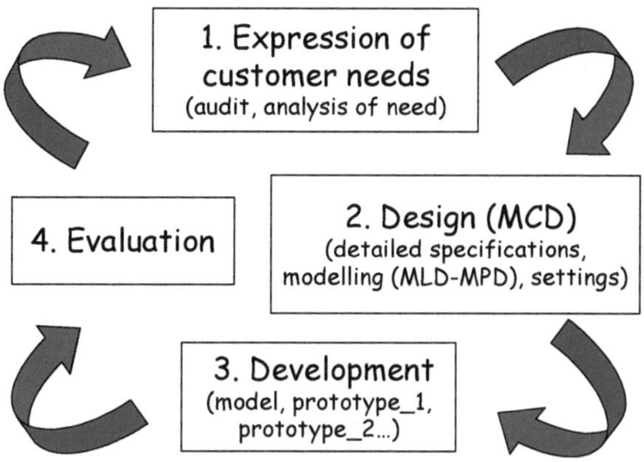

Fig. 1. Iterative and incremental approach to deploy PLM solution [1].

account. One problem stems from the uniqueness and the diversity of each solution. Other one concerns the fact that views and semantics between the different actors of the project are often different: customers/users are functional and business oriented, while the editor is faced with structural and technological issues. This often leads to a misunderstanding underlying and creates difficulties during the specifications validation step.

This approach is not efficient yet and causes significant delays on the initial planning. To reduce and optimize the analysis of expectations for each new project and to increase the efficiency of the procedure for solutions deployment we proposed to develop a new approach [1]. Our objective was to facilitate the preliminary analysis of the system and the characterization of users' expectations and needs. This approach was developed with LASCOM a French PLM editor and was inevitably "editor oriented". In a nutshell, approach optimizes audit and analysis of need for PLM editor (time reduction) and creates a dependency relationship between customer and PLM editor. In this case, SMEs could be reluctant to approach PLM editors and prefer to keep a relative autonomy towards editors. SMEs need time to understand and integrate PLM system and are often suspicious about editors' intentions. To limit harmful effects of a too PLM editor centered approach we propose in this paper an process to enable companies to understand PLM concept, express their needs and define their own specifications in autonomy before calling a PLM editor. Our approach is composed with 4 steps in order to formalize the needs of the company before the first meetings with the PLM editor (Fig. 2):

- First step: understanding the organization of R&D process, to model the existing organization without considering a "PLM editor centered" vision,
- Second step: understanding the philosophy of PLM approach, to appreciate and estimate possible impacts of the PLM in the company,
- Third step: considering users in the PLM deployment, to favor acceptation,
- Fourth step: formalization of the needs and definition of the preliminary specifications of a solution which could be an adapted one for the company.

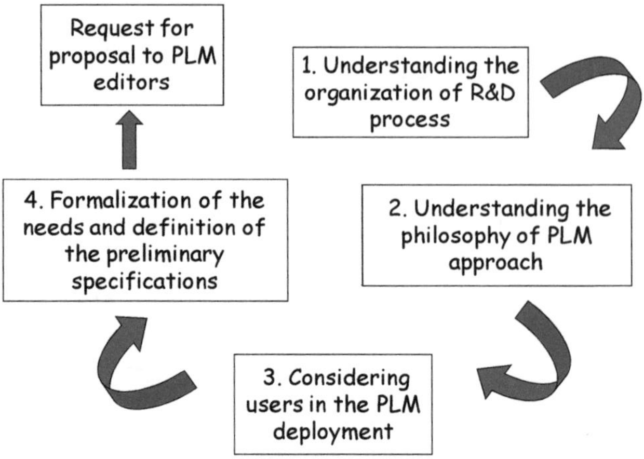

Fig. 2. Internal process to study relevance of PLM solution deployment in a company.

In this paper we present our approach through the real case study of Poult, a French producer of biscuits, which decided to improve its research and development process in 2014 and initiated a reflection on the opportunity to use a PLM system. This SME has ever had experiences with different PLM editors and preferred to preliminary work with our research team in order to anticipate and limit difficulties before send a request of proposal to PLM editors again. The paper is structured in order to show our progressive approach to help members of the team "PLM project" (managers of R&D, production, marketing, quality and purchasing departments, R&D assistant, Ms. PLO - PhD student). First section describes the initial vision of the R&D process to be improved. Second section shows how Poult progressively understands PLM concepts and adapts them. Following section presents work in progress which concerns a user centered approach to precisely specify users' needs. Finally, last section concludes and states futures works.

2 First Step: Understanding the Organization of R&D Process

Poult is a French producer of biscuits which decided to improve its research and development process in 2014. R&D process essentially concerns development of new product or evolution of an existing one. Product could be developed for Poult's label or for other customers' labels. Poult controls technical activities to create biscuits but has many difficulties to control and manage data generated during R&D activities. That the reason why managers decided to study the opportunity to deploy a PLM system in the company to allow data management and increase efficiency of R&D phases. As the R&D process was not really formalized first step of our collaboration concerned global identification and definition of principal activities of the R&D process. This process begins when customer sends specifications of the expected biscuit and finishes when the industrial production of the biscuit starts (Table 1). In first time, the vision is quite global because it is relatively unusual for Poult to express its R&D organization.

Table 1. Preliminary description of the Poult's R&D process activities and tasks.

Activity	Task	Actor involved
Customer's or internal (Poult's project) request for proposal	NPD request	Customer
	Request validation	"Product family" (R&D, marketing, trade, production)
	Feasibility survey	
	Feasibility survey validation	
Internal review	Product brief definition	Marketing
	Packaging brief definition	Development pack
	Brief definitions validation	"Product family"
First testing	Preliminary testing definition	R&D project manager, production manager
	Orders of specific ingredients	R&D project manager, supply chain manager
	Specific ingredients reception	R&D assistant, storekeeper
Lab and industrial testing	Testing definition (formulation of the recipe)	R&D project manager
	Cost price calculation	
	Testing of the recipe	R&D project manager, production
	Control of products	
	Tasting (internal tasting)	R&D project manager, R&D assistant
	Testing validation	"Product family"
Internal validation	Conformity validation	R&D project manager, quality
	Provisory labeling card edition	R&D project manager
	Global cost price analysis	Trade department
	Physiochemical analysis	External lab
Sampling for the customer	Customer's sampling production	R&D project manager, R&D assistant
	Customer's sampling validation	
	Customer's sampling sending	
	Customer's acceptance	Customer
Final customer's validation	Internal and external panels	Customer
	Final recipe validation	
Industrialization		

3 Second Step: Understanding the Philosophy of PLM Approach

Preliminary description of the R&D process (Table 1) is useful to partially understand R&D process but it has to evolve to be more operational with a view to a PLM system deployment. So, second step of our collaboration was to switch from a classical "*activities*" model to a "*product lifecycle*" model. As the main problem for SMEs in the exploitation of a PLM system is the lack of models to represent the product lifecycle [5], start of this step was not easy. Discussion with project team members leaded to guide our reflection on the use of ontologies to provide an answer to the need for a clear understanding of product lifecycles phases [6] and the need of system interoperability [7]. Several ontologies [8] or researches [9] exist and have been presented to members of the project with a view to build a common semantic and a share understanding of model. These exchanges allow us to find an agreement and we decide to exploit Bruno *et al.*'s ontology and UML model [5]. Bruno *et al.* developed in 2015 their reference ontology for PLM which clearly makes appear PLM concepts (Table 2) and relationships between each on them (white classes - Fig. 3). POULT chooses to use this ontology because it is based on a serious analysis of existing ontologies and it is considered as understandable and well-adapted to the company thanks to the use of UML.

Our experience with POULT puts in evidence the difficulty to identify ontology and models to present PLM philosophy and concepts to people in charge of a PLM project in a company. Thanks to such an experience, we are working on an approach to define

Table 2. Description of PLM concepts [5]

Concept	Description
Product	A generic term for whatever is produced by a process and serves a need or satisfies a want
Customer	The reference person of a company that ordered a product
Project	The term used by a company to indicate the collaboration with a customer for the developing of a product. Each project refers to one product and is connected with one customer
Product component	One of the hardware, electronic or software that makes up a product. A component may be subdivided into other components, which combine into sub-assemblies and assemblies to define product. Each product can be made of several components, and the same component can be used by different products
Material	The material of which a product or a product component is made of
Physical characteristic	The physical characteristic of a product or product component
Unit	The unit in which the Physical characteristic is measured
Activity	An action executed during the product lifecycle of a specific product that can be univocally and un-ambiguously identified
File	Electronic data managed and stored as a single object
Document	A uniquely-identified block of information that can be composed by several files
Tool	A software tool used to produce a file, for which the name and the version have to be specified
Resource	An entity that is involved in the execution of an activity. A resource can be of two kinds: person or machine
Role	The term used to define a specific set of skills and responsibilities associated with the employees of the company

and select possible combinations (ontology + models) depending on the company context to express the plhilosophy of PLM approach. We will present our propositions in a future paper which will be focused on more conceptual aspects of our research.

Thanks to Bruno *et al.*'s propositions we create a common vision of a PLM system between team project members and researchers. Moreover, such description of PLM concepts and ULM class diagram were very helpful for the team which has been able to define its own description of PLM concepts and UML class diagram adapted to Poult. All Bruno *et al.*'s classes have been conserved (or slightly evolved) and 10 new classes complete the UML class diagram to be closed to the Poult's reality. New classes represent particularity of Poult or food industry. Poult considers a product as a quadruplet [recipe + raw materials + ingredients + packaging] and data associated to this quadruplet are managed separately. So these classes appear in the new version of the diagram. Moreover, food industry has specific rules to ensure quality during all the production process for the final users. These rules oblige Poult to manage precisely specific data (machine characteristic, supplier characteristics, etc.). These classes also complete the UML diagram. Table 3 provides a description of these new classes and Fig. 3 shows an UML class diagram of PLM adapted to Poult (added classes in grey).

4 Third Step: Considering Users in the PLM Deployment

The UML class diagram adapted to Poult shows how project team members have understood PLM. They evolve from a global vision of the R&D process of Poult to a more operational vision which integrates PLM concepts. Thanks to such representation architecture of PLM system appears. As deployment and implementation of an effective solution not only consists in selecting and installing software but also in obtaining the users acceptance, we have to focus now on final users of the PLM system. The understanding of user's needs and expectations is a critical phase for the deployment of such solutions. Nevertheless, much of the traditional research on software project management does not consider users' expectation correctly and neglects to ask project managers about their perspectives and ideas on how to manage projects [10]. This crucial step depends on the ability to understand and consider users' expectations [11] and to analyze, co-ordinate and control the collaboration between the numerous users concerning by the project: strategic/tactical decision-makers, project managers, designers, experts from different disciplines and with different experiences, external partners, etc. The views and semantics between the different actors of the project are often different. Customers are functional and business oriented, while the editor is faced with structural and technological issues. This often leads to a misunderstanding underlying and creates difficulties during the specifications validation step. To reduce these difficulties, we developed in 2012 an "editor" oriented approach to facilitate exchanges between PLM editors and customers [1, 2]. Our objective was to make easier the preliminary analysis of the system and the characterization of users' expectations and needs. This approach is based on the use of mind map and persona to progressively define users' profiles and expectations.

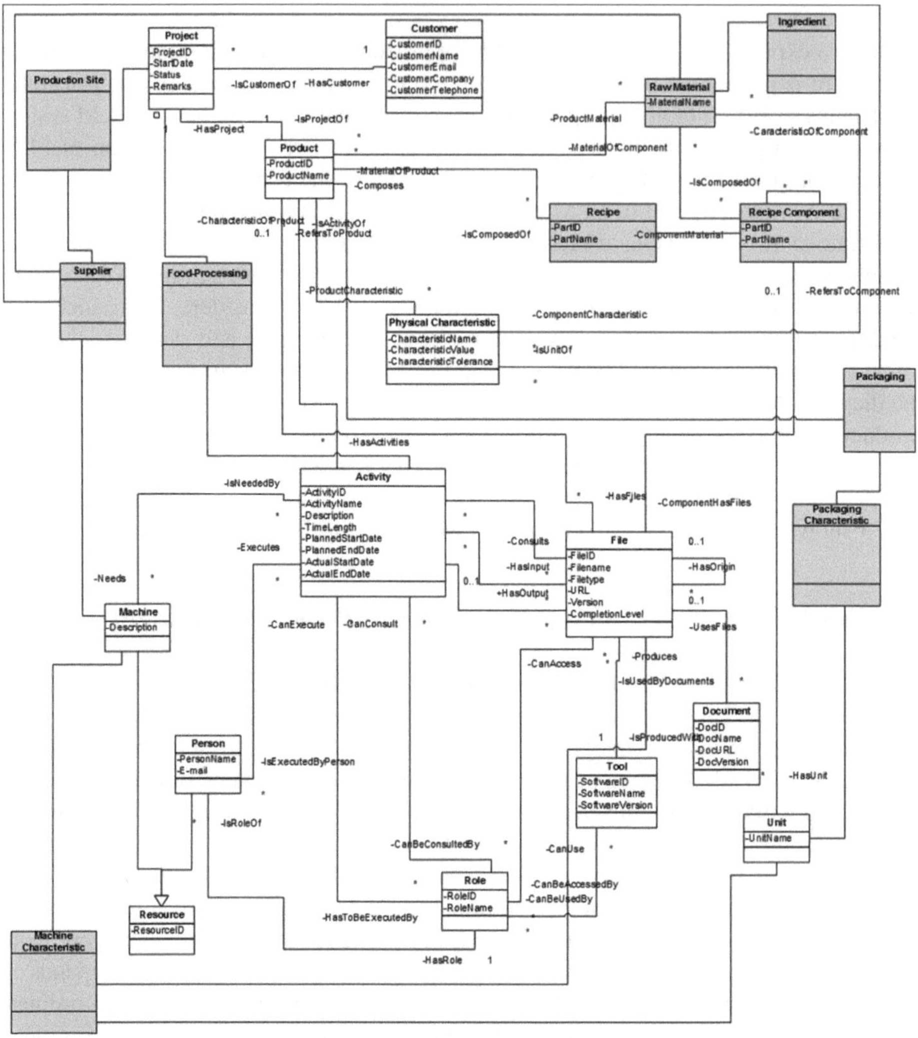

Fig. 3. ULM class diagram of PLM adapted to Poult.

When a project starts editor initializes a specific map for the customer (Fig. 4). Four branches structure the map:

- Enterprise modelling which regroups data concerning the customer (structural and functional organizations, actors implied in the project, etc.). This branch evolves and is more and more precise according to project evolution.
- Follow-up of the contributions allows project manager to have a trace of each action realized during the project. The aim of this branch is to be able to follow each evolution of the project in term of “who decided what?”

Table 3. Description of additional PLM concepts adapted to Poult (food industry).

Concept	Description
Food-processing (to complete product)	R&D department could develop new product (i.e. new biscuits) or new food-processing. So, a class "Food-processing" has been created to clearly make appear these two kinds of production
Production site (to complete customer)	A product or a food-processing could be ordered by a customer or by Poult's production site. So, a class "Production site" has been created to make appear these two kinds of prime contractor
Recipe and recipe component (to complete product component)	Poult's products are identified thanks to a "recipe" and a recipe is composed with components. That the reason why the class "product component" evolved to be "recipe" and "recipe component" classes. A product has only one recipe which can be made of several components, and the same component can be used by different products
Raw material and ingredient (substitute material)	In food industry the term "raw material" is preferable to "material". Raw material can be made of several "ingredient". Combination of ingredients in a raw material is an important data to respect food regulations
Packaging	Product is one or more biscuits plus a specific packaging. Poult manages its biscuit and its packaging separately so a specific class has been created for "packaging"
Packaging characteristic	The different characteristic of a packaging
Supplier	In food industry, all components have to be controlled. One performance indicator to be controlled is "who supply the component"? "Supplier" and associated characteristics are important data to be managed by PLM
Machine characteristic	Food industry rules oblige to manage data about machines used to produce biscuit. Objective is to ensure quality of the process on the whole for final users. So, Poult has to manage data associated to its machines

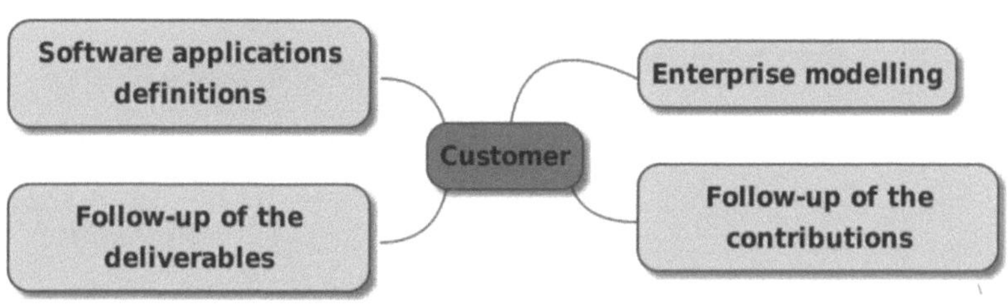

Fig. 4. Global architecture of a map dedicated to a customer.

- Follow-up of the deliverables regroups all the documents which are produced during the project. This branch helps editor and customer to judge if the progress of the project according to the common deadlines fixed from the start of the project.
- Software applications definitions is the branch in which we fond all the versions of the software developed during the project.

Each actor of PLM editor which is involved in the project completes his part of the map. Information concerning customer and project lifecycle (activities and associated documents) are in the map and each steps of the software development are capitalized and reusable. Relationships exist between elements of branches to obtain a global and dynamic vision of the structure of the system. Such a simplified representation makes easier relationships between editor and customer [1]. A map is associated to one project and to one customer. When the PLM is deployed it is easy to maintain solution because editor has customers' data in the map and an evolution of the map is quickly reverberated in the PLM system. Concerning Poult, we have organized interviews of each potential user since few weeks in order to complete the branch "enterprise modeling" (Fig. 5). Interviews are in progress and the branch evolves. Other branches cannot be completed, they concern PLM editor and no one is selected yet. When team project members will estimate that they have a clear vision of PLM concepts, of their needs and of the specifications of the solution, they will formalize all of these data (step 4 – Fig. 2) and send a request for proposal to PLM editors.

Fig. 5. Preliminary description of the production site of Montauban.

5 Conclusion

Collaboration with LASCOM until 2012 allows us to develop a specific approach to model system in which a PLM solution has to be deployed. Aware about limits of this approach we confront since 2015 our propositions to the reality in a SME, Poult, a French biscuit producer. In this paper, we present the progress of the project with Poult. We describe the progressive and relatively autonomous approach we propose to PLM project team members of Poult: 1. Understanding the global organization of the R&D department. 2. Understanding the philosophy of the PLM approach to develop a model adapted to the SME and coherent with PLM concepts. 3. Considering users in the PLM deployment to define precisely specifications and increase the degree of acceptance. Even if this approach seems to be a top-down one it is more complex in reality. As it is very collaborative and participative, it is a hybrid approach between top-down and bottom-up. Team members are implicated but users are very concerned too. Formalisms used to support each step seems to be adapted to users' expectations (SADT for first step – not presented here, Bruno's model of PLM concepts and UML class diagram for second step and mind map for third step). The next step is the definition of the specification to write the request for proposal to PLM editors. As objective is to start PLM deployment in 2017, it looks obvious that the request for proposal will be send during summer 2016.

References

1. Baczkowski, M.: Amélioration du processus de déploiement d'une solution PLM par l'utilisation de cartes heuristiques et de persona: cas LASCOM. Thesis of the University of Bordeaux (2012)
2. Baczkowski, M., Robin, V., Rose, B.: Using of the concepts of roles and context in a project management/PLM Solution: the real case study of LASCOM. In: 11th Biennial Conference on Engineering Systems Design and Analysis (ASME-ESDA2012), Nantes, France (2012)
3. Stark, J.: Product Lifecycle Management: 21st Century Paradigm for Product Realization. Springer, London (2005)
4. El Kadiri, S., Pernelle, P., Delattre, M., Bouras, A.: Current situation of PLM systems in SME/SMI: survey's results and analysis. In: Proceedings of the 6th International conference Conf Product Lifecycle Management (2009)
5. Bruno, G., Antonelli, D., Villa, A.: A reference ontology to support product lifecycle management. 9th CIRP Conference on Intelligent Computation in Manufacturing Engineering, in Procedia CIRP, vol. 33, pp. 41–46 (2015)
6. McKenzie-Veal, D., Hartman, N.W., Springer, J.: Implementing Ontology-Based Information Sharing in Product Lifecycle Management. Academia.edu, San Francisco (2010)
7. Abdul-Ghafour, S.: Integration of product models by ontology development. In: IEEE International Conference on Information Reuse and Integration (2012)
8. Jurisica, I., Mylopoulos, J., Yu, E.: Ontologies for knowledge management: an information systems perspective. Knowl. Inf. Syst. **6**, 380–401 (2004)
9. Lacombe, C.: Contribution à une méthodologie et une modélisation pour accompagner les petites entreprises dans l'étude de leur organisation afin de spécifier leurs besoins et sélectionner une solution ERP. Thesis of the University of Bordeaux (2016)

10. Rose, J., Pedersen, K., Hosbond, J.H., Kraemmergaard, P.: Management competences, not tools and techniques: a grounded examination of software project management at WM-data. Inf. Soft. Technol. **49**(6), 605–624 (2007)
11. Petter, S.: Managing user expectations on software projects: lessons from the trenches. Int. J. Proj. Manag. **26**(7), 700–712 (2008)

Model of Monetarisation of the Non-availability of Intralogistics Systems for the Evaluation of System Design Alternatives

Friederike Rechl(✉), Konstantin Krebs, and Willibald A. Günthner

FML – Institute for Materials Handling, Material Flow, Logistics, Technical University of Munich, Garching, Germany
{rechl,kontakt}@fml.mw.tum.de, konstantinkrebs@googlemail.com

Abstract. Intralogistics systems secure the internal flow of materials and are a success factor for handling and producing companies. In general, the objective of analysing life-cycle costs is to economically evaluate system design alternatives aiming at supporting investment decisions. One essential influence factor of operating costs, and thus life-cycle costs, is the availability. The non-availability significantly influences the operating costs, e.g. repairs or loss of revenues. A research field that has not been investigated in the field of intralogistics is the monetarisation of non-availability. An appropriate cost model is therefore necessary. As a result, the costs of non-availability can be evaluated monetarily as a function of time. With the help of such a monetary parameter, financial risks can already be detected during the planning phase. This paper models an approach of the monetarisation of the non-availability of intralogistics systems as an economical evaluation indicator during the planning phase.

Keywords: Intralogistics systems · Cost-effectiveness · Planning · Non-availability · Investment decision

1 Motivation and Initial Situation

Intralogistics systems have become a key competition factor caused by their function of securing the internal flow of material and goods and therefore by increasing cost pressure [1]. Consequently, the requirements concerning availability and cost-effectiveness of those systems have grown as well. In the field of plants and machines, several research studies prove that it is less the investment, and more the operating costs, which are responsible for the majority of the total life-cycle costs (LCC) [2]. For that reason, the planning and projection of those systems have become more important as the operating costs in particular are significantly influenced by the choice of constructive characteristics and the operational strategy.

A research field, which has not been investigated yet, is the monetarisation of the non-availability (NA) of intralogistics systems. Due to the fact that failures can cause high additional costs in the operating phase (e.g. repairs or loss of revenues), an

R. Harik et al. (Eds.): PLM 2016, IFIP AICT 492, pp. 523–536, 2016.
DOI: 10.1007/978-3-319-54660-5_47

appropriate calculation model is necessary in order to economically evaluate the NA. With the help of such a model, the NA can be expressed monetarily and financial risks can already be detected in the planning phase.

This paper models an approach for the monetarisation of the NA of intralogistics systems. Consequently, the model can already provide an evaluation parameter for comparing system design alternatives in the planning phase.

2 Objective and Procedure

The objective of this paper is the design of a calculation model for the costs of the NA of intralogistics systems as an evaluation parameter of system design alternatives during the planning phase.

Firstly, the term of costs of the NA in the field of intralogistics is defined. Secondly, the current state-of-the-art including approaches for LCC calculation, cost calculation concerning failures and a description of availability concerning operating costs is presented. Thirdly, the system boundary is set concerning the model building with the help of a conveyor and storage technology aspects, as well as a process-based description. Based on that, the monetarisation model and the needed input parameters are presented. Finally, the application of the model is described and the results evaluated with the help of a planning example.

3 Term Definition of the Costs of Non-availability

As regards the NA, several terms in respect of the costs exist. Gudehus [3] introduced the term, shortage costs, which includes loss of profits, contribution margin loss and delivery delay penalties. For the existing approaches in this field, the focus is often set on profit losses. An NA causes the NA of goods if a buffer cannot intercept the goods. Depending on the nature of the company, customers who cannot be supplied, recourse to competitors. This view is especially useful for manufacturing companies. Even a partial loss through reduced revenues or penalties for delay is conceivable.

The shortage costs include so-called opportunity costs (OC), such as lost profits, as described above. In this paper, the objective is set on the costs of NA including OC. Accordingly, the model considers not only the operating costs, which are directly caused by the NA, or are generated during the NA, but also the OC as a consequence.

4 State-of-the-Art

Derived from the definition of availability, the cost of the NA of intralogistics systems can be defined as a monetary measure of the time-dependent, non-functional and therefore unavailable state of a system. [4]

The NA of intralogistics systems can be significantly influenced by the extent of incurred maintenance activities. The extent of NA is visible in the magnitude of repairs, which appear as operating costs. For this reason, the DIN 60300-3-3 recommends considering the availability as costs in economical evaluations. [5]

With regard to the prognosis of maintenance costs, several approaches exist in the field of machines and plants. Compared to the intralogistics, the maintenance costs have been focused and were therefore investigated further. Currently, the topic of maintenance in the field of intralogistics is limited to statutory maintenance measures (e.g. DIN EN 15635) [6].

Other existing models of maintenance cost calculation are mainly of a stochastic nature. Works by Dhillon [7], Fürnrohr [8], Ostwald and McLaren [9] and Fritz [10] can be named. Dhillon presents models for the calculation of preventive and corrective maintenance expenses. The cost models are essentially based on a component-specific failure rate [7]. In comparison, Fleischer and Wawerla [11] provide a generic approach for estimating the distribution function of a system's repairs based on the mentioned failure rate distribution and on a Monte Carlo simulation to determine the total LCC. In his thesis on stochastic models for forecasting the LCC of complex systems, Fürnrohr shows similar concepts [8]: also based on the concept of a failure rate, Elsayed [12] describes a system reliability estimation for time-independent and default-related models. In contrast to this, Lad and Kulkarni [13] highlight maintenance planning based on the plant structure (e.g. as in regard to equal parts) and present here a model which aims to calculate failure-based follow-up costs.

In practice, the most commonly used approaches are the models provided by the VMDA [14]. Accordingly, the total maintenance and repair costs are tripartite: inspection, planned maintenance, as well as repairs.

The costs of inspection (IH1) are defined as [14]:

$$IH1 = \sum (IH1.1 \cdot (IH1.2 \cdot IH1.6 + IH1.3 + IH1.4 \cdot IH1.5)). \tag{1}$$

with the frequency per year *IH1.1* [number], the required time *IH1.2* [h], the material costs *IH1.3* [€], the average resource time effort *IH1.4* [h], the hourly rate of the resource *IH1.5* [€/h] and the hourly rate of the maintenance personnel *IH1.6* [€/h].

The cost of the planned maintenance (IH2) (see formula (2)), which is similar to the calculation procedure of IH1, also strongly depends on the frequency per year (*IH2.1*). Furthermore, the work effort in hours (*IH2.2*) and the hourly rate of the employee (*IH2.6*) are needed. In addition, the resource costs have to be determined with the help of the hourly resource rate (*IH2.5*) and the resource time effort per process (*IH2.4*). Finally, the material costs (*IH2.3*) are added.

$$IH2 = \sum (IH2.1 \cdot (IH2.2 \cdot IH2.6 + IH2.3 + IH2.4 \cdot IH2.5)). \tag{2}$$

The costs of repair (IH3) are directly determined by the availability [15]:

$$IH3 = \sum (\frac{D2}{IH3.1} \cdot (IH3.2 \cdot IH3.6 + IH3.3 + IH3.4 \cdot IH3.5)). \tag{3}$$

Decisive for the calculation is the mean time between repair operations (*IH3.1*). This corresponds to the *MTBF* value (mean time between failures). In addition, the workload per repair process in hours (*IH3.2*) is required, which is expressed by the value *MDT* (mean down time). Moreover, the cost of materials (*IH3.3*), resource costs (*IH3.4*, *IH3.5*) and the hourly rate of the maintenance engineer (*IH3.6*) must be known.

As regards the economic assessment of NA, there are several approaches in the literature. Here, according to the aforementioned concept of Gudehus, the shortage costs are calculated with the help of the ability to deliver products and the shortage costs per product. However, a specific calculation procedure is not described. [3] In a work by Dervisopoulos et al. [15], the consideration of the shortage costs to evaluate the LCC is emphasised, but here, too, a specific calculation procedure is not given.

A concrete calculation method of the shortage costs is presented by Kulkarni und Lad [13] in which the expected total failure costs $E[TC]$ of a component during a defined period is determined by using the expected number of failures $E[N(T)]$ and costs per failure $E[C]$ [13]. According to Höck [16], another calculation model is based on the average output quantity, multiplied by the value in monetary units W_{piece} [€/piece].

The short overview on existing models of the costs of NA shows that there are very different approaches when a calculation procedure is not given or the focus is set on follow-up costs. The existing models are not analogous. Furthermore, the mentioned approaches focus on the field of machines and plans. Höck uses, in principle, the capital, which is bound by non-expelled products. Gudehus and Kulkarni use a vague amount of shortage costs per unit for which, however, an explicit calculation rule is also not given; they even propose the use of empirical values or estimations. This underlines the need for a standardised approach to the monetarisation of the costs of NA as a planning parameter in the field of intralogistics.

5 Definition of the System Boundary

As regards the model, the focus is set on automated material handling systems. The system boundary includes process-oriented automatic storage and retrieval of handling units (HU) in or from the automatic high-bay warehouse (HBW), or the mini-load system (MLS) from or to the transfer point of the automatic conveyor technology. As regards the pack conveyor technology, the personnel costs of the employee are considered in the analysis. The personnel costs of the employee who performs the uptake and release of HU are taken into account, because the employee works directly on the conveyor technology and thus in a stationary workplace. Costs of forklifts, trucks, etc., are not considered.

Process-based, the system boundary can be described as follows. Figure 1 shows an example of the described technology and interfaces within the system boundary. The introduction of HU in the system is carried out on the *A-point*. From there, HU are transported on pallets with pallet conveyor technology in an HBW and stored. The racks are served by one or more stacker cranes (SC) in one or more aisles. The SC are specifically selected for each rack facility. Packs are brought and stored over pack conveyor technology in an MLS. From HBW, HU can be transported via pallet conveyor technology to the *E-point* and then abandon the system, the same applies for HU from MLS concerning pack conveyor technology. A detailed overview of the described conveyor and storage technology is shown in (Fig. 2).

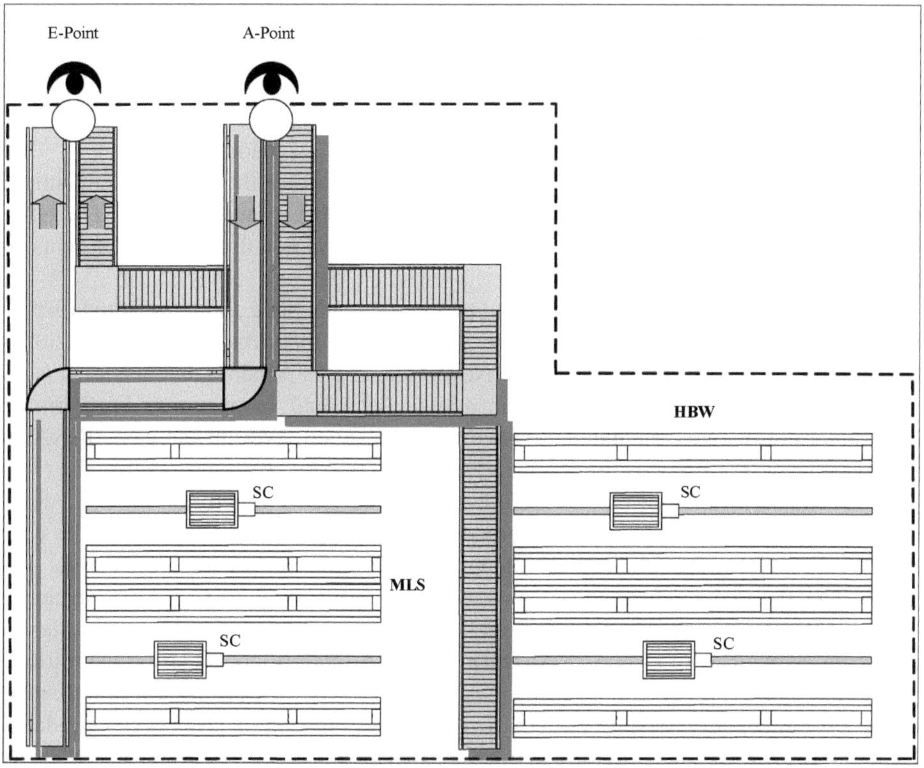

Fig. 1. Schematic representation of an exemplary system boundary including the *A* and *E-Point*, the *high-bay warehouse* and the *mini-load system* with their *stacker cranes* and the appropriate *conveyor technology*. A detailed overview of the described conveyor and storage technology is shown in the following figure.

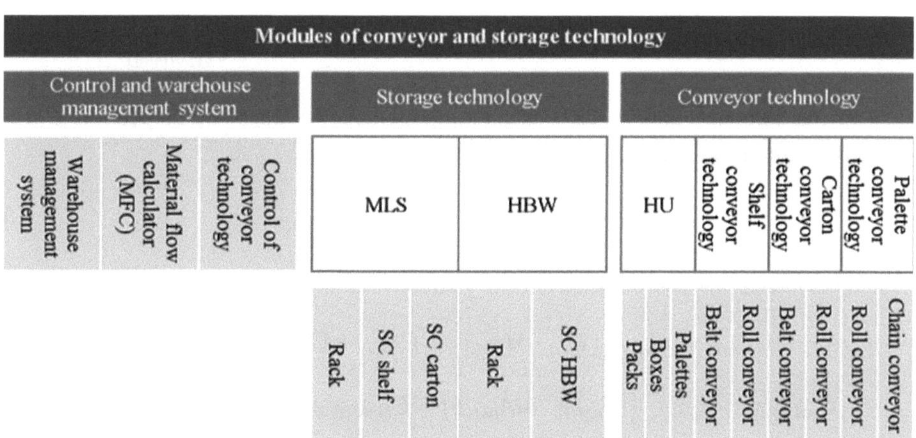

Fig. 2. Exemplary *modules* of *conveyor* and *storage technology* within the system boundary. The grey ones are the *modules*. The arrangement of *modules* is used for the generation and understanding of the cost model of non-availability in Sects. 6 and 7, especially in Sect. 7.2.

6 Calculation Model Building of the Costs of Non-availability

For the model generation, those LCC are identified first, which are caused by NA or are generated time-based during the NA. In other words, these are the operating costs during the time slice of the NA. Second of all, the OC are added.

As regards the first step, it can be excluded that, during the procurement, implementation and removal phases, costs are generated which are caused by NA. The NA is therefore only relevant during the operating phase of a system, thus only these costs are tested for their NA dependence.

The cost calculation of inspection and planned maintenance are not affected directly by the NA (see Sect. 4, formulas (1) to (3)). High availability may be the result of frequent maintenance and repair works. Nevertheless, it is possible that a system is not available even in the case of regular maintenance and inspections. Furthermore, inspection and planned maintenance have to be executed, even in the case of NA. In addition, the costs of repairs are relevant for the cost model. As regards formulae (1) to (3), only the calculation of repairs includes a variable based directly on the NA, which is the *MTBF* value. However, as explained, in addition to the costs of repair, the costs of inspection (IH1) and planned maintenance (IH2) must be considered as well.

Besides the maintenance and repair costs, there are further LCC, which are caused by the NA or are generated during an NA. Energy costs are incurred during the operation, as well as in case of NA. During the NA, energy costs can be even lower. Other LCC are the space and surface costs independently incurred by the functionality of the system. Finally, despite the NA, personnel and insurance costs are engendered.

The OC, which are consequential costs due to the NA, are implemented in the model as well. Due to the fact that the OC depend on several factors and aspects, they are considered in the model as a variable $C_{opportunity_{(t)}}$ depending time-based on the NA.

The calculation of the annual cost of NA C_{NA} of intralogistics systems can thus be summarised as follows:

$$C_{NA_{(t)}} = C_{MR} + C_{energy} + C_{surface} + C_{space} + C_{personnel} + C_{insurance} + C_{opportunity}. \tag{4}$$

The maintenance and repair costs $C_{MR_{(t)}}$ include the costs of inspection $C_{I(t)(i)}$, planned maintenance $C_{pM(t)(i)}$ and repairs $C_{R(t)(i)}$:

$$C_{MR_{(t)}} = C_{I(t)(i)} + C_{pM(t)(i)} + C_{R(t)(i)}. \tag{5}$$

with (based on formulae (1) to (3))

$$C_{I(t)(i)} = n_{I(i)} \cdot \left[\left(T_{I(i)} \cdot MA_{I(i)}\right) + C_{MI(i)} + \left(T_{BMI(i)} \cdot BM_{I(i)}\right)\right]. \tag{6}$$

$$C_{pM(t)(i)} = n_{pM(i)} \cdot \left[\left(T_{pM(i)} \cdot MA_{pM(i)}\right) + C_{MpM(i)} + \left(T_{BMpM(i)} \cdot BM_{pM(i)}\right)\right]. \tag{7}$$

$$C_{R(t)(i)} = \frac{T_B}{MTBF_{(i)}} \cdot \left[\left(MDT_{(i)} \cdot MA_{R(i)} \right) + C_{MR(i)} + \left(T_{BMR(i)} \cdot BM_{R(i)} \right) \right]. \qquad (8)$$

with

i = Control variable of module i (see Fig. 2)
$C_{I(t)(i)}$ = Inspection costs of the module i [€]
$n_{I(i)}$ = Frequency of inspection [number]
$T_{I(i)}$ = Time effort per inspection [h]
$MA_{I(i)}$ = Employee hourly rate for inspection [€/h]
$C_{MI(i)}$ = Material costs per inspection [€]
$T_{BMI(i)}$ = Resource time effort per inspection [h]
$BM_{I(i)}$ = Resource hourly rate per inspection [€/h]
$C_{pM(t)(i)}$ = Cost of planned maintenance of module i [€]
$n_{pM(i)}$ = Frequency of planned maintenance [number]
$T_{pM(i)}$ = Time effort per planned maintenance [h]
$MA_{pM(i)}$ = Employee hourly rate for planned maintenance [€/h]
$C_{MpM(i)}$ = Material costs per planned maintenance [€]
$T_{BMpM(i)}$ = Resource time effort per planned maintenance [h]
$BM_{pM(i)}$ = Resource hourly rate per planned maintenance [€/h]
$C_{R(t)(i)}$ = Repair costs of module i [€]
T_B = Annual operating hours [h]
$MTBF_{(i)}$ = $MTBF$ of module i [h]
$MDT_{(i)}$ = MDT of module i [h]
$MA_{R(i)}$ = Employee hourly rate for repair [€/h]
$C_{MR(i)}$ = Material costs per repair [€]
$T_{BMR(i)}$ = Resource time effort per repair [h]
$BM_{R(i)}$ = Resource hourly rate per repair [€/h]

Overall, the formula for calculating the total annual costs C_{NA} of an intralogistics system with I modules is:

$$\begin{aligned} C_{NA} = \sum_{i=1}^{I} & n_{I(i)} \cdot \left[\left(T_{I(i)} \cdot MA_{I(i)} \right) + C_{MI(i)} + \left(T_{BMI(i)} \cdot BM_{I(i)} \right) \right] \\ & + n_{pM(i)} \cdot \left[\left(T_{pM(i)} \cdot MA_{pM(i)} \right) + C_{MpM(i)} + \left(T_{BMpM(i)} \cdot BM_{pM(i)} \right) \right] \\ & + \frac{T_B}{MTBF_{(i)}} \cdot \left[\left(MDT_{(i)} \cdot MA_{R(i)} \right) + C_{MR(i)} + \left(T_{BMR(i)} \cdot BM_{R(i)} \right) \right] \\ & + C_{energy_{(i)}} + C_{surface_{(i)}} + C_{space_{(i)}} + C_{personnel_{(i)}} + C_{insurance_{(i)}} \\ & + C_{opportunity_{(i)}}. \end{aligned} \qquad (9)$$

If the number of inspections per year ($n_{I(i)}$) is increased, a higher value of the $MTBF_{(i)}$ value can be expected. The following section demonstrates the application of the calculation model. Furthermore, the model is assessed based on a practical example.

7 Application of the Model Based on a Practical Example

The calculation model of the costs of NA of intralogistics systems is demonstrated and evaluated with the help of a practical planning example in this section. For this, the cost and planning data of an intralogistics system of a company from 2009 to 2014 are available. The system comprises a tray warehouse, an MLS and an HBW.

7.1 Procedure of Data Collection

As can be seen from the calculation approach in formula (9), data on the maintenance and repairs, energy consumption, surface and space costs, as well as personnel and insurance costs, are required. The OC are considered as a variable. The cost data in respect of the insurance, the personnel, the surface and space can be taken out of the planning and implementation documents. Energy costs were modelled based on the description of the used conveyor and storage technology components with their technical information, as well as on two research works [17, 18]. The maintenance and repair cost data are accessible in the firm's ERP[1] system.

7.2 Analysis of Data and Determination of Module Cost Data

First of all, the used storage and conveyor technology based on the raw data are categorised. They are divided into so-called *modules,* being equal to the scheme of conveyor and storage in Fig. 2. Overall, there are thus nine modules:

- Pallet conveyor technology (chain and roll)
- Carton conveyor technology (roll and belt)
- Shelf conveyor technology (roll and belt)
- HBW SC
- MLS carton SC
- MLS shelf SC

As regards the presented cost model in formula (9), the generation of cost data is as follows. The costs of inspection, planned maintenance and repair are charged as a flat rate, since no dedicated data on hourly rates, resource costs and material costs are known. Furthermore, a differentiation between the costs of inspection and planned maintenance cannot be made. The cost shares for each module (e.g. palette conveyor technology chain) are considered proportionally. The weighting is determined by the ratio of the total number of executed activities to the total number of the module group (e.g. palette conveyor technology).

As regards the calculation of energy costs, it should be noted that the energy consumption needs to be specified both under load, and in standby mode. The total energy consumption of the conveyor technology in standby is specified per metre. Knowing the length of the module means that the standby energy consumption per year

[1] Enterprise resource planning.

can be calculated. The energy costs are then calculated by multiplying the energy consumption with the energy price.

Since the annual administrative overheads (AO) are only known for the entire system, they must be divided between the conveyor technology and racks, including the SC. For this purpose, the ratio of the investment costs of the conveyor technology and racks in respect to SC are determined and the AO are divided accordingly. The proportion of AO is then spread over the surface of the modules in order to obtain the surface cost rate. To calculate the surface costs, the surface of each module has to be determined. The width of modules is known and is multiplied by the length. In the case of SC, the length corresponds to the length of the rack aisle.

The annual personnel costs are calculated based on the time slice of NA ($MDT_{(i)}$), the number of employees and the employee hourly rate:

$$C_{personnel_{(i)}} = \sum_{i=1}^{I} MDT_i \cdot number\ of\ employees \cdot hourly\ rate. \tag{10}$$

The insurance costs are determined in a similar way to the AO. Higher investment costs require higher insurance rates, so the approach is justified. The insurance costs of SC components can thus be directly specified. For the conveyor modules, the insurance costs are standardised to metres and then multiplied by the length.

Based on the aggregation of the data, cost data sheets can be provided for each module. Hence, these data sheets include the input data for the calculation model of the costs of NA (see formula (9)).

In the case of planning, the idea of generating such modules is to provide building blocks. Planning alternatives can be easily created with these blocks. The modules can be arranged as needed with their specific cost data. Based on the arranged modules, the planning alternative can be evaluated economically. As a result, this flexible approach helps with generating several system planning alternatives in order to compare them in matters of the costs of NA. The costs of possible NA can therefore be estimated quickly. This evaluation parameter gives hints about the economic extent of costs in the case of NA and is therefore an essential factor in investment decisions. An example of a cost data sheet for modules is shown in Table 1.

7.3 Calculation of the Costs of Non-availability in a Planning Case

With the help of an exemplary planning case, the calculation model of the costs of NA as an evaluation parameter concerning two system alternatives, A and B, is demonstrated. The generated model (see formula (9)) and the module concept (Sect. 7.2) are used for this.

In the planning case of an HBW, there are two possible alternatives (see Fig. 3). In system A, via chain conveyor (CC A) pallets are transported to roll conveyor (RC A). The RC distributes the pallets on three aisles of an HBW, which are served by the SC A1, A2 and A3 operating parallel. The transfer devices between RC and SC are not considered. In system B, the transport of pallets is also carried on a chain conveyor CC B.

Table 1. Example of a *cost data* sheet for *modules* (e.g. *pallet conveyor with chain* and *roll,* as well as *stacker cranes* in the *high-bay warehouse*).

Module / Cost data (annual)	*Pallet conveyor*		HBW SC
	Chain	Roll	
MTBF [h]			
MDT [h]			
Availability η [%]			
Costs per unplanned maintenance [€]			
Costs per inspection [€]			
Frequency of inspection per year [1/year]			
Width of the module [m]			
Procurement costs per metre [€/m]			
Procurement costs of the module [€]			
Life-time [years]			
Procurement costs of the module per year [€/a]			
Energy consumption (standby) per metre [kWh/m]			
Energy consumption of the module [kWh]			
Energy price [€/kWh]			
Energy costs of the module [€]			
Required surface [m²]			
Surface cost rate [€/m²]			
Surface costs of the module [€]			
Insurance costs per metre [€/m]			
Insurance costs of the module [€]			
Length of the module [m]			
Personnel hourly cost rate [€/h]			
Number of employees [number]			

Compared to A, the racks comprise four aisles with four SC. With the help of the calculation approach of formula (9), it should be investigated if an additional aisle in the rack system is cost-effective as regards a possible NA. The two system alternatives therefore have to be compared economically with regard to the costs of NA, and the costs of NA $C_{NA_{(A)}}$ and $C_{NA_{(B)}}$ have to be determined.

The availability of system A is given as 99.702209% and as 99.702222% of system B which proves to be less of a difference. The specific availability of A and B was determined with the help of the single availabilities of modules and the Boolean notation [19].

The calculation of the costs of NA follows the approach of formula (9). The inspection costs of each module include the costs of planned maintenance and are given as a lump sum, which is multiplied by the number of inspections per year in respect of the planned maintenance works. The number of repairs is the ratio of operating period

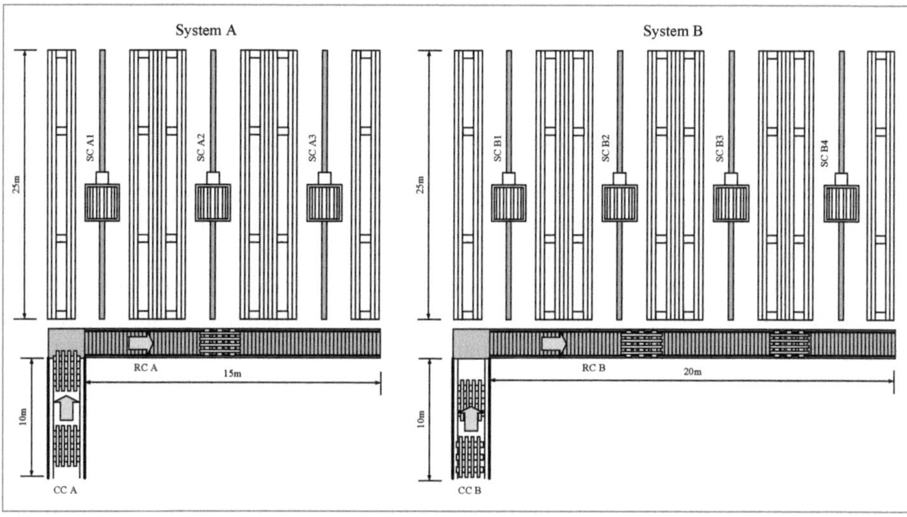

Fig. 3. Schematic representation of *system* alternatives, *A* and *B: A* and *B* differ with an additional aisle in *system B*.

T_B to *MTBF* which is multiplied by the cost rates for repairs. The cost rates for energy, surface, space, personnel and insurance are then added. The OC are implemented as a variable $C_{opportunity_{(t)(A,B)}}$. In total, the annual costs of the NA of the two alternatives are:

$$C_{NA_{(A)}} = 701,198.08\,€ + C_{opportunity_{(t)(A)}} \text{for system A and} \tag{11}$$

$$C_{NA_{(B)}} = 848,792.17\ € + C_{opportunity_{(t)(B)}} \text{for system B.} \tag{12}$$

The realisation of alternative B with an improved availability can be justified if

$$C_{NA_{(B)}} \leq C_{NA_{(A)}} \tag{13}$$

$$C_{opportunity_{(t)(A)}} - C_{opportunity_{(t)(B)}} \geq 147,594.09\ € \tag{14}$$

The results show that the implementation of an additional aisle with one SC causes a minimal improvement of the total availability. If the difference of the OC of A and B is higher than the difference of the NA-dependent LCC, the realisation of B can be justified even in the case of a higher investment for B. The OC of B can be assumed smaller than that of A because of the improved throughput and capacity so that losses of revenues or penalties should be compensated.

As a result, it has to be investigated whether the lower costs of NA towards a higher availability of the system is an adequate option regards the OC. Higher storage and retrieval performance enabled by the additional SC can generate higher revenues which may reduce OC and therefore the costs of NA.

As regards this planning example, the implementation of an additional aisle can be justified in respect of the requirements of formula (14).

7.4 Discussion of the Results and Evaluation of the Model

The database, which is used to determine the module cost data, is extensive, but not all the required input variables can be derived from it. In addition, assumptions are made, which should be examined in detail and confirmed. This includes the assumption of considering AO as surface costs. The space costs are not considered due to lack of data. The database also refers to a specific project and to a comparatively short period. In particular, data for maintenance and repair should be generated and analysed over longer periods, ideally over the entire life-cycle. Furthermore, the calculation of the OC is decisive – this does, however, comprise several problems and challenges because a standardised approach for its calculation does not exist.

By increasing the database, further modules, such as conversion devices and sequencers, as well as other conveyor system modules and SC, can be integrated into the module kit. For example, a corporate database of modules with cost data sheets based on the actual costs thus enables an approach for modelling more complex system planning alternatives. Nevertheless, this approach does provide a quick, low-effort way to evaluate systems with regard to their availability and cost-effectiveness in relation to a possible NA.

With the help of the model, NA can be recorded and evaluated in monetary units. The consideration and reduction of these costs are necessary, especially against the background of competitiveness. Intralogistics costs are therefore not only operating costs, but also the costs of non-operation with their financial consequences, which should be considered in terms of a larger logistical framework. When comparing planning alternatives, conclusions can be made as to whether an intralogistics system is cost-effective, also in the case of NA. Furthermore, it can be investigated whether additional modules, like the additional aisle in the planning example, are economically worthwhile.

8 Summary and Outlook

The aim of this paper was to develop a model for calculating the costs of the NA of intralogistics systems. The procedure of model generation, a definition of the costs of NA, the state-of-the-art and the system boundary were presented. In the state-of-the-art, the various concepts for the costs of NA were defined in order to clearly distinguish the subject matter. Existing models for the costs of NA and maintenance cost calculation were described. The existing maintenance cost models were used as a basis for the generation of the NA cost model.

Then, a holistic calculation model for the costs of NA as a monetarisation approach was developed. This calculation model allows the generation of an evaluation parameter in addition to the criterion of LCC, in order to select and compare system planning alternatives. The model comprises costs which are caused by NA, or which are generated during the NA, with their consequential costs.

The model's application, as well as the data acquisition, have been demonstrated with the help of a planning example. The modules and module cost data sheet generation were discussed in detail. Based on the exemplary module kit, system alternatives were able to be mapped. In the example, the costs of NA were calculated for two planning alternatives and evaluated.

In a critical analysis of the results, the potential of the approach can be identified. By extending and validating the database, it is possible to introduce additional modules of intralogistics systems. Furthermore, a standardised approach for calculating the OC has to be generated. For validation, the use of sensitivity analysis is recommended. The costs of NA should be used as an additional criterion to the LCC within the assessment of planning alternatives aiming at investment decision making in terms of a larger logistical framework.

Acknowledgments. The authors are grateful for the support of the Dr. Friedrich Jungheinrich Foundation. Any opinions, findings, conclusions or recommendations expressed in this paper are those of the writers.

References

1. Weber, J.: Logistikkostenrechnung: Kosten-, Leistungs- und Erlösinformationen zur erfolgsorientierten Steuerung der Logistik. Springer, Heidelberg (2012)
2. Doha, A., Das, A., Pagell, M.: The influence of product life cycle on the efficacy of purchasing practices. Int. J. Oper. Prod. Manag. **33**(4), 470–498 (2013)
3. Gudehus, T.: Logistik: Grundlagen - Strategien - Anwendungen. Springer, Berlin (2010)
4. Verein Deutscher Ingenieure: Availability of Transport and Storage Systems including Subsystems and Elements (VDI 3581). Beuth, Berlin (2004)
5. Deutsches Institut für Normung e.V.: Dependability Management: Part 3-3: Application Guide: Life Cycle Costing (DIN 60300-3-3). Beuth, Berlin (2005)
6. Deutsches Institut für Normung e.V.: Steel Static Storage Systems: Application and Maintenance of Storage Equipment (DIN 15635). Beuth, Berlin (2009)
7. Dhillon, B.: Life Cycle Costing for Engineers. CRC Press, Boca Raton (2010)
8. Fürnrohr, M.: Stochastische Modelle zur Prognose von Lebenszykluskosten komplexer Modelle: Dissertation. Universität der Bundeswehr, München (1992)
9. Ostwald, P., McLaren, T.: Cost Analysis and Estimating for Engineering and Management. Pearson Prentice Hall, Upper Saddle River (2004)
10. Fritz, A.: Berechnung und Monte-Carlo Simulation der Zuverlässigkeit und Verfügbarkeit technischer Systeme: Dissertation. Universität Stuttgart, Stuttgart (2001)
11. Fleischer, J., Wawerla, M., Niggeschmidt, S.: Machine life cycle cost estimation via monte-carlo simulation. In: Takata, S., Umeda, Y. (eds.) Advances in Life Cycle Engineering for Sustainable Manufacturing Businesses: Proceedings of the 14th CIRP Conference on Life Cycle Engineering, pp. 449–453. Springer, London (2007)
12. Elsayed, E.: Reliability Engineering. Wiley, Hoboken (2012)
13. Lad, B., Kulkani, M.: Integrated reliability and optimal maintenance schedule design: a life cycle based approach. Int. J. Prod. Lifecylce Manag. **3**, 78–90 (2008)

14. Verband Deutscher Maschinen- und Anlagenbau e. V.: Forecasting Model for Lifecycle Costs of Machines and Plants (VDMA 34160). Beuth, Berlin (2006)
15. Dervisopoulos, M., Schatka, A., Torney, M.: Life Cycle Costing im Maschinen- und Anlagenbau. Ind. Manag. **22**, 55–58 (2006)
16. Höck, M.: Dienstleistungsmanagement aus produktionswirtschaftlicher Sicht. Betriebswirtschaftliche Forschung zur Unternehmensführung. Deutscher Universitätsverlag, Wiesbaden (2005)
17. Günthner, W.A., Habenicht, S.: Erweiterte Logistikplanung unter Einbeziehung des Energieverbrauchs: Forschungsbericht der AiF-Forschungsvereinigung Bundesvereinigung Logistik e. V. (BVL), Berlin (2013)
18. Günthner, W.A., Habenicht, S., Ertl, R.: Analytische Energiebedarfsermittlung von Intralogistiksystemen in der Planungsphase: Tagungsband WGTL-Kolloquium, 77–90, Garching (2013)
19. Verein Deutscher Ingenieure: Boolean Model (VDI 4008). Beuth, Berlin (1998)

Industry 4.0

Smart Manufacturing: Characteristics and Technologies

Sameer Mittal, Muztoba Ahmad Khan, and Thorsten Wuest(✉)

Department of Industrial and Management Systems Engineering,
West Virginia University, Morgantown, WV, USA
{samittal,mdkhan}@mix.wvu.edu, thwuest@mail.wvu.edu

Abstract. The purpose of this paper is to collect and structure the various features of Smart Manufacturing (SM). Researchers have previously identified various characteristics and technologies of Smart Manufacturing System (SMS); this paper collects, discusses and merges some of those characteristics and technologies available in the current body of knowledge. In the future, it is expected that this selection of characteristics and technologies will help to compare and distinguish other initiatives like Industry 4.0, smart factory, intelligent manufacturing, distributive manufacturing, etc. which are frequently used synonymous with SM. The result of this paper is a comprehensive list of characteristics and technologies that are associated with a SMS. As many of the listed items show variating overlaps, certain technologies and characteristics are merged and clustered. This results in a set of five defining characteristics and ten technologies that are considered relevant for a SMS. The authors hope to provide a basis for a broad and interdisciplinary discussion within the SM community about the defining technologies and characteristics of a SMS.

Keywords: Smart Manufacturing · Characteristics and technologies · Industry 4.0 · Smart factory · Intelligent manufacturing

1 Introduction

Smart Manufacturing (SM) has significant gained momentum in industry and academia in recent years. SM is set of practices that use networked data and information technology [1, 2] to architect the future manufacturing systems. Many manufacturing systems are presenting themselves as Smart Manufacturing Systems (SMS). However, there is still a lack of commonly accepted understanding what defines a manufacturing system as being 'smart'.

What aspects make a manufacturing system smart? Literature suggests to consider these aspects in the form of characteristics and technologies. Only two papers were found relevant to the list of characteristics and technologies associated with smart manufacturing when we used "Smart Manufacturing" as the search term in the electronic journals of Taylor and Francis, Science Direct, Wiley, Emerald and Springer. We did the same at Google and Google Scholar, and found only one relevant journal paper and few grey papers published by NIST (National Institute of Standards and Technology) and SMLC (Smart Manufacturing Leadership Coalition). In this study, we

R. Harik et al. (Eds.): PLM 2016, IFIP AICT 492, pp. 539–548, 2016.
DOI: 10.1007/978-3-319-54660-5_48

focused on characteristics and technologies of only SMS; and kept characteristics and technologies associated with Industry 4.0, smart factory and other such manufacturing initiatives out of our focus. The reason is, that this allows us to create a comprehensive list of SM-specific characteristics and technologies, which later may be compared to the aforementioned other concepts to analyze the similarities and differences among them.

This paper starts with the literature review of a comprehensive list of various characteristics and technologies that are associated with SMS. Later on, it discusses the individual characteristics and technologies and suggests a clustering based on their definition. Finally it concludes by presenting a more compact list of characteristics and technologies that are associated with SM as a basis for further discussion within the SM community.

2 Literature Review

Various researchers have identified different characteristics and technologies associated with SMS. Some of these characteristics and technologies have been specifically mentioned as such and the authors identified others by thoroughly going through the content. Depending on the application of SM, it may need a different set of characteristics and technologies. Therefore, the question arises if a SMS has to incorporate all of the identified characteristics and technologies simultaneously or if it is enough to define a manufacturing system as smart when only a certain selection is employed.

A characteristic is a property that is peculiar to something and can be varied to make elements look similar or different for example modularity, heterogeneity, flexibility, etc. Technology on the other hand is the use of science for practical purposes for example data analytics, 3-D printing, etc. Technology are also the identifiable parts of a larger construction that can provide a particular function or a group of related functions. This paper presents a discussion on various SM related characteristics and technologies that have been defined in the following section.

Table 1 presents a list of 19 characteristics identified in literature defining a SMS. The last column 'Cluster' in Table 1 will be elaborated in the discussion section. In Table 1 the characteristics have been shown in *italic font* and the technologies have been represented in **bold font** to make the paper more communicative to the readers.

Table 2 presents a list of 19 technologies that are associated with SMS. The last column in Table 1 has been framed after the discussion. Similar to the previous Table 1, certain items can be identified as being rather closely related. This is partly due to different authors using different terminology but also the level of detail the authors chose to describe relevant subcategories of technologies. This issue will be addressed in the following discussion section. As in Table 1, the technology cluster in Table 2 are shown in bold.

The items presented in the Tables 1 and 2 are derived from various literature sources. As mentioned, this leads to some of these items being similar. In the next section, we present a perspective on how we may cluster different characteristics and technologies.

Table 1. List of characteristics associated with a Smart Manufacturing System.

Sl. No.	Characteristic	Reference(s)	Cluster
1	Digital Presence	[3, 4]	*Context Awareness*
2	Modularity	[4]	*Modularity*
3	Heterogeneity	[3, 4]	*Heterogeneity*
4	Scalability	[3, 4]	**Intelligent Control**
5	Context Awareness	[4]	*Context Awareness*
6	Autonomy	[3, 4]	**Intelligent Control**
7	Adaptability	[3]	**Intelligent Control**
8	Robustness	[5]	**Intelligent Control**
9	Flexibility	[6]	**Intelligent Control**
10	Fully Automated	[6]	**Intelligent Control**
11	Asset Self-awareness	[5]	*Context Awareness*
12	Interoperability	[3, 4]	*Interoperability*
13	Networkability	[4]	*Interoperability*
14	Information Appropriateness	[5]	*Interoperability*
15	Integrability	[5]	*Interoperability*
16	Sustainability	[5]	**Energy saving/Energy Efficiency**
17	Compositionality	[3]	*Compositionality*
18	Composability	[3]	*Modularity*
19	Proactivity	[5]	**Intelligent Control**

Table 2. List of technologies associated with a Smart Manufacturing system.

S. No.	Technology	Reference(s)	Cluster
1	Intelligent	[6]	**Intelligent Control**
2	Intelligent Control	[6]	**Intelligent Control**
3	Energy Saving/Energy Efficiency	[3, 7, 6]	**Energy saving/Energy Efficiency**
4	Cyber Security	[7, 5]	**Cyber Security**
5	Holograms	[6, 7]	**Visual Technology**
6	VR (Virtual Reality)	[7]	**Visual Technology**
7	AR (Augmented Reality)	[7]	**Visual Technology**
8	Real-time Communication	[6]	**Cloud Manufacturing**
9	Big Data	[6]	**Data Analytics**
10	Cyber-Physical Infrastructure	[3, 5, 6]	**CPS/CPPS**
11	CPS(Cyber Physical Systems)/CPPS (Cyber Physical Production Systems)	[6, 7]	**CPS/CPPS**
12	IoT/IoS/IIoT	[6, 7]	**IoT/IoS**
13	Advanced Manufacturing	[3]	
14	Cloud Computing/Cloud Manufacturing	[6, 7]	**Cloud Manufacturing**
15	3- D Printing/Additive Manufacturing	[6, 7]	**3- D Printing/Additive Manufacturing**
16	Tracking and Tracing	[6]	**Smart Product/Part**
17	Smart Sensors	[6]	**Smart Product/Part**
18	Smart Product/Part	[6]	**Smart Product/Part**
19	Data Analytics	[3, 4]	**Data Analytics**

3 Discussion

The presented characteristics and technologies have been mentioned and described in current SM literature. However, the detailed definitions of these characteristics and technologies suggest that some of them might be synonyms of each other and some of these may be merged to present a more focused result. In the following, the previously identified characteristics and technologies (Tables 1 and 2) will be critically discussed and a clustering is proposed to develop a more comprehensive and targeted list. This is depicted in the fourth column in Tables 1 and 2, which indicates the suggested clusters for each characteristic and technology. In the forthcoming analysis, the following format has been chosen for better illustration and transparency: characteristic cluster has been given the *italics font* whereas the technology cluster has been mentioned in **bold font**; similarly, to enhance the readability of the paper we have discussed them using the italics and bold fonts respectively.

3.1 Characteristics Clusters

Context Awareness: Context awareness is an important characteristic of a SMS [4, 8] and it can be seen as a combination of different attributes. Identity- A SMS should have a unique identity. As a SMS often operates in a digital environment, we may say that a SMS should have its own *digital presence* [4] and therefore digital presence is inherent when we consider context awareness. Location- It is used to describe the physical location of the system itself or subsystems within Status. This is used to describe the present state of the activities that are being carried within the SMS. *Asset self-awareness* will also mean that the SMS should be able to know about its present state [5]. Time: The SMS should be able to define its timely priorities, and it might even need to consider the local time.

Modularity: Modularity is the property of a system, by virtue of which a unit can be decomposed into components that can be combined to form different configurations [4]. *Composability* is the property of the system when it could be developed from its sub-systems [3]. As both of these properties consider a unit being made from sub-units and by modularity we can have a different unit arising, therefore composability may be considered as a part of modularity.

Heterogeneity: Heterogeneity considers the diversity and dissimilarities in the units and components. However, it does not consider the combination of units and as a result it should be considered as a separate characteristic [4].

Compositionality: Compositionality is the property that deals with the understanding of the whole system based on the definition of its components and the combination of the constituents [3]. As, neither modularity nor heterogeneity deal with the system or component definitions compositionality should be considered as a separate characteristic.

Interoperability: Interoperability is the characteristic due to which units would be able to exchange and share information with each other [4, 3]. With the help of *networkability,* systems are able to collaborate in different process related aspects and for this collaboration they have to allow each other to share and exchange their information [4]. Therefore, networkability is covered by interoperability. *Information appropriateness,* describes that information is available, accessible and understandable when needed; this should be a characteristic of information to be shared otherwise the information will be of no use [5]. *Integrability* is the characteristic due to which different units can be integrated, but two units are integrated if they have an access to each other's information and therefore this characteristic is included in interoperability [5]. However, integrability is different from modularity because modularity combines the systems physically resulting into a new configuration, whereas integrability is inclined towards the exchange of information between two systems and therefore it is a part of interoperability.

3.2 Technologies Clusters

Intelligent Control: An important characteristic of manufacturing is that the systems are very quick to response. Papers referred to this response using different words. *Scalability* is considered as the property by which it can easily handle the fluctuations in load [4], by *adaptability* it can decide about its own diagnosis, prognosis, and the best system performance even when it has uncertain information [9], a machine has *robustness* when under uncertain conditions it can perform well [5] and it possesses *flexibility* when it can adapt to changes in the external environment [10]. With the help of **intelligent** technology a system is able to change its action based on its own experience [11] and it has **intelligent control** technology than it can make use of artificial intelligence techniques to control its mechanisms [11]. These characteristics and technologies converge towards being responsive to changes and may use artificial intelligence techniques for doing so and therefore, they should be considered as a part of Intelligent Control. A manufacturing unit possess *autonomy* if (a) it can adapt with feedback and pursue its activities to achieve the objective [4] and (b) the unit wants the feedback mechanism to work it will need the technology of intelligent control therefore autonomy should be a part of intelligent control. A system is said to be *fully automated* if it can do its own work completely but the extent of automation may vary from system to system. For a system to be fully automated it will also need some intelligent control mechanisms and more sophisticated are the control mechanisms the degree of automation would increase. Therefore, fully automated should also be covered by intelligent control. *Proactivity* is the characteristic that can help units to eliminate failures before they happen by sensing the situation [5]. As, this characteristic considers sensing and controlling the mechanism of system, it will need intelligent control mechanism and therefore we can consider it as a part of intelligent control. But, proactivity senses the present situation that might involve data so this characteristic might be involved in the data analytics cluster as well.

Energy Saving/Energy Efficiency: Products and processes are said to possess *sustainability* if they are reusable and they cause minimum environmental footprints [5] thus making the products and processes more economical, social and environment friendly. **Energy saving/Energy Efficiency** is the technology due to which the energy required to provide a product and service can be reduced and various studies have been done to decrease the use of energy in manufacturing systems [7]. If a system can reuse its products then the amount of energy required will decrease and therefore sustainability can be arguable seen as part of energy saving. Although, researchers have considered energy saving/energy efficiency on par with the other technologies, it should be rather considered as a necessity for any manufacturing system and not only SMS. The choice of terminology 'energy saving' as a technology was derived from literature.

Cyber Security: Data should be secured from cyber threats. As SM is largely based on digitization and data based services, **cyber security** becomes an important technology for SMS [8]. Even though this also involves data, it should still be considered separate from interoperability because interoperability is about data sharing and availability whereas this is about data privacy and security.

Visual Technology: Hologram is the technology that makes use of a 3-D image formed by a light field in a three dimensional space [12]; **Virtual Reality (VR)** is a technology that creates 3-D image with the help of a computer and it can be interacted with the help of electronic devices and the user can feel as if he has been "immersed in a synthesized environment" [13, 14]; **Augmented Reality (AR)** is a technology that can superimpose a computer generated 3-D numerical format in the real world, but one cannot interact with it [15, 16]. Since all these technologies deal with the visual representation of an object they may be considered as a part of the **visual technology** cluster [15].

Data Analytics: Big data is the technology that can analyze large data sets including real-time data that is difficult to analyze by traditional methods; **data analytics** deal with turning the volume, variety, velocity and veracity of data into actions and insights in a manufacturing system [3, 16]. As **data analytics** can deal with a very high volume of data so big data can be placed under it and it can even deal with a high velocity of data therefore it can communicate in real-time with the customers.

Cyber Physical Infrastructure: Cyber-physical System (CPS)/Cyber-Physical Production Systems (CPPS) are the same [3] and they are *the technology used by computer algorithms to solve physical mechanisms* [17]; **CPPS** is an applied form of **CPS** in production [18]. We will consider all these technologies as **CPS**.

IoT/IoS: The **IoT** enables the communication between physical and internet-enabled devices [7] and when **IoT** capabilities are seen as services they are referred as **IoS** [19]. Although both **CPS** and **IoT/IoS** consider physical world but the computer algorithms may or may not use the internet. There are examples when CPS has been considered as a foundation for **IoT/IoS** [20]. But they might not always help each other so they are considered as separate technologies in this case. In this paper we are considering IoT as ubiquitous in the global sense and as a combination of national IoT, industrial IoT and local IoT [21].

Advanced Manufacturing: Advanced Manufacturing is the technology that can integrate technology based production systems like FMS (Flexible Manufacturing System), RMS (Reconfigurable Manufacturing System), CIM (Computer Integrated Manufacturing), Additive Manufacturing etc. [22]. Overall, advanced manufacturing may be understood as an integration of different production technologies and therefore it should not be considered as a technology for Smart Manufacturing. Rather it could be an important discussion if various advanced manufacturing systems could be referred to as SMS. One possible distinction is that SM are reliable on data analytics and the advanced manufacturing is more physical manufacturing-technology focused.

Cloud Manufacturing: Cloud Manufacturing is driven by **cloud computing** [16] that can, e.g., use real-time demand to decide the production planning and scheduling. **Data analytics** may be considered as a part of cloud manufacturing, but as the applications of data analytics are so diverse that we should not consider it to be a part of cloud manufacturing. **Real-time communication** is the technology that would enable the users to exchange data with the systems in real-time. As it involves exchange of information between system and humans therefore it is not a part of interoperability.

3-D Printing/Additive Manufacturing: 3-D Printing/Additive Manufacturing is the technology that can print a 3-D image into an object with the help of laser beam, electron beam etc., as the objects are printed layer by layer therefore this technology is also referred as additive manufacturing [8]. **Additive Manufacturing** is often referred to as being part of the **Advanced Manufacturing** domain [22].

Smart Products/Parts: *Tracking and tracing* is the technology due to which one can find the past and present locations of unique objects as information carrying identities [23]. But we need some (sensing) technology which can help to monitor tracking and tracing, and these sensors are referred as **smart sensors**; when the smart sensors, have processors and software for an efficient exchange of data they are called as **smart products/parts.** IT has not been considered as a separate technology as almost all other technologies need inputs from it. It may be argued that tracking and tracing is to be considered as a characteristic or a technology, but as it has been finally kept under a technology group and it has been considered as a technology [6]. *Tracking and tracing* could also be considered as *Tracking and tracing in Real-time* but in this paper **Real-time communication** is considered as a separate technology placed under Cloud Manufacturing and therefore it is rather referred as Tracking and tracing.

From our discussion we can observe that there are many characteristic act as the building block for a technology and therefore we have less number of characteristics and more number of technologies. It can also be seen that the cluster **intelligent control** consists of six characteristics namely *scalability*, *adaptability*, *flexibility, autonomy*, *fully automated*, *proactivity* and 2 technologies **intelligent** and **intelligent control**; making it the biggest cluster. It has also been discussed that why some of the technologies like **data analytics** and **cloud manufacturing** that have many common elements are being considered as separate?

Commercial implementation of SM for 4 different kind of industries has also been presented in the literature [1]. NIST has also presented some of the characteristics and technologies discussed in this paper and considered as standards. The list of aggregated characteristics and technology clusters presented in this paper is expanding on the basic ones presented in [24]. A landscape consisting of standards has also been suggested for reaching the goal of SM [24]. The standards are presented in terms of the three lifecycle dimensions: product, production system and business. Later, the standards that are present today and the one that are required in the future for establishing an SM are analyzed. These characteristics and definitions are from a small set of research and there might be some others which were not reviewed and in future we plan to consider a more comprehensive list.

4 Conclusion

This paper identified, discussed and clustered characteristics and technologies that define a Smart Manufacturing System (SMS). Overall, it was found that there are five characteristics, namely context awareness, modularity, heterogeneity, interoperability and compositionality, and ten technologies, namely intelligent control, energy saving/energy efficiency, cyber security, CPS/CPPS, visual technology, IoT/IoS, cloud computing/cloud manufacturing, 3-D printing/additive manufacturing, smart product/part and data analytics, that are required in a SMS. These characteristics and technologies can also be used to classify a manufacturing system as smart. With the help of this list of characteristics and technologies we can classify if the initiatives like Industry 4.0, and manufacturing systems like smart factory, intelligent manufacturing, distributive manufacturing, etc. are similar, and if by what degree, to smart manufacturing. In this paper, we can also observe that there is a smaller number of clustered characteristics compared to the number of clustered technologies. One possible explanation for this is, that technologies needed some characteristics as their inputs and it would have been redundant to consider such characteristics separately, for example the characteristics scalability, flexibility, adaptability, robustness, autonomy, fully automated and proactivity were clustered in the technology intelligent control. However, for the same reason we do not have technology/technologies clustering into a characteristic. It was also discussed why advanced manufacturing is a manufacturing system itself and should not be considered as a part of technologies.

The resultant list is to be understood as a first step in defining a comprehensive list of commonly agreed upon SM characteristics and technologies. The authors encourage industry and academic SM professionals to provide feedback in order to develop this list further. This can lead to a further expansion or reduction of the list. A similar development is expected if new SM literature will be published in the future containing additional characteristics and technologies.

A limitation of this paper is that, while extracting the characteristics and technologies from literature sources where they were not directly mentioned and classified as such, the subjective perspective of authors plays a part in the decision of choosing either technology or characteristic as the defining element. The clusters made here were made by the knowledge and perspective of the authors. Some of the characteristics and technologies were listed in the literature but there definitions were not provided and therefore these characteristics and technologies were defined from other papers and author's knowledge. The authors tried to increase the transparency of the clustering by explaining the reasoning of the decisions. However, this paper is understood as a first step towards a commonly accepted list of defining characteristics and technologies for Smart Manufacturing. Readers are actively encouraged to provide feedback and challenge the selection.

References

1. Davis, J., Edgar, T., Graybill, R., Korambath, P., Schott, B., Swink, D., Wang, J., Wetzel, J.: Smart manufacturing. Ann. Rev. Chem. Biomol. Eng. **6**, 141–160 (2015)
2. Smart Manufacturing Leadership Coalition. https://smartmanufacturingcoalition.org/. Accessed 30 May 2016
3. Rachuri, S.: Smart manufacturing systems design and analysis. In: National Institute of Standards and Technology (2015)
4. Kühnle, H., Bitsch, G.: Smart manufacturing units. In: Kühnle, H., Bitsch, G. (eds.) Foundations and Principles of Distributed Manufacturing, pp. 55–70. Springer, New York (2015)
5. Smart Process Manufacturing Engineering Virtual Organization Steering Committee: Smart Process Manufacturing: An Operations and Technology Roadmap. Full Report (2009)
6. Park, J., Lee, J.: Presentation on Korea smart factory program. In: 12th International Conference on Advances in Production Management Systems. Accessed 8 Sept 2015
7. Kang, H.S., Lee, J.Y., Choi, S., Kim, H., Park, J.H., Son, J.Y., Do Noh, S.: Smart manufacturing: past research, present findings, and future directions. Int. J. Precis. Eng. Manuf.-Green Technol. **3**, 111–128 (2016). Springer, Berlin
8. Abowd, G.D., Ebling, M., Hung, G., Lei, H., Gellersen, H.W.: Context- aware computing. IEEE Pervasive Comput. **1**, 22–23 (2002)
9. Zuehlke, D.: SmartFactory—towards a factory-of-things. Annu. Rev. Control **34**, 129–138 (2010)
10. De Weck, O.L., Ross, A.M., Rhodes, D.H.: Investigating relationships and semantic sets amongst system lifecycle properties (Ilities). In: Third International Engineering Systems Symposium CESUN, vol. 1, pp. 18-20 (2012)
11. Stengel, R.: Robotics and Intelligent Systems! (2015)
12. Matsushima, K., Nakahara, S., Arima, Y., Nishi, H., Yamashita, H., Yoshizaki, Y., Ogawa, K.: Computer holography: 3D digital art based on high-definition CGH. J. Phy.: Conf. Ser. **415**, 12–53 (2013). IOP Publishing
13. Steuer, J.: Defining virtual reality: dimensions determining telepresence. J. Commun. **42**, 73–93 (1992)
14. Earnshaw, R.A.: Virtual reality systems. Academic Press, Cambridge (2014)
15. Azuma, R.T.: A survey of augmented reality. Teleoperators Virtual Environ. **6**, 355–385 (1997)
16. Yu, C., Xu, X., Lu, Y.: Computer-integrated manufacturing, cyber-physical systems and cloud manufacturing-concepts and relationships. Manuf. Lett. **6**, 5–9 (2015)
17. Lee, E.A.: Cyber physical systems: design challenges. In: 11th IEEE International Symposium on Object Oriented Real-Time Distributed Computing, pp. 363–369 (2008)
18. Monostori, L.: Cyber-physical production systems: roots, expectations and R&D challenges. Procedia CIRP **17**, 9–13 (2014). Elsevier

19. Alberti, A.M., Singh, D.: Internet of things: perspectives, challenges and opportunities. In: International Workshop on Telecommunications, pp. 1–6 (2013)
20. Klotzer, C., Pflaum, A.: Cyber-physical systems as the technical foundation for problem solutions in manufacturing, logistics and supply chain management. In: 5th International Conference on Internet of Things (IOT), pp. 12–19. IEEE (2015)
21. Ning, H., Wang, Z.: Future internet of things architecture: like mankind neural system or social organization framework? Commun. Lett. **15**, 461–463 (2011)
22. Tao, F., Cheng, Y., Zhang, L., Nee, A.Y.C.: Advanced manufacturing systems: socialization characteristics and trends. J. Intell. Manuf. **1**, 1–16 (2014)
23. Paunescu, D., Stark, W.J., Grass, R.N.: Particles with an identity: tracking and tracing in commodity products. Powder Technol. **291**, 344–350 (2016)
24. Lu, Y., Marris, K.C., Frechette, S.: Current Standards Landscape for Smart Manufacturing Systems. (NISTIR 8107) (2016). doi:10.6028/NIST.IR.8107

Role of Industrial Internet Platforms in the Management of Product Lifecycle Related Information and Knowledge

Karan Menon(✉), Hannu Kärkkäinen, and Jayesh Prakash Gupta

Tampere University of Technology, Tampere, Finland
{karan.menon,hannu.karkkainen,jayesh.gupta}@tut.fi

Abstract. This paper addresses the data, information and knowledge management challenges in product lifecycle management (PLM) using novel industrial internet/industry 4.0/cyber-physical system platforms. PLM is quite seminally related to data, information and knowledge, and about getting these properly to serve a company's business and product development as well as to create value for the customer. We analyze Industry platforms, that are enabled by industrial internet based technologies as well as certain collaboration and social media platforms that help solving certain PLM challenges. This analysis will allow companies to make informed decisions while selecting platforms to solve their PLM challenges.

Keywords: Industrial internet · Industry4.0 · Platform · PLM PLM challenges

1 Introduction

Product lifecycle management (PLM) can be defined as a systematic and controlled concept for managing product related information and products throughout the whole product lifecycle [1]. PLM is quite seminally about data, information and knowledge, and about getting these properly to serve a company's business and product development (e.g. [2–4]), as well as to create value for the customer [2].

However, there are various challenges related to accessing and managing all relevant data, information and knowledge related to products' lifecycle, which is often due to the fact that such relevant information may be dispersed among a number of various actors, who also have their personal conception of the product and its performance [5]. Relatively recently, it has been understood that various technologies and approaches related to Internet of Things and Industrial Internet, such as sensors, machine-to-machine communication and various types of platforms can, however, offer quite important and novel solutions to the management of product lifecycle information, such as providing access and real-time insights to the data of many PLM-related actors.

For instance, the flow of real time data from the various sensors across the value chain will enable for the first time the chance to observe the entire value chain instantly. This will enable the optimization of the entire value chain rather than some part of

R. Harik et al. (Eds.): PLM 2016, IFIP AICT 492, pp. 549–558, 2016.
DOI: 10.1007/978-3-319-54660-5_49

it [6]. Hence, industrial internet will go way beyond the traditional factory automation and will reduce the transaction costs for every transaction in the value chain. Yet, partly due to the recent maturation of many industrial internet related technologies and concepts, there is relatively little research that study the possibilities of industrial internet to PLM field. One of such topic is the role of various types of industrial internet- related platforms to enhancing the management of relevant data, information and knowledge related to products' lifecycle and different lifecycle phases.

The significance of platforms has grown increasingly (e.g. [7]). Importantly, platforms and platform-like digital services can provide new ways to access and accelerate the capturing of data and converting it into insightful information and knowledge. The role of various platforms, industrial internet–related platforms in particular, in the context of PLM and in facilitating the management of product lifecycle information has not been studied previously, according to our survey of current PLM and industrial internet literature [2, 6, 8, 9].

Thus, we have come up with the following research questions which will be addressed in this study:

- Which kinds of PLM related data, information and knowledge management challenges are addressed by novel platforms in industrial internet?
- How do the industrial internet platforms address the information and knowledge management issues in product lifecycle management?

To address the above research questions, this study will try to discover and analyse novel types of platforms from academic literature as well as other relevant sources. Selection of different types of platforms for further analyses, and evaluation of their capabilities to address the various challenges related to the management of data, information and knowledge in PLM context will be done.

2 PLM and Product Lifecycle Management Challenges

Product lifecycle management (PLM) can be defined as a systematic and controlled concept for managing product related information and products throughout the whole product lifecycle [10]. However, the focus of our study lies essentially in the management of data, information and knowledge related to products and product lifecycle, not e.g. product management as such. PLM aims to provide a shared platform for effectively capturing, representing, organizing, retrieving and reusing product-related lifecycle information across companies, and to support the integration of the existing software systems. PLM is often seen essentially as PLM software (either essentially a single PLM solution, or a large group of different types of solutions, such as PDM, CRM, ERP, excel sheets, various collaboration tools etc.). Commonly, however, PLM can be seen as a larger PLM concept which involves e.g. people, processes and technological solutions (e.g. [2, 11]). In our study, we focus on the latter, more extensive concept of PLM.

There are a number of different types of challenges related to the management of product lifecycle information. We will review some of the major challenges here, and analyse in later sections how such challenges can be dealt with through the novel possibilities of Industrial internet and specifically the identified various Industrial internet platforms. Here, we focus on the important overall challenges of PLM that can most probably be addressed through means of Industrial internet and Industrial internet platforms, not e.g. topics related to standards.

There are various PLM-related literature reviews and outlook or survey-type of articles (e.g. [1, 5, 8, 12, 13]) and other found relevant generic articles on the broad topic of data, information and knowledge management in PLM context. The many challenges in the management of data, information and knowledge in PLM context are rooted in the long lifecycles of products (e.g. [14]); the transfer of information between product lifecycle phases (beginning, middle and end of life) and so-called "closed-loop" PLM (e.g. [1]); problems related to the extended enterprise and the collaboration and communication of companies, customers and other relevant actors with relevant expertise and knowledge during the lifecycle (e.g. [15]); the real-time accessing, transfer, management, aggregation and analytics of all different types of data, information and knowledge needed in PLM, including structured, not structured and even tacit knowledge of employees (e.g. [15]) as well as making sense of the data and connecting it to the decision making of various PLM-related processes. The goals and challenges of PLM might be very different in different types of companies, e.g. project-based or one-of-the-kind organizations vs. mass-customized or many-of-the-kind organizations (e.g. [4, 5]). The interoperability of Information Systems throughout the product's life cycle is primordial for a successful Product Lifecycle Management approach. The ability of two (or more) systems to communicate, cooperate and exchange services and data, thus despite the differences in languages, implementations, executive environments and abstraction models [12].

3 Industrial Internet Platforms

3.1 Types of Platforms

Platforms on a very broad level can be divided into "internal" or firm level platforms and "external" or ecosystem level (industry wide) platforms. This broad classification allows us to place external or industry platforms as key enablers for enhancement in the management of data, information and knowledge during the lifecycle of a product.

We take the definition of Industry Platform by [7]. According to them, *"industry platforms are defined as products, services, or technologies developed by one or more firms, and which serve as foundations upon which a larger number of firms can build further complementary innovations and potentially generate network effects."* External or Industry platforms are probably most relevant forms of platforms in the context of PLM, because they can enhance the management of data, information and knowledge not only internally, but also amongst the various organizational actors throughout the lifecycle phases (BOL, MOL, EOL).

In case of Industry or external platforms, there are differences in the degree of platforms' *openness meaning* how 'open' the platform is in order to let third party developers and companies to make applications over the platform using the data and information from the platform [7, 16]. In an external platform the degree of openness can vary on a number of factors or dimensions [7]: the access to information in the platform to build applications can vary, the rules that allow the usage of platform can differ, and even the fee to get the access (license fee) can change. The more open the platform is in these three dimensions, the more easily it is for the different parties to access and share the relevant data through the platform.

3.2 Industrial Internet Platform Functionalities

Industrial internet, Industry 4.0 and CPS can be collectively defined as industrial systems that integrate computational and physical capabilities of machines in order to provide advanced analytics and interact with humans [9, 17–20]. In this study, we define industrial internet platforms as platforms which adhere to the general definition of industry platform (as in Sect. 3.1) and the industrial internet definition mentioned above.

In the context of product lifecycle management (PLM), there has been a marked shift in its vision, which would ideally mean the ability to access, manage and control product related information across various phases of lifecycle [5]. In case of PLM, industrial internet platforms can provide the real time management of data and information flows and help in the data-information-knowledge (D-I-K) transformations along all the phases of product lifecycle.

The industrial internet platforms can access data from different sensors, actuators, enterprise systems, social media and other novel data sources [21, 22]. The industrial internet platform is able to aggregate data into a single database which can be stored, either in dedicated in-house servers or with other third party cloud storage providers [19, 23]. This organised data can be used, for example, by technicians to remotely monitor the condition of machine without physically being present [24], the data can also be run through machine learning algorithms to predict the health condition of a machine and notify the concerned technician to make an informed decision about the need to have the machine maintenance [25]. The data, via the platform, can provide different analytics like descriptive, predictive and prescriptive to create proper infographics which facilitate experienced knowledge workers [18]. Consider the example of a new industrial internet platform based risk assessment solution in Oil & Gas sector, which allows real time visual representation of risks to oil pipeline, based on internal and external environment factors. These infographics provide the experienced pipeline operators a new way to check pipeline integrity. [26] In many cases the industrial internet platforms enable development of applications (“apps”) on top of the platform. These applications help in sharing the relevant information between the different actors and can also help in sense-making [27].

Today, there is a plethora of platforms available. We selected a subset of platforms that enable efficient and real time management of data, information and knowledge over various lifecycle phases. These platforms were searched from mainly academic articles (example [17, 28–31]) and other relevant sources which reviewed characteristics of platforms, functionalities of platforms and data and information management perspective of platforms. Some platforms, such as Exosite and IndustryHack, were added into this pool because they were discovered to be interesting in some of their characteristics. From this subset a large pool was selected based on the following inclusion criteria:

1. Platforms that are relevant to industrial internet and cater to manufacturing and industrial companies.
2. Platforms that are international. This allows various actors involved in the lifecycle of the product to use them from different geographical locations.
3. Platforms that satisfy the definition of External/industry platforms [7] that allow the inter-organizational collaboration to manage data, information and knowledge.

Table 1 above shows the examples of various platforms in the domain of Industrial internet/Industry4.0/CPS [9, 17], Internet of Things (IoT). [28, 31], social media platforms in manufacturing industrial companies [32], crowdsourcing and collaboration platforms [33]. These examples are not an exclusive list of platforms but they are representatives of the domains.

Table 1. Large pool of industry platforms by their domain

Division by domain	Platform examples
Industrial internet/Industry 4.0/cyber physical system (CPS) platforms	General Electric's Predix, Microsoft Azure, Cyberlighting's Cyberville, Schneider Electric's Wonderware, SAP Hana Cloud Platform (Connected Manufacturing & Predictive Maintenance and services), Bosch Production & Logistics, LifeCycle Care (Your KoneCranes + TrueConnect), John Deere Forest Insight
Internet of things platforms	PTC-Thingworx, IBM BlueMix, Exosite, Google Brillo, Sap IoT Platform, Intel IoT, Salesforce IoT Cloud
Social media platforms in manufacturing industrial companies	Yammer, LinkedIn, Twitter
Crowdsourcing & collaboration platforms	IndustryHack, GrabCad, Innocentive

4 Analysis of Industrial Internet Platforms from PLM Perspective

In order to do an in depth analysis of industrial internet platforms from the perspective of PLM, we further selected 10 platforms (see Table 2), that represent different platform domains and have unique features as platforms, considering especially their capabilities to address various challenges (drawn from Sect. 2, and represented as the major evaluation criteria in Table 2). We further selected 5 platforms (see Table 3), that provide analysis to highlight the effects on management of data, information and knowledge across various PLM phases using industrial internet as a technology enabler.

Table 2. Platform analysis based on industrial internet based on data, information and knowledge

Industrial internet based Information and knowledge functionalities	GE-Predix	MyJohnDeere	Bosch IoT Suite	Sap-Hana Cloud	Microsoft Azure	PTC-ThingWorx	Cyberlighting-CyberVille	Industry Hack	Yammer
Data Access & Collection	++	++	++	+	+	--	--	++	--
Data Aggregation & Sharing	++	+	+	++	++	++	+	--	--
Data Storing	+	+	+	+	+	--	--	--	--
Analytics & Visualizations	+	+	+	+	+	++	++	+	--
Information Sharing	+	+	+	+	+	+	+	+	+
Sense making	--	+	--	--	--	--	--	++	++

-- Not present

+ Present

++ Unique Feature

In Table 2, IndustryHack is a unique actor as it uses the concept of hackathon [34] in industrial setting to bring together outside experts who can help in rapid prototyping [35] and present a proof of concept for the given industrial problem. In terms of data access, Predix, MyJohnDeere and Bosch IoT Suite have the unique advantage of providing their own sensors which can work in different environments [9, 21, 26]. These platforms have capability to directly access a new source of data which is not possible for platforms which don't provide their own hardware (example sensors, actuators). On the other hand, IndustryHack collects data in terms of a pool of experts which can collaborate with industries in the hackathons. Hana, Azure, Predix, Thingworx also allow the real time data integration with data from novel data sources like social media [28–30]. This kind of combination of data can lead to creation of new information. Platform like Cyberville provides feature like multilayered 3D view of complex network in real time. Thingworx lowers technological complexities for users through codeless mashup capabilities. This enables easy creation of variety of visual infographics. [29, 31] in business context, sense making needs experts who can help in making quality decisions after an informed sense making process (Namvar et al. [27]). While sense making is enabled by most of the platforms in the above list. Platforms like Yammer (microblog) and IndustryHack directly support sense-making by bringing together relevant experts to make sense of provided information.

Table 3 provides detailed analysis of 5 platforms that address the challenges of PLM in the context of data information and knowledge management. Platforms have different degrees of openness [7]: Access to data and information, Rules governing the platform and cost of access to data and information. Cyberville is open from the viewpoint of DIK in a way that it follows the open source standards of the internet technology. Access to data information and knowledge across the life cycle phases and

Table 3. Detailed analysis of industrial internet platforms in the context of PLM

<table>
<tr><td colspan="2">Platforms to be analyzed →</td><td rowspan="2">GE Predix</td><td rowspan="2">Microsoft Azure</td><td rowspan="2">PTC ThingWorx</td><td rowspan="2">MyJohnDeere</td><td rowspan="2">CyberVille-CyberLighting</td></tr>
<tr><td>Criteria for analysis ↓</td><td>Detailed criteria for analysis ↓</td></tr>
<tr><td>Openness of the platform</td><td>Access to information</td><td>High</td><td>High</td><td>High</td><td>Low</td><td>Medium</td></tr>
<tr><td rowspan="2">Level of openness – low, medium & high</td><td>Cost of access</td><td>High</td><td>High</td><td>Medium</td><td>Low</td><td>Low</td></tr>
<tr><td>Control in terms of rules to use the platform</td><td>High</td><td>Low (users can decide about data access)</td><td>Low (users can decide about data access)</td><td>High</td><td>Low</td></tr>
<tr><td rowspan="3">Used in product lifecycle phases</td><td>BOL</td><td rowspan="3">Across and within all phases</td><td rowspan="3">Across and within all phases</td><td>No</td><td rowspan="3">Across and within all phases</td><td>No</td></tr>
<tr><td>MOL</td><td rowspan="2">Across and within MOL and EOL</td><td>Extensively in MOL</td></tr>
<tr><td>EOL</td><td>Less in EOL</td></tr>
<tr><td>Interoperability between different information systems</td><td>Yes/no</td><td>Yes</td><td>Yes</td><td>Yes</td><td>Yes</td><td>Yes</td></tr>
<tr><td rowspan="2">Real time monitoring/analytics</td><td>Basic</td><td rowspan="2">Advanced</td><td rowspan="2">Advanced</td><td rowspan="2">Advanced</td><td rowspan="2">Advanced</td><td rowspan="2">Basic</td></tr>
<tr><td>Advanced</td></tr>
<tr><td rowspan="2">On-demand tailored solutions</td><td>Demand-side user (end user)</td><td>Yes</td><td>Yes</td><td>Yes</td><td>Yes</td><td>Yes</td></tr>
<tr><td>Supply-side (application developer)</td><td>No</td><td>Yes</td><td>Yes</td><td>No</td><td>Yes</td></tr>
</table>

within the different phases (in case of Closed Loop PLM) is the key to the value creation from product related lifecycle data, information and knowledge [8]. MyJohnDeere is a kind of a platform that enables the product manufacturer to tap into all the data and information throughout the lifecycle phases and also access within different lifecycle phases. Interoperability [12] which is one of the key issues in all industry softwares (for example PLM, PDM, CRM, ERP) is solved by the use of industrial internet platforms by the use of plugins. In order to create value of data and information it is important to get this data and information in real time and provide analytics based on this data in real time as well. GE Predix and Microsoft Azure kinds of industrial internet platform have incorporated Big Data technologies in the platform architecture to enable real time monitoring as well as analytics [9, 26, 28]. One of the key differentiator between traditional industry softwares and platforms like PTC Thingworx, Cyberville, GE Predix is the availability of On-demand tailored solutions [29, 31] or "apps" which result into a marketplace. These "apps" or applications create value of data, information and knowledge for the platform users. The popularity and acceptance of this marketplace generates network effects for the platform [7].

5 Discussion and Conclusion

The challenges with the management of data, information and knowledge in case of PLM is a very important area of research. Problems such as real-time data access, transfer, management and analytics are some of the challenges that need to be solved efficiently. Industrial internet platforms address to the challenges of data information and knowledge during and within the PLM phases. Most of the platforms are efficient and similar in the storing the data and sharing information. Platforms like IndustryHack that allow tapping into outside experts while Yammer is centered on supporting collaboration between experts enable the sense-making of the data and information. Advanced analytics like the multi-layered real-time 3D visualization and mashup kind of applications (for analytics) is enabled by industrial internet platforms. The On-demand tailored solutions help visualize and manage data and information using portable devices (mobile phones, smart watches) which the large PLM and PDM systems do in a restricted manner.

Our purpose was to analyse and understand the potential role of II platforms in the management of product lifecycle related information and knowledge. From our analyses, first, we can conclude that there exist quite different types of external industry platforms with different emphases in their capability of addressing various types of PLM challenges. In addition to IoT platforms, industry 4.0 platforms and CPS platforms, these include also crowdsourcing and social media platforms that can address some of the relevant PLM challenges that others are not well-positioned to do, such as tapping into external knowledge resources and helping to make sense of various existing data. The analysis, in overall, demonstrates that many of the platforms seem to cater for the PLM challenges in rather different and unique manner compared to traditional PLM software, even if various PLM software have recently adopted platforms features and even developed their own app store solutions. This uniqueness is related to for instance enhanced interoperability and the ability to make use of novel data sources in a flexible and real-time manner. Second, we claim that industrial internet platforms can and should, in many cases, be adopted to allow more extensive and useful management of all relevant data from the lifecycle, and combined to existing PLM software through the platforms' capabilities to connect to external software and hardware. We believe that such platforms, when selected in an informed manner, can have even a significant role in enhancing the management of product lifecycle related information and knowledge. Simultaneously, companies should be careful when selecting platforms (as well as any other software solutions), because switching to other software can be difficult later on due to the path-dependency of the decisions.

A small or medium sized company might want to select a platform based on open source standards and open interfaces, such as CyberVille- Cyberlighting, while a large established company might prefer a more mature and developed platform like Predix or ThingWorx. Companies should also take care to make a decision which suits the core objectives of PLM in the longer term, defining these objectives carefully before the decision.

References

1. Kadiri, S.E., Kiritsis, D.: Ontologies in the context of product lifecycle management: state of the art literature review. Int. J. Prod. Res. **53**(18), 5657–5668 (2015)
2. Schuh, G., Rozenfeld, H., Assmus, D., Zancul, E.: Process oriented framework to support PLM implementation. Comput. Ind. **59**(2–3), 210–218 (2008)
3. Kärkkäinen, H., Pels, H.J., Silventoinen, A.: Defining the customer dimension of PLM maturity. In: Rivest, L., Bouras, A., Louhichi, B. (eds.) PLM 2012. IAICT, vol. 388, pp. 623–634. Springer, Heidelberg (2012). doi:10.1007/978-3-642-35758-9_56
4. Kärkkäinen, H., Myllärniemi, J., Okkonen, J., Silventoinen, A.: Maturity assessment for implementing and using product lifecycle management in project-oriented engineering companies. Int. J. Electron. Bus. **11**(2), 176–198 (2014)
5. Terzi, S., Bouras, A., Dutta, D., Garetti, M., Kiritsis, D.: Product lifecycle management – from its history to its new role. Int. J. Prod. Lifecycle Manag. **4**(4), 360–389 (2010)
6. Buda, A., Främling, K., Borgman, J., Madhikermi, M., Mirzaeifar, S., Kubler, S.: Data supply chain in industrial internet. In: 2015 IEEE World Conference on Factory Communication Systems (WFCS), pp. 1–7 (2015)
7. Gawer, A., Cusumano, M.A.: Industry platforms and ecosystem innovation. J. Prod. Innov. Manag. **31**(3), 417–433 (2014)
8. Jun, H.-B., Kiritsis, D., Xirouchakis, P.: Research issues on closed-loop PLM. Comput. Ind. **58**(8–9), 855–868 (2007)
9. Agarwal, N., Brem, A.: Strategic business transformation through technology convergence: implications from General Electric's industrial internet initiative. Int. J. Technol. Manag. **67** (2–4), 196–214 (2015)
10. Saaksvuori, A., Immonen, A.: Understanding the product lifecycle. Prod. Lifecycle Manag. 191–206 (2008)
11. Batenburg, R., Helms, R.W., Versendaal, J.: PLM roadmap: stepwise PLM implementation based on the concepts of maturity and alignment. Int. J. Prod. Lifecycle Manag. **1**(4), 333–351 (2006)
12. Elheni-Daldoul, D., Le Duigou, J., Eynard, B., Hajri-Gabouj, S.: Enterprise information systems' interoperability: focus on PLM challenges. In: Emmanouilidis, C., Taisch, M., Kiritsis, D. (eds.) APMS 2012. IAICT, vol. 398, pp. 184–191. Springer, Heidelberg (2013). doi:10.1007/978-3-642-40361-3_24
13. Ming, X.G., Yan, J.Q., Lu, W.F., Ma, D.Z.: Technology solutions for collaborative product lifecycle management–status review and future trend. Concurr. Eng. **13**(4), 311–319 (2005)
14. Ball, A., Ding, L., Patel, M.: An approach to accessing product data across system and software revisions. Adv. Eng. Inform. **22**(2), 222–235 (2008)
15. Ameri, F., Dutta, D.: Product lifecycle management: closing the knowledge loops. Comput.-Aided Des. Appl. **2**(5), 577–590 (2005)
16. Eisenmann, T.R.: Managing proprietary and shared platforms. Calif. Manag. Rev. **50**(4), 31–53 (2008)
17. Hermann, M., Pentek, T., Otto, B.: Design principles for industrie 4.0 scenarios. In: 2016 49th Hawaii International Conference on System Sciences (HICSS), pp. 3928–3937 (2016)
18. Lee, J., Bagheri, B., Kao, H.-A.: A cyber-physical systems architecture for industry 4.0-based manufacturing systems. Manuf. Lett. **3**, 18–23 (2015)
19. Evans, P.C., Annunziata, M.: Industrial internet: pushing the boundaries of minds and machines. Gen. Electr. **26** (2012)
20. Lansiti, M., Lakhani, K.R.: Digital ubiquity: how connections, sensors, and data are revolutionizing business. Harv. Bus. Rev. **92**(11), 90–99 (2014)

21. Porter, M.E., Heppelmann, J.E.: How smart, connected products are transforming companies. Harv. Bus. Rev. **93**(10), 96–114 (2015)
22. Porter, M.E., Heppelmann, J.E.: How smart, connected products are transforming competition. Harv. Bus. Rev. **92**(11), 64–88 (2014)
23. Lee, I., Lee, K.: The Internet of Things (IoT): applications, investments, and challenges for enterprises. Bus. Horiz. **58**(4), 431–440 (2015)
24. Lesjak, C., Ruprechter, T., Haid, J., Bock, H., Brenner, E.: A secure hardware module and system concept for local and remote industrial embedded system identification. In: Proceedings of the 2014 IEEE Emerging Technology and Factory Automation (ETFA), pp. 1–7 (2014)
25. Lee, J., Kao, H.-A., Yang, S.: Service innovation and smart analytics for industry 4.0 and big data environment. Procedia CIRP **16**, 3–8 (2014)
26. Winnig, L.W.: GE's big bet on data and analytics. MIT Sloan Manag. Rev. **57**(3), Spring 2016
27. Namvar, M., Cybulski, J.L., Perera, L.: Using business intelligence to support the process of organizational sensemaking. Commun. Assoc. Inf. Syst. (2015). Accepted Publication
28. Derhamy, H., Eliasson, J., Delsing, J., Priller, P.: A survey of commercial frameworks for the Internet of Things. In: 2015 IEEE 20th Conference on Emerging Technologies Factory Automation (ETFA), pp. 1–8 (2015)
29. Heo, Y.J., Oh, S.M., Chin, W.S., Jang, J.W.: A lightweight platform implementation for Internet of Things. In: 2015 3rd International Conference on Future Internet of Things and Cloud (FiCloud), pp. 526–531 (2015)
30. Familiar, B.: IoT and microservices. In: Familiar, B. (ed.) Microservices, IoT, and Azure, pp. 133–163. Springer, Heidelberg (2015)
31. Weinberger, M., Köhler, M., Wörner, D., Wortmann, F.: Platforms for the Internet of Things : an analysis of existing solutions. Presented at the 5th Bosch Conference on Systems and Software Engineering (BoCSE), Ludwigsburg (2014)
32. Jussila, J.J., Kärkkäinen, H., Aramo-Immonen, H.: Social media utilization in business-to-business relationships of technology industry firms. Comput. Hum. Behav. **30**, 606–613 (2014)
33. Howe, J.: Crowdsourcing: a definition. In: Crowdsourcing: Why the Power of the Crowd is Driving the Future of Business, 02 June 2006
34. Raatikainen, M., Komssi, M., dal Bianco, V., Kindstöm, K., Järvinen, J.: Industrial experiences of organizing a hackathon to assess a device-centric cloud ecosystem. In: 2013 IEEE 37th Annual Computer Software and Applications Conference (COMPSAC), pp. 790–799 (2013)
35. Gunasekaran, A.: Agile manufacturing: enablers and an implementation framework. Int. J. Prod. Res. **36**(5), 1223–1247 (1998)

Diverse Scope Coordination in Design Management

Shuichi Fukuda(✉)

System Design and Management, Keio University, Yokohama, Japan
shufukuda@gmail.com

Abstract. This is a position paper to share our experience how Lazy Evaluation approach in AI is useful for team decision making with members with diverse knowledge and experience from many different fields. For example, Industrie 4.0 is a German proposal of a new framework to team up SMEs in order to cope with the frequent and extensive changes today. Until recently, we could fight with 11 best players, but today we need to fight with best 11. If the situations do not change then best players in each position can form a good team and win. But just as soccer demonstrates, such fixed formation does not work anymore. All players have to changes their roles flexibly and adaptively in response to the change. But unlike soccer where a goal is very clear, engineering teams need to determine a common goal first of all. But the greatest difficulty is members have different knowledge and experience, especially so when members come from different fields. Thus, how we can coordinate their diverse scopes and come up with an identical scope which satisfy all members and which leads to fruitful collaboration is a big challenge. This paper describes how Lazy Evaluation is effective for negotiation among members with diverse knowledge and experience and for coming up with an identical goal toward fruitful collaboration.

Keywords: Design management · Diverse members · Scope coordination · Lazy evaluation · Satisficing

1 Design Scope Coordination

Although there are many papers on design management, there are very few on design scope coordination. For example, in project management, work scope and product scope are taken up. Work scope is about how to run the project and product scope is what product to produce. Although there are detailed discussion about how these scopes should be executed, how the scope should be framed is not well discussed.

But most important issue is how we frame our scope. This is essentially the same problem as has been discussed in AI research field as the Frame Problem. "The Frame Problem is the challenge of representing the effects of action in logic without having to represent explicitly a large number of intuitively obvious non-effects in AI, but it can be regarded as a more general problem of How do we account for apparent ability to make decisions on the basis only of what is relevant to an ongoing situation without having explicitly to consider all that is not relevant?" [1].

R. Harik et al. (Eds.): PLM 2016, IFIP AICT 492, pp. 559–566, 2016.
DOI: 10.1007/978-3-319-54660-5_50

Design scope coordination is a typical example of the Frame Problem. With the progress of engineering and with the quickly spreading diversification and personalization, engineering problems cannot be solved without involvement of many experts from many different fields. Thus, what becomes important, but is not taken up for discussion is how we fill up their differences and reach a final goal acceptable to all members involved.

In project management, PMBOK [2] plays an important role, but it does not describe these diverse "common senses". And when they discuss parameters such as functional, design, etc., the scope is already fixed. The most important issue how we can frame our strategic scope is not discussed enough.

Pre-stage of Project Management becomes, however, increasingly important especially in PLM, because PLM requires very broad knowledge and experience across many different fields as it requires not only knowledge about design, manufacture, but also operation, i.e., it covers a very broad context.

2 Increasing Importance of Decision Making

This issue boils down to the problem of how we make decisions. Most of the research on project management and related works are dealing with the problems after a decision is made. But decision making in cases which relate to a wide variety of fields and broad contexts must be accepted by all members concerned who come from diverse fields. Of course, all members do not share the same knowledge and experience. They have their own views and even the same knowledge is used differently from field to field. So scope coordination for decision making is increasing its importance. Then, how can we overcome such difficulties and make appropriate decisions in an age of increasing diversification and personalization?

3 Lazy Evaluation

If we look back and consider how we make decisions, we soon realize that we do not make decisions all at once. The more difficult the problem is, the more time or stages we take to come up with the final decision. In other words, the larger problem space is, the more time or stages we need to fix our scope. In fact, when the problem space is very large, we cannot make decisions rationally due to such problems of combinatorial explosion, computational complexity, etc., and we have to look for satisficing as Herbert Simon pointed out [3]. Interestingly enough, another economist John Keynes pointed out economic agents make decisions rationally for short term expectations, but when it comes to long term, they rely on their confidence [4]. Thus, how we can let members feel satisfied and how they can agree upon the final goal with confidence is most crucial in team decision making with members from diverse fields.

The difficulty of decision making in a problem relating to diverse fields is scopes are different from member to member so that they are not identical. Of course, members do their best to increase the overlapping common area, but no matter how much efforts they may pay to increase it, there still remains areas which are not covered by all members (Fig. 1). The most important thing is how we can find a common area, or intersection if we use set theory term, among all members involved with satisfaction and with confidence.

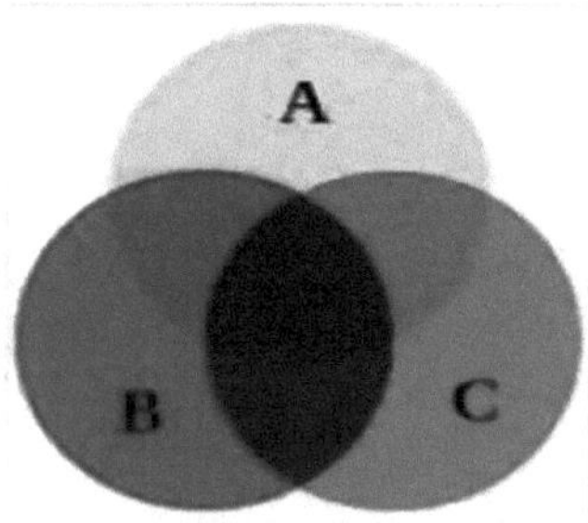

Fig. 1. Intersection

If this common area or intersection can be found easily, then there is no problem. There might be slight differences, for example, regarding the definition of parameters, etc., among diverse members, but such small discrepancies can be easily solved if detailed discussion is made. Although it may take time, it is essentially not different from one time decision making.

Such one time decision making can be done when the problem is not so much complicated or large. Essentially rational approaches can be applied and the problem will be solved.

But when the problem relates to a wide variety of fields, such rational approaches cannot be applied and we have to introduce multi-stage decision making and repeat the process of convincing members that the line of reasoning is adequate. If the problem is small and simple, members can understand the line of reasoning easily and although it may take time, we can reach the common goal.

What makes multi-stage decision making difficult which relates to a wide variety of fields is there are issues which some of the members cannot understand at some stages, because the lines of reasoning vary from field to field. These members have to wait until the reasoning comes to the stage when they understand how the problem is going to be solved. When the reasoning comes to the stage they can understand, they can express their views and opinions and ask for revision, etc., based on their own knowledge and experience.

Then, how can we deal with this problem of multi-stage decision making in a situation where the problem is related to many diverse fields?

Lazy evaluation is the answer to this problem. We postpone our decision until later stage when we can make a decision. When the discussion comes to the stage you understand, then you can express your opinion and demand, if necessary, to change the conclusion which is obtained through the previous stages or give advice to improve the conclusion, based on your own field. And in the worst case, when you cannot understand the whole process, the constraints must be relaxed and repeat such trial and error approach from the first until every member understands the line of reasoning and can agree upon the final decision. This way, the final conclusion is reached by unanimous agreement of all members (Fig. 2).

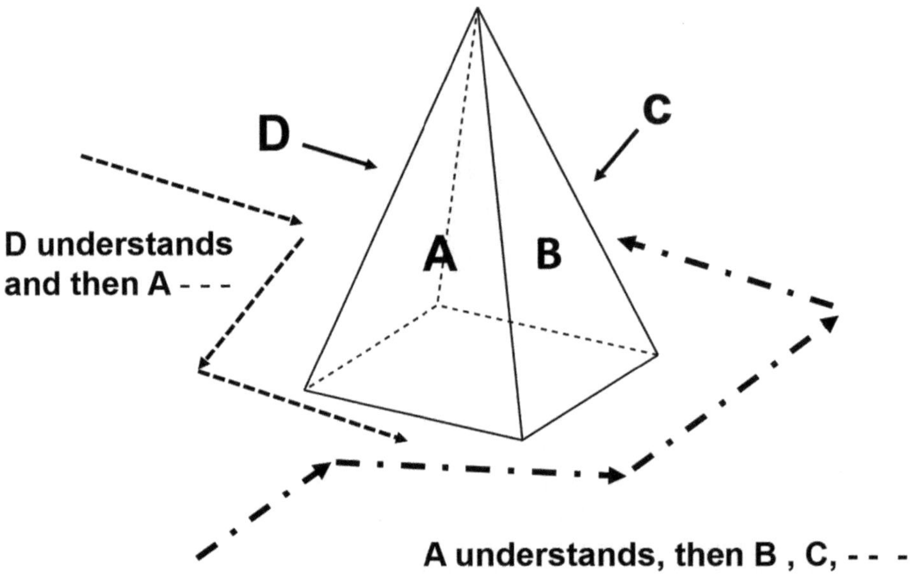

Fig. 2. Illustrative explanation of lazy evaluation used for team decision making with diverse members with diverse backgrounds

In other words, the common area or interaction varies with how the discussion goes on. In rational approaches, the common area or interaction does not change. But in the case of multi-stage decision making with diverse members, we have to note that the common area or the common goal varies from case to case. If some members are taking the initiative, the goal would reflect their knowledge and experience more.

Thus multi-stage decision making in a team with diverse members from diverse backgrounds is nothing other than negotiation. We have to remember negotiation comes first before collaboration. In other words, when the problem cannot be solved rationally, we have to resort to negotiation among members from diverse fields. But how we can negotiate to arrive at the common goal by coordinating the scope is not well discussed.

Thus, this final solution may not be the optimum in the strict sense, but it is a *satisficing* solution. Herbert Simon pointed out that if the number of variables is too many, we cannot find the optimum mathematically due to such a problem of computational complexity, etc. so that we have to satisfy ourselves with the notion of *satisficing*. The term *Satisficing* is a combination of satisfy and suffice and it means satisfy enough [3].

To understand Simon's idea better, let us consider global optimization. Although the optimum can be obtained rationally if it is local optimization, we cannot obtain such a mathematically accurate optimum, when it comes to global optimization. Take Simulated Annealing for example. We repeat searching many times to reach an optimum, but it is nothing other than to regard the highest (or the lowest) one as the optimum, because we have repeated so many searches. There is no mathematical guarantee that it is the highest. We only believe or would like to believe it is the highest because we tried so many times. Thus, global optimization just makes us emotionally satisfied. It is nothing other than satisficing.

Lazy Evaluation is a method originally proposed in programming language theory. The primary reason why it was invented was to reduce the running time and to increase performance, because it avoids repeated evaluation. But the point which this paper emphasizes is very much different. This approach works very well for negotiation for decision making for a team with members of many different backgrounds.

Lazy evaluation permits very flexible and adaptable line of reasoning. Thus, it provides us with a tool to reach emotionally satisfied conclusions. Again, this approach is useful to convince every member of a team with different backgrounds that the line of reasoning is adequate and their knowledge and experience are duly reflected in the final conclusion so that they accept it with enough satisfaction. But we have to remember that nobody sees or understands the whole picture. So this approach is completely different from an approach to construct a meta-level knowledge and experience representation for decision making.

4 System to Produce Welding Procedure Specification

This chapter describes our past experience of producing a legal document called Welding Procedure Specification. We formed a consortium with about 12 industry members with the leadership of Welding Research Institute, Osaka University. The members include Nippon Steel, Mitsubishi Heavy Industry, Kawasaki Heavy Industry, Kobe Steel, Toyo Engineering, Shimizu Corporation, IHI, Shin-Meiwa, etc. Their fields are heavy industries, shipbuilding, airplanes, automobiles, etc.

As is well known, welding requires a wide variety of knowledge and experience such as material, electrical, mechanical, etc. and its application areas are also diverse such as civil, architectural, transportations, etc. But to carry out welding, there are legal rules which require us to specify how welding will be done.

These rules about welding are different from country to country. American Welding Society introduces such concepts as welding of box-type components and sets down legal rules to apply to welding of boxes. Such boxes are used for containers, and used as components in ships, truck, etc. So such legal rules based on structural modules can be applied in a straightforward manner.

But in Japan, welding rules are set based upon the concept of weldline. Thus, we have to work out rules for each case because weldments vary widely from structure to structure and from product to product. Japanese rules pay attention only to welding, and they do not take into consideration such constraints as structures, etc. So industries have to form Welding Procedure Specification (WPS) to demonstrate that the welding they are going to perform follows the legal rules of Japanese welding rules and in addition that their way is reasonable enough from other respects.

This process of producing WPS, however, used to be a world of the rule of thumb. When industries worked in their own fields and their products and services were not so much diversified as they are today, the rule of thumb worked well.

But when shipping business was very bad in Japan, their welding department attempted to secure employment of their welders by receiving orders from other industries such as construction, etc. But they could not. This is because they relied too much on their rule of thumb and this rule does not work in other industries. Such failures prompted them to introduce a more rational and versatile approach.

To respond to their request, we developed an AI-based system which adopts Lazy Evaluation and Constraint Management [5–7].

The system itself is not special in the sense of programming. But we paid out chief attention to how members will feel satisfied with the flow of reasoning. We constructed a knowledge and experience representation, by noting that members with adjacent area can communicate easily. By putting together such member to member pieces together, we come up with the final representation as shown in Fig. 3. Then, we adopted Lazy Evaluation technique to utilize this representation.

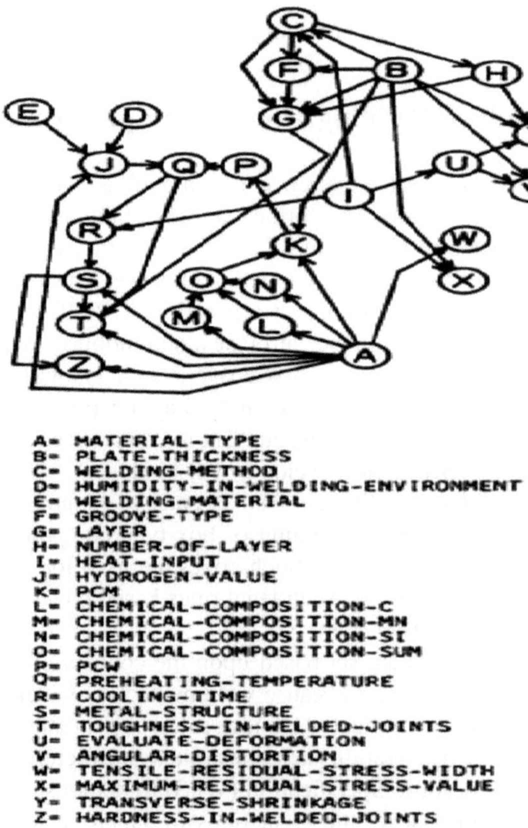

Fig. 3. Knowledge and experience representation for welding procedure specification

This system met industry needs and it was adopted by many major Japanese industries. Their fields include Shipbuilding, Building, Construction, Machinery, etc., although each industry customized it to meet their needs. But the basic structure is the same. Their system introduced Lazy Evaluation. They are being used today, although they are updated of course.

This demonstrates how such a system was needed and desired by industries. But at that time, industries were working in their own fields and there were few problems which required such a wide variety of knowledge and experience as in welding, so they could manage to solve the difficulty by accumulating experience.

But with quickly increasing diversification, the walls between industries are falling quickly apart and industries have to collaborate across many different areas. Thus, the need for more adaptable and flexible decision making tools are increasing rapidly.

Although the time we developed the system and the time Japanese industries started to use our system in welding was long time ago, before such diversification as we see today started, such needs were present in such a multi-expertise field as welding because it relates to many different fields so that collaborative decision making is called for.

The technique or programming of Lazy Evaluation can be easily found in AI literatures. What this paper emphasizes is that it can be used very effective for another application, i.e., negotiation before collaboration, although it was originally developed for programming efficiency.

The need for such a system for supporting decision making among members from widely different fields is quickly increasing, such as in Industrie 4.0 [8]. Although the system we developed was only for welding, the basic framework certainly works for other applications. As the number of variables are rapidly increasing and the backgrounds of participating members are quickly diversifying, such an approach to reach a strategic goal acceptable by all members is increasing its importance.

5 Summary

Increasing diversification and personalization call for collaboration among many members from many different fields. And the more diversified the requirements become, the more difficult it becomes to reach a common strategic goal acceptable to all members, because knowledge and experience are different from field to field and sometimes the same knowledge is used in a different way.

Therefore, how we can coordinate their different scopes and come up with an identical scope is a great challenge and its solution is strongly called for. In other words, negotiation is needed for satisficing and convincing collaboration.

This paper points out by sharing our experience in welding that Lazy Evaluation, which is one of the AI techniques for computer processing efficiency, can be used in a very different way. It is very effective for negotiation to come up with an identical scope and to determine a common goal which is satisficing and convincing to all members.

As Industrie 4.0 indicates, our world is moving more toward best 11 from 11 best, as American football coach Knuth Rockne pointed out. It is no more the time if we assemble 11 best players, we can win. We have to consider how we can utilize the presently available resources to the maximum. Rockne demonstrated his belief by bringing University of Notre Dame from the bottom to the top. This can also be observed in soccer. Situations change so frequently and widely in today's soccer so that it becomes increasingly important how we can form a strategy flexibly and adaptively to the changes.

Another important point is as everything is speeding up these days, we do not have enough time to develop new technology to cope with the changing situations. Thus, what we need now is "Do what you can, with what you have, where you are" as Theodore Roosevelt said. We have to utilize the current resources to the maximum in order to achieve the goal. We have to form a well working team, but with the available members.

Lazy Evaluation can be used, in spite of its misleading name, to arrive at a common goal shared by all member quickly and to satisfice them all. Although it was originally a technique to facilitate processing speed on a computer, but what this paper emphasizes is that it can be used for facilitating negotiation before collaboration.

References

1. Stanford Encyclopedia of Philosophy. http://plato.stanford.edu/entries/frame-problem. Accessed 14 Apr 2016
2. A Guide to the Project Management Body of Knowledge (PMBOK Guide), Fourth Edition. http://www.works.gov.bh/English/ourstrategy/Project%20Management/Documents/Other%20PM%20Resources/PMBOKGuideFourthEdition_protected.pdf. Accessed 14 Apr 2016
3. Simon, H.A.: Rational choice and the structure of the environment. Psychol. Rev. **63**(2), 129–138 (1956)
4. Keynes, J.M.: The General Theory of Employment, Interest and Money. Palgrave Macmillan, Basingstoke (1936)
5. Fukuda, S., Maeda, A., Kimura, M.: Development of an expert system for weld design support. Trans JSME (A) **52**(476), 1183–1190 (1986). (in Japanese)
6. This system was awarded by Okada Memorial Foundation (1986)
7. The development of this system led to Lifetime Achievement Award, ASME CIE Division in 2015
8. Securing the Future of German Manufacturing Industry Recommendations fr Implementing the Strategic Initiative INDUSTRIE 4.0 – Final Report of Industrie 4.0 Working Group. http://www.acatech.de/fileadmin/user_upload/Baumstruktur_nach_Website/Acatech/root/de/Material_fuer_Sonderseiten/Industrie_4.0/Final_report__Industrie_4.0_accessible.pdf. Accessed 14 April 2016

Metrics, Standards and Regulation

Developing a Unified Product Lifecycle Management Value Model

Abram L.J. Walton[1(✉)], Michael W. Grieves[2], Darrel L. Sandall[3], and Matthew L. Breault[4]

[1] Director of Center for Lifecycle and Innovative Management, Florida Institute of Technology, Melbourne, FL, USA
awalton@fit.edu

[2] Executive Director of Center for Advanced Manufacturing and Innovative Design, Florida Institute of Technology, Melbourne, FL, USA
mgrieves@fit.edu

[3] College of Business, Florida Institute of Technology, Melbourne, FL, USA
dsandall@fit.edu

[4] Researcher, Florida Institute of Technology, Melbourne, FL, USA
mbreault2008@my.fit.edu

Abstract. With the understanding of the enormous economic value inherent in next generation products, business enterprises repeatedly describe the value metrics and Return On Investment (ROI) of Product Lifecycle Management (PLM) as difficult to assess, thus confounding their ability to quickly and strategically make decisions. Given that PLM initiatives are such sizable investments and interdisciplinary, executives are struggling to agree upon value metrics to measure throughout the project to understand an accurate value created. Thus a shortage of known ROI information is available to make the case for financing a PLM project; moreover unique industry and organizational variables make it unfeasible for companies to easily benchmark competitors and predetermine the values gained. A literature review reveals a void of information relative to quantifiable value metrics and ROI of PLM. This article proposes a framework to use Grounded Theory research methodology to capture value metrics and formulate models, contributing to future organizational decisions on PLM implementations.

Keywords: Product lifecycle management · PLM · ROI · Value · Grounded theory · Internet of Things

1 Introduction

Product lifecycle management (PLM) is often cited as one of the most important strategic capital investments product-based companies can make, resulting in a boosted and sustained competitive advantage (e.g. decreasing product time-to-market, increasing reuse during new product development, and increasing the capacity for change control) when implemented in a holistic approach [1]. Yet, due to the size of the investment and the interdisciplinary impact of PLM, executives are struggling to make the case for financing a PLM project as there is a shortage of known Return On

R. Harik et al. (Eds.): PLM 2016, IFIP AICT 492, pp. 569–578, 2016.
DOI: 10.1007/978-3-319-54660-5_51

Investment (ROI) or similar value metric information available. Unique industry and organizational variables make it unfeasible for companies to easily benchmark competitors and predetermine the values gained [2]. Issues related to how firms measure performance are not isolated to technologically driven firms. Rather, nearly every organization is facing increasing pressure to justify Information Technology (IT) decisions and to quantify how a new system will change human-computer interactions, and ultimately affect the bottom line. An organization's ability to innovate depends not only on the overarching system and IT infrastructure, but how humans employ the system to maximize innovation. Advancements in PLM and their implications for an ever evolving and changing workforce require that organizations embrace and employ effective decision making methodologies.

This article explains the challenges executive management face understanding the values of PLM. A literature review reveals the lack of value metrics for companies attempting to determine the value created from their PLM investments. Reviewing previously published value metrics for IT systems creates a baseline for our research on the value of PLM. Future exhaustive research using Grounded Theory will allow for the creation of effective models and organic theories from data gathered on proposed value metrics of PLM. The specific value metrics captured and components analyzed are set forth in this article.

2 Review of Literature

An extensive search conducted for publications directly relating to the value metrics of PLM produced no results. This exposes a clear gap in the field of knowledge. Metrics for understanding value created by PLM have not been documented and executives are struggling to gather information supporting their PLM investments and mitigating the risks of future investments [3]. This research proposes to fill the void of information. Investigating publications concerning value metrics and models of IT systems can be used as a starting point for value metrics for PLM. These publications were chosen based on their relativity to the scope of research and their number of recitations reflecting their applicability into industry.

2.1 Value Metrics of IT Systems

In the Harvard Business Review article "Six IT Decisions Your IT People Shouldn't Make," Ross and Weill [4] wrote that the most frequent complaints they heard from top executives were about struggling to calculate payback on IT, realizing the business value from high priced technology, and justifying ongoing increases in IT spending. Their research reveals that companies successfully managing IT investments lead to returns that are as much as 40% higher than those of their competitors [4]. Due to advancements in IT systems and PLM solutions, this delta, based on returns 40% greater than those of competitors, created by successful management will arbitrate companies' ability to survive in the future.

Weill and Olson [5] analyzed a diverse group of case studies relating to IT investments such as Supply Chain Management (SCM), Customer Relationship Management (CRM), and Enterprise Resource Planning (ERP) systems. They established connections between the IT investment objectives and the performance measures that should be tracked per each investment. Three main connections were established: revenue growth rates should be a performance measure for strategic IT investments, return on assets [6] should be a performance measure for informational IT investments, and indirect labor should be a performance measure for transactional IT investments.

Nine years later, Weill and Broadbent [6] expounded on the above mentioned reference to include their fourth IT investment area of infrastructure. They subsequently created a new model containing the four types of IT investments and their corresponding value added areas, as shown in Fig. 1.

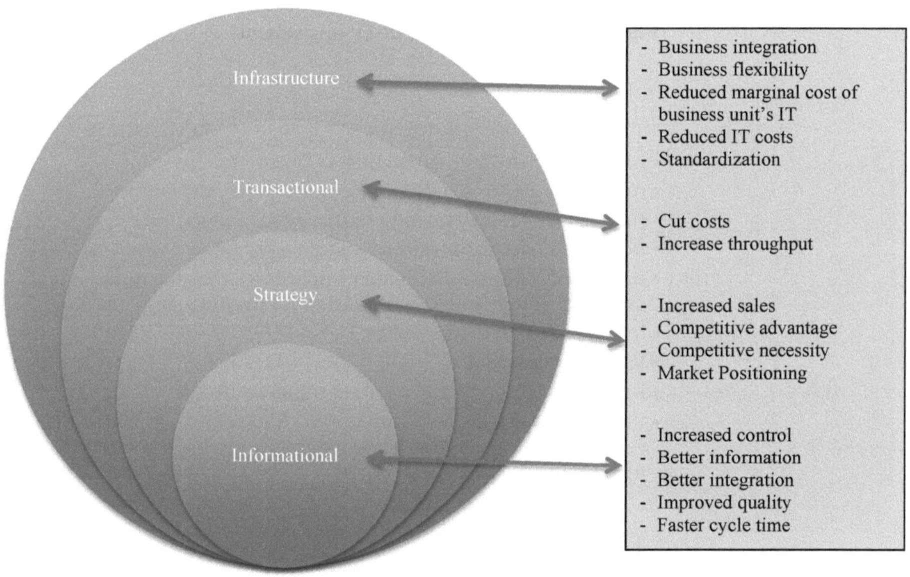

Fig. 1. IT investment area model

During the IT system investment justification process, ROI is often a discussion point since it is a widely used metric. Parker [7] details a method to calculate ROI for IT projects in which he places tangible benefits into five major categories as shown in Fig. 2.

Further outlined in Fig. 3: Non-tangible benefits of IT investment are the non-tangible, yet highly important benefits. Parker [7] suggests that these should not be placed in ROI calculations due to their difficulty to financially quantify.

Beyond the benefits factored into the ROI calculation, there are three other considerations that need to be made. Timeframe, Consistency, and Precision are additional relevant factors. Timeframe is the period in which those benefits are calculated for and

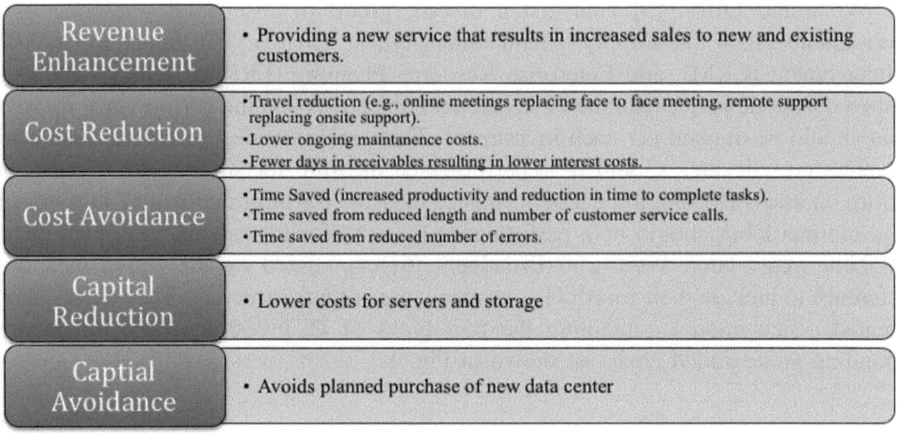

Fig. 2. Tangible benefits of IT investment

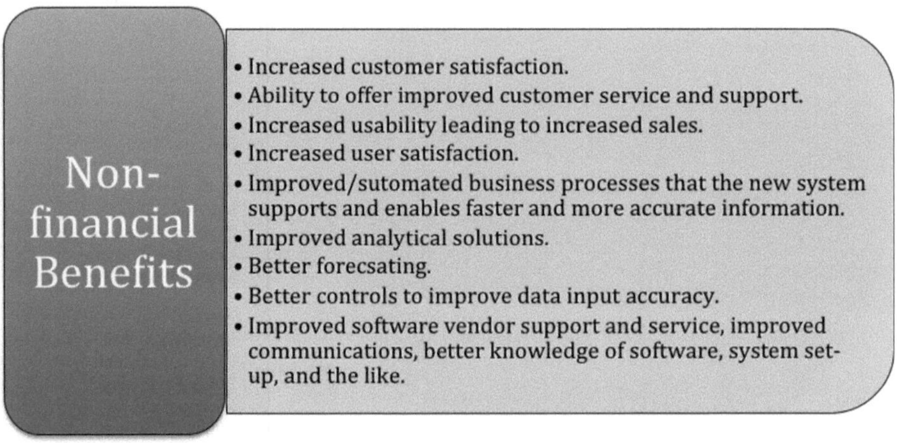

Fig. 3. Non-tangible benefits of IT investment

Parker recommends this to be around five years for IT systems. Consistency refers to aspects like inflation, taxation, and other assumptions being kept uniform across all IT system project calculations to maintain equal evaluations. Precision is describing all dollar values with a balance of certainty and accuracy and maintaining regularity for all IT investment decisions.

Wen and Yen [8] reviewed the most commonly accepted methodologies for measuring IT investment payoffs. The evaluation methods include ROI, Cost-Benefit Analysis (CBA), Return On Management (ROM), and Information Economics (IE). The tangible benefits cited above by Broadbent, Olsen, Parker, and Weill can be defined as the profit or return and then can be divided by the investment required for the ROI calculation. Further time value functions are applied to provide deeper analytical framework. Net Present Value (NPV) and Discounted Cash Flow (DCF) are additional

ROI methods dependent upon an interest rate to perform the calculation. These methods are predominantly used for tangible, quantitative benefits; however, the intangible benefits are better used for CBA, ROM, and IE.

The CBA approach is ideal for two main complications. They include quantifying the value of benefits that do not flow back to the investor, and identifying the market value of costs and benefits from intangible factors. CBA requires an agreement on the measures of value for intangible benefits. If there is disagreement on the appropriate values then one of the following methods should be used. ROM uses a simple ratio of productivity as "output/input." Strassmann [9] defines the output as the delta between the direct operating costs and the value added due to direct labor. Simons and Dávila [10] express it as productive organizational energy released divided by management time and attention invested. The advantage of the ROM method is that it can focus on the contributions of IT to the management process [8]. The IE method is analogous to the CBA method with the addition of a ranking and scoring technique of intangibles and risk factors associated with the IT investment. The justifications have been made for systems such as ERP, CRM, and SCM; however, the cross-functional impact of PLM is problematic for executives making the case for financing a PLM project [2].

3 Why Is PLM Value Hard to Calculate?

Research by Walton and Tomovic [2] explains, "the benefits of PLM are difficult to assess because the same benefit can be expressed as a function of time, cost, quality, or a combination thereof" [2]. PLM projects, like many other cross-functional implementations with interwoven components and processes, require combined and synchronous attention to all phases. Implementations that lack these combined foci stem from misguided perceptions about the intricacies and interdependencies in foundational PLM modules, which creates negative business outcomes in myriad areas involving people, practices, processes, and technology [11]. Subsequently, having expended millions of dollars for technological infrastructure implementation, education, and service, senior-level executives are eager to see trustworthy and unbiased data supporting their investments in PLM. Furthermore, without knowing the bottom-line impact of PLM on cost-savings and revenue-generation, executives are unable to precisely estimate the level of risk associated with future PLM investments [12].

These imprecise estimates stem from the lack of baseline data, which creates the struggle of determining ROI during, throughout, and after the project roll out. Additionally, the absence of baseline data and the inability to calculate post implementation ROI contributes to the overall deficiencies of market data attempting to place a value of PLM, which only serve to exacerbate the challenge of obtaining buy-in for a PLM implementation project from the corporation's most senior executives [13]. Resultantly, numerous enterprises scramble to collect the data during the implementation and after rollout because, over the lifecycle of the project, the priority is generally on issue and risk mitigation rather than on gathering data to justify the platform-decision that has already been made. After the rollout, teams resort to focusing on employing the full measure of the new platform and the temporary resources assigned during the implementation are moved on to other projects [14]; thus, data collection continues to be an area lacking both internal to corporations and even more so in the industry at-large. Despite the fact that there are no widely cited failures in PLM implementations, the issues related to there being a dearth of data showing PLM's value. This exacerbates the struggle companies face in quantifying PLM's benefits, and thus the adage, 'you cannot manage what you do not measure' [15] encapsulates an executive board's ability to justify their decision to implement PLM. Synonymous to this issue, since there are no widely cited failures, a lack of focus on optimization also exists because implementations are repeatedly seen as successful, so a strong enough urgency has not been created for implementation optimisation.

In order to resolve these challenges, enormous amounts of resources have been expended by companies, vendors, and academicians alike, with an aim of creating maturity models, benchmarking systems, and implementation indexes [2, 16, 17]. Nonetheless, there are still myriad reports and complaints from industry executives who express distress about the gap between published models for ROI and the models' inapplicability to their companies [18–20]. Worse yet, perceptions regarding reported benefits from vendors or consultants are often viewed with skepticism and bias [21–23], and executives argue that due to the enormous monetary costs of a PLM implementation, a company's key decisions cannot be left up to what could be viewed as biased information. Despite the published benefits, the true value or ROI for any particular organization cannot be predetermined, which hinders the decision-making and selection process. Moreover, since the benefits of PLM are often organizationally-specific, they do not easily correlate from one enterprise to another due to copious organizational variables (e.g. industry, company size, market segment, and business process maturity). This further hinders executives attempting to triangulate the value. This research aims to bridge the gap between the benefits of PLM and the creation of value and ROI for organizations implementing PLM.

4 Research Plan

As highlighted earlier, many quantitative research studies have been performed for the valuing of IT systems [6–8]. In contrast, our PLM value metric research will follow a qualitative research methodology. Silverman explains that "the papers in qualitative journals do not routinely begin with a hypothesis, the 'cases' studied are usually far fewer in number and the authors' interpretation is carried on throughout the writing" [24]. Sociologists Glaser and Strauss created grounded theory when they explicated the qualitative research strategies that they had used in their studies of how staff organized care of dying patients in hospitals [25]. Since 1967, the method has proved valuable through different industries, and is an inductive, iterative, interactive, and comparative method geared towards theory construction [26]. This approach produces a theory representative of the data that has been gathered and systematically analyzed during the research process.

Our data collection will consist of released information concerning product-producing companies within Fortune's list of the 1000 largest companies in the U.S. based on revenues for 2014. The information is generally published by four entities: the company, the company's PLM vendor, a PLM consulting firm that has experience with the company, or conference presentations and proceedings documenting the company's PLM information. Unavoidably, there are biases in the information released from these sources. This bias will remain within the research data collection pool; however, throughout the initial and focused coding periods we will sieve out as much as possible.

The analysis for determining the value metrics of PLM will consist of coding data in two phases, initial coding and focused coding. Glaser states that initial coding, sometimes known as open coding, asks these questions of the data: what is actually happening in the data, what are these data a study of, and what category does this case, segment, or statement of data indicate [25]? These questions will be answered by reviewing the data word-by-word, line-by-line, paragraph-by-paragraph, or incident-by-incident. Focused coding will be more exclusive and conceptual than initial coding. Performing focused coding amalgamates and explains larger segments of data. This will normally create categories for the grounded theory to be constructed upon. Charmaz suggests making the following comparisons during focused coding: comparing different people, comparing data from the same individuals at different points in time, comparing specific data with the criteria for the category, and comparing categories in the analysis with other categories [27]. Coding will create impressions for ideas, thoughts, or connections, which then leads to theoretical sampling.

Glaser and Strauss define theoretical sampling as "the process of data collection for generating theory whereby the analyst jointly collects, codes, and analyzes his data and decides what data to collect next and where to find them" [25]. This iterative process of gathering data, coding, and theoretical sampling will be performed until there is a saturation of data and all new information stops yielding any new theories. Since grounded theories are derived from data, they can be safe guides for the operation by the establishment of a deeper understanding and insight [28]. The research methodology for the discovery of value metrics for PLM will be Grounded theory approached as described by Silverman [24], Glaser and Strauss [25], Takhar-Lail [28] and Charmaz [26].

The goal of this research is to bridge the gap between the various value metric frameworks proposed in a variety of industry and academically generated literature and the current struggles that industry executives face when making strategic investments for PLM implementations. It provides a novel process to view the value of PLM and takes the research to a degree of understanding, in which, meaning can be given to the collected raw data. The research will gather benefits and costs of PLM implementations from numerous industries and markets. Due to the disparate nature of all the benefits and costs from different companies, after being collected, the data will undergo coding and analysis based on specific organizational variables to determine the value of each instance. These values will be put into a framework to help companies not only in their investment justification processes, but also in their post project value realization process. The multitude of the analysis may be outside of typical geometric spacing (e.g. Fig. 4

The analysis will generate multidimensional models (i.e. possible utilizing greater than three dimensions) [29] analyzing factors such as industry, company size, PLM use case, solution provider, business case, and value of each instance. This research stands to provide companies a tool and a valuable road map to determine the value of their PLM strategies. Furthermore, by having the ability to extrapolate data within the

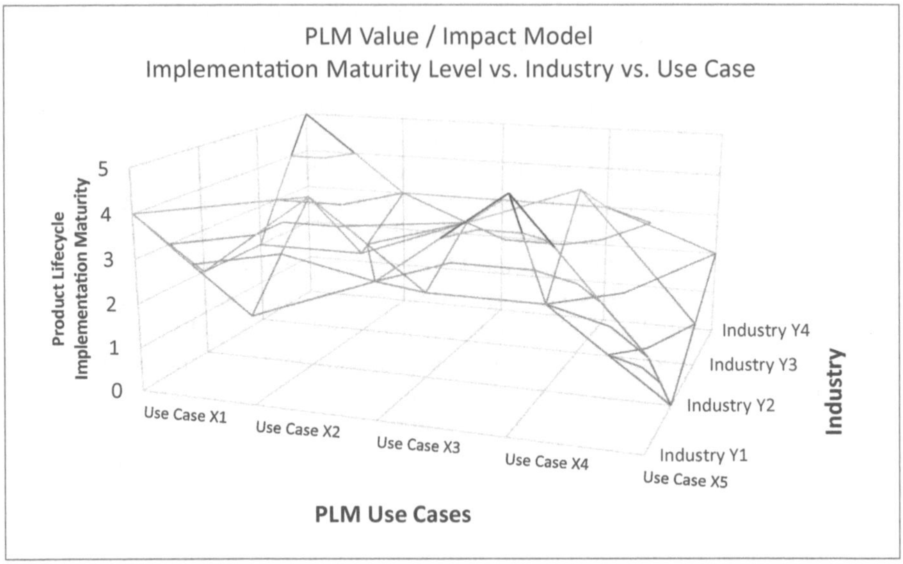

Fig. 4. Example of PLM value/impact model

model, companies will be able to better pinpoint PLM use-cases that are optimized for their industry and company size, allowing them to make well-informed decisions on their investment directions.

5 Limitations

The data collected for on-going and future research outlined in this paper is subject to natural biases due to the source of gathering information. The publishing bodies' best interest is to represent the benefits and accomplishments as triumphantly as possible without misrepresenting or being deceitful. The rhetoric and the reality of the information gathered will be coded carefully in an effort to eliminate all bias; however, we will not know for sure the extent of the biases represented.

6 Conclusion

The investment size and interdisciplinary impact of PLM create a need for higher probability of success for executives making the case for financing a PLM project. PLM implementations on the whole have a shortage of known ROI information available and the academic research to date has not addressed the challenges that industry executives are facing. Thus, the vast collection of PLM instances gathered by the proposed future research will allow for extrapolation of unique industry and organizational variables making it feasible for companies to easily benchmark competitors and predetermine the values gained.

References

1. Grieves, M.: Product Lifecycle Management: Driving the Next Generation of Lean Thinking. McGraw Hill Professional, New York (2006)
2. Walton, A.L.J., Tomovic, C.L., Grieves, M.W.: Product lifecycle management: measuring what is important - product lifecycle implementation maturity model. In: Bernard, A., Rivest, L., Dutta, D. (eds.) 2013 10th IFIP WG 5.1 International Conference on Product Lifecycle Management for Society, Nantes, France, pp. 406–421. Springer, Heidelberg (2013)
3. Tomovic, C., et al.: Measuring the impact of product lifecycle management: process plan, waste reduction and innovations conceptual frameworks, and logic model for developing metrics. In: Tomovic, M., Wang, S. (eds.) Product Realization, pp. 1–14. Springer, Heidelberg (2009)
4. Ross, J., Weill, P.: Six IT decisions your IT people shouldn't make. Harvard Bus. Rev. **80**, 84–91 (2002)
5. Weill, P., Olson, M.H.: Managing investment in information technology: mini case examples and implications. MIS Q. **13**(1), 3–17 (1989)
6. Weill, P., Broadbent, M.: Leveraging the New Infrastructure: How Market Leaders Capitalize on IT. Harvard Business Press, Brighton (1998)
7. Parker, J. Calculating ROI on Information Technology Projects (2012). (cited 29 Nov 2015)
8. Wen, H.J., Yen, D.D., Lin, B.: Methods for measuring information investment payoff. Hum. Syst. Manag. **17**(2), 145–163 (1998)
9. Strassmann, P.A.: Information Payoff: The Transformation of Work in the Electronic Age. The Free Press, New York (1985)
10. Simons, R., Dávila, A.: How high is your return on management? (cover story). Harvard Bus. Rev. **76**(1), 70–80 (1998)
11. Marien, E.J.: Meeting the product lifecycle challenge, p. 50+ (2006)
12. Tomovic, C., et al.: Development of product lifecycle management metrics: measuring the impact of PLM. Int. J. Manuf. Technol. Manag. **19**(3/4), 167–179 (2010)
13. Voskuil, J.: Getting buy-in-ROI. In: PI Congress. PI Congress, Chicago (2013)
14. Graeb, R.: How to measure the value of PLM solutions. in: http://blogs.ptc.com/. (2013) http://blogs.ptc.com/2013/08/05/how-to-measure-the-value-of-plm-solutions/
15. Deming, W.E.: Out of the Crisis, vol. 510. Massachusetts Institute of Technology, Center for Advanced Engineering Study, Cambridge, MA (1986)
16. Batenburg, R., Helms, R., Versendaal, J.: PLM roadmap: stepwise PLM implementation based on the concepts of maturity and alignment. Int. J. Prod. Lifecycle Manag. **1**(4), 333–351 (2006)
17. Savino, M.M., Mazza, A., Ouzrout, Y.: PLM maturity model: a multi-criteria assessment in southern Italy companies. Int. J Oper. Quant. Manag. **18**(3), 159–180 (2012)
18. Sevenler, K.: PLM roadmap: xerox development and deployment. In: PI Congress, Chicago (2013)
19. Davin, J.: Deckers brands' business transformation journey. In: PI Congress, Chicago (2013)
20. Stark, J.: Product Lifecycle Management-Volume 1: 21st Century Paradigm for Product Realisation. Springer, Cham (2015)
21. Aras: Engineering definition and supply chain BOM management for complex configurations: ge aviation. In: Aviation, G. (ed.). Aras.com (2013)
22. Oracle: Oracle agile PLM for the medical device industry. In: Oracle Executive Brief (2012)
23. Siemens: Shanghai Yanfeng Johnson Controls Seating: Reaping the rewards of worldwide concurrent design (2012). Siemens: Siemens.com/teamcenter
24. Silverman, D.: Interpreting Qualitative Data. Sage, Thousand Oaks (2015)

25. Glaser, B., Strauss, A.L.: The Discovery of Grounded Theory. Aldine De Gruyter, New York (1967)
26. Charmaz, K.: Constructing Grounded Theory: A Practical Guide Through Qualitative Analysis. Introducing Qualitative Methods Series. Sage, Thousand Oaks (2006)
27. Charmaz, K., Smith, J.: Qualitative psychology a practical guide to research methods. Grounded Theory, pp. 81–110. Sage, Thousand Oaks (2003)
28. Takhar-Lail, A.: Market Research Methodologies: Multi-method and Qualitative Approaches. IGI Global, Hershey (2014)
29. Gorbach, I., Berger, A., Melomed, E.: Describing multidimensional space. In: Microsoft SQL Server 2008 Analysis Services Unleashed. Sams (2008)

Identifying PLM Themes, Trends and Clusters Through Ten Years of Scientific Publications

Felix Nyffenegger[1(✉)], Louis Rivest[2], and Christian Braesch[3]

[1] HSR, Rapperswil, Switzerland
felix.nyffenegger@hsr.ch
[2] ETS, Montreal, Canada
louis.rivest@etsmtl.ca
[3] Université Savoie Mont-Blanc - SYMME, Annecy, France
christian.braesh@univ-smb.fr

Abstract. PLM encompasses a wide array of expertise, from designing green products to digital factories, with perspectives ranging from an IT standpoint to business strategies, encompassing products, processes and services. Hence, identifying the contours of PLM as a science through the themes, trends and clusters of its scientific literature is very challenging. At the same time, being able to portray PLM will benefit the PLM community, including researchers and practitioners, and should help foresee its future. This work examines PLM research bibliometric trends over the last ten years. We review the scientific literature published in English from 2005 to 2014 in peer-reviewed journals and conferences. Paper keywords are analyzed so as to identify trends and reveal the clusters of related themes based on the occurrences of words and the frequency of associations between them. Amongst the findings we observe that PLM coverage is both very large (2847 keywords being used over a decade) and very thin (2134 of these keywords appear only once in the decade). We also observe that the keyword showing the highest increase is Building Information Modeling (BIM).

Keywords: Bibliometric analysis · PLM · Review · Mapping study · Trends · Overview

1 Introduction

Product Lifecycle Management (PLM) has gained momentum over roughly the last 15 years, both in industry and in the research community. It can be stated that PLM encompasses a vast array of expertise, from designing green products to continuous manufacturing processes management, and that its perspectives range from Information Technology (IT) and Knowledge representation to Management-oriented works. This variety makes it challenging to define the contour of the very nature of PLM today and where it is headed.

This paper therefore presents a mapping of the PLM scientific literature published from 2005 to 2014 in peer-reviewed conferences and journals. It focuses on assessing a decade of PLM-related research work so as to establish a portrait of what themes and

R. Harik et al. (Eds.): PLM 2016, IFIP AICT 492, pp. 579–591, 2016.
DOI: 10.1007/978-3-319-54660-5_52

topics researchers have been working on over the last decade and detect underlying trends, if any. This paper also examines some clusters of themes and topics that are connected within PLM by studying the relationships between keywords found in the PLM literature. The first section reviews the literature relevant to our work. The methodology used for paper selection and the analysis technique are presented next, followed by the highlights of our findings. These findings are then analyzed and discussed, and we end with some conclusions and views on future work.

2 Related Research

Kitchenham [1] distinguishes *systematic literature reviews* from *mapping studies*. While the former aim at answering specific research questions, mapping studies are suitable to answer general questions, which are more relevant to research trends. Mapping studies aggregate and classify the relevant literature. One important factor for a mapping study is that a stringent search process be used.

Shepperd [2] suggests elaborating systematic reviews in the following steps: problem formulation, locating evidence, appraising evidence quality, evidence synthesis and interpretation and lastly, reporting. Our working methodology implements all of these steps, as described below.

Aside from the scientific literature that may guide our work towards constructing a high quality mapping study, we also searched for general PLM literature reviews or state-of-the-art summaries, and found very few. Bhatt et al. [3] published a PLM review in 2015 identifying some of the most frequent PLM research themes, but it was limited to papers published in PLM International Conference (IC) proceedings.

In 2015, Varandas et al. [4] published an analysis of PLM literature published from 2006 to 2010, with a focus on the concepts of Product Life Cycle Management, New Product Development, Environmental Sustainability and their interfaces (in Portuguese). Also in 2015, Mas et al. [6] published a review of PLM from the perspective of its impact on the aerospace industry in which they presented selected PLM topics from the developments in aerospace over roughly the last fifty years. Just a few years earlier (in 2013), Nappi and Rozenfeld [5] published a PLM literature review focusing on sustainability performance indicators.

Cao and Folan [7] reviewed the evolution of Product Life Cycle literature from 1950 to 2009, showing how it led to PLM. In 2005, Ming et al. [8] also presented a PLM review, which now dates back to over a decade. Some papers have promising titles but their contents do not help us in our work [9, 10].

The excellent paper from Terzi et al. [11] shares some of our aims and describes the constituent elements of PLM, and classifies them into three fundamentals themes: information and communication technologies, business processes, and methodologies. The findings presented below could clearly be classified along the same lines.

None of the above-mentioned papers exposes global PLM themes, trends and clusters over the years through a systematic PLM literature review based on keywords analysis. Hence, this paper offers a unique, fact-based, perspective on PLM.

3 Research Objective

Our objective is to draw a general portrait of PLM scientific literature over the last decade. This general portrait is designed to:

- identify the major themes being studied in the PLM scientific literature, thereby revealing what researchers consider to be part of PLM science;
- identify trends amongst these major themes so as to recognize both the 'rising stars' and those that are in decline over a ten-year period;
- identify in what countries PLM research is being conducted and observe if this research effort is stable, declining or increasing, by country; and
- identify clusters of ideas that are logically connected within the PLM domain.

From there, we should be able to answer, in a next step, questions such as: is CAD (Computer-Aided Design), as a topic, at the heart of PLM? Is BIM (Building Information Modeling) equivalent to PLM but applied exclusively to construction?

The working methodology established to achieve our objectives is described in the next section.

4 Methodology

This study addresses trends in the research fields of PLM and its objectives have a general character. Thus a mapping study was selected as the general methodology to achieve our goal. As noted by Kitchenham [1], particular care has to be taken with a proper selection process to identify the relevant literature and a well-defined and reliable classification system.

We should stress here that even though mapping studies traditionally include a step for the classification of the collected information based on the domain knowledge of experts, the working methodology adopted here avoids any such biased classification. Hence, the general steps suggested by Shepperd [2] for unbiased evidence based studies were followed. The procedures and methods for locating evidence, appraising evidence quality and evidence synthesis and interpretation for this study are explained in the following sections.

For this initial study we decided that the entity of evidence is keywords. We argue that the authors are best qualified to explain their own work based on keywords and, thus, this is an adequate starting point to analyze what topics are being researched and how they are linked to each other. Keywords may be biased by trends or explicit calls for conferences. This effect should be considered when interpreting the results. In upcoming works, the analysis is planned to be extended to abstracts or even full paper texts, rather than keywords only; those efforts would more precisely reveal the publications' contents.

4.1 Paper Selection

Paper selection was conducted in three steps. First, a set of selection criteria was established and appropriate databases were searched for relevant papers. The duplicates from different sources were identified and eliminated in the second step. In the third and final selection step, the publication guidelines of the corresponding journals and conferences of all the remaining papers were checked to assure an acceptable scientific standard. These criteria include a neutral (not vendor-influenced) publisher and a peer-review process.

The following selection criteria were used for paper selection:

1. Must be in English;
2. Must have an abstract;
3. Must have keywords[1];
4. Must have a date (at least the year) of publication;
5. Paper must be published between 1.1.2005 and 31.12.2014;
6. Must have PLM or *Product Lifecycle Management* (or any alternative spelling such as Product life-cycle management) in the title, keywords, abstract, or title of the proceedings or journal; and
7. Paper must be peer reviewed in a conference or a journal.

Criteria 6 implies that all papers included in our work could be said to be 'PLM-tagged research'. Hence, papers that could have otherwise been classified as belonging to PLM because of their content, such as, for example, 'collaboration and interoperability in product development', were not included if they were not PLM-tagged by their authors. As a consequence, all publications included in our analysis are considered as PLM-related by their authors. This is consistent with our intent to delineate the nature of PLM research.

Papers for this study were selected from four sources:

- International Journal of Product Lifecycle Management (IJPLM);
- Product Lifecycle Management International Conference (PLM IC);
- Web of Science and Science Direct – These databases are two of the largest database for scientific publications.

It can be emphasized that all the papers from the IJPLM and PLM IC satisfy all our criteria, even when a paper does not use PLM in its title or keywords. In addition, keywords added by editors had to be removed for our study, since our hypothesis is based on author's keywords.

4.2 Appraising and Improving Data Quality

Several steps were taken so as to appraise and improve the quality of our data. As mentioned above, we tried to execute these steps with a minimum of bias. Initially all records were captured into Zotero as a common literature database, where we could identify (and eliminate) duplicates. Next, data exporting was done in order to process the data. Finally, the processed data was merged into the final database with a schema that supports our analysis. The merging and creation of the final database was done

[1] About 60 papers published by ASME were not included because no keywords were available.

automatically by an algorithm developed for that purpose. This algorithm follows the rules identified during the steps of metadata alignment, data enrichment and keyword normalization, as explained below. The automation of this process allows the full process to be repeated in the future, so as to easily include new publications and keep our database up to date.

The most critical step was normalization. The journal and proceedings names, and most importantly, the keywords had to be transferred into a normalized form. This transformation included some interpretation by the authors. However, we conducted this step following a clear set of rules.

- **Metadata alignment** - Metadata from the different sources needed to be aligned, so that equivalent fields of different records have the same meaning, such as, for example, a journal's name or the name of a conference.
- **Metadata enrichment** - Since we aimed to offer a geographic perspective to our data, the publications needed geo location. Hence, each publication was tagged by the country of the first author's institution.
- **Normalization** – A critical step in our analysis was the normalization: Each keyword was translated into a normalized form, so that keywords with the same meaning are unique. We needed to select and apply some rules for this process, including:
  - American English is chosen over Britain English (e.g. 'modelling' is normalized to 'modeling', 'visualisation' to 'visualization', etc.);
  - Plurals become singular except when a word is usually used in plural, such as 'logistics';
  - Lifecycle is always written as one word.

Particular care was spent on acronyms. The same acronym can have different meanings, and tracing back from the acronym to the correct keyword led at least to searching through a paper's abstract.

4.3 Synthesis and Interpretation

An efficient method with which to present aggregated data from different perspectives and at different levels is necessary to allow its interpretation. At this stage we decided on three main perspectives: geographic distribution, a co-occurrence based keyword graph, and the trends of keywords based on their 10 years' of history.

Geographic Distribution. As mentioned above, during data quality improvement, we added a country of origin to each publication, according to first author affiliation. Hence, we can provide histograms showing the evolution of the number of publications per year per country over the selected ten-year period.

Building Clusters Based on a Co-occurrence Network Co-occurrence networks are used to visualize the connections between concepts expressed by terms in text sources. In this context, co-occurrence is defined as the paired presence of two terms in a specified unit of text. Two co-occurring terms can be called "neighbors" and these are grouped into "neighborhoods" based on their interconnections.

In this study, two keywords become neighbors if they appear in the same publication. A co-occurrence network then helps to visualize the relationships between keywords and highlights clusters of keywords by identifying their neighborhood. As suggested by Li et al. [12], in our keyword co-occurrence network each keyword is represented by a node. The size of a node correlates to the number of total *occurrences* of a keyword in all publications. Co-occurrence relationships are represented as edges; hence the number of co-occurrences of a given pair of keywords influences the *weight* of this edge. McSweeney [13] and the community around the graph visualization tool Gephi [14] discuss different alternatives to measuring the importance of a node in a graph. For our purpose, the most appropriate measure seems to be the *degree*. The degree corresponds to the number of edges that are attached to a node. Nodes with a high degree play a central role in the network.

To identify clusters, we decided to focus on first-level neighborhoods (all direct co-occurrences of a specific keyword). We used the ForcAtlats2 algorithm [15] to lay out our graph. However, if all nodes and edges are visualized, the graph becomes a so-called "hairball". To remove complexity from the graph and thereby reveal clusters, controlling the displayed nodes by filtering the degrees and the occurrences of nodes is essential, as shown below.

Analyzing Trends. A third perspective on the data is to extract keyword trends. The trend is retrieved by looking at the number of their occurrences per year in a histogram. The linear regression of this histogram gives us an indication about the trend of each keyword. However, the number of occurrences per year per keyword is, in many cases, rather low, so the measure of a trend by linear regression must be looked at critically. In future work, we will extend the study to abstracts or full paper texts, and so the results might be more robust.

5 Some Results and Findings

5.1 General Findings

Table 1 below summarizes the number of contributions considered in the review according to the criteria described above (peer-review, presence of keywords, etc.), and their sources. We observe that IJPLM is by far the leading PLM journal with 45% of the papers published (146 out of 326), followed by Computers in Industry with 12% (38) of the journal contributions.

The PLM International Conference series is the major scientific PLM conference with 69% (571 out of 827) of the conference papers; the second one having published only 1% (10) of these contributions.

5.2 Analysis from Geographical Data

Each of the 1153 scientific contributions was associated to the country of the first author's institution. A few observations can be made. First, France is the top contributor with 206 papers over the 2005–2014 period. Bhatt et al. made a similar

Table 1. Number of scientific contributions and their sources

Property	Figure
Number of publications	1153
Number of journals involved	63
Number of publications from journals	326
Top 3 journals	International journal of PLM (146)
	Computers in industry (38)
	Computer-aided-design (13)
Number of conferences involved	153
Number of publications from conferences	827
Top 3 conferences	International conference on PLM (571)
	CIRP design conference (10)
	International conference on digital enterprise technology (9)
Number of normalized keywords	2847

observation while considering only contributions to the PLM International Conference [3]. Germany is second with 160 contributions. Italy and China are next with 96 contributions each.

Histograms expressing the evolution of contributions by country over time (Fig. 1) suggest that scientific production from France is maintained over the ten-year period. The same could be stated for Germany and Italy, even though peaks can be observed. These peaks correspond with the country hosting the PLM IC (France 2013; Germany 2010; Italy 2007). We also note that the number of contributions from the USA seems to have decreased in the second half of the ten-year period.

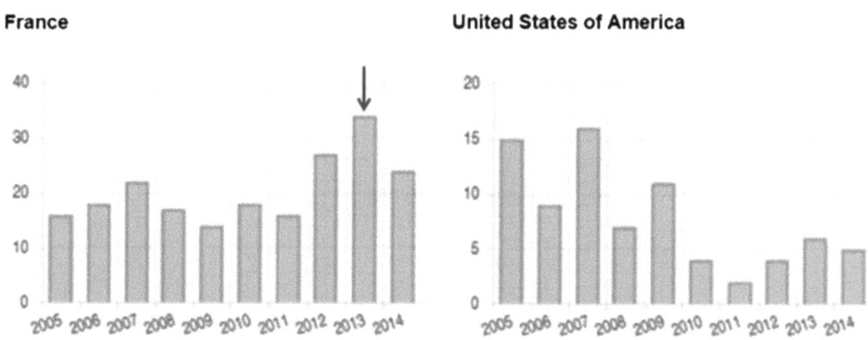

Fig. 1. Contributions by France and USA over the 2005–2014 period

5.3 PLM Themes as Revealed by Keywords

As indicated in Table 1, the 1153 papers that met our criteria used a total of 2847 normalized keywords. Figure 2 shows the distribution of the normalized keywords

Fig. 2. Distribution of normalized keywords degree

degree. The figure shows a distinct L-shape since some keywords are very common, while most of them only occur in a single paper. In fact, 2134 normalized keywords are used only once in the 1153 papers, while 713 were used more than once. Hence, it could be argued that the PLM community is spread both wide and thin.

Table 2 shows the list of the 15 top-ranking keywords, based on their degree, found in the considered literature. We should note that the Keyword *PLM* (normalized as '*product lifecycle management*') is not used by all papers; this can be deemed as reasonable for papers published via a medium dedicated to PLM (IJPLM and PLM IC) where PLM as a keyword may be considered implicit.

Table 2. Top - ranking normalized keywords and their degree

Rank	Name	Degree
1	product lifecycle management	585
2	product development	144
3	ontology	114
4	knowledge management	111
5	product data management	109
6	product design	101
7	computer aided design	101
8	interoperability	93
9	collaboration	80
10	product lifecycle	74
11	collaborative design	72
12	concurrent engineering	70
13	new product development	65
14	product lifecycle management system	58
15	lifecycle assessment	58

Considering that both *ontology* and *knowledge management* refer to **Knowledge Management**, it is reasonable to consider that this is a fundamental topic to PLM (ranks 3 and 4). In a similar manner, *product development*, *product design* and *new product development* all refer to **Product Development**, which is clearly a topic of importance to PLM (ranks 2, 6 and 13). And last and not surprisingly, *interoperability*, *collaboration*, *collaborative design* and *concurrent engineering* all refer to **Collaboration**, which is important to PLM (ranks 8, 9, 11 and 12). It can also be stated that *product data management* and *computer aided design* are two classes of tools that are central to PLM.

These top-ranking keywords describe PLM in a very generic way. Hence, keywords that appear farther down on the list are 'less obvious' and may describe second-level ideas. For example, *product lifecycle management system* (rank 14) is a subset of *product lifecycle management.* Thus, filtering out the top level keywords helps unveil the less obvious topics. This filtering is illustrated later where we show how the *computer aided design* cluster is revealed.

5.4 PLM Trends as Revealed by Keyword Evolution Over Time

Having collected the occurrences of each keyword over the ten-year period, it is possible to detect trendy keywords (or rising stars). Among all the normalized keywords, *building information modeling* is the one with the highest slope and is, hence, the top rising star of PLM. This can be explained by the fact that special sessions on BIM were organized at PLM IC in 2013 and 2014, which basically indicates that the PLM community now includes BIM within its perimeter of interest (Fig. 3).

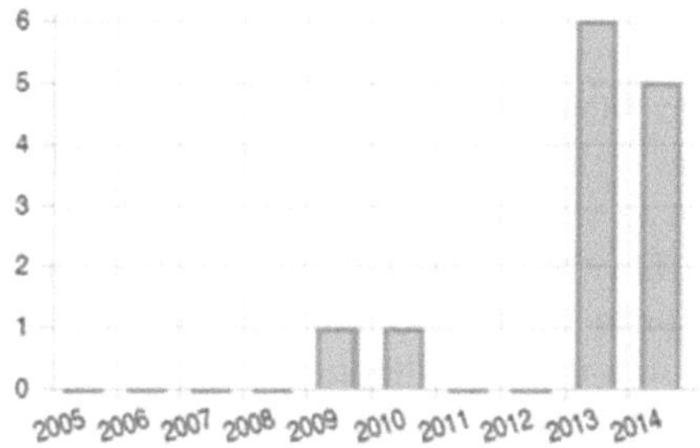

Fig. 3. Occurrences of *Building Information Modeling* as a keyword

Besides, neither *Industry 4.0* nor *Industrie 4.0* appears amongst the keywords. *Internet of things* appears once a year from 2011 to 2014, for a total of four occurrences.

5.5 PLM Clusters as Revealed by Keywords Co-occurrences

The normalized keywords collected from the selected papers were analyzed for co-occurrences. Keywords do co-occur if they are used by a given paper. Co-occurrences naturally lead to clusters of usually associated keywords. Figure 4 shows the 'hairball' corresponding to all 713 normalized keywords with at least 2 occurrences, and the

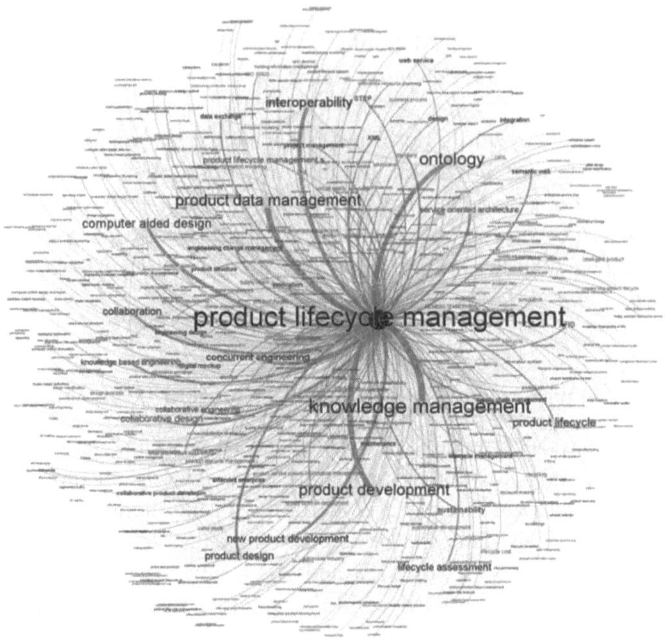

Fig. 4. The PLM graph ('hairball') of keywords co-occurrences

connections between them. Major PLM clusters are revealed by the thickness of the edge between a pair of nodes as well as the size of the fonts used to display the keywords.

Further filtering helps to reveal clusters. For example, Fig. 5 shows the keywords with a degree less than 102 (which serves to hide the five top keywords from Table 2) and an occurrence superior to 10. This tool reveals the clusters of keywords associated with a specific one. The first-level neighbors of *computer aided design* are displayed, hence revealing the CAD cluster. Interestingly, but not surprisingly, this cluster includes *STEP*, *digital mockup*, *data exchange*, *collaboration* and *product design*, amongst others.

Figure 6 shows the cluster around *building information modeling*, previously identified as a rising star. This cluster reveals that *building information management* has a strong connection with *building information modeling*, and that *digital mockup* is connected with *maintenance* (but not with design), suggesting that the considered scientific literature sees *digital mockup* as a tool for *building maintenance*, but that using digital mockups for building design is not explored. Of course, the reader should remember that the BIM literature surveyed here is limited to a small number of papers that were PLM-tagged so as to be included in our work. Hence, this cluster tells a story about BIM/PLM research, one that would probably differ if based on 'pure' BIM literature.

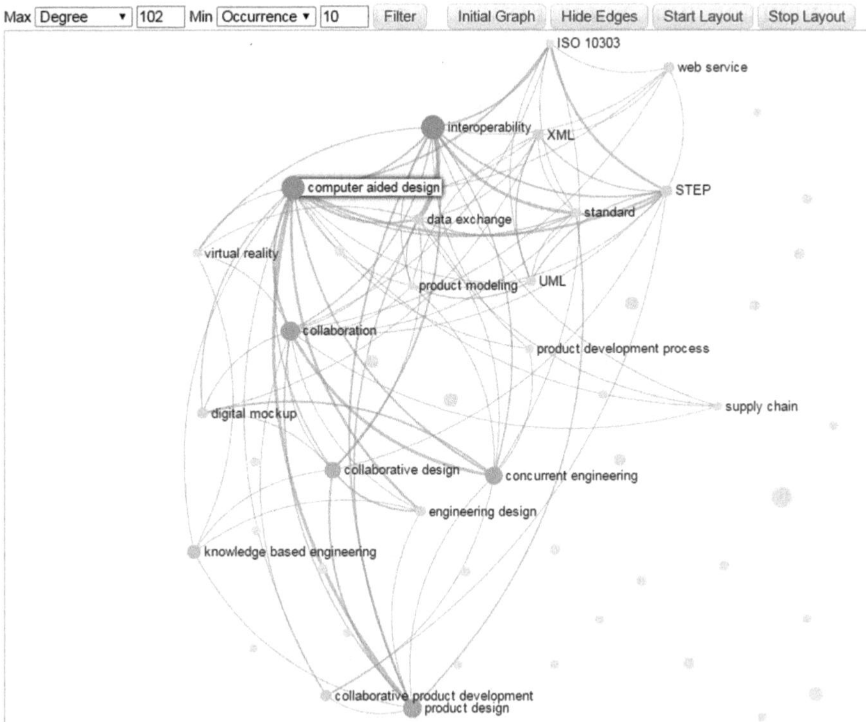

Fig. 5. *Computer aided design* cluster of keywords

Fig. 6. *Building information modeling* cluster of keywords

6 Conclusion and Some Future Work

This paper presents a method to analyze a large corpus of 10 years of scientific publications in order to characterize PLM. The 1153 publications included in this corpus were filtered according to a list of criteria, such as peer-review. The proposed approach builds on keywords selected by the authors of these publications. These keywords were normalized to limit variations due to American or British English, and so on. That process yielded a total of 2847 normalized keywords, 2134 of them used only once. It can be concluded from these numbers, and from the L-shape distribution of the normalized keywords, that PLM as a research domain has a coverage that is both wide and thin. It would be interesting to conduct similar analysis on other research domains so as to compare the distribution of keywords.

Characterizing PLM through normalized keywords also allows to observe the evolution of keywords over a ten-year period, and to identify the keywords that are gaining or declining in popularity. The data clearly shows, for example, that 'building information modeling' is now being considered as a part of PLM by its community of researchers.

The presented work also used the co-occurrences of keywords in a given paper so as to capture relations between keywords. If multiple papers use the same pair of normalized keywords, the intensity of this relation is reflected in this association. We are therefore able to identify keywords that belong to the same cluster as well as the intensity of the pairs within clusters. In future work we will characterize clusters related to any significant keyword and even compare clusters. We can even envision characterizing the evolution of clusters over time.

One challenge of the selected approach is that the number of occurrences of keywords is low and hence compromises the statistics and trends. However, this limitation could be overcome by conducting a similar analysis of abstracts and even full-text analyses. Amongst the other steps of this ongoing project, publications from 2015 will be added, and the graphic analysis tools will eventually be made available to colleagues through a dedicated website.

References

1. Kitchenham, B.A., Budgen, D., Brereton, P.: The value of mapping studies: a participant-observer case study. In: Proceedings of the 14th International Conference on Evaluation and Assessment in Software Engineering, British Computer Society (2010)
2. Shepperd, M.: Combining evidence and meta-analysis in software engineering. In: Lucia, A., Ferrucci, F. (eds.) ISSSE 2009-2011. LNCS, vol. 7171, pp. 46–70. Springer, Heidelberg (2013). doi:10.1007/978-3-642-36054-1_2
3. Bhatt, S., Tseng, F.H., Maranzana, N., Segonds, F.: Scientometric study of product lifecycle management international conferences: a decade overview. In: Bouras, A., Eynard, B., Foufou, S., Thoben, K.-D. (eds.) PLM 2015. IAICT, vol. 467, pp. 672–683. Springer, Heidelberg (2016). doi:10.1007/978-3-319-33111-9_61

4. Varandas Junior, A., Miguel, P.A.C., Carvalho, M.M., Zancul, E.S.: Product life cycle management and product development: bibliometric analysis and literature classification. Production **25**(3), 510–528 (2015). (São Paulo)
5. Nappi, V., Rozenfeld, H.: Sustainability performance indicators for product lifecycle management. In: 22nd International Congress of Mechanical Engineering (COBEM) (2013)
6. Mas, F., Arista, R., Oliva, M., Hiebert, B., Gilkerson, I., Rios, J.: A review of PLM impact on US and EU aerospace industry. Procedia Eng. **132**, 1053–1060 (2015)
7. Cao, H., Folan, P.: Product life cycle: the evolution of a paradigm and literature review from 1950–2009. Prod. Plan. Control Manag. Oper. **23**(8), 641–662 (2012)
8. Ming, X.G., Lu, W.F., Yan, J.Q., Ma, D.Z.: Towards collaborative innovation via product lifecycle management (PLM): status review and technology trend. In: ASME 2005 International Design Engineering Technical Conferences and Computers and Information in Engineering Conference (2005)
9. Laumond, J.P.: Motion planning for PLM: state of the art and perspectives. Int. J. Product Lifecycle Manag. (IJPLM) **1**(2), 129–142 (2006)
10. Antti, P., Rissanen, N., Vainio, V.: PLM state of the practice and future challenges in globally networked manufacturing companies. In: The 1st PDM Forum for Finland-Russia Collaboration, Lappeenranta (2013)
11. Terzi, S., Bouras, A., Dutta, D., Garetti, M., Kiritsis, D.: Product lifecycle management – from its history to its new role. IJPLM **4**(4), 360–389 (2010)
12. Li, H., An, H., Wang, Y., Huang, J., Gao, X.: Evolutionary features of academic articles co-keyword network and keywords co-occurrence network: based on two-mode affiliation network. Physica A: Stat. Mech. Appl. **450**, 657–669 (2016)
13. McSweeney, P.J.: Gephi network statistics. In: Google Summer of Code 2009 Project Proposal (2009)
14. Heymann, S.: Gephi Statistics. https://github.com/gephi/gephi/wiki/Statistics. Accessed 23 Feb 2016
15. Jacomy, M., Venturini, T., Heymann, S., Bastian, M.: ForceAtlas2, a continuous graph layout algorithm for handy network visualization designed for the Gephi software. PLoS ONE **9**(6), e98679 (2014). doi:10.1371/journal.pone.0098679

Performance Analysis of CyberManufacturing Systems: A Simulation Study

Zhengyi Song and Young B. Moon(✉)

Department of Mechanical and Aerospace Engineering, Syracuse University, Syracuse, USA
{zsong04,ybmoon}@syr.edu

Abstract. CyberManufacturing System (CMS) is an advanced vision for future manufacturing where physical components are fully integrated and seamlessly networked with computational processes, forming an on-demand, intelligent and communicative manufacturing resource and capability repository with optimal, sustainability-oriented manufacturing solutions. CMS utilizes recent developments in Internet of Things, Cloud Computing, Fog Computing, Service-Oriented Technologies, etc. Manufacturing resources and capabilities can be encapsulated, registered and connected to each other directly or through the Internet, thus enabling intelligent behaviors of manufacturing components and systems such as self-awareness, self-prediction, self-optimization, and self-configuration among others. This research presents a definition of CMS, an architecture and unique functions of CMS, and performance analysis of CMS using simulation models. Five examples have been developed and used for illustration and validation of CMS. The results show significant improvement in enhanced functionality and cooperative performance.

Keywords: CyberManufacturing System · Cloud Manufacturing · Cyber-Physical System · Modeling and Simulation

1 Introduction

CyberManufacturing System is a vision for future manufacturing where physical components are fully integrated and seamlessly networked with computational processes, forming an on-demand, intelligent and communicative manufacturing resource and capability repository with optimal, sustainability-oriented manufacturing solutions. By leveraging recent developments in Internet of Things, Cloud Computing, Fog Computing, Cyber-Physical System, Service-Oriented Technologies, Modeling and Simulation, Virtual Reality, Embedded Systems, Sensor Networks, Wireless Communications, Machine Learning, Data Analytics, Advanced Manufacturing Processes, etc., CMS performs as a convergence of promising and advanced Information and Communication Technologies. Particularly, Cyber-Physical System helps CMS enable manufacturing resources and capabilities to be sensed and connected to each other offline or online (Fig. 1).

Among the previous implemented manufacturing systems, FMS (Flexible Manufacturing System) consists of CNC machines connected by automated material-handling

R. Harik et al. (Eds.): PLM 2016, IFIP AICT 492, pp. 592–605, 2016.
DOI: 10.1007/978-3-319-54660-5_53

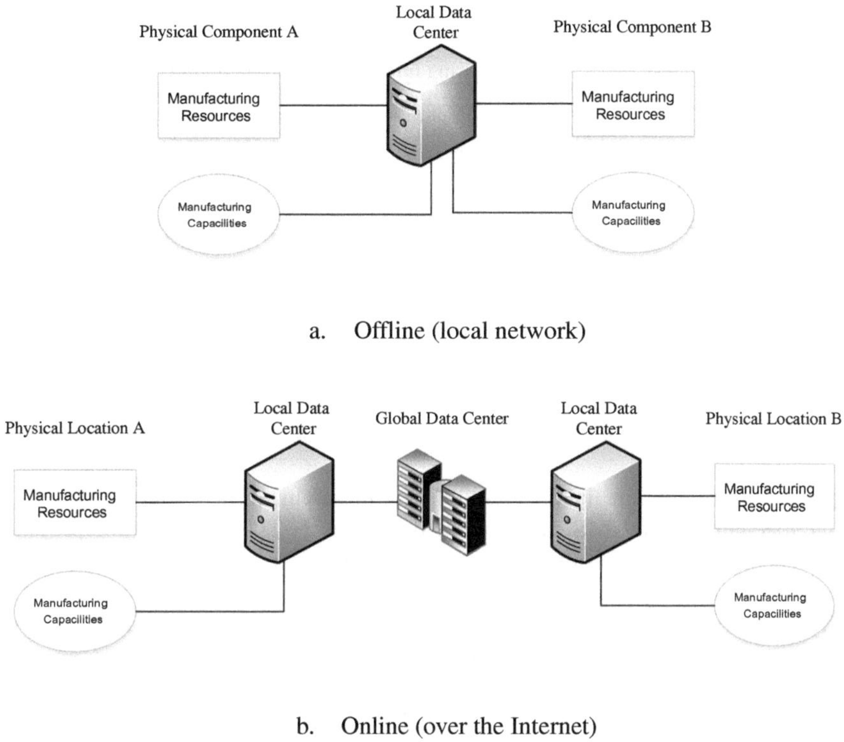

Fig. 1. CMS network

system, controlled by computer to create an integrated system for processing palletized parts across various work stations in the systems [1]. However, the design of FMSs, which is based on the machines tools and technological components available on-site, restricts the variety of the parts to be manufactured [2], whereas CMS coordinates a pool of potentially unlimited shared, reconfigurable and scalable manufacturing resources and capabilities. Furthermore, in FMS, the automation and flexibility in control are not designed to utilize recent developments in big data analytics.

In the environment of CMS, manufacturing components and systems operate in an intelligent way and own functions such as self-awareness, self-prediction, self-optimization, and self-configuration. Various initiatives in different countries have been created to reflect and recognize this future vision, including "*Industrie 4.0*" by Germany [3], "*Monozukuri*" by Japan [4], "*Factories of the Future*" by EU [5], and "*Industrial Internet*" by GE [6].

CMS integrates complete information of product life cycle activities and manufacturing component activities by harnessing and taking advantage of the development of advanced communication and sensor techniques. CMS possesses useful characteristics such as service-orientated manufacturing, proactive and preventive maintenance (Table 1).

Table 1. Supporting techniques, information coverage and characteristics of CMS

Support Techniques	Manufacturing Information	CMS Service Characteristics
Sensor Network	Product Lifecycle Activities	Service-orientated Manufacturing
Embedded Systems	Opportunity Identification	Virtual Manufacturing
Virtual Realty	Concept Development	Real Time Simulation
Modeling and Simulation	Manufacturing Processes	Networked Manufacturing System
Fog Computing	Inventory Design	Proactive and Preventive Maintenance
Cloud Computing	Supply Chain Management…	Energy Management
Data Mining and Analytics	Manufacturing Component Activities	Fleet Tracking
Machine Learning	Manufacturing Operations	Supply Optimization
Advanced Manufacturing Processes	Availability	Prediction and Clustering
Service-orientated Technologies	Planned Maintenance	
	Product Quality…	

2 Architecture of CMS

The proposed architecture in this section is a hierarchical structure for showing the internal mechanism of CMS, as illustrated in Fig. 2. This architecture provides as step-by-step guidance for companies or manufacturers to set up CMSs or migrate to CMSs from current manufacturing systems. In this architecture, the both ends of CMS - the physical provider layer and application/user layer - possess less fixed components and structure but more adaptability. However, the intermediate layers - core services layer - stay in a steady state and only vary by adding or removing storage or computing power. Additional intermediate or supporting components or layers can be added to the structure based on the business needs, user requirements or research emphases.

This architecture consists of five layers, mainly divided by the substances, pivotal activities and major enabling techniques within each layer. Interlinked relationships between layers also show all the possible interactive activities and information or material flow across layers. By organizing the manufacturing resources and capabilities and linking them by informational components following the proposed architecture, a CMS can thus be established and generates expected benefits.

2.1 Application/User Layer

This layer is intended to directly communicate with the users, including product developer, designer and consumers. Product development and manufacturing missions are two main issues to be addressed in this layer, depending on different phases of product life cycle. These tasks and missions are published to the application interface layer and a list of favorable solutions with auxiliary information or finished products will be returned or delivered for selection or picked up by the users, respectively.

2.2 Application Interface Layer

This layer plays a connecting role between application/user layer and core service layer, acting as a buffer of inventory and information processing. If the mission

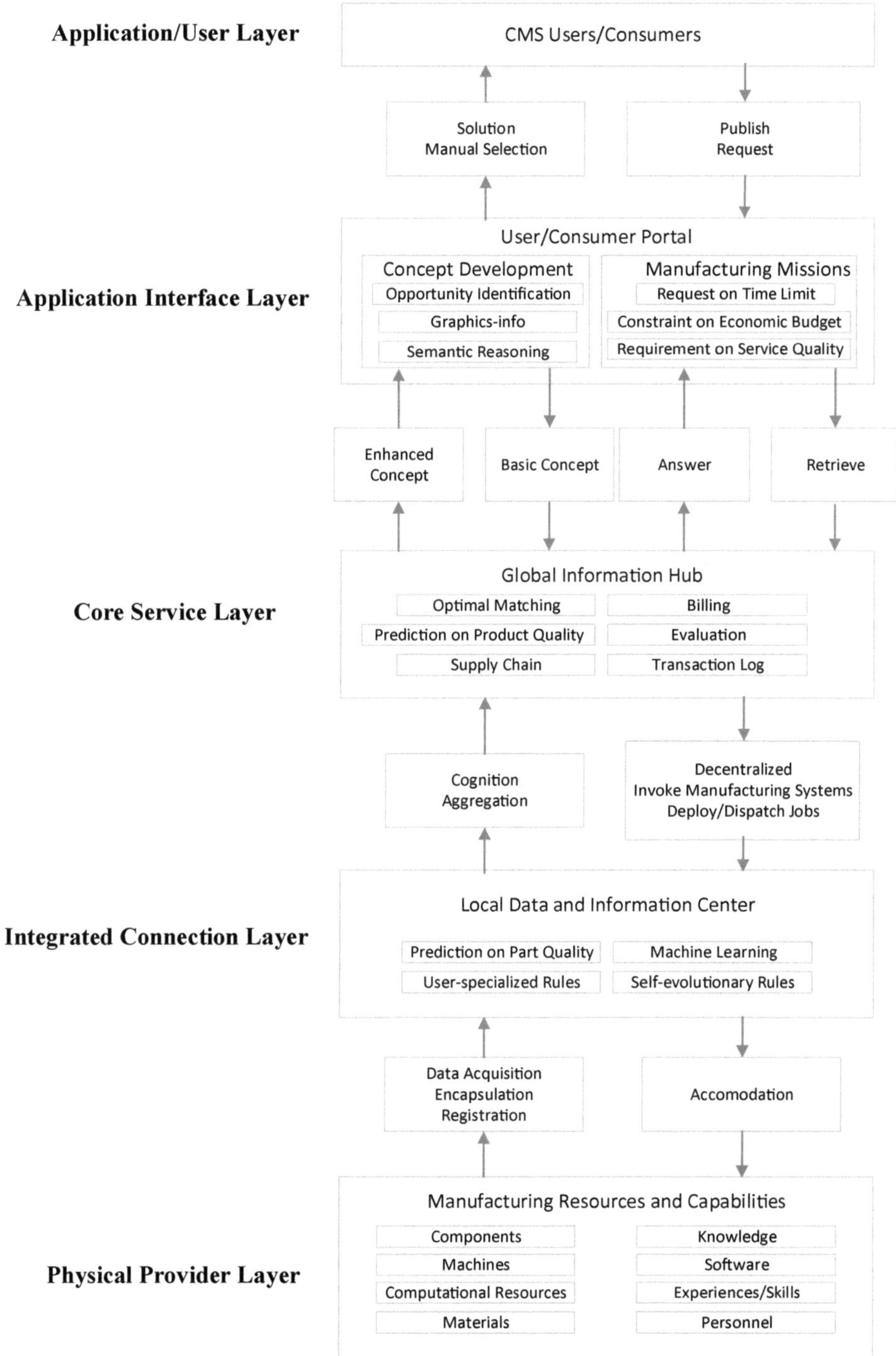

Fig. 2. CMS hierarchical architecture

required from application/user Layer originates from the concept developing stage, opportunities will first be identified. After that, information will be extracted if the opportunity is estimated feasible. Initial concept will be formed and then iterated and enhanced. Similarly, during the manufacturing stage, manufacturing mission will be described, digitalized for quoting and answering, bargaining, and then supervised by manufacturing processes virtualization and visualization.

2.3 Global Core Service Layer

In this layer, a global information hub with powerful storage and computation capability aggregates all the information of registered products' life cycle activities and manufacturing units in the cyber system, together with logistics information and transaction log by utilizing big data analytics technique [7]. The main function of this layer is to optimally evaluate and match manufacturing resources and capabilities along the fleet, record manufacturing behaviors and transaction activities in a global scale, where CMS adopts the mechanism of Network Manufacturing and Manufacturing Grid.

2.4 Integrated Connection Layer

Integrated connection layer serves as the local analysis and self-control center. The main activity of this layer is the encapsulation of physical manufacturing units of factory floor into meaningful information. Compared with the fully global control implemented in Cloud Manufacturing, the existence of this layer of hierarchically controlling helps avoiding the unnecessary trivial communication and controlling of the units in factory units over the cyber informational center, which significantly improves the response speed and communication efficiency. By forming a local self-control manufacturing system, manufacturing units' accommodation, job dispatch and quality prediction will become faster and more accurate. Furthermore, supervisory self-control rules and parameters will initially be set by human but will perform self-evolutionarily according to the information learnt by data acquisition from physical provider layer in sequencing system control.

2.5 Physical Provider Layer

Physical provider layer is for all manufacturing components, equipment and personnel in a factory level. The conditions of each manufacturing units might be directly measured by diverse sensors, like presence sensor and RFID, or obtained from controller or enterprise manufacturing systems, such as ERP, MES, SCM and CMM [8, 9]. This advanced sensor deployment is the infrastructure of this layer and control activities are operated by actuators executed by the signal feedback from local data and self-control center.

3 Functions of CMS

A CMS exhibits five important functions that represent all the behaviors and characteristics (Table 2). The numbering sequence is based on the implementation layer where a function is enabled. Starting from 1st to 5th, the function is moving toward core service layer and becomes more accessible to big data analytics and utilizing machine learning algorithm. Real-time acquisition, big data analytics, useful information elicitation, behavior learning, prediction and physical actuation enable all the five functions. These five functions of CMS integrate the manufacturing activities and provide a step-by-step guideline for executing CMS.

Table 2. Main enabling techniques, main benefits and main applications of five functions

Functions	Main enabling technique	Main benefits	Main application
1. Self-monitoring	Monitoring system; sensor deployment	Reduce WIP inventory; increase productivity	Machine failure; fluctuation in customer's demands; assembly recipe missing
2. Self-awareness	Expert-defined rule; user-defined rule; controller parameter	Save mode switching time	Switch of the working modes of the manufacturing components
3. Self-prediction	Advanced sensor deployment; adaptive machine learning algorithm	Increase of product quality; decrease of finish time; decrease of waiting time	Products with high quality requirement; products in large batch size and of tool-consuming
4. Self-optimization	Cloud-based data analytics	Reduce finish time	Products with requirement on manufacturing finish time
5. Self-configuration	Sensor deployment; manufacturing missions description framework	Increase the utilization of manufacturing components in factory floor	Machine in low occupation but with high cost in setup

4 CMS Functions in Life Cycle of Product

The above five CMS functions are implemented in different stages in product life cycle. Self-prediction comes firstly in aggregating resource and allocation of manufacturing jobs. Then self-optimization provides optimal matching of manufacturing units and self-configuration enables waiting missions ready but this function is actually implemented in later manufacturing phase. Self-awareness will be ready for any modification of the working mode of local manufacturing resources and capabilities clusters. Finally, self-monitoring will supervise the functions of all the solution arrangements in the lowest level and latest phase. The working phases of CMS for each function are shown in Fig. 3.

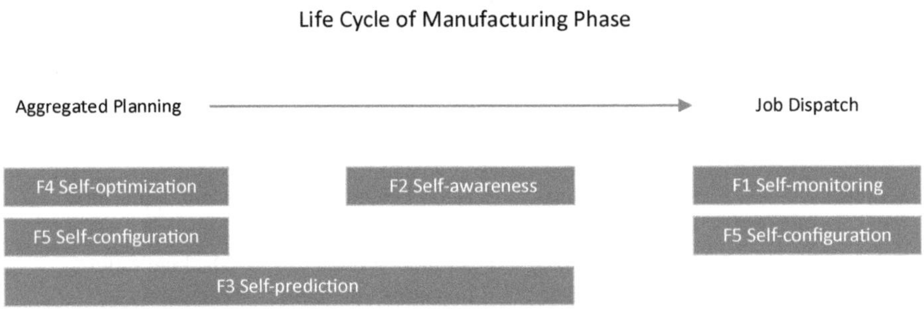

Fig. 3. Working phase of CMS function in product life cycle

5 CMS Performance Research

In order to quantitatively and comprehensively evaluate the performance of CMS, performance evaluation and behavior studying of CMS have been conducted.

5.1 Simulation-Based Evaluation

Simulation is a powerful tool in studying various complex manufacturing systems by mimicking the real system and exploring scenarios, and thus can be used to evaluate manufacturing system solutions, concepts and scenarios before implementing them in actual world [10, 11]. Various simulation tools can be used to support manufacturing system operation through data-driven decision making. Simulation studies generate data in cycle time, throughput, WIP inventory and bottleneck position. Their results can be used for physical layout design of factory floor, control policies, scheduling and routing strategy, diagnosis and other system configurations of manufacturing systems, and corresponding post what-if analysis for optimization.

Among various simulation methods, Agent-based Modeling and Simulation (ABMS), Discrete-Event Modeling and Simulation (DEMS) and System Dynamics Modeling and Simulation (SDMS) are commonly used. Among them, DEMS provides a dynamic simulation on the servicing time, utilization and bottleneck identification, which provides manufacturing system performance evaluation. Based on that, a combination of DEMS and other analysis tools can provide a broader view, more holistic and comprehensive approach with finer resolution of the results of manufacturing systems' performance. This combination has been applied in the implementation for seeking solution or detecting bottlenecks on current manufacturing systems [12, 13]. Furthermore, CMS is currently only a vision and thus has not been fully realized in industry field yet. Therefore, simulation approach is considered most appropriate and qualified method.

5.2 Examples

In this section, hypothetical examples with different scenarios are used to capture the performance in each phase along manufacturing activities. Simple but representative products, a plastic storage box, a shaft for gear box and a drone, are selected to illustrate the performance of implementation of each function. The manufacturing processes of the storage box are shown in Fig. 4. The bill of material of the plastic box, shaft and drone are shown in Tables 3, 4 and 5, respectively. Processing time of manufacturing a drone is given after that, and the information partially from the paper [14]. The processing time is estimated by *WILLIT 3D PRINT* and the transfer time is estimated by *GOOGLE MAP*. Both are open source applications.

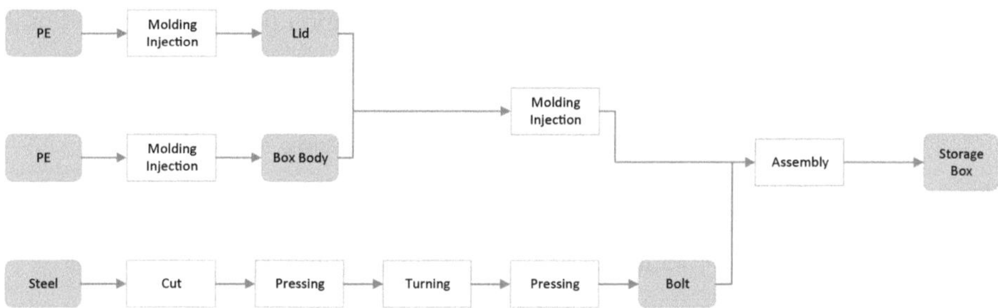

Fig. 4. Manufacturing processes of storage box

Table 3. BOM of the storage box

Name	Material	Number	Weight	Total weight
Lid	PE	1	0.033 kg	0.033 kg
Box body	PE	1	0.012 kg	0.012 kg
Bolt	steel	4	0.002 kg	0.008 kg
Assembly	PE 0.45 kg; steel 0.008 kg			

Table 4. BOM of the shaft and support information

Name	Material	Batch size	Roughness requirement	Total weight
Shaft	Steel	8000	3.6 μm	0.004 kg

Table 5. Bill of material of drone

Part	Dimension	Processing time	Number
Propeller	160 × 4	20 min	4
Legs	10 × 4	15 min	4
Arm	90 × 4	15 min	4
Frame body	35 × 1	2 h	1
Shield	35 × 1	20 min	1
Frame body bottom	60 × 1	15 min	1
Gimbal	–	2 h	1
Outsourced part assembly	Assembly other parts	Assembly time	Number
Motor	12 h	15 min	4
Navigation board	18 h	10 min	1
Main board	18 h	10 min	1
Camera	18 h	10 min	1
Batteries	20 h	6 min	1
Control board	20 h	7.5 min	1

According to [14], the processing time and transportation time are estimated in the Table 6.

Table 6. Processing time and transportation time of drone

Process	Time or duration	Process	Time or duration
Load raw material	5 min	Transport parts to final assembly line	10 min
3D printer failure	30 min	3D printer repair	15 min
Transport assemble to warehouse	15 min	Adjust assembly line	15 min
Switch to assembly other products	15 min	Transport assembly to customer	10 h

Based on the manufacturing information of above three products, 5 scenarios serving for the evaluation of each function are created and summarized in the Table 7.

Table 7. Hypothetical example studying summary

Functions	Examples
Self-monitoring	Example 1 failure of tapping in bolt manufacturing
Self-awareness	Example 2 set-up of threading in bolt manufacturing
Self-prediction	Example 3 turning tool remaining life prediction in shaft manufacturing
Self-optimization	Example 4 Optimization in plastic box body inspector selection
Self-configuration	Example 5 inspection of the molding injection parts

6 Result and Analysis

Table 8 shows all the simulation results based on the scenario setting in the previous chapters. Due to the limited space of this paper, the result shows the most critical indicator for measuring and evaluating the performance of each function.

Table 8. Summary of simulation result

Example	1	2	3	4	5	
Object	Box body	Bolt	Finish time	Box body	Box body	Lid
Indicator	Number In Queue	Number destroyed (productivity)	Finish time (/h)	Time in system (/s)	Number destroyed (productivity)	
Comparison	CMS – traditional	CMS – traditional	CMS – traditional	CMS – traditional	CMS – traditional	
Test	Paired-t	Paired-t	Paired-t	Paired-t	Paired-t	
Length	4 h	1 min	70 h	4 h	1 h	
Sample Size	100	100	100	100	100	
t-value	–20.845	1.3432	–301.97	–21.552	1.2189	1.42
P-value	2.2e-16	0.1823	2.2e-16	2.2e-16	0.2258	0.1587
C.I.	(–1.15, –0.95)	(–0.19 0.99)	(–27.14, –26.78)	(–20.23, –16.82)	(–5.24, 21.94)	(–4.14, 25.00)
Difference Mean	–1.05	0.4	–27	–18.53	8.35	10.43

6.1 Self-monitoring

In this example, real-time monitoring guarantees the information accurately and quickly conveying among the others components, and the action of starting or stopping of production branch in system is actuated with no delay. In this example, the average number of box body in the production system is selected for showing the performance of the system since the main benefits is to reduce the WIP inventory. Seen from the comparison results, self-monitoring brings significant decrease in waiting items. Even though the absolute storage space saved is less than 2 items, the saving in buffer or storage of the whole system will be significantly accumulated in the networked environment.

6.2 Self-awareness

In this example, the threading machine will not be ready until the arrival of first part from inspection process, from the viewpoint of traditional in-house manufacturing. Self-awareness function of CMS will save the time on set-up preparation by arousing them in advance upon the detection of coming parts. The benefit mainly shows as the increase of productivity or saving of time. The result shows the difference is not significant since the saving of preparation time or other working mode switching time of one component makes little effect compared with other uncertainties in a production line, such as downtime and stochastic processing time, etc. However, the accumulation of this time saving in production system will greatly shorten the final finishing time.

6.3 Self-prediction

In this example, prediction on tool life and avoidance on possible occurrence of tool breakdown or repair time will significantly save total manufacturing time and the unnecessary loss of tools. Manufacturing time can be used to represent the benefits. Seen from the result, a significant time saving has been achieved.

6.4 Self-optimization

Traditionally, the mission will be more likely to be evenly or randomly assigned to all the available equipment in the factory floor. In CMS, a list of available and favorable manufacturing resources will be ranked and sorted by multi-criteria specified by manufacturing tasks. A smart matching of manufacturing resources may bring either significantly increased productivity output given a fixed manufacturing time or a shorter finishing time given a batch size. Moreover, the variance brought by uncertainties in production system will be greatly reduced by real-time sensor system and dynamic optimization arrangement.

6.5 Self-configuration

In manufacturing systems, bottleneck processes usually stay in occupied status while the rest processes are always starving. For starving manufacturing components in cyber system, a list of manufacturing missions from the cyber information center are on hold and waiting to be processed, resulting in maximization of these components' utilization. In this example, the inspection worker is overqualified for only coping with inspection mission of box body. The waiting task assigned from cyber center is lid inspection. The result shows a slight increase of productivity of box body, which validates the premise that the current manufacturing mission will not be influenced. In the same time, the production line also makes accomplishment of checking 10 lids by utilizing the idle time of the inspector. The results illustrate that this function not only helps manufacturing units to fully achieve current manufacturing goals, but also makes some extra progresses in on other manufacturing missions (Fig. 5).

In order to quantify the performance change by migrating to CMS, an index system has been developed (Table 9).

According to the developed coefficients table, the improved performance can be aggregated as in the Table 10.

From the results, reduction on waiting time, inventory cost, storage space, and increase on productivity and product quality are shown as the main benefits of CMS. Even though not in the same significance level, these key performances indicators

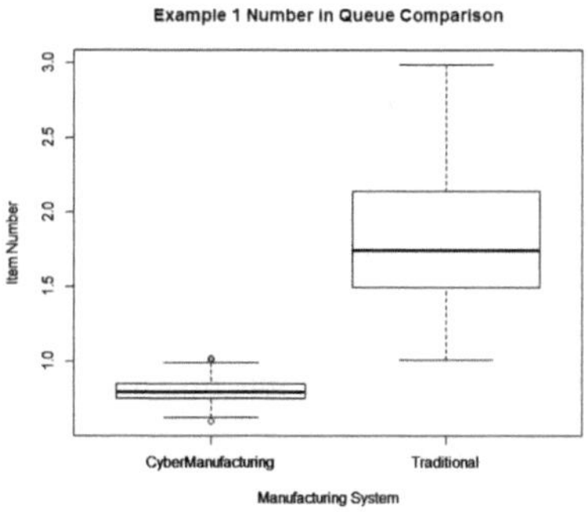

a. Example 1

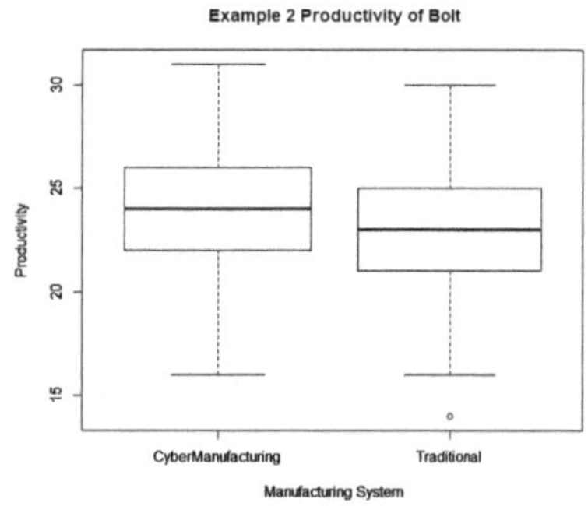

b. Example 2

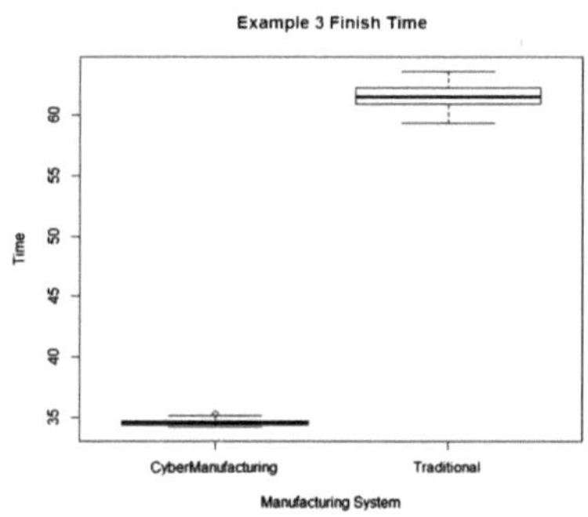

c. Example 3

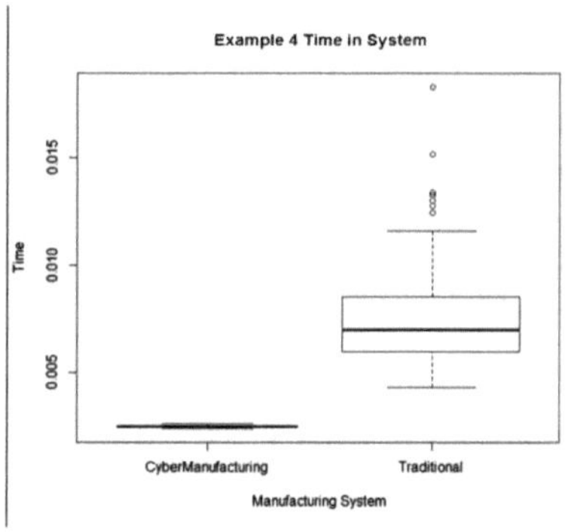

d. Example 4

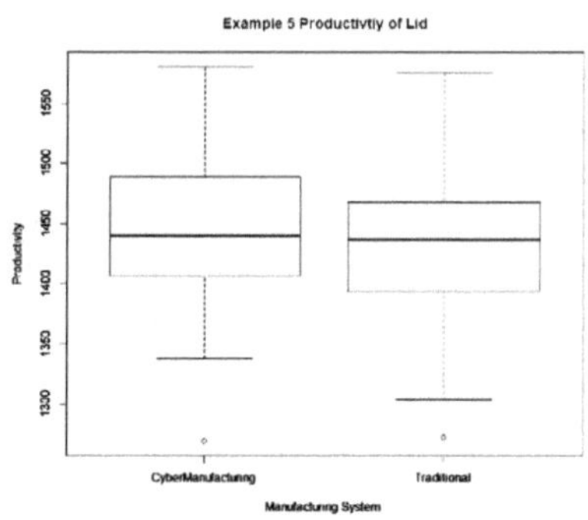

e. Example 5

Fig. 5. Simulation result boxplots

Table 9. Performance indices metrics coefficients table

	Lid	Box body	Box assembly	Bolt	Shaft
Product revenue ($\$/unit$)	P_{Lid}	$P_{Box\ Body}$	P_{Box}	P_{Bolt}	P_{Shaft}
Time cost ($\$/(s \cdot unit)$)	TC_{Lid}	$TC_{Box\ Body}$	TC_{Box}	TC_{Bolt}	TC_{Shaft}
Waiting storage space cost ($\$/unit$)	SC_{Lid}	$SC_{Box\ Body}$	SC_{Box}	SC_{Bolt}	SC_{Shaft}

Table 10. Summary of benefits by implementing CMS function in examples

Example	Function	Time length or batch size	Benefits(/$)
Ex. 1	Self-monitoring	4 h	$1.05 * SC_{BoxBody}$
Ex. 2	Self-awareness	1 min	$0.4 * P_{Bolt}$
Ex. 3	Self-prediction	8000 units	$27 * TC_{Shaft}$
Ex. 4	Self-optimization	4 h	$106560 * TC_{BoxBody}$
Ex. 5	Self-configuration	1 h	$10.43 * P_{Lid} + 8.35 * P_{BoxBody}$

measured by evaluation framework shows the change and improvement when migrating to CMS from solely in-house traditional manufacturing system. By rapid communication and adaptive behavior learning in different levels, quick accommodation, better manufacturing mission dispatch, optimal manufacturing component utilization will be achieved.

7 Discussion and Conclusion

CMS is new concept and requires additional work on its definitions and implementation details. This research covers from definition, architecture, uniqueness, functions, performance evaluation and simulation studying, forming a multi-facet, comprehensive learning on CMS. Integrating all the necessary manufacturing information, CMSs give better solution in solving the bottleneck in material and energy consumption, increase of manufacturing efficiency and pricing strategy.

This work provides explorative insights into behavior pattern and characteristics of CMS thus performance assessment with preliminary benefits analysis related with leveraging CMSs. However, more comprehensive models are needed for further studying the working pattern and whole behaviors of CMS. More work and devotion in this area will enable the CyberManufacturing to be quickly developed into a well-defined manufacturing system. This research will convince researchers of the general benefits brought by CMS and enlighten them to further and deeper pursue understanding and application of CMS.

References

1. Browne, J., Dubois, D., Rathmill, K., Sethi, S.P., Stecke, K.E.: Classification of flexible manufacturing systems. FMS Mag. **2**(2), 114–117 (1984)

2. Kusiak, A.: Application of operational research models and techniques in flexible manufacturing systems. Eur. J. Oper. Res. **24**(3), 336–345 (1986)
3. Wan, J., Cai, H., Zhou, K.: Industrie 4.0: enabling technologies. In: 2014 International Conference on Intelligent Computing and Internet of Things (ICIT), pp. 135–140. IEEE (2015)
4. Aoki, K., Staeblein, T., Tomino, T.: Monozukuri capability to address product variety: a comparison between Japanese and German automotive makers. Int. J. Prod. Econ. **147**, 373–384 (2014)
5. Mavrikios, D., Papakostas, N., Mourtzis, D., Chryssolouris, G.: On industrial learning and training for the factories of the future: a conceptual, cognitive and technology framework. J. Intell. Manuf. **24**(3), 473–485 (2013)
6. Posada, J., Toro, C., Barandiaran, I., Oyarzun, D., Stricker, D., De Amicis, R., Vallarino, I.: Visual computing as a key enabling technology for industrie 4.0 and industrial internet. IEEE Comput. Graphics Appl. **35**(2), 26–40 (2015)
7. Wu, D., Rosen, D.W., Wang, L., Schaefer, D.: Cloud-based design and manufacturing: a new paradigm in digital manufacturing and design innovation. Comput.-Aided Des. **59**, 1–14 (2015)
8. Moon, Y.B.: Enterprise Resource Planning (ERP): a review of the literature. Int. J. Manage. Enterp. Dev. **4**(3), 235–264 (2007)
9. Lee, J., Bagheri, B., Kao, H.A.: A cyber-physical systems architecture for industry 4.0-based manufacturing systems. Manuf. Lett. **3**, 18–23 (2015)
10. Boulonne, A., Johansson, B., Skoogh, A., Aufenanger, M.: Simulation data architecture for sustainable development. In: Proceedings of the 2010 Winter Simulation Conference (WSC), pp. 3435–3446. IEEE. (2010)
11. Heilala, J., Vatanen, S., Tonteri, H., Montonen, J., Lind, S., Johansson, B., Stahre, J.: Simulation-based sustainable manufacturing system design. In: Winter Simulation Conference, WSC 2008, pp. 1922–1930. IEEE (2008)
12. Widok, A.H., Schiemann, L., Jahr, P., Wohlgemuth, V.: Achieving sustainability through a combination of LCA and DES integrated in a simulation software for production processes. In: Proceedings of the Winter Simulation Conference, p. 155. Winter Simulation Conference (2012)
13. Mani, M., Johansson, B., Lyons, K.W., Sriram, R.D., Ameta, G.: Simulation and analysis for sustainable product development. Int. J. Life Cycle Assess. **18**(5), 1129–1136 (2013)
14. Wu, D., Rosen, D.W., Schaefer, D.: Scalability planning for cloud-based manufacturing systems. J. Manuf. Sci. Eng. **137**(4), 040911 (2015)

A Spatio-Temporal Product Lifecycle Network Representation

Kumari Moothedath Chandran, Amaresh Chakrabarti(✉), and Monto Mani

Centre for Product Design and Manufacturing, Indian Institute of Science, Bangalore, India
{kumari,ac123,monto}@cpdm.iisc.ernet.in

Abstract. Product lifecycle is a complex network with large supply chains from multiple organisations. Lifecycle assessment of products of organisations with globally dispersed manufacturing supply chains and international market involves various spatial and temporal constraints. Even though organisations have data of their global supply chains, data is typically stored textually as spreadsheets, or visually as process flow charts. Visual representation of this large data using flow charts makes it complex and difficult to read and interpret. A decluttered, simplified product lifecycle data representation method is presented in this paper, which is developed for use alongside an LCA tool.

Keywords: Spatio-temporal network · Product lifecycle mapping · Global manufacturing

1 Globally Dispersed Product Lifecycle

Geographically dispersed manufacturing makes the lifecycle of a product from an organisation a large network with global supply chains. Companies build or acquire manufacturing facilities in different countries based on strategic business reasons. For example, General Electric Aviation headquartered in Ohio, USA, opened a component manufacturing, service, support and sales centre in 2010 in Singapore to cater to the Asia-Pacific region as well as the international market [1]. Original Equipment Manufacturers (OEM) source around 80% of the value of the final manufactured product from outside their companies [2]. Apple iPhone manufacturing involves nine different companies from the USA, China, Korea, Japan, and Germany [3]. Hence, understanding the lifecycle of a company's product with globally dispersed manufacturing supply chain, market and service networks, involves spatial and temporal data. Decision to select manufacturing locations by companies are based on specification satisfaction, quality, cost of manufacturing, shipping costs and time, and process scheduling. Individuals—employees of companies with global manufacturing networks, component manufacturers, and material suppliers—do not have an understanding of where they stand, and how crucial the role they play is with respect to the product lifecycle network. This is not due to non-availability of information; but rather due to the complexity of information in the way it is currently stored. The following

R. Harik et al. (Eds.): PLM 2016, IFIP AICT 492, pp. 606–617, 2016.
DOI: 10.1007/978-3-319-54660-5_54

quote from Lewis E Platt, former CEO of HP illustrates this difficulty. "If HP knew what HP knows, we would be three times as profitable" [4].

Even though organisations have record of their global supply chains, these are most often stored textually in the form of spreadsheets, or visually as process flow charts. Commercially available PLM tools (e.g. Enovia, Teamcentre) store these data in the form of textual records attributed to product geometry. LCA software (e.g. SimaPro) do not capture company data, but prompts the tool user to select equivalent processes from commercially available LCA databases (e.g., Eco-invent) and displays the environmental impact values of the product. Neither PLM nor LCA tools provide a complete understanding of the product lifecycle network. A product's lifecycle with global manufacturing, distribution, use, re-use and disposal network involves geographically dispersed processes across time zones and lifecycle phases. Hence it involves spatial and temporal information of these processes. A spatio-temporal product lifecycle representation method is presented in this paper, which is developed for use alongside an LCA tool.

2 Information Visualisation in Product Lifecycle

Visualisation is the process or activity by which non-visual information is converted to a visual form [5–8]. Companies use Gantt charts and flow charts to understand process sequences and identify critical processes for project scheduling and planning purposes. These diagrams capture the temporal and sequential dependencies of processes involved. The spatial aspects are not reflected in Gantt or flow chart diagrams. For example, Gantt charts would look the same whether two sequential processes were to take place in the same location or in two different continents, as long as the duration of these processes remained the same. Flow charts do not represent actual process durations involved unlike in Gantt charts, and do not show spatial information. A process flow chart would hence appear the same, irrespective of the variations in process durations, and whether individual processes took place across the globe or in the same plant. It merely shows the sequence or processes. Such oversimplification in visualisation leaves out essential information needed for decision making by an individual. One is unable to evaluate the real world reasons for supply chain disruptions or delays - for example, a natural calamity in the location where components are manufactured; a political scenario which led to closure of a factory; an increase in cost due to local economic conditions; an environmental law which prevented the functioning of a manufacturing plant due to its emissions, etc. Such aspects involving legislations, and demand for sustainable activities are increasing the complexity of product design [9–11]. Companies in high technology industries face challenges due to product complexity and globally dispersed product design activities [9, 12].

Geographic Information System (GIS) tools in logistics (E.g. ArcGIS) map supply chain information on a two-dimensional map. An example of how such a mapping would look for the Boeing 747-8's manufacturing network is shown in Fig. 1. More information layers can be added on GIS tools over the 2D base map which would be displayed in the form of text or tables. GIS tools do not capture temporal dimensions of individual processes and their sequences like in Gantt and flow charts. However, they capture time indirectly through real time tracking for shipments.

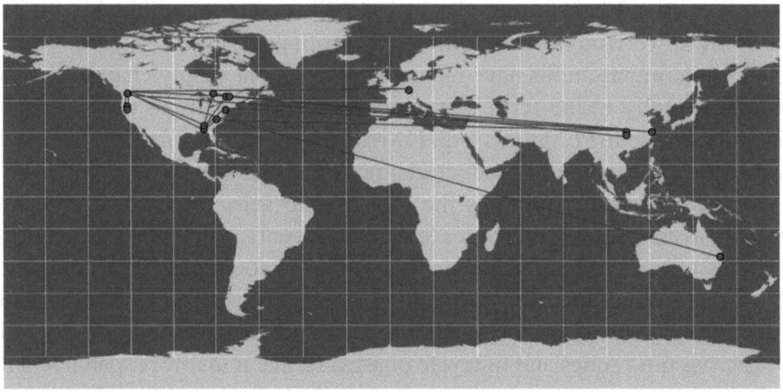

Fig. 1. Manufacturing network of Boeing 747-8. (Data sourced from a video documentary, and online sources [13]. Assumptions of locations and values are made for representation purposes.)

The Material Flow Analysis (MFA) method, which is based on material flows and mass balance of a system boundary, uses flow charts with stock quantities alongside for visual representation of data. An example of Titanium fan blade manufacturing process for Rolls-Royce Trent 1000 engines used in Boeing 787 Dreamliner is shown in Fig. 2. This diagram captures the process sequence along with stock quantities of inputs and outputs. The MFA flowchart does not provide information on locations at which the processes took place, locations from where the inputs were sourced, locations where the waste generated were disposed, and locations where the recycled stocks were used. MFA flowcharts do not provide temporal information of processes as well. Sankey diagrams and bar charts are used by LCA tools (for e.g. SimaPro) to show the environmental impact and emission values. An example of Rolls-Royce Trent 1000 engine manufacturing process is depicted in a Sankey diagram in Fig. 3. The Sankey diagram shows process-wise environmental impacts; the thicker the line, the higher the impacts are, and vice versa. This depiction is end-product focussed and does not show the spatial or temporal dependencies of the processes involved.

Other visual representations used in manufacturing and production planning and other spatio-temporal representations are reviewed elsewhere [14]. Most of these representations become complex and cluttered while representing large datasets of

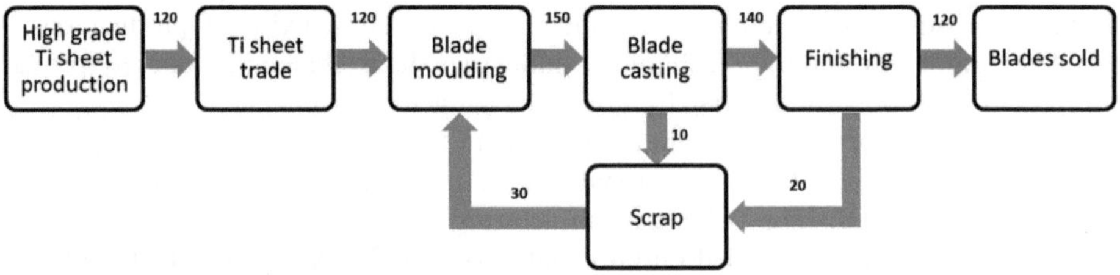

Fig. 2. Material flow of Titanium blade manufacturing process for Rolls-Royce Trent 1000 engine. (Data sourced from a video documentary, and online sources [13]. Assumptions of locations and values are made for representation purposes.)

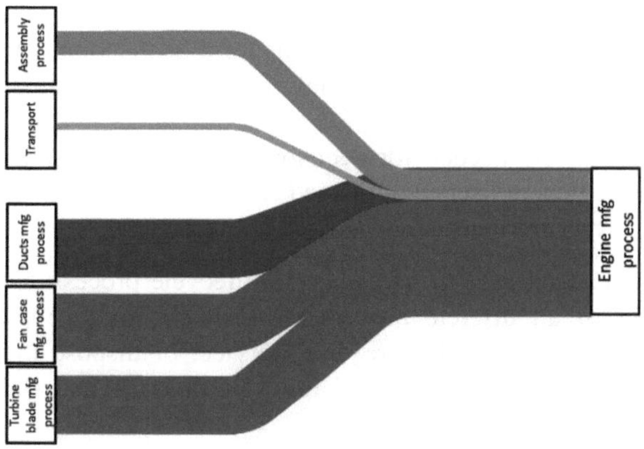

Fig. 3. Sankey diagram showing LCA results of manufacturing processes for Rolls-Royce Trent 1000 engine. (Data sourced from a video documentary, and online sources [13]. Assumptions of locations and values are made for representation purposes.)

product lifecycle information. GIS based tools when used for product lifecycle data, display many criss-crossing lines connecting locations in maps where the user cannot comprehend the entire network. MFA flowcharts if drawn for entire product lifecycle, will have many processes with arrows in different directions and stock quantities. The flowchart size will be large and a user can get confused while following the arrows going back and forth. Sankey diagram for LCA results of a product lifecycle will have large number of processes with criss-crossing lines of varying thicknesses and colours. A decluttered and simplified product lifecycle data representation method with spatial and temporal information is necessary for better understanding and decision making involved with global supply chain networks. One such representation is proposed in this paper, which is developed for use in an LCA tool.

3 Proposed Space-Time Network Method

The need for a new visual representation arose when the data of geographically dispersed manufacturing, lifecycle processes, inventories, and environmental impacts associated with them had to be analysed to aid decision making, while using an LCA tool under development for a sponsored project from industry. Potential first tier end users of the tool include design engineers, department heads, project managers, R&D personnel and top-management. Second tier end users of the LCA tool would be component manufacturers, suppliers, partnering companies for sub-assembly manufacturing. The LCA results would be used for discussions with end users in order to optimize a product's global supply chain network for reducing environmental impacts. These results would also be useful in discussions with third tier users, e.g. factory floor employees. Since geographically dispersed supply chain involves working with people from different countries, the challenges involved with this are: (a) the data and results must be easy to comprehend for people from varying educational backgrounds; (b) it should be readable irrespective of linguistic barriers across regions; (c) compatibility of the data representation method for use in print form at locations or situations where there are no computers or devices to display the data, such as small-scale manufacturing units in developing countries.

The information layers needed for decision-making were arrived at based on the information the three tiers of users would need and how the challenges described above can be overcome. The information needed are as follows:

(a) *Lifecycle processes and their sequence:* A lifecycle process sequence is defined here as a set of all discrete processes which should take place in a desired sequence in order to manufacture, use, service, or dispose the product. It is a superset of processes involved in all lifecycle phases—material, manufacturing, assembly, transport, use, re-use/disposal.
(b) *Spatial and temporal information of lifecycle processes:* Spatial information includes locations of lifecycle processes—city and country names, or geographic co-ordinates. Temporal information includes durations of each process.
(c) *Inputs and Outputs for each lifecycle process:* Inputs and outputs include material, energy and information, e.g. material resources, products, electricity, fuels and lubricants.
(d) *Equipment and People:* Equipment are machinery involved in order to carry out a process. For e.g., large machines, computing, sensing and testing devices, and transport devices such as trolleys, cranes, and automobiles.
(e) *LCA results:* LCA results can be in the form of single point values or ranges for each process involved.

A new representation named Space-Time Network (STN) Method was designed based on the objectives and the information to be represented. Figure 4 describes the

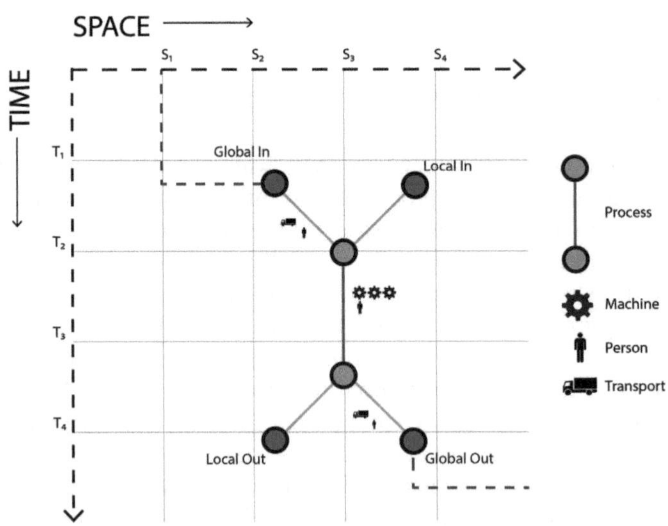

Fig. 4. Basic elements of a Space-Time Network Graph

basic elements of STN method. The STN method uses an inverted graph to plot space along the x-axis, and time along the inverted y-axis. The unit of x-axis are the geographic co-ordinates of the locations involved. Every unique geographic co-ordinate value is allotted one unit position in the x-axis. The order of placing the locations is based on the West to East - North to South Rule (WENS Rule) explained below:

1. Successive positions in the x-axis from left to right in the STN graph will be allotted in the order of appearance of the longitude values from West to East in a world map.
2. If two or more geographic co-ordinates have the same longitude value, the successive positions in the x-axis from left to right will be allotted in the order of appearance of latitude values from North to South in a world map.

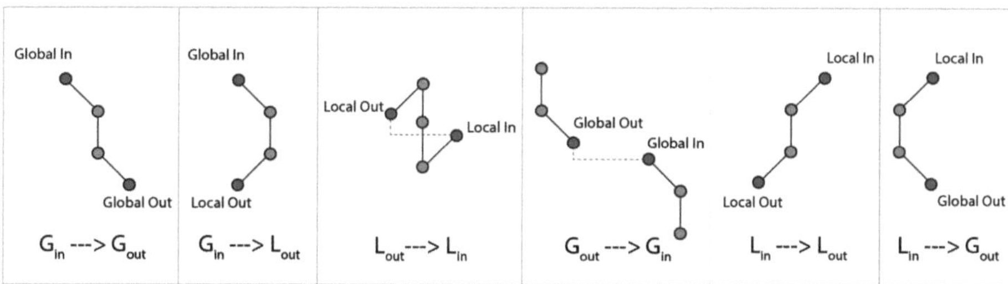

Fig. 5. Possible combinations of input-output scenarios represented using connectors in STN graph

This rule makes it easier for anyone to mark the x-axis positions by just looking at a commonly used world map. A world map is used along with STN graph to map the locations from the 2D maps to the x-axis unit positions of STN graph. The example in Fig. 6 illustrates this. The WENS Rule eliminates the clutter of criss-crossing lines as observed in GIS based tools (see Fig. 1). The unit of time in STN graph can vary depending on the unit of process durations for each product lifecycle. The unit can be in seconds for a product with a shorter production time and lifecycle; it can be in days or months for products with longer production time and lifecycle. Absolute time can be used as well to represent the durations.

Each process is represented in an STN graph as a straight line with its x-axis representing the location of the process (Fig. 4). The y-axis or the length of the line signifies the duration of the process. The diagonal lines in Fig. 4 are connectors. Global connectors (Global In and Global Out) and local connectors (Local In and Local Out) are used to link process chains and material flows, between two locations and the same location respectively. The connectors are drawn as notations, and it is represented using a diagonal line of uniform length and angle with two nodes (start and end). The orientation of the connectors are different depending on the type of connector. There are four connector types:

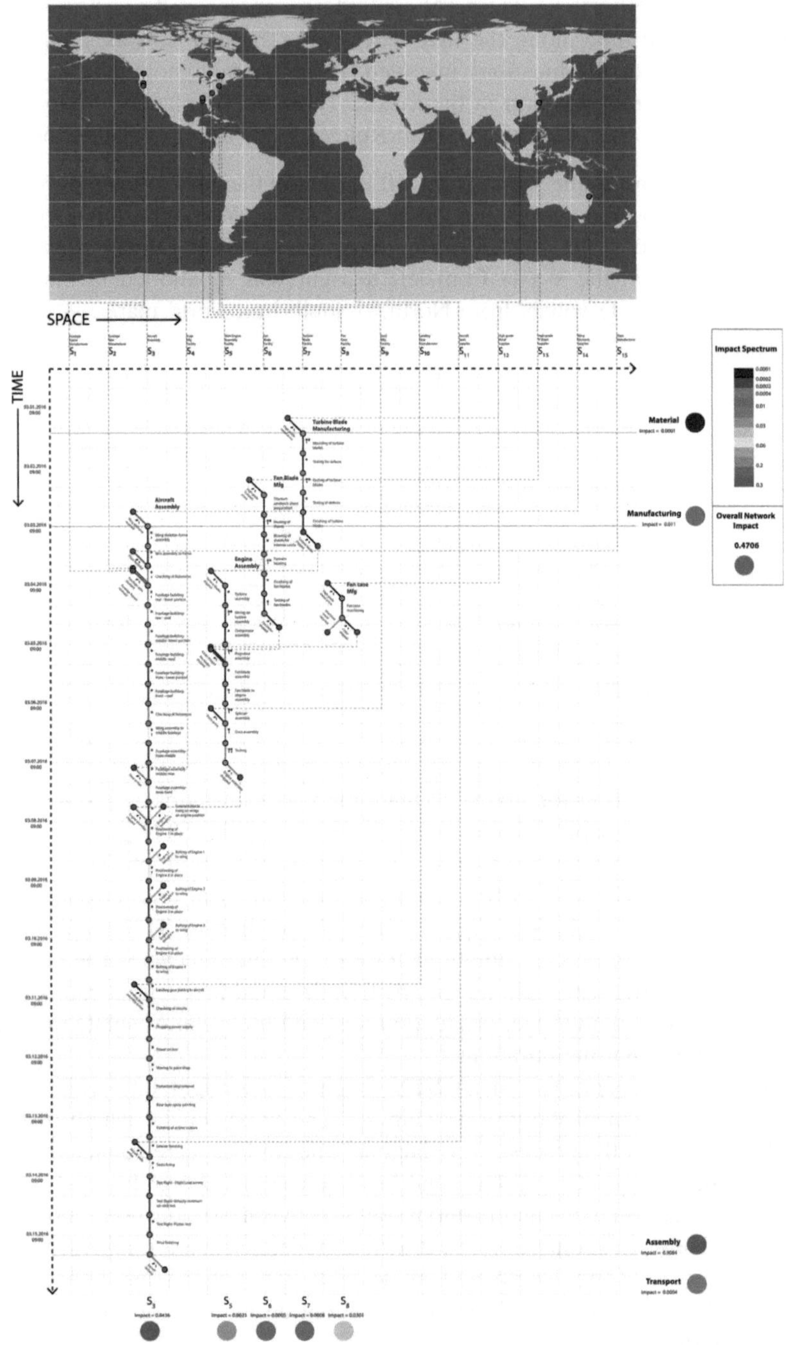

Fig. 6. Space-Time Network representation of Boeing 747-8. (Impact values are only for indicative purposes). Figure 7 shows an enlarged image of a portion of this diagram. (Color figure online)

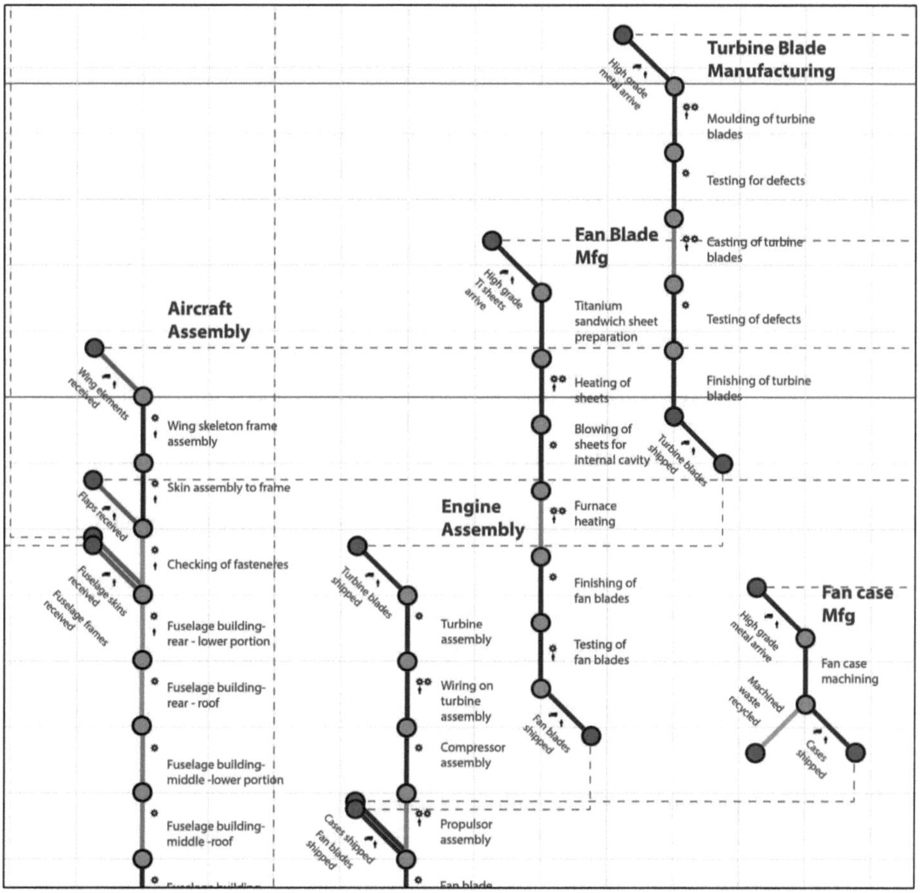

Fig. 7. Enlarged portion of the STN representation of Boeing 747-8 example in Fig. 6.

1. *Global In*, G_{in}: a connector to the left drawn at the start node of a process. G_{in} denotes, the process to which it is connected receives input material sourced from another location.
2. *Global Out,* G_{out}: a connector to the left drawn at the end node of a process. G_{out} denotes, the process to which it is connected has an output to be shipped to another location.
3. *Local In,* L_{in}: a connector to the right drawn at the start node of a process. L_{in} denotes, the process to which it is connected receives an input sourced from the same location.
4. *Local Out,* L_{out}: a connector to the right drawn at the end node of a process. L_{out} denotes, the process to which it is connected has an output which is either locally discarded, or goes for recycling.

Different combinations of input-output scenarios exist in a product lifecycle and supply chain. Every possible scenario can be depicted using these four connectors as shown in Fig. 5. What each of these scenarios signify is explained in Table 1. The connectors eliminate the issue of clutter due to criss-crossing of lines in GIS based or any map based representations. The connectors enable the network to expand as more information becomes available, without having to redraw the rest of the graph. The equipment and people involved are shown, using graphic symbols of gear and human respectively, next to each process. The count of the symbols denote the equipment and people count in each process. Transportation involved in G_{in} and G_{out} is shown using a truck symbol next to these connectors.

Table 1. Meaning of connector combinations with respect to input-output scenarios

Connector combinations	Meaning
G_{in} - G_{out}	Receiving raw materials/products/finished goods from another location and shipping the finished product to another location
G_{in} - L_{out}	Products/Materials from other locations received as an input and output disposed locally
L_{out} - L_{in}	An output is recycled and is reused by receiving it as an input to another process
G_{out} – G_{in}	Output in the form of raw materials/products/finished goods are shipped to another location where it is an input to a process
L_{in} - L_{out}	Locally sourced material is used as an input to a process and its output is locally disposed or recycled
L_{in} - G_{out}	Locally sourced material is used as an input to a process and its output is shipped to another location

The logic of plotting an STN graph is described below:
Here, S denotes *space*; t, *time*; P, *process*; Out, *output*; Inp, *input.*

1. S_i (t) is a location point in the space-time co-ordinate at a given point of time. The co-ordinate values of the point S_i (t) will be (S_i, t_i), where i = 1, 2, 3…
2. A process, P_{ij} is defined by a pair of 2 points (S_i, t_i) and (S_j, t_j) where $t_j > t_i$; i = 1, 2, 3…; j = 1, 2, 3…
3. A G_{out} or G_{in} is a process, P_{ij}, defined by a set of 2 points, (S_i, t_i) and (S_j, t_j); where $t_j > t_i$; $S_i \neq S_j$; i = 1, 2, 3…; j = 1, 2, 3…
4. An L_{in} or L_{out} is a process, P_{ij} defined by a set of Input-Output values of P_{ij} and its succeeding process P_{jk} such that{Out P_{ij}} $\neq$ {Inp P_{jk}}; where $S_{ij} = S_{jk}$; $t_k > t_j > t_i$; i = 1, 2, 3…; j = 1, 2, 3…; k = 1,2,3,…

The basic elements of the STN graph have been described in this section. The next section explains how the STN graph depicting LCA results can be plotted, using an example of product supply chain and lifecycle network.

3.1 Example of Boeing 747-8 Using STN Method

An example of Boeing 747-8's supply chain network, involving processes from the life cycle phases of material, manufacturing, assembly and transport, is demonstrated using the STN method. Data for this was accumulated by transcribing documentary videos of Boeing 747-8 and GE engine manufacturing [15, 16], and from information available in company websites [17]. The data displayed is not an accurate representation of The Boeing Company's actual supply chain network. Assumptions have been made for demonstration purposes of the STN method. The Boeing 747-8 has 6 million parts, most of which arrive just-in time [15]. The major subassemblies for the Boeing 747-8 are the GE Engines GE nx-2B, wing elements, landing gear and structural elements. All of these are sourced from different plants and locations. The major components for GE nx-2B engines are turbine blades, fan cases and fan blades, which are sourced from different companies or manufactured at plants at different locations. The aircraft assembly, engine manufacturing, turbine blade, fan blade and fan case manufacturing for engine assembly are demonstrated in this example using the STN graph (see Fig. 6).

The range of impact values from LCA results are categorised into a colour spectrum (see Fig. 6, right side). The LCA value for each process is checked against this colour spectrum and the corresponding colours are used for the process lines. The overall impact of the lifecycle network is shown on the right side (see Fig. 6, below colour spectrum). The overall impact is shown in a circle, with the impact value depicted using the corresponding colour from the spectrum. The lifecycle phase-wise aggregated impact values are shown on the right side in a colour coded circle depicting its value, with a red line depicting the end of each phase. Each lifecycle phase is demarcated with respect to the product for which the lifecycle is evaluated, which in this example is the Boeing 747-8 aircraft. Space-wise aggregation of LCA results are shown using colour coded circles (as per the spectrum) at the end of each x co-ordinate position, which denotes the corresponding locations.

4 Advantages and Limitations of STN Method

A manufacturing plant has machines running continuously and simultaneously, producing parts and products in batches. At every instance of time, different batches of products are at varying degrees of completion. The STN method, by focussing on one manufacturing lot, produces a clear picture of a product's lifecycle network and its dependencies across different locations and processes. From Fig. 6, one could distinguish 5 different chains showing processes taking place in 5 locations. The STN method also carries the good aspects of the commonly used graphical representations which are: the sequence from material flow analysis, geographic tagging from GIS, use of colours in Sankey diagrams for LCA results, and temporal information and process dependencies from Gantt charts. The material flow is captured, without having to show the quantities, by use of G_{in}, G_{out}, L_{in} and L_{out}. The colour coding of processes, and space-wise and lifecycle phase-wise aggregation of LCA results enable users to locate the individual process, or location, or the life-cycle phase, which contribute to higher environmental impacts. With this knowledge, decision makers have better chance to optimise the network effectively for reducing the environmental impacts. Alternative lifecycle networks can be compared easily using this method. Two networks can be compared, or the same network can be optimised for reducing environmental impacts, till the desired values are achieved.

The STN graph can be used for an entire product lifecycle or for individual life-cycle phases. It can also be drawn for an individual factory, where each zone is represented by different points in the x-axis. STN graph captures the real scenario when it comes to recycle-reuse-disposal phase. In most representations in PLM and LCA, re-cycle and re-use phases are depicted as a loop connecting the manufacturing process. In reality and in STN method, the L_{out} (discarded outputs) join as L_{in} (recycled inputs in this case) at the next point in space and time where those processes that take them as input actually occurs.

The STN method supports addition of more supply chain and life cycle data into the network as more information becomes available. The whole product lifecycle can be built in a modular manner, and each supplier, or component manufacturer can contribute its data to add to the network. The network can be easily drawn by hand for quick discussions and modification. The STN method is compatible to print media. There is no loss of data when the STN graph is printed in colour. Black and white prints show the geographically dispersed lifecycle network.

The STN method is not a replacement for existing supply chain and logistics tools that handle large amounts of logistics related information including part numbers, real time tracking etc. This method is useful for the intended users as explained earlier for decision making purposes related to the product supply chain and lifecycle. The STN method have been presented to industry representatives, who acknowledged the potential usefulness of the method. User surveys of end users are planned to be carried out to estimate the level of understanding and ease of use of STN method compared to other graphical representations.

5 Conclusions

According to Winston [18], finding appropriate representation is a major part of a problem solving effort. A good representation 'makes important things explicit' and exposes 'the natural constraints inherent in the problem' [18, 19]. The STN method proposes an information visualisation approach to graphical problem solving in the product lifecycle related domain. Supply chain infographics convey data in pictorial manner, but the ability to create good infographics depends on the skill of the designer. The STN graph is a generic and replicable design, from which the relationships between processes, locations, and network dependencies can be interpreted and extrapolated. An implementation of the STN method is currently being tested for its efficacy.

Acknowledgments. The authors acknowledge the contribution of The Boeing Company, USA for providing financial support under contract PC36018 at SID, IISc.

References

1. GE Aviation Press Release. GE Aviation Produces New Components at its Singapore Facility, 02 February 2010
2. Adam, C., Robinson, P.: Manufacturing in the 21st century: an holistic future. Aust. Q. **66** (3), 17–36 (1994)
3. Xing, Y., Detert, N.: How the iPhone widens the United States trade deficit with the People's Republic of China. In: ADBI Working Paper 257. Asian Development Bank Institute, Tokyo (2010)
4. Preis, A., Beaulieu, M.: The role of knowledge management in aircraft product development. In: PLM 2012 Keynote Presentation (2010)
5. Meyer, J.-A.: The acceptance of visual information in management. Inf. Manag. **32**, 275–287 (1997)
6. Rosenblum, L., Brown, B.: Visualization. IEEE Comput. Graph. Appl. **12**(4), 18–20 (1992)
7. Krrmker, D.: Visualisierungssysteme. Springer, Berlin (1992)
8. Charwat, H.: Lexikon der Mensch-Maschine-Kommunikation. Oldenbourg, München/Wien (1992)
9. Gmelin, H., Seuring, S.: Achieving sustainable new product development by integrating product life-cycle management capabilities. Int. J. Prod. Econ. **154**, 166–177 (2014)
10. Bevilacqua, M., Ciarapica, F., Giacchetta, G.: Development of a sustainable product lifecycle in manufacturing firms: a case study. Int. J. Prod. Res. **45**(18–19), 4073–4098 (2007)
11. Hu, G., Bidanda, B.: Modeling sustainable product lifecycle decision support systems. Int. J. Prod. Econ. **122**(1), 366–375 (2009)
12. Grieves, M.: Product Lifecycle Management: Driving the Next Generation of Lean Thinking. McGraw-Hill, New York (2006)
13. How To Build 787 Dreamliner Jet Engine. https://youtu.be/_30T6MqdSlw. Accessed 15 Apr 2016
14. Chandran, K.M., Mani, M., Chakrabarti, A.: A spatio-temporal network representation for manufacturing. In: Chakrabarti, A. (ed.) ICoRD 2015. SIST, vol. 35, pp. 459–470. Springer, Heidelberg (2015). doi:10.1007/978-81-322-2229-3_39
15. Boeing 747–8. National Geographic Megastructures Documentary. https://youtu.be/fv5a26Aoi7wboeing. Accessed 15 Apr 2016
16. GEnx-2B. GE Aviation. https://youtu.be/sv5C5I67SNA. Accessed 15 Apr 2016
17. Boeing 747. http://www.airframer.com. Accessed 15 Apr 2016
18. Winston, P.H.: Artificial Intelligence, 2nd edn. Addison-Wesley, Reading (1984)
19. Yuan, M., Mark, D.M., Egenhofer, M.J., Peuquet, D.J.: Extensions to geographic representations. In: A Research Agenda for Geographic Information Science, pp. 129–156. CRC, Boca Raton (2004)

Product, Service and Systems

An IoT Fueled DSS for MOL Marine Auxiliaries Management

Moritz von Stietencron[1(✉)], Karl A. Hribernik[1], Carl Christian Røstad[2], Bjørnar Henriksen[2], and Klaus-Dieter Thoben[1,3]

[1] BIBA - Bremer Institut für Produktion und Logistik GmbH, University of Bremen, Hochschulring 20, 28359 Bremen, Germany
{sti,hri,tho}@biba.uni-bremen.de
[2] SINTEF Technology and Society, S.P. Andersens vei 5, 7465 Trondheim, Norway
{carl.c.rostad,bjornar.henriksen}@sintef.no
[3] Faculty of Production Engineering, University of Bremen, Badgasteiner Straße 1, 28359 Bremen, Germany

Abstract. The producers of marine auxiliaries face the challenge, that they need to adapt their middle-of-life activities to the otherwise defined and often not well communicated schedules of the ships, which are carrying their products. This paper presents both the methodological approach to a solution and its prototypical implementation in a specific use case. The solution presented is utilizing the Internet of Things (IoT) and the data that is constantly being produced by the ships through the Automatic Identification System (AIS) to help overcome this problem.

Keywords: Internet of Things · AIS · PLM · MOL · Marine industry

1 Introduction

The management of middle-of-life (MOL) actions is a challenging task for the producers of marine auxiliaries. While this may be found true for many knowledge intensive products, there are a couple of unique restrictions that apply in the marine domain. However, with the wake of the Internet of Things (IoT) also new possibilities for overcoming these problems are emerging.

In this paper we are presenting an IoT based approach to intelligent management of MOL activities for marine auxiliaries and their producers. Based on the general motivation, related work and presentation of the methodology, a specific implementation for a decision support system based on data from the AIS (Automatic Identification System) network is presented. The paper concludes with a summary of the findings and an outlook to future work.

R. Harik et al. (Eds.): PLM 2016, IFIP AICT 492, pp. 621–630, 2016.
DOI: 10.1007/978-3-319-54660-5_55

2 Background and Motivation

The suppliers of auxiliary components in the shipbuilding domain share the problem, that while their products may be important to the operation of the ship, they regularly do not have a high enough significance to influence possible schedules and locations for middle of life (MOL) activities, such as maintenance, repair and overhaul (MRO) on their products. With regards to the tight operation schedules of their containing product, the ship, the auxiliaries' suppliers are thus at the mercy of the shipowning company.

As a direct influence on the ships schedule for MOL activities is not possible, the auxiliaries producers have to adapt their actions to the ships schedules. The traditional practise requires the producers to manually identify the products which require service or for which additional offerings can be made and contact the respective shipowning companies to ask for available time slots. These time slots have are usually during cargo handling in port. An overview of these information over multiple shipowners and ports to streamline schedules is often already outdated before it has been fully compiled in the traditional manner.

Due to these problems some producers of marine auxiliaries have begun to use AIS based online systems like MarineTraffic[1] to track the relevant ships and identify their next port calls. However, this practise either binds the users to the consumer oriented user interface offered for free or at little costs by the service providers or invokes high costs for data acquisition and integration into the enterprise systems.

The solution proposed in this paper tries to overcome these problems and offer a cost effective and efficient way for marine auxiliaries producers to manage MOL activities on their products.

3 Related Work

This section gives an overview of the related work of the scientific community on the main technologies and topics relevant to the methodology described in the succeeding chapter.

3.1 PLM – Product Lifecycle Management

The production engineering perspective on Product Lifecycle Management (PLM) [1] often divides the products lifecycle into the following three main phases: beginning-of-life (BOL), middle-of-life (MOL) and end-of-life (EOL) [2]. While the BOL with steps such as product development, production and distribution and the EOL with the reverse logistics are regularly of little interest to the customer or end user, the MOL phase and its contents are in direct interaction with the user [3].

This high degree of user control imposes a barrier to frequent interaction of product and producer. This is even increased in control and security sensitive industries like the marine sector.

[1] http://www.marinetraffic.com/.

However, for closed-loop PLM it is crucial to combine information flows of as many product phases as possible [4]. Thus the integration of the MOL phase as the regularly longest phase is of high importance.

3.2 Servitization

The term “servitization” has been established by Vandermerwe and Rada [5] and characterizes the change of the producers business model from product sales towards the conversion of service offers along the entire product lifecycle. These service offerings can be both product extending as well as product maintaining (e.g. MRO). Servitization can be pursued due to different reasons of economic, environmental or strategic perspectives [6]. For knowledge intensive products servitization (by the producer) is traditionally a wide spread approach to supplying the customer with the through-life services he and his product need. Marine auxiliaries can be included in this consideration as they regularly have to fulfill strict regulations both in production as well as during service.

3.3 Digitized Products

The process of collecting, storing and analysing data from customers and end-users of products and services with the goal to discover new needs or identify changes in usage patterns is called informatization by [7]. Informatization is done to enhance existing offers or the related service-level agreements (SLAs) back to the customer. [7] systematise this process as an information feedback loop beginning with collecting and storing data from customers, analysing it to create data about them, and providing information about new service offerings back to the customer, after which the loop is repeated. As systems of product-services (PSS) are seldom provided by an individual company, and the economics of scale in the networked economy stem from the size of the supporting network [8], multiple information feedback loops are opened amongst the stakeholders in the PSS network.

One emerging source of information for these feedback loops is the result of the increasing digitalization of products, services and PSS. According to [9], digitalized products are those, which have seven material properties: *programmability, addressability, senseability, memorability, communicability, traceability,* and *associability*. This enables a loose coupling across the four layers of a digital service architecture, which includes devices, networks, services and contents. Other authors have previously developed concepts for “digitalized” products, such as smart or intelligent products. These are physical products which may be transported, processed or used and which comprise the ability to act in an intelligent manner. McFarlane et al. define the Intelligent Product as *“a physical and information based representation of an item […] which possesses a unique identification, is capable of communicating effectively with its environment, can retain or store data about itself, deploys a language to display its features, production requirements, etc., and is capable of participating in or making decisions relevant to its own destiny”* [10]. The degree of intelligence an intelligent product may exhibit varies from simple data processing to complex proactive behaviour [11]. Digitized or intelligent products can thus make use e.g. of RFID, sensors and embedded computing to collect information about their usage, service, maintenance, upgrading, decommissioning and disposal throughout their lifecycles and feed it back to stakeholders responsible for the PSS offer.

3.4 IoT – Internet of Things

The product services of the 21st century are broadly supported by and reliant on the internet [12]. This trend is dramatically increased by the possibilities of the Internet of Things (IoT).

The Internet of Things can be seen as an evolution of the "old" human driven internet towards an internet which is driven by inanimate objects – things [13]. Originating in the wake of radio frequency identification (RFID) technology the IoT encompasses every object that participates in data exchange with other systems. It does not make any difference whether this exchange is multilateral or not, neither what sort of system is observed [14]. In practice this means, that both embedded systems with advanced on-board intelligence as well as simple data processing or forwarding can be part of the internet of things as long as data exchange is conducted automatically.

3.5 AIS – Automatic Identification System

The Automatic Identification System (AIS) for ships was developed as a system to make ship traffic safer by avoiding accidents due to human errors or technological insufficiencies like impaired radar sight [15, 16]. The International Maritime Organisation issued a guideline for its use in 2002 [17] and thus forced the mass introduction of the system.

The AIS messages are sent automatically at a defined interval and can be received and read by anyone within the proximity of the sender as the VHF radio technology is used. Typically, a range of 10 to 20 nautical miles can be reached but this strongly depends on the hardware choice and geographical parameters [18]. The standardized AIS messages convey information about the ship, its position and also its current voyage [15].

Since its initial development one and a half decades ago both the capabilities and uses of the AIS have been constantly extended. For example, satellite based AIS (S-AIS) can now also cover the oceans beyond the reach of shore based receivers [19]. The data which is being generated by hundreds of thousands of ships every minute is also put to use in increasingly various fashions. From collision avoidance systems [20] over marine traffic engineering and harbour traffic management [21] to homeland security applications [22, 23] the applications are still mostly confined to the original idea of AIS – increasing security, safety and efficiency of the vessel and the traffic system.

4 Methodology

This section describes the methodology used to address the problem stated in the second chapter by applying the technologies and concepts introduced in the preceding section.

4.1 Approach

A six step approach was chosen and prototypically implemented in a use case. Figure 1 below gives an overview of the process.

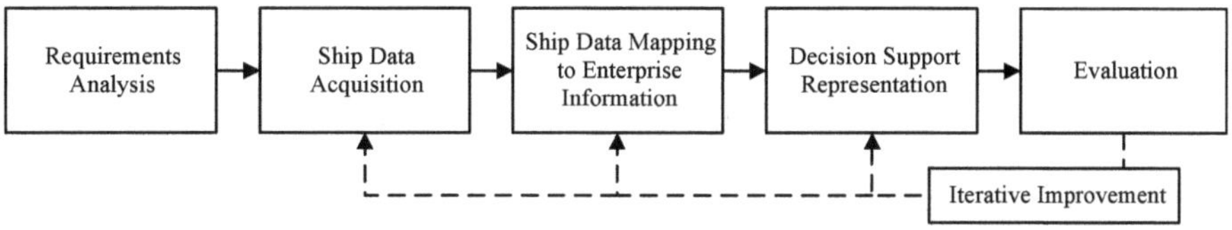

Fig. 1. Block diagram of the chosen methodology

The following subsections illustrate the use case and the steps taken during prototypical implementation.

4.2 Use Case

TeamTec AS is a Norwegian producer of marine auxiliaries. Its main products are incinerators for on-board waste treatment, stripping ejectors (fluid driven jet pumps) and ballast water treatment system. It has over 30 years of history and thousands of products installed on ships worldwide. The TeamTec incinerators are high knowledge products which are serviced only by TeamTec or affiliated service providers. With a very high number of concerned shipowning companies the administrative effort to coordinate MOL activities on their products is immense. While TeamTec has for many years been recording information from all lifecycle phases about their products on item-level, the access to updated information regarding the containing ship is completely manual up to now.

The available lifecycle data is managed in an ERP system but the ships schedules are retrieved manually from various AIS based internet services and compiled in spreadsheets to be followed up on.

4.3 Prototypical Implementation

The implementation process at TeamTec was conducted during the research project "Innovativ Kraft" funded by the Research Council of Norway, following the steps presented in Sect. 4.1.

Requirements Analysis. During several meetings the requirements towards the DSS were recorded. Involved were the process owners and experts for information technology and industrial process design. The identified main objectives for the DSS are summarized in the following table together with their criticality.

In a feasibility study it was found that the three objectives with regards to the data content (O1–O3) can be achieved by the use of AIS data. It was also found, that the three technical objectives (O4–O6) can be best implemented in an individual server application, which can be operated via a web user interface.

Ship Data Acquisition. The commercial access to AIS data streams is as previously stated regularly linked to a substantial recurring fee to other internet service providers. As the relevant AIS information (see Table 1, O1 and O2) are rather static during a single voyage, uniform AIS coverage over the whole sea surface is not required in this use case. Thus the utilization of a S-AIS services is not needed. After a market analysis it was decided to join the AISHub Data Sharing Network[2].

Table 1. Summary of main objectives identified during requirements analysis.

Objective no.	Objective content	Criticality
O1	Information about next port of call	High
O2	Information about estimated time of arrival	High
O3	Search/order by IMO number	Medium
O4	Flexible data mapping with enterprise data	High
O5	Low total cost of ownership	Low
O6	Data ownership	Medium

By providing one AIS data stream to the AISHub any member gains access to the combined stream of all members' receivers, providing access to AIS data concerning over 23500 vessels including the rights to commercial use of the data. Figure 2 shows the coverage of both the BIBA AIS station as well as the AISHub total feed.

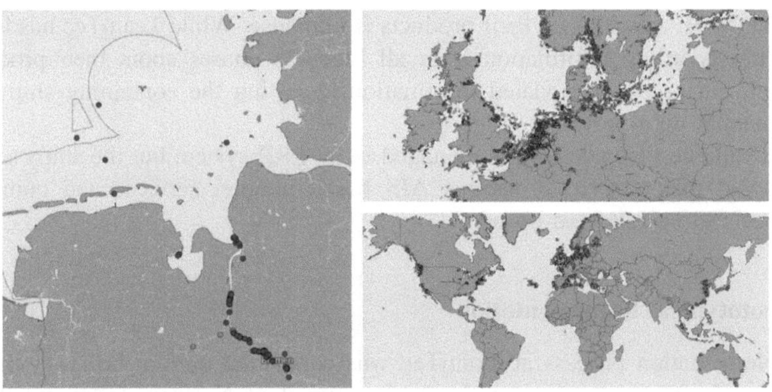

Fig. 2. Coverage maps of the BIBA feed (left) and the AISHub feed (right)

Due to its inland location for the BIBA AIS station, a directional antenna was chosen together with an internet enabled receiver which forwards the received data from the AIS radio system to the AISHub servers.

The incoming data is filtered for the relevant ships and stored in a database.

[2] http://www.aishub.net/.

Ship Data Mapping to Enterprise Information. The identification of the relevant ships is based on the company database which holds the IMO number as means of identification of the product containing ship. Against this data set, which is updated once new ships have been added to the ERP system, the incoming AIS stream will be compared and only the messages concerning the relevant ships is further processed.

The stored information from the ERP system and the AIS system are linked via the project reference. On the ERP system it links to all information regarding the product and its lifecycle data, while on the AIS system it links to the installation and subsequently to the ship. However, it must be noted, that this is a n − 1 relationship, as one ship can have multiple installations.

Decision Support Representation. From the combined information a number of views can be generated. At the current state three main views have been implemented:

The *vessel list* view gives an overview of the vessels registered in the system with some details for vessel identification and the project reference. It also allows manual editing and the addition and removal of vessels. Figure 3 gives an example of this view.

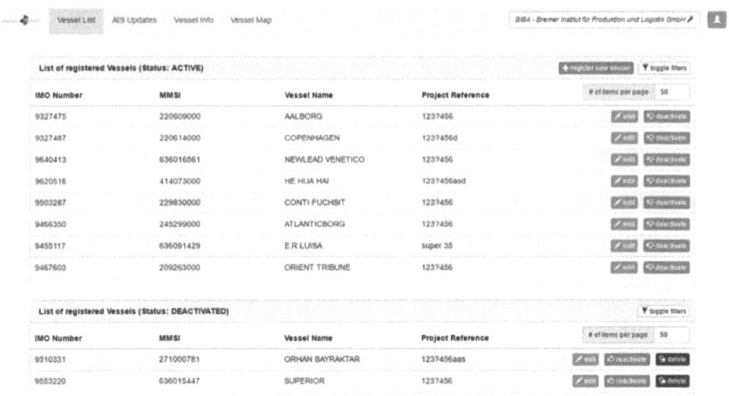

Fig. 3. Screenshot of the vessels listings.

The *vessel information* view shows the current AIS data sets for the vessels and gives information about the current location, next port of call and estimated time of arrival of the vessel.

Finally, the *vessel map* gives an overview of the positions of all selected ships on a world map. This map can also be adjusted to show the next destinations of the ships. Furthermore, a heat map layer can be activated on the map, to allow for easy analysis of the main areas of travel of the company's products. Figure 4 gives an example of the heat map view.

Filters can be applied on all views to allow for quick navigation even in large amounts of data.

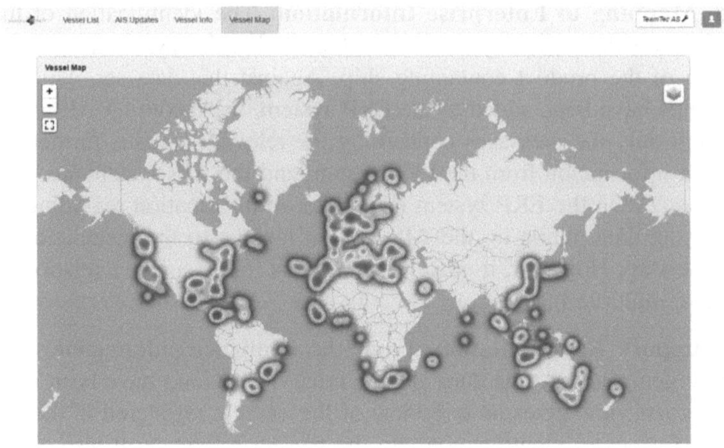

Fig. 4. Screenshot of the current positions of approximately 6000 selected vessels displayed as heat map.

Evaluation and Iterative Improvement. For the evaluation of the system the progress of the development has been presented during multiple meetings. The feedback was collected and included in the ongoing development process.

5 Results

The ongoing evaluation of the system has shown that the system presented has the potential of significant improvements in both efficiency and resource effectivity. The objectives set at the beginning of the implementation can be met throughout.

It is estimated that for TeamTec the productive implementation would save multiple hours of daily work time. More important however it would allow for a better customer service due to easily enabling coordinated requests to the shipowning companies and a significant decrease in maintenance personnel travels.

6 Conclusion and Outlook

This paper has documented the methodological approach to the problem of middle-of-life actions (MOL) management for marine auxiliaries producers. The producers face the challenge, that they need to adapt their maintenance activities to the otherwise defined but miscommunicated schedules of the ships, which are carrying their products. The presented system provides a solution utilizing the Internet of Things (IoT) and the data that is constantly being produced by the ships through the Automatic Identification System (AIS).

The system evaluations have found that the system holds significant potential for the use case companies as most likely also for many other companies in the sector, However, from the prototypical implementation presented in this paper to the productive implementation some further adjustments need to be made.

Furthermore, the identification of further going objectives has already begun. One research topic to be considered is how the solution can be best applied to a group of companies in order to leverage the effects of joint MOL actions. From the data analytics point of view, it can also be investigated how the MOL actions management can be further optimized by including historical data from the ships.

Another research direction will be how to extend the basic IoT functionalities that are being used in the system at the moment to the use of product embedded information devices which can supply product state information. This could greatly enhance the current solution and enable more effective and efficient MOL actions like predictive maintenance.

Acknowledgments. This work was partially funded by The Research Council of Norway within the project "Innovativ Kraft" (project no. 235708). The authors would like to thank TeamTec AS for the support and openness in the preparation of this paper.

References

1. Sundin, E.: Life-cycle perspectives of product/service-systems: in design theory. In: Sakao, T., Lindahl, M. (eds.) Introduction to Product/Service-System Design, pp. 31–49. Springer, Heidelberg (2009)
2. Kiritsis, D., Bufardi, A., Xirouchakis, P.: Research issues on product lifecycle management and information tracking using smart embedded systems. Adv. Eng. Inform. **17**, 189–202 (2003)
3. Hribernik, K.A., von Stietencron, M., Hans, C., Thoben, K.-D.: Intelligent products to support closed-loop reverse logistics. In: Hesselbach, J., Herrmann, C. (eds.) Glocalized Solutions for Sustainability in Manufacturing, pp. 486–491. Springer, Heidelberg (2011)
4. Jun, H.B., Kiritsis, D., Xirouchakis, P.: Research issues on closed-loop PLM. Comput. Ind. **58**, 855–868 (2007)
5. Vandermerwe, S., Rada, J.: Servitization of business: adding value by adding services. Eur. Manag. J. **6**, 314–324 (1989)
6. Neely, A.: Exploring the financial consequences of the servitization of manufacturing. Oper. Manag. Res. **1**, 103–118 (2009). doi:10.1007/s12063-009-0015-5
7. Opresnik, D., Hirsch, M., Zanetti, C., Taisch, M.: Information – the hidden value of servitization. In: Prabhu, V., Taisch, M., Kiritsis, D. (eds.) Advances in Production Management Systems: Sustainable Production and Service Supply Chains, pp. 49–56. Springer, Heidelberg (2013)
8. Kelly, K.: New Rules for the New Economy. Penguin, London (1999)
9. Yoo, Y., Henfridsson, O., Lyytinen, K.: Research commentary-the new organizing logic of digital innovation: an agenda for information systems research. Inf. Syst. Res. **21**, 724–735 (2010)
10. McFarlane, D., Sarma, S., Chirn, J.L., Wong, C.Y., Ashton, K.: Auto ID systems and intelligent manufacturing control. Eng. Appl. Artif. Intell. **16**, 365–376 (2003). doi:10.1016/S0952-1976(03)00077-0
11. Kärkkäinen, M., Holmström, J., Främling, K., Artto, K.: Intelligent products—a step towards a more effective project delivery chain. Comput. Ind. **50**, 141–151 (2003). doi:10.1016/S0166-3615(02)00116-1

12. Thoben, K.-D., Wortmann(Hans), J.C.: The role of IT for extended products' evolution into product service ecosystems. In: Emmanouilidis, C., Taisch, M., Kiritsis, D. (eds.) Advances in Production Management Systems: Competitive Manufacturing for Innovative Products and Services, pp. 399–406. Springer, Heidelberg (2012)
13. Ashton, K.: That "internet of things" thing. RFiD J. **22**, 97–114 (2009)
14. Atzori, L., Iera, A., Morabito, G.: The internet of things: a survey. Comput. Netw. **54**, 2787–2805 (2010)
15. Harati-Mokhtari, A., Wall, A., Brooks, P., Wang, J.: Automatic identification system (AIS): data reliability and human error implications. J. Navig. **60**, 373–389 (2007). doi:10.1017/S0373463307004298
16. IALA: IALA Technical Clarifications on ITU Recommendation ITU-R M.1371-1, Edition 1.4 (2003)
17. IMO - International Maritime Organization. Guidelines for the Onboard Operational Use of Shipborne Automatic Identification Systems (AIS) (2002)
18. Eriksen, T., Høye, G., Narheim, B., Meland, B.J.: Maritime traffic monitoring using a space-based AIS receiver. Acta Astronaut. **58**, 537–549 (2006). doi:10.1016/j.actaastro.2005.12.016
19. Narheim, B., Olsen, O., Helleren, O., Olsen, R., Beattie, A., Zee, R.: A Norwegian satellite for space-based observations of AIS in the high north. In: AIAA/USU Conference on Small Satellites (2008)
20. Mou, J.M., van der Tak, C., Ligteringen, H.: Study on collision avoidance in busy waterways by using AIS data. Ocean Eng. **37**, 483–490 (2010). doi:10.1016/j.oceaneng.2010.01.012
21. Lin, C., Dong, F., Le, J., Wang, G.: AIS system and the applications at the harbor traffic management. In: 4th International Conference on Wireless Communications, Networking and Mobile Computing, WiCOM 2008, pp. 1–3 (2008)
22. Zhu, F.: Mining ship spatial trajectory patterns from AIS database for maritime surveillance. In: 2011 2nd IEEE International Conference on Emergency Management and Management Sciences (ICEMMS), pp. 772–775 (2011)
23. Tetreault, B.J.: Use of the Automatic Identification System (AIS) for maritime domain awareness (MDA). In: Proceedings of MTS/IEEE OCEANS, vol. 2, pp. 1590–1594 (2005)

Lifecycle Management in the Smart City Context: Smart Parking Use-Case

Ahmed Hefnawy[1,3](✉), Taha Elhariri[1], Abdelaziz Bouras[2,3], Chantal Cherifi[1], Jeremy Robert[4], Sylvain Kubler[4], and Kary Främling[5]

[1] DISP Lab, Université Lumière Lyon 2, Lyon, France
{ahmed.hefnawy,taha.elhariri, chantal.cherifi}@univ-lyon2.fr
[2] DCSE, College of Engineering, Qatar University, Doha, Qatar
abdelaziz.bouras@qu.edu.qa
[3] Ministry of Transport and Communications (MoTC), Doha, Qatar
[4] Interdisciplinary Centre for Security, Reliability and Trust, University of Luxembourg, Luxembourg City, Luxembourg
{jeremy.robert,sylvain.kubler}@uni.lu
[5] Aalto School of Science and Technology, Espoo, Finland
kary.framling@aalto.fi

Abstract. Lifecycle management enables enterprises to manage their products, services and product-service bundles. IoT and CPS have made products and services smarter by closing the loop of data across different phases of lifecycle. Similarly, CPS and IoT empower cities with real-time data streams from heterogeneous objects. Yet, cities are smarter and more powerful when relevant data can be exchanged between different systems across different domains. From engineering perspective, smart city can be seen as a System of Systems composed of interrelated/interdependent smart systems and objects. To better integrate people, processes, and systems in the smart city ecosystem, this paper discusses the use of Lifecycle Management in the smart city context. Considering the differences between ordinary and smart service systems, this paper seeks better understanding of lifecycle aspects in the smart city context. For better understanding, some of the discussed lifecycle aspects are demonstrated in a smart parking use-case.

Keywords: Product Lifecycle Management · Service Lifecycle Management · Closed loop lifecycle management · System of Systems · Smart city

1 Introduction

Lifecycle Management is a concept [1] that evolved in 1990 s to improve several engineering aspects of an enterprise to manage its products across their lifecycles [2]. As per Li et al. [3], Product Lifecycle Management (PLM) is ideally used to manage the knowledge intensive process consisting mainly of market analysis, product design and process development, product manufacturing, distribution, product in use, post-sale service, and recycling. Despite what its name implies, PLM is not only about

R. Harik et al. (Eds.): PLM 2016, IFIP AICT 492, pp. 631–641, 2016.
DOI: 10.1007/978-3-319-54660-5_56

manufactured products; Stark [4] extends the definition of "product" to include services, package of services or a bundle of products and services. Isaksson et al. [5] also see "service" as part of the wider concept of "product".

The transformation from product-oriented to more service-oriented economies is part of a complete "servitization" revolution, with more than 70% of global workers engaged in service tasks [6]. Therefore, traditional product-centric sectors evolve into service-centric sectors in order to meet the new challenges, with the aim to put customers and users at the center of their business models [7]. Through servitization, companies seek unique selling proposition for their products, in which the physical artifact is extended by a surrounding provision of services, thus defining the concept of Product–Service System (PSS) [8].

The advancement of ICT and the evolvement of Internet of Things (IoT) and Cyber Physical Systems (CPS) have made ordinary products smarter. Kiritsis [10] argues that smart products allow monitoring new parameters of the product and its environment along different phases of lifecycle. Similarly, IoT and CPS have an enabling role in public services in the city environment, and can exist in many forms [12]. The simplest form of CPS is the form of single objects, like sensors and actuators that collect data and execute commands respectively. CPS can also be in the form of smart systems that address domain-specific issues, like transportation, parking, energy, lightening, etc.

As it was proposed in previous research in [12–14], and in line with ambitions of many cities and states around the world, there is a need for a more holistic vision of smart city as a complete ecosystem. This paper carries on the proposed lifecycle approach to ensure systematic involvement and seamless flow of information between different stakeholders of the smart city ecosystem. Nevertheless, this holistic vision of smart city implies interrelations and interdependence between multiple smart systems that in many cases are independently developed, operated and managed [15]. Hence this paper proposes a step further to extend lifecycle functionalities to smart cities, in order to exchange not only generated data but also system data, versions, variants and business processes. This research aims to understand some lifecycle aspects in the smart city context, considering some features like heterogeneity of data sources, interdependence between smart systems and integration between cyber and physical components.

The remainder of this paper consists of four sections. Section 2 presents the different types of lifecycle management in the manufacturing and servitization context. Section 3 projects lifecycle management aspects on smart city systems and explains the proposed meaning of different lifecycle components and functionalities in the smart city context. Section 4 demonstrates the lifecycle approach in a smart parking use-case. Section 5 includes discussion and future work.

2 Lifecycle Management in Manufacturing and Servitization Context

The term lifecycle management has been mostly associated with "Product", in Product Lifecycle Management (PLM) and "Service", in Service Lifecycle Management (SLM). However, bi-directional coordination and interaction between PLM and SLM is needed for Product-Service Systems (PSS) [28], in which a manufacturing company sets its market proposition on extending the traditional functionality of its products by incorporating additional services for reaching new market competitive advantages [6]. As per the definitions listed in Table 1, "service" can be seen as a sub-set of "product"; and PSS can be seen as extended "Product", where the product is a complex result of tangible and intangible components. Yet, due to the evolutionary process towards servitization, SLM and PLM-SLM are particularly required to address the special features of service systems and product service systems respectively.

Table 1. Scope of lifecycle management based on definitions of product, service and PSS.

	Definition/Scope
Product (PLM)	An output that results from a process. Products can be tangible or intangible, a thing or an idea, hardware or software, information or knowledge, a process or procedure, a service or function, or a concept or creation (ISO 9001:2000) [5]
Service (SLM)	An activity done for others with an economic value and often done on a commercial basis [6]
PSS (PLM-SLM)	An extended product, where the product is a complex result of tangible and intangible components [9]

PLM is commonly referred to as a strategic approach that incorporates the management of data associated with products of a particular type, and perhaps the versions and variants of that product type, as well as the business processes that surround it [11]. As illustrated in Fig. 1, PLM has three main phases [2]: Beginning of Life (BOL), Middle of Life (MOL), and End of Life (EOL) [3].

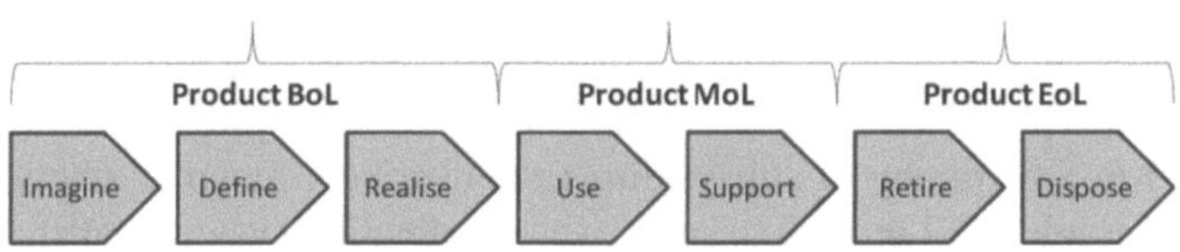

Fig. 1. Phases of PLM [28].

SLM is conceptually similar to PLM, however it manages the lifecycle of services instead of tangible products. SLM is part of Service Science, Management and Engineering (SSME); it creates a connection between Management and Engineering [28]. As illustrated in Fig. 2, SLM can be characterized by the same three main phases, like PLM: BOL, MOL, and EOL [16, 17].

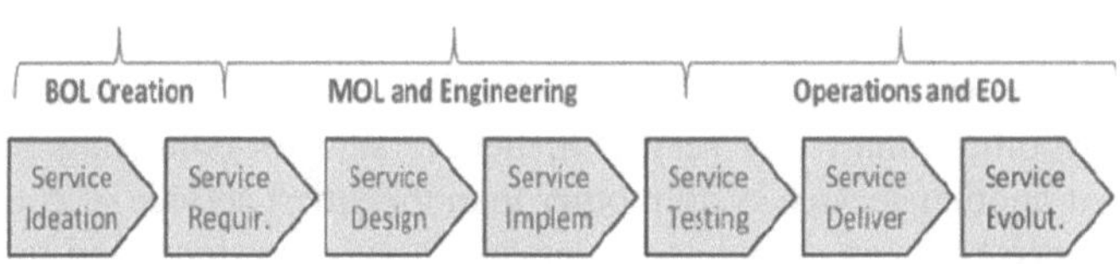

Fig. 2. Phases of SLM [28].

PSS. As part of the servitization trend, manufacturing companies extend their traditional products by incorporating additional services. This approach supports the development of service-oriented sectors, switching the emphasis from the "sale of products" to the "sale of use" and reshaping the same concept of customer values, from "possession" to "utilization" [6, 26]. Ownership stays with manufacturers who provide and guarantee functions/solutions instead of products; hence, efficient use, maintenance and repair, in MOL, are becoming prevailing in the value chain [5]. Figure 3, illustrates the different phases of PSS Lifecycle.

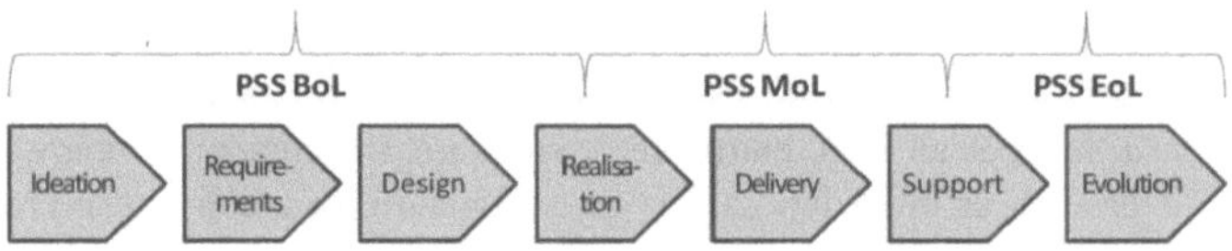

Fig. 3. PSS lifecycle model [28].

3 Lifecycle Management in the Smart City Context

3.1 Smart City Context

Smart city is a composition of smart objects, smart systems, and smart services that focus on problems and issues that arise in service sectors, like transport, logistics, energy, waste management [18, 19]. Yet, smart city as a complete ecosystem goes beyond conventional product systems, service systems or PSS [20, 21]. Smart city service systems are particularly featured with being technology-intensive, information-driven, productivity-focused, customer-centric, innovative, modular, service-based, inter-disciplinary, heterogeneity, etc [22]. Moreover, smart city is a System of Systems (SoS), where individual, heterogeneous, functional service systems are linked together and organized in a hierarchy of subsystems to realize new features/functionalities [15, 17, 27]. For example, [20] propose a smart waste collection system that enable dynamic scheduling and routing of waste trucks. The proposed system features data exchange between waste management, surveillance/monitoring and transportation/routing smart systems. Another example, from [19], a CCTV camera video stream to feed to a video processing algorithm that extracts information such as numbers of cars/people/objects in a given street. Authors propose a middleware layer for selection and discovery of the appropriate data sources.

Like other engineering systems, smart city service systems share similar lifecycle concerns [3], like deployability, disposability, engineerability, maintainability, operatability, procureability, producibility, etc. Yet, the SoS feature of smart city brings some more concerns. One of the concerns, the loose coupling of information sources from real-time intelligence functions (i.e. the collected data for certain smart service can be used by other smart city services); hence, sensors collecting particular data might be part of another service system other than the smart service of concern. In such a case, dependence between connected smart city service systems and traceability and trustworthiness of data across these systems should be addressed.

3.2 Smart City Lifecycle Management (SCLM)

Lifecycle Management is proposed to be used in the smart city context to manage data, versions, variants and business processes associated with heterogeneous, uniquely identified connected objects. Nonetheless, extending lifecycle management concepts to smart cities requires special type of lifecycle management, where many of the aspects are defined/redefined to consider the particular features that differentiate the smart city context from manufacturing and servitization context. Table 2 summarizes some of the relevant aspects of SCLM.

Table 2. Different aspects of Smart City Lifecycle Management (SCLM).

Aspect	Description
Phases	To allow evolutionary development of smart city, in most cases, smart city is composed of independently developed, operated and managed service systems. Therefore, SCLM has no clear phases similar to PLM/SLM; instead, each component of the smart city has its own lifecycle; and, smart city components can be at different phases - BOL, MOL and EOL - in the same time. Therefore, the lifecycle of smart city is a lifecycle of lifecycles
Bill of Materials (BOM)	BOM is a hierarchical structure showing the components that make up the end item [14]. The end item in this case can be a smart city service system or a smart city SoS. In the smart city context, smart objects can be repurposed and reused [23]. Therefore, BOM in the smart city context should allow for loose-coupling, modularity, composability, scalability, interdependency and dynamic complexity [24, 25]
Object/Service/ System data	The interdependence between different smart systems in the smart city context, as detailed in hierarchy structure of BOM, gives the right to interdependent systems to exchange product/service/system data that should be generated and used across lifecycle phases. Archiving and traceability requirements vary from one industry to another. Smart Object/Service/System data can be in various states, including in-work, in-process, in-review, released, as-designed, as-planned, as-built, as-installed, as-maintained, and as-operated [14]
Ownership and Rights	Ownership in the smart city context is an important issue. In light of heterogeneity, repurposing and reusing of data sources, certain components can belong to multiple smart systems. Due to the dynamic complexity of smart city, rights may change during lifecycle. Rights include rights to access, create and modify data, and also rights to approve and promote
Policies and Regulations	Smart city is subject to many policies and regulations related to the different utilities infrastructure, public services and applications. Cyber security, resiliency of ICT connectivity infrastructure and user data privacy are of absolute importance
Versions, Variants and Options	During SCLM phases, smart city components can be modified or upgraded, particularly software components. Smart city components can have multiple versions, options, variants, releases and alternatives
Processes	Processes include problem report, engineering change process and enterprise notification process. For these processes, it's absolutely important to define actors and roles. In the smart city context, processes include notifications, verifications and approvals between actors from different domains

4 Smart Parking: Use-Case

To better understand some of the abovementioned SCLM aspects, this section carries on the use-case, presented in [13], for smart parking system. The proposed scenario was examined in collaboration with the on-going H2020 project named "bIoTope"[1] to use the O-MI/O-DF standards to exchange data between different nodes in the proposed smart parking system. Meanwhile, Aras Innovator® was used to examine some life-cycle management functionalities in the proposed case. This paper focuses only on the lifecycle aspect of the smart parking system.

As detailed in [13], the proposed smart parking system allocates parking spaces to users, based on the preferred entrance and eligibility to use allocated spots for people with disability. In this paper, we propose to use smart parking systems in FIFA World Cup 2022 stadia in Qatar. The main functions of the proposed system include: booking of parking spaces in-advance through online booking; parking space allocation as close as possible to entrance leading to the booked seat; fast track car entrance through gates that are equipped with plate number reader and only open to eligible cars; another plate number reading at each parking space to alert user in case of parking in a wrong space (not the allocated parking space). Figure 4 presents the high-level illustration of the proposed smart parking system.

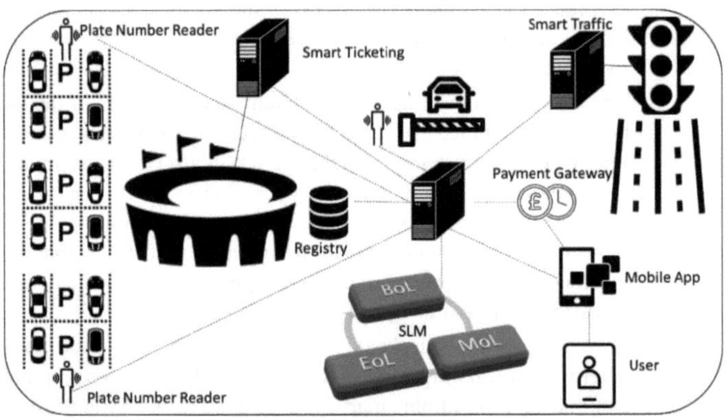

Fig. 4. Smart parking: high-level illustration.

BOM. To develop the BOM, during the BoL, we detailed a hierarchical structure of the components that make up the smart parking system. The smart parking system was structured in zones (1…n); each zone has one gate equipped with plate number reader; and certain number of parking spaces (1…j), each has its plate number reader. Figure 5 shows a snapshot from BOM. Aras Innovator® was used for two purposes, first is to build and manage BOM; second is to export BOM in O-DF structure as XML file to build O-DF object tree. Figure 5 is a screenshot from Aras Innovator®, showing the

[1] http://biotope.cs.hut.fi/.

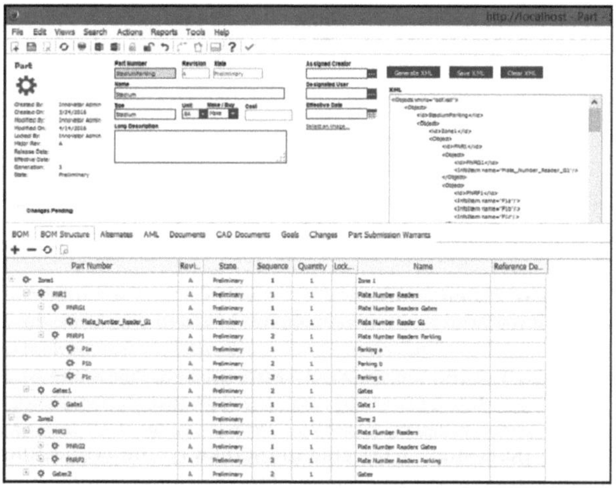

Fig. 5. BOM: screenshot from aras innovator®.

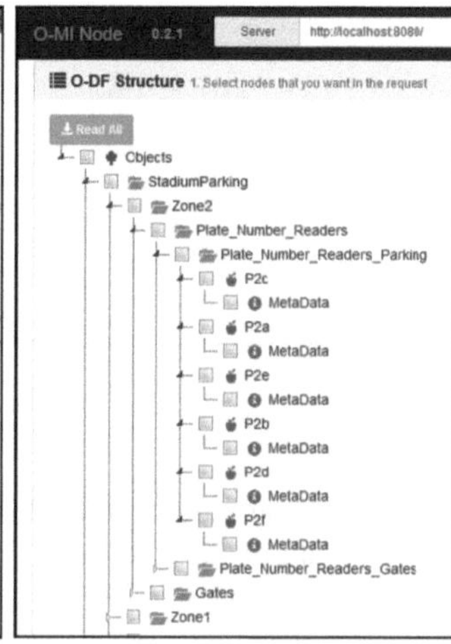

Fig. 6. O-DF object tree.

user interface for smart parking system; and Fig. 6 shows the implementation of the O-DF structure into the smart parking O-MI node which relies on the first reference implementation of O-MI/O-DF standards.

Versions, Variants and Options. During MoL, the BoM may be updated using the same methodology, presented in Figs. 5 and 6, as new versions, variants and options evolve. Normally, new versions, variants and options evolve to add new functionalities or to address certain problems. For this purpose, we denoted the smart parking system, as explained above, as version (V 1.0). We proposed a new scenario of users parking in parking spaces different than their allocated ones, disregarding the red light alert. For this, Problem Reports (PRs) were developed by parking zone administrators in three different stadia reporting the same problem. PRs were reviewed and verified by chief of staff in stadia. The manager of smart parking has approved PRs, as per the PR process shown in Fig. 7.

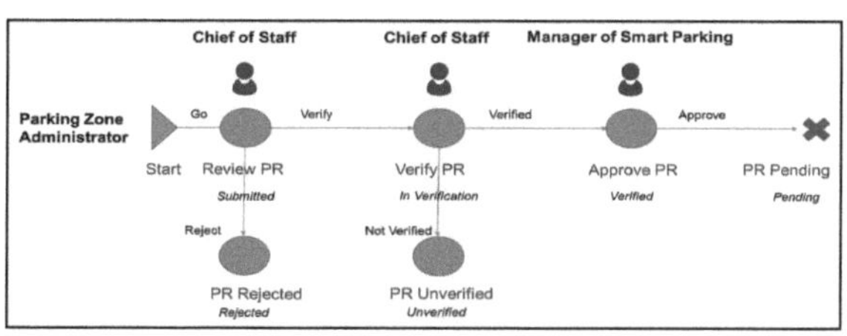

Fig. 7. PR process.

As a response to the above mentioned PRs, an Engineering Change Request (ECR) was developed to overcome the mentioned problem, as per the ECR process shown in Fig. 8. The proposed solution was to add surveillance cameras to monitor

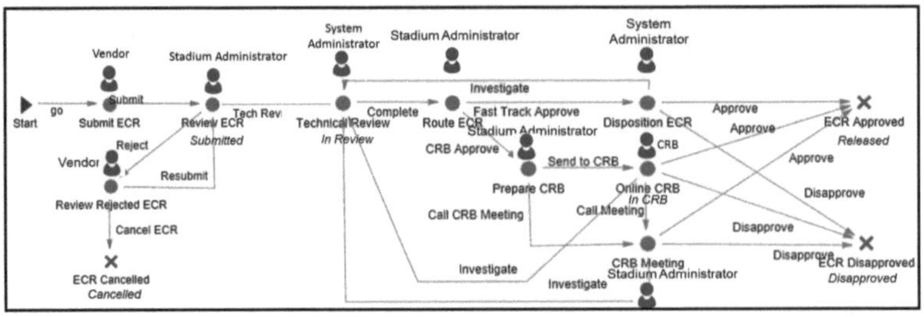

Fig. 8. ECR workflow process.

violent parking cars in order to file cases against these cars. One stadium has rejected the ECR and decided to keep (V 1.0) smart parking system while dealing with the PR by increasing the number of security personnel who can immediately intervene and request violent cars to use their allocated parking spaces. The second stadium has approved the ECR through a fast track approval. Hence, the smart parking system evolved to version (V 2.0); accordingly, the BOM should be updated by adding 1 camera to each parking zone. The third stadium has approved the ECR and requested to add an option to connect the smart parking system with the traffic department system so that the applicable fine will go directly to the traffic department upon capturing the violent car. Hence, a new variant will evolve (V 2.1). Due to the relationship with other systems, the ECR in the last scenario should go through the Change Request Board (CRB) approval route that involve all relevant stakeholders.

The Enterprise Change Notice (ECN) is a process by which changes are implemented within the smart parking system, as shown in Fig. 9. The change, in case of (V 2.0) and the variant (V 2.1), is the addition of cameras, as new parts to all parking zones. The ECN process is used to take the new parts from preliminary lifecycle state to a released lifecycle state. The relevant PRs and ECR can be attached to the ECN for tracking and reporting.

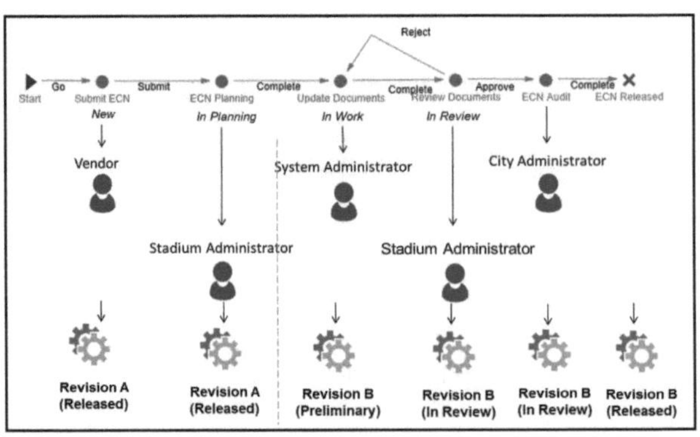

Fig. 9. ECN workflow process.

Aras Innovator® was used to build the BoM at the BoL; manage PRs, ECR and ECN processes and accordingly update the BOM, during MoL. Hence, Aras Innovator® can be used as a master tool to manage all lifecycle aspects, across different phases, including BOM development and changes in case of new versions and/or variants.

5 Discussion and Future Work

As lifecycle management has enabled large enterprises to better manage their products, services and product-service bundles; similarly, lifecycle management can enable city operators to better manage public services and supporting infrastructure. The wide spread of IoT technologies and CPS systems in the city environment closes lifecycle data/information loops across different phases and between heterogeneous objects/ systems. From engineering perspective, smart city as a service system has some features like heterogeneity and loose-coupling of data sources; complexity of systems and composability of parts; customer oriented and service based systems. For these particular features, this paper proposed Smart City Lifecycle Management (SCLM) to be used in the smart city context, instead of the general PLM and SLM.

This paper has described some aspects of SCLM, namely Phases; Bill of Materials (BOM); Object/Service/System data; Ownership and Rights; Policies and Regulations; Versions, Variants and Options; and, Processes. For better understanding, some SCLM aspects were demonstrated through a smart parking use-case.

The vision of applying lifecycle management in the smart city domain(s) is to better integrate people, processes, and systems; and assure information consistency, traceability, and long-term archiving. To achieve such a holistic vision of complete smart city ecosystem, there is a need for two types of data to be exchanged. First, data collected from heterogeneous data sources that can be used in different domains. Second, system data that include BOM, versions, variants, stats and other lifecycle related data. Future work will include expanding the use-case to ensure exchange of the two types of data between different systems in the smart city. Another required effort is to build general smart city BOM that includes as much as possible categories and parts that compose a smart city.

References

1. Zhang, H., Sekhari, A., Ouzrout, Y., Bouras, A.: PLM components monitoring framework for SMEs based on a PLM maturity model and FAHP methodology. J. Mod. Proj. Manag. **2** (1), 109–119 (2014)
2. Zhang, H., Ouzrout, Y., Bouras, A., Savino, M.: Sustainability consideration within product lifecycle management through maturity models analysis. Int. J. Serv. Oper. Manag. **19**(2), 151–171 (2014)
3. Li, J., Tao, F., Cheng, Y., Zhao, L.: Big data in product lifecycle management. Int. J. Adv. Manuf. Technol. **81**(1), 667–684 (2015)
4. Stark, J.: Product Lifecycle Management: 21 Century Paradigm for Product Realization, 2nd edn. (2011)

5. Isaksson, O., Larsson, T.C., Öhrwall Rönnbäck, A.: Development of product-service systems: challenges and opportunities for the manufacturing firm. J. Eng. Des. Spec. Issue Prod.-Serv. Syst. **20**(4), 329–348 (2009)
6. Sassanelli, C., Pezzottac, G., Rossi, M., Terzia, S., Cavalieric, S.: Towards a lean product service systems (PSS) design: state of the art, opportunities and challenges. Procedia CIRP **30**, 191–196 (2015)
7. Freitag, M., Kremer, D., Hirsch, M., Zelm, M.: An approach to standardize a service life cycle management. In: Enterprise Interoperability. John Wiley & Sons, Ltd., Chichester (2013)
8. Garetti, M., Rosa, P., Terzi, S.: Life cycle simulation for the design of product-service systems. Comput. Ind. **63**, 361–369 (2013)
9. Cassina, J., Cannata, A., Taisch, M.: Development of an extended product lifecycle management through service oriented architecture. In: The 1st CIRP Industrial Product-Service Systems (IPS2) Conference, Cranfield University, 1–2 April 2009
10. Kiritsis, D.: Closed-loop PLM for intelligent products in the era of the internet of things. Comput.-Aided Des. **43**, 479–501 (2010)
11. Främling, K., Kubler, S., Buda, A.: Universal messaging standards for the IoT from a lifecycle management perspective. IEEE Internet Things J. **1**(4), 319–327 (2014)
12. Hefnawy, A., Bouras, A., Cherifi, C.: Lifecycle based modeling of smart city ecosystem. In: IKE 2015: The 14th International Conference on Information and Knowledge Engineering, Las Vegas, 27–30 July 2015
13. Hefnawy, A., Bouras, A., Cherifi, C.: IoT for smart city services: lifecycle approach. In: The International Conference on Internet of things and Cloud Computing (ICC 2016), Cambridge, 22–23 March 2016
14. Hefnawy, A., Bouras, A., Cherifi, C.: Integration of smart city and lifecycle concepts for enhanced large-scale event management. In: IFIP PLM 2015 International Conference, Doha 19–21 October 2015
15. Lopes, J., Pineda, R.: Service systems engineering applications. In: Conference on Systems Engineering Research (CSER 2013), 19–22 March 2013
16. Mahut, F., Bricogne, M., Daaboul, J., Eynard, B.: Servicization of product lifecycle management: towards service lifecycle management. In: IFIP PLM 2015 International Conference, Doha, 19–21 October 2015
17. Freitag, M., Stadler, S.: Requirements for a service lifecycle management. In: Conference Paper: Fraunhofer IAO, January 2013
18. Cavalieri, S., Pezzotta, G.: Product–service systems engineering: state of the art and research challenges. Comput. Ind. **63**(4), 278–288 (2012)
19. Poncela, J., et al.: Smart cities via data aggregation. Wirel. Pers. Commun. **76**(2), 149–168 (2014)
20. Jin, J., Gubbi, J., Marusic, S., Palaniswami, M.: An information framework for creating a smart city through internet of things. IEEE Internet Things J. **1**(2), 112–121 (2014)
21. Sum, J.: Service systems engineering: framework & systems modeling. Institute of Technology Management, National Chung Hsing University Taichung 40227, Taiwan ROC, January 2014
22. BKCASE Editorial Board. The Guide to the Systems Engineering Body of Knowledge (SEBoK), v.1.3. R.D. Adcock (EIC). The Trustees of the Stevens Institute of Technology, Hoboken (2014)
23. Tao, F., Zuo, Y., Xu, L., Lv, L., Zhang, L.: Internet of things and BOM-based life cycle assessment of energy-saving and emission-reduction of products. IEEE Trans. Ind. Inform. **10**(2), 1252–1261 (2014)

24. Böhmann, T., Leimeister, J., Möslein, K.: Service systems engineering. Bus. Inf. Syst. Eng. **6**, 73–79 (2014). doi:10.1007/s12599-014-0314-8
25. Silcher, S., Minguez, J., Scheibler, T., Mitschang, B.: A service-based approach for next-generation product lifecycle management. In: IEEE IRI 2010, Las Vegas, Nevada, USA, 4–6 August 2010
26. Schmidt, D., Malaschewski, O., Fluhr, D., Mörtl, M.: Customer-oriented framework for product-service systems. In: 7th Industrial Product-Service Systems Conference-PSS, Industry Transformation for Sustainability and Business, Procedia CIRP30, pp. 287–292 (2015)
27. IEEE-Reliability Society. Technical Committee on "Systems of Systems" – White Paper, October 2014
28. Wiesner, S., Freitag, M., Westphal, I., Thobena, K.: Interactions between service and product lifecycle management. In: 7th Industrial Product-Service Systems Conference- PSS, Industry Transformation for Sustainability and Business. Procedia CIRP30, pp. 36–41 (2015)

Error Generation, Inventory Record Inaccuracy (IRI) and Effects on Performance: A Dynamic Investigation

Wissam EL Hachem[1], Ramy Harik[2(✉)], and Joseph Khoury[3]

[1] Department of Operations Management, ESSEC Business School, Paris, France
Wissam.elhachem@essec.edu

[2] Department of Mechanical Engineering, School of Engineering and Computing, University of South Carolina, Columbia, SC, USA
harik@cec.sc.edu

[3] Methode Electronics Inc., Gau-Algesheim, Germany
Joseph.khoury@methodegermany.com

Abstract. One of the aspects of a good inventory control system is low Inventory Record Inaccuracy (IRI). IRI control ought to be an integral part of PLM by helping to further streamline the production, transportation and service stages. This paper contributes to the expanding debate on linking error generation to Inventory Record Inaccuracy (IRI) and its ensuing effects on performance. Methods of discovering and eliminating the root causes of IRI are presented. A System Dynamics (SD) simulation model is used to examine and confirm the substantial impact of error generation and IRI on workflow. The results of the model show that even a small undetected source of IRI can accumulate and eventually destabilize the entire system.

Keywords: Supply chain · Inventory control · Error generation Inventory record inaccuracy · System Dynamics

1 Introduction

Inventory management is of prime importance for businesses with any kind of inventory, especially those that deal with physical assets. Inventory management and Product Lifecycle Management (PLM), which include production and transportation stages of a product, are closely related where the former is an integral part of the latter. In this paper, the focus is on manufacturing and assembly plants and their inventory management techniques, specifically, record inaccuracies and performance measurements. Companies base their inventory and production decisions on inventory reports of stock levels as generated by information systems. These reports could have errors as discrepancies between actual inventory levels and reported system levels are often reported [2, 12]. The issue of record inaccuracy is not limited to manufacturing industry alone as it is also prevalent in sectors such as retailing and banks. Inventory Control and in particular Inventory Record Accuracy are central to any supply chain initiative and their success is

R. Harik et al. (Eds.): PLM 2016, IFIP AICT 492, pp. 642–651, 2016.
DOI: 10.1007/978-3-319-54660-5_57

a pre-requisite for supply chain collaboration initiatives. Inaccurate inventory records cause a significant drop in company's profits by as much as millions of dollars [7, 11]. This is caused by either excess or shortage in inventory of certain parts which eventually leads to low service levels. Hence, controlling IRI is crucial in PLM.

This paper will contribute to the emerging debate on the effects of Inventory Record Inaccuracy (IRI) on performance. It will do so by thoroughly defining and discussing IRI in Sect. 2 before presenting a System Dynamics model to investigate the dynamics of error generation and its impact on performance in Sect. 3. Contributions and limitations are outlined in Sect. 4 before concluding in Sect. 5.

2 Inventory Record Inaccuracy (IRI)

Inventory management can be complex in nature. Practices such as ABC and similar ones are important yet they are not capable of forecasting the dynamics involved in inventory management. Some programs like MRP and ERP are quite effective in controlling inventory. But, in addition to these programs, dynamic production simulation models could also be beneficial. They offer a more holistic view as seen through hands-on model building experience which helps users to understand unique nuances of the systems adopted in their respective company. An example of such simulation models will be discussed in Sect. 3.

Along with simulation tools, inventory scanning technologies have also proven to be useful, in particular, Radio Frequency Identification (RFID). For inventory control, case-level tagging has the best quality-to-cost ratio [3].

Mere implementation of the cited inventory control systems is insufficient to yield good results. All these systems are dependent on the availability of accurate information including identity, status and location of components. Having inaccurate records will result in wrong order decisions (overstocking or under stocking) which jeopardizes the profits of the company.

2.1 What is IRI?

IRI is the discrepancy between the system level and the actual level of inventory. There could be overstated inventory when the systems show more than the physical inventory or understated inventory when the systems show less than actual physical inventory levels in the stores [8]. The ratio of over and understated inventory varies between different types of businesses, however quite often they are equal [5, 6]. There are two types of variance, Net Variance (Eq. 1) and Gross Variance (Eq. 2), as well as two measurements types, dollar based and count based.

$$\text{Net Variance} = \sum (\text{System Inv Level} - \text{Store Inv Level}). \quad (1)$$

$$\text{Gross Variance} = \sum \text{abs}(\text{System Inv Level} - \text{Store Inv Level}). \quad (2)$$

Dollar based measurements are typically used by auditors in their calculations at an aggregate level, where overstated and understated discrepancies do not matter as long as they almost cancel each other out. This is similar to the Net Variance construct. Count based measurements are typically used by operations managers to maintain an accurate view of their stock keeping unit (SKU) levels. Count based is similar to the Gross Variance construct.

2.2 Importance of IRI

IRI tracking has financial as well as operational benefits. Some of the financial reasons are minimizing over or under payment of taxes and thus avoiding negative economic repercussions [10]. There are several operational reasons to support the importance of IRI tracking. First, inaccurate records will eventually lead to stockouts (Overstated levels generate phantom inventory delaying the trigger to order new inventory) or overstocking (understated levels leads to hidden inventory and the ordering of excessive levels) [9]. Second, fixing inventory records is time and labor consuming reducing efficiency. Third, production control systems are very much sensitive to IRI [1]. Fourth, inventory control software such as ERP requires high inventory accuracy (above 95%).

2.3 Causes of IRI

Inventory record inaccuracy has many root causes. Most of them are either process related or volume related. In the process related category, with every step in the manufacturing and allied processes, there is a probability of error. Ways to reduce errors include reducing number of transactions and simplifying processes as much as possible. In the volume related category, larger volumes imply more transactions, and consequently more chances of errors. To reduce source of errors, methods such as backflushing, bill of material (BOM) simplification and Kanban can be adopted.

Figure 1 presents a causal loop diagram (CLD) depicting some of the dynamics of inventory record errors. A causal loop diagram (CLD) links variables that have a

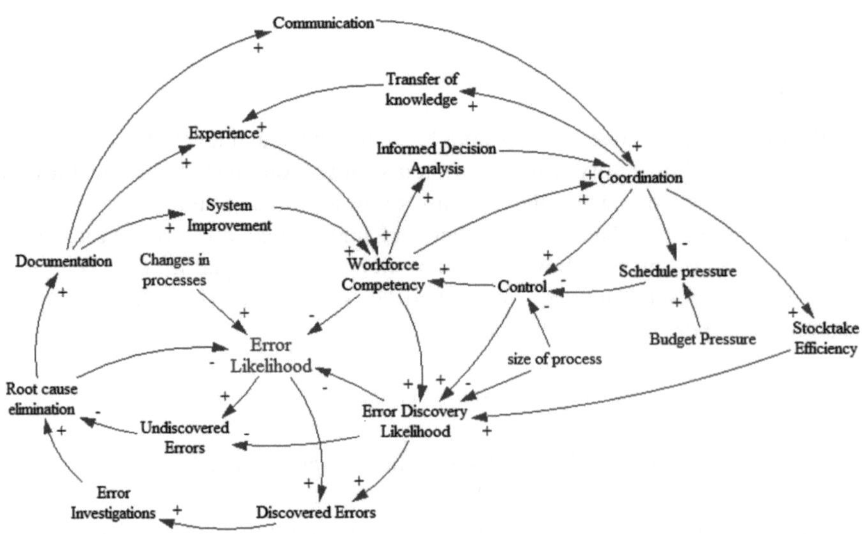

Fig. 1. Inventory record error dynamics

hypothesized direct or indirect causal relationship to a target variable whose behavior is being investigated. A model of inventory error generation will be discussed in Sect. 3.

A company has several ways to improve inventory accuracy. Some firms tackle this issue by eliminating the root causes and some others aim for better error discovery and correction. This is done through cycle counting (Geographic method, Random Sampling, ABC…), stocktaking (Quarterly or Yearly), control charts (particularly attribute charts), investigating behavioral root causes (prominent in activities such as Order Picking) and transaction reduction (simpler BOM's, Kanban, Backflushing).

3 Dynamic Behavior and Performance Measurement

The dynamics in inventory management are complex and therefore, simulation is needed for better control. MRP and ERP are widely used software that are quite efficient in inventory management. However, these software applications most often require customization to fit the needs of particular firms. This could be problematic as their users might introduce complicated constraints and objectives if they do not perfectly understand the underlying logic behind these applications. In this section we will present a sample simulation model that follows the methodology of System Dynamics (SD). The model will present a structure that partially explains error generation and has the potential to advance a firm's knowledge of its inventory system by offering a "hands-on" model building experience.

Error generation with regard to inventory records is quite complex and it has many different root causes as well as many different solutions. A simple model that follows the System Dynamics (SD) methodology has been constructed that illustrates error generation inside a company and its impact on work completion given limited resources (mainly workers). The structure of the model can be applied to both operational errors for manufacturing throughput as well as to warehousing, shipping and receiving errors for IRI. This paper will apply the model within an IRI context.

The basic concept of the model is that a company has a certain number of units to process per month. There are errors in the processing which results in under 100% completion rate along with additional rework even after costly workforce expansion and improvement programs. The model tackles some of the loops in the inventory dynamics model using the causal loop diagram (CLD) as given in Fig. 1. The stocks and flows (S&F) model was built using the iThink software and its CLD is given in Fig. 2.

Model Explanation. Every two variables are linked together by an arrow which has either a positive "+" or a negative "−" polarity (Fig. 3). The sign of the polarity is determined following the "ceteris paribus" principle, meaning by setting everything else as constant. The "+" polarity as in Fig. 3 means that if Variable A increases, Variable B will increase and vice versa. The "−" polarity means that if Variable C increases, Variable D will decrease and vice versa.

The main components of the model are explained next. Every worker has a standard workload capacity (for example 20 units/employee) that he/she can process per month. Given a certain workforce number (for example 100 employees), a certain

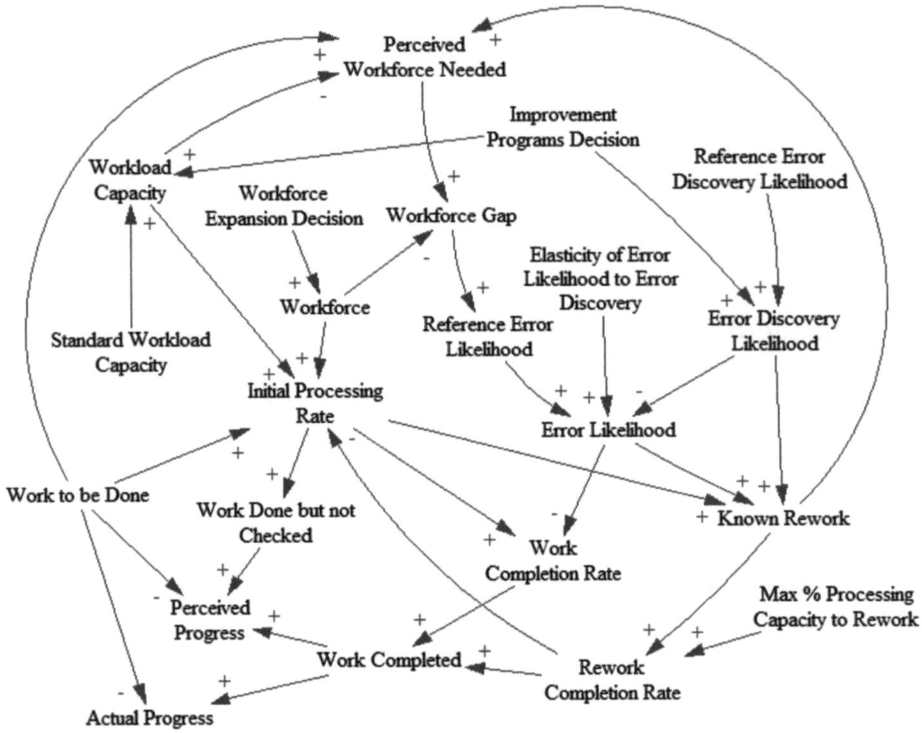

Fig. 2. Error generation CLD

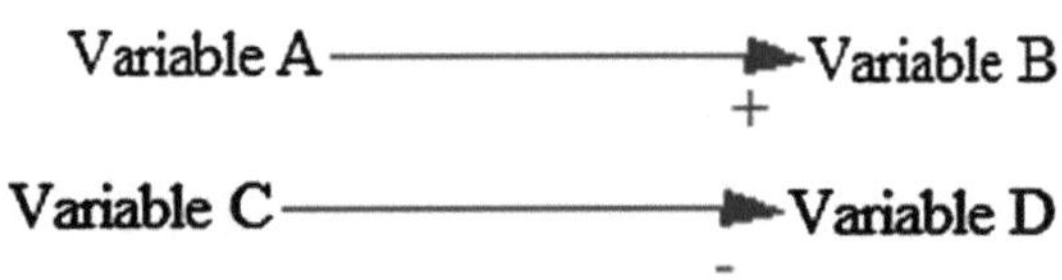

Fig. 3. CLD polarity

processing capacity is determined (in our example its 2000 units). Given a certain volume of work to be done and a workload capacity, a certain number of workforce is perceived able to finish the work (here its 100 employees).

Based on this, the company can choose to modify its current number of workers to match with the perceived workforce number or to leave it constant as it is. A positive gap between the needed number of workers and the actual number will result in an increased pressure on the existing workers and will lead to an increase in error generation:

A minimum 5% reference error likelihood is present even when gap is zero to account for the many other sources of error generating factors. A maximum limit of 25% errors is placed to keep error generation levels to a reasonable level. These error levels can be changed to suit each specific industry and its production lines/methods.

There is as an error discovery likelihood that counteracts error generation. The reference error discovery likelihood is placed at 90%, which implies that 90% of all errors can be discovered.

Since there are errors in the processing of the units with a 90% error discovery rate, there will be known rework. The known rework will require processing again. It is assumed that all of the rework will be done correctly with no possibility for errors at this stage. The rework will require some of the workers to devote their time to it. It is assumed that rework will have priority over initial processing, meaning if there are workers available, some or all of them will be devoted to rework.

In the model, there is a "max % processing capacity to rework" that limits the percentage of workers that will devote their time for rework. Currently it is set to a full 100%. So if there are 10 workers available, and there is rework that requires 10 workers, all workers will be devoted for the rework. This can be modified if needed in the structure of the model by setting a "max % processing capacity to rework" lower than 1. Hence the initial processing rate has to take into account the rework completion rate.

The units that are successfully processed from the beginning are the "work completion rate". Work completed will be summation of both the work completion rate and of the rework completion rate:

$$\text{Work completed} = \text{rework completion rate} + \text{work completion rate.} \tag{3}$$

Out of the total errors that are generated, 90% of them are discovered. Meaning 10% of the errors are not discovered by the company and will wrongfully show up as completed. Hence a discrepancy between perceived progress and actual progress arises:

$$\text{Perceived Progress} = (\text{work done but not checked} + \text{work completed}) \div \text{Cumulative Work to be done.} \tag{4}$$

$$\text{Actual Progress} = \text{work completed} \div \text{cumulative work to be done.} \tag{5}$$

If there is a 5% error likelihood with 90% error discovery likelihood, then 0.5% of the work is never properly done, which will cost the company a lot of money either in lost revenue or added expenses of costly rework. Perceived progress is an erroneous 100% if there is no workforce gap.

The company will need to deploy some strategy to counteract the error generation. In this model, the major driver of error generation is the workforce gap. Hence the company has to always make sure that it has enough workers to handle the amount of work to process. The two main feedback loops of error generation in the model are presented in Fig. 4.

One Loop is a Reinforcing Loop for Known Rework, meaning an increase in the Known Rework will lead to an even bigger increase later on. The other loop is a Balancing loop, meaning an increase in Known Rework will lead to its decrease later on. The two policies of Improvement Programs and Workforce Expansion are also illustrated in Fig. 4 with red links. The two policies work as follows:

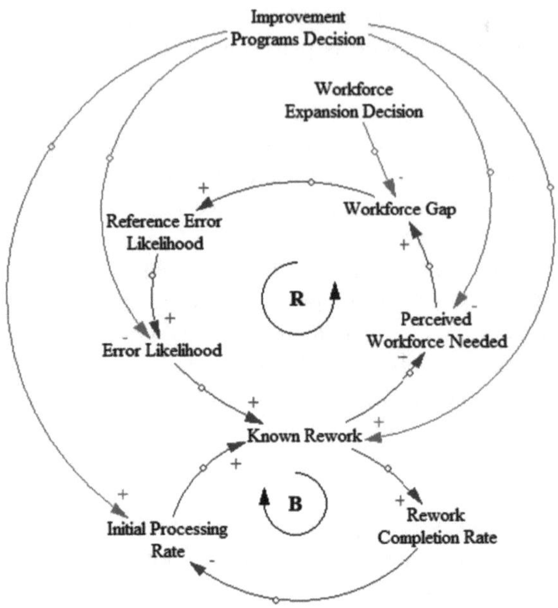

Fig. 4. Error generation main loops and policies (Color figure online)

- Workforce expansion: Even with an initial gap of zero, given a minimum 5% error likelihood, there will be rework to be done which would require workers. Hence the need to hire more people. This would keep the gap at zero keeping the error percentage from rising above 5%.
- Improvement programs: Improvement programs could involve one or more of the following methods: lean manufacturing techniques, new scanning technology, or stocktake standardization. Lean techniques and new scanning technology would increase workload capacity as well as error discovery.

If improvement programs are introduced, workload capacity is increased by one additional unit to 21 units/employee which would increase the Initial processing rate and decrease the perceived workforce needed. Also, error discovery would increase by 5% increasing Known Rework. By increasing error discovery, error likelihood would drop as well.

The Improvement Programs policy will strengthen the balancing loop by increasing the Initial Processing Rate as well as increasing known rework through higher error discovery. This policy however will have a conflicting role concerning the reinforcing loop. It will decrease the Perceived Workforce Needed as well as the Error Likelihood slowing down the reinforcing loop while strengthening it by increasing the Initial Processing Rate and Known Rework. One or both of these policies should be implemented from the start to prevent an escalation in error generation.

Model Behavior. Let us run the model for 36 months under different scenarios. Please note that this model does not take into consideration constraints such as hiring, firing and training times. Figures 5 and 6 show the outcomes.

Scenario 1 is for Workforce Expansion: If the company decides to hire more people from the beginning to close the gap between workforce and perceived workforce needed, the actual progress would fall before rising back to 0.993 by the end. The perceived workforce needed would increase to 127 before falling back to 105.

Scenario 2 is for Improvement Programs: If the company decides to implement improvement programs from the beginning (it is assumed that they are effective immediately), the actual progress would stay constant at 0.9974 which is the maximum progress that can be made given the undiscovered errors. The perceived workforce needed is a constant at 99 because the workload capacity is now higher.

Scenario 3 is when both policies are delayed by 5 months: If the company decides to delay its workforce expansion and improvement programs policies by 5 months, the actual progress would fall to 0.798 before rising back up to 0.995. The perceived workforce would increase to 170 before falling back down to 99.

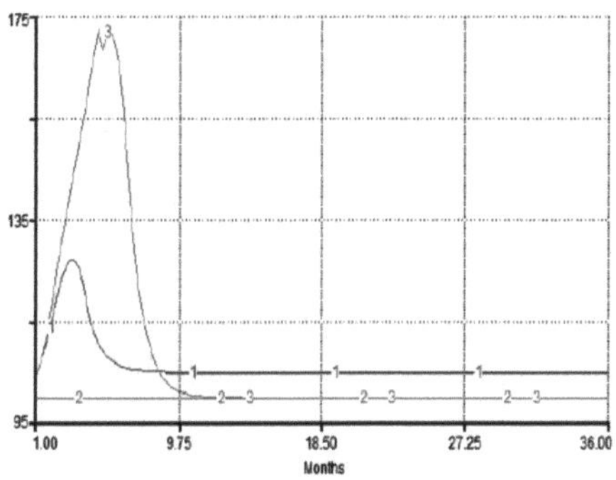

Fig. 5. Workforce needed scenarios

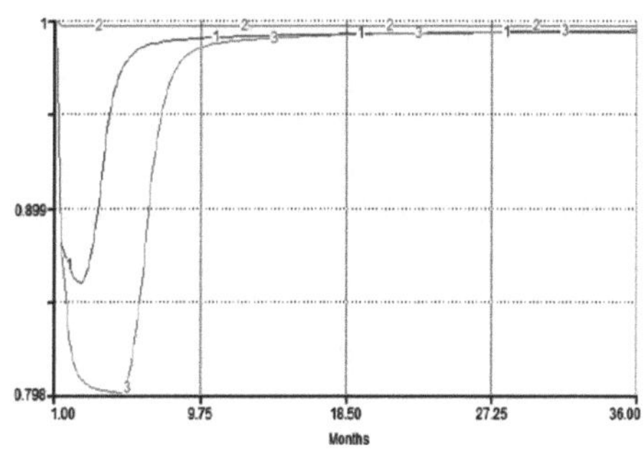

Fig. 6. Actual progress scenarios

In scenario 3 with a delay of 5 months before implementing the policies, errors would accumulate leading to higher error likelihoods which would require even more workers to devote their time to rework, thereby reducing the initial processing capacity and increasing the work to be done.

4 Contributions and Limitations

The paper presents a detailed yet concise overview of IRI with all the key terms and techniques that one might need. This is a rarely discussed topic in the literature and hence the paper would prove useful to researchers and managers.

The paper presents novel and relevant diagrams and models in Sect. 3 that offer insights into the dynamics at play in error generation and IRI. The results of the error generation and IRI models with the suggested policies help the reader in understanding the complexity of the topic and how simple and small errors can lead to big repercussions. However these are initial models and they portray simplified realities where some of the constraints have been relaxed. Further efforts are still needed to capture and incorporate more of the dynamics involved into the presented models. Mental models at play in such complex environments might provide crucial tips into the root causes of such discrepancies [4]. The challenge would be how to capture all of these factors while preserving the simplicity of the models and their ability to offer actionable analytics for practitioners. Naturally, optimization efforts to achieve the best mix of different performance indicators are the next step after having finalized the structure of the models.

As a next step, the presented model can be incorporated into larger models which represent entire supply chains and consequently the transportation and service stages of PLM would be tackled as well versus only the production stage in this paper.

5 Conclusions

Inventory control is fundamental for any company that deals with any kind of inventory. An implicit assumption of perfect information on the state of the inventory given by inventory information systems has been proven to be wrong. Error generation which leads to IRI have many root causes and there are several methods to counter-act it. Every company has to consider each of these methods such as cycle counting, stocktaking and simulation in its efforts to minimize IRI. This paper compiles some of the techniques that can be used in these efforts and it presents as well models that capture some of the dynamics that give rise to error generation and IRI. It is important to recognize that perfect information is not possible and zero errors is an idealistic goal that could backfire by setting off a vicious dynamic chain of reactions. A properly conceived plan has to be carefully set with the help of simulation tools. This would improve our understanding of the repercussions of policies and bridge the gap between achieved results and desired goals.

References

1. Chan, F., Wang, Z.: Robust production control policy for a multiple machines and multiple product-types manufacturing system with inventory inaccuracy. Int. J. Prod. Res. **52**(16), 4803–4819 (2014)
2. DeHoratius, N., Raman, A.: Inventory record inaccuracy: an empirical analysis. Manag. Sci. **54**(4), 627–641 (2008)
3. Delen, D., Hardgrave, B., Sharda, R.: RFID for better supply-chain management through enhanced information visibility. Prod. Oper. Manag. **16**(5), 613–624 (2007)
4. EL Hachem, W., Khoury, J., Harik, R.: Mental Model Moderation Modification and Managing (5M) framework: a system dynamics and Brunswikian lens model approach to complex decision making. In: Proceedings of International Conference on Industrial Engineering and Operations Management, pp. 1–10. IEEE, Dubai (2015)

5. Hardgrave, B., Aloysius, J., Goyal, S.: RFID-enabled visibility and retail inventory record inaccuracy: experiments in the field. Prod. Oper. Manag. **22**(4), 843–856 (2013)
6. Hardgrave, B., Aloysius, J., Goyal, S.: Does RFID improve inventory accuracy? A preliminary analysis. Int. J. RF Technol. **1**(1), 44–56 (2008)
7. Hollinger, R.C., Davis, J.L.: National retail security survey report. Department of Sociology and the Center for Studies in Criminology and Law, University of Florida (2001)
8. Khader, S., Rekik, Y., Botta-Genoulaz, V., Campagne, J.: Inventory management subject to multiplicative inaccuracies. Int. J. Prod. Res. **52**(17), 5055–5069 (2014)
9. Nachtmann, H., Waller, M., Rieske, D.: The impact of point-of-sale data inaccuracy and inventory record data errors. J. Bus. Log. **31**(1), 149–158 (2010)
10. Rekik, Y., Sahin, E.: Exploring inventory systems sensitive to shrinkage - analysis of a periodic review inventory under a service level constraint. Int. J. Prod. Res. **50**(13), 3529–3546 (2012)
11. Rossetti, M.D., Buyurgan, N., Bhonsle, A., Gumrukcu, S., Chittoori, K.: An analysis of the effect of inventory record inaccuracy in a two-echelon supply chain. Int. J. Invent. Res. **1**(2), 174–208 (2010)
12. Raman, A., DeHoratius, N., Ton, Z.: Execution: the missing link in retail operations. Calif. Manag. Rev. **43**(3), 136–152 (2001)

Author Index